Readings on
the psychology
of women

Readings on the psychology of women

Edited by *Judith M. Bardwick*

HARPER & ROW, Publishers

New York   Evanston   San Francisco   London

Readings on the psychology of women

To Abe and Ethel: with Love!

Contents

PART III   The Traditional Role: Gratifications, Frustrations, and Stresses

PART IV   The Women's Liberation Movement

Preface

Feminine rage and accusations—and occasionally the backlash of traditionalists—dominate the media. Book stores suddenly have new collections of Women's Liberation books and Sex Role has hit the best seller list. This is a different book: it is an academic's collection of theory and research papers from the professional literature of psychology, sociology, anthropology, endocrinology, obstetrics, and psychosomatics. This collection is primarily intended to generate discussion in class and research in the professions.

The impetus for organizing this collection came, largely, from my feeling that in my book Psychology of Women *I omitted topics that would distract from the theory I was trying to develop. But in a collection of papers one is not so restricted; one can range widely and need not be so constrained. These papers range from abstract theoretical analyses to clinical observations, to experimental reports, and to a few more personal statements. I have enjoyed the luxury of including things we really don't know very much about—but should.*

A book of readings doesn't have the clear organization and obvious unifying theme of a book written by a single author. This is especially true when the papers were not initially written for the collection. I have tried to provide some unity through the introductions that precede each section. In preparing the introductory essays I was stunned to discover how thematically unified these papers are. Probably a reflection of our current preoccupations, all of these papers bear upon questions of contemporary role expectations, conflicts, and status.

Questions like these never have definitive answers. Even in science, answers always reflect the expectations of scientists of some particular persuasion in a specific era who are using the methodologies available and acceptable to them. The answers, like the questions of science, change as method and theory evolve. Only if one recognizes the tentative nature of a "fact" can approaches to answers be beneficially derived from data.

Because rhetoric, passion, and extremism characterize most of what has been recently published, this is, at first glance, a duller book, an academician's book. Though quieter, I think in the long run this is the more enduring and the more fascinating approach.

Judith M. Bardwick

Acknowledgments

My thanks are extended to Noel C. Hicks who was my assistant in the preparation of this book. Without Noel's intelligent dedication this book would not yet be completed.

My admiration and very real gratitude are extended to the contributors whose papers make up this book. That these papers are outstanding and important should be clear to the reader. What will not be so obvious is that these contributors are pioneers, who offered data and theory where there was none. Not many years ago I used to receive phone calls about my seminar on the psychology of women. "But there is no psychology of women!" was a frequent comment. That's right. There wasn't. But there will be.

Part I

The development of sex differences

The first section of this collection contains papers about the development of sex differences. Always with us is the temptation to simplify and assume either a position based upon constitutional determinism (with a little socialization thrown in), or one based on environmental determinism (with a nod toward some unexplicated physiological factors). The antiquated nature-nurture controversy is a phoenix of a cliché that continuously experiences vigorous rebirth. But the question doesn't have an either-or answer. We need to know the response characteristics of an organism, the origins of these potentials, how these potentials affect the organism's behaviors, and the responses characteristically elicited from that organism by its environment.

John Money is particularly interested in the genetic, fetal, hormonal, and central nervous system factors that may be related to homosexuality, bisexuality, and heterosexuality. In his paper we find that the origins of sexual identity and behavior are based, in extraordinarily complex ways, on the interactions of constitutional factors and the sexual designation in which a child is reared. Much of the physiological information is new, based upon recent improvements in measurement techniques. The information is congruent with animal data (see the paper by Mitchell) and, particularly in extreme examples, clarifies the role of physiological factors as they affect the central nervous system and therefore the organism's response capacities.

Sex differences seem to begin to develop prior to birth. This means that even at birth the organism has tendencies with which it responds to external stimuli in complex interaction. (If only we really understood what those words really describe!) Response tendencies are what are reinforced, punished, or ignored. These interactions are seen in Moss' paper, where the sex, age, and state of the infant influenced the mother's response to her baby.

Early differences result in early inequities. The majority of the sex differences seen in young children show that the male child is at a significant disadvantage. Singer, Westphal, and Niswander report that males, from birth to four years, have significantly higher incidence of abnormalities and it is probable that there are constitutional, notably genetic, factors underlying this phenomenon.

Interaction between biological tendencies and maternal responses to the infant are found in studies of primates as well as infants. Mitchell observed that while most of the mother's responses to her infant monkey were not sex-typed, there are sex-typed responses, and they are very likely to have important consequences upon the development of aggression, independence, and perhaps vocalization—personality variables that conspicuously and significantly differentiate between men and women and girls and boys.

Observing infants at three weeks and at three months, Moss found that males slept less and cried more during observations than did females and this contributed to their experiencing a more stimulating interaction with their mothers. When the state of the infant was controlled for, most sex differences were no longer statistically significant (with the important exception that mothers imitate the vocalizations of girls more than boys). When controlling for the state of the infant makes sex differences disappear, it seems possible that differences in state—

irritability, arousability, motor activity, passivity, and the like—may be the basic, original differences between the sexes.

However, in a sex-linked interaction the mothers in Moss' study increased their contact with their daughters when they were irritable but decreased their contact with their three-month-old sons, even though the boys were more irritable. Moss suggests that the less organized physiological functions of the male may make him less able to respond favorably when his mother intervenes and thus his behavior is less reinforcing for her. At first, in earliest infancy, the response of the mother is shaped by that of the child, and subsequently, even at three months, the child responds to the behaviors of the mother. Moss contends that children whose behavior evokes appropriate responses from their mothers will become more amenable to social reinforcement and will manifest high degrees of attachment behavior. This, we know, usually describes girls.

The same characteristic sex differences in dependence upon the mother, activity level, and amount of vocalization, were observed in thirteen-month-old children by Goldberg and Lewis. Like Moss, they found that when the children were six months old, mothers touched, talked to, and handled their daughters more than their sons. When the children were thirteen months old, the daughters touched and talked to their mothers more than the sons did. Furthermore, the boys were more independent, more exploratory, and generally more vigorous, preferring toys requiring gross motor activity. These behavior differences, common in the sexes when they are older, were already present in the first year, and may be related to the quality of the relationship of the mother and child at six months. Remembering the previous papers, sex differences are present at three weeks and probably at birth. These characteristic behaviors or states are responded to differentially by mothers (and fathers and siblings), increasingly so as the child grows older.

Maccoby's chapter summarizes sex differences in intellectual functioning and explores behavioral differences as they correlate with characteristic personality variables and socialization experiences. Differences between boys and girls increase as they grow older, and Maccoby specifies the cognitive differences between the sexes, relating them to differences in personality, especially to differences in impulse control, anxiety, aggression and competitiveness, the motive to achieve, traits of masculinity and femininity, and dependence, independence, and passivity. Consistent with the other papers in this section (and in the sections that follow), Maccoby evaluates the data and finds it probable that the major differences are significantly related to boys' greater independence and activity and to girls' greater passive-dependency and conformity. The experimental findings, in Maccoby's opinion, support the idea that environmental factors, especially those embedded in parent-child relations, significantly affect the child's intellectual performance. But it is not simple—the same environmental input affects the sexes differently, thus making it clear that there is a complex interaction between an innate temperament that is more characteristic of one sex than the other, and environmental effect.

In Douvan's paper we continue to explore characteristic personality differences between the sexes. These differences maximize during adolescence and have enormous effects upon achievement aspirations, career commitments, role-related anxieties and dominant goals, and the personality characteristics brought to the role. Whereas the major psychological task of the male adolescent is the development of internal values and controls, girls are far less preoccupied with evolving personal, individual standards and values. Adolescent girls, like little girls, continue to look outside, to their parents (and teachers and friends), for rewards, punishments, and identity. The critical integrating variable in the personality of girls is their interpersonal skill and sensitivity. The reliance on the interpersonal rather than the internal, serves as a source of esteem and affirmation of the self, but is simultaneously the major point of feminine vulnerability.

Socialization pressures increase enormously in adolescence, pushing teenagers to conformity with adult sex roles. Now ambivalence characteristically increases in girls who experience the power of society's preference for male achievements while girls are increasingly motivated to succeed in their traditional feminine role. Very significantly, in terms of future role choices, during adolescence the internalization of the dominant cultural values leads girls to fear success in the job market because it threatens their concept of femininity. Thus the majority of adolescent girls withdraw from visible competitive achievement and this means that their commitment to work, success, and a professional identity is less than that of boys. One cannot overestimate the importance of this psychological development. It is the subject of part II.

1 Sexual dimorphism and homosexual gender identity

John Money

Whatever the degree of an individual's homosexual commitment, the behavior concerned may be in some degree hereditary, constitutional, and biological in its determination, and in some degree environmental, learned, and sociological. It is not a question of either/or with respect to each of these categories, or a question of how much; the basic question is, Which type? The chronic and obligative, essential or idiopathic homosexual may be a product of the confluence of heredity and environment, constitution and learning, biology and sociology. Likewise with the transitory, facultative, optional, and induced homosexual.[1]

In the etiology of homosexuality, one may look for prenatal preordained factors either in the genetic code or in the metabolism of the intrauterine environment. It is remotely possible that one may find also a factor associated with birth—or birth injury. Postnatally, one must look for critical period experiences or exposures that may leave a permanent imprint. One needs an open mind regarding the nature of such experiences. For all that is known at present, these factors may range from a specific nutritional insufficiency to deprivation of sensory stimulation, as in congenital hearing loss, to pathology of behavioral interaction within the family, or to incapacity to relate freely with children of similar age.

Despite the fact that science and medicine do not yet have the answer to what determines psychosexual differentiation as homosexual, heterosexual, or bisexual, the body of knowledge is constantly expanding. The remainder of this paper reviews the present state of knowledge regarding genetic, fetal, hormonal, and central nervous system factors that may be related to behavioral homosexuality.

Cytogenetics: the sex chromosomes

The discovery that a difference between the sexes is visibly evident in individual cells of the body dates from as recently as 1949. It was then that Barr and Bertram at London, Ontario, discovered the sex-chromatin spot (Moore, 1966), since known as the Barr body, present in the nucleus of cells from female mammals but not in those from males Subsequently, it was discovered that the cells of certain morphologic-appearing males, namely those with Klinefelter's syndrome, have a Barr body in them. The significance of this finding remained obscure until after 1956, at which time it first became possible actually to visualize and count the chromosomes in a single cell (see reviews by Bartalos & Baramki, 1967; Ferguson-Smith, 1961; Hirschhorn & Cooper, 1961; Sohval, 1961). The chromosome count of a phenotypic male with Klinefelter's syndrome shows him to have a supernumerary X chromosome. Instead of the normal male count of 44 + XY chromosomes or the normal female count of 44 + XX, the Klinefelter male has 44 + XXY (47, XXV). In some cases, there is more than one supernumerary X chromosome. To the extra X chromosome is attributed responsibility for the stigmata of the syndrome: namely, a tendency to cunuchoidism of body build; late onset of puberty; weak pubertal virilization with possible breast development, as in a female; small penis, small sterile testes, and subnormal libido or sexual drive. The central nervous system seems also to be involved: Witness an elevated frequency of the occurrence of mental deficiency and of various forms of psychopathology. The latter includes psychosexual pathologies, despite the low power of sexual drive, including homosexuality and its related conditions of transvestism and transexualism (Money & Pollitt, 1964).

It cannot be said that the extra X chromosome of Klinefelter's syndrome induces a degree of psychic femininity in all affected individuals, but only that the incidence of effeminancy is increased. Some individuals escape entirely. The best way to make sense of this state of affairs is to postulate a genetically determined condition of vulnerability to error in psychosexual differentiation. The developmental period of greatest risk would appear to be postnatal,

Reprinted from John Money, "Sexual Dimorphism and Homosexual Gender Identity," *Psychological Bulletin*, 74:6, 1970, pp. 425-440. Copyright 1970 by the American Psychological Association, and reproduced by permission. Supported by Research Grants 2R01-HD 00325 and 5K03-HD 18635, United States Public Health Service.

during the preschool years, which is when psychosexual differentiation chiefly is accomplished (Money, Hampson, & Hampson, 1955, 1957). At this time all development is susceptible to influence from the social environment—for example, the acquisition of a native language. That the differentiation of a gender identity is also powerfully influenced by social experience can be clearly demonstrated in certain cases of hermaphroditism (see subsequent discussion). As in the case of a native language, however, the process of psychosexual differentiation is clearly one of interactionism between brain and social stimulus. The child with injury to language centers of the dominant hemisphere may be defective in language acquisition. One cannot be very specific about the human brain in matters of psychosexual identity, except to note that psychosexual changes may, in rare instances, be associated with temporal lobe malfunction or injury; and that these changes sometimes are reversed as a consequence of successful brain surgery (Blumer, 1969; Epstein, 1961, 1969). It may also be of significance that not only psychosexual pathology, but also electroencephalographic abnormality (Hambert & Frey, 1964) has an elevated frequency incidence in Klinefelter's syndrome.

Other syndromes in which the sex chromosomes are implicated are the female triple-X syndrome, Turner's syndrome, and the XYY syndrome in males (Bartalos & Baramki, 1967; Gardner, 1969; Wilkins, 1965). Triple-X females are morphologically and psychosexually unremarkable.

Patients with Turner's syndrome are morphologic females who are dwarfed, without gonads, and subject to a variety of other birth defects. The chromosomal error is most typically an absence of one of the pair of X chromosomes (45, X). Girls with this condition need hormonal replacement therapy at the age of puberty in order to mature sexually. Psychosexually they represent virtually the obverse of homosexuality which is conspicuous by its absence in this syndrome. The girls not only conform to the style of femininity idealized in our cultural definitions of femininity, but they also are (long before they know the prognosis of their condition) maternal in their childhood play and adult aspirations. This very complete feminine gender identity and absence of homosexual traits may have its origins in a total absence of gonadal hormones during fetal development, so that there is no malelike hormonal effect on the sex-regulating centers of the developing brain (Ehrhardt, 1969; Money & Mittenthal, 1970).

The XYY syndrome (see review by Money, Gaskin, & Hull, 1970) has so recently been discovered that information regarding gender identity in men with this chromosomal aberration (47, XYY) is still tentative. The condition became noteworthy after it was found to be frequent among tall and slender men detained in institutions for delinquents and criminals. Therefore, it has been conjectured that the extra Y chromosome may have some bearing on poorly regulated or impulsive behavior, sexual behavior included. The incidence of homosexual experience is high among institutionalized XYY males and occurs also when they are not institutionalized.

The examination of syndromes gives one-half of the story (the half that is traditionally neglected) of the relationship between genetics, specifically chromosomal genetics, and homosexuality. The other half of the story comes from testing a sample group of homosexuals themselves.

Nuclear sex-chromatin surveys of homosexuals and eonists have disclosed no discrepancies between them and control groups of men with normal masculine gender identity (Bleuler & Wiedemann, 1956; Pare, 1956; Raboch & Nedoma, 1958). In chromosome counting, there are no reports of discrepancies consistently related to homosexuality or to either the transvestite or transsexual form of eonism (Pritchard, 1962), though there are known sporadic combinations of either homosexuality or eonism with the XXY chromosome complex of Klinefelter's syndrome (as discussed earlier in this review). Though the total number of cases studied has been modest, deviations from normal expectancy have always been in patients whose other clinical signs indicated the probability of a cttigebetuc error in advance of the actual test. Homosexual men whose physical examination reveals no bodily abnormality have not been found to have a Barr body, indicative of an extra X chromosome; nor when the more time-consuming chromosome count has been performed have chromosomal errors been directly visualized. Since men with the XYY syndrome were overlooked until recent years, one must allow the possibility that a chromosome-counting (karyotyping) survey of a large sample of homosexuals might disclose some hitherto unsuspected abnormality in some individuals. Meantime, on the basis of techniques so far employed, there is no way of implicating an error of the chromosomes themselves in the etiology of ordinary homosexuality. Whether genes rather than entire chromosomes may be implicated is an altogether different matter. There is no technique yet available for visualizing, counting, or otherwise directly implicating certain genes in the etiology of anything. Such implication must always be by inference, is only rarely possible, and has not yet been achieved in any part of behavior genetics, to say nothing of sexual behavior genetics.

Statistical genetics

The attempt to implicate hereditary mechanisms in homosexuality at the genic, if not the chromosomal, level long antedates the new era of cytogenetics. The older, statistical methods are those of the sex ratio, ordinal position, and twin comparisons.

In sex-ratio studies, the male:female ratio in the sibships of male homosexuals was compared with the expected ratio of 106:100 (Darke, 1948; Jensch, 1941a, 1941b; Kallman, 1952; Lang, 1940; Slater, 1958). Each study turned up a different ratio, some with and some without statistical significance, ranging from 106:100 in Darke's small sample to 125:100 in Kallman's twin study. The most often quoted study is that of Lang, based on 1,015 cases. His ratio was 121:100, which could be subdivided to 128:100 for those cases over the age of 25, and to 113:100 for the younger age group. It is possible that the results of all these studies have no more significance than if the figures had been drawn from a random number table, a procedure which sometimes yields statistically significant differences. On the other hand, the results may reflect a tendency for homosexual men to have more brothers in the family than expected. In this case, the findings may signify not a genetic predisposition to homosexuality, but a tendency for an effeminate gender identity to develop more easily in boys whose families have a shortage of sisters and daughters. From this latter point of view, it is provocative that Slater found a brother:sister ratio in the families of male exhibitionists of 109:144—an excess of female sibs to form an audience for their show-off brother!

Extending his observations from family constellation to ordinal position of siblings, Martensen-Larsen (1957) somewhat casually reported findings on a sample of 63 homosexuals, which not only confirmed a preponderance of brothers over sisters, but also showed the homosexuals to have a predominance of ordinal position in the lowest third of the sibship. There was also a preponderance of brothers in the families of the 42 fathers and 21 grandfathers studied, whereas the 25 grandmothers and 45 mothers had a preponderance of sisters. In the 44 homosexual women and the 39 of their mothers and 16 maternal grandmothers studied, sisters predominated in the sibships with no data reported for the fathers. The homosexual women came from the upper and lower thirds of the sibship more often than the middle.

In the matter of ordinal position, Slater's data (1958, 1962) showed that compared to exhibitionists, homosexuals tended to be born late in the sibship and of older mothers.

Another type of study purporting to implicate a genetic mechanism for homosexuality is that of Kallman (1952) on homosexual twins. Kallman reported a high degree of concordance for homosexuality in each of 37 pairs of identical monozygotic twins. The figure for fraternal dizygotic twins was quite different. There were 26 such pairs of twin brothers studied, with the index case known to be overtly homosexual; 58% of the dizygotic co-twins revealed no evidence of homosexual experience after the age of adolescence, whereas the remaining 42% ranged over the full scale of 1 to 6 on the Kinsey homosexuality ratings. Only 11.5% of the co-twins (3 of 26) were homosexual enough to get a rating as high as 5 or 6 (which requires a high or exclusive degree of homosexuality for at least 3 years between the ages of 16 and 35). Kinsey's corresponding percentage for ratings of 5 or 6 in the general male population was 10%.

Kallman's identical twins were not reared apart. Their concordance for homosexuality may, therefore, represent a tendency in monozygotic twins to be replicas of one another while growing up and responding to their jointly shared life experiences. In this case, their homosexuality would not be a primary genetic unfolding, but secondary to the unison in which the pair encountered life's transactions.

A further word of caution, applicable not only to homosexual but to all twin studies, is very much in order; namely, identical twins are not necessarily cytogenetically identical. That is to say, twins who qualify as identical by all the usual criteria (including blood type, dermatoglyphics, and skin transplant) may not have the same number of chromosomes. This surprising finding has emerged from the study of mongolism (trisomy-21) and Turner's syndrome, when identical and apparently monozygous twins proved to be cytogenetically discordant (Bruins, van Bolhuis, Bijlsma, & Nijenhuis, 1963; Lejeune, Lafourcade, Schärer, de Wolff, Salmon, Haines, & Turpin, 1962; Ross, Tijo, & Lipsett, 1969; Russell, Moschos, Butler, & Abraham, 1966; Turpin, Lejeune, Lafourcade, Chigot, & Salmon, 1961). These findings may require a rather extensive revision of current concepts of perfect genetic identity in monozygous twins, since they may be identical for all but one chromosome or one pool of genes. The missing (or added) part of the genetic code may be the very part that makes all the difference with respect to the trait, like homosexuality, which is the subject of behavioral interest in a twin study.

Fetal differentiation of sexual morphology

In clinical medicine and experimental biology, the principles governing sexual differentiation of the embryo and fetus (see review by Federman, 1967) have been elucidated during the past quarter century. Errors of differentiation, notably in both clinical and experimentally induced hermaphroditism, are important to the theory of homosexuality. In some instances these errors result in what is, in effect, homosexuality by experiment or by experiment of nature.

In the development of the embryo, nature's first choice or primal impulse is to differentiate a female. The anlagen of the sex organs when they first appear are identical for both sexes. The principle of differentiation is always that to obtain a male, something must be added. Subtract that something, and the result will be a female. Castrate the fetus in utero prior to the critical period when sexual morphology will be differentiated, and all the offspring, whether genetic males or females, will be born with female external gentalia. The first demonstration of this principle was by means of surgical castration of fetal rabbits (Jost, 1961). Jost's original work was in the early 1950s. The same effect can now be achieved nonsurgically by means of functional hormonal castration (Neumann & Elger, 1966). The hormone used is cyproterone acetate, an antiandrogen or androgen antagonist. Injected into the pregnant mother, it reaches the fetus and renders all of its cells androgen insensitive. Thenceforth, those cells of a genetic male dependent on male hormone, in order to differentiate the masculine sexual morphology, behave as if they were in a genetic female. The result is that a genetic male animal is born with the perfect facsimile of external female morphology, including a vagina large enough in adulthood for copulation. The gonads are testes. The uterus and fallopian tubes are absent, as in a normal male. The embryonic differentiation of these organs is not under the control of androgen. They therefore do not develop under the influence of antiandrogen. At puberty, the testes will function in the normal male fashion. To obtain a feminizing puberty, they will need to be removed or their influence counteracted by further administration of antiandrogen. Then female hormones will need to be administered. Properly regulated in the female fashion, the animals (rats) used in Neumann's experiment exhibited estrus, behaving in mating in a manner indistinguishable from normal females, and were accepted as such by normal males in the colony.

These antiandrogenized rats are an experimental counterpart of a human clinical condition, the syndrome of androgen insensitivity or testicular feminization (Federman, 1967, Chapter 8). Children born with this syndrome are a perfect female facsimile, externally. Therefore, they are invariably assigned as females. Their gonads are two testes, always lacking spermatogenesis, which may be completely undescended or may push down toward the labia. The uterus is vestigial, making menstruation impossible. Either menstrual failure or the lumps of the testes in the groins are the usual reason for referral and diagnosis. The vagina in some cases is too short for comfortable intercourse and so will need surgical lengthening in middle teenage or sometime later. The onset of puberty is at the usual time and is invariably feminizing, since the cells of the body are unable to respond to the normal masculine output of androgen from the testes. They respond instead to the normal amount of estrogen produced in a male by the testes, which is enough to produce a degree of feminization so complete as to be quite compatible with a career as a fashion model. It is a characteristic of the syndrome that the girls are tall. Some of them are unable to grow sexual or axillary hair. The nature of the resistance to androgen at the cellular level is unknown, but is presumed to be enzymatic—either a missing enzyme or a superfluous and toxic one. The condition is hereditary, probably a sex-linked dominant, being found in the aunts, nieces, cousins, and siblings of affected individuals. Psychosexual differentiation is invariably feminine, usually uncompromisingly feminine, with a strong degree of maternalism which makes for very good adoptive motherhood (Money, Ehrhardt, & Masica, 1968).

Human beings with the androgen insensitivity syndrome and antiandrogenized rats make it very clear, for those who ever doubted it after the opening sections of this paper, that genetic sex alone does not exercise a direct and peremptory power over psychosexual differentiation. The genetic sex difference can express itself in psychosexual differentiation only if the intervening steps of hormonal and morphological differentiation follow a phylogenetically prescribed course. Quite possibly, neural differentiation within the brain is yet another necessary intervening step (see subsequent discussion).

There is a semantic and conceptual lesson to be learned from women with the androgen insensitivity syndrome. Genetically and gonadally they are male. Therefore, when they marry a man, both partners are in a relationship of genetic and gonadal homosexuality. Morphologically, hormonally, and psychosexually, they are heterosexual in their relationship. Legally and in the popular conscience also they are heterosexual, for the evidence of common sense is that two people are homosexual not when they have the same chromosomal sex or the same hidden sexual structures internally, but when they have the same copulatory organs externally, and a psychosexual disposition to use them in an erotic relationship together.

Genetic males who qualify as females have their counterpart in genetic females who qualify as males. This latter condition is found clinically in human beings, as is its counterpart, and it can also be induced experimentally in animals by injection of the pregnant mother with male sex hormone. In human beings the condition of complete masculinization occurs sometimes in the adrenogenital syndrome of female hermaphroditism (Federman, 1967, Chapter 9; Money, 1968b). The source of excess fetal androgens is from the baby's own adrenal cortex which, on the basis of a genetically recessive trait, functions abnormally. From its undifferentiated state, the genital tubercle enlarges to become a penis instead of a clitoris. The skin that would have constituted the hood of the clitoris and the labia minora, follows the masculine alternative of wrapping around the penis and fusing to form the urethal tube. The labioscrotal folds do not stay divided to form labia majora, but fuse in the midline to form an empty scrotum. The gonads are ovaries and remain internal. The uterus opens into a shortened vagina which opens into the urethra near the neck of the bladder, instead of having an external opening in the normal position adjacent to the urinary orifice.

This same masculinized sexual anatomy can be found also in genetic females whose mothers were given one of the new synthetic progestins to prevent miscarriage. Rather rarely when they are administered, these hormones which have an androgenic biochemical structure will have an androgenic physiologic effect on the female fetus.

As may be expected, some of these masculinized genetic females with a penis pass as cryptorchid males and are declared and reared as boys (Money, 1955). Some of them may escape further medical attention until they are too old for a sex reannouncement. They remain living as boys and are given the appropiate hormonal therapy to prevent early virilization and the various other signs and symptoms associated with the adrenogenital syndrome, if they have that diagnosis. Additional surgical treatment is also given to prevent the pubertal appearance of menstrual bleeding, spontaneously, in the progestin-induced syndrome and, as a sequel to cortisone therapy in the adrenogenital syndrome, if such has been instituted. Such boys are also given androgenic hormonal therapy to induce masculine pubertal development. So regulated surgically and hormonally, these patients differentiate a masculine psychosexual identity.

The sexual behavior in adulthood of experimentally masculinized genetic female animals will depend partly on the regime of hormonal regulation on which they are maintained. The most data have come from guinea pigs and rats (see review by Money, 1965). The general trend was for their behavior to resemble more closely that of normal male than normal female controls, but their scores were not identical with those of normal males. The rhesus monkey has also been used in these masculinizing experiments, but the animals are still too scarce or too young for all the critical questions to have been answered regarding adult sexual behavior. In childhood, however, the masculinized girl monkeys behaved like tomboys, engaging in more rough and tumble play than the normal controls, plus more initiation of play, and more threats, chasing play and sexual play with attempted mounting.

One should not look too closely for an etiologic comparison between a genetic female with a penis and a typical female homosexual, since the latter differentiates a psychosexual identity as the possessor not of a penis, but a normal female vulva. A more fair comparison might be between a female homosexual and a genetic female fetally exposed to androgen without getting a penis, or one whose masculinized, or partially masculinized external genitals were surgically corrected at birth. There are cases, clinical and experimental, that more or less fulfill this requirement. The same holds true in the analogous comparison of the androgen insensitivity syndrome with typical male homosexuality. But more about this in the next section.

Sex differentiation and brain

The most up-to-the-minute new knowledge in sex research concerns a sex difference in the influence of fetal hormones on that part of the brain, the hypothalamus, which will subsequently regulate the cycles of sexual functioning in the female or their absence in the male. (See reviews by Doerner, 1967; Harris, 1964; Money, 1965; Neumann, Steinbeck, & Hahn, in press.) The work of several different investigators in this country and Europe has converged to produce this new knowledge, most of it obtained from species that manifest the phenomenon of estrus. The basic principle to emerge is the same as that which applies to the differentiation of genital morphology (see earlier discussion in this review), namely, that nature's basic premise is to make a female. To make a male, something must be added. Once again, that something is male sex hormone. When radioactive-labeled male hormone is administered to the fetus either through the mother or directly, in the case of the rat which is born immature, its uptake can be traced to various organs, including cells in the hypothalamus. When the hormone is administered within the time limit of the effective critical period in development, then if the fetus is a genetic female, the hypothalamic nuclei will be masculinized. In consequence, these cells will never, in the future, be able to release their neurohumoral messages to the pituitary in the cyclic fashion characteristic of the female. Like the male, the animal will therefore always be uncyclical, though unlike the male will most likely be in a state of constant estrus but without ovulation. In addition, because other nearby hypothalamic nuclei that regulate sexual behavior in phase with the sexual cycle will have been affected by the male sex hormone, the animal's sexual behavior will not conform to that of the normal female. Typically, the animal will be disoriented and disorganized in its sexual response, or will repulse the male.

The converse of this story is found in the male that is castrated before the critical period when androgen should leave its imprint on the hypothalamus. Animals so treated show, when they are tested by means of an ovarian graft implanted behind the lens of the eye, that the pituitary functions cyclically, in the female fashion. The ovarian graft can be seen to pass through ovarian cycles as in a normal female. In sexual behavior in adulthood, these early castrated animals are significantly more feminine in their responses to mounting by intact males than are their experimental controls, though they are likely to be sexually apathetic unless first primed with estogen and progesterone or, paradoxically, with testosterone (see reviews by Whalen, 1968; Gorski, in press).

In the foregoing experiments, interference with the normal progress of growth and development occurred after the fetuses had passed through the phase of external sex-organ differentiation. In gross external anatomy, they appeared normal. Only their pituitary-gonadal cycling was abnormal and also their behavior. If the experimental interference with normal fetal development is timed earlier, then the morphologic differentiation of the external organs is rendered hermaphroditic and abnormal, as in the extreme cases of antiandrogenization and masculinization already described. Rodent females exposed to androgen from this earlier stage until after birth, and not subsequently castrated, reject the male in adulthood, and display more masculine mounting behavior toward receptive females than do their normal controls. Antiandrogenized males, their testes intact, show bisexual behavior in adulthood, dependent on the sex of the partner (Neumann & Elger, 1965).

Phylogenetically, it is a big leap from estrous rodents to menstrual primates, especially with respect to a system so species-variable as the reproductive system. One may not draw parallels and inferences indiscriminately. For example, in the rhesus monkey and in man, fetal exposure of the female to androgen does not predictably interfere with the pituitary's regulation of normal menstrual cycling. Provided the evidence is interpreted with caution, however, there are some inferences to be made regarding the masculinization of behavior in human females fetally exposed to androgen, as in congenital virilizing adrenal hyperplasia (the adrenogenital syndrome of female hermaphroditism) and girls with progestin-induced masculinized genitalia.

For present purposes, the most instructive human cases are those in which the condition was recognized at birth and the necessary hormonal and surgical corrections immediately instituted (Ehrhardt, Epstein, & Money, 1968; Ehrhardt & Money, 1967). Under these circumstances, the possible effect of a prenatal masculinizing effect on the central nervous system is not contaminated by either the postnatal effect of masculine-looking abnormal genitalia or by the presistence of incongruous hormonal function.

In both groups of girls, there was a high incidence of tomboyism as defined by themselves, their mothers, and their playmates—far higher than found in the control group. This tomboyism manifested itself primarily in athletic energy expenditure that included, but was not restricted to, boys' sports and activities. Boys' toys were preferred over dolls. The rehearsal of motherhood in childhood play was missing or low in the priority of interests. In anticipating the future, romance and marriage, though not ruled out, were subordinated to career ambitions. Girlhood clothing and hair style showed a marked preference for utilitarianism and functionalism rather than being chic, pretty, or fashionably feminine. There was no evidence of a directly or incipiently lesbian type of erotic interest—simply a low priority rating for interest in boys as compared with the control group. An unexpected side-finding was an excessively high incidence of high IQs, which probably is not attributable to an artifact of sampling.

In the clinical study of human beings, there are no male counterparts to the above groups, namely, genetic males who were antiandrogenized or unandrogenized prenatally and then hormonally and surgically remasculinized for assignment at birth. The nearest approximation is found in cases of agenesis of the penis which may be total, or the organ may be a microphallus with or without hypospadias. At birth, some children of this type are assigned and surgically corrected as females. Others are assigned as males. Some few of them may ultimately request to be reassigned as females, but the majority will accept themselves in the sex of original assignment (Money, unpublished data).

In each foregoing type of case, it does seem likely that there may be some residual influence of the hormonal effect on the developing fetal brain—probably the hypothalamus but possibly also the temporal lobe. The residual effect does not, however, automatically dictate the postnatal differentiation of a gender identity as a homosexual. Postnatal events exercise their own power on gender identity differentiation. Nonetheless, one may be justified in making the inference that had the fetally masculinized girls been assigned and corrected as boys, they would not have had much difficulty in differentiating psychosexually as boys. There are indeed cases, as is evident from the next section of this review, where such has been observed. The same thing holds in converse for the incompletely masculinized boys.

As applied to homosexuality, these clinical findings suggest that an apparently normal baby destined to be a homosexual may have some hidden predisposition, perhaps lurking in the neurohumoral system of the brain, that makes him or her more vulnerable to differentiate a psychosexual identity as a homosexual—not in any preordained, automatic, or mechanistic sense, but only if the social environment happens to provide the right confluence of circumstances.

Sex assignment and gender identity

None of the foregoing evidence regarding genetic or fetal-hormonal influences on sex differences in morphology or neural organization is incompatible with the evidence of an extraordinary contribution from the postnatal environment of social exposure to the differentiation of a person's gender identity. There is no more convincing evidence of the power of social interaction on gender-identity differentiation than in the case of congenital hermaphrodites who are of the same diagnosis and similar degree of hermaphroditism, but are differently assigned and with a different postnatal medical and life history (Money, 1963b, 1970a; Money & Ehrhardt, 1968). It is possible, for example, to have four genetic females, each ultimately diagnosed as having the adrenogenital syndrome of female hermaphroditism: one is assigned as and reared as a girl, one as a boy, one provisionally as a boy, and one provisionally as a girl. The subsequent medical and social histories differ, relative to

the sex of assignment or provisional assignment and rearing. Psychosexual differentiation takes place, respectively, in the four cases as feminine, masculine, ambivalently wanting to be changed to a girl, and ambivalently wanting to be changed to a boy (Money, 1968c, 1970b, and unpublished case histories).

The lesson of these four cases does not need to be belabored. They indicate that the outcome in psychosexual differentiation was entirely independent of genetic sex which was the same in all four, and also independent of hormonal sex—the boy who changed to live as a girl was already prematurely and strongly virilized (as is usual in the syndrome) before cortisone therapy was instituted to induce breast development, menstruation, and ovulation. The first two cases illustrate also the congruence between sex of assignment and the differentiation of gender identity when the parents and other significant people in the social environment are not ambivalent about the sex to which their child belongs, whereas the second two cases illustrate what may happen when the opposite is true.

Requests for sex reassignment among hermaphrodites are the exception rather than the rule. The request may be from male to female or vice versa, irrespective of genetic or gonadal sex, but requests from female to male are more common. There is a good explanation for this preponderance of female to male requests. Such requests are typically made by individuals with a large and visible phallus who were not surgically feminized early in life, and so grew up with visible evidence of ambiguity. At puberty, further masculinization is evidenced, regardless of genetic sex, because female hermaphrodites with a large, phallic-looking clitoris typically have the virilizing adrenogenital syndrome (untreated); and in males, the larger the unfinished hermaphroditic penis, the greater the chance that they will virilize at puberty instead of feminize or remain eunuchoid.

There is, at the present stage of medical history, a rather remote possibility that some few male hermaphrodites without a large phallus and not puberially masculinized, may, if reared as a girl, feel like a lesbian who should have been a boy. Many if not all of such cases, however, have a history of undercurrents of ambiguity in the minds of the parents as to their true sex. The preponderance of evidence from hermaphroditism relative to the theory of homosexuality points to the importance of subtleties in the sex rearing in shaping the differentiation of gender identity as male, female, or ambivalent.

Postpubertal hormonal differences

It has long been taught that childhood is a period of hormonal dormancy, but that belief is currently open to doubt and reexamination, particularly in the wake of a new technique (Raiti & Davis, 1969; Raiti, Johanson, Light, Migeon, & Blizzard, 1969; Raiti, Light, & Blizzard, 1969) for measuring the pituitary gonadotrophic hormones that stimulate the ovaries and testes. Changes in the level of these hormones, follicle stimulating hormone (FSH) and luteinizing hormone (LH), are detectable in advance of clinically evident puberty. Nonetheless, the chief fact of puberty is the release of sex hormones by the gonads.

Contrary to popular belief, males and females make some of all three sex hormones, androgen, estrogen, and progestin. The difference between the sexes is not absolute and all-or-none, but a matter of relativity or degree. Further, in biochemical structure, the sex hormones are all "first cousins." It is possible for the body to convert one into the other. Alternatively, it may retain a surplus of a hormone or its precursor which might be destroyed. For example, in males estrogen produced by the testes should be destroyed in the liver. Failure of this mechanism may be responsible for some cases of breast development (gynecomastia) in adolescent boys.

In the 1940s, the era when the sex hormones had first been synthesized, there was a flurry of excitement concerning the relationship of the level of hormones in the blood or urine to homosexuality (male) and heterosexuality; and conversely, concerning the use of hormones in the treatment of homosexuality (see review by Money, 1961). The excitement was all doomed to disappointment. Methods of measurement were crude then. In the present day of more refined measurement techniques, no one is very interested in large-scale studies of homosexual blood and urine, since detailed individual studies, for example, of spermatic vein blood taken from a male transexual at operation, indicate that there is no reason to suspect a statistical difference from hormone levels in control blood and urine (Migeon, Rivarola, & Forest, 1969).

Clinically, it is true that some homosexuals have a history of chromosomal error, sexual birth deformity, undescended testes, small penis, delayed puberty, gonadal insufficiency, poorly developed or contradictory sexual dimorphism of body build, gynecomastia (in boys), and hirsuitism (in girls). But the frequency of any one of these disorders among homosexuals is so sporadic as to not create special hormonal research vigilance at the present time. Conversely, the incidence of homosexuality in the clinical population of each one of the listed disorders is so sporadic that one cannot seriously entertain the hypothesis of a primary hormonal cause-effect link between the physical symptoms, on the one hand, and homosexuality on the other. If there is any link, it is more likely to be secondary. There is far and away more homosexuality among organists, hairdressers, actors, interior decorators, or antique dealers than among patients with any given endocrine diagnosis! One may fairly safely interpret today's clinical evidence to mean that the sex-hormone levels of adulthood have very little to do with the etiology of homosexuality.[2]

The story with regard to therapy is a little different, insofar as male hormone administered to either a male or female homosexual, enhances the level of libido and leads to a probable increase in homosexual activity. Androgen is a libido-enhancing hormone for both sexes (Everitt & Herbert, 1969; Herbert, 1970; Money, 1961). By contrast, estrogen is a functional castrating agent in the male. It thus may lower the intensity of libido and lead to a decrease of sexual initiative and activity. In effect, it is an erotic tranquilizer in the male. Its therapeutic use is limited by its promotion of breast growth,[3] which is a positive advantage in the case of the male transexual who is not disturbed by

having his sexual initiative reduced by estrogen therapy. In the female, estrogen appears to be more important to the cycle of nidation and gestation than to libido and eroticism per se, except that the unestrogenized vagina is unlubricated and painful in intercourse.

Neuroperceptual sex differences

Knowledge of differences between the sexes at the neuropsychologic—neurosensory, neuroperceptual, or neurocognitional—level is fragmentary, being mostly derived from anecdotal observations with only a few systematic observations or experiments. The earliest systematic data are those from the Kinsey interviews (Kinsey, Pomeroy, Martin, & Gebhard, 1953). They point to a higher frequency of erotic (genitopelvic) arousal in the male than the female, in response to visual and narrative erotic stimuli. The relative frequencies varied in accordance with the type of stimulus and, no doubt, in accordance with individual preference and personal history.

A more recent study and an experimental one is that of Schmidt and Sigusch (1970). Using a specially prepared movie demonstrating sexual relations, they found that college women responded sexually to this form of erotic stimulation in a fashion similar to men.

When men and women are sexually aroused by visual or narrative material, the nature of the carry-through may be different. Men are, in the popular view, more readily aroused than women to a casual or promiscuous liason, if such is available. Women are more dependent on long-term romantic and sentimental ties with a partner, especially in connection with stimulation through the tactile senses.[4]

There is another potential sex difference in response to the visual image. Men respond to a visual image, for example a pinup girl, as to a substitute object of sexual desire. Women may respond to the same stimulus, but not, if they do, as to an object of desire: the woman projects herself into the image and becomes the seductive one. Men, in general, do not project themselves into a picture of a man in this way. Only the homosexual man responds to pictures of other males, and then as sexual objects.

Apart from the preferred sex of the image, homosexuals do not, so far as is known, differ from other members of their morphologic sex in response to visual or narrative erotic stimulation. There is some evidence (Money & Brennan, 1969; Money & Primrose, 1969) to indicate that transsexuals, despite the intensity of their identification with the sex of their desired reassignment, also do not differ from members of their morphologic sex of birth in visual and narrative erotic responsivity.

Another line of evidence supporting a sex difference in erotic arousal pertains to dreams. The Kinsey studies showed that only 37% of women reported orgasm dreams, whereas 83% of men did. Further, in women, dreams culminating in orgasm occurred with greatest frequency between the ages of 30 and 50, but in men they occurred during the immediate postpubertal teens and the 20s. On the basis of anecdotal impression, a similar difference holds up in a comparison of homosexual women and men. Obviously a systematic study is needed.

Perceptual distractibility is another variable that shows a sex difference. More than the female, the male in his erotic pursuits is fairly promiscuously distractible from one love object to another, especially over a period of time, except perhaps when he is in the vortex of having just fallen desperately in love. The female is more steadfastly tied to a single romantic object or concept. In the act of copulation, by contrast, it is the male who has a singleness of purpose, perhaps oblivious even to noxious stimuli, and who is likely to be unable to continue if successfully distracted by a competing stimulus. The sex difference appears to hold widely in the animal kingdom (Beach, 1947, p. 264). Horsley Gantt (1949), director emeritus of the well known Pavlovian Laboratories at Johns Hopkins, wrote:

A marked difference between the male and female cat is that the female's interest in food is not inhibited by the sexual excitation of copulation, for she, as well as a bitch, will accept food not only after coitus, but even during the act! . . . The female is, however, much more strongly oriented about the off-spring than about the sexual act; she undergoes a great inhibition of conditional reflexes and of some unconditional reflexes postpartum, a fact which has been demonstrated several times in my laboratory with dogs [p. 37].

The male's ready arousal by perceiving a new erotic stimulus perhaps relates to his greater expenditure of energy in the service of sexual searching, pursuit, and consummation. Expenditure extends also to adventurous exploratory roaming, to assertiveness and aggression, and to the defense of territorial rights.

Once again, there is no systematic evidence concerning homosexuals and their ratings on these variables of distractibility and energy expenditure. Students of homosexuality would probably agree, however, that male and female homosexuals are not different from ordinary males and females regarding distractibility. In energy expenditure, there is quite possibly a difference with regard to aggression and territorial rights, insofar as certain rather languid, strongly female-identifying homosexual males are persecuted by their age-mates in childhood because they do not fight for a position in the boyhood pecking order. The relationship of this nonbelligerency to the nervous system is still conjectural.

The sense of smell (see reviews by Money, 1960, 1963a) is characterized by a rather remarkable sex difference which is hormone controlled. Smell acuity, at least for some compounds appears to be regulated by estrogen level. Women generally have greater acuity than men. There may be some exceptions but acuity is at its peak for most women when they are not in their progestin (menstruating) phase of the menstrual cycle. Their acuity is lost after ovariectomy, but regained if they are given estrogen. In male rats, estradiol (an estrogen) will suppress acuity completely. Castration will lessen, but not abolish, an adult male rat's capacity to distinguish the estrous female from the diestrous; male juveniles have a little of this discriminatory ability. Surgical removal of the pituitary gland suppresses ovarian function and brings about loss of the sense of smell. There is a rare clinical syndrome (Kallman's syndrome), more frequent in males than females, in which congenital absence of the sense of smell is a pathognomonic sign, along with hypogonadism and sterility.

Whether all these data on the sense of smell have any bearing on homosexuality is not known. One possibility that might warrant further investigation pertains to neonatal life and early childhood. Perhaps human sex differences in the sense of smell are already in evidence at the age when, in some lower mammals, smell is the mechanism for bonding the mother-child relationship. One might conjecture that a neutral impairment in the baby's sense of smell or in the mother's stimulus (too much or too little, or the wrong odor), or even in the father's stimulus, will perhaps lead to an error in psychosexual differentiation. The extraordinary potency of odors in regulating body function in mammals was not known until Parkes and Bruce (1961) published their findings. They showed that an odor may be a pheromone (a long-distance exciter) for mammals as well as insects. They demonstrated that if a newly mated female mouse was exposed to the smell of an alien stud male, for an appropriate number of hours, or even to the box in which he had been caged, then she would fail to implant the eggs, would fail even to have the expected pseudopregnancy, but would return to estrus as though coitus had not occurred.

The effect of odor was further demonstrated; crowding female mice together in small groups induced pseudopregnancies and, in large groups anestrus. These effects could be prevented by excision of the olfactory bulbs or by individual housing. Overcrowding of both sexes together is known to produce a range of social pathologies in rats (Calhoun, 1962), including destructive attack on subordinates, starvation of subordinates, male cannibalism of the young, and male homosexuality. Moreover, overcrowding of female mice during pregnancy was shown (Keeley, 1962) to have an adverse effect on the offspring as manifested in behavioral development. The mechanism of transmission is presumably hormonal.

Clearly, pheromonal and density research are pertinent for further research on the genesis of psychosexual differentiation. The sex-difference effect of vocal sound in the neonatal and early childhood period might also be looked into, and the sense of touch as experienced in rocking, patting, stroking, cuddling, clinging, and nestling.

Brain and dimorphism of gender identity

The differentiation of one gender identity instead of the other may follow a paradigm not unlike that of the development of the internal sexual morphology (Money, 1968b). Two separate anatomic systems exist, the Wolffian and the Muellerian, both of which are intact early in embryonic development. Under hormonal influence, one system proliferates at a critical point in development into the functional organs of one sex, and the other regresses to a vestigial state. The correct balance is not always maintained, as in the sexual ambiguity of hermaphroditism where both systems may appear in an incomplete form. An analogous ambiguity in psychosexual differentiation might result in sexual deviations such as homosexuality, transvestism, or more rarely, transsexualism.

In the world of a growing child, both male and female systems of behavior exist as models, carrying a positive or negative valence according to the sex of the child's rearing. Whatever may be the possible unlearned assistance from constitutional sources, the child's psychosexual identity is not written, unlearned, in the genetic code, the hormonal system or the nervous system at birth. The child becomes conditioned to adhere to the positive model, that is, the one congruous with his rearing which, in the normal course of events, is congruous with his anatomy. There are some children who very early encounter difficulty with the positive model and a correct gender identity. The signs may be unmistakably manifested as young as the age of 3. For most children, however, positive and negative are clearly distinguishable. The model belonging to the other sex takes on a negative valence and is a constant reminder of how *not* to act. With its negative valence this opposite-sex model does exist in the brain, however, as a neurocognitional entity. For those individuals destined to be heterosexual and incapable of homosexual acts, under any circumstances, the negative valence will be incapable of lifting. For other individuals the negative valence may never become properly established. These are the individuals who will trace their homosexuality as far back as they can remember. For yet other individuals, the negative valence may be unstable so that the opposite-sex model of gender identity may, under special circumstances, become operational. These special circumstances may be developmental or in response to a traumatic emotional event. They may be the product of brain pathology: homosexuality or other forms of sexual pathology, quite incongruous with the earlier life history, may appear in cases of deteriorative or senile brain disease. There could conceivably, if one interpolates from brain stimulation experiments on animals, be special experimental circumstances which would induce homosexuality in human beings. The special circumstances which render operational the opposite-sex model are, for certain individuals social—though the model's operation is only in fragmented form. These are the circumstances in which some people are able to temporize with homosexuality while heterosexually deprived, or chiefly for purposes of financial gain.

Investigation of the origin and regulation of the activating and inhibiting mechanisms in the hypothalamus and elsewhere in the human brain still remains to be undertaken. In the future, it may be found that a theory of neural inhibition can be extended to include a faulty postnatal inhibitory mechanism in homosexuals which allows opposite-sex behavior patterns, including those built up through social learning, to be activated. The activation of dormant, sexually dimorphic behavior was demonstrated experimentally in the rat by Fisher (1966). Male sexual behavior was elicited from either male or female animals. Fisher injected sodium testosterone sulfate directly through a microcanula implanted in the midlateral preoptic region of the hypothalamus. Similar implants of testosterone in the medial preoptic region produced maternal-like behavior. Again, the effect was obtained in either male or female animals.

The operational existence of the two sex models, or rather the patient's version of them, is nicely evident in some cases of transsexual homosexualism. In what are probably only rare cases, the two models may be activated in alternating episodes of short duration. Each is identified by a separate name, as in one case, Marylou and Robert. In this case, Marylou went into a kind of staring trance when she was questioned about Robert's sex-reassignment operation, which was taboo knowledge for her. From the trance Robert emerged, with his different, deep-pitched speaking voice and his more down-to-earth ways. Marylou was coy and demure. She was gradually taking over. Robert believed that she would soon displace him completely.

The trancelike phenomenon ushering in an alternation of personality is not common among transsexuals who, by the very nature of their condition, usually stabilize as fulltime members of their reassigned sex. Nontranssexual transvestite homosexuals more frequently alternate their egos, episodically, along with their clothes. One such patient would take on his alternate personality, Pattie, in a kind of metamorphosis from Jack to Pattie as he sat before the mirror while dressing and applying makeup.

A great many transsexual homosexuals claim that they have always had only one personality, namely, the feminine one for as long as they can remember. Usually there is no one to dispute them—no one who observed them sufficiently closely over the years to be able to detect and report a personality change. Occasionally, one has the chance to follow a transsexual over the years. There was one patient in whom the feminine personality appeared only episodically at first, and not when the patient was dressed in boys' clothes which was, by family edict, most of the time. Over a period of 3 years, Tommy, also known as Kelvin, phased out as Kathryn, was then old enough to be independent of family, and established herself on a full-time basis, completely sure that she would eventually get surgically transformed. Kathryn had a different speaking voice than Tommy, more high-pitched and with a minimal lisp. She was also different in demeanor, being more languid and tender in nature.

There are reports in the literature to indicate that, occasionally, a change of personality toward transvestism may have its onset in conjunction with the development of temporal lobe seizures (Epstein, 1961). In one case, the change was reversed by a temporal lobectomy which got rid of both the seizures and the transvestism.

This case is a reminder that in the absence of seizures, one does not yet know anything of the neurophysiology of the phenomenon of multiple personality or dissociation, or of the emergence of an alternate personality, as in transsexualism, transvestism, or other manifestations of homosexuality. It is there, however, in the developmental neurophysiology and neuropsychology of behavior that the answer will one day be found to lie.

The male transsexual, being the extreme form of homosexual that he is, is able to live, work, think and make love as a woman. His female personality is, in part, his developmental conception of those traits and behavior patterns which typically constitute femininity. It is a conception that excludes some traits, such as an urge to fondle the newborn, and a propensity to erotic arousal less by visual and narrative stimuli than by touch, because those traits are intrinsic to feminine experience unfamiliar to him. The male transsexual conforms to the conception of femininity he has assimilated, however, until by most standards, his personality—*her* personality—is female and is completely dissociated from male identity. There is no more extraordinary example of what homosexuality means and of how the human organism can react.

NOTES

1. Exactly the same statements may be made of the heterosexual.
2. A special case might be made for women with the congenital adrenogenital syndrome who, in the era before cortisone therapy, reached adulthood heavily masculinized by their own adrenal androgens. Among a group of 23 such women, 10 could report having dreamed bisexually, and 4 of the 10 had had bisexual experience (Ehrhardt, Evers, & Money, 1968). These women were all markedly masculinized before birth, however, as well as subsequently, so the possible relationship between male hormone and masculine (homosexual) behavior cannot be attributed to a pubertal and adult hormonal effect per se.
3. Two other steroids have the same antiandrogenic and erotictranquilizing effect without inducing breast growth. They are cyproterone acetate and medroxyprogesterone acetate. Both have been used, in recent therapeutic investigations, for the successful regulation of criminal sexual behavior in sex-offender disorders (Laschet, 1969; Money, 1968a, 1970b).
4. There is some conversely corroborative evidence from the hormonally virilized women referred to in Footnote 2. These women reported a ready arousal from visual and narrative, as well as tactile stimulation (Ehrhardt, Evers, & Money, 1968).

REFERENCES

Bartalos, M., & Baramki, T. A. *Medical cytogenetics.* Baltimore: Williams and Wilkins, 1967.
Beach, F.A. A review of physiological and psychological studies of sexual behavior in mammals. *Physiological Reviews*, 1947, **27**, 240-307.
Bleuler, M., & Wiedemann, H. R. Chromosomengeschlecht und Psychosexualitact. *Archiv für Psychiatrie und Zietschrift Neurologie*, 1956, **195**, 14-19.
Blumer, D. Transsexualism, sexual dysfunction and temporal lobe disorder. In R. Green & J. Money (Eds.), *Transsexualism and sex reassignment.* Baltimore: John Hopkins Press, 1969.
Bruins, J. W., van Bolhuis, J., Bijlsma, J. B., & Nhenhuis, L. E. Discordant mongolism in monozygotic twins? *Genetics Today. Proceedings of the XI International Congress of Genetics, The Hague, Netherlands.* Vol. 1. New York: Macmillan, 1963. (Abstract 16.26)
Calhoun, J. B. Population density and social pathology. *Scientific American*, 1962, **206**, 139-148.
Darke, R. A. Heredity as an etiological factor in homosexuality. *Journal of Nervous and Mental Disease*, 1948, **107**, 251-268.
Doerner, G. Tierexperimentelle Untersuchungen zur Frage einer hormonellen Pathogenese der Homosexualitact. (Animal experimental studies on the question of a hormonal pathogenesis of homosexuality.) *Acta Biologica et Medica Germanica*, 1967, **19**, 569-584.
Ehrhardt, A. A. Zur Wirkung foetaler Hormone auf Intelligenz und gescgkecgtssoezifisches Verhalten. (The effect of fetal hormones on intelligence and gender identity.) Inaugural-Dissertation zur Erlangung des Doktorgrades der Philosophischen Fakultact der Universitact Duesseldorf, Duesseldorf, West Germany, 1969.
Ehrhardt, A. A., Epstein, R., & Money, J. Fetal androgens and female gender identity in the early-treated adrenogenital syndrome. *Johns Hopkins Medical Journal*, 1968, **122**, 160-167.
Ehrhardt, A. A., Evers, K., & Money, J. Influence of androgen and some aspects of sexually dimorphic behavior in women with the late-treated adrenogenital syndrome. *Johns Hopkins Medical Journal*, 1968, **123**, 115-122.
Ehrhardt, A. A., & Money, J. Progestin-induced hermaphroditism: IQ and psychosexual identity in a study of ten girls. *The Journal of Sex Research*, 1967, **3**, 83-100.
Epstein, A. Relationship of fetishism and transvestism to brain and particularly to temporal lobe dysfunction. *Journal of Nervous and Mental Disease*, 1961, **133**, 247-254.
Epstein, A. Disordered human sexual behavior associated with temporal lobe dysfunction. *Medical Aspects of Human Sexuality*, 1969, **3**, 62-68.
Everitt, B. F., & Herbert, J. Adrenal glands and sexual receptivity in female rhesus monkeys. *Nature*, 1969, **222**, 1065-1066.
Federman, D. D. *Abnormal sexual development, a genetic and endocrine approach to differential diagnosis.* Philadelphia: W. B. Saunders, 1967.
Ferguson-Smith, M. A. Chromosomes and human disease. In A. G. Steinberg (Ed.), *Medical genetics.* New York: Grune & Stratton, 1961.
Fisher, A. Chemical and electrical stimulation of the brain in the male rat. In R. A. Gorski & R. E. Whalen (Eds.), *Brain and behavior.* Vol. 3 *The brain and gonadal function.* Berkeley: University of California Press, 1966.
Gantt, W. H. Psychosexuality in animals. In P. H. Hoch & J. Zubin (Eds.), *Psychosexual development in health and disease.* New York: Grune & Stratton, 1949.
Gardner, L. I. (Ed.) *Endocrine and genetic diseases of childhood.* Philadelphia: W. R. Saunders, 1969.
Gorski, R. A. Gonadal hormones and the perinatal development of neuroendocrine function. In L. Martini & V. F. Ganong (Eds.), *Frontiers of neuroendocrinology.* New York: Oxford University Press, 1971, in press.
Hambert, G., & Frey, T. S. The electroencephalogram in the Klinefelter syndrome. *Acta Psychiatrica Scandinavica*, 1964, **40**, 28-36.
Harris, G. W. Sex hormones, brain development and brain function. *Endocrinology*, 1964, **75**, 627-648.
Herbert, J. Hormones and reproductive behavior in rhesus and talapoin monkeys. *Journal of Reproduction and Fertility*, 1970 (Suppl. 11), 119-140.
Hirschhorn, K., & Cooper, H. L. Chromosomal aberrations in human disease. *The American Journal of Medicine*, 1961, **31**, 442-470.
Jensch, K. Zur Genealogie der Homosexualitact. *Archiv für Psychiatrie und Nervenkrankheiten*, 1941, **112**, 527-540. (a)
Jensch, K. Weiterer Beitrag zur Genealogie der Homosexualität. *Archiv für Psychiatrie und Nervenkrankheiten*, 1941, **112**, 679-696. (b)
Jost, A. The role of the fetal hormones in prenatal development. *Harvey Lectures*, Series 55, 1961, 201-226.
Kallman, F. J. Comparative twin study on the genetic aspects of male homosexuality. *Journal of Nervous and Mental Disease*, 1952, **115**, 283-298.
Keeley, K. Prenatal influence on behavior of offspring of crowded mice. *Science*, 1962, **135**, 44-45.
Kinsey, A. C., Pomeroy, W. B., Martin, C. F., & Gebhard, P. H. *Sexual behavior in the human female.* Philadelphia: W. B. Saunders, 1953.
Lang, T. Studies on the genetic determination of homosexuality. *Journal of Nervous and Mental Disease* 1940, **92**, 55-64.
Laschet, U. Die Anwendbarkeit von Antiandrogen in der Humanmedizin. *Saarlaendisches Aerzteblatt*, 7, July, 1969.
Lejeune, J., Lafourcade, J., Schärer, K., de Wolff, E., Salmon, C., Haines, M., & Turpin, R. Monozygotisme hétérocaryote: jumeau normal et jumeau trisomique 21. *Comptes Rendus de l'Académie des Sciences*, 1962, **254**, 4404-4406.
Martensen-Larsen, O. The family constellation and homosexualism. *Acta Genetica et Statistica Medica*, 1957, **7**, 445-446.
Migeon, C. J., Rivarola, M. A., & Forest, M. G. Studies of androgens in male transexual subjects; effects of estrogen therapy. In R. Green & J. Money (Eds.), *Transsexualism and sex reassignment.* Baltimore: Johns Hopkins Press, 1969.
Money, J. Hermaphroditism, gender and precocity in hyperadrenocorticism: Psychologic findings. *Bulletin of The Johns Hopkins Hospital*, 1955, **96**, 207-226.
Money, J. Components of eroticism in man: Cognitional rehearsals. In J. Wortis (Ed.), *Recent advances in biological psychiatry.* New York: Grune & Stratton, 1960.
Money, J. Components of eroticism in man. I: The hormones in relation to sexual morphology and sexual desire. *The Journal of Nervous and Mental Disease*, 1964, **132**, 239-248.
Money, J. Cytogenetics and psychosexual incongruities, with a note on space-form blindness. *American Journal of Psychiatry*, 1963, **119**, 820, 827.(a)
Money, J. Developmental differentiation of femininity and masculinity compared. In S. M. Farber & R. H. L. Wilson (Eds.), *Man and civilization.* New York: McGraw-Hill, 1963. (b)
Money, J. Discussion. In R. P. Michael (Ed.), *Endocrinology and human behavior.* London: Oxford University Press, 1968. (a)
Money, J., *Sex errors of the body.* Baltimore: Johns Hopkins Press, 1968. (b)
Money, J. Psychologic approach to psychosexual misidentity with elective mutism: Sex reassignment in two cases of hyperadrenocortical hermaphroditism. *Clinical Pediatrics*, 1968, **7**, 331-339. (c)
Money, J. Matched pairs of hermaphrodites: Behavioral biology of sexual differentiation from chromosomes to gender identity. *Engineering and Science* (California Institute of Technology), 1970, **33**, 34-39. (a)
Money, J. Use of an androgen-depleting hormone in the treatment of male sex offenders. *Journal of Sex Research*, 1970, **6**(3), in press. (b)

Money, J., & Brennan, J. G. Sexual dimorphism in the psychology of female transsexuals. In R. Green & J. Money (Eds.), *Transsexualism and sex reassignment.* Baltimore: Johns Hopkins Press, 1969. Money, J., & Ehrhardt, A. A. Prenatal hormonal exposure: Possible effects on behavior in man. In R. P. Michael (Ed.), *Endocrinology and human behavior.* London: Oxford University Press, 1968.

Money, J., Ehrhardt, A. A., & Masica, D. N. Fetal feminization induced by androgen insensitivity in the testicular feminizing syndrome: Effect on marriage and maternalism. *The Johns Hopkins Medical Journal,* 1968, 123, 105-114.

Money, J., Gaskin, R. J., & Hull, H. Impulse, aggression and sexuality in the XYY syndrome. *St. John's Law Review,* 1970, 44, 220-235.

Money, J., Hampson, J. G., & Hampson, J. L. Hermaphroditism: Recommendations concerning assignment of sex, change of sex, and psychologic management. *Bulletin of The Johns Hopkins Hospital,* 1955, 97, 284-300.

Money, J., Hampson, J. G., & Hampson, J. L. Imprinting and the establishment of gender role. *Archives of Neurology and Psychiatry,* 1957, 77, 333-336.

Money, J., & Mittenthal, S. Lack of personality pathology in Turner's syndrome: Relation to cytogenetics, hormones and physique. *Behavior Genetics,* 1970, 1, 43-56.

Money, J., & Pollitt, E. Cytogenetic and psychosexual ambiguity: Klinefelter's syndrome and transvestism compared. *Archives of General Psychiatry,* 1964, 11, 589-595.

Money, J., & Primrose, C. Sexual dimorphism and dissociation in the psychology of male transsexuals. In R. Green & J. Money (Eds.), *Transsexualism and sex reassignment.* Baltimore: Johns Hopkins Press, 1969.

Moore, K. L. (Ed.) *The sex chromatin.* Philadelphia: W. B. Saunders, 1966.

Neumann, F., & Elger, W. Physiological and psychical intersexuality of male rats by early treatment with an antiandrogenic agent (1,2α-methylene-6-chloro-Δ"-hydroxyprogesterone acetate). *Acta Endocrinologica* 1965 (Supple. 100), 174.

Neumann, F., & Elger, W. Permanent changes in gonadal function and sexual behavior as a result of early feminization of male rats by treatment with an antiandrogenic steroid. *Endokrinologie* 1966, 50, 209, 225.

Neumann, F., Steinbeck, H., & Hahn, J. D. In *Hormones and brain differentiation.* Oxford: Pergamon, in press.

Pare, C. M. B. Homosexuality and chromosomal sex. *Journal of Psychosomatic Research,* 1956, 1, 247-251.

Parkes, A. S., & Bruce, H. M. Olfactory stimuli in mammalian reproduction: Odor excites neurohumoral responses affecting oestrus, pseudopregnancy, and pregnancy in the mouse. *Science,* 1961, 134, 1049-1054.

Pritchard, M. Homosexuality and genetic sex. *Journal of Mental Science,* 1962, 108, 616-623.

Raboch, J., & Nedoma, K. Sex chromatin and sexual behavior. A study of 36 men with female nuclear pattern and of 194 homosexuals. *Psychosomatic Medicine,* 1958, 20, 55-59.

Raiti, S., & Davis, W. T. The principles and application of radioimmunoassay with special reference to the gonadotropins. *Obstetrical and Gynecological Survey,* 1969, 24, 289-310.

Raiti, S., Johanson, A., Light, C., Migeon, C. J., & Blizzard, R. M. Measurement of immunologically reactive follicle-stimulating hormone in serum of normal male children and adults. *Metabolism,* 1969, 18, 234-240.

Raiti, S., Light, C., & Blizzard, R. M. Urinary follicle-stimulating hormone excretion in boys and adult males as measured by radioimmunoassay. *Journal of Clinical Endocrinology and Metabolism,* 1969, 29, 440-445.

Ross, G. T., Tjio, J. H., & Lipsett, M. B. Cytogenetic studies of presumptive monozygotic twin girls discordant for gonadal dysgenesis. *Journal of Clinical Endocrinology and Metabolism,* 1969, 29, 440-445.

Russell, A., Moschos, A., Butler, L. J., & Abraham, J. M. Gonadal dysgenesis and its unilateral variant with testis in monozygous twins: Related to discordance in sex chromosomal status. *Journal of Clinical Endocrinology and Metabolism* 1966, 26, 1282-1292.

Schmidt, G., & Sigusch, V. Psychosexuelle Stimulation durch Filme: Geschlechtsspezifische Unterschiede. (Psychosexual stimulation with movies: Sex specific differences.) In *Tendenzen der Sexualforschung.* Stuttgart: Ferdinand Enke, 1970, in press.

Slater, E. The sibs and children of homosexuals. In D. R. Smith & W. A. Davidson (Eds.), *Symposium on nuclear sex.* New York: Interscience Publishers, 1958.

Slater, E. Birth order and maternal age of homosexuals. *Lancet* 1962, 1, 69-71.

Sohval, A. R. Recent progress in human chromosome analysis and its relation to the sex chromatin. *American Journal of Medicine,* 1961, 31, 397-441.

Turpin, R., Lejeune, J., Lafourcade, J., Chigot, P., & Salmon, C. Présomption de monozygotisme en dépit d'un dimorphisme sexuel: sujet masculin XY et sujet neutro, Haplo X. *Comptes Rendus de l'Acad*émie des Sciences, 1961, 252, 2945-2946.

Whalen, R. E. Differentiation of the neural mechanisms which control gonadotropin secretion and sexual behavior. In M. Diamond (Ed.), *Perspectives in reproduction and sexual behavior.* Bloomington: Indiana University Press, 1968.

Wilkins, L. *The diagnosis and treatment of endocrine disorders in childhood and adolescence.* (3rd ed.) Springfield, Ill.: Charles C Thomas, 1965.

2 *Sex differences in the incidence of neonatal abnormalities and abnormal performance in early childhood*

Judith E. Singer
Milton Westphal
Kenneth R. Niswander

Reprinted from Judith E. Singer, Milton Westphal, and Kenneth R. Niswander, "Sex Differences in the Incidence of Neonatal Abnormalities and Abnormal Performance in Early Childhood," Child Development, 39, 1968, pp. 103-122. ©1968 by the Society for Research in Child Development, Inc. This is a report from the Collaborative Study of Cerebral Palsy. The Collaborative Study of Cerebral Palsy, Mental Retardation and Other Neurological and Sensory Disorders of Infancy and Childhood is supported by the National Institute of Neurological Diseases and Blindness. The following institutions participate: Boston Lying-in Hospital; Brown University; Charity Hospital, New Orleans; Children's Hospital of Buffalo; Children's Hospital of Philadelphia; Children's Medical Center, Boston; Columbia University; Johns Hopkins University; University of Minnesota; Medical College of Virginia; New York Medical College; Pennsylvania Hospital; University of Oregon; University of Tennessee; Yale University; and the Perinatal Research Branch, NINDB. This study was supported by grant NB-02404 from the National Institutes of Health and by similar grants to the other participating institutions. Milton Westphal is presently at Medical College of South Carolina, Judith E. Singer's address: Child Development Program, Buffalo's Children's Hospital, 219 Bryant Street, Buffalo, New York 14222.

Introduction

Many clearcut, significant sex differences have been described in human disease, development, and behavior. The majority of these differences show the male to be at a disadvantage. More males are conceived than females (Rhodes, 1965; Shettles, 1961; Szilard, 1960), but this preponderance is decreased by the higher abortion and stillborn rates for males (Baumgartner, Pessin, Wegman, & Parker, 1950; Childs, 1963; Rhodes, 1965). In the neonatal period males have more morbidity and a higher mortality rate than females (Baumgartner et al., 1950; Childs, 1963). Surviving males continue to be at a disadvantage. They are more susceptible to many diseases (Childs, Cantolino, & Dyke, 1962; Kravitz, 1965; Gexon, Hatch, Rycheck, & Rogers, 1963), and they grow and mature physically more slowly than females (Bayer & Bayley, 1963; Watson & Lower, 1951 p. 171). Learning and behavior disorders are more frequent among males than females (Bentzen, 1963), and a higher percentage of males are mentally defective (Everhart, 1960; Sinks & Powell, 1965). In performance, measured by the IQ and school achievement, males are at a disadvantage (Ames & Ilg, 1964; Bayne & Clark 1959; Darley & Winitz, 1961; Honzik, 1963; Jones, Gross, & VanWhy, 1960; Parsley, 1964; Sinks & Powell, 1965; Wisenthal, 1965).

Data from the Collaborative Study of Cerebral Palsy allow detailed investigation of sex differences. This study is being conducted at 13 collaborating institutions across the United States and includes a wealth of data on prenatal, perinatal, and neonatal variables and subsequent development and performance of participating patients. This paper reports an analysis of sex differences of Study patients in physical, neurological, and pyschological development from birth to 4 years.

Method

SUBJECTS

Data were available on 15,000 patients in the first year of life. Data on later development on this population were not yet available, so performance at 3 and 4 years of age was obtained for a small number of cases at individual participating institutions. The Collaborative Study population is 55 percent Negro and has over 95 per cent ward patients. A more detailed picture of the Collaborative Study population and structure has been described elsewhere (Berendes, 1966).

PROCEDURE

The data analyzed consisted of:

1. Ratings of 187 possible neonatal abnormalities listed on a neonatal summary evaluation filled out by a Study pediatrician.

2. Ratings of mental, fine-motor, gross-motor, and social-emotional development plus the overall summary from the 8-month psychological examination. These ratings are made by a Study psychologist trained in the use of a special project research form of the Bayley Scales of Infant Development.

3. Overall evaluation on the 12-month neurologic examination made by a Study pediatric neurologist or pediatrician trained in infant neurology.

4. Overall summary of the first year of life made by a Study pediatric neurologist or pediatrician trained in infant neurology.

5. Global evaluation and sum of subscale ratings from the 36-month speech-and-hearing examination. This examination was specifically designed for project use and is administered and scored by a specially trained speech-and-hearing examiner.

6. Global evaluation, IQ, and rating of mental, fine-motor, gross-motor, concept formation, and behavioral development on the 48-month psychological examination. This examination is administered and scored by a Study psychologist trained in the use of a special project research examination composed of such standard tests as the Stanford Binet Intelligence Scale, the Graham Blocks Concept Formation Test, and several motor coordination tests.

On all of these examinations, ratings may be "normal," "suspect," or "abnormal." Standards or guidelines, derived from present data, were used for these ratings with some examiner subjectivity permitted. Reliability studies have shown high interinstitution and interexaminer reliability. For convenience in description and statistical analyses, examiners' ratings of "suspect" and "abnormal" were combined into a single "abnormal" category and compared with ratings of "normal." The significance of abnormal versus normal findings in males and females was determined by the χ^2 technique.

Results

Sex differences in performance of 15,000 children in the first year of life are shown in Table 1. On the 8-month examination, significant sex differences were found on all scales—mental, fine-motor, gross-motor, social-emotional, and overall summary. Males had significantly poorer scores on all scales except the social-emotional. On the 12-month neurological examination, males had significantly more abnormal ratings than did females ($p < .01$), and the sex difference in the incidence of abnormalities listed in the

TABLE 1   *Performance in First Year of Life (N = 15,000)*

	Per cent abnormal		
Performance measures	Male	Female	χ^2
8-month mental	7.9	6.8	9.11*
8-month fine motor	15.0	11.0	64.54**
8-month gross motor	15.7	12.7	33.98**
8-month social emotional	7.7	9.4	16.81**
8-month final diagnosis	15.5	12.5	26.25**
12-month neurological	8.9	7.8	8.17*
First year summary	65.0	26.6	39.8**

* $p < .01$.
** $p < .001$.

TABLE 2   *Three-Year Speech and Hearing (N = 100)*

	Per cent abnormal		
Scale	Male	Female	χ^2
Global rating	23.4	4.8	4.58*
Sum of subscale ratings	12.6	6.6	3.72

* $p < .05$.

TABLE 3   *Four-Year Psychological Examination—Buffalo Population (N = 71)*

	Per cent abnormal		
Scale	Male	Female	χ^2
Mental (IQ 80)	7.1	0	1.05
Fine motor	24.1	4.7	4.20*
Gross motor	21.4	2.3	4.82*
Concept formation	17.8	0	5.61*
Behavior	44.8	7.1	11.88**
Global	37.9	2.3	13.01***

* $p < .05$.
** $p < .01$.
*** $p < .001$.

TABLE 4   *Four-Year Psychological Examination—Buffalo Population (N = 71)*

	Mean		
Subtest	Male	Female	t Value[a]
Stanford-Binet IQ	106.5	110.9	1.17
Graham blocks	33.9	38.6	2.60**
Wallen pegboard	21.0	18.4	1.84*
Bead stringing	9.1	10.1	1.61
Maze drawing	1.9	1.1	2.23*
Copy forms	1.8	2.1	2.15*
Line-walk	6.4	8.1	2.10*
Ball catch	2.1	2.4	1.40
Hopping	1.3	2.6	2.97**

[a] One-tailed.
* $p < .05$.
** $p < .01$.

TABLE 5   *Four-Year Psychological Examination—Buffalo, Philadelphia, and Boston Populations (N = 471)*

	Per cent abnormal		
Scale	Male	Female	χ^2
Total scale	18	12	12.89**
Mental	14	15	.00
Fine motor	31	19	7.88*
Gross motor	9	7	.5
Concept formation	11	6	3.33
Behavior	18	15	.5
Global	23	15	.01

* $p < 01$.
** $p < 001$.

summary of the first year of life was significant at the .001 level. Of 248 possible abnormalities, 65 per cent were found to have a higher incidence among males whereas only 26.6 per cent had a higher incidence among females.

Analyses of ratings from the 36-month speech-and-learning examination on a sample of one hundred children in the Buffalo population are shown in Table 2. Excluded from the sample were three males and one female who spoke foreign languages. Global scores were not obtained for six males and two females who did not give adequate cooperation. Among the remaining 88 children, males had significantly more abnormal global ratings than did females ($p < .05$). On the subscales ratings, 12.6 per cent of the males and 6.6 per cent of the females were given abnormal ratings, but this difference was not statistically significant.

The data on the 48-month psychological examination were analyzed in two parts. First, 71 4-year examinations done at the Buffalo project center were analyzed for sex differences in the individual test items, the subscale ratings, and the global evaluation. Examination of 29 males and 42 females in the Buffalo sample showed significant sex differences on all subscales, with males performing less well than females (See Table 3). To determine whether performance on the individual test items showed these same differences, means were obtained for male and female performance on each test on the 4-year examination battery. As shown in Table 4, females did better than males on all scales. Sex differences in IQ on the Stanford Binet were not significant, though the mean IQ for females (110.9) was higher than for males (106.5). On the other eight subtests, the sex differences were statistically significant on six scales ($p < .05$) and approached significance on the other two ($p < .06$ and $< .07$). Thus, the Buffalo sample of 71 4-year examinations showed clear, consistent, and significant sex differences.

In order to test whether the findings in the Buffalo population of private patients would be substantiated in (a) a larger population and (b) different project populations, data supplied on 260 cases from the Philadelphia project center and 100 cases from the Boston project center were analyzed. The sex differences were not as large in the other populations as in Buffalo but they were still apparent. The combined samples showed a higher incidence of abnormality among males than among females on all scales except the mental scale as shown in Table 5. However, the difference was statistically significant only for the fine-motor scale. Of the 15 subscale ratings, 5 from each of the three institutions, 11 showed a higher incidence of abnormalities for males. When these 15 subscales ratings were totalled, it was found that 18 per cent of all ratings given to males and 12 per cent of all ratings given to females were abnormal ($p < .001$).

The tendency for males to have more abnormal ratings was present at all institutions, but the degree of sex differences was most marked in the Buffalo population. It is interesting to note that the higher the mean IQ of the population the greater the sex difference. Table 6 shows that the Buffalo population had the highest mean IQ and the greatest sex difference, while the Philadelphia population had the lowest mean IQ and the smallest sex difference.

Thus, on the performance measures significant sex differences (showing males to have poorer performance) were found on the 8-month, 12-month, 36-month, and 48-month examinations and the 1-year summary.

Awareness of these sex differences leads to a search for cause. Although inherent, environmental, and test standardization variables may, at least in part, contribute to sex differences in performance, our data do not allow analysis of their effect. Our data do, however, allow analysis of sex differences in neonatal variables.

Pasamanick's Theory of the continuum of reproductive casualty (Pasamanick & Knoblock, 1960) suggests that if large sex differences are present in perinatal experience, later sex differences in performance could be attributed to either pre- or perinatal experience. Our data show clear and significant sex differences in perinatal experience. Condition at birth, as measured by the Apgar rating (Apgar, 1953), shows a significant sex difference. Males had significantly more low (< 6) Apgar scores than did females ($p < .001$). Out of 187 abnormalities listed on the Collaborative Study neonatal summary form, 71.8 per cent occurred predominantly among males, 25.1 percent among females and 3.1 per cent had equal sex distribution. This sex difference was statistically significant at the .001 level as shown in Table 7. Thus, males have more abnormalities in the neonatal than do females.

Previous studies (Berendes, 1964; Robinson & Robinson, 1965; Wiener, Rider, Oppel, Fischer, & Harper, 1965) have shown that birthweight has a major effect both on neonatal condition and future performance. Our data showed a significant relation between sex and birthweight, the males being heavier, but no relation between sex and gestational interval. It is interesting to note that although males have a birthweight advantage they still have more abnormalities and poorer performance. Table 8 shows that sex differences in performance in the first year of life remain when birthweight is controlled. Note that the differences are most marked for birthweight over 2,500 grams and decrease somewhat in the 2,000-2,500 gram group.

TABLE 6   Four-Year Psychological Examination (N = 471)

Locations	Per cent abnormal		Difference (Male-Female)	Mean IQ
	Ratings across all scales			
	Male	Female		
Buffalo	18.1	4.4	13.9	109.7
Boston	10.5	7.5	3.0	107.5
Philadelphia	18.8	17.9	.9	89.3

TABLE 7   Neonatal Condition (N = 15,000)

Measures	Per cent abnormal		χ^2
	Male	Female	
Apgar < 6	4.4	3.5	14.75*
Neonatal summary[a]	71.1	25.1	41.0*

[a]Per cent abnormalities predominantly male versus predominantly female.
* $p < .001$

TABLE 8   Significance Levels for χ^2 Values for Sex Differences by Birthweight (N = 15,000)

Measures	Birthweight			
	2,001 grams	2,001-2,500 grams	2,501 grams +	Total
Apgar at 5 minutes	n.s.	n.s.	***	***
12-month neurological	*	n.s.	**	**
8-month final diagnosis	**	**	***	***
8-month mental	**	n.s.	***	**
8-month fine motor	*	***	***	***
8-month gross motor	**	***	***	***
8-month social emotional	n.s.	n.s.	***	***

NOTE.—Sex × Birthweight: $\chi^2 = 40 26$, $p < .001$. Sex × Gestation: $\chi^2 = .05$.

Discussion

The sex differences described in this report have implications for test standardization, for the use of controls in longitudinal studies of development, and for the understanding of mechanisms of reproductive casualty. First the existence of sex differences in performance indicates a need for test standardization by sex; male performance should not be evaluated by the same standards as female performance. Second, studies of relation between perinatal distress and later development must include controls for sex in order to balance the biasing effect of overselection of males in the distressed group. Third, the etiologic mechanisms of these sex differences, once understood, may prove to have general application to the genesis of poor performance.

Fundamentally, sex differences must have their origin in the genetic code. The increased incidence of abnormal performance among males may: (*a*) result directly from genetic difference, (*b*) result from obstetric problems which have a genetic cause, (*c*) result from neonatal distress of primary or secondary genetic origin, (*d*) result from destructive maternal attitudes arising out of a stressing perinatal experience.

Details of the mechanisms behind sex differences are obscure. Possibilities include: (*a*) the presence of deleterious genetic material on the Y chromosome, (*b*) the relative lack in the male of beneficial genetic material on the X chromosome, and (*c*) immunologic incompatibility between the male fetus and his female mother.

Knowledge of the activity of genetic material on the Y chromosome is very limited, but the X chromosome has been shown to have loci controlling the production of certain fractions of gamma globulin and some enzymes (Davidson, 1964; Gitlin, Gross, & Janeway, 1959). According to the Lyon Theory (Davidson, 1964), one X chromosome in each cell becomes pycnotic in early gestation forming a Barr body. The genes on the pycnotic chromosome are partially functional or nonfunctional in the resulting cell line. Since the X chromosome lost in each cell line is apparently chosen at random, the female organism has active genetic material from both maternal and paternal X chromosomes while the male organism has chromatin from only the maternal X. Thus the female has a greater opportunity to benefit from a variety of genetic material.

Renkonnen (Renkonnen & Makela, 1962) has suggested that certain females may become sensitized to male fetuses. He supports this hypothesis with statistical evidence showing a nonrandom occurrence of families with male children early in the birth order and only female children later. While other explanations are available, the possibility of sensitization of the mother to substances produced under control of genes on the Y chromosome must be considered. Such sensitization might result in rejecting of the male fetus, accounting for the higher abortion rate in males. It also might cause nonlethal damage to the fetus resulting in an increased incidence of poor performance among males.

REFERENCES

Ames, L. B., & Ilg, F. L. Sex differences in test performance of matched girl-boy pairs in the five-to-nine-year-old range. *Journal of Genetic Psychology*, 1964, 104, 25-34.

Apgar, V. A proposal for a new method of evaluation of the newborn infant. *Current Researches in Anesthesia and Analgesia*, 1953, 32, 260-267.

Baumgartner, L., Pessin, V., Wegman, M., & Parker, S. Weight in relation to fetal and newborn mortality; influence of sex and color. *Pediatrics*, 1950, 6, 329-342.

Bayer, L. A., & Bayley, N. Growth pattern shifts in healthy children: spontaneous and induced. *Journal of Pediatrics*, 1963, 62, 631-645.

Bayne, A. W., & Clark, J. R. Secular change in the intelligence of eleven-year-old Aberdeen school children. *Human Biology*, 1959, 31, 325-333.

Bentzen, F. Sex ratios in learning and behavior disorders. *American Journal of Orthopsychiatry*, 1963, 33, 92-98.

Berendes, H. W. Obstetrical complications and mental deficiency. Paper presented at International Copenhagen Congress on the Scientific Study of Mental Retardation, Denmark, August, 1964.

Berendes, H. W. The structure and scope of the collaborative project on cerebral palsy, mental retardation, and other neurological sensory disorders of infancy and childhood. In S. Chipman, A. Lilienfeld, B. Greenberg, & J. Donnelly (Eds.), *Research methodology and needs in perinatal studies*. Springfield, Ill.: Thomas, 1966. Pp. 118-139.

Childs, B. Genetic origin of some sex differences among human beings. *Pediatrics*, 1963, 35, 798-812.

Childs, B., Cantolino, S., & Dyke, M. K. Observations on sex differences in human biology. *Bulletin of the Johns Hopkins Hospital*, 1962, 110, 134-144.

Darley, F. L., & Winitz, H. Comparison of male and female kindergarten children on the WISC. *Journal of Genetic Psychology*, 1961, 99, 41-49.

Davidson, R. The Lyon hypothesis. *Journal of Pediatrics*, 1964, 65, 765-775.

Everhart, R. W. Literature survey of growth and developmental factors in articulatory maturation. *Journal of Speech and Hearing Disorders*, 1960, 25, 59-69.

Gitlin, D., Gross, P. A. M., & Janeway, C. A. The gamma globulins and their clinical significance. *New England Journal of Medicine*, 1959, 260, 21-27, 72-76, 121-125, 170-178.

Honzik, M. P. A sex difference in the age of onset of parent child resemblance in intelligence. *Journal of Educational Psychology*, 1963, 54, 231-237.

Jones, R. L., Gross, F. P., & VanWhy, E. L. A longitudinal study of reading achievement in a group of adolescent institutionalized mentally retarded children. *Training School Bulletin*, 1960, 57, 41-47.

Kravitz, H. Sex distribution of hospitalized children with acute respiratory diseases, gastroentertis and meningitis. *Clinical Pediatrics*, 1965, 4, 485-491.

Parsley, K. M., Jr. Further investigation of sex differences in achievement of under-, average-, and over-achieving students within five I.Q. groups in grades four through eight. *Journal of Educational Research*, 1964, 57, 268-270.

Pasamanick, B., & Knoblock, H. Brain damage and reproductive casualty. *American Journal of Orthopsychiatry*, 1960, 30, 298-305.

Renkonnen, K. O., & Makela, L. R. Factors affecting human sex ratio. *Nature* (London) 1962, 308-309.

Rhodes, P. Sex of the fetus in ante partum hemorrhage. *Lancet*, 1965, 2, 718-719.

Robinson, N.M., & Robinson, H. B. A follow-up study of children of low birth weight and control children at school age. *Pediatrics*, 1965, 35, 425-433.

Shettles, L. B. Conception and birth sex ratios. *Obstetrics and Gynecology*, 1961, 18, 123-127.

Sinks, M. B., & Powell, M. Sex and intelligence as factors in achievement in reading in grades four through eight. *Journal of Genetic Psychology*, 1965, 106, 67-79.

Szilard, L. Dependence of the sex ratio at birth on the age of the father. *Nature* (London), 1960, 86, 649-650.

Thompson, T. J., Gexon, H. M., Hatch, T. F., Rycheck, R. R., & Rogers, K. D. Sex distribution of staphyloccus aureus colourization and disease in newborn infants. *New England Journal of Medicine*, 1963, 269, 337-341.

Watson, E. H., & Lower, G. H. *Growth and development of children*. Chicago: Year Book Publishers, 1951.

Wiener, G., Rider, R. V., Oppel, W. C., Fischer, L. K., & Harper, P. A. Correlates of low birth weight: psychological status at six to seven years of age. *Pediatrics*, 1965, 35, 434-444.

Wisenthal, M. Sex differences in attitudes and attainment in junior schools. *British Journal of Educational Psychology*, 1965, 35, 79-85.

TABLE 1   Median Frequencies of Maternal Behaviors toward Male and Female Infants and Probability Levels of Wilcoxon Tests

Maternal behavior	0-3 Months		Sex difference	3-6 Months		Sex difference	Age difference P	
	M	F	(P)	M	F	(P)	M	F
1. Approach	50.5	58.0		11.0	13.0		.01	.01
2. Withdraw	50.0	17.5	*	33.0	23.5			
3. Visual orient	860.5	887.5		632.5	768.0			
4. Oral explore	26.5	39.0		13.5	9.5		.01	.01
5. Manual explore	31.5	40.0		3.5	5.0		.01	.01
6. Nonspecific contact	70.0	90.0	*	35.5	38.5		.01	.01
7. Retrieve	48.5	70.5		1.5	3.5		.01	.01
8. Embrace	1,210.0	1,432.5	*	353.5	323.5		.01	.01
9. Clasp	32.5	44.0	*	23.5	28.5		.05	
10. Restrain	24.5	63.5	.05	0.0	1.0		.01	.01
11. Reject	23.5	16.5		44.5	27.0		.05	
12. Groom	164.0	189.5		32.5	75.5	*	.01	.02
13. Clasp-pull-bite	25.0	17.0		33.0	28.0			
14. Retrieval grimace	12.5	11.5		0.0	0.5		.02	.05
15. Threat	23.0	54.5		85.5	79.0		.01	
16. Present	6.5	4.0		9.0	5.0	.01		

* Significant at the .05 level by a one-tailed Wilcoxon test.

significantly in the second 90 days, but for mothers of male infants only. Mothers of males showed a significant increase in rejection and threat in the second 90-day block.

Infant behaviors

Male and female infants differed significantly in only one mother-directed behavior: clasp-pull-bite (see Table 2). Male infants exhibited this behavior significantly more often than did females.

Reliable decreases with age occurred for both male and female infants in the following categories: embrace, ventral contact, and nipple contact. Significant increases for both sexes were observed in approach, withdraw, and nonspecific contact. Females showed stable increases in coo, visual

orient, oral explore, and manual explore, and significant decreases in gross body contact and clasping, while males exhibited a significant increase in clasp-pull-biting.

Nonpunitive physical contact

Two general categories involving the total frequency of nonpunitive physical contact were devised combining several behaviors: (a) infant-initiated nonpunitive physical contact included embraces, oral explores, manual explores, nonspecific contacts, gross body contacts, ventral contacts, nipple contacts, and clasp; and (b) mother-initiated nonpunitive physical contact included embraces, oral explores, manual explores, nonspecific contacts, retrievals, clasps, restrains, and grooms. Female infants received more non-

TABLE 2   Median Frequencies of Infant Behaviors toward Mother and Probability Levels of Wilcoxon Tests

Infant behavior	0-3 Months		Sex difference	3-6 Months		Sex difference	Age difference P	
	M	F	(P)	M	F	(P)	M	F
1. Embrace	1,331.0	1,371.5		326.0	492.0		.01	.01
2. Coo	25.0	29.5		72.5	67.5			.05
3. Approach	341.0	330.0		658.0	469.5		.03	.01
4. Withdraw	4.0	5.0		40.0	38.5		.01	.01
5. Visual orient	433.5	428.5		668.5	706.0			.01
6. Oral explore	119.5	126.5		40.0	51.5			.01
7. Manual explore	51.0	64.5		32.5	36.0			.01
8. Nonspecific contact	463.0	516.5		947.5	712.5		.01	.05
9. Gross contact	117.0	166.5		167.5	96.5			.05
10. Ventral contact	1,957.5	1,843.5		537.5	868.5		.01	.01
11. Nipple contact	1,801.0	1,693.5		553.0	739.5		.01	.01
12. Clasp	269.5	338.5		191.5	158.5			.01
13. Submit	5.5	6.0		4.5	4.0			
14. Clasp-pull-bite	1.5	3.5		6.5	3.5	.01	.01	

TABLE 3   *Median Frequencies of Nonpunititive Physical Contact and Probability Levels of Wilcoxon Tests*

	0-3 Months		Sex difference (P)	3-6 Months		Sex difference (P)	Age difference (P)	
	Male Infant	Female Infant		Male Infant	Female Infant		Male Infant	Female Infant
Mother initiated	1,764.5	1,985.5	.05	461.5	634.5		.01	.01
Infant initiated	6,126.5	6,543.5		3,205.0	3,409.5		.01	.01

punitive physical contact from their mothers during the first 3 months than did male infants (see Table 3), and female infants seemed to reciprocate with a higher frequency of nonpunitive physical contact than did the male infants, although the latter difference was not significant.

Discussion

If protection can be defined as close nonpunitive physical contact, the mothers protected the female infants more than the males. The frequencies of maternal restraint observed also supported this notion. The female infants both received and reciprocated more positive physical contact than did the males. The mothers of males did not differ significantly from the mothers of females in the amount of punishment administered to the infants, but they promoted independence in their male offspring by not restraining them and by withdrawing from them. Higher activity in the male infants might have accounted for at least part of the depressed positive maternal contact. Male infants in the field have been reported to leave their mothers sooner than female infants (Itani, 1959), but Jensen et al. (1967) reported that the *mothers* of males as well as the male infants themselves withdrew from contact more frequently than mothers of females during the first 15 weeks of life. This finding was partially corroborated in the present report. The mothers apparently play an active role in promoting differential amounts of independence in the two sexes. The females remain closely attached to the mothers; the males interact more frequently with other members at the periphery of the troop. Field studies have described the behavioral repertoire of the female infants as being centered in the mature females and particularly in their own mothers (DeVore, 1963; Jay, 1963). The males, on the other hand, became the recipients of more social exploration and grooming from other members of the troop than did the female infants (Boelkins, personal communication, 1967). Differential activity levels again may account for some of this difference, but most of the grooming and exploration directed toward male infants by other members of the troop has been reported to occur when the infants were in physical contact with the mother (R. C. Boelkins, personal communication). There were apparently three behaviors which promoted independence in the male: (*a*) the mother's early withdrawal from contact with the male infant, (*b*) the high interest of the other troop members in the male infant, and (*c*) the male infant's own striving for independence from the mother.

Despite the relatively low level of positive physical con-

tact between male infants and their mothers, the physical interaction that did occur was quite intense. Mothers of males were more frequently involved in bouts of social play with their infants, and this play involved vigorous bouncing and wrestling. Although these interactions were not observed frequently, even between males and their mothers, they were almost never seen between females and their mothers. In addition, mothers of males sexually presented more often to their infants than did mothers of females, and the only two infants aggressed by their mothers were males.

This high intensity of maternal interaction with the male infant can apparently be exaggerated when the mother has been socially deprived early in life. In the jungle-reared mothers of the present study, significant infant sex differences were not found in the frequencies of punishment. However, Arling (personal communication) observed that maternal punishment increased to the point of brutality in rhesus monkeys that had been socially deprived. In eight out of nine of Arling's brutal animals, the maternal brutality was directed toward a male infant.

In the present study, most infant-directed behaviors decreased from the first 90-day block to the second. However, there were some exceptions, such as punishing, rejection, and threats, which have been described as good indicants of the mother's transition into a second maternal stage (Hansen, 1966). Both the frequency and the form of maternal punishment changed with the age of the infant. Gentle mouthing by the mother occurred frequently in the first 90 days but changed in quality to biting in the second 90-day block, while rejection gradually increased over time. Hansen (1966) reported similar changes. The maternal convulsive jerk, a response which usually occurred when the infant bit the nipple, disappeared completely in the second 90-day block of the present study, and the pattern of mouthing and jerking slowly gave way to rejecting or pushing the infant away in the second 90 days. The increased frequency of male infant punishment administered by the mothers of the present study in the second 90 days was undoubtedly related to the increasing frequency of male infant clasp-pull-bites directed toward the mothers.

Mother-directed behaviors involving prolonged contact (e.g., embrace, ventral contact, nipple contact) decreased sharply in the second 90 days of life, while noncontact or brief-contact behaviors increased. There was a transition for both mother and infant away from an attachment restricted to physical contact to one including sensory and motor communicative skills. Coo vocalizations and visual orients increased with age in the infant, while threats and presents increased in the mothers. Coo vocalizations generally occurred more frequently in juvenile females than in juvenile males (Mitchell, in press), but this sex difference was not yet evident at 6 months of age.

In humans, it has been generally believed that sex differences are to a large extent experientially determined by a process called "sex-typing" (see Mussen, Conger, & Kagan, 1963, p. 286). The present data suggest that experiential variables may also influence the sex role of the monkey. A previous experiment at Wisconsin (Chamove, Harlow, & Mitchell, 1967) reported differential maternal-like infant-directed behaviors in sexually immature male and female monkeys. The females typically exhibited maternal-like affiliative patterns toward infants, whereas the males exhibited patterns of indifference or hostility. Such differences were observed in monkeys over a wide range of social rearing conditions but have been conspicuously absent in monkeys reared in social isolation (Mitchell, in press). These apparently biological sex differences become more marked in monkeys who have experienced real monkey mothering.

Generally speaking, in the rhesus monkeys, and probably in all primates, the mother's relations with the male and the female infant are very much alike. However, the differences that do exist may be crucial to the long-term development of the primate. For example, one would predict from the above data that overprotective mothering would lead to more social retardation in the male than in the female. A recent project at the Wisconsin Primate Laboratory found that overprotective primiparous mothering did in fact retard male infants more than female infants. Primiparous mothered males played very little and cooed very frequently (Mitchell, Ruppenthal, Raymond, & Harlow, 1966).

These two behavioral patterns are characteristically female. Differences in mother-infant interaction apparently engender differential long-term effects along a male-female continuum of behavior.

REFERENCES

Alexander, B. K. The effects of early peer deprivation on juvenile behavior of rhesus monkeys. Unpublished doctoral dissertation, University of Wisconsin, 1966.

Arling, G. L. Effects of social deprivation on maternal behavior of rhesus monkeys. Unpublished Master's thesis, University of Wisconsin, 1966.

Chamove, A. C., Harlow, H. F., & Mitchell, G. D. Sex differences in the infant-directed behavior of preadolescent rhesus monkeys. *Child Development*, 1967, 38, 329-335.

DeVore, I. T. Mother-infant relations in baboons. In H. Rheingold (Ed.). *Maternal behavior in mammals.* New York: Wiley, 1963. Pp 305-335.

Griffin, G. A. The effects of multiple mothering on the infant-mother and infant-infant affectional systems. Unpublished doctoral dissertation, University of Wisconsin, 1966.

Hansen, E. W. The development of maternal and infant behavior in the rhesus monkey. *Behaviour*, 1966, 27, 107-149.

Itani, J. Paternal care in the wild Japanese monkey, *Macaca fuscata* Primates, 1959, 2, 61-93.

Jay, P. Mother-infant relations in langurs. In H. Rheingold (Ed.), *Maternal behavior in mammals.* New York: Wiley, 1963. Pp. 287-304.

Jensen, G. D., Bobbitt, R. A., & Gordon, B. N. Sex differences in social interaction between infant monkeys and their mothers. In J. Wortis (Ed), *Recent advances in biological psychiatry.* Vol 9. New York: Plenum, 1966. Pp. 283-293.

Jensen, G. D., Bobbitt, R. A., & Gordon, B. N. The development of maternal independence in mother-infant pigtailed monkeys, *Macca nemestrina.* In S. A. Altmann (Ed.), *Social communication among primates.* Chicago: University of Chicago Press, 1967. Pp 43-53.

Mitchell, G. D. Persistent behavior pathology in rhesus monkeys following early social isolation. *Folia primatologica*, in press.

Mitchell, G. D., Ruppenthal, G. C., Raymond, E. J., & Harlow, H. F. Long-term effects of multiparous and primiparous monkey mother rearing. *Child Development*, 1966, 37, 781-791.

Mussen, P. H., Conger, J. J., & Kagan, J. *Child development and personality.* New York: Harper & Row, 1963.

4 Sex, age, and state as determinants of mother-infant interaction

Howard A. Moss

A major reason for conducting research on human infants is derived from the popular assumption that adult behavior, to a considerable degree, is influenced by early experience. A corollary of this assumption is that if we can precisely conceptualize and measure significant aspects of infant experience and behavior we will be able to predict more sensitively and better understand adult functioning. The basis for this conviction concerning the enduring effects of early experience varies considerably according to the developmental model that is employed. Yet there remains considerable consensus as to the long term and pervasive influence of the infant's experience.

Bloom (1964) contends that characteristics become increasingly resistant to change as the mature status of the

Edited from Howard A. Moss, "Sex, Age, and State as Determinants of Mother-Infant Interaction," Merrill-Palmer Quarterly, 13 : 1, 1967, pp. 19-36. Presented at the Merrill-Palmer Institute Conference on Research and Teaching of Infant Development, February 10-12, 1966, directed by Irving E. Sigel, chairman of research. The conference was financially supported in part by the National Institute of Child Health and Human Development. The author wishes to express his appreciation to Mrs. Helene McVey and Miss Betty Reinecke for their assistance in preparing and analyzing the data presented in this paper.

characteristic is achieved and that environmental effects are most influential during periods of most rapid growth. This is essentially a refinement of the critical period hypothesis which argues in favor of the enduring and irreversible effects of many infant experiences. Certainly the studies on imprinting and the effects of controlled sensory input are impressive in 'this respect (Hess, 1959; White and Held, 1963). Learning theory also lends itself to support the potency of early experience. Since the occurrence of variable interval and variable ratio reinforcement schedules are highly probable in infancy (as they are in many other situations), the learnings associated with these schedules will be highly resistant to extinction. Also, the pre-verbal learning that characterizes infancy should be more difficult to extinguish since these responses are less available to linguistic control which later serves to mediate and regulate many important stimulus-response and reinforcement relationships. Psychoanalytic theory and behavioristic psychology probably have been the most influential forces in emphasizing the long-range consequences of infant experience. These theories, as well as others, stress the importance of the mother-infant relationship. In light of the widespread acceptance of the importance of early development, it is paradoxical that there is such a dearth of direct observational data concerning the functioning of infants, in their natural environment, and in relation to the primary caretakers.

Observational studies of the infant are necessary in order to test existing theoretical propositions and to generate new propositions based on empirical evidence. In addition, the infant is an ideally suitable subject for investigating many aspects of behavior because of the relatively simple and inchoate status of the human organism at this early stage in life. Such phenomena as temperament, reactions to stimulation, efficacy of different learning contingencies, perceptual functioning, and social attachment can be investigated while they are still in rudimentary form and not yet entwined in the immensely complex behavioral configurations that progressively emerge.

The research to be reported in this paper involves descriptive-normative data of maternal and infant behaviors in the naturalistic setting of the home. These data are viewed in terms of how the infant's experience structures potential learning patterns. Although the learning process itself is of primary eventual importance, it is necessary initially to identify the organizational factors, in situ, that structure learning opportunities and shape response systems.

A sample of 30 first-born children and their mothers were studied by means of direct observations over the first 3 months of life. Two periods were studied during this 3-month interval. Period one included a cluster of three observations made at weekly intervals during the first month of life in order to evaluate the initial adaptation of mother and infant to one another. Period two consisted of another cluster of three observations, made around 3 months of age when relatively stable patterns of behavior were likely to have been established. Each cluster included two 3-hour observations and one 8-hour observation. The 3-hour observations were made with the use of a keyboard that operates in conjunction with a 20-channel Esterline-Angus Event Recorder. Each of 30 keys represents a maternal or infant behavior, and when a key is depressed it activates one or a combination of pens on the recorder, leaving a trace that shows the total duration of the observed behavior. This technique allows for a continuous record showing the total time and the sequence of behavior. For the 8-hour observation the same behaviors were studied but with the use of a modified time-sampling technique. The time-sampled units were one minute in length and the observer, using a stenciled form, placed a number opposite the appropriate behaviors to indicate their respective order of occurrence. Since each variable can be coded only once for each observational unit, a score of 480 is the maximum that can be received. The data to be presented in this paper are limited to the two 8-hour observations. The data obtained with the use of the keyboard will be dealt with elsewhere in terms of the sequencing of events.

The mothers who participated in these observations were told that this was a normative study of infant functioning under natural living conditions. It was stressed that they proceed with their normal routines and care of the infant as they would if the observer were not present. This structure was presented to the mothers during a brief introductory visit prior to the first observation. In addition, in order to reduce the mother's self-consciousness and facilitate her behaving in relatively typical fashion, the observer emphasized that it was the infant who was being studied and that her actions would be noted only in relation to what was happening to the infant. This approach seemed to be effective, since a number of mothers commented after the observations were completed that they were relieved that they were not the ones being studied. The extensiveness of the observations and the frequent use of informal conversation between the observer and mother seemed to contribute further to the naturalness of her behavior.

The observational variables, mean scores and sample sizes are presented in Table 1. These data are presented separately for the 3-week and the 3-month observations. The inter-rater reliabilities for these variables range from .74 to 1.00 with a median reliability of .97. Much of the data in this paper are presented for males and females separately, since by describing and comparing these two groups we are able to work from an established context that helps to clarify the theoretical meaning of the results. Also, the importance of sex differences is heavily emphasized in contemporary developmental theory and it is felt that infant data concerning these differences would provide a worthwhile addition to the literature that already exists on this matter for older subjects.

The variables selected for study are those which would seem to influence or reflect aspects of maternal contact. An additional, but related consideration in the selection of variables was that they have an apparent bearing on the organization of the infant's experience. Peter Wolff (1959), Janet Brown (1964), and Sibylle Escalona (1962) have described qualitative variations in infant state or activity level and others have shown that the response patterns of the infant are highly influenced by the state he is in (Bridger, 1965). Moreover, Levy (1958) has demonstrated that maternal behavior varies as a function of the state or

TABLE 1   Mean Frequency of Maternal and Infant Behavior at 3 Weeks
             and 3 Months

Behavior	3-week observation		3-month observation[a]	
	Males [b] (N = 14)	Females (N = 15)	Males [b] (N = 13)	Females (N = 12)
Maternal variables				
Holds infant close	121.4	99.2	77.4	58.6
Holds infant distant	32.2	18.3	26.7	27.2
Total holds	131.3	105.5	86.9	73.4
Attends infant	61.7	44.2	93.0	81.8
Maternal contact (holds and attends)	171.1	134.5	158.8	133.8
Feeds infant	60.8	60.7	46.6	41.4
Stimulates feeding	10.1	14.0	1.6	3.6
Burps infant	39.0	25.9	20.9	15.3
Affectionate contact	19.9	15.9	32.8	22.7
Rocks infant	35.1	20.7	20.0	23.9
Stresses musculature	11.7	3.3	25.8	16.6
Stimulates/arouses infant	23.1	10.6	38.9	26.1
Imitates infant	1.9	2.9	5.3	7.6
Looks at infant	182.8	148.1	179.5	161.9
Talks to infant	104.1	82.2	117.5	116.1
Smiles at infant	23.2	18.6	45.9	46.4
Infant variables				
Cry	43.6	30.2	28.5	16.9
Fuss	65.7	44.0	59.0	36.0
Irritable (cry and fuss)	78.7	56.8	67.3	42.9
Awake active	79.6	55.1	115.8	85.6
Awake passive	190.0	138.6	257.8	241.1
Drowsy	74.3	74.7	27.8	11.1
Sleep	261.7	322.1	194.3	235.6
Supine	133.7	59.3	152.7	134.8
Eyes on mother	72.3	49.0	91.0	90.6
Vocalizes	152.3	179.3	207.2	207.4
Infant smiles	11.1	11.7	32.1	35.3
Mouths	36.8	30.6	61.2	116.2

[a] Four of the subjects were unable to participate in the 3-month observation. Two moved out of the area, one mother became seriously ill, and another mother chose not to participate in all the observations.

[b] One subject who had had an extremely difficult delivery was omitted from the descriptive data but is included in the findings concerning mother-infant interaction.

activity level of the infant. Consequently, we have given particular attention to the variables concerning state (cry, fuss, awake active, awake passive, and sleep) because of the extent to which these behaviors seem to shape the infant's experience. Most of the variables listed in Table 1 are quite descriptive of what was observed. Those which might not be as clear are as follows: *attends infant*—denotes standing close or leaning over infant, usually while in the process of caretaking activities; *stimulates feeding*—stroking the infant's cheek and manipulating the nipple so as to induce sucking responses; *affectionate contact*—kissing and caressing infant; *stresses musculature*—holding the infant in either a sitting or standing position so that he is required to support his own weight; *stimulates/arouses infant*—mother

provides tactile and visual stimulation for the infant or attempts to arouse him to a higher activity level; and *imitates infant*—mother repeats a behavior, usually a vocalization, immediately after it is observed in the infant.

The sex differences and shifts in behavior from 3 weeks to 3 months are in many instances pronounced. For example, at 3 weeks of age mothers held male infants about 27 minutes more per 8 hours than they held females, and at 3 months males were held 14 minutes longer. By the time they were 3 months of age there was a decrease of over 30% for both sexes in the total time they were held by their mothers. Sleep time also showed marked sex differences and changes over time. For the earlier observations females slept about an hour longer than males, and this difference

TABLE 2   *Changes in Behavior between 3 Weeks and 3 Months (N = 26)*

Maternal variables	t-values	Infant variables	t-values
Higher at 3 weeks:		*Higher at 3 weeks:*	
Holds infant close	4.43****	Cry	2.84***
Holds infant distant	.56	Fuss	1.33
Total holds	4.00****	Irritable (cry and fuss)	1.73*
Maternal contact		Drowsy	9.02****
(holds and attends)	.74	Sleep	4.51****
Feeds infant	3.49***		
Stimulates feeding	3.42***		
Burps infant	3.28***		
Rocks infant	1.08		
Higher at 3 months:		*Higher at 3 months:*	
Attends infant	5.15****	Awake active	2.47**
Affectionate contact	2.50**	Awake passive	5.22****
Stresses musculature	3.42***	Supine	1.75*
Stimulates/arouses infant	2.63**	Eyes on mother	3.21***
Imitates infant	4.26****	Vocalizes	3.56***
Looks at infant	.38	Infant smiles	6.84****
Talks to infant	2.67**	Mouths	3.69***
Smiles at infant	4.79****		

* $p < .10$ ** $p < .05$ *** $p < .01$ **** $p < .001$

tended to be maintained by 3 months with the female infants sleeping about 41 minutes longer. Again, there was a substantial reduction with age in this behavior for both sexes; a decrease of 67 and 86 minutes in sleep time for males and females, respectively. What is particularly striking is the variability for these infant and maternal variables. The range for sleep time is 137-391 minutes at 3 weeks and 120-344 minutes at 3 months, and the range for mother holding is 38-218 minutes at 3 weeks and 26-168 minutes for the 3-month observation. The extent of the individual differences reflected by these ranges seems to have important implications. For instance, if an infant spends more time at a higher level of consciousness this should increase his experience and contact with the mother, and through greater learning opportunities, facilitate the perceptual discriminations he makes, and affect the quality of his cognitive organization. The finding that some of the infants in our sample slept a little over 2 hours, or about 25% of the observation time and others around 6 hours or 75% of the time, is a fact that has implications for important developmental processes. The sum crying and fussing, what we term irritability level of the infant, is another potentially important variable. The range of scores for this behavior was from 5-136 minutes at 3 weeks and 7-98 at 3 months. The fact that infants are capable through their behavior of shaping maternal treatment is a point that has gained increasing recognition. The cry is a signal for the mother to respond and variation among infants in this behavior could lead to differential experiences with the mother.

Table 2 presents *t* values showing changes in the maternal and infant behaviors from the 3-week to the 3-month observation. In this case, the data for the males and females are combined since the trends, in most instances, are the same for both sexes. It is not surprising that there are a number of marked shifts in behavior from 3 weeks to 3 months, since the early months of life are characterized by enormous growth and change. The maternal variables that show the greatest decrement are those involving feeding behaviors and close physical contact. It is of interest that the decrease in close contact is paralleled by an equally pronounced increase in attending behavior, so that the net amount of maternal contact remains similar for the 3-week and 3-month observations. The main difference was that the mothers, for the later observation, tended to hold their infants less but spent considerably more time near them, in what usually was a vis-à-vis posture, while interacting and ministering to their needs. Along with this shift, the mothers showed a marked increase in affectionate behavior toward the older infant, positioned him more so that he was required to make active use of his muscles, presented him with a greater amount of stimulation and finally, she exhibited more social behavior (imitated, smiled, and talked) toward the older child.

The changes in maternal behavior from 3 weeks to 3 months probably are largely a function of the maturation of various characteristics of the infant. However, the increased confidence of the mother, her greater familiarity with her infant, and her developing attachment toward him will also account for some of the changes that occurred over this period of time.

By 3 months of age the infant is crying less and awake more. Moreover, he is becoming an interesting and responsive person. There are substantial increases in the total time spent by him in smiling, vocalizing, and looking at the mother's face, so that the greater amount of social-type behavior he manifested at three months parallels the increments shown in the mother's social responsiveness toward him over the same period. The increase with age in the time

TABLE 3   *Correlations between Observations at 3 Weeks and at 3 Months (N = 26)*

Maternal variables	r =	Infant variables	r =
Holds infant close	.23	Cry	.28
Holds infant distant	.04	Fuss	.42**
Total holds	.18	Irritable (cry and fuss)	.37*
Attends infant	.36*	Awake active	.25
Maternal contact		Awake passive	.26
(holds and attends)	.25	Drowsy	.44**
Feeds infant	.21	Sleep	.24
Stimulates feeding	.37*	Supine	.29
Burps infant	.20	Eyes on mother	− .12
Affectionate contact	.64****	Vocalizes	.41**
Rocks infant	.29	Infant smiles	.32
Stresses musculature	.06	Mouths	− .17
Stimulates/arouses infant	.23		
Imitates infant	.45**		
Looks at infant	.37*		
Talks to infant	.58***		
Smiles at infant	.66****		

*p < .10   ** p < .05   *** p < .01   **** p < .001

the infant is kept in a suspine position also should facilitate his participation in vis-à-vis interactions with the mother as well as provide him with greater opportunity for varied visual experiences.

Table 3 presents the correlations between the 3-week and the 3-month observations for the maternal and infant behaviors we studied. These findings further reflect the relative instability of the mother-infant system over the first few months of life. Moderate correlation coefficients were obtained only for the class of maternal variables concerning affectionate-social responses. It thus may be that these behaviors are more sensitive indicators of enduring maternal attitudes than the absolute amount of time the mother devoted to such activities as feeding and physical contact. The few infant variables that show some stability are, with the exception of vocalizing, those concerning the state of the organism. Even though some of the behaviors are moderately stable from three weeks to three months, the overall magnitude of the correlations reported in Table 3 seem quite low considering that they represent repeated measures of the same individual over a relatively short period.

Table 4 presents *t*-values based on comparisons between the sexes for the 3-week and 3-month observations. A number of statistically significant differences were obtained with, in most instances, the boys having higher mean scores than the girls. The sex differences are most pronounced at 3 weeks for both maternal and infant variables. By 3 months the boys and girls are no longer as clearly differentiated on the maternal variables although the trend persists for the males to tend to have higher mean scores. On the other hand, the findings for the infant variables concerning state remain relatively similar at 3 weeks and 3 months. Thus, the sex differences are relatively stable for the two observations even though the stability coefficients for the total sample are low (in terms of our variables).

In general, these results indicate that much more was happening with the male infants than with the female infants. Males slept less and cried more during both observations and these behaviors probably contributed to the more extensive and stimulating interaction the boys experienced with the mother, particularly for the 3-week observation. In order to determine the effect of state we selected the 15 variables, excluding those dealing with state, where the sex differences were most marked and did an analysis of covariance with these variables, controlling for irritability and another analysis of covariance controlling for sleep. These results are presented in Table 5. When the state of the infant was controlled for, most of the sex differences were no longer statistically significant. The exceptions were that the *t*-values were greater, after controlling for the state, for the variables "mother stimulates/arouse" was obtained for the males and the higher score for "imitates" by the females. The variable "imitates" involves repeating vocalizations made by the child, and it is interesting that mothers exhibited more of this behavior with the girls. This response could be viewed as the reinforcement of verbal behavior, and the evidence presented here suggests that the mothers differentially reinforce this behavior on the basis of the sex of the child.

In order to further clarify the relation between infant state and maternal treatment, product-moment correlations were computed relating the infant irritability score with the degree of maternal contact. The maternal contact variable is based on the sum of the holding and attending scores with the time devoted to feeding behaviors subtracted out. These correlations were computed for the 3-week and 3-month observations for the male and female samples combined and separate. At 3 weeks a correlation of .52 (p < .01) was obtained between irritability and maternal contact for the total sample. However, for the female subsample this correlation was .68 (p < .02) and for males of only .20 (non. sig.). Furthermore, a somewhat similar pattern occurred for the correlations between maternal contact and infant irritability for the 3-month observation. At this age the correla-

TABLE 4   Sex Differences in Frequency of Maternal and Infant Behaviors at 3 Weeks and 3 Months

Maternal variables	t-values		Infant variables	t-values	
	3 weeks	3 months		3 weeks	3 months
Male higher:			*Male higher;*		
Holds infant close	1.42	1.52	Cry	1.68	1.11
Holds infant distant	2.64**		Fuss	2.48**	3.47***
Total holds	1.65	1.12	Irritable (cry and fuss)	2.23**	2.68**
Attends infant	2.66**	1.10	Awake active	1.66	.57
Maternal contact			Awake passive	2.94***	1.77*
(holds and attends)	2.09**	1.57	Drowsy		.41
Feeds infant	.06	.27	Supine	2.30**	1.07
Burps infant	1.67	.69	Eyes on mother	1.99*	.75
Affectionate contact	.90	1.00	Mouths	.64	
Rocks infant	1.21				
Stresses musculature	2.48**	1.67			
Stimulates/arouses infant	2.20**	1.53			
Looks at infant	1.97*	1.36			
Talks to infant	1.02	.79			
Smiles at infant	.57				
Female higher:			*Female higher:*		
Holds infant distant		.05	Drowsy	.03	
Stimulates feeding	.62	1.47	Sleep	3.15***	2.87**
Rocks infant		.82	Vocalizes	1.34	.23
Imitates infant	.80	1.76*	Infant smiles	.02	.08
Smiles at infant		.44	Mouths		2.57**

* $p < .10$ ** $p < .05$ *** $p < .01$

TABLE 5   Sex Differences after Controlling for Irritability and Sleep Time through Analysis of Covariance[a]

Maternal or infant behaviors	Sleep time controlled for		Sex with higher mean score	Irritability controlled for		Sex with higher mean score
	3 weeks	3 months		3 weeks	3 months	
Variables	t	t		t	t	
Holds infant close	.30	1.22		.64	1.70	
Holds infant distant	.59	− .20		.92	− .20	
Total holds	.43	.88		.86	1.08	
Attends infant	1.12	1.36		1.91*	.94	Males
Maternal contact						
(holds and attends)	.62	1.04		1.20	1.12	
Stimulates feeding	.55	−1.12		−.09	−1.06	
Affectionate contact	−.46	.91		.56	1.27	
Rocks	.35	−.70		.44	−1.44	
Stresses musculature	1.84*	.71	Males	1.97*	1.40	
Stimulates/arouses infant	2.09**	1.82*	Males	2.43**	2.31**	Males
Imitates infant	−.91	−2.73**	Females	−.63	−2.14**	Females
Looks at infant	.58	1.35		1.17	1.02	
Talks to infant	−.48	.24		.70	.59	
Infant supine	.82	−.03		1.36	.69	
Eyes on mother	.37	.58		1.76*	−.37	Males

[a] A positive t-value indicates that males had the higher mean score, and a negative t-value indicates a higher mean score for females.

* $p < .10$ ** $p < .05$

tion is .37 ($p < .10$ level) for the combined sample and .54 ($p < .05$ level) for females and $-.47$ ($p < .10$ level) for males. A statistically significant difference was obtained ($t = 2.40$, $p < .05$ level) in a test comparing the difference between the female and male correlations for the 3-month observation. In other words maternal contact and irritability positively covaried for females at both ages; whereas for males, there was no relationship at 3 weeks, and by 3 months the mothers tended to spend less time with the more irritable male babies. It should be emphasized that these correlations reflect within group patterns, and that when we combine the female and male samples positive correlations still emerge for both ages. Since the males had substantially higher scores for irritability and maternal contact than the females, the correlation for the male subject does not strongly attenuate the correlations derived for the total sample, even when the males within group covariation seems random or negative. That is, in terms of the total sample, the patterning of the males scores is still consistent with a positive relationship between irritability and maternal contact.

From these findings it is difficult to posit a causal relationship. However, it seems most plausible that it is the infant's cry that is determining the maternal behavior. Mothers describe the cry as a signal that the infant needs attention and they often report their nurturant actions in response to the cry. Furthermore, the cry is a noxious and often painful stimulus that probably has biological utility for the infant, propelling the mother into action for her own comfort as well as out of concern for the infant. Ethological reports confirm the proposition that the cry functions as a "releaser" of maternal behavior (Bowlby, 1958; Hinde, et al., 1964; Hoffman, et al., 1966). Bowlby (1958) states:

It is my belief that both of them (crying and smiling), act as social releasers of instinctual responses in mothers. As regards crying, there is plentiful evidence from the animal world that this is so: probably in all cases the mother responds promptly and unfailingly to her infant's bleat, call or cry. It seems to me clear that similar impulses are also evoked in the human mother. . . .

Thus, we are adopting the hypothesis that the correlations we have obtained reflect a causal sequence whereby the cry acts to instigate maternal intervention. Certainly there are other important determinants of maternal contact, and it is evident that mothers exhibit considerable variability concerning how responsive they are to the stimulus signal of the cry. Yet it seems that the effect of the cry is sufficient to account at least partially for the structure of the mother-infant relationship. We further maintain the thesis that the infant's cry shapes maternal behavior even for the instance where the negative correlation was noted at 3 months for the males. The effect is still present, but in this case the more irritable infants were responded to *less* by the mothers. Our speculation for explaining this relationship and the fact that, conversely, a positive correlation was obtained for the female infants is that the mothers probably were negatively reinforced for responding to a number of the boys but tended to be positively reinforced for their responses toward the girls. That is, mothers of the

more irritable boys may have learned that they could not be successful in quieting boys whereas the girls were more uniformly responsive (quieted by) to maternal handling. There is not much present in our data to bear out this contention, with the exception that the males were significantly more irritable than the girls for both observations. However, evidence that suggests males are more subject to inconsolable states comes from studies (Serr and Ismajovich, 1963; McDonald, Gynther, and Christakos, 1963; Stechler, 1964) which indicate that males have less well organized physiological reactions and are more vulnerable to adverse conditions than females. The relatively more efficient functioning of the female organism should thus contribute to their responding more favorably to maternal intervention.

In summary, we propose that maternal behavior initially tends to be under the control of the stimulus and reinforcing conditions provided by the young infant. As the infant gets older, the mother, if she behaved contingently toward his signals, gradually acquires reinforcement value which in turn increases her efficacy in regulating infant behaviors. Concurrently, the earlier control asserted by the infant becomes less functional and diminishes. In a sense, the point where the infant's control over the mother declines and the mother's reinforcement value emerges could be regarded as the first manifestation of socialization, or at least represents the initial conditions favoring social learning. Thus, at first the mother is shaped by the infant and this later facilitates her shaping the behavior of the infant. We would therefore say, that the infant, through his own temperament or signal system contributes to establishing the stimulus and reinforcement value eventually associated with the mother. According to this reasoning, the more irritable infants (who can be soothed) whose mothers respond in a contingent manner to their signals should become most amenable to the effects of social reinforcement and manifest a higher degree of attachment behavior. The fact that the mothers responded more contingently toward the female infants should maximize the ease with which females learn social responses.

This statement is consistent with data on older children which indicate that girls learn social responses earlier and with greater facility than boys. (Becker, 1964). Previously we argued that the mothers learned to be more contingent toward the girls because they probably were more responsive to maternal intervention. An alternative explanation is that mothers respond contingently to the girls and not to the boys as a form of differential reinforcement, whereby, in keeping with cultural expectations, the mother is initiating a pattern that contributes to males being more aggressive or assertive, and less responsive to socialization. Indeed, these two explanations are not inconsistent with one another since the mother who is unable to soothe an upset male infant may eventually come to classify this intractable irritability as an expression of "maleness."

Although we have shown that there is a covariation between maternal contact and infant irritability and have attempted to develop some theoretical implications concerning this relationship, considerable variability remains as to how responsive different mothers are to their infants' crying behavior. This variability probably reflects differences in maternal attitudes. Women who express positive feelings about babies and who consider the well-being of the infant to be of essential importance should tend to be more responsive to signals of distress from the infant than women who exhibit negative maternal attitudes. In order to test this assumption, we first derived a score for measuring maternal responsiveness. This score was obtained through a regression analysis where we determined the amount of maternal contact that would be expected for each mother by controlling for her infant's irritability score. The expected maternal contact score was then subtracted from the mother's actual contact score and this difference was used as the measure of maternal responsivity. The maternal responsivity scores were obtained separately for the 3-week and the 3-month observations. The parents of 23 of the infants in our sample were interviewed for a project investigating marital careers, approximately 2 years prior to the birth of their child, and these interviews provided us with the unusual opportunity of having antecedent data relevant to prospective parental functioning. A number of variables from this material were rated and two of them, "acceptance of nurturant role," and the degree that the baby is seen in a "positive sense" were correlated with the scores on the maternal responsivity measure.[1] Annotated definitions of these interview variables are as follows:

"Acceptance of nurturant role" concerns the degree to which the subject is invested in caring for others and in acquiring domestic and homemaking skills such as cooking, sewing, and cleaning house. Evidence for a high rating would be describing the care of infants and children with much pleasure and satisfaction even when this involves subordinating her own needs.

The interview variable concerning the "degree that the baby is seen in a positive sense" assesses the extent to which the subject views a baby as gratifying, pleasant and non-burdensome. In discussing what she imagines infants to be like she stresses the warmer, more personal, and rewarding aspects of the baby and anticipates these qualities as primary.

Correlations of .40 ($p < .10$ level) and .48 ($p < .05$ level) were obtained between the ratings on "acceptance of nurturant role" and the maternal responsivity scores for the 3-week and 3-month observations, respectively. The "degree that the baby is seen in a positive sense" correlated .38 ($p < .10$ level) and .44 ($p < .05$ level) with maternal responsivity for the two ages. However, the two interview variables were so highly intercorrelated ($r = .93$) that they clearly involve the same dimension. Thus, the psychological status of the mother, assessed substantially before the birth of her infant, as well as the infant's state, are predictive of her maternal behavior. Schaffer and Emerson (1964) found that maternal responsiveness to the cry was associated with the attachment behavior of infants. Extrapolating from our findings, we now have some basis for assuming that the early attitudes of the mother represent antecedent conditions for facilitating the attachment behavior observed by Schaffer and Emerson.

In conclusion, what we did was study and analyze some of the factors which structure the mother-infant relationship. A central point is that the state of the infant affects the quantity and quality of maternal behavior, and this in turn would seem to influence the course of future social learning. Furthermore, through controlling for the state of the infant, we were able to demonstrate the effects of pre-parental attitudes on one aspect of maternal behavior, namely, the mother's responsiveness toward her infant. Many investigators, in conducting controlled laboratory studies, have stressed that the state of the infant is crucial in determining the nature of his responses to different stimuli. This concern is certainly highly relevant to our data, collected under naturalistic conditions.

NOTES

1. Dr. Kenneth Robson collaborated in developing these variables and made the rating.

REFERENCES

Becker, W. C. Consequences of different kinds of parental discipline. In M. L. Hoffman & Lois W. Hoffman (Eds.), *Review of child development research: I* New York: Russell Sage Found. 1964. Pp. 169-208.

Birns, B. Individual differences in human neonates response to stimulation. *Child Develpm.*, 1965, 36, 249-256.

Bloom, B. S. *Stability and change in human characteristics.* New York: Wiley, 1964.

Bowlby, J. The nature of a child's tie to his mother. *Internat. J. Psychoanal.*, 1958, 39, 350-373.

Bridger, W. H. Psychophysiological measurement of the roles of state in the human neonate. Paper presented at Soc. Res. Child Develpm., Minneapolis, April, 1965.

Brown, Janet L. States in newborn infants. *Merrill-Palmer Quart.*, 1964, 10, 313-327.

Escalona, Sibylle K. The study of individual differences and the problem of state. *J. Child Psychiat.*, 1962, 1, 11-37.

Fantz, R. Pattern vision in newborn infants. *Science*, 1963, 140, 296-297.

Hess, E. H. Imprinting. *Science*, 1959, 130, 133-141.

Hinde, R.A., Rowell, T. E., & Spencer-Booth, Y. Behavior of living rhesus monkeys in their first six months. *Proc. Zool. Soc., London*, 1964, 143, 609-649.

Hoffman, H., et al. Enhanced distress vocalization through selective reinforcement. *Science*, 1966, 151, 354-356.

Lennenberg, E. H., Rebelsky, Freda G., & Nichols, I. A. The vocalizations of infants born to deaf and to hearing parents. *Vita Humana*, 1965, 8, 23-37.

Leuba, C. Toward some integration of learning theories: The concept of optimal stimulation. *Psychol. Rep.*, 1955, 1, 27-33.

Levy, D. M. *Behavioral analysis.* Springfield, Ill.: Charles C. Thomas, 1958.

McDonald, R. L., Gynther, M. D., & Christakos, A. C. Relations between maternal anxiety and obstetric complications. *Psychosom. Med.*, 1963, 25, 357-362.

Moss, H. A. Coping behavior, the need for stimulation, and normal development. *Merrill-Palmer Quart.*, 1965, 11, 171-179.

Murphy, Lois B., et al. *The widening world of childhood.* New York: Basic Books, 1962.

Noirot, Eliane. Changes in responsiveness to young in the adult mouse: the effect of external stimuli. *J. comp. physiol. Psychol.*, 1964, 57, 97-99.

Razran, G. The observable unconscious and the inferable conscious in current Soviet psychophysiology: Interoceptive conditioning, sematic conditioning, and the orienting reflex. *Psychol Rev.*, 1961, 68, 81-146.

Rheingold, Harriet L. The modification of social responsiveness in institutional babies. *Monogr. Soc. Res. Child Develpm.*, 1956, 21, No. 2 (Serial No. 23).

Schaffer, H. R. & Emerson, Peggy E. The development of social attachments in infancy. *Monogr. Soc. Res. Child Develpm.*, 1964, 29, No. 3 (Serial No. 94).

Serr, D. M., & Ismajovich, B. Determination of the primary sex ratio from human abortions. *Amer. J Obstet Gyncol.* 1963, 87, 63-65.

Stechler, G. A longitudinal follow-up of neonatal apnea. *Child Develpm.*, 1964, 35, 333-348.

Stechler, G. Paper presented at Soc. Res. Child Develpm., Minneapolis, April, 1965.

White, B. L. & Held, R. Plasticity in perceptual development during the first six months of life. Paper presented at Amer. Ass. Advncmnt. Sci., Cleveland, Ohio, December, 1963.

White, R. W. Motivation reconsidered: the concept of competence. *Psychol. Rev.*, 1959, 66, 297-323.

Wolff, P. H. Observations on newborn infants. *Psychosom. Med.* 1959, 21, 110-118.

5 Play behavior in the year-old infant: early sex differences[1]

Susan Goldberg
Michael Lewis

Until recently, the largest proportion of studies in child development gave attention to nursery and early grade school children. The literature on sex differences is no exception. A recent book on development of sex differences which includes an annotated bibliography (Maccoby, 1966) lists fewer than 10 studies using infants, in spite of the fact that theoretical discussions (e.g., Freud, 1938 [originally published in 1905]; Piaget, 1951) emphasize the importance of early experience. Theoretical work predicts and experimental work confirms the existence of sex differences in behavior by age 3. There has been little evidence to demonstrate earlier differentiation of sex-appropriate behavior, although it would not be unreasonable to assume this occurs.

Recently, there has been increased interest in infancy, including some work which has shown early sex differences in attentive behavior (Kagan and Lewis, 1965; Lewis, in press). The bulk of this work has been primarily experimental, studying specific responses to specific stimuli or experimental conditions. Moreover, it has dealt with perceptual-cognitive differences rather than personality variables. There has been little observation of freely emitted behavior. Such observations are of importance in supplying researchers with the classes of naturally occurring behaviors, the conditions under which responses normally occur, and the natural preference ordering of behaviors. Knowledge of this repertoire of behaviors provides a background against which behavior under experimental conditions can be evaluated.

The present study utilized a free play situation to observe sex differences in children's behavior toward mother, toys, and a frustration situation at 13 months of age. Because the Ss were participants in a longitudinal study, information on the mother-child relationship at 6 months was also available. This made it possible to assess possible relations between behavior patterns at 6 months and at 13 months.

Method

SUBJECTS

Two samples of 16 girls and 16 boys each, or a total of 64 infants, were seen at 6 and 13 months of age ($\pm$ 6 days). All Ss were born to families residing in southwestern Ohio at the time of the study. All were Caucasian. The mothers had an average of 13.5 years of schooling (range of 10-18 years) and the fathers had an average of 14.5 years of schooling (range of 8-20). The occupations of the fathers ranged from laborer to scientist. Of the 64 infants, 9 girls and 10 boys were first-born and the remaining infants had from 1 to 6 siblings.

THE 6-MONTH VISIT

The procedure of the 6-month visit, presented in detail in Kagan and Lewis (1965), included two visual episodes and an auditory episode where a variety of behavioral responses were recorded. The infant's mother was present during these procedures. At the end of the experimental procedure, the mother was interviewed by one of the experimenters, who had been able to observe both mother and infant for the duration of the session. The interviewer also rated both mother and infant on a rating scale. The items rated for the infant included: amount of activity, irritability, response to mother's behavior, and amount of affect. For the mother, the observer rated such factors as nature of handling, amount of playing with the baby, type of comforting behavior, and amount of vocalization to the baby. Each item was rated on a 7-point scale, with 1 indicating the most activity and 7 the least. For the purpose of this study, it was necessary to obtain a measure of the amount of physical contact the mother initiated with the child. Since scores on the individual scales did not result in sufficient variance in the population, a composite score was obtained by taking the mean score for each mother over all three of the touching-the-infant scales. These included:

This research was conducted at the Fels Research Institute and was supported in part by grants HD-00868, FR-00222, and FR-05537 from the National Institute of Mental Health, U.S. Public Health Service. Editorial assistance was supported by research grant 1 P01 HD01762 from the National Institute of Child Health and Human Development. Portions of this paper were presented at the 1967 meeting of the Society for Research in Child Development, New York. We would like to thank Lynn Godfrey, Cornelia Dodd, and Helen Campbell for their aid in data analysis. Author Lewis' address: Center for Psychological Studies, Educational Testing Service, Princeton, New Jersey 08540.

amount of touching, amount of comforting, and amount of play. The composite touch scores (now called the amount of physical contact) resulted in a sufficiently variable distribution to be used for comparison with the 13-month touch data.

THE 13-MONTH VISIT

Kagan and Lewis (1965), who employed the same 64 infants for their study, described the procedures used at 6 months, which were similar to those of the present (13-month) study. The only addition was a free play procedure, which will be discussed in detail below.

The playroom, 9 by 12 feet, contained nine simple toys: a set of blocks, a pail, a "lawnmower," a stuffed dog, an inflated plastic cat, a set of quoits (graduated plastic doughnuts stacked on a wooden rod), a wooden mallet, a pegboard, and a wooden bug (a pull toy). Also included as toys were any permanent objects in the room, such as the doorknob, latch on the wall, tape on the electrical outlets, and so forth. The mother's chair was located in one corner of the room.

PROCEDURE

Each S, accompanied by his mother, was placed in the observation room. The mother was instructed to watch his play and respond in any way she desired. Most mothers simply watched and responded only when asked for something. The mother was also told that we would be observing from the next room. She held the child on her lap, the door to the playroom was closed, and observation began. At the beginning of the 15 minutes of play, the mother was instructed to place the child on the floor.

MEASUREMENT

Two observers recorded the S's behavior. One dictated a continuous behavioral account into a tape recorder. The second operated an event recorder, which recorded the location of the child in the room and the duration of each contact with the mother.

Dictated recording.—During the initial dictation, a buzzer sounded at regular time intervals, automatically placing a marker on the dictated tape. The dictated behavioral account was typed and each minute divided into 15-second units, each including about three typewritten lines. The typed material was further divided into three 5-second units, each unit being one typed line. Independent experimenters analyzed this typed material. For each minute, the number of toys played with and amount of time spent with each toy was recorded.

Event recorder.—To facilitate recording the activity and location of the child, the floor of the room was divided into 12 squares. For each square, the observer depressed a key on the event recorder for the duration of time the child occupied that square. From this record it was possible to obtain such measures as the amount of time spent in each square and the number of squares traversed. A thirteenth key was depressed each time the child touched the mother. From this record, measures of (a) initial latency in leaving the mother, (b) total amount of time touching the mother, (c) number of times touching the mother, and (d) longest period touching the mother were obtained.

TABLE 1 Summary of Infant Behavior to Mother in Free Play Session

Behavior	Girls	Boys	p
Touching mother:			
$\bar{x}$ latency in seconds to return to mother	273.5	519.5	<.002
$\bar{x}$ number of returns	8.4	3.9	<.001
$\bar{x}$ number of seconds touching mother	84.6	58.8	<.03
Vocalization to mother:			
$\bar{x}$ number of seconds vocalizing to mother	169.8	106.9	<.04
Looking at mother:			
$\bar{x}$ number of seconds looking at mother	57.3	47.0	<.09
$\bar{x}$ number of times looking at mother	10.8	9.2	NS
Proximity to mother			
$\bar{x}$ time in squares closest to mother	464.1	351.4	<.05
$\bar{x}$ time in squares farthest from mother	43.8	44.3	NS

The data analysis presented in this report provides information only on sex differences (a) in response to the mother and (b) in choice and style of play with toys. Other data from this situation are presented elsewhere (Lewis, 1967).

Results

RESPONSE TO MOTHER (13 MONTHS)

Open field.—Boys and girls showed striking differences in their behavior toward their mothers (see Table 1). First, upon being removed from their mothers' laps, girls were reluctant to leave their mothers. When Ss were placed on the floor by their mothers, significantly more girls than boys returned immediately—in less than 5 seconds ($p < .05$ for both samples by Fisher Exact Probability Test). This reluctance to leave their mothers is further indicated by the time it took the children to first return to their mothers. Girls, in both samples, showed significantly shorter latencies than boys. Out of a possible 900 seconds (15 minutes), girls returned after an average of 273.5 seconds, while boys' average latency was nearly twice as long, 519.5 seconds. This difference was highly significant ($p < .002$, Mann-Whitney U test). All significance tests are two-tailed unless otherwise specified.

Once the children left their mothers, girls made significantly more returns, both physical and visual. Girls touched their mothers for an average of 84.6 seconds, while boys touched their mothers for only 58.8 seconds ($p < .03$, Mann-Whitney U test). Girls returned to touch their mothers on an average of 8.4 times, and boys 3.9 times ($p < .001$, Mann-Whitney U test). For the visual returns, the number of times the child looked at the mother and the total amount of time spent looking at the mother were

TABLE 2   Summary of Infant Behavior during Barrier Frustration

Behavior	Girls	Boys	p
$\bar{x}$ number of seconds crying	123.5	76.7	<.05
$\bar{x}$ number of seconds at ends of barrier	106.1	171.0	<.001
$\bar{x}$ number of seconds at center	157.7	95.1	<.01

obtained from the dictated material. The mean number of times girls looked at the mother was 10.8 (as compared with 9.2 for boys), a difference which was not significant. The total amount of time looking at the mother was 57.3 seconds for girls and 47.0 seconds for boys ($p < .09$, Mann-Whitney U test).

Finally, vocalization data were also available from the dictated material. The mean time vocalizing to the mother was 169.8 seconds for girls and 106.9 seconds for boys ($p < .04$, Mann-Whitney U test).

Another measure of the child's response to his mother was the amount of physical distance the child allowed between himself and his mother. Because the observers recorded which squares the child played in, it was possible to obtain the amount of time Ss spent in the four squares closest to the mother. The mean time in these squares for girls was 464.1 seconds; for boys, it was 351.4 seconds ($p < .05$, Mann-Whitney U test). Moreover, boys spent more time in the square farthest from the mother, although the differences were not significant.

Barrier frustration.—At the end of the 15 minutes of free play, a barrier of mesh on a wood frame was placed in such a way as to divide the room in half. The mother placed the child on one side and remained on the opposite side along with the toys. Thus, the child's response to stress was observed.

Sex differences were again prominent, with girls crying and motioning for help consistently more than boys (see Table 2). For both samples, amount of time crying was available from the dictated record. Girls' mean time crying was 123.5 seconds, compared with 76.7 seconds for boys ($p < .05$, Mann-Whitney U test). Boys, on the other hand, appeared to make a more active attempt to get around the barrier. That is, they spent significantly more time at the ends of the barrier than girls, while girls spent significantly more time in the center of the barrier—near the position where they were placed ($p < .01$, Mann-Whitney U test).

TOY PREFERENCE (13 MONTHS)

A second area of experimental interest was toy preference. When the nine toys were ranked in order of the total amount of time they were played with, girls and boys showed similar patterns of preference.

Table 3 presents each toy and the amount of time it was played with. Play with the dog and cat were combined into one category. The toys which were used most were the lawnmower, blocks, and quoits, and those that were used least were the stuffed dog and cat. On a *post hoc* basis, it seems as if the toys which received the most attention were those that offered the most varied possibilities for manipulation.

Although there were no sex differences in overall toy

TABLE 3   Mean Time Playing with Toys, by Sex

	Girls	Boys	p
Total time with:			
Mallet	51.7	60.8	
Bug	50.2	45.3	
Pail	34.6	22.9	
Blocks	126.5	77.5	<.03
Lawnmower	220.3	235.6	
Cat plus dog (combined)	31.0	9.1	<.01
Quoits	122.7	130.3	
Pegboard	37.2	28.7	<.05
Nontoys	6.9	31.0	<.005
Putting toys in pail	28.2	43.0	
Banging toys	19.7	34.8	<.05
Lawnmowing on other toys	2.8	9.8	
Other manipulation of two toys	28.2	10.3	<.05

preference, there were significant sex differences in the amount of time spent with individual toys and in the ways toys were used. Girls played with blocks, pegboard, and with the dog and cat (the only toys with faces) more than boys did ($p < .03$, $p < .03$, $p < .01$, respectively, Mann-Whitney U test).

In terms of style of play, there were also sex differences. Observation of girls' play indicates that girls chose toys which involved more fine than gross muscle coordination, while for boys, the reverse was true—building blocks and playing with dog and cat versus playing with mallet and rolling the lawnmower over other toys. Moreover, boys spent more time playing with the nontoys (doorknob, covered outlets, lights, etc.; $p < .005$, Mann-Whitney U test).

In terms of overall activity level, boys were more active than girls. Girls tended to sit and play with combinations of toys ($p < .05$, Mann-Whitney U test), while boys tended to be more active and bang the toys significantly more than girls ($p < .05$, Mann-Whitney U test). In addition, the children were rated by two observers on the vigor of their play behavior; a rating of 1 was given for high vigor, 2 was given for medium vigor, and 3 for low vigor. These ratings were made from the dictated material for each minute, so that the final score for each S represented a mean of 15 vigor ratings. The interobserver reliability was $\rho = 0.78$. They boys played significantly more vigorously than girls (mean for boys was 2.45, varying from 1.2 to 3.0; for girls, the mean was 2.65, varying from 1.9 to 3.0 [$p < .05$, Mann-Whitney U test]). This vigor difference was also seen in the style of boys' play; for example, boys banged with the mallet and mowed over other toys. Thus, there were not only significant differences in the choice of toys, but also in the way the toys were manipulated. The data indicate that there are important and significant sex differences in very young children's response to their mothers, to frustration, and in play behavior.

Mother-infant touch (6 months).—One possible determinant of the child's behavior toward the mother in the playroom is the mother's behavior toward the child at an earlier age. The 6-month data indicated that mothers of girls touched their infants more than mothers of boys. On the composite score, where 1 indicated most touching and

7 least, there were twice as many girls as boys whose mothers were rated 1-3 and twice as many boys as girls whose mothers were rated 5-7 ($p < .05, \chi^2$ test). Moreover, mothers vocalized to girls significantly more than to boys ($p < .001$, Mann-Whitney U test), and significantly more girls than boys were breast-fed rather than bottle-fed ($p < .02$, Mann-Whitney U test). Thus, when the children were 6 months old, mothers touched, talked to, and handled their daughters more than their sons, and when they were 13 months old, girls touched and talked to their mothers more than boys did. To explore this relationship further, mothers were divided into high, medium, and low mother-touch-infant groups (at 6 months), with the extreme groups consisting of the upper and lower 25 per cent of the sample. For the boys at 13 months, the mean number of seconds of physical contact with the mother indicated a linear relation to amount of mother touching (14, 37, and 47 seconds for the low, medium, and high mother-touch groups, respectively; Kruskal-Wallis, $p < .10$). Thus, the more physical contact the mother made with a boy at 6 months, the more he touched the mother at 13 months. For the girls, the relation appeared to be curvilinear. The mean number of seconds of touching the mother for the low, medium, and high mother-touch groups was 101, 55, and 88 seconds, respectively (Kruskal-Wallis, $p < .10$). The comparable distribution for number of seconds close to the mother was 589, 397, and 475 seconds (Kruskal-Wallis, $p < .03$). A girl whose mother initiated very much or very little contact with her at 6 months was more likely to seek a great deal of physical contact with the mother in the playroom than one whose mother was in the medium-touch infant group.

Observation of the mothers' behavior when their infants were 6 months old revealed that five of the seven mothers of girls who showed little physical contact were considered by the staff to be severely rejecting mothers. The data suggest that the child of a rejecting mother continues to seek contact despite the mother's behavior. This result is consistent with Harlow's work with rejected monkeys (Seay, Alexander, & Harlow, 1964) and Provence's work with institutionalized children (Provence, 1965; Provence & Lipton, 1962) and suggests that the child's need for contact with his mother is a powerful motive.

Discussion

Observation of the children's behavior indicated that girls were more dependent, showed less exploratory behavior, and their play behavior reflected a more quiet style. Boys were independent, showed more exploratory behavior, played with toys requiring gross motor activity, were more vigorous, and tended to run and bang in their play. Obviously, these behavior differences approximate those usually found between the sexes at later ages. The data demonstrate that these behavior patterns are already present in the first year of life and that some of them suggest a relation to the mother's response to the infant in the first 6 months. It is possible that at 6 months, differential behavior on the part of the mother is already a response to differential behavior on the part of the infant. Moss (1967) has found behavioral sex differences as early as 3 weeks. In interpreting mother-infant interaction data, Moss suggests that maternal behavior is initially a response to the infant's behavior. As the infant becomes older, if the mother responds contingently to his signals, her behavior acquires reinforcement value which enables her to influence and regulate the infant's behavior. Thus, parents can be active promulgators of sex-role behavior through reinforcement of sex-role-appropriate responses within the first year of life.

The following is offered as a hypothesis concerning sex-role learning. In the first year or two, the parents reinforce those behaviors they consider sex-role appropriate and the child learns these sex-role behaviors independent of any internal motive, that is, in the same way he learns any appropriate response rewarded by his parents. The young child has little idea as to the rules governing this reinforcement. It is suggested, however, that as the child becomes older (above age 3), the rules for this class of reinforced behavior become clearer and he develops internal guides to follow these earlier reinforced rules. In the past, these internalized rules, motivating without apparent reinforcement, have been called modeling behavior. Thus, modeling behavior might be considered an extension or internalization of the earlier reinforced sex-role behavior. However, it is clear that the young child, before seeking to model his behavior, is already knowledgeable in some appropriate sex-role behavior. In that the hypothesis utilizes both early reinforcement as well as subsequent cognitive elaboration, it would seem to bridge the reinforcement notion of Gewirtz (1967) and Kohberg's cognitive theory (1966) of identification.

The fact that parents are concerned with early display of sex-role-appropriate behavior is reflected in an interesting clinical observation. On some occasions, staff members have incorrectly identified the sex of an infant. Mothers are often clearly irritated by this error. Since the sex of a fully clothed infant is difficult to determine, the mistake seems understandable and the mother's displeasure uncalled for. If, however, she views the infant and behaves toward him in a sex-appropriate way, our mistake is more serious. That is, the magnitude of her displeasure reveals to us the magnitude of her cognitive commitment to this infant as a child of given sex.

Regardless of the interpretation of the observed sex differences, the free play procedure provides a standardized situation in which young children can be observed without interference from experimental manipulation. While behavior under these conditions may be somewhat different from the young child's typical daily behavior, our data indicate that behavior in the play situation is related to other variables, that behavior can be predicted from earlier events, and that it is indicative of later sex-role behavior. The results of the present investigation as well as the work of Bell and Costello (1964), Kagan and Lewis (1965), and Lewis (in press) indicate sex differences within the first year over a wide variety of infant behaviors. The fact that sex differences do appear in the first year has important methodological implications for infant research. These findings emphasize the importance of checking sex differences before pooling data and, most important, of considering sex as a variable in any infant study.

NOTES

1. Stanley B. Messer and Michael Lewis replicated these sex differences in a sample of children from a lower socio-economic background. Messer, S. B. and Lewis, M., "Social Class and Sex Differences in the Attachment and Play Behavior of the Year-Old Infant," *Merrill-Palmer Quarterly*, in press.

REFERENCES

Bell, R. Q., & Costello, N. S. Three tests for sex differences in tactile sensitivity in the newborn. *Biologia Neonatorum*, 1964, 1, 335-347.
Freud, S. Three contributions to the theory of sex. Reprinted in *The basic writings of Sigmund Freud*. New York: Random House, 1938.
Gerwitz, J. The learning of generalized imitation and its implications for identification. Paper presented at the Society for Research in Child Development Meeting, New York, March, 1967.
Kagan, J., & Lewis, M. Studies of attention in the human infant. *Merrill-Palmer Quarterly*, 1965, 11, 95-127.
Kohlberg, L. A cognitive-developmental analysis of children's sex role concepts and attitudes. In E. Maccoby (Ed.), *The development of sex differences*. Stanford, Calif.: Stanford University Press, 1966.
Lewis, M. Infant attention: response decrement as a measure of cognitive processes, or what's new, Baby Jane? Paper presented at the Society for Research in Child Development Meeting, symposium on "The Role of Attention in Cognitive Development," New York, March, 1967.
Lewis, M. Infants' responses to facial stimuli during the first year of life. *Developmental Psychology*, in press.
Maccoby, E. (Ed.) *The development of sex differences*. Stanford, Calif: Stanford University Press, 1966.
Moss, H. Sex, age and state as determinants of mother-infant interaction. *Merrill-Palmer Quarterly*, 1967, 13(1), 19-36.
Piaget, J. *Play, dreams and imitation in childhood*. New York: Norton, 1951.
Provence, S. Disturbed personality development in infancy: a comparison of two inadequately nurtured infants. *Merrill-Palmer Quarterly*, 1965, 2, 149-170.
Provence, S., & Lipton, R. C. *Infants in institutions*. New York: International University Press, 1962.
Seay, B., Alexander, B. K., & Harlow, H. F. Maternal behavior of socially deprived rhesus monkeys. *Journal of Abnormal and Social Psychology*, 1964, 69(4), 345-354.

6 Sex differences in intellectual functioning

Eleanor E. Maccoby

This chapter will present and evaluate several possible explanations of the differences found between the performances of boys and girls on a variety of intellectual tasks. As a preliminary step the findings concerning sex differences in average proficiency on these tasks will be briefly summarized. Then any sex differences in the way intellectual performance correlates with other variables (such as personality factors and socialization experiences) will be discussed. And finally, these findings will be considered in the light of known or inferred differences in situations or demands impinging upon the two sexes, to see whether these might influence the nature of intellectual development.

Sex differences in average performance

Several detailed reviews of the differences between the sexes in average performance on tests of abilities are available in the literature (Anastasi, 1958; Terman and Tyler, 1954), and the results of the studies included in these reviews as well as those appearing more recently are summarized in the bibliography at the end of this volume. The relevant studies will not be completely referenced here. The primary conclusions to be drawn from them are:

(1) *General intelligence*. Most widely used tests of general intelligence have been standardized to minimize or eliminate sex differences. Whether differences are found on any particular test will depend on the balance of the items— whether there are more items of a kind on which one sex normally excels. There is a tendency for girls to test somewhat higher on tests of general intelligence during the preschool years, boys during the high school years. There is a possibility that the latter finding is in part a function of differential school dropout rates; more boys drop out, leaving a more highly selected group of boys in high school. But some longitudinal studies in which the same children have been tested repeatedly through their growth cycle show greater gains for boys than girls. Sontag et al. (1958) and Elbert and Simmons (1943) both report this finding; Bayley (1956, 1957) does not. The changes in tested intelligence that occur during late adolescence and adulthood appear to favor men somewhat; that is, women decline somewhat more, or gain somewhat less, depending on the test used (Terman and Oden, 1947; Bradway and Thompson, 1962; Bayley and Oden, 1955; Haan, 1963).

(2) *Verbal ability*. Through the preschool years and in the early school years, girls exceed boys in most aspects of verbal performance. They say their first word sooner, articulate more clearly and at an earlier age, use longer sentences, and are more fluent. By the beginning of school, however, there are no longer any consistent differences in vocabulary. Girls learn to read sooner, and there are more

Reprinted from The Development of Sex Differences, *edited by Eleanor E. Maccoby, pp. 25-36, 38-44, 46-55, with the permission of the publishers, Standard University Press. © 1966 by the Board of Trustees of the Leland Stanford Junior University.*

boys than girls who require special training in remedial reading programs; but by approximately the age of ten, a number of studies show that boys have caught up in their reading skills. Throughout the school years, girls do better on tests of grammar, spelling, and word fluency.

(3) *Number ability.* Girls learn to count at an earlier age. Through the school years, there are no consistent sex differences in skill at arithmetical computation. During grade school years, some studies show boys beginning to forge ahead on tests of "arithmetical reasoning," although a number of studies reveal no sex differences on this dimension at this time. Fairly consistently, however, boys excel at arithmetical reasoning in high school, and the differences are substantially in favor of men among college students and adults. In a longitudinal sample, Haan finds men accelerating more than women in arithmetical ability during early adulthood.

(4) *Spatial ability.* While very young boys and girls do not differ on spatial tasks such as form boards and block design, by the early school years boys consistently do better on spatial tasks, and this difference continues through the high school and college years.

(5) *Analytic ability.* This term has several meanings. It is used to refer to the ability to respond to one aspect of a stimulus situation without being greatly influenced by the background or field in which it is presented. In this sense, it is equivalent to what Witkin calls "field independence." On measures of this trait, such as the Embedded Figures Test and the Rod and Frame Test, boys of school age score consistently and substantially higher than girls (Witkin et al., 1954). Sigel et al. (1963), however, did not find sex differences on an embedded-figures test among a sample of five-year-olds, nor did Maccoby et al. (1965) among four-year-olds.

A related meaning of "analytic ability" is concerned with modes of grouping diverse arrays of objects or pictures. People who group "analytically"—put objects together on the basis of some selected element they have in common (e.g., all the persons who have a hand raised)—have been shown to be less influenced by background conditions in recognition tests, and hence are analytic in the Witkin sense as well. Boys more commonly use analytic groupings than do girls. How early this difference emerges is still an open question. Sigel did not find sex differences in grouping behavior among four- and five-year-olds. Kagan et al. (1963) did find clear sex differences among children in the second to fourth grade.

(6) *"Creativity."* There are relatively few studies comparing the sexes on aspects of creativity, and the outcome depends on the definition of the term. If the emphasis is on the ability to break set or restructure a problem, there is a tendency for boys and men to be superior, particularly if the problem involves a large perceptual component. Breaking set is involved in the tasks used to measure "analytic ability," discussed above, and in some of the tests that have a high loading on the space factor.

If creativity is thought of in terms of divergent, as distinct from convergent, thinking (see Guilford, 1956), the evidence appears to favor girls somewhat, although the findings are not consistent. A task requiring children to think of

ways in which toys could be improved showed that in the first two grades of school, each sex was superior when dealing with toys appropriate to its own sex, but by the third grade, boys were superior on both feminine and masculine toys. On the other hand, girls and women do better on a battery of divergent tasks measuring the variety of ideas produced for the solution of verbally presented problems (Klausmeier and Wiersma, 1964; Trembly, 1964).

(7) *Achievement.* Girls get better grades than boys throughout the school years, even in subjects in which boys score higher on standard achievement tests. In adulthood, after graduation from school, men achieve substantially more than women in almost any aspect of intellectual activity where achievements can be compared—books and articles written, artistic productivity, and scientific achievements. A follow-up study of gifted children showed that while gifted boys tended to realize their potential in their occupations and creative output, gifted girls did not.

How large are the group differences summarized above? It is difficult to find a satisfactory answer to this question, for some studies report that a difference between the sexes is statistically significant, without giving the actual magnitude of the mean scores that are being compared. Even when mean scores are given, there is a problem of the meaning of the units on the scale—whether they are equal throughout the scale. With these reservations in mind, existing information does suggest that sex differences in spatial ability and in some aspects of analytic ability are substantial from the early school years on, and that sex differences in mathematical reasoning by high school age are also substantial, while differences in verbal ability are less marked. But on all measures reported, there is considerable overlap between the distribution of scores of the two sexes.

Correlations between intellectual performance and personality characteristics

So far, we have been summarizing the known differences between the sexes in their average performance on a variety of tasks. But this, of course, does not provide a complete account of sex differences. Even on tests where the distribution of scores is the same for the two sexes (in mean and standard deviation), the array of scores will often correlate differently with other variables for boys and girls (Sigel, 1964). We will now examine what is known concerning the linkages between performance on intellectual tasks and other characteristics, especially personality characteristics, to see whether the nature of these linkages is different for the two sexes.

IMPULSE CONTROL

For the present, we will use the term "impulse" to designate high levels of undirected activity and the inability to delay or inhibit behavior that is incompatible with goal-directed activity. We assume that the ability to persist at a task involves inhibition of competing response tendencies, hence we include both "distractability" and low task persistance as indicating lack of impulse control.

Sigel et al. (1963) report a study of children four to five years old, in which observational measures were taken of

(1) emotional control, (2) cautiousness, and (3) attentiveness. In addition, each child was given a grouping test, in which he had to select from an array of pictures the one that was most like a standard. Some children adopted a "descriptive part-whole" grouping style (called analytic responses by Kagan et al., 1963). The sexes did not differ on Sigel's three measures of impulsiveness. But for boys, the frequency of analytic grouping was positively correlated with emotional control, cautiousness, and attentiveness, while for girls these correlations were negative. That is, the girl who used this grouping style was impulsive, the boy controlled.

A similar result was obtained by Kagan et al. (1964), working with the Fels longitudinal sample. He reports a correlation of .45 between "emotional control" and the use of analytic concepts in a grouping test for boys, while the corresponding correlation for girls is −.20.

In a study by Sutton-Smith et al. (1964) it was found that adopting a winning strategy in a game of tick-tack-toe (previously found to correlate with I.Q.) was characteristic of girls who were aggressive, dominant, and hyperactive, while the boys who adopted a winning strategy at this game were not especially active and showed a preference for "conceptual recreations."

Murphy (1962) reports that, for boys, a measure of "coping" is correlated with "the ability to balance gratification and frustration" (which we may take to be a measure of impulse control); for girls, these two variables are not correlated. Among girls, on the other hand, coping is positively correlated with speed or tempo of behavior, a factor that does not relate to coping among boys.

Kagan and Moss, in their longitudinal study (1962) done at the Fels Institute, report that measures of hyperkinesis (high levels of undirected activity) during childhood correlate negatively with adult intellectual interests for men, while the correlation is slightly positive for women. It appears, then, from these varied studies, that impulsiveness is a negative factor for at least some aspects of intellectual development in boys, but for girls it is a less negative—and perhaps even a positive—factor.

FEARFULNESS AND ANXIETY

The Kagan and Moss study also dealt with the relationship between fearfulness and intellectual development. Boys who were timid and cautious in early childhood had higher I.Q.'s and developed greater intellectual interests in adulthood; for girls, the correlations between fearfulness and measures of intellectual performance were zero or negative. For example, timidity, measured during the 10-14 year age period, correlated −.63 with the degree of intellectual interests the girl displayed in adulthood, while the comparable figure for boys was .26. Bayley and Schaefer (1964) working with a different longitudinal sample, find timidity and reserve to be negative factors for both sexes, but especially so for boys during middle childhood and adolescence. The correlations they report between I.Q. and absence of shyness in earlier childhood, however, are more positive for girls than for boys, and hence more consistent with the Kagan and Moss findings. It may be that the

relationship between timidity and intellectual performance is highly age-specific, and more so for boys than for girls.

Correlations between measures of anxiety and measures of aptitude or achievement are substantially negative for girls and women, while the correlations are either low negative, zero, or positive for boys and men. The evidence fairly consistently points to this difference in the role anxiety plays for the two sexes (Davidson and Sarason, 1961; Iscoe and Carden, 1961; Russell and Sarason, 1965; Walter et al., 1964), although there is one set of contrary findings (French, 1961).

AGGRESSION AND COMPETITIVENESS

In one study (Maccoby and Rau, 1962), aggressiveness, as measured by a peer-nomination technique in classrooms of fifth-grade children, was negatively related (slightly but significantly, r = −.27) to a measure of total intelligence (PMA) for boys, and unrelated to this measure for girls. And in the same study, anxiety over aggression was positively related to intelligence for boys (r = .39), unrelated for girls. In the Fels sample (Moss and Kagan 1962) nonphysical aggression was positively related to I.Q. among girls, unrelated among boys. E. K. Beller (1962) found, in a sample of five- and six-year-old children, a strong negative relationship between aggressiveness and performance on an embedded-figures test for boys, while these variables were uncorrelated for girls. As previously noted, Sutton-Smith's findings on a winning game strategy yielded positive correlations with aggressiveness for girls, but not for boys. Thus aggressiveness appears to be more of an inhibitor, or less of a facilitator, for intellectual development among boys than among girls.

In the Fels sample, competitiveness was found to correlate with I.Q., and with progressive increases in I.Q., for both sexes, but the correlations are higher for girls than boys (Sontag et al., 1958; Moss and Kagan, 1962).

LEVEL OF ASPIRATION AND ACHIEVEMENT MOTIVATION

The evidence is not clear whether boys or girls have a higher correlation between ability (as measured by I.Q. tests) and achievement. Phillips et al. (1960), working with seventh-grade children, found the correlation to be higher for boys. Coleman (1961) reports that among high school students, boys named as "best scholar" had higher I.Q. scores than girls so named, despite the fact that the girls had higher average I.Q. scores in the population studied. He suggests that girls of this age are caught up in a "double bind." They wish to conform to their parents' and teachers' expectations of good academic performance, but fear that high academic achievement will make them unpopular with boys. As a result of these dual pressures, Coleman suggests, the brightest girls do creditably in school but less than their best. On the other hand, the brightest boys feel free to excel in scholarship and do so in fact.

Terman and Oden's follow-up study of gifted children (1947) disclosed that, for girls, there was no relationship between the level of occupational achievement and I.Q. as measured during the school years, while for boys this correlation was substantial. There is evidence that girls who are underachievers in high school usually begin to be so at about the onset of puberty (Shaw and McCuen, 1960), while for boys underachievement in high school usually has an earlier onset. This contrast is a further indication that the achievement drop-off among girls as they reach maturity is linked to the adult female sex role.

While additional studies contrasting age levels are needed to confirm the point, it appears that the social pressures to do well or poorly in school may have a reverse time sequence for the two sexes. As noted above, the pressures on bright girls not to do as well as they can tend to be augmented in adolescence, so that correlations between ability and achievement ought to be higher during the early school years. By contrast, peer-group pressures on boys in the early school years are often (though not always) in the direction of achievement in sports and other nonacademic pursuits; and boys of this age are frequently engaged in efforts to achieve autonomy, especially in relation to their mothers, with the result that they are less willing than girls to accede to the demands of their predominantly female teachers. In adolescence, however, especially for middle-class boys, the pressures for college entrance and professional preparation begin to be felt, with the result that the more intelligent boys begin to buckle down at this time. Even in high school, however, the boys' more autonomous approach to their school work is indicated in the greater selectivity of their efforts: boys are likely to do well in subjects that interest them and poorly in subjects that bore them, while girls tend to perform uniformly in all their school subjects (Coleman, 1961).

One factor that may operate to produce a higher correlation between aptitude and performance for boys throughout the school years is that boys appear to evaluate their own abilities and performance more realistically than girls. Crandall et al. (1962) asked children how well they expected to do on a new task they were about to undertake. Among boys, the brighter the boy, the better he expected to do on the new task (r = .62). Among girls, the brighter the girl the *less* well she expected to do on a new task (r = −.41). Furthermore, when the children were asked whether they believed that their score on a task was mostly a function of their own efforts, or a matter of chance or luck, the brighter boys more often believed that success was an outcome of their own efforts. Among the girls, there was no relationship between I.Q. and belief in self-responsibility versus chance. P. S. Sears (1963) similarly found a positive correlation between a measure of intelligence and boys' self-appraisal of their own abilities, while these variables were essentially uncorrelated for girls.

There is some evidence that girls appear to be more afraid of failure, and more disorganized by it, than boys. Harmatz (1962), working with college students, found that when women were working on a fairly difficult task and were told that they were not doing well on it, both their level of aspiration and their performance declined, as compared with a control group of women who did not receive this negative feedback. This is consistent with McClelland's (1953) finding that among women the level of achievement motivation (as reflected in TAT stories) is not affected by

an "arousal" treatment involving academic competition, while among men it is increased. Moriarty (1961) observed the task orientation and coping behavior of a group of preschool children while they were taking individually administered intelligence tests. She found that while girls initially approached the task in a more organized way, as the tasks became harder and failures were encountered, the girls became less integrated in their performance and more desirous of leaving the field than did boys.

Murphy (1962) makes a similar observation concerning the behavior of children of nursery school age during an intelligence test: "Confronted with difficulty, a larger number of boys became more active in expressing autonomy, while girls tended to become more passive." (p. 210.) Crandall and Rabson (1960), working with children ranging in age from three to nine years, found that when children were offered the choice of returning either to tasks at which they had previously failed or to tasks at which they had previously succeeded, girls more often chose to repeat their earlier successes, while boys tended to prefer working further on tasks they had not mastered previously. The evidence is not entirely consistent, however. Yonge (1964), working with college men and women, found that when given insoluble problems presented as an I.Q. test, women attempted more problems but made more errors. The increased error rate may indicate some disorganization of behavior under failure, and this would be consistent with earlier findings; but the increase in number of problems attempted does not reflect the usual pattern of decreased level of aspiration with failure among women. Perhaps the Yonge findings are a function of a highly selected sample. In any case, the bulk of the findings seem to indicate that boys are more likely to rise to an intellectual challenge, girls to retreat from one. What may be a physiological indicator of this phenomenon was noted by Leiderman and Shapiro (1963) in their study of autonomic responses during group problem solving with an ambiguous task. While being rewarded for initiations of a solution, the Galvanic Skin Potential of female subjects decreased, that of male subjects increased.

SEX-TYPING

"Masculinity" and "femininity" have been measured in a number of ways. Some of the standard measures have a single scale running from masculine to feminine. Others (Brim, 1958; Oetzel, 1961) measure masculinity and femininity independently, so that it is possible for an individual to obtain a high score on both measures if he possesses traits commonly labeled as characteristic of the two different sexes. Using the latter kind of measure, Oetzel found that, among fifth-grade boys, total PMA scores were positively correlated with femininity and slightly negatively correlated with masculinity; in other words, the brighter boys were considerably more feminine and slightly less masculine than their less intelligent peers. Among girls, however, total PMA scores were slightly positively correlated with both masculinity and femininity. This means that the high I.Q. girl is likely to be dominant and striving (characteristics labeled "masculine"), but she may also act more "grown-up" and be more anxious to do things for other people than her less intelligent peers (behaviors normally classified as "feminine").

The Fels longitudinal study (Moss) reports that a young child's interest in the games and activities characteristic of the opposite sex is positively correlated with I.Q.; that is, the brighter girls are more likely to enjoy baseball and other boys' games, while the brighter boys will more often engage in feminine activities.

Both Barron (1957) and MacKinnon (1962) report that men who are outstanding in originality or creativity score more toward the feminine end of an M-F scale than do their less creative counterparts. This difference, they say, reflects a greater breadth of interests among creative men; for example, such men have aesthetic interests, which are usually included as feminine indicators on an M-F scale because women are, on the average, more likely than men to have strong aesthetic interests.

Bieri (1960) studied sex-typing in relation to performance on an embedded-figures test. He found that men who obtained high scores on this test (and hence would be labeled "analytical") revealed identification with their mothers rather than their fathers on the semantic differential. Analytical female subjects, by contrast, were characterized by a high level of identification with their fathers. This latter finding is consistent with the observations of Plank and Plank (1954), who studied the autobiographies of a group of outstanding women mathematicians, and found that there was evidence in all of them of a strong attachment to, and identification with, their fathers rather than their mothers.

The studies cited so far indicate that analytic thinking, creativity, and high general intelligence are associated with cross-sex-typing, in that the men and boys who score high are more feminine, and the women and girls more masculine, than their low-scoring same-sex counterparts. There are a few exceptions in the literature to this generalization. Milton (1957) correlated scores on the Terman-Miles M-F scale with scores on problems requiring restructuring and breaking set, and found that the more masculine subjects of both sexes did best on these problems. In a study of young boys, Anastasiow (1963) administered a toy-preference test of sex-typing and ease of learning first-grade-level reading and arithmetic, with the high-masculine group doing best on school tasks, the high-feminine next best, and the intermediate group least well. So the evidence for boys is somewhat equivocal (the differences perhaps being a function of how sex-typing is measured), although the weight of evidence does support an association between femininity and intellectual performance. For girls and women, the evidence consistently points to masculinity as a correlate of intellectuality.

It is important to note, however, that this cross-sex typing does not imply that intellectual individuals are sexually uninterested in, or unattractive to, the opposite sex. It merely means that they share more of the interests and activities normally characteristic of the opposite sex.

DEPENDENCY, PASSIVITY, AND INDEPENDENCE

For both sexes, there is a tendency for the more passive-dependent children to perform poorly on a variety of intellectual tasks, and for independent children to excel. However, for some kinds of tasks, the relationships are stronger for boys than for girls, and for others the reverse is true. In the Fels longitudinal study, observational measures of dependency were taken, and were then related to I.Q. (Moss and Kagan, 1962). For boys, the correlations ranged from zero to slightly positive. For girls, they were negative; that is, the less dependent girls were the brighter ones.

Also using the Fels sample, Sontag et al. (1958) studied the personality factors associated with progressive increases in I.Q., and found that independence was a factor for both sexes, but that the relationship was considerably stronger for boys. Bieri, studying the correlation of performance on the Embedded Figures Test with "acceptance of authority," found that subjects who refuse to accept authority do considerably better on the EFT; this was true for subject of both sexes, but the relationship was even greater for the male subjects. Nakamura (1958) gave his subject a set of problems requiring restructuring for their solution. He also gave the subjects a perceptual test in which they could either rely upon their own judgments or go along with the rigged consensus of a group of observers. The subjects who did best on the restructuring problems were those who resisted the conformity pressures in the perceptual situation, and, again, the correlation was higher for male subjects.

Witkin (1962) summarizes the work done by himself and others relating analytic perceptual style (field independence) to a variety of indicators on the dependence-independence dimension. The evidence he cites is impressive in showing that both global (field dependent) perceivers and those who have difficulty breaking set in problem solving are dependent in their interpersonal relations, suggestible, conforming, and likely to rely on others for guidance and support. Most of Witkin's work has been done with boys alone, so we do not have evidence from this source concerning sex differences that may exist in the magnitude of the relationship between an analytic cognitive style and an independent orientation toward others.

Possible causal factors of sex differences in intellectual abilities

The research summarized so far has shown that (1) there are a number of aspects of intellectual performance on which the sexes differ consistently in the average scores obtained, and that (2) whether or not there is a difference in average performance on a given task, there are some substantial sex differences in the intercorrelations between intellectual performance and other characteristics of the individual or his environment. We turn now to an examination of several possible explanations for these differences.

DEVELOPMENTAL TIMETABLE

Physiologically, girls mature faster than boys. And because certain aspects of intellectual development cannot occur until the relevant physical structures are complete, we might expect girls to develop some abilities earlier than boys. For example, at birth the cortical structures relevant to speech are not fully formed. Insofar as speech must wait until they are, we might expect girls to talk sooner than boys. The physiological timetable, of course, determines not only the individual's rate of development in early life but also the age at which he reaches his optimum level, the duration of his stay at this level, and the time of onset and the rate of the aging process. The fact that females mature faster during the first part of the life cycle does not necessarily imply that they begin to age sooner, although they may, despite their greater average longevity.

The sex differences found in general intelligence during the early part of the life span, insofar as these differences may be determined from tests standardized to minimize them, do seem to parallel the physiological trends. That is, girls get off to a faster start in language and in some other aspects of cognitive performance. Moreover, parent-child resemblances in intelligence set in earlier for girls than boys. The sexes are very similar during the early and middle school years, and then boys begin to forge ahead in some ability areas during the high school years. But Bayley (1956) has shown that the rate of intellectual growth is unrelated to the rate of physical growth if one scores both in terms of the per cent of mature growth attained. Hence it does not appear that there is any single developmental timetable controlling both physical and mental growth. Even if some of these differences could be accounted for in terms of different developmental timetables, it is doubtful whether some of the major differences we have noted could be so explained. It is difficult to see, for example, why maturational factors should produce greater differences between the sexes in spatial than verbal performance. Nor why a fast-developing organism should show different kinds of relationships between intellectual functions and personality traits than a slow-developing organism. We must therefore turn to different explanatory concepts.

DIRECT EFFECTS OF SEX-TYPED INTERESTS

Perhaps the explanation for the differences we have noted is very simple: members of each sex are encouraged in, and become interested in and proficient at, the kinds of tasks that are most relevant to the roles they fill currently or are expected to fill in the future. According to this view, boys in high school forge ahead in math because they and their parents and teachers know they may become engineers or scientists; on the other hand, girls know that they are unlikely to need math in the occupations they will take up when they leave school. And adult women, most of whom become housewives or work at jobs that do not make many intellectual demands, decline in measures of "total intelligence" because such tests call upon skills that are not being used by adult women as extensively as they are used by adult men. As far as women's lack of creativity and intellectual productivity is concerned, we could argue that women are busy managing households and rearing children, and that these activities usually preclude any serious commitment to other creative endeavors. Undoubtedly, matters of opportunity and life setting play a very large role in the relative accomplishments of the two sexes. That this is not the whole story, however, is suggested by a study of Radcliffe Ph.D.'s (1956), in which it was found that the women Ph.D.'s who had taken academic posts had published substantially less than their male counterparts, and that this was just as true of unmarried academic women as it was of

married ones. Thus women who are as well off as men (or perhaps better off) with respect to alternative demands on their time are nevertheless less productive. It is difficult to attribute this fact to anything about the professional roles they currently occupy. If their behavior is role-determined, it must be determined by sex roles established or anticipated earlier in life.

Some of the major sex differences we have noted—some appearing at a fairly early age—do not appear to have any direct relevance to adult sex roles, actual or anticipated. Does a girl of nine do poorly on an embedded-figures test because she thinks that this kind of skill is not going to be important for her later on in life, and well on a spelling test because she thinks this kind of skill is going to be important. It is doubtful whether either children or adults see those ability areas where we have detected the greatest sex differences as sex-role specific. This is not to say that sex-typing is irrelevant to intellectual development. But it is doubtful whether the sex differences in spatial ability, analytic style, and breaking set can be understood in terms of their greater direct relevance to the role requirements of one sex or the other.

OPPORTUNITIES TO LEARN

Do the sexes differ in their opportunities to learn the skills and content of the ability areas where stable sex differences have been found? It has been widely assumed that girls' early verbal superiority might be due to their spending more time with adults, particularly with their mothers. From research on birth order and experimental studies of the effects of verbal interaction with adults in language acquisition, it may be safely inferred that the amount of a child's contact with adults does influence his language development. Preschool girls are kept at home with their mothers, the argument goes, while boys are allowed to go out to play with age-mates. As a result, girls have more opportunity to develop language skills. But when children enter school, and boys are exposed to intensive stimulation from the teacher, they catch up. A weakness of this argument is that it does not explain why boys catch up in vocabulary and reading comprehension, but not in fluency, spelling, and grammar. And furthermore, we lack direct evidence that preschool girls are kept at home more. Although it fits our stereotypes of the two sexes to think of girls as more protected, we must consider the possibility that girls may actually be given more freedom than boys. Because girls mature faster, perhaps parents can trust them sooner than boys to play away from home with little adult supervision. We simply lack information on this point.

Similarly, it has been suggested that boys acquire greater spatial and perceptual-analytic ability because they have more opportunity to manipulate objects. Again, we have no evidence that this is so. It is true that if one watches nursery school children at play, one is more likely to find boys building with blocks and girls placing doll furniture in a doll house or pretending to cook with beaters and bowls; but it is difficult to see why one of these kinds of object manipulation should lead to greater spatial ability than the other. We know little about what kinds of learning experiences are involved when a child dissects stimuli (as the analytical, field-independent child does) instead of responding to them globally, but it is difficult to see why sheer quantity of stimulus exposure should make a difference beyond a certain point. That is, it is reasonable to suppose that a child who is subjected to severe stimulus deprivation may find it difficult to make fine perceptual discriminations, and hence might perceive more globally. But normally reared children of both sexes have considerable opportunity to move about in space and explore a variety of objects. We suspect that exposure to a variety of stimuli is a necessary but not sufficient condition for the development of an analytic cognitive style, and that children of both sexes, if they grow up in a normal environment, will have enough stimulus contact to permit, if not ensure, this development.

"IDENTIFICATION" AND MODELING

It has been thought that girls may be more verbal and boys more quantitative because children tend to model themselves primarily upon the same-sex parent (Carlsmith, 1964). Since mothers are typically more verbal and fathers typically more skilled at quantitative tasks, the argument goes, modeling the same-sex parent will produce differential patterns of abilities in boys and girls.

There are a number of difficulties with this explanation of the typical sex differences in ability profiles. Not all aspects of intellectual functioning are susceptible to modeling. Vocabulary and verbal fluency are aspects of a parent's intellectual equipment that a child can copy. Normally, his spelling is not. Yet girls maintain superiority throughout the school years in spelling and fluency, though not in vocabulary. Much of a parent's quantitative reasoning is done covertly, so that it is not accessible for copying, and very little spatial thinking is communicated from parent to child. Yet it is in spatial performance that we find the most consistent sex differences.

Sex differences in verbal ability occur at a very early age, long before the child is able to identify which parent is the same sex as himself, and long before he begins to copy same-sex models differentially (see Kohlberg's chapter in this volume). Sex differences in verbal ability decline during the age period when the rise of identification and differential modeling ought to increase them. And consistent sex differences in quantitative ability do not appear until adolescence, long after the time when boys and girls have begun to prefer same-sex models. For these reasons we do not believe that the identification hypothesis provides an adequate explanation of the sex differences in ability profiles noted at the beginning of this chapter.

SEX-TYPED PERSONALITY TRAITS
AS MEDIATING PROCESSES

Numerous studies have shown that girls are more conforming, more suggestible, and more dependent upon the opinion of others than boys. And as mentioned earlier in this chapter, a number of studies have demonstrated that these very personality traits are associated with (1) field dependency (global perceiving), and (2) lack of ability to break set or restructure in problem solving. Witkin et al. (1962) have suggested that herein lies the explanation of sex differences in field independence and analytic style—that girls are more field-dependent and less analytical because of their greater conformity and dependency.

Why should there be any relationship between the cluster of personality dispositions that we may call the dependency cluster and individuals' characteristic modes of dealing with a stimulus array? Two possible reasons suggest themselves. First, an individual who is dependent and conforming is oriented toward stimuli emanating from other people; perhaps he finds it difficult to ignore these stimuli in favor of internal thought processes. Analytic thinking appears to require more internal "processing"; Kagan et al. (1963) have shown it to be associated with longer reaction times than global responding. Dependent children have been shown to be more distractible (Rau, 1963); their internal processing is interrupted, perhaps because of their greater orientation toward external interpersonal cues. This orientation probably helps them in certain kinds of intellectual performance; they should do better in recognizing names and faces, for example. But tasks calling for sequential thought may be hindered by a heavy reliance on external, interpersonal cues.

A second and related reason why one might expect to find a connection between the independence-dependence personality dimension and the mode of dealing with a stimulus array in problem solving has to do with activity. The dependent-conforming person is passive, waiting to be acted upon by the environment. The independent person takes the initiative. Intellectual tasks differ in how much activity they require, so that the passive person is more at a disadvantage on some tasks than others. Vocabulary tests, for example, depend upon previously established associations, and therefore involve less trial and error than tasks that require restructuring or finding the answer to a previously unsolved problem.

We are postulating, then, that dependency interferes with certain aspects of intellectual functioning. But there are other aspects of intellectual performance that dependency may facilitate—achievement, for example, Sears (1963) has found that, among girls, projective measures of "need affiliation" are positively related to academic achievement; in other words, achievement efforts can be motivated by a desire for social approval, and in the Sears work this proved to be true to a greater degree for girls than boys.

On the basis of the above considerations, we find it plausible to believe that some of the sex differences outlined in the first section of the chapter may be traced to boys' greater independence and activity, girls' greater conformity and passive-dependency. We do not know whether these personality differences between the sexes are in any degree innate, or whether they are entirely a product of the social learning involved in the acquisition of sex roles; but we do suggest that the existence of the differences may have a bearing upon the intellectual development of the two sexes.

We noted earlier that there were several traits, such as impulsiveness, aggression, and hyperkinesis, which appeared to be positive correlates for girls and negative ones for boys. Kagen, Moss, and Sigel (1963) first called attention to these differences, saying, "It is possible that analytic and non-analytic responses are the product of different causal agents in boys and girls. Specifically, motoric impulsivity may be one of the primary antecedents of nonanalytic, undifferentiated conceptual responses." (p. 111.)

How can a mediating process facilitate or inhibit intellectual growth for one sex and not the other? We do not think it necessary to suppose that different psychological principles govern the intellectual development of the two sexes; therefore we would like to explore two alternative possibilities to explain these opposite-direction effects. The first is that we have not been measuring comparable processes in the two sexes, and that when we specify the variables more exactly, same-direction correlations will emerge. For example, when we measure total activity level, we might get opposite correlations for the two sexes between activity level and measures of intellectual performance, but a high total activity level may have a different "meaning" for the two sexes, in the sense that it forms part of a different constellation of attributes. There is some indication from recent study on activity level (Maccoby et al., 1965) that this is the case. But if we measure a selected aspect of activity, such as the ability to inhibit motor movement or the amount of intersituational variation in activity, we can and do obtain correlations with intellectual performance that are similar for both sexes. It is also possible that scores on total aggression will not relate clearly to intellectual performance, while scores that reflect whether the aggression is directed and instrumental would do so. If these distinctions were made in the measurement of aggression, the sex differences in the way aggression correlates with cognitive performance might well disappear.

The second possible explanation of these opposite-direction correlations involves an assumption of curvilinearity. Let us assume that there is a single personality dimension, running from passive and inhibited at one end of the scale to bold, impulsive, and hyperactive at the other. A tentative hypothesis might be that there is a curvilinear relationship between this dimension and intellectual performance, so that both the very inhibited and the very bold will perform less well, while those who occupy the intermediate positions on the inhibited-impulsiveness dimension will perform optimally. We suggest further that boys and girls, on the average, occupy different positions on the dimension we have described. There is reason to believe that boys are more aggressive, more active, and less passive than girls. Whether the differences are innate or the outcome of social learning is not so important here. The situation that we hypothesize may be graphed as follows:

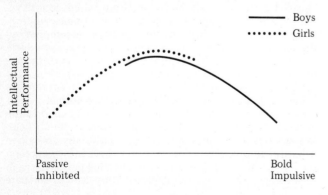

If the hypothesis holds, it would follow that for optimum intellectual performance, most girls need to become less passive and inhibited, while most boys need to become less impulsive. However, for those girls who do happen to be highly impulsive (as much so as the average boy, or even more so), impulsiveness should be a negative factor, as timidity should be for those boys at the passive end of the scale.

A parallel analysis may be made of anxiety as it affects intellectual performance in the two sexes. There is substantial evidence (beginning with the theoretical formulation of the problem by Taylor and Spence, 1952) that the relation of anxiety to performance is curvilinear. Either very high or very low levels of anxiety interfere with performance on a variety of tasks; intermediate levels facilitate performance. If women and girls have a high base level of anxiety, then increases in anxiety above their base level will frequently carry them past the optimum point of the curve, and result in inhibition or disorganization of performance. If boys and men have a low base level of anxiety, increases in anxiety will more often either improve performance, or move them through the middle portions of the curve where changes in performance would not be found.

In evaluating this hypothesis, we must first ask whether the two sexes do in fact differ in their base level of anxiety. As may be seen from the summary in the Oetzel bibliography, there is very strong evidence for greater anxiety in girls when anxiety is measured with paper-and-pencil tests like the CMAS or TASC. However, the tendency for girls to score higher in anxiety on these tests has been attributed to their greater willingness to admit to such feelings, and is not conclusive evidence that any more basic difference exists. The answer to the question will no doubt depend upon how anxiety is defined. In two studies that measure physiological reactions to stress (Sontag, 1947; Berry and Martin, 1957), females were found to have greater autonomic reactivity. Jersild and Holmes (1935) presented standardized fear situations in a laboratory situation to children of nursery school age, and obtained higher average "fear" scores for girls than boys. Some unpublished work by Kagan done with infants during the first year of life shows that when girls are set down on the floor in a strange room, they cling to the mother's leg longer before crawling away to explore objects; also they are more upset when placed behind a barrier so that the mother is visible but inaccessible. Harlow's finding that monkeys go to the mother for contact comfort when presented with fear stimuli gives us some basis for inferring that the behavior of the infants in Kagan's study was motivated by timidity—i.e., that the girls are more frightened than the boys by the strange situation in which they have been placed. With these various pieces of evidence in mind, we believe it to be a reasonable hypothesis that girls do have a higher base anxiety level than boys, so that increments from this base level might be expected to have a different effect for the two sexes.

We have so far discussed two "personality" dimensions that might bear a curvilinear relation to intellectual performance: anxiety, and a dimension running from inhibited-passive to bold-impulsive. Neither of these dimensions is precisely defined; if we wish to test the validity of the formulation, we must specify more exactly the behavioral dispositions that distinguish the sexes and bear the hypothesized curvilinear relation to intellectual performance. We must note, for example, that although the sexes do differ on such aspects of "impulsivity" as frequency of temper tantrums, aggression, and activity, they do not consistently differ on the "reflectivity-impulsivity" dimension (Kagan et al., 1964), so that this aspect of impulsivity would not be relevant to the explanation of sex differences offered here. Further differentiation will also be needed on the "intellectual performance" dimension. It is quite possible, for example, that "analytic style" and performance on spatial tests are related to impulsiveness or anxiety in the manner described, while certain apsects of verbal ability are not.

Genetic versus environmental contributions

In the preceeding section, we have discussed sex differences in personality traits as possible mediators of differences in intellectual performance. Assuming that the evidence is sufficient to convince the reader that there is indeed a substantial probability that such attributes as fearfulness, impulsiveness, independence, etc., do have a bearing on intellectual functioning, then it may be valuable to consider briefly the origins of the sex differences in these personality traits, with a view to discovering if the intellectual characteristics of either sex are likely to change as cultural conditions change. To what extent are boys more active or more aggressive because they are trained to adopt these socially defined sex-appropriate characteristics, and to what extent are they more active because of a substratum of biological determination with which environmental inputs must interact? Mischel [in his analysis] has taken a social-learning point of view, arguing that the known socialization inputs to the two sexes are sufficiently different in the appropriate ways to produce known sex differences in dependency and aggression (and by implication in other personality traits as well). Hamburg, on the other hand, has presented evidence that in primates sex-specific hormones govern not only specifically sexual behavior, but also various kinds of social behavior. Male-hormone treatment administered to a pregnant animal increases the incidence among the female offspring of rough-and-tumble play, and decreases the tendency to withdraw from the initiations, threats, and approaches of others. An interesting point emerging from Hamburg's report is that sex differences in social behavior may be related to endocrine influences even though there is no detectable sex difference in hormone concentrations at the time the behavior is observed. This point is important because of the fact that present methods of measurement do not reveal any differences between young boys and girls in the concentration of male or female hormones present in their bodies, even though their social behavior might suggest the presence of such a difference. This might be taken to mean that the differences in social behavior could not be a product of differential hormonal factors in the two sexes. Hamburg points to the possibility that hormonal "sensitization" during the prenatal period may contribute to the arousal of sex-appropriate behavior later in the life cycle, when the specific hormone concentrations are no longer present.

D'Andrade, analyzing the cross-cultural evidence in his chapter, notes that certain temperamental differences seem to be cross-culturally universal, and are found even in societies where most of the usual environmental pressures toward sex-typing are absent (e.g., the Kibbutzim in Israel). He also suggests that certain differential behavior in the two sexes is directly conditioned by such physical differences as size, strength, and biological role in the bearing and suckling of children; these differences are then generalized to similar activities and become institutionalized in occupational roles and other cultural prescriptions, in preparation for which anticipatory sex-typing occurs in childhood.

Let us assume, then, that the sex-typed attributes of personality and temperament which we have found to be related to intellectual functioning are the product of the interweaving of differential social demands with certain biological determinants that help to produce or augment differential cultural demands upon the two sexes. The biological underpinnings of the social demands for sex-typed behavior set modal tendencies for cultural demands, and set limits to the range of variation of these demands from one cultural setting to another. Still, within these limits considerable variation does occur, between families, between cultures, and in the nature of the behavior that a social group stereotypes as "feminine" or "masculine." Is there any evidence that such variations are associated with the nature or quality of intellectual performance in the two sexes?

In an attempt to measure cultural influences outside the home, Minuchin (1964) compared the performances of boys and girls in "modern" and "traditional" schools. In this study, an effort was made to control for social class and intellectual ability of the children, in order to isolate the effects of the two school atmospheres. In the traditional school, behavior was more sex-typed during play sessions than in the modern school. And in intellectual tasks, there were greater sex differences in problem solving and coding tasks in the traditional schools than in the modern ones. These findings would be consistent with the hypothesis that strong social demands for sex-typed behavior, such as aggression in boys and conformity-passivity in girls, play a role in producing some of the sex differences we have seen in intellectual performance. The proof of this point, however, would rest on experimental attempts to change the nature of intellectual performance through changes in the social expectations for sex-typed behavior. Only one attempt of this kind has been reported. Carey (1955) attempted to improve problem-solving behavior by changing "attitudes" toward such behavior. Group discussions directed toward improving the subjects' self-confidence in problem-solving tasks were held; these discussions emphasized the fact that it was socially acceptable to excel at problem solving. The discussion sessions improved the performance of college women but not of college men, suggesting that beliefs that skill in problem solving was not appropriate behavior had been an impediment to the normal performance of women but not of men. More such experimental evidence is needed to provide information on the difficulties and possible effects of influencing culturally prescribed behavior. It would be valuable, too, to have information on the extent of sex differences in intellectual performance in societies with high sex-role differentiation, and to compare these findings with similar findings for societies in which sex-role differentiation is minimized.

The findings on socialization practices within families, as they relate to intellectual development in the two sexes, point first of all to the fact that the environmental factors embodied in parent-child interaction do indeed make a difference in the child's intellectual performance. But more importantly, these findings indicate that the same environmental input affects the two sexes differently, and that different factors are associated with optimal performance for boys and girls. The brighter girls tend to be the ones who have not been tied closely to their mother's apron strings, but have been allowed and encouraged to fend for themselves. The brighter boys, on the other hand, have had high maternal warmth and protection in early childhood. We find, then, that environmental effects are not merely something added to, or superimposed upon, whatever innate temperamental differences there are that affect intellectual functioning. Rather, there is a complex interaction. The two sexes would appear to have somewhat different intellectual strengths and weaknesses, and hence different influences serve to counteract the weaknesses and augment the strengths.

REFERENCES

Anastasi, Anne. (1958) *Differential psychology* (3rd ed.). New York: Macmillan.

Anastasiow, N. (1963) The relationship of sex role patterns of first-grade boys to success in school. Unpublished doctoral dissertation, Stanford University.

Barron, F. (1957) Originality in relation to personality and intellect. *J. Pers.*, 25, 730-42.

Bayley, Nancy. (1956) Individual patterns of development. *Child Developm.*, 27, 45-74.

——, (1957) Data on the growth of intelligence between 16 and 21 years as measured by the Wechsler-Bellevue Scale. *J. genet. Psychol.*, 90, 3-15.

——, and Melita H. Oden. (1955) The maintenance of intellectual ability in gifted adults. *J. Geront.*, 10, 91-107.

——, and E. S. Schaefer. (1964) Correlations of maternal and child behaviors with the development of mental abilities: data from the Berkeley Growth Study. *Soc. Res. Child Developm. Monogr.*, 29, No. 6, 3-79.

Beller, E. K. (1962) A study of dependency and aggression in early childhood. Progress Report, Project M-849, Child Development Center, New York, N.Y.

Berry, J. L., and B. Martin. (1957) GSR reactivity as a function of anxiety, instructions and sex. *J. abnorm. soc. Psychol.*, 54, 9-12.

Bieri, J. (1960) Parental identification, acceptance of authority, and within-sex differences in cognitive behavior. *J. abnorm. soc. Psychol.*, 60, 76-79.

Bradway, Katherine P., and Clare W. Thompson. (1962) Intelligence at adulthood: a 25-year follow-up. *J. educ. Psychol.*, 53, 1-14.

Brim, O. G. (1958) Family structure and sex role learning by children: a further analysis of Helen Kock's data. *Sociometry*, 21, 1-16.

Carey, Gloria L. (1955) Reduction of sex differences in problem solving by improvement of attitude through group discussion. Unpublished doctoral dissertation, Stanford University.

Carlsmith, Lynn. (1964) Effect of early father absence on scholastic aptitude. *Harvard educ. Rev.*, 34, 3-21.

Coleman, J. S. (1961) *The adolescent society.* Glencoe, Ill.: The Free Press.

Crandall, V. J., Rachel Dewey, W. Katkovsky, and Anne Preston. (1964) Parents' attitudes and behaviors and grade school children's academic achievements. *J. genet. Psychol.*, 104, 53-66.

——, W. Katkovsky, and Anne Preston. (1962) Motivational and ability determinants of young children's intellectual achievement behaviors. *Child Developm.*, 33, 643-61.

——, and A. Rabson. (1960) Children's repetition choices in an intellectual achievement situation, following success and failure. *J. genet. Psychol.*, 97, 161-68.

Davidson, K. S., and S. B. Sarason. (1961) Test anxiety and classroom observations. *Child Developm.*, 32 199-210.

Ebert, Elizabeth, and Katherine Simmons. (1943) The Brush Foundation study of child growth and development. I: Psychometric tests. *Soc. Res. Child Developm. Monogr.*, 8, No. 2.

French, J. W. (1961) A study of emotional states aroused during examinations. College Entrance Examination Board, Research and Development Reports. March 1961, R.B., 61-66.

Guilford, J. P. (1956) The structure of intellect. *Psychol. Bull.*, 53, 267-93.

Haan, Norma. (1963) Proposed model of ego functioning: coping and defense mechanisms in relationship to I.Q. change. *Psychol. Monogr.*, 77, No. 571.

Harmatz, M. G. (1962) Effects of anxiety, motivating instructions, success and failure reports, and sex of subject upon level of aspiration and performance. Unpublished master's thesis, University of Washington.

Honzig, Marjorie P. (1957) Developmental studies of parent-child resemblance in intelligence. *Child Developm.*, 28 (2), 215-27.

Iscoe, I., and Joyce A. Carden. (1961) Field dependence, manifest anxiety, and sociometric status in children. *J. consult. Psychol.*, 25, 184.

Jersild, A. T., and F. B. Holmes. (1935) Children's fears. *Child Developm. Monogr.*, No. 20, 1-356.

Kagan, J., and H. A. Moss (1962) *Birth to maturity.* New York: John Wiley & Sons.

——, H. A. Moss, and I. E. Sigel. (1963) The psychological significance of styles of conceptualization. In J. C. Wright and J. Kagan (eds.), Basic cognitive processes in children. *Soc. Res. Child Developm. Monogr.*, 28, No. 2.

——, Bernice L. Rosman, Deborah Day, Albert J. and W. Phillips. (1964) Information processing in the child: significance of analytic and reflective attitudes. *Psych. Monogr.*, 78, No. 1.

Klausmeier, H. J., and W. Wiersma. (1964) Relationship of sex, grade level, and locale to performance of high I.Q. students on divergent thinking tests. *J. educ. Psychol.*, 55, 114-19.

Leiderman, P. H., and D. Shapiro. (1963) A physiological and behavioral approach to the study of group interaction. *Psychosom. Med.*, 25, 146-57.

Maccoby, Eleanor E. Woman's intellect. (1963) In S. M. Farber and R. L. Wilson (eds.), *The potential of woman.* New York: McGraw-Hill.

——, Edith M. Dowley, J. W. and R. Degerman. (1965) Activity level and intellectual functioning in normal preschool children. *Child Developm.*, 36, 761-70.

——, J. W. Hagen, L. W. Sontag, and J. Kagan. (1963) Unpublished report, Laboratory of Human Development, Stanford University.

——, and Lucy Rau. (1962) Differential cognitive abilities. Final report, Cooperative research project No. 1040, Owen House, Stanford University.

MacKinnon, D. W. (1962) The nature and nurture of creative talent. *Amer. Psychologist*, 17, 484-95.

McClelland, D., J. W. Atkinson, R. A. Clark, and E. L. Lowell. (1953) *The achievement motive.* New York: Appleton-Century-Crofts.

Milton, G. A. (1957) The effects of sex-role identification upon problem-solving skill. *J. abnorm. soc. Psychol.*, 55, 208-12.

Minuchin, Patricia. (1964) Sex role concepts and sex typing in childhood as a function of school and home environments. Paper presented at American Orthopsychiatric Association, Chicago.

Moriarty, A. E. (1961) Coping patterns of preschool children in response to intelligence test demands. *Genet. Psychol. Monogr.*, 64, 3-127.

Moss, H. A., and J. Kagan. (1958) Maternal influences on early I.Q. scores. *Psychol Rep.*, 4, 655-61.

——, and J. Kagan. (1962) Unpublished manuscript.

Murphy, Lois B. (1962) *The widening world of childhood.* New York: Basic Books.

Nakamura, C. Y. (1958) Conformity and problem solving. *J. abnorm. soc. Psychol.*, 56, 315-20.

Oetzel, Roberta. (1961) The relationship between sex role acceptance and cognitive abilities. Unpublished master's thesis, Stanford University.

Phillips, B. N., E. Hindsman, and C. McGuire. (1960) Factors associated with anxiety and their relation to the school achievement of adolescents. *Psychol Rep.*, 7, 365-72.

Plank, Emma H., and R. Plank. (1954) Emotional components in arithmetic learning as seen through autobiographies. In R. S. Eissler et al. (eds.), *The psychoanalytic study of the child*, Vol. IX. New York: International Universities Press.

Radcliffe committee on graduate education for women. (1956) *Graduate education for women.* Cambridge: Harvard University Press.

Rau, Lucy. (1963) Interpersonal correlates of perceptual-cognitive functions. Paper presented at Society for Research in Child Development, San Francisco.

Russell, D. G., and E. G. Sarason. (1965) Test anxiety, sex, and experimental conditions in relation to anagram solution. *J. Pers. soc. Psychol.*, 1, 493-96.

Sears, Pauline S. (1963) The effect of classroom conditions on the strength of achievement motive and work output on elementary school children. Final report, Cooperative research project No. 873, Stanford University.

Shaw, M. C., and J. T. McCuen. (1960) The onset of academic under-achievement in bright children. *J. educ. Psychol.*, 51, 103-8.

Sigel, I. (1964) Sex differences in cognitive functioning re-examined: a functional point of view. Paper presented at Society for Research in Child Development, Berkeley, California.

——, P. Jarman, and H. Hanesian. (1963) Styles of categorization and their perceptual, intellectual, and personality correlates in young children. Unpublished paper, Merrill-Palmer Institute.

Sontag, L. W. (1947) Physiological factors and personality in children. *Child Develpm.*, 18, 185-89.

——, C. T. Baker, and Virginia A. Nelson. (1958) Mental growth and personality development: a longitudinal study. *Soc. Res. Child Develpm. Monogr.*, 23, No. 68.

Sutton-Smith, B., V. J. Crandall, and J. M. Roberts. (1964) Achievement and strategic competence. Paper presented at the Eastern Psychological Association, April 1964.

Taylor, Janet A., and K. W. Spence. (1952) The relationship of anxiety level to performance in serial learning. *J. exp. Psychol.*, 44, 61-64.

Terman, L. M., and Melita H. Oden. (1947) *The gifted child grows up.* Stanford: Stanford Univer. Press.

Terman, L. M., and Leona E. Tyler. (1954) Psychological sex differences. In L. Carmichael (ed.), *Manual of child psychology* (2nd ed.). New York: John Wiley & Sons.

Trembly, D. (1964) Age and sex differences in creative thinking potential. Paper presented at the American Psychological Association's annual convention.

Walter, D., Lorraine S. Denzler, and E. G. Sarason. (1964) Anxiety and the intellectual performance of high school students. *Child Develpm.*, 35, 917-26.

Witkin, H. A., R. B. Dyk, H. F. Faterson, D. R. Goodenough, and S. A. Karp. (1962) *Psychological differentiation.* New York: John Wiley & Sons.

——, Helen B. Lewis, M. Herzman, Karen Machover, Pearl B. Meissner, and S. Wapner. (1954) *Personality through perception.* New York: Harper.

Yonge, G. D. (1964) Sex differences in cognitive functioning as a result of experimentally induced frustration. *J. exp. Educ.*, 32, 275-80.

7 *Sex differences in adolescent character processes*

Elizabeth Douvan

According to psychoanalytic theory, adolescence represents a recapitulation of the Oedipus conflict. The relative calm and control achieved during latency suffer a disruption at this point because of the re-emergence of intense sexual impulses, and the child is plunged once more into Oedipal conflict.

Several critical new features mark this re-enactment of the Oedipal drama, however, and distinguish it from its earlier counterpart. The ego of the puberal child, enriched and articulated during latency, is in a more advantageous position in relation to the impulses than it was in the Oedipal phase. For during its struggle with impulses the ego has gained an ally in the agency of the super-ego. And the fact of genital capability opens for the child new possibilities for resolving conflict. The male child need not simply repress his love for the mother and gain mastery of his ambivalence and fears through identification. He may now seek substitutes for the mother, substitutes who are suitable love objects. Though he may identify with the father in a more or less differentiated fashion, he need not use identification as a global defense against overpowering fear of the rival father, since the father is no longer his rival in the same crucial way.

Part of the outcome of the adolescent struggle is the renegotiation of the ego—super-ego compact: that is, a change in character. As part of the process of remodeling his original identifications, the child establishes a set of values and controls which are more internal and personal than earlier ones and which reflect his new reality situation as an adult.

This is the developmental task and context facing the adolescent boy. But what of the task confronting the girl at this period? With what resources and what history does she enter adolescence? Analytic theory, though wanting in specificity, gives us some broad clues about this development, its unique characteristics, and the ways in which it differs from development in the male child.

First, we expect that super-ego is less developed in women (and in adolescent girls). Since the little girl has no decisive motive force comparable to the boy's castration anxiety, she does not turn peremptorily against her own instinctual wish nor form the same critical and definite identification with the like-sexed parent. Her motives for internalizing the wishes of important adults are fear and loss of love and a sense of shame. According to Deutsch (1), an important step in the socialization of girls occurs when the father enters an agreement with the little girl whereby he exchanges a promise of love for her forfeiture of any direct expression of aggressive impulses.

A significant difference may be noted at this point: the boy who has accomplished the Oedipal resolution now has an *internal* representative of the parents which he must

Reprinted from Elizabeth Douvan, "Sex Differences in Adolescent Character Processes," Merrill-Palmer Quarterly, Vol. 6, pp. 203-211. This article is based on a paper read at the American Psychological Association meetings, September, 1957.

placate and which serves as a source of reinforcement for his acts. The little girl, on the other hand, continues to look to the parents as the source of reward and punishment since her identifications are only partial and primitive.

At adolescence this difference has a critical significance: the boy enters the adolescent contest with an ego that is reinforced by a strong ally, a vigorous super-ego. And in reworking the relation between the ego and the impulses, there is an internal criterion by which the boy judges the new arrangement. His new values and controls are an individual accomplishment and are judged, at least in part, by individual standards. The girl meets the rearoused instincts of adolescence with an ego only poorly supported by partial identifications and introjects. She still needs to rely heavily on externally imposed standards to help in her struggle with impulses.

With this formulation as a starting point, we made a number of predictions about sex differences in character development and looked at data from two national sample surveys of boys and girls in the 14- to 16-year age group for tests of our predictions.[1] Specifically, we explored the following conceptions:

1. Adolescent girls will show less concern with values and with developing behavior controls than will boys; that is, character will show rapid development in boys during adolescence, while girls will be less preoccupied with establishing personal, individual standards and values.

2. Personal integration around moral values, though crucial in the adjustment of adolescent boys, will not predict adjustment in girls. Rather, sensitivity and skill in interpersonal relationships will be critical integrative variables in adolescent girls and will predict their personal adjustment.

Our studies yield substantial support for the first speculation. Girls are consciously less concerned about developing independent controls than boys are. They are more likely to show an unquestioned identification with, and acceptance of, parental regulation. They less often distinguish parents' standards from their own, and they do not view the parents' rules as external or inhibiting as often as boys do. Boys more often tell us they worry about controls—particularly controls on aggression; when we ask them what they would like to change about themselves, the issue of controls again emerges as an important source of concern. More important, perhaps, as evidence of their greater involvement in building controls, we find that boys tend to conceive parental rules as distinctly external, and, to some extent, opposed to their own interests. So when we ask why parents make rules, boys underscore the need to control children (e.g., to keep them out of trouble). Girls reveal an identification with the parents when they say that parents make rules to teach their children how to behave, to give them standards to live by, to let children know what is expected of them. Boys think of rules as a means of restricting areas of negative behavior, while girls more often see them as a means of directing and channeling energy.

In answer to all of our questions about parental rules, boys repeatedly reveal greater differentiation between their own and their parents' standards.[2]

One of the most impressive indications of the difference

between boys and girls in their stance toward authority comes from a series of projective picture-story questions. At one point in this series a boy or girl is shown with his parents, and the parents are setting a limit for the child. We asked respondents to tell what the child would say. A quarter of the boys questioned the parental restriction—not with hostility or any sign of real conflict, but with a freedom that implies a right to question—while only 4 per cent of the girls in the same age group responded in this way. On the other hand, a third of the girls reassured the parents with phrases like "don't worry," or "you know I'll behave, I'll act like a lady"; the boys almost never gave answers comparable to these.

Both of these response types reveal a respect for one's own opinions. They both indicate autonomy, but very different attitudes toward parental rules: the boy openly opposes; the girl not only acquiesces to, but reinforces the parents' regulation.

Girls are more authority reliant than boys in their attitudes toward adults other than their parents. And we find lower correlations among internalization items for girls, indicating less coherence in internalization for them than for boys.

These are examples of differences that support the claim that boys are actively struggling with the issue of controls, that they are moving in a process of thrust and counterthrust toward the construction of personal, individuated control systems more conscious and rational than previous global identifications; and that girls, on the other hand, are relatively uninvolved in the struggle and maintain a compliant-dependent relationship with their parents.

The second hypothesis suggested at the beginning of this paper deals with the significance of progress in internalization for the personal integration and adjustment of boys and girls. Having found that girls are less urgently struggling for independent character, we wonder what this means about their general ego development and integration. Are girls relatively underdeveloped in these areas as well as in independence of character?

The analysis we have done to date indicates that the second alternative is at least a viable hypothesis. In an analysis of extreme groups, we find that the well-internalized boy is characterized by active achievement strivings, independence of judgment, a high level of energy for use in work and play, and self-confidence combined with realistic self-criticism. He is well developed in the more subtle ego qualities of organization of thought and time-binding. They boy who has not achieved internal, personal controls and who responds only to external authority is poorly integrated, demoralized, and deficient in all areas of advanced ego functioning (Table 1).

Again, we ask, what does girls' relatively common reliance on external controls mean about their ego integration? We find when we analyze extreme groups of girls that internalization of individual controls is no guarantee of ego development, and that girls who are dependent on external controls do not show the disintegration and demoralization that mark the noninternalized boy. In short, internalization of independent standards is not an efficient predictor of ego organization or ego strength in girls.

TABLE 1   *Extreme Groups on an Internalization Index Compared on Measures of Other Ego Variables (Boy Sample)*

Selected measures of ego variables	Internalization index		Chi square	P level
	High	Low		
I. Achievement				
a. prefer success to security	.64	.47	8.140	< .01
b. choose job aspiration on achievement criteria	.78	.62	9.331	< .01
c. choose job aspiration because of ease of acquiring job, minimum demands	.01	.13	13.758	< .001
d. upward mobile aspirations	.70	.53	7.158	< .01
II. Energy level				
a. high on index of leisure engagements	.49	.40	2.729	< .10 > .05
b. belong to some organized group	.77	.65	5.50	< .05
c. hold jobs	.63	.42	12.576	< .01
d. date	.66	.52	6.007	< .05
III. Autonomy				
a. rely on own judgment in issues of taste and behavior	.40	.20	12.786	< .01
b. have some disagreements with parents	.67	.49	12.804	< .01
c. choose adult ideal outside family	.23	.14	4.547	< .05
d. have no adult ideal	.07	.16	8.621	< .01
e. authority reliant in relation to adult leaders	.23	.54	28.544	< .001
IV. Self-confidence				
a. high on interviewer rating of confidence	.43	.22	11.213	< .01
b. low on interviewer rating of confidence	.16	.35	14.205	< .001
c. high on rating for organization of ideas	.65	.43	9.861	< .01
d. low on rating for organization of ideas	.08	.28	19.006	< .001
V. Self-criticism				
a. wish for changes that can be effected by individual effort	.36	.12	16.22	< .001
b. wish for changes that cannot be effected by individual effort	.14	.30	12.613	< .01
c. no self-change desired	.27	.42	7.498	< .05
VI. Time perspective				
a. extended	.44	.28	7.604	< .05
b. restricted	.14	.33	15.721	< .01

NOTE.—The Internalization Index is based on responses to three questions: (a) What would happen if parents didn't make rules? (b) When might a boy (girl) break a rule? (c) one of the picture-story items: What does the boy (girl) do (when pressed by peers to ignore a promise to parents)? External responses are those which see children obeying only out of fear, breaking rules when they think they will not be caught, relying exclusively on externally imposed guides. Internal responses, in contrast, reveal a sense of obligation or trust about promises given, consider rules unbreakable except in emergencies when or they are for some other reason less critical than other circumstances, and think that children would rely on their own judgment were parental authority no longer available. Subjects who gave internal responses to two or three questions are included in the High category; those who gave two or more external responses are grouped in the Low Internalization category.

There are several possible explanations for this absence of significant association in girls. High internalization in girls may not reflect independence of standards. Deutsch (1) has observed girls' greater capacity for intense identification, compared to boys; and we may have in the girls' apparently well-internalized controls a product of fusion with parental standards rather than a differentiated and independent character. Moreover, dependence on external standards is the norm for girls in adolescence. Parents are permitted and encouraged to maintain close supervision of the growing girl's actions. Under these circumstances, compliance with external authority is less likely to reflect personal pathology or a pathological family structure.

To this point, then, we have seen that girls are less absorbed with the issue of controls, and that the successful internalization of controls is less crucial for their integration at this age than it is for boys.

We speculated that the critical integrating variable for the girl is her progress in developing interpersonal skill and sensitivity. A striking continuity in feminine psychology lies in the means of meeting developmental crises. In childhood, adolescence, and adulthood the female's central motive is a desire for love, and her means of handling crises is to appeal for support and love from important persons in her environment. This contrasts with the greater variety of methods—of mastery and withdrawal—that the male uses in meeting developmental stresses. The girl's skill in pleading her cause with others, in attracting and holding affection, is more critical to her successful adaptation.

We designed a test of the importance of interpersonal development in boys and girls. Again, taking extreme groups, those who reveal relatively mature attitudes and skills in the area of friendship and those who are impressively immature, we compared performance in other areas of

TABLE 2   *Extreme Groups on an Interpersonal Development Index Compared on Measures of Other Ego Variables (Girl Sample)*

Selected measures of ego variables	Interpersonal development index			
	High	Low	Chi square	P level
I. *Energy level*				
a. high on index of leisure engagements	.41	.27	9.335	< .01
b. belong to some organized group	.97	.75	37.012	< .001
c. hold jobs	.60	.51	2.444	< .10 > .05
d. date	.81	.66	10.98	< .01
II. *Self-confidence*				
a. high on interviewer rating of confidence	.47	.32	9.071	< .01
b. low on interviewer rating of confidence	.17	.30	11.522	< .01
c. high on interviewer rating for poise	.38	.14	29.613	< .001
d. low on interviewer rating for poise	.14	.29	15.072	< .001
III. *Time perspective*				
a. extended	.50	.37	8.621	< .01
b. restricted	.04	.13	12.714	< .01
IV. *Organization of ideas*				
a. high on interviewer rating	.51	.34	12.401	< .01
b. low on interviewer rating	.14	.28	13.168	.001
V. *Feminine identification*				
a. high on index of traditional feminine orientation	.37	.11	37.93	.001
b. choose own mother as an ideal	.48	.30	14.14	.001

NOTE.—The Interpersonal Development Index is based on responses to three questions: (a) Can a friend ever be as close as a family member? (b) What should a friend be or be like? (c) What makes a girl (boy) popular with other girls (boys)? Answers counted highly developed are those that stress intimacy, mutuality, and appreciation of individuality and individual differences. Our High category consists of subjects who gave such answers to all three questions. The Low group comprises youngsters who gave no such answers to any of the three critical items.

ego development. With girls we found clear relationships between interpersonal development and the following ego variables: energy level, self-confidence, time-perceptive and organization of ideas, and positive feminine identification (Table 2).

Interpersonal skill in boys is not significantly related to activity level, time-binding, self-confidence, or self-acceptance. In short, it does not assert the same key influence in the ego integration of boys that it does in feminine development.

What significance do these findings have? What are the sources of the differences we have observed, and what do they mean about the later settlement of character issues in the two sexes in adulthood?

Differences in character processes in boys and girls probably reflect both basic constitutional and developmental differences between the sexes and also variation in the culture's statement of character crises for boys and girls.

Perhaps the most crucial factor leading to boys' precocity in moral development is the more intense and imperious nature of the impulses they must handle. The sexual impulses aroused in the boy at puberty are specific and demanding and push to the forefront the need for personal controls which accommodate his sexual needs. Acceptance of parental standards or maintenance of the early identification-based control would require denial of sexual impulses, and this is simply not possible for the boy after puberty.

The girl's impulses, on the other hand, are both more ambiguous and more subject to primitive repressive defenses. She has abandoned aggressive impulses at an earlier phase of development and may continue to deny them. Her sexual impulses are more diffuse than the boy's and can also more readily submit to the control of parents and to the denial this submission may imply.

The ambiguity of female sexual impulses permits adherence to earlier forms of control and also makes this a comfortable course since their diffusion and mystery implies a greater danger of overwhelming the incompletely formed ego at adolescence. Freud noted the wave of repression that occurs in females at puberty and contrasted it to the psychic situation of the boy (5).

Additional factors leading to postponement of character issues in girls are their greater general passivity and their more common tendency toward intensive identifications in adolescence and toward fantasy gratification of impulses.

I would like to mention one final point which, I think, has critical implications for character development in girls. Building independent standards and controls (i.e., settling an independent character) is part of the broader crisis of defining personal identity. In our culture there is not nearly as much pressure on girls as on boys to meet the identity challenge during the adolescent years. In fact, there is a real pressure on the girl *not* to make any clear settlement in her identity until considerably later. We are all familiar with the neurotic woman who, even in adulthood, staunchly resists any commitment that might lead to self-definition and investment in a personal identity, for fear of restricting the range of men for whom she is a potential marriage choice. This pattern, it seems, reflects forces that are felt more or less by most girls in our culture. They are to remain fluid and malleable in personal identity in order to adapt to the needs of the men they marry. Too clear a self-definition during adolescence may be maladaptive. But when broader identity issues are postponed, the issues that might lead to differentiation of standards and values are also postponed. I do not, then, feel with Pope that most women have no character at all. I do think that in all likelihood feminine character develops later than masculine character, and that adolescence—the period we ordinarily consider *par excellence* the time for consolidation of character—is a more dramatic time for boys than for girls.

NOTES

1. The studies were conducted at the Survey Research Center of the University of Michigan. Respondents were selected in a multi-stage probability sampling design, and represent youngsters of the appropriate age in school. Each subject was interviewed at school by a member of the Center's Field Staff; interviews followed a fixed schedule and lasted from one to four hours. For details about the studies, and copies of the complete questionnaire, readers may refer to the basic reports (2, 3).

2. In the full series, we asked respondents why parents make rules, what would happen if they didn't, when a boy might break a rule, whether the respondent himself had ever broken a rule, and what kind of rule he would never break. For exact phrasing and order of questions, the reader may refer to the basic study reports (2, 3).

REFERENCES

1. Deutsch, Helene. *The psychology of women.* New York: Grune and Stratton, 1944. 2 vols.
2. Douvan, Elizabeth, and Kaye, Carol. *Adolescent girls.* Ann Arbor, Mich.: Survey Research Center, University of Michigan, 1956.
3. Douvan, Elizabeth, and Withey, S. B. *A Study of adolescent boys.* Ann Arbor, Mich.: Survey Research Center, University of Michigan, 1955.
4. Fenichel, O. The pregenital antecedents of the Oedipus complex. *Int. J. Psychoanal.,* 1931, 12, 141-166.
5. Freud, S. Female sexuality. *Int. J. Psychoanal.,* 1932, 13, 281-297.

Part II

Socialization, cultural values, and the development of motives

The fact that the ten papers in this section were written by people of different academic backgrounds makes the consistency of the observations and conclusions impressive. Although angry members of the Women's Liberation movement shake their fists at external causes, these papers make it clear that it is the internalization of the culture's traditional roles for women that renders ambivalence and thus role conflict inevitable. Obviously external factors such as the structures of society and prejudiced expectations lead, in reality, to discriminatory practices. But the core of conflict and ambivalence can be understood as psychological phenomena.

The question is, how does society socialize its members so that the majority of adults come close to the idealized norms of that society, and what are the conditions and the processes by which the norms are forced to change? Using an interactive model, that is the topic of the paper by Bardwick and Douvan. It is our feeling that until puberty girls are reared permissively, developing a "bi-sexual" identity, rewarded for traditional femininity and for successful competitive achievement. With puberty, permissiveness ends. In adolescence those competitive skills that were a route to rewards from others are often punished, one's striving qualities go underground, and "femininity" as a traditional role becomes a goal to be earned. For girls still in a competitive milieu, there is a long delay in evolving a definition of the self, an emphasis on an identity defined by one's relationships with others, a honing of skills that make one desirable, a plasticity of personality that makes one adaptable. But adolescence is too late for the development of a simple concept of the self. While focusing upon the traditional role, middle-class girls have simultaneously internalized the values and the goals of the dominant masculine-achieving-independent culture and have participated successfully within it in school.

The most recent information I have seen, a 1971 dissertation[1] analyzing data collected in 1968 and 1969, shows the duality of identity very clearly. Women entering the University of Michigan were asked what kind of marital, parental, and career status they wanted "fifteen years from now." Seventy-six percent of the respondents wanted to be married and 54.8% wanted a career too. Reinterviewed at the end of their freshman year, 85.7% wanted to be married and 62.9% wanted a career too. That probably reflects the values of the college population—"bi-sexually" reared women want to participate in traditional and achieving roles. Women are angered when they are forced to choose one role, which means choosing one aspect of the self, thus denying a major component of one's personality. Actually, as Bardwick and Douvan have written, it is not quite that simple. Personality characteristics of men make it more probable that they will achieve when the task requires autonomy and competitiveness.

Komarovsky's classic paper was published in 1946 and is based upon data collected in 1942 and 1943. It is stunning to realize the consistency of role conflict for women. In the early forties, Komarovsky found the same societal dynamics, the same adjustments, lies, and resentments that are the subject of so much inquiry now. There were then and are now two roles present in the social environment of college women. The goals within each role are mutually exclusive, and the personality qualities each evokes are so different that what is an asset in one role is a liability in the other. In this paper we can see clearly the attempt to make oneself more desirable by hiding abilities—a fusion of adaptability and perjury likely to lead to self-contempt and rage.

Horner's paper summarizes the results of several studies in which she found that a critical barrier to women's success in competitive academic or occupational roles lies in their internal fear of success. The motive to avoid success evolves when one feels that succeeding in competition would result in social rejection and/or feelings of being unfeminine. The women most afraid of success prove to be those who are most capable of achieving. Horner's data, some collected in 1970, reveal the same feelings of frustration, hostility, aggression, bitterness, and confusion that characterized Komarovsky's students. The bitterness and anger is the result not of simply being shut out of participation in the competitive occupational sphere, but from needing to accomplish the traditional role, giving priority to it, and thus being one's own executor of the demise of a large part of the self—at least in behavior on the outside. Those girls who do not experience a fear of success, are, in Horner's data, those whose motives to achieve are low. Those girls have no trouble in competitive situations probably because for most of them, they have no history of success and no expectation of it. Both Horner and Tangri[2] found that the fear of success increases from the freshman to the junior year (and to graduate school) and that able girls, selected for their academic ability, change their plans to what they perceive is a less ambitious, more feminine career. This change characterizes girls fearful of success; those low in fear of success change much less. The single most important factor in arousing fear of success is the girl's perception of the attitude of her male peers. The single best predictor of the behavior of women is the attitude of the man with whom they are involved. Fear of success is another facet of the female's use of the interpersonal as her major route to identity and the changes in self because of the vulnerabilities involved.[3]

In studies using black men and women, Horner found a reversal, that is, that fear of success was more characteristic of black men than black women. Comparing white and black female college students, Weston and Mednick found fewer fear-of-success responses among blacks, which suggests that black college women do not experience the same fear of success in intellectually competitive situations that many whites do. Although this study did not find class differences within the sample of black women, a study of black upper-middle-class sorority women at the University of Michigan resulted in fear-of-success scores quite like those of whites. Thus although the dynamics of black society may have placed a premium on successful achievement among black women (which results in the low fear-of-success scores), successful participation in middle-class American society evokes the characteristic middle-class fear of success among women.

In the first part of her paper, Rossi thoroughly documents the participation of American women in the technical and atypical professions of engineering, medicine, and science. The small percentage of women involved is well known. Analyzing the barriers to participation in these careers, Rossi notes that easy solutions, such as increasing stipends, child care facilities, changing tax laws, and retraining older women, are not likely to make much difference. From study of the characteristics of outstanding scientists, Rossi concludes that if a woman is to be a scientist and not a (passive) lab assistant, she must be high in intellectual ability, fiercely persistent in work goals, extremely independent, and basically asocial. These qualities characterize relatively few men and far fewer women. The evolution of these personality qualities in large numbers of girls would require a revolution in child-rearing.

In all of these papers, again and again, the idea repeats: significant changes in role participation will require significant changes in the socialization of our youth (of both sexes) and in most if not all of our cultural institutions.

Rossi concludes her paper by citing data from her large-scale study of college women, pointing out that most of them saw the idea of success for themselves as success achieved through the accomplishments of their husbands and children. But four out of five of those respondents reserved their admiration for other women who had achieved outstandingly within *a demanding profession. Although not participating themselves, they nonetheless provide a widespread base of sympathetic approval for those who are pioneers.*

The next two papers examine the characteristics of women who did not fear success but, instead, trained for a profession and are committed to achieving. The paper by Simon, Clark, and Galway is a report of the employment positions, salaries, and publication productivity of male and female Ph.D.'s. The study reveals that the greatest number of publications were produced by married women—more than unmarried women or males! That is logical if you assume that the most common and logical route to the development of self-esteem and confidence among American women is marriage and maternity, which are perceived as the major tasks of early adulthood. In addition, we might surmise that the very atypical women who achieve that level of professionalism are more highly motivated than the average male. Nonetheless, it does disturb one's stereotype! Also unexpected is the paper's conclusion that though there are some differences between the woman Ph.D and her male counterpart, the differences are relatively small and are decreasing. "The woman Ph.D appears to be an accepted professional colleague"—due presumably to her productivity and professionalism.

It is especially interesting to note that over 95% of the male Ph.D's in the sample were married, but only 50% of the women were. Among the women who were married, 80% were married to professional men. In addition to the observation in the paper that women are expected to marry up in social class, which clearly restricts the appropriate population of men for women Ph.D's, the self-confidence of the man is probably a factor. As women may fear their loss of femininity because of success, so men may fear their emasculation when women are their professional equals or superiors. Like educated black women, female Ph.D's may have difficulty finding similarly trained, confident partners.

When Helson investigated the personality characteristics of women mathematicians she found them very like the scientists described in Rossi's paper. Women mathematicians genuinely valued intellectual and cognitive matters, were intellectually able, valued their independence and autonomy, their dependability and responsibility, their objectivity and rationality. Those who were acknowledged as creative mathematicians were more original, intellectual, narcissistic, and unconventional than the others.

Of all the possible variables, differences in personality characteristics most significantly differentiated creative from noncreative mathematicians. One has a global impression that creative women, even more than creative men, are not only unconventional, rebelliously independent, narcissistic, and free to reject outside influences, but also flexible, self-directed, and strongly abstract in interests. In this and other studies by Helson the same constellation recurs among creative women. Creative, achieving women are often ambivalent toward their mothers and identify with fathers who use intellectual activity to express themselves and give purpose to their lives, and who have strong symbolic interests and a need for autonomy.

In general, creativity and achievement seem to require, at a minimum, some independence from loving, accepting, judging parental figures.

In the remaining two papers of this section, we will return to the study of sex roles, but with a more sociological perspective than before. In the paper by Angrist we are reminded that role is an underdefined, overused, ill-conceptualized abstraction. We persist in speaking as though there were single models of sex role, but no role is ever really isolated. We are all many-faceted actors in a complex society, participants in many roles, carriers of diverse labels, enactors of multiple behaviors, still with a core of "I." That there is little consensus today on the content of sex roles for women reflects a weakness in definition, an acknowledgment of multiplicity, and is a reflection of the changing, blurred, and variable forms of women's roles. Using the term frequently we forget that sex role is an abstraction, a construct, a simplification of a much more complex reality. As Angrist says, "the individual rarely, if ever, behaves just as a man or woman. Rather, sex modifies, sometimes strongly, sometimes weakly, whatever social interactions or relationships he is engaged in."

Using data from college women, Angrist supports her contention that the socialization of women and the multiplicity of choices within the female sex role lead to a logical flexibility of role behaviors that are realistically adapted to changes in women's roles over their life span. This may explain why many women seem less conflicted than simplified theory leads us to expect. That is, Angrist suggests that women experience less role conflict to the extent that they perceive themselves as having alternatives and options as the contingencies of their lives change.

We have noted that the presence or absence of fear of success in women is linked to the perceived attitude of a boyfriend, husband, or father. We have also noted that the best single predictor of a woman's behavior is her perception of the attitude of the man with whom she is involved. Bailyn's paper examines the importance of the husband's life style, attitudes, and goals, particularly as they affect role behaviors and marital happiness. In the sample of British couples whom Bailyn interviewed, a career or family orientation apparently was not important in deciding whom to marry. This means that career-oriented men were no more likely to marry traditional wives than were family-oriented men and that women who preferred to integrate a career with a family did not show a preference for men who emphasized career or family. But the meshing of career and family orientations of both partners was crucially important in affecting the happiness of the marriage. Actually, it was the husband's orientation that was decisive. The husband's values and his orientation to integrating family and work influenced the happiness of the marriage and was particularly decisive in regard to his wife's attempt to have both a career and a satisfying marriage. That the husband's—never the wife's—values are determinative, suggests that for those who marry, traditional dependence and adaptability are still characteristic even of working women, even if they are career oriented (too).

NOTES

1. Delsa Diane Hatch, "Differential Personal Change of Males and Females in Two College Environments" (Ph.D. dissertation, University of Michigan), page 73.
2. Sandra Tangri, "Innovation in Occupational Choice" (Ph.D. dissertation, University of Michigan, 1969).
3. During the spring of 1971 two of my graduate students gave Horner's cues to samples of undergraduates. Instead of getting high percentages of fear-of-success responses they were getting answers like, "Anne's parents were both physicians and it was expected that she would go to medical school." Then there would often be a self-conscious inquiry of whether the interviewer had seen the Horner article in *Psychology Today*. It seems to me that given the critical importance of the fear of success, especially in the light of Women's Liberation, girls may be experiencing pressures to acknowledge their ambivalence and confront their fears. An equally tenable explanation lies in the hypothesis that sharp students outwit psychologists when the theory and techniques of measurement are known.

8 *Ambivalence: the socialization of women*

Judith M. Bardwick
Elizabeth Douvan

"What are big boys made of? What are big boys made of?"

Independence, aggression, competitiveness, leadership, task orientation, outward orientation, assertiveness, innovation, self-discipline, stoicism, activity, objectivity, analytic-mindedness, courage, unsentimentality, rationality, confidence, and emotional control.

"What are big girls made of? What are big girls made of?"

Dependence, passivity, fragility, low pain tolerance, nonaggression, noncompetitiveness, inner orientation, interpersonal orientation, empathy, sensitivity, nurturance, subjectivity, intuitiveness, yieldingness, receptivity, inability to risk, emotional liability, supportiveness.[1]

These adjectives describe the idealized, simplified stereotypes of normal masculinity and feminity. They also describe real characteristics of boys and girls, men and women. While individual men and women may more resemble the stereotype of the opposite sex, group differences between the sexes bear out these stereotypic portraits. How does American society socialize its members so that most men and women come close to the society's ideal norms?

Reprinted from Judith M. Bardwick and Elizabeth Douvan, "Ambivalence: the Socialization of Women," Chapter 9 of Woman in Sexist Society, *pp. 147-159, edited by Vivian Gornick and Barbara K. Moran, © 1971 by Basic Books, Inc., Publishers, New York.*

From infancy children have behavioral tendencies that evoke particular types of responses from parents, older siblings, and anyone else who interacts with the child. Such responses are a function of both individual values—whether the particular person values outgoing extroverted behavior, for example—and widespread social values of acceptable child behavior. Socialization refers to the pressures—rewarding, punishing, ignoring, and anticipating—that push the child toward evoking acceptable responses.

Comparisons between boys and girls in infancy and the earliest childhood years reveal modal differences between the sexes. Boys have higher activity levels, are more physically impulsive, are prone to act out aggression, are genitally sexual earlier, and appear to have cognitive and perceptual skills less well-developed than girls of the same age. Generally speaking, girls are less active physically, display less overt physical aggression, are more sensitive to physical pain, have significantly less genital sexuality, and display greater verbal, perceptual, and cognitive skill than boys.[2]

All impulsive, aggressive children are forced to restrain these tendencies since running away, biting, kicking, publicly masturbating, and other similar behaviors are injurious either to the child and his playmates or the pride of his parents. It is critically important to the development of sex differences that these tendencies are more typical of boys than of girls. In addition, girls' more mature skills enable them to attend to stimuli, especially from other people, more swiftly and accurately than boys.[3] Girls are better at analyzing and anticipating environmental demands; in addition, they have greater verbal facility. Girls' characteristic behavior tends to disturb parents less than boys' characteristic behavior. The perceptual, cognitive, and verbal skills which for unknown reasons are more characteristic of girls enable them to analyze and anticipate adult demands and to conform their behavior to adult expectations.[4] This all means that if the socialization demands made upon boys and girls were actually the same, girls would be in a better position to cope with the world than are boys.

While these differences in response tendencies would be sufficient to result in group differences between boys and girls, another factor adds to the probability of sex differences. Many characteristic responses are acceptable in girls, ranging from the very feminine through the athletic tomboy. For boys, neither the passive sissy nor the aggressive and physical "bad boy" are acceptable. From around the age of two to two and a half, when children are no longer perceived as infants but as children, more boys than girls experience more prohibitions for a wider range of behavior. In addition, and of special importance, dependent behavior, normal to all young children, is permitted for girls and prohibited for boys. Thus, girls are not encouraged to give up old techniques of relating to adults and using others to define their identity, to manipulate the physical world, and to supply their emotional needs.[5]

When people find their ways of coping comfortable and gratifying, they are not motivated to develop new techniques which in the long run might be far more productive. All very young children are dependent on adults for their physical well-being and for the knowledge that they exist and have value. Girls' self-esteem remains dependent upon other people's acceptance and love; they continue to use the skills of others instead of evolving their own. The boy's impulsivity and sexuality are sources of enormous pleasure independent of anyone else's response; these pleasures are central to the early core-self. Negative sanctions from powerful adults against masturbation, exploration, and physical aggression threaten not only the obvious pleasures, but, at heart, self-integrity. Thus, boys are pressured by their own impulses and by society's demands to give up depending predominantly on the response of others for feelings of self-esteem. Adult responses are unpredictable and frequently threatening. Forced to affirm himself because of the loss of older, more stable sources of esteem, the boy begins, before the age of five, to develop a sense of self and criteria of worth which are relatively independent of others' responses. He turns to achievements in the outer and real world and begins to value himself for real achievements in terms of objective criteria.

On the other hand, neither the girl's characteristic responses nor widespread cultural values force her to give up older, more successful modes of relating and coping. Her sexuality is neither so genital nor so imperative,[6] but, rather, an overall body sensuality, gratified by affection and cuddling. Since girls are less likely to masturbate, run away from home, or bite and draw blood, their lives are relatively free of crisis until puberty. Before that girls do not have to conform to threatening new criteria of acceptability to anywhere near the extent that boys do. When boys are pressured to give up their childish ways it is because those behaviors are perceived as feminine by parents. Boys have to earn their masculinity early. Until puberty, femininity is a verbal label, a given attribute—something that does not have to be earned. This results in a significant delay in the girl's search for identity, development of autonomy, and development of internal criteria for self-esteem. Because they continue to depend on others for self-definition and affirmation and are adept at anticipating other people's demands, girls are conformist. Girls are rewarded by good grades in school, parental love, teacher acceptance, and peer belonging. As a result, girls remain compliant and particularly amenable to molding by the culture.[7]

Longitudinal studies which measure the same people from earliest childhood through adulthood reveal that some characteristics remain stable over the life span in both sex groups, while other traits change.[8] While activity level and the tendency to be extroverted or introverted are rather stable in both sexes, other dimensions like passivity-dependence and aggression may remain stable or change depending on sex. There are significant correlations over the life span for aggression in males and passivity and dependency in females; on the other hand, passivity and dependency in males and aggression in females show no consistency over the life span. These psychological dimensions change or remain constant depending on whether individual inclinations threaten idealized cultural concepts of masculinity and femininity.[9] Aggression in boys is permitted and encouraged and only the form is socialized; dependence and passivity in girls is permitted and encouraged, and only the form is altered. Sex differences in infancy and childhood are enlarged through socialization.

Schools are generally feminine places,[10] institutions where conformity is valued, taught largely by conformist women. The course content, the methods of assessing progress, and the personal conduct required create difficulties for boys who must inhibit impulsivity, curb aggression, and restrain deviance. The reward structure of the school system perpetuates the pattern set by relationships with the parents—boys are further pressured to turn to their peers for acceptance and to develop internal criteria and objective achievements; girls are further urged to continue the nondeviant, noninnovative, conformist style of life.

Girls are rewarded with high grades in school, especially in the early years of grammar school. What do girls do especially well in? What are they being asked to master? Grammar, spelling, reading, arithmetic—tasks that depend a great deal upon memorization and demand little independence, assertiveness, analysis, innovativeness, creativity.[11] The dependent, passive girl, cued into the affirming responses of teachers, succeeds and is significantly rewarded in school for her "good" behavior and her competent memorizing skills.

It appears that until puberty academically successful girls evolve a "bisexual" or dual self-concept. Both sexes are rewarded for achievement, especially academic achievement. Girls, as well as boys, are permitted to compete in school or athletics without significant negative repercussions. The girl who is rewarded for these successes evolves a self-concept associated with being able to successfully cope and compete. While there are no negative repercussions and there is a high probability of rewards from parents and teachers as long as her friends are similarly achieving, this girl will also feel normally feminine (although questions of femininity are probably not critically important in self-evaluation of prepubertal girls unless they are markedly deviant). With the onset of the physical changes of puberty, definitions of normalcy and femininity change and come precipitately closer to the stereotype. Now behaviors and qualities that were rewarded, especially successful competing, may be perceived negatively.[12] Femininity also becomes an attribute that has to be earned—this task is made crucially difficult because of the girl's ambivalent feelings toward her body.[13]

The maturation of the girl's reproductive system brings joy and relief, feelings of normalcy, and the awareness of sexuality. Simultaneously, in normal girls the physical changes are accompanied by blood and pain, the expectation of body distortion in pregnancy, the threat of the trauma of birth, and the beginning of sexual desirability. In addition, the physical changes of menstruation are accompanied by significant and predictable emotional cycles sufficiently severe to alter the perception of her body as secure or stable.[14] Simultaneously joyful and fearful, the young adolescent girl must begin to evolve a feminine self-concept that accepts the functions and future responsibilities of her mature body; at the same time these physical changes are cues for alterations in the demands made upon her by the culture.[15] From the very beginning of adolescence girls, as potential heterosexual partners, begin to be punished for conspicuous competing achievement and to be rewarded for heterosexual success. Socialization in adolescence empha-

sizes the use of the cosmetic exterior of the self to lure men, to secure affection, to succeed in the competition of dating. At the same time the girl is warned not to succeed too much: conspicuous success in competitive dating threatens her friendships with girls. She learns in puberty that she is likely to be punished for significant competition in either of her important spheres.

Thus, for a long time, even the girls who are competitive, verbally aggressive, and independent can feel normal, but with the onset of puberty girls are faced with their first major crises: they must come to terms with and find pleasure in their physical femininity and develop the proper psychological "femininity." Since they are still primarily cued to others for feelings of esteem, and largely defined by interpersonal relations, under the stress of their evolving, incomplete feminine identity, most girls conform to the new socialization criteria. While girls characteristically achieved in grade school because of rewards for this "good" behavior from others (rather than for achievement's own sake), in adolescence the establishment of successful interpersonal relationships becomes the self-defining, most rewarding, achievement task.[16] When that change in priorities occurs—and it tends to be greatest in the later years of high school, and again in the later years of college—personal qualities, such as independence, aggression, and competitive achievement, that might threaten success in heterosexual relationships are largely given up.

While boys are often afraid of failing, girls are additionally afraid of succeeding.[17] The adolescent girl, her parents, her girl friends, and her boy friends perceive success, as measured by objective, visible achievement as antithetical to femininity. Some girls defer consciously, with tongue in cheek, but the majority, who were never significantly aggressive, active, or independent, internalize the norms and come to value themselves as they are desired by others. The only change from childhood is that the most important source of esteem is no longer the parents but the heterosexual partner.

The overwhelming majority of adolescent girls remain dependent upon others for feelings of affirmation. Unless in early life the girl exhibited the activity, aggression, or sexuality usually displayed by boys, and thereby experienced significant parental prohibitions, there is little likelihood that she will develop independent sources of esteem that refer back to herself. Instead, the loss of love remains for her the gravest source of injury to the self and, predictably, she will not gamble with that critical source of esteem.[18]

In the absence of independent and objective achievements, girls and women know their worth only from others' responses, know their identities only from their relationships as daughters, girl friends, wives, or mothers and, in a literal sense, personalize the world. When we ask female college students what would make them happy or unhappy, when would they consider themselves successful, both undergraduate and graduate students reply: "When I love and am loved; when I contribute to the welfare of others; when I have established a good family life and have happy, normal children; when I know I have created a good, rewarding stable relationship."[19] During adolescence as in childhood, females continue to esteem themselves insofar as they are esteemed by those with whom they have emotional relationships. For many women this never changes during their entire lifetime.

Girls are socialized to use more oblique forms of aggression than boys, such as the deft use of verbal injury or interpersonal rejection. Their aggression is largely directed toward people whose return anger will not be catastrophic to self-esteem—that is, other females. In their relationships with their fathers and later with their boy friends or husbands, girls do not threaten the important and frequently precarious heterosexual sources of love. Instead, aggression is more safely directed toward other women with whom they covertly compete for love. In relationships between men, aggression is overt and the powerful relationships are clear; female aggression is covert, the power relationships rarely admitted. With the denial of disguise of anger, a kind of dishonesty, a pervasive uncertainty, necessarily creeps into each of a woman's relationships, creating further anxiety and continued or increased efforts to secure affection. The absence of objective success in work makes girls invest in, and be unendingly anxious about, their interpersonal worth. Women use interpersonal success as a route to self-esteem since that is how they have defined their major task. If they fail to establish a meaningful, rewarding, unambivalent love relationship, they remain cued into the response of others and suffer from a fragile or vulnerable sense of self. Those who are secure enough, who have evolved an identity and feeling of worth in love relationships, may gamble and pursue atypical, nontraditional, competitive, masculine achievements.

According to Erik Erikson, the most important task in adolescence is the establishment of a sense of identity. This is more difficult for girls than for boys. Because her sexuality is internal, inaccessible, and diffuse, because she feels ambivalent toward the functions of her mature reproductive system, because she is not punished for her impulsivity, because she is encouraged to remain dependent, a girl's search for her feminine identity is both complex and delayed. To add to her problems, she is aware both of the culture's preference for masculine achievements and of the fact that there is no longer a single certain route for achieving successful femininity. The problem grows ever more complex, ever more subtle.

In these affluent times middle-class girls are apparently not punished simply for being girls. They are not prohibited from going to college, seeking school office, or achieving honors. Marriage and maternity are held out as wonderful goals, not necessarily as inhibiting dead ends. Although girls are rewarded for conformity, dependence, passivity, and competence, they are not clearly punished for the reverse. Until adolescence the idea of equal capacity, opportunity, and life style is held out to them. But sometime in adolescence the message becomes clear that one had better not do too well, that competition is aggressive and unfeminine, that deviating threatens the heterosexual relationship.[20] Masculinity is clearly defined and earned through individual competitive achievement. For the girl overt freedoms, combined with cultural ambiguity, result in an unclear image of femininity. As a result of vagueness about how to become feminine or even what is feminine, the girl responds to the single clear directive—she withdraws from what is clearly masculine. In high school and increasingly in college, girls cease clearly masculine pursuits and perceive the establishment of interpersonal goals as the most salient route to identity.[21] This results in a maximization of interpersonal skills, an interpersonal view of the world, a withdrawal from the development of independence, activity, ability, and competition, and the absence of a professional work commitment.

The personality qualities that evolve as characteristic of the sexes function so as to enhance the probability of succeeding in the traditional sex roles. Whether you are male or female, if you have traditionally masculine personality qualities—objectivity rather than subjectivity, aggression rather than passivity, the motive to achieve rather than a fear of success, courage rather than conformity, and professional commitment, ambition, and drive[22]—you are more likely to succeed in masculine roles. Socialization enhances initial tendencies; consequently, relatively few women have these qualities.

Thus, the essence of the problem of role conflict lies in the fact that up until now very few women have succeeded in traditionally masculine roles, not only because of disparagement and prejudice, but largely because women have not been fundamentally equipped and determined to succeed. Some women's tragedy is their desire to succeed in competitive achievement and their contempt for the traditional role for which they are better equipped.

It is probably not accidental, therefore, that women dominate professions that utilize skills of nurturance, empathy, and competence, where aggressiveness and competitiveness are largely dysfunctional.[23] These professions, notably teaching, nursing, and secretarial work, are low in pay and status. The routes to occupational success for women are either atypical and hazardous or typical, safe, and low in the occupational hierarchy. (It is interesting to note that in the USSR where over 70 percent of the physicians are women, medicine is a low-status occupation.)

In spite of an egalitarian ideal in which the roles and contributions of the sexes are declared to be equal and complementary, both men and women esteem masculine qualities and achievements. Too many women evaluate their bodies, personality qualities, and roles as second-rate. When male criteria are the norms against which female performance, qualities, or goals are measured, then women are not equal. It is not only that the culture values masculine productivity more than feminine productivity. The essence of the derogation lies in the evolution of the masculine as the yardstick against which everything is measured. Since the sexes are different, women are defined as not-men and that means not good, inferior. It is important to understand that women in this culture, as members of the culture, have internalized these self-destructive values.[24]

What we have described is ambivalence, not conflict. Conflict is the simultaneous desire to achieve a stable and rewarding heterosexual relationship (and the rest of the female's traditional responsibilities and satisfactions) and to participate fully in competitive achievement and succeed. Conflict, in this sense, is understandable as a vying between traditional and nontraditional roles, between affiliative and achievement motives. (Most women resolve this potential difficulty by defining affiliation as achievement.) Ambivalence is clearly seen in the simultaneous enjoyment of one's feminine identity, qualities, goals, and achievements and the perception of them as less important, meaningful, or satisfying than those of men. Girls envy boys; boys do not envy girls.

The culture generally rewards masculine endeavors and those males who succeed—who acquire money, power, and status, who enjoy an easy and free sexuality, who acquire and produce things, who achieve in competition, who produce, who innovate and create. By these criteria, women have not produced equally. The contributions that most women make in the enhancement and stabilization of relationships, their competence and self-discipline, their creation of life are less esteemed by men and women alike. It is disturbing to review the extent to which women perceive their responsibilities, goals, their very capacities, as inferior to males; it is similarly distressing to perceive how widespread this self-destructive self-concept is. Society values masculinity; when it is achieved it is rewarded. Society does not value femininity as highly; when it is achieved it is not as highly rewarded.

Today we have a peculiar situation in which sex-role stereotypes persist and are internalized by adults and children, yet the labor force includes thirty-one million working women and the college population is almost half women.[25] The stereotype persists because there is always cultural lag, because few women achieve markedly responsible or powerful positions, and because the overwhelming majority of working women perceive themselves as working in order to benefit the family.[26] In general, working women do not see work as an extension of egocentric interests or as the fulfillment of achievement ambitions, but as another place in which more traditional motives are gratified.

Perhaps the percentage of the female population who have had at least some college and who have achieved and been rewarded in the educational system faces the most difficult problems.[27] Some part of this population has evolved—normally and not as a compensatory function—self-concepts and motives that take for granted the value of marriage and maternity, but also include individuality, creativity, independence, and successful competitive achievement. These characteristics become criteria by which the excellence of the self is measured. It is obvious that these characteristics are not highly functional within the traditional role, and moreover, cannot truly be achieved within the traditional female role. There would be no conflict if competitive achievement were the only aspect of these women's self-concept, but it is not. Characteristically, normal girls simultaneously put priority upon successful heterosexual relationships, which lead to the establishment of the nuclear family and traditional responsibilities.[28] Most girls effect a compromise, recognizing the hierarchy of their motivations and the appropriateness of their heterosexual desires. They tend to marry, work for a few years, and then start having babies. Inexperienced and unprepared, they tell themselves that the traditional role is creative and fulfilling. But creativity and fulfillment are hard to distinguish under the unending and repetitive responsibilities of diapers, dishes, and dusting. They tell themselves that when the children enter school they will reenter the labor force or the university. For these women, who have internalized the unequal evaluation of roles, who have developed needs to achieve, who have been rewarded because of their achievements, the traditional role is inadequate because it cannot gratify those nonnurturant, nonsupportive, nondependent, nonpassive aspects of the self.

Very few young women understand the very real limits upon achieving imposed by maternity, because they traditionally have had little experience with traditional role responsibilities before they marry. Typically, girls do not ask why there are so few female role models around who succeed in work while they have young children. While children are a real achievement, a source of joy and fulfillment, they are also time-consuming and energy-depleting, a major source of responsibility and anxiety. In today's child-centered milieu, with the decline of the extended family and the dearth of adequate child-care facilities, the responsibility for childrearing falls directly on the mother alone.

Success in the traditional tasks is the usual means by which girls achieve feelings of esteem about themselves, confidence, and identity.[29] In general they have continued, even as adults, to esteem themselves as they are valued by others; that source of esteem is interpersonal, best earned within the noncompetitive, nonaggressive traditional role. Without independent, objective competitive achievements, confidence is best secured within the traditional role—in spite of the priority given to masculine achievements. Whether or not the woman is achievement-oriented, her years of major childrearing responsibilities result in a decline in old work skills, a loss of confidence that she can work, a fear of failing within a competitive milieu that she has left. In other words, not only have specific techniques been lost or new data become unfamiliar, withdrawal from a competitive-achievement situation for a significant length of time creates the conviction that she is not able.

The very characteristics that make a woman most successful in family roles—the capacity to take pleasure in family-centered, repetitive activities, to sustain and support members of the family rather than pursuing her own goals, to enhance relationships through boundaryless empathy—these are all antithetical to success in the bounded, manipulative, competitive, rational, and egocentric world of work.[30] Because they are not highly motivated and because they are uncertain about what is normal or desirable, many women do not work. Even those who do continue to feel psychologically responsible for the maintenance of the family and are unwilling to jeopardize family relationships. Most work at jobs that contribute to family vacations, college fees, or the general family budget.[31] Even women who pursue a career or profession, rather than merely holding a meaningless job, assume the responsibility for two major, demanding roles. Rather than make this commitment, many women professionalize their voluntary or club activities, bringing qualities of aggression, competitiveness, and organizing skills to these "safer" activities.

Women tend not to participate in roles, or seek goals that

threaten their important affiliative relationships because in those relationships they find most of their feelings of esteem and identity. This perpetuates psychological dependency which may be functional in the relationships but injurious to the self-concept of those who have internalized the values of the culture. Undeniably, it is destructive to feelings of esteem to know that you are capable and to be aware that you are not utilizing much of your potential.[32] The question of whether nontraditional success jeopardizes feelings of femininity has not yet been answered. Most women today would not be willing to achieve a greater success than their husbands. In this tradition-bound, sex-stereotyped culture, even though millions of women are employed, old values are internalized and serve as criteria for self-evaluation.

Neither men nor women entering marriage expect the sexes to share equally in privileges and responsibilities. Very few couples could honestly accept the wife's having the major economic responsibility for the family while the husband deferred to the demands of her work. Few individuals could reverse roles without feeling that he is not "masculine," and she is not "feminine."[33] Masculinity and femininity are aspects of the self that are clearly tied to roles—which role, how typical or deviant, how well accomplished, the extent of the commitment.

Yet a new reality is emerging today, for this is an era of changing norms. Although the unidimensional stereotype still persists and remains partially viable, it is also simplistic and inaccurate. Both men and women are rejecting the old role allocations which are exaggerated and costly because they push men and women into limited slots solely on the basis of sex. But an era of change results in new uncertainties and the need to evolve new clear criteria of masculinity and femininity, which can be earned and can offer feelings of self-esteem to both sexes.

The socialization model is no longer clear; in its pure form it exists primarily in media, less in life. Since almost half of American women work, the percentage rising with the rising level of education, it is clear that, at least for educated middle-class women, the simplistic stereotype is no longer valid. Similarly we find that more men are rejecting success as the sole source of esteem or masculinity. The male turning toward his family reflects his need not to be bound or limited by the unidimensional role model. For both sexes this is a period of change in which both old and new values coexist, though the visible norms derive from the old model. Today's college students seem to be more aware than the generation that preceded them of the consequences of role choice; they seem to be evolving a goal in which men are more nurturant than they were, while females are freer to participate professionally without endangering the male's esteem.

Both the work and the housewife roles are romanticized, since romanticism is enhanced when reality does not intrude. Women glorify work when and because they do not participate in it. Role conflict for women is largely a feeling of having been arbitrarily shut out from where the action is—a reaction to a romanticized concept of work and a reaction against the reality of the repetitive world of child care. Frustration is freely available to today's woman: if she participates fully in some professional capacity she runs the risk of being atypical and nonfeminine. If she does not achieve the traditional role she is likely to feel unfulfilled as a person, as a woman. If she undertakes both roles, she is likely to be uncertain about whether she is doing either very well. If she undertakes only the traditional role she is likely to feel frustrated as an able individual. Most difficult of all, the norms of what is acceptable, desirable, or preferable are no longer clear. As a result, it is more difficult to achieve a feminine (or masculine) identity, to achieve self-esteem because one is not certain when one has succeeded. When norms are no longer clear, then not only the "masculine" achieving woman but also the nonworking traditionally "feminine" woman can feel anxious about her normalcy, her fulfillment. Many women try to cope with their anxiety by exaggerating, by conforming to stereotyped role images. When one is anxious or uncertain about one's femininity, a viable technique for quelling those anxious feelings is an exaggerated conformity, a larger-than-life commitment to *Kinder, Küche, Kirche*. In this way a woman creates images, sending out clarified and exaggerated cues to others. Thus, the message is clear and she can be more certain that the feedback will assure her of her femininity.

It is easy to be aware of the discrepancy between the stereotyped norm and the reality. People are not simple. Whenever one sees a total investment or role adoption in its stereotyped, unidimensional form, one suspects a flight from uncertainty about masculinity or femininity. During a period of transition one can expect to see increasing numbers of women quelling anxiety by fleeing into a unidimensional, stereotyped femininity. As new norms gain clarity and force, more flexible roles, personalities, and behaviors will evolve. Role freedom is a burden when choice is available but criteria are unclear; under these circumstances it is very difficult to know whether one has achieved womanhood or has dangerously jeopardized it.

NOTES

1. J. Silverman, "Attentional Styles and the Study of Sex Differences," in D. Mostofsky, ed., *Attention: Contemporary Studies and Analysis* (New York: Appleton-Century-Crofts, in press): H. A. Witkin et al., *Personality through Perception: An Experimental and Clinical Study* (New York: Harper, 1954); J. Kagan, "Acquisition and Significance of Sex Typing and Sex Role Identity," in M. L. Hoffman and L. W. Hoffman, eds., *Review of Child Development Research* (New York: Russell Sage Foundation, 1964), 1:137-167; L. M. Terman and L. E. Tyler, "Psychological Sex Differences," in L. Carmichael, ed., *A Manual of Child Psychology*, 2nd ed. (New York: John Wiley, 1954), ch. 19; E. Douvan and J. Adelson, *The Adolescent Experience* (New York: John Wiley, 1966).

2. Silverman, *op. cit.*, Terman and Tyler, *op. cit.*; R. Q. Bell and N. S. Costello, "Three Tests for Sex Differences in Tactile Sensitivity in the New Born," *Biologia Neonatorum* 7 (1964): 335-347; R. Q. Bell and J. F. Darling, "The Prone Head Reaction in the Human Neonate: Relation with Sex and Tactile Sensitivity," *Child Development* 36 (1965):943-949; S. M. Garn, "Roentgenogrammetric Determinants of Body Composition," *Human Biology* 29 (1957): 337-353; J. Kagan and M. Lewis, "Studies of Attention in the Human Infant," *Merrill-Palmer Quarterly* 2 (1965): 95-127; M. Lewis, J. Kagan, and J. Kalafat, "Patterns of Fixation in the Young Infant," *Child Development* 37 (1966): 331-341; L. P. Lipsitt and N. Levy, "Electrotactual Threshold in the Human Neonate," *Child Development* 30 (1959): 547-554.

3. Kagan and Lewis, *op. cit.*; Lewis, Kagan, and Kalafat, *op. cit.* In spite of this initial advantage which might be thought to lead, logically and inevitably to high achievement investment, girls' socialization ends without realization of this early promise. J. Veroff, "Social Comparison and the Development of Achievement Motivation," in C. Smith, ed., *Achievement Related Motives in Children*

(New York: Russell-Sage Foundation, 1969); pp. 46-101, suggests that the period of optimal generalization of the achievement motive is early, about the age of four or five. At this time girls are better at the truly critical tasks of speaking, comprehending, and remembering. But these accomplishments are taken for granted by children, who strive rather to tie shoelaces, ride bicycles, climb trees, and jump rope—all physical accomplishments. In other words, at the time when the motive for achievement is learned and generalized, the children themselves define physical tasks as important. Girls' greater cognitive and verbal skills do not, therefore, contribute to the development of a higher achievement motivation.

4. E. Maccoby, ed., *The Development of Sex Differences* (Stanford: Stanford University Press, 1966).

5. J. M. Bardwick, *The Psychology of Women* (New York: Harper & Row, 1971).

6. Helene Deutsch, *Psychology of Women* (New York: Grune & Stratton, 1944), vol. 1; K. Horney, "On the Genesis of the Castration Complex in Women," *International Journal of Psychoanalysis 5* (1924): 50-65.

7. Douvan and Adelson, *op. cit.*

8. N. Bayley, "Consistency of Maternal and Child Behaviors in the Berkeley Growth Study," *Vita Humana 7* (1964): 73-95; M. P. Honzik and J. W. MacFarlane, "Prediction of Behavior and Personality from 21 months to 30 years," unpublished manuscript, 1963; J. Kagan and H. A. Moss, *Birth to Maturity* (New York: John Wiley, 1962); E. S. Schaefer and N. Bayley, "Maternal Behavior, Child Behavior, and Inter-correlations from Infancy through Adolescence," *Monograph of the Society for Research on Child Development 28* (1963), serial no. 87.

9. Kagan and Moss, *op. cit.*

10. H. S. Becker, "Social Class Variations in One Teacher-Pupil Relationship," *Journal of Educational Sociology 25* (1952): 451-465.

11. Maccoby, *op. cit.*

12. M. S. Horner, "Fail: Bright Women," *Psychology Today 3* (November 1969): 36.

13. Bardwick, *op. cit.*; E. Douvan, "New Sources of Conflict at Adolescence and Early Adulthood," in Judith M. Bardwick et al, *Feminine Personality and Conflict* (Belmont, Calif.: Brooks/Cole, in press).

14. M. E. Ivey and J. M. Bardwick, "Patterns of Affective Fluctuation in the Menstrual Cycle," *Psychosomatic Medicine 30* (1968): 336-345.

15. Douvan, *op. cit.*

16. J. G. Coleman, *The Adolescent Society* (New York: Free Press, 1961).

17. Horner, *op. cit.*

18. Deutsch, *op cit.*; Douvan and Adelson, *op. cit.*

19. J. Bardwick and J. Zweben, "A Predictive Study of Psychological and Psychosomatic Changes Associated with Oral Contraceptives," mimeograph, 1970.

20. M. Komarovsky, *Women in the Modern World* (Boston: Little Brown, 1953).

21. *Ibid.*; R. Goldsen, M. Rosenberg, R. Williams, E. A. Suchman, *What College Students Think* (Princeton, N.J.: Van Nostrand, 1961); Coleman, *op. cit.*; N. Sanford, *The American College* (New York: John Wiley, 1962).

22. T. Parsons, "Age and Sex in the Social Structure of the United States." *American Sociological Review 7* (1942): 604-616.

23. M. Mead, *Male and Female* (New York: William Morrow, 1949).

24. Bardwick, *op. cit.*; Mead, *op. cit.*

25. R. E. Hartley, "Children's Concept of Male and Female Roles," *Merrill-Palmer Quarterly 6* (1960): 153:163.

26. F. I. Nye and L. W. Hoffman, *The Employed Mother in America* (Chicago: Rand-McNally, 1963).

27. R. Baruch, "The Achievement Motive in Women: Implications for Career Development," *Journal of Personality and Social Psychology 5* (1967): 260-267.

28. Bardwick, *op. cit.*

29. Douvan and Adelson, *op. cit.*

30. D. L. Gutmann, "Woman and Their Conception of Ego Strength," *Merrill-Palmer Quarterly 11* (1965): 29-240.

31. Nye and Hoffman, *op. cit.*

32. G. Gurin, J. Veroff, and S. Feld, *Americans View Their Mental Health* (New York: Basic Books, 1960).

33. D. J. Bem and S. L. Bem, "Training the Woman to Know Her Place," based on a lecture delivered at Carnegie Institute of Technology, October 21, 1966, revised 1967.

9 Cultural contradictions and sex roles

Mirra Komarovsky

Profound changes in the roles of women during the past century have been accompanied by innumerable contradictions and inconsistencies. With our rapidly changing and highly differentiated culture, with migrations and multiplied social contacts, the stage is set for myriads of combinations of incongruous elements. Cultural norms are often functionally unsuited to the social situations to which they apply. Thus they may deter an individual from a course of action which would serve his own, and society's, interests best. Or, if behavior contrary to the norm is engaged in, the individual may suffer from guilt over violating mores which no longer serve any socially useful end. Sometimes culturally defined roles are adhered to in the face of new conditions without a conscious realization of the discrepancies involved. The reciprocal actions dictated by the roles may be at variance with those demanded by the actual situation. This may result in an imbalance of privileges and obligations[1] or in some frustration of basic interests.

Again, problems arise because changes in the mode of life have created new situations which have not as yet been defined by culture. Individuals left thus without social guidance tend to act in terms of egotistic or "short-run hedonistic" motives which at times defeat their own long-term interests or create conflict with others. The precise obligation of a gainfully employed wife toward the support of the family is one such undefined situation.

Finally, a third mode of discrepancy arises in the existence of incompatible cultural definitions of the same social

Reprinted from Mirra Komarovsky, "Cultural Contradictions and Sex Roles," American Journal of Sociology, 52:3, Nov. 1946, pp. 184-189.

situation, such as the clash of "old-fashioned" and "radical" mores, of religion and law, of norms of economic and familial institutions.

The problems raised by these discrepancies are social problems in the sense that they engender mental conflict or social conflict or otherwise frustrate some basic interest of large segments of the population.

This article sets forth in detail the nature of certain incompatible sex roles imposed by our society upon the college woman. It is based on data collected in 1942 and 1943. Members of an undergraduate course on the family were asked for two successive years to submit autobiographical documents focused on the topic; 73 were collected. In addition, 80 interviews, lasting about an hour each, were conducted with every member of a course in social psychology of the same institution—making a total of 153 documents ranging from a minimum of five to a maximum of thirty typewritten pages.

The generalization emerging from these documents is the existence of serious contradictions between two roles present in the social environment of the college woman. The goals set by each role are mutually exclusive, and the fundamental personality traits each evokes are at points diametrically opposed, so that what are assets for one become liabilities for the other, and the full realization of one role threatens defeat in the other.

One of these roles may be termed the "feminine" role. While there are a number of permissive variants of the feminine role for women of college age (the "good sport," the "glamour girl," the "young lady," the domestic "home girl," etc.), they have a common core of attributes defining the proper attitudes to men, family, work, love, etc., and a set of personality traits often described with reference to the male sex role as "not as dominant, or aggressive as men" or "more emotional, sympathetic."

The other and more recent role is, in a sense, no *sex* role at all, because it partly obliterates the differentiation in sex. It demands of the woman much the same virtues, patterns of behavior, and attitude that it does of the men of corresponding age. We shall refer to this as the "modern" role.

Both roles are present in the social environment of these women throughout their lives, though, as the precise content of each sex role varies with age, so does the nature of their clashes change from one stage to another. In the period under discussion the conflict between the two roles apparently centers about academic work, social life, vocational plans, excellence in specific fields of endeavor, and a number of personality traits.

One manifestation of the problem is in the inconsistency of the goals set for the girl by her family.

Forty, or 26 per cent, of the respondents expressed some grievance against their families for failure to confront them with clear-cut and consistent goals. The majority, 74 per cent, denied having had such experiences. One student writes:

How am I to pursue any course single-mindedly when some way along the line a person I respect is sure to say, "You are on the wrong track and are wasting your time." Uncle John telephones every Sunday morning. His first question is: "Did you go out last night?" He would think

me a "grind" if I were to stay home Saturday night to finish a term paper. My father expects me to get an "A" in every subject and is disappointed by a "B." He says I have plenty of time for social life. Mother says, "That 'A' in Philosophy is very nice dear. But please don't become so deep that no man will be good enough for you." And, finally, Aunt Mary's line is careers for women. "Prepare yourself for some profession. This is the only way to insure yourself independence and an interesting life. You have plenty of time to marry."

A Senior writes:

I get a letter from my mother at least three times a week. One week her letters will say, "Remember that this is your last year at college. Subordinate everything to your studies. You must have a good record to secure a job." The next week her letters are full of wedding news. This friend of mine got married; that one is engaged; my young cousin's wedding is only a week off. When, my mother wonders, will I make up my mind? Surely, I wouldn't want to be the only unmarried one in my group. It is high time, she feels, that I give some thought to it.

A student reminisces:

All through high school my family urged me to work hard because they wished me to enter a first-rate college. At the same time they were always raving about a girl schoolmate who lived next door to us. How pretty and sweet she was, how popular, and what taste in clothes! Couldn't I also pay more attention to my appearance and to social life? They were overlooking the fact that this carefree friend of mine had little time left for school work and had failed several subjects. It seemed that my family had expected me to become Eve Curie and Hedy Lamar wrapped up in one.

Another comments:

My mother thinks that its very nice to be smart in college but only if it doesn't take too much effort. She always tells me not to be too intellectual on dates, to be clever in a light sort of way. My father, on the other hand, wants me to study law. He thinks that if I applied myself I could make an excellent lawyer and keeps telling me that I am better fitted for this profession than my brother.

Another writes:

One of my two brothers writes: "Cover up that high forehead and act a little dumb once in a while"; while the other always urges upon me the importance of rigorous scholarship.

The students testified to a certain bewilderment and confusion caused by the failure on the part of the family to smooth the passage from one role to another, especially when the roles involved were contradictory. It seemed to some of them that they had awakened one morning to find their world upside down: what had hitherto evoked praise and rewards from relatives, now suddenly aroused censure. A student recollects:

I could match my older brother in skating, sledding, riflery, ball, and many of the other games we played. He enjoyed teaching me and took great pride in my accomplishments. Then one day it all changed. He must have suddenly become conscious of the fact that girls ought to be feminine. I was walking with him, proud to be able to make long strides and keep up with his long-legged steps when he turned to me in annoyance, "Can't you walk like a lady?" I still remember feeling hurt and bewildered by his scorn, when I had been led to expect approval.

Once during her freshman year in college, after a delightful date, a student wrote her brother with great elation:

"What a beautiful evening at ——— fraternity house! You would be proud of me, Johnny, I won all ping-pong games but one!"

"For heaven's sake," came the reply, "when will you grow up? Don't you know that a boy likes to think he is better than a girl? Give him a little competition, sure, but miss a few serves in the end. Should you join the Debate Club? By all means, but don't practice too much on the boys." Believe me I was stunned by this letter, but then I saw that he was right. To be a success in the dorms one must date, to date one must not win too many ping-pong games. At first I resented this bitterly. But now I am more or less used to it and live in hope of one day meeting a man who is my superior so that I may be my natural self.

It is the parents and not the older sibling who reversed their expectations in the following excerpt:

All through grammar school and high school my parents led me to feel that to do well in school was my chief responsibility. A good report card, an election to student office, these were the news Mother bragged about in telephone coversations with her friends. But recently they suddenly got worried about me: I don't pay enough attention to social life, a woman needs *some* education but not that much. They are disturbed by my determination to go to the School of Social Work. Why my ambitions should surprise them after they have exposed me for four years to some of the most inspired and stimulating social scientists in the country, I can't imagine. They have some mighty strong arguments on their side. What is the use, they say, of investing years in training for a profession, only to drop it in a few years? Chances of meeting men are slim in the profession. Besides, I may become so preoccupied with it as to sacrifice social life. The next few years are, after all, the proper time to find a mate. But the urge to apply what I have learned, and the challenge of this profession is so strong that I shall go on despite the family opposition.

The final excerpt illustrates both the sudden transition of roles and the ambiguity of standards:

I major in English composition. This is not a completely "approved" field for girls so I usually just say "English." An English Literature major is quite liked and approved by boys. Somehow it is lumped with all the other arts and even has a little glamour. But a composition major is a girl to beware of because she supposedly will notice all your grammar mistakes, look at your letters too critically, and consider your ordinary speech and conversation as too crude.

I also work for a big metropolitan daily as a correspondent in the city room. I am well liked there and may possibly stay as a reporter after graduation in February. I have had several spreads [stories running to more than eight or ten inches of space], and this is considered pretty good for a college correspondent. Naturally, I was elated and pleased at such breaks, and as far as the city room is concerned I'm off to a very good start on a career that is hard for a man to achieve and even harder for a woman. General reporting is still a man's work in the opinion of most people. I have a lot of acclaim but also criticism, and I

find it confusing and difficult to be praised for being clever and working hard and then, when my efforts promise to be successful, to be condemned and criticized for being unfeminine and ambitious.

Here are a few of these reactions:

My father: "I don't like this newspaper setup at all. The people you meet are making you less interested in marriage than ever. You're getting too educated and intellectual to be attractive to men."

My mother: "I don't like your attitude toward people. The paper is making you too analytical and calculating. Above all, you shouldn't sacrifice your education and career for marriage."

A lieutenant with two years of college: "It pleased me greatly to hear about your news assignment—good girl."

A Navy pilot with one year of college: "Undoubtedly, I'm old fashioned, but I could never expect or feel right about a girl giving up a very promising or interesting future to hang around waiting for me to finish college. Nevertheless, congratulations on your job on the paper. Where in the world do you get that wonderful energy? Anyway I know you were thrilled at getting it and feel very glad for you. I've an idea that it means the same to you as that letter saying 'report for active duty' meant to me."

A graduate metallurgist now a private in the Army: "It was good to hear that you got that break with the paper. I am sure that talent will prove itself and that you will go far. But not too far, as I don't think you should become a career woman. You'll get repressed and not be interested enough in having fun if you keep after that career."

A lieutanant with a year and a half of college: "All this career business is nonsense. A woman belongs in the home and absolutely no place else. My wife will have to stay home. That should keep her happy. Men are just superior in everything, and women have no right to expect to compete with them. They should do just what will keep their husbands happy."

A graduate engineer—my fiancé: "Go right ahead and get as far as you can in your field. I am glad you are ambitious and clever, and I'm as anxious to see you happily successful as I am myself. It is a shame to let all those brains go to waste over just dusting and washing dishes. I think the usual home life and children are small sacrifices to make if a career will keep you happy. But I'd rather see you in radio because I am a bit wary of the effect upon our marriage of the way of life you will have around the newspaper."

Sixty-one, or 40 per cent, of the students indicated that they have occasionally "played dumb" on dates, that is, concealed some academic honor, pretended ignorance of some subject, or allowed the man the last word in an intellectual discussion. Among these were women who "threw games" and in general played down certain skills in obedience to the unwritten law that men must possess these skills to a superior degree. At the same time, in other areas of life, social pressures were being exerted upon these women to "play to win," to compete to the utmost of their abilities for intellectual distinction and academic honors. One student writes:

I was glad to transfer to a women's college. The two years at the co-ed university produced a constant strain. I am a good student; my family expects me to get good marks. At the same time I am normal enough to want to be invited to the Saturday night dance. Well, everyone knew that on that campus a reputation of a "brain" killed a girl socially. I was always fearful lest I say too much in class or answer a question which the boys I dated couldn't answer.

Here are some significant remarks made from the interviews:

When a girl asks me what marks I got last semester I answer, "Not so good—only one 'A'," When a boy asks the same question, I say very brightly with a note of surprise, "Imagine, I got an 'A!' "

I am engaged to a southern boy who doesn't think too much of the woman's intellect. In spite of myself, I play up to his theories because the less one knows and does, the more he does for you and thinks you "cute" into the bargain. . . . I allow him to explain things to me in great detail and to treat me as a child in financial matters.

One of the nicest techniques is to spell long words incorrectly once in a while. My boyfriend seems to get a great kick out of it and writes back, "Honey, you certainly don't know how to spell."

When my date said that he considers Ravel's *Bolero* the greatest piece of music ever written, I changed the subject because I knew I would talk down to him.

A boy advised me not to tell of my proficiency in math and not to talk of my plans to study medicine unless I knew my date well.

My fiancé didn't go to college. I intend to finish college and work hard at it, but in talking to him I make college appear a kind of a game.

Once I went sailing with a man who so obviously enjoyed the role of a protector that I told him I didn't know how to sail. As it turned out he didn't either. We got into a tough spot, and I was torn between a desire to get a hold of the boat and a fear to reveal that I had lied to him.

It embarrassed me that my "steady" in high school got worse marks than I. A boy should naturally do better in school. I would never tell him my marks and would often ask him to help me with my homework.

I am better in math than my fiancé. But while I let him explain politics to me, we never talk about math even though, being a math major, I could tell him some interesting things.

Mother used to tell me to lay off the brains on dates because glasses make me look too intellectual anyhow.

I was once at a work camp. The girls did the same work as the boys. If some girls worked better, the boys resented it fiercely. The director told one capable girl to slow down to keep peace in the group.

How to do the job and remain popular was a tough task. If you worked your best, the boys resented the competition; if you acted feminine, they complained that you were clumsy.

On dates I always go through the "I-don't-care-anything-you-want-to-do" routine. It gets monotonous but boys fear girls who make decisions. They think such girls would make nagging wives.

I am a natural leader and, when in the company of girls, usually take the lead. That is why I am so active in college activities. But I know that men fear bossy women, and I always have to watch myself on dates not to assume the "executive" role. Once a boy walking to the theater with me took the wrong street. I knew a short cut but kept quiet.

I let my fiancé make most of the decisions when we are out. It annoys me, but he prefers it.

I sometimes "play dumb" on dates, but it leaves a bad taste. The emotions are complicated. Part of me enjoys "putting something over" on the unsuspecting male. But this sense of superiority over him is mixed with feeling of guilt for my hypocrisy. Toward the "date" I feel some contempt because he is "taken in" by my technique, or if I like the boy, a kind of a maternal condescension. At times I resent him! Why isn't he my superior in all ways in which a man should excel so that I could be my natural self? What am I doing here with him, anyhow? Slumming?

And the funny part of it is that the man, I think, is not always so unsuspecting. He may sense the truth and become uneasy in the relation. "Where do I stand? Is she laughing up her sleeve or did she mean this praise? Was she really impressed with that little speech of mine or did she only pretend to know nothing about politics?" And once or twice I felt that the joke was on me: the boy saw through my wiles and felt contempt for me for stooping to such tricks.

Another aspect of the problem is the conflict between the psychogenetic personality of the girl and the cultural role foisted upon her by the milieu.[2] At times it is the girl with "masculine" interests and personality traits who chafes under the pressure to conform to the "feminine" pattern. At other times it is the family and the college who thrust upon the reluctant girl the "modern" role.

While, historically, the "modern" role is the most recent one, ontogenetically it is the one emphasized earlier in the education of the college girl, if these 153 documents are representative. Society confronts the girl with powerful challenges and strong pressure to excel in certain competitive lines of endeavor and to develop certain techniques of adaptations very similar to those expected of her brothers. But, then, quite suddenly as it appears to these girls, the very success in meeting these challenges begins to cause anxiety. It is precisely those most successful in the earlier role who are now penalized.

It is not only the passage from age to age but the moving to another region or type of campus which may create for the girl similar problems. The precise content of sex roles, or, to put it another way, the degree of their differentiation, varies with regional, class, nativity, and other subcultures.

Whenever individuals show differences in response to some social situation, as have our 153 respondents, the question naturally arises as to the causes. It will be remembered that 40 per cent admitted some difficulties in personal relations with men due to conflicting sex roles but that 60 per cent said that they had no such problems. Inconsistency of parental expectations troubled 26 per cent of the students.

To account for individual differences would require another study, involving a classification of personalities in relation to the peculiar social environments of each. Generally speaking, it would seem that it is the girl with a "middle-of-the-road personality" who is most happily adjusted to the present historical moment. She is not a perfect incarnation of either role but is flexible enough to play both. She is a girl who is intelligent enough to do well in school but not so brilliant as to "get all 'A' 's"; informed and alert but not consumed by an intellectual passion; capable but not talented in areas relatively new to women; able to stand on her own feet and to earn a living but not so good a living as to compete with men; capable of doing some job well (in case she does not marry or, otherwise, has to work) but not so identified with a profession as to need it for her happiness.

A search for less immediate causes of individual reactions would lead us further back to the study of genesis of the personality differences found relevant to the problem. One of the clues will certainly be provided by the relation of the child to the parent of the same and of the opposite sex. This relation affects the conception of self and the inclination for a particular sex role.

The problems set forth in this article will persist, in the opinion of the writer, until the adult sex roles of women are redefined in greater harmony with the socioeconomic and ideological character of modern society.[3] Until then neither the formal education nor the unverbalized sex roles of the adolescent woman can be cleared of intrinsic contradictions.

NOTES

1. Clifford Kirkpatrick, "The Measurement of Ethical Inconsistency in Marriage," *International Journal of Ethics*, XLVI (1936), 444-60.
2. Margaret Mead, *Sex and Temperament in Three Primitive Societies* (New York: Morrow & Co., 1935).
3. See excellent discussion in Talcott Parsons, "Age and Sex in the Social Structure of the United States," *American Sociological Review*, VII (1942), 604-16, and in the same issue, Ralph Linton, "Age and Sex Categories," pp. 589-603, and Leonard S. Cottrell, Jr., "The Adjustment of the Individual to His Age and Sex Roles," pp. 617-20.

10   *The motive to avoid success and changing aspirations of college women*

Matina Horner

It has been about seven years when, in an attempt to explain the major unresolved sex differences in previous research on achievement motivation, I first proposed the presence of the "motive to avoid success" as a "Psychological barrier to achievement in women." I suggested, at that time, that women are anxious about success, and that the motive to avoid success exists and receives its impetus from the expectancy held by most women that success, especially in competitive achievement situations, will be followed by negative consequences for them. Among these are social rejection and feelings of being unfeminine or inadequate as a woman.

This concept was developed within the framework of an Expectancy-Value theory of motivation which argues that the most important factors determining the arousal of one's motives and thereby the ultimate strength of one's motivation and the direction of his behavior are:

1) the *expectations* or beliefs one has regarding the nature and likelihood of the consequences of his actions and
2) the value of these consequences to him in light of his particular personality and motives.

With this in mind, it is important to emphasize the idea that to say that women have a "motive to avoid success," i.e., a disposition or tendency to become anxious about

"achieving" because they anticipate or expect negative consequences because of success—is not at all the same as saying that they have a "will to fail," i.e., a motive to approach failure. Unfortunately this has become an increasingly common misinterpretation of my conceptualization of the "motive to avoid success." The presence of a "will to fail" would imply that women actively seek out failure because they anticipate or expect positive consequences from failing. Quite the contrary, I have argued that it is precisely those women who most want to achieve and who are most capable of achieving who experience the detrimental effects of a "fear of success." Their positive achievement-directed tendencies are inhibited by the presence of the motive to avoid success because of the arousal of anxiety about the negative consequences they expect will follow success. Although there may well exist such a thing as a motive to approach failure—a will to fail—it is not conceptually the same as the variable which I have called the "motive to avoid success," and should not be confused with it. Both theoretically and with regard to behavioral implications, the two are quite independent.

Unfortunately in American society even today femininity and competitive achievement continue to be viewed as two desirable but mutually exclusive ends, just as they were in 1949 when Margaret Mead pointed out that "each step

Reprinted from Matina Horner, "The Motive to Avoid Success and Changing Aspirations of College Women," Women on Campus: 1970 a Symposium, pp. 12-23, by permission of the Center for the Continuing Education of Women, Ann Arbor, Mich.

forward as a successful American, regardless of sex, means a step back as a woman." Thus the active pursuit of success is hindered and the actual level of performance attained by many otherwise achievement-motivated and able young women does not reflect their true abilities. When success is likely or possible, these young women, threatened by the negative consequences they expect to follow success, become anxious, and their positive achievement strivings become thwarted.

Thus, their abilities, interests, and intellectual potential remain inhibited and unfulfilled. But, at what cost? Toward the end of this chapter we shall consider a recent analysis of some of our data which show that this lack of fulfillment does not occur without a price, a price paid in feelings of frustration, hostility, aggression, bitterness, and confusion, which are clearly manifested in the fantasy productions of these young women. In the course of our work it has become increasingly clear that once the motive to avoid success is aroused, it exerts a powerful impact on one's achievement strivings. In the initial study it was the only one of the four psychological variables assessed (i.e., the motive to achieve, to avoid failure, to affiliate with others, and resultant achievement motive) which predicted female performance. (Horner, 1968) The girls high in the motive to avoid success performed at a significantly lower level in a mixed-sex competitive achievement situation than they did subsequently in a strictly non-competitive but achievement-oriented situation, in which the only competition involved was with the task and one's internal standards of excellence.

Those low in the motive to avoid success on the other hand performed at a higher level in the competitive condition, as did most of the men in the study. The results of the study suggested very clearly that girls, especially those with a high motive to avoid success, would be least likely to develop their interests and explore their intellectual potential when competing against others, especially against men, because the expectancy of negative consequences associated with success would be greatest under such conditions. It should be pointed out that it was only after a measure of the individual differences in the strength of the motive to avoid success was developed and used in the analysis that the results for the women in this study became at all meaningful or clear.

For those who are not familiar with the way in which presence of the motive to avoid success is assessed, let me briefly summarize. (Horner, 1968, 1970) Individual differences in the strength of the motive to avoid success are determined by the presence of "fear of success imagery" in thematic stories written by subjects in response to a verbal lead connoting a high level of accomplishment, particularly in a mixed-sex competitive achievement situation. Thematic apperceptive imagery connoting "Fear of Success" is defined as that in which statements are made showing:

1) the presence of anticipation of negative *consequences* or *affect* because of the success, including fear of being socially rejected, fear of losing one's friends or one's eligibility as a date or marriage partner, and fear of becoming isolated, lonely, or unhappy as a result of success.

2) any direct or indirect expression of conflict about the success, such as doubting or wondering about one's femininity or normality, or feeling guilty and in despair about the success.

3) denial of effort or responsibility for attaining the success, sometimes using psychologically ingenious means to change the content of the cue or simply by saying "it is impossible."

4) bizarre or inappropriate responses to the cue frequently filled with hostility or confusion, as for instance in the story in which Anne is "attacked and maimed for life" for her accomplishment.

In the first study the verbal lead used to assess the presence of "Fear of Success" for women/men was: "At the end of first term finals Anne/John finds herself/himself at the top of her/his medical school class." In that study more than 65% of the 90 female stories written compared with less than 10% of the 88 male stories written contained imagery connoting Fear of Success. The significant sex differences observed in presence of fear of success imagery ($p = \; < .0005$) have been maintained in all subsequent samples of white men and women studies with the only major change being an increase among white males in fear of success in the last two years. (Horner 1972, in press)

In our studies using black samples Heming and I have found a reversal in the presence of fear-of-success imagery, fear of success being more characteristic of the black men than of the black women tested. An interesting reversal in attitudes toward achievement occurs in our data when race role is imposed upon sex role. This is manifested in a comparison of the presence of fear-of-success imagery when both race and sex of the samples are controlled:

| White Men 10% | Black Men 67% |
| White Women 64% | Black Women 29% |

It has become quite clear from the various samples tested that one's disposition to accept success as a truly positive experience, enhancing self-esteem is by and large a function of how consistent this success is with one's internalized standards and expectations, one's stereotypes, of appropriate sex and/or race role identity and behavior. Our data show that despite a recent surge of interest in the "liberated generation" or the counterculture stressing the removal of unfair prejudices and boundaries of all sorts, conceptions of race and sex roles in particular are so deeply ingrained and historically rooted that they have remained rigid. Thus, despite recent advances in legal and educational opportunities, they psychologically bar many young men and women from taking full advantage of these changes. At any rate for most black men and white women, the attainment of success and/or leadership is seen as an unexpected event, making them the object of competitive assault or social rejection. Some examples from Black Male Stories:

Sam is on the spot. He is "top gun" and he knows that his fellow students, intensely competitive as they are, will be out to "gun him down" academically to dethrone him.

Sam has really booked in order to combat the "niggers ain't shit" syndrome most whitey's have . . . A lot of white boys will jump out of H . . . C. . . . The Professors will of course make sure that Sam is not Number 1 the following term.

Sam has found himself at the top of his class. Sam has perhaps cheated, lied and finagled his way to this point.

Many theoretically important and relevant parallels exist between our samples of white women and black men which are of interest here, some of which I will return to in a latter part of the paper. Most of my comments today will, however, be directed toward understanding the impact of the motive to avoid success on the changing aspirations of college women. The data from our black samples which is very exciting and a significant part of our work on fear of success deserves to and will be treated as whole in a separate paper now in preparation. It is perhaps important to note here that we have detected an increase in fear of success among black women in the past year as a function of their involvement in the black movement.

I have argued that the motive to avoid success is a *latent*, stable, personality disposition, acquired early in life in conjunction with sex and now race role standards and sexual and/or racial identity. It was, therefore, important to begin to determine when, for whom, at what age, and under what circumstances this disposition is aroused and then serves to inhibit the achievement strivings of women. Some of our later work will be directed toward how it is acquired. It is, of course, consistent with Expectancy-Value theory to argue that the motive to avoid success is more likely to be aroused in high achievement-oriented, high-ability women than in low-achievement-oriented, low-ability women. After all, only for those women who desire and/or can realistically expect to achieve success does the expectancy of negative consequences because of success become meaningful. These are important issues and therefore, one of the major reasons for several of the subsequent studies that have been done was simply to observe the incidence of fear of success imagery in female subjects at different ages and at different education, occupational, and ability levels. The incidence of the motive to avoid success has ranged from a low of 47 per cent in a 7th grade junior high school sample to a high of 86.6 per cent in two of the subsequent samples tested: first, a sample of current law school students, and second, a sample of secretaries, all of whom were very able high school graduates. In each of the college samples tested fear-of-success imagery has ranged from 60 per cent in a sample of college freshmen at a large midwestern university to 85 per cent in a sample of very high ability juniors at an outstanding eastern coed university where the emphasis on achievement is very high.

In several of these studies the content of the verbal lead used was altered so as to make the situation described more consistent and meaningful with respect to the age, educational level, and occupation of the subjects being tested. For instance, in the junior high and high school levels, the cue used was:

Sue has just found out that she has been made valedictorian of her class.

For the secretaries in the sample the cue was:

Mary's boss has been permanently transferred to the California branch of the company she works for. The board of directors has chosen Mary above many of its other junior executives to take over his highly valued position.

It is of interest to note that regardless of the specific cue used, the responses of the older, more successful women—for instance, those among our sample of present law school students and graduates compared with those of our younger college and high school students—were characterized by a concern with and an awareness of some of the *reality*-based sources of the Motive to Avoid Success and reflected the actual price one must pay for overcoming societal pressures and pursuing one's interests despite them. For example, in response to a cue about a successful female law partner came the following response from a young female attorney (a recent law school graduate):

Unmarried, probably because most men can't handle the emotional threat posed by such a bright, aggressive girl. She's attractive, well-dressed but rather hard. Comes on too strong. Has developed a defensive attitude towards men and people in general because of having to defend her right to be a lawyer. She is of course very able.

The high, if anything increasing, incidence of fear of success imagery found in our studies indicates the extent to which women have incorporated society's attitudes and then tend to evaluate themselves in terms of these attitudes which stress the idea that competition, success, competence, and intellectual achievement are basically inconsistent with femininity. The emphasis on the new freedom of women has not done away with this tendency, anymore than have the vote, trousers, cigarettes, and even similar standards of sexual behavior. If anything, the attitudes seem to be intensifying. In *The Return of the Cave Woman* Margaret Mead has pointed out that women are not using their personal potential in the general community even to the degree that society would presently allow. One might speculate about how much of this problem is attributed to the high incidence of the motive to avoid success that we have observed. There is mounting evidence in our data suggesting that many achievement-oriented American women, especially those high in the motive to avoid success, when faced with the conflict between their feminine image and developing their abilities and interests, compromise by disguising their ability and abdicating from competition in the outside world. They are convinced "that it is more important to *BE* a woman, i.e., to live through and for others, than to become some kind of specialist, therefore, most young girls, especially in college, are prepared unconsciously if not consciously to surrender chances for personal distinction so as to be fairly sure of pleasing a larger range of men." These attitudes are reflected in the high incidence of the motive to avoid success and ultimately in the significant and *increasing* absence of capable and trained American women from the mainstream of thought and achievement in the society. This withdrawal exists despite the removal of many previous legal and educational barriers and despite the presence of more opportunities for women.

In light of the terrible loss of human potential and economic resources reflected by this pattern of behavior, it seemed particularly important for us to look more intensely and critically at the factors which tend to arouse the motive to avoid success and those most effective in minimizing its influence. We therefore undertook several studies[1] at an outstanding eastern college for women, a school at which the students are chosen primarily because of their high ability, achievement, motivation, and previous success. Most of the students arrive at the school very ambitious and committed to the idea of distinguishing themselves in a future career, even if they are not exactly sure what it will be. But, as we will see from the data, by the time they are juniors, most have changed their plans toward a less ambitious, more traditionally feminine direction. Sandra Tangri, in 1969, found such a trend in her University of Michigan coeds.

The incidence of Fear of Success was 75 per cent in the first pilot sample tested, and 85 per cent in a second sample. The experimental portion of the second study is just now being completed. Thus only the admittedly limited, nonetheless interesting, data of the pilot study have been analyzed and will be discussed here in any detail.

Using a questionnaire and intensive interviews we tried to explore the elements present during the college experience, both personal and situational, which arouse the motive to avoid success. Particular attention was paid as to how this motive influences the educational and career aspirations of these bright and highly motivated young women at a time in our society when self-actualization and equality of women is drawing much public attention. All the girls in the sample were doing well and had grade points of B- or better. Nevertheless, 12 of the 16 or 75% of these girls showed evidence of high fear of success. They manifested their anxiety about success in such reported behaviors as:

1) refusing to divulge the fact that they are doing well or have received an "A," preferring instead to make their failures known. The more successful they were the less likely they were to say so. For instance, all three of the girls who had straight A averages would prefer to tell a boy that they have gotten a "C" than an "A." Most of the girls with B-s preferred to report an "A."

2) changing their majors and future career plans toward what *each of them considers to be for her (and this is important) a more traditional, appropriately feminine and less ambitious one.*

Just how important it is to attend to each individual's subjective expectations and evaluation of certain careers was clearly emphasized by the subject who changed her career goals from medicine to law because she thought:

Law school is less ambitious, it doesn't take as long . . . is more flexible in terms of marriage and children. It is *less masculine* in that it is more accepted for girls to go to law school.

The others who changed their aspirations from law school to "teaching" or "housewife" apparently do not hold the same expectations about a law career.

Several of the girls indicate that they have given up the idea of a career at all and a couple even plan to quit school. Only 2, or about 12 per cent, of the sample have in the course of their education in fact changed their plans toward a more ambitious, more traditionally masculine direction. Although several of the girls have started out majoring in the natural sciences, with the intent of pursuing a medical career, all are now, as juniors, majoring in appropriately female areas such as English, fine arts, French and history. This pattern reflects what I have at other times indicated:

namely, that no one feels badly about nor seriously objects to a higher education in a woman provided the objective is to make her a more interesting and enlightened companion, wife, and/or mother. The objections, the negative consequences arise only when the objectives become more personal and career oriented, especially in non-traditional areas.

Individual differences in the motive to avoid success were very effective in predicting these patterns of behavior. Whereas more than 90 per cent of those who showed evidence of high fear of success (11 out of 12) changed their aspirations toward a more traditional direction, less than 25% of those low in fear of success did so.

A similar relationship is observed between individual differences in the motive to avoid success and responses to the question, "Are you more likely to tell your boyfriend or boys in your classes that you have gotten an A or a C?" Whereas 100 per cent of those low in fear of success would be more likely to report an A, sometimes with some explanation, only 33 per cent of those high in fear of success would do so.

Two of the factors considered as potentially the ones arousing the fear of success and thus negatively influencing the achievement strivings of these girls were the parental attitudes and those of the male peers toward appropriate sex role behavior. Many of the girls substantiated Komarovsky's argument that in the later college years girls experience a sudden reversal in what parents applaud for them. Whereas they have previously been applauded for academic success, these girls now find themselves being evaluated "in terms of some abstract standard of femininity with an emphasis on marriage as the appropriate goal for girls of this age." One says:

There is a lot of pressure from my mother to get married and not have a career. *This is one reason I am going to have a career* and wait to get married. . . . There is also some pressure from my father to get married, too.

There was, apparently, no relationship between such shifts in parental attitudes and fear of success. Nor did there appear, as you can see from that statement, to be any direct indication that parents had influenced anyone to turn away from a role-innovative type of career. If anything the influence appears to be in the opposite direction as in the above example. Some girls report being motivated for careers by the negative examples set by their mothers.

My mother is now working as a secretary, but she didn't work until now. I don't want to end up like that.

Another reason (I am going to have a career and wait to get married) is a reaction to my mother's empty life.[2]

On the other hand, the attitude of male peers toward the appropriate role of women, which they apparently do not hesitate to express, appears to be the most significant factor in arousing the motive to avoid success in these girls. The girls who showed evidence of anxiety about success and social rejection and had altered their career aspirations toward a more traditional direction were either not dating at all (interestingly enough, it was the three girls with the all A averages who were not dating at all) or were dating men who do not approve of "career women." When asked, for instance, how the boys in their lives feel about their aspirations, even the less ambitious goals, a frequent response—in fact, the most common response—was: "They laugh." Others were:

He thinks it's ridiculous for me to go to graduate school or law school.

He says I can be happy as a housewife and I just need to get a liberal arts education.

He wants a wife who will be a mother full time until the kids are grown.

I am turning more and more to the traditional role because of the attitudes of my boyfriend and his roommates. I am concerned about what they think.

This last comment is consistent with the idea that women are dependent on others for their self-esteem and have difficulty believing they can function well autonomously. This is again reflected in a statement made by one of the girls high in fear of success who is planning to leave college:

I have a lot of ideas about what I'd like to do (water sculpture presently)—but I'm waiting around for a man, and that makes me mad. I think that when I find someone I will be able to get involved in something. I need someone to respect me and what I want to do, to lend importance to what I sense is important.

The girls on the other hand who were either low in fear of success, or high in fear of success but continuing to strive for innovative careers, were either engaged to or seriously dating men who were not threatened by this success and in fact expected it of them, and provided much encouragement for them. This was reflected in such statements as:

He wants me to be intelligent. It is a source of pride *to him* that I do so well.

I would have to explain myself if I got a C. I want him to think I'm as bright as he is.

He thinks it would be a good idea for me to go to law school.

He feels very strongly that I should go to graduate school to get a Master's degree. He does not want to feel that he has denied me a complete education.

It is interesting to note that one of the factors distinguishing the couples in this second group from those in the first is a mutual understanding that the boy is the more intelligent of the two. "He's so much smarter . . . competition with him would be hopeless." This fact or belief seems to be sufficient to keep the motive from being aroused and affecting behavior.

In the first group there exists a tension between the two rooted in the fear that *she* is the more intelligent one. Other important factors seem to be based on how threatening the boyfriend sees her present and future success to be to *his* . . . i.e., are they in the same school, taking the same courses, planning to go to the same graduate school or to have the same career?

He is going to medical school, too, and we take some of the same courses. I don't compete with him, but he competes

with me. I usually do better than he does and this depresses him. He resents the fact that I do better.

The significance of male attitudes in determining the arousal of fear of success and its impact on behavior has been substantiated in a subsequent study in which the sex role attitudes of the male friends of the girls in the sample were actually assessed and proved to be the most significant factor accounting for the presence or absence of fear of success in the girls. We are currently trying to determine whether these male attitudes will predict to decremental change in the performance of the girls when competing against the men compared to their own previous level of non-competitive performance.

I have already indicated that when success is likely or possible, threatened by the negative consequences they expect to follow success because it would imply a violation of sex role boundaries, young women become anxious and their positive achievement strivings and aspirations become thwarted. But at the beginning I suggested that this does not occur without a price—a price paid in feelings of frustration, hostility, aggression, etc. I'd like to briefly now consider the data reflecting this emotional cost. A comparison of the thematic apperceptive stories written by young college women differing in strength of the "motive to avoid success" in response to the cue, "Anne is sitting in a chair with a smile on her face," help make this quite evident. Whereas more than 90% of those low in fear of success wrote positive, primarily affiliative stories centering on such things as dates, engagements, forthcoming marriages as well as a few on successful achievements, less than 20% of those high in fear of success wrote stories of this type. The rest of the responses, if not bizarre, were replete with negative affiliative imagery centering on hostility toward or manipulation of others.

I think the stories speak for themselves: let me give you a few examples. Here are stories by girls low in fear of success:

1) Anne's boyfriend has just called her. Not really boyfriend—a boy she really has wanted to go out with for ages. Anne is a very goodlooking girl—but never thought Mr. X would call her.

She sees Mr. X in classes and she really thinks he is fine. She's really wanted to have a date with him for over 1 year now—and her day has finally come.

Oh boy. I'm so excited, what shall I wear. I wonder if I should buy something new to wear. Will he like me? I am so excited. Anne is very happy.

Anne will have a marvelous time on her date and hope and pray that Mr. X will take her out again.

2) Anne is happy—she's happy with the world because it is so beautiful. It's snowing, and nice outside—she's happy to be alive and this gives her a good warm feeling. Anne did well on one of her tests, likes most of her classes in college. She hopes that if she has done well in the past she will continue to in her class. She wants to go into a subject she can do well in, she wants to major in a field she's good in and likes. She doesn't want to be a flunkie. She'll go into

her field, if not this one, another one which she will take next year—if everything works out, she'll be happy. She can then repay her parents for everything they've done.

3) Anne is sitting in a chair. She is very happy. Her mother walks into the room, and Anne tells her mother that her boyfriend has called, . . . they become engaged, set their wedding date.

Compare these with typical stories written by girls high in fear of success:

1) Anne is recollecting her conquest of the day. She has just stolen her ex-friend's boyfriend away, right before the high school senior prom. Anne was jealous of her friend's popularity and when they decided not to associate with each other, Anne decided to do something to really get back at her friend—take her boyfriend. Anne is thinking that she has proven herself equal to her friend socially. She wanted to hurt her and succeeded by taking the boyfriend away. Anne will lose him because he'll find out how sneaky and underhanded she is. They will go to the prom but it will end there.

2) Anne is waiting for the cab to come to take her to the Markley mixer where she wants to meet new people. She is thinking of the fun she'll have and thinking of encountering her ex-boyfriend who is president of the mixer. She had really liked her ex-boyfriend and since they broke up she really wanted to show him she can meet new boys and have fun with others besides him. She will meet another boy at the dance who showers her with his attention and she willingly and happily flaunts this boy in front of her ex-boyfriend. The new boy calls her later but she finds she doesn't really like him and only used him to show her ex-boyfriend.

3) Anne is at her father's funeral. . . . She knows it is unseemly to smile but she cannot help it. Anne is fighting to keep from laughing. Her brother Ralph pokes her in fury but she is uncontrollable. Her mother is sobbing and unaware of Anne's behavior. Anne rises dramatically and leaves the room, stopping first to pluck a carnation from the blanket of flowers on the coffin.

The differences in the two kinds of stories are, I think, very clear. One can only speculate about how much of what was expressed in fantasy is a true reflection of the actual behavior or intents of these young women, and if these responses do in fact accurately reflect their behavior, what the consequences of such behavior might be for them. One of the things that makes this a particularly interesting area to pursue is that a consistent pattern has been found in our black data, i.e., black men with low fear of success characteristically wrote stories of romance and often of success to the smile cue while high fear-of-success men wrote stories of the manipulative variety:

He is watching a group of people argue. They are the people he hates. The people have fought against this man for some time and won. He is happy because he made them split and argue. He wants them to go on fighting.

John is happy cause it's all over finally. He had been talking to Jean for at least two months and things had been going his way. John met her at a party and made a bet with some friends that he could really buckle her knees. . . .

In light of the high and if anything increasing incidence of the motive to avoid success in our data it seems apparent that most otherwise achievement-motivated young white women when faced with a conflict between their feminine image and expressing their competences or developing their abilities and interests adjust their behaviors to their internalized sex role stereotypes. A parallel situation seems to exist for young black men who seem to adjust their behaviors to internalized race role stereotypes. In order to feel or appear more feminine women disguise their abilities and withdraw from the mainstream of thought, non-traditional aspiration, and achievement in our society. As the data indicate however this does not occur without a high price, a price paid by the individual in negative emotional and interpersonal consequences and by the society in a loss of valuable human and economic resources. Kai Erikson in *Wayward Puritans* (1966) has argued that "The chief ways that individuals in a group learn about the norms of that group may be from boundaries made salient by those who violate them. The cost of boundary violation may be illustrated through the isolation, chastisement or ill fortune of the deviant." Perhaps the expectation or anticipation of negative consequences because of success that we have found in our fear of success stories among both our white and black samples were realistically learned in just this way. Much work clearly remains to be done.

NOTES

1. The data in the first study was gathered and initially analyzed by Miss Molly Schwern for her junior honors project.

2. It is of interest to note here that the majority of the girls in our college samples who were high in fear of success came from middle or upper middle class homes. The fathers were successful professional or business men who were better educated than their mothers. Both parents encouraged and rewarded academic success with a high premium placed on education, factors which McClelland has shown in *The Achieving Society* lead to the development of a high motive to achieve. Only later do these girls experience the reversal in attitude discussed previously. The girls low in fear of success come from primarily lower and lower middle class homes in which the fathers have not been successful.

REFERENCES

Atkinson, J. W., and Feather, M. T. 1966. *A theory of achievement motivation.* New York: John Wiley & Sons.
Horner, M. 1968. Sex differences in achievement motivation and performance in competitive and non-competitive situations. Unpublished doctoral dissertation, University of Michigan.
Horner, M. 1970. Femininity and Successful Achievement: A Basic Inconsistency, Ch. 3 in Bardwick, Douvan, Horner, and Gutmann, *Feminine Personality and Conflict.* Belmont, Calif: Brooks/Cole.
Horner, M. 1970. The motive to avoid success and changing aspirations of college women. Unpublished, preliminary draft.
Horner, M. and Rhoem. 1968. The motive to avoid success as a function of age, occupation and progress at school. Unpublished research report.
Komarovsky, Mirra. 1959. Functional analysis of sex roles. *Amer. Soc. Rev. 15:* 508-516.
Lipinski, E. G. 1965. Sex-role conflict and achievement motivation in college women. Unpublished doctoral dissertation, University of Cincinnati.
Mead, Margaret. 1949. *Male and Female.* New York: Morrow. Also New York: Dell (Laurel Edition), 1968.
Schwenn, M. 1970. Arousal of the motive to avoid success. Unpublished junior honors paper. Harvard University.
Tangri, S. 1969. Role-innovation in occupational choice. Unpublished doctoral dissertation. University of Michigan.

11 Race, social class, and the motive to avoid success in women

Peter J. Weston
Martha T. Mednick

Horner (1968) successfully reconciled some of the confusion in research on achievement motivation in women by postulating and demonstrating an avoidance motive called the motive to avoid success (M-s).[1] This psychological barrier to intellectual achievement is defined as "the expectancy or anticipation of negative consequences as a result of success in competitive achievement situations." In the case of women, the specific negative consequences may be social rejection by men, loss of affection, friendship or one's datable or marriageable quality (Horner, 1968, p. 22)." According to Horner, when a girl achieves intellectually, she anticipates that she will be regarded as unfeminine. Horner's data support the existence of such a motive in fantasy productions; she also successfully predicted women's problem solving behavior in intellectually competitive situations by using M-s scores. Tangri (1969) also demonstrated that senior level college women express M-s with greater frequency than do junior level girls.

It has been observed by a number of investigators that the motivations and aspirations expressed by black women follow a different pattern than those expressed by white women (Moynihan, 1965; Frazier, 1939, 1962; Pettigrew, 1965). Forces inherent in the social system have had a deleterious effect on black family life as evidenced, for example, by the high percentage of black families headed by women (Clark, 1965; U. S. Department of Labor, 1965). It is commonly asserted that this has resulted in a sex-role identity pattern in which women are more dominant and aggressive and permitted, and indeed, encouraged to be aspiring and intellectually striving. This overt image is partially confirmed by studies of aspirations of black high school students in which girls express higher aspirations than boys (Thompson, 1965); black parents' aspirations for their daughters are higher than for their sons. This finding was not obtained by Gurin and Katz (1966) in their massive study of motivation and level of aspiration in students in Southern black colleges in which college women expressed lower aspirations than the men, seemingly following the pattern of the larger society. The aspirations of these women seemed to be a reflection of the women's realistic perceptions of the opportunities available to them. We maintain, however, that while a girl may lower and be realistic about her aspirations, she may nevertheless main-tain fantasies of success and achievement and not avoid dominance and aggressive intellectual mastery. Furthermore, the dynamics involved in her achievement orientation may still be quite different from those of the white women. With this in mind, a series of studies have been undertaken with the goal of exploring the personality and motivational dynamics influencing expressed aspirations and actual career planning in black college women.

A few words must be added about the variable of social class. The possibility of social class differences among black women must be anticipated. The black middle class has been described as "out-middle classing" white middle class in terms of their values. Furthermore, since middle class life is generally more male dominated and family life more stable (Frazier, 1962), it is reasonable to expect that the black middle class college women will be less dominant and striving than her lower class counterpart.

The present study simply sought to compare black women with white women, not on aspirations, but in fantasy productions to a situation with an intrinsic theme of intellectual competition.

The following hypotheses were tested:

1. Black college women will exhibit fewer M-s responses than white college women.

2. Lower class black women will have fewer M-s responses than middle class black women.

Method

SUBJECTS

The Ss were 63 undergraduate women enrolled at Bluefield State College and 22 enrolled at American University.[2] The breakdown of these Ss by race and social class is

TABLE 1   Number of Subjects from Each School by Race and Social Class

Race	American University		Bluefield State	
	Middle class	Lower class	Middle class	Lower class
Black	10	1	22	28
White	11	0	13	0

Reprinted from Peter J. Weston and Martha T. Mednick, "Race, Social Class, and the Motive to Avoid Success in Women," Journal of Cross-Cultural Psychology, 1:3, Sept. 1970, pp. 284-291. Based on the thesis by the senior author submitted to Howard University in partial fulfillment of the requirements for the M.A. in Psychology.

given in Table 1. Social class was determined by occupation and educational level of the parents.

MATERIALS

Verbal TAT cues such as those used by Horner and a brief questionnaire requesting socio-economic information were administered to each subject. The four cues in order of presentation were as follows:

1. After first term finals, Anne finds herself at the top of her medical school class.
2. A young woman is talking about something important with an older person.
3. Jennifer has just been informed that her three-act play will be produced in New York this coming season.
4. Susan is sitting in a chair with a smile on her face.

Cues 1 and 3 were designed to elicit success imagery while cues 2 and 4 were non-arousal or neutral cues and, as such, were not scored for M-s but served as buffers in the experimental situation.[3]

PROCEDURE

The Ss were seated in a classroom and given a questionnaire containing the four verbal cues. The cues were presented in the order stated above. All Ss received the following instructions:

You are going to see a series of verbal leads or cues and I would like you to tell a story that is suggested to you by each one. Try to imagine what is going on in each. Then tell what the situation is, what led up to the situation, what the people are thinking and feeling and what they will do. In other words, write as complete a story as you can, a story with plot and characters. You will have twenty seconds to look at each verbal cue and then five minutes to write your story about it. Write your first impressions and work rapidly. I will keep time and tell you when it is time to finish your story and to get ready for the next cue. Remember there are no right or wrong answers or kinds of stories, so please feel free to write whatever story is suggested to you when you look at a cue. Spelling, punctuation, and grammar are not important. What is important is to write out as fully and as quickly as possible the story that comes into your mind as you imagine what is going on in each cue.

Thus, the Ss were required to write brief five-minute stories in response to each of the four cues which were observed for twenty seconds. The stories were written around the following four questions spaced on an answer sheet:

1. What is happening? Who are the persons?
2. What has led up to this situation? What has happened in the past?
3. What is being taught? What is wanted? By whom?
4. What will happen? What will be done?

The instructions given are standard for the TAT; their general tone is to urge the Ss to produce stories and not to think in terms of right or wrong answers.

The M-s scores were obtained from a content analysis of the fantasies. The first and third cues were scored for M-s independently by two trained raters using the coding directions described by Horner (1968). A general decision was made concerning the presence or absence of M-s imagery and only results agreed upon by both raters were considered.[4] Any imagery (i.e., statement in the story) which suggested or anticipated negative consequences as a result of success was considered fear-of-success imagery. More specifically, this meant that someone in the story was being placed in an undesirable or negative situation (e.g., losing the friendship of close associates, being socially rejected especially by men, feeling guilt, despair, or doubting one's normality or femininity) because of success in an intellectually competitive situation.

Thus, in scoring the stories for M-s when there was negative imagery reflecting concern about the success, the following scoring criteria were used:

a. negative consequences because of the success
b. anticipation of negative consequences because of the success
c. negative affect because of success
d. instrumental activity away from present or future success
e. any direct expression of conflict about success.

Also scored was any evidence of:

f. denial of the situation described by the cue
g. bizarre, inappropriate, unrealistic or non-adaptive responses to the situation described by the cue.

No score was given when the stories contained no indication of negative consequences, negative effect or concern about negative consequences of success. This comprised the "low M-s" category in analysis. A score of 1 indicated that the S's responses reflected mild concern about possible negative consequences of success while a score of 2 was given when there was mention of severe negative consequences of success.[5] Scores of 1 and 2 comprised the "high M-s" category. A score of 3 was assigned to those stories of a bizarre, inappropriate or unrealistic nature. These stories were not used in the analysis of M-s.

After writing the stories, each S was asked to answer the questionnaire described above. The designation of social class level was determined on the basis of the answers to those questions.

Results

The M-s data were evaluated separately for each success cue and for the two schools. These means and standard deviations are presented in Table 2.

The significance level of all group differences were evaluated by means of the Fisher Exact Probability Test (1956). Table 3 shows the findings from the Bluefield and American University samples.

The hypothesis with regard to race differences was supported for both cues and at both schools. Class differences within the Black group were not significant, in contradiction to our second hypothesis. This, of course, was only observed at Bluefield State, but was consistent for both cues. It should be noted that partial replication of these data has been obtained on three additional samples. In a master's thesis by Bright conducted at Howard University

TABLE 2   M-s Means and Standard Deviations for the Two Schools and the Two Cues

| | Bluefield State | | | | | | American University | | | | | |
| | Cue 1 | | | Cue 3 | | | Cue 1 | | | Cue 3 | | |
Race and class	N	M	SD	N	M	SD	N	M	SD	N	M	SD
White middle	13	1.25	.59	13	.73	.75	11	1.13	.73	11	.44	.50
Black middle	22	.16	.49	22	.11	.31	10	.30	.64	10	0	0
Black lower	28	.24	.42	28	0	0	1	0	0	1	0	0

TABLE 3   Motive to Avoid Success as Related to Race and Social Class

| | Bluefield State sample | | | | American University sample | | | |
| | Cue 1 | | Cue 3 | | Cue 1 | | Cue 3 | |
Race and class	High M-s	Low M-s	High M-s	Low M-s	High M-s	Low M-s	High M-s	Low M-s
White middle	11	1	6	5	6	2	4	5
Black middle	2	17	2	16	2	8	0	9
	$\rho = .00001$		$\rho = .018$		$\rho = .28$		$\rho = .041$ ($\alpha = .05$)	
Black lower	6	19	0	19	NR[2]	NR	NR	NR
Black middle	2	17	1	16	NR	NR	NR	NR
	$\rho = .170$		$\rho = .23$					

Note —   Fisher probability test used for all analyses.
[1] $\alpha = .05$ for all tests
[2] NR — no respondents

in 1970, 28% of 125 women tested (all black) manifested M-s on the "Anne" cue. In additional studies at other black schools in the Southeast, Puryear (M. S. Thesis, 1971) found a similar rate (N = 165). In all cases incidence of M-s and social class level were unrelated. The point should also be made that with these additional samples the experimenter was a woman, in contrast with the first, wherein the instruments were administered by a man.

Discussion

The race difference hypothesis was supported; social class, on the other hand, does not seem to affect M-s imagery. This held for both cues and both schools.

The stories of black Ss displayed very little M-s. The following are examples of stories written by these Ss. A response to cue 1:

Anne is very pleased because upon completion of finals she finds herself at the top of her medical school class. Anne has studied diligently for long and hard hours. She has always wanted to be a part of the medical profession. Although she studied constantly, she never dreamed of being number one in her class. She wants to pursue a medical career and she is convinced that she can master the work. Her parents and boyfriend will be proud of her. She will continue in medical school, graduate and go on to become a leader in her profession.

Another example of a response to cue 3:

Jennifer has majored in drama school. Although she is only a junior, she has been writing little three-act plays, one of which has brought her much success. She is, of course, delighted because she never anticipated that any of her work would ever be produced. Jennifer had fancied herself more as an actress than a playwrite. She will continue to write more plays. Eventually, Jennifer will write and star in her own productions, moving on to Hollywood, making motion pictures and receiving an Oscar.

In contrast, the display of fear of success imagery is quite clear in the stories of white Ss. Examples of such stories are the following: Typical responses to cue 1:

Anne and her fellow classmates are sitting around 'shooting the bull.' Final exams, naturally, is the topic of discussion. Two or three people seem to dominate the conversation, and Anne is sitting quietly off to one side, her facial expression is one of mixed emotions. Anne has always been a good student and medicine is her 'tning.' She has worked many long and hard hours to achieve the goal she has reached, with very little time for fun. Anne wonders whether it is really worth it, as she seems to be left out of the 'fun crowd' and ignored by the guys because she is a 'brain.' The only time she is noticed is when someone needs help with homework. Anne will let her studies go and become a party girl.

and

Anne is in George Washington Medical School. The persons involved are the ten girls and fifty guys in Anne's first year in medical class. Anne graduated at the top of her class at Jackson College for Women. She was an anthropology major. Anne's friends and parents are proud. Some of the guys in her class are jealous and there's some tension in the class.

Anne will marry Jack, a second year medical student and she won't finish medical school.

A response to cue 3:

Jennifer has worked very hard to achieve this success despite lack of encouragement from Bill, her boyfriend. Bill feels that success will change her. She will go to New York and her play will be a flop. She will come back to Bill. However, Bill is engaged. Jennifer realizes her mistake and lost dream and becomes a nun.

Horner (1968) has suggested that the high M-s found in white S is probably due to the aggressive overtones of intellectual competition needed for success in these areas, since aggression has been socially linked to a lack of femininity and its display is seen as leading to negative consequences (i.e., social rejection). The present findings suggest that success in intellectually competitive situations does not elicit similar fear in the black college woman. This may be related to the different sex role patterns since, as noted above, the nature of American society has placed black women in more dominant roles than those assumed by black men or by white women. Accordingly, intellectual mastery is not threatening and professional achievement may in fact not lead to rejection by the male. A successful woman is an economic asset and attractive rather than threatening to a black man. Hence, success as here projected is not to be feared. It may also be argued that the aspirations depicted in these situations are so unrealistic for any black person that the girls do not actually project themselves into their stories, do not identify with the characters and therefore have nothing to fear. For the present this must stand as an alternative explanation though there is some evidence that this is not the case. It would be difficult to argue that the American University sample sees such career goals as completely unattainable. While the Bluefield women may view themselves, as well as their potential husbands, as being unlikely to achieve high status professional careers, the girls attending a white urban university may have realistic aspirations of this sort. It is interesting to note here that in a study of black upper-middle class sorority women attending the University of Michigan, M-s scores matched those of white women on that campus, indicating that at some point up the social-educational status ladder fears of such success may appear.[6] We are now proceeding with several studies designed to illuminate the dynamics of M-s in these women as well as their actual career aspirations and the degree of their commitment to these aspirations. Problem solving performance of high and low M-s scorers in competition with men will be examined. Of course, if low M-s is simply a result of the unreality of the goals implied in the cue, and fear of being intellectually dominant over men does exist, this should be demonstrated in a face to face competitive task.

A final comment about the absence of social class differences needs to be made. It has been suggested (Horner, personal communication) that a black woman needs to be of upper-middle or upper class status before a fear of success is generated. The Michigan findings tend to support this notion but we could not examine this in our data. Social class differences will be examined in more detail in data about to be collected at Howard University.

NOTES

1. This study addresses itself to a comparison of women from several cultural subgroups within the American (U.S.) society. Cross-society or national comparisons are projected for future research by the second author.

2. Bluefield State is a four-year liberal arts college in West Virginia whose undergraduate population is approximately 50.8% black. (U.S. Department of Health, Education and Welfare, 1967; Bluefield Registrar's Office, 1969). The undergraduate population of American University (Washington, D.C.) is 4-4.8% black (Statistical Office, American University, 1969).

3. The use of verbal cues appear as effective in eliciting imagery as the TAT pictures and have been used by numerous investigators (Atkinson, Horner, Tangri, McClelland, 1959; Bachman et al., 1967). Of course, these are ideally suited to studies in which race comparisons are to be made, since the problem of changing the pictures of identity figures does not arise.

4. For the sample of 85 Ss the raters agreed upon 91.8% of the responses to cue 1; there was 81.2% agreement on responses to cue 3.

5. There were seven such stories in the Bluefield sample: five were in response to cue 1 and two to cue 3. No such stories appeared in the American University sample.

6. Personal communications from Matina S. Horner and Sandra G. Tangri.

REFERENCES

Clark, Kenneth B. *Dark ghetto.* New York: Harper and Row, 1965.
Davis, A., & Havighurst, R. J. Social class and color differences in child-rearing. In C. Kluckhohn, H. A. Murray, & D. M. Schneider (eds.), *Personality in nature, society and culture.* (third ed.) New York: Alfred A. Knopf, 1959, chap. 18.
Frazier, E. F. *Black bourgeoisie.* New York: Collier Books, 1962.
Gurin, P., & Katz, D. *Motivation and aspiration in the Negro college.* Final report, U.S. Department of Health, Education and Welfare, 1966.
Horner, M. S. Sex differences in achievement motivation and performance in competitive and non-competitive situations. Unpublished doctoral dissertation, University of Michigan, 1968.
Moynihan, D. P. *The Negro family.* Washington, D.C.: Office of Policy Planning and Research, United States Department of Labor, 1965.
Pettigrew, L. *A profile of the Negro American.* Princeton: D. Van Nostrand Company, 1964.
Siegel, S. *Non-parametric statistics for the behavioral sciences.* New York: McGraw-Hill, 1956.
Tangri, Sandra S. Role-innovation in occupational choice among college women. Unpublished doctoral dissertation, University of Michigan, 1969.
Thompson, D. In Moynihan, D. (Ed.), *The Negro family.* U.S. Department of Labor, 1965.
United States Department of Labor. *The Negroes in the United States: their economic and social situations.* Bulletin No. 1511, U.S. Department of Labor, 1965.
United States Department of Labor. *Extent of unemployment among non-white men, 1955-63.* Bureau of Labor Statistics, 1965.
Weston, P. J. *Race, social class and the motive to avoid success in women.* Unpublished Master's Thesis, Howard University, 1969.

12 Barriers to the career choice of engineering, medicine, or science among American women

Alice S. Rossi

The reasons for accepting the view that more women should enter science, engineering, and medicine may flow from concern with (1) individual personal satisfaction and (2) the enlargement of the minority women represent in these fields and national interest in manpower utilization to (3) a radical transformation of the relations between the sexes as part of an ideology of sex equality. In my own view, all three reasons are of equal importance. Furthermore, in the paper to follow, my intent is to be provocative, and to insist that many areas of seeming peripheral significance are actually at the root of our topic. Let me start therefore with a few of the propositions I shall make and examine, so that you may know, in advance of the analysis, what certain of my conclusions and convictions are.

Men believe, and women accept their belief, that woman's role should be selfless, dedicated to being man's helpmeet, and any work or career on the part of women should fill in the gaps of time and energy left over from their primary obligations as wives and mothers. This adaptive role is compatible with a job as a laboratory assistant, engineering aide, or medical technician, but not with responsible careers as scientist, engineer, or doctor, except for those rare Amazons among us who can live two lifetimes in one.

Part-time employment is this generation's false panacea for avoiding a more basic change in the relations between men and women, a means whereby, with practically no change in the man's role and minimal change in the woman's, she can continue the same wife and mother she has been in the past, with a minor appendage to these roles as an intermittent part-time professional or clerical worker.

Campaigns to increase the support and encouragement given to the *college-age* woman to enter the sciences, engineering, or medicine can only effectively reach and help the young woman who is already interested and prepared by a background in science and mathematics to take advantage of opportunities offered her in college. Such women are a tiny minority of their sex, whose experiences at much earlier ages have set in motion an abiding interest in things generally disapproved of for girls in our society. College freshmen do not shift from fine arts to chemistry, or from journalism to engineering, except in rare instances. Hence efforts to be really effective must concentrate on much earlier stages of life and must involve fundamental changes in the rearing of girls and boys.

Studies and observations show that the contemporary college woman persists in wanting a mate more intelligent than herself whom she can "look up to" and thus vicariously experience life and work in his shadow. This is a natural consequence of childhood tears, coquetry, "good" behavior, and dependence on close interpersonal ties. Beneath her jeans and plaid shirt, the girl within has not changed very much from her grandmother in crinoline and lace. Unless enough women want as a mate an intellectual peer and a tender comrade in life and work, few will aspire to or persist in the more demanding professions, and fewer still will make notable contributions to their fields.

The present pattern of women's participation in science and engineering

An examination of the 1965 census data on occupations and sex shows that women accounted for 65 per cent of the increase to the labor force between 1950 and 1960.[1] A few occupations have actually changed from predominantly masculine fields to feminine fields; e.g., the percentage of bank tellers who are women has increased from 45 to 69 per cent, of hucksters and peddlers from 14 to 59 per cent (e.g., "Avon Calling"), of teachers outside the elementary, high school, and college levels (adult education, technical and private schools) from 26 to 61 per cent.[2] There has been no such dramatic change among the professional and technical occupations that concern us: here women represent not 65 but 26 per cent of the increase during the decade of the fifties. This means that in many occupations the number of women has risen strikingly over the decade, but the increase of men has been so much greater that the proportion women represent of the total employed in the field has actually declined. The field of mathematics is a good illustration of this: there has been a 210 per cent increase in the number of women, but the number of men in mathematics increased 428 per cent, with the result that

Edited from Alice S. Rossi, "Barriers to the Career Choice of Engineering, Medicine, or Science Among American Women," in Jacquelyn A. Mattfeld and Carol G. Van Aken, eds., Women and the Scientific Professions, *1965, pp. 51-127, by permission of the M.I.T. Press, Cambridge, Massachusetts.*

TABLE 1   *Women Employed in Science, Engineering, Medicine, and Technical Occupations, 1950 and 1960*

Selected Occupations	Per cent female		Per cent increase 1950 to 1960		Total number	
	1960	1950	Men	Women	1960	1950
Natural scientists						
Total	9.9	11.4	30.0	10.4	149,330	116,918
Agricultural scientists	5.2	5.3	27.6	23.3	7,895	6,200
Biological scientists	26.7	29.2	56.6	38.2	13,937	9,215
Chemists	8.6	10.0	13.5	−3.6	83,420	74,637
Geologists and geophysicists	2.3	5.6	81.1	−27.3	18,551	10,598
Mathematicians	26.4	38.0	428.1	209.8	7,527	1,691
Physicists	4.2	6.5	92.5	20.2	13,941	7,422
Miscellaneous	9.8	15.9	−39.1	−65.1	4,059	7,155
Engineers						
Total	0.8	1.2	64.3	11.0	860,949	526,179
Aeronautical	1.6	1.9	193.9	144.1	51,703	17,650
Chemical	0.9	1.9	27.3	−38.4	41,026	32,543
Civil	0.6	1.6	26.2	−54.7	155,173	124,225
Electrical	0.8	1.2	74.3	19.1	183,887	105,887
Industrial	2.1	1.2	139.5	358.8	97,458	40,278
Mechanical	0.3	0.5	40.9	−8.7	158,188	122,440
Metallurgical	0.9	2.0	51.0	−25.7	18,459	12,346
Mining	0.3	0.8	−14.3	−61.5	12,084	14,155
Sales	0.3		129.1		56,836	24,734
Not elsewhere classified	0.8	2.3	108.7	−31.4	86,135	41,921
Physicians and surgeons	6.8	6.1	18.1	32.0	228,926	192,520
Technicians						
Medical and dental	62.4	56.7	56.2	98.6	138,162	76,662
Electrical and electronic	4.6		643.1		91,463	11,738
Other engineering and physical sciences	12.8	18.0	114.7	43.0	183,609	90,995
Not elsewhere classified	23.6	34.1	309.4	144.7	65,723	18,605

[a] Per cent not shown where less than 0.01.

[b] Per cent increase not shown where less than 0.1 or where base is less than 100.

(Source: U.S. Bureau of the Census, *Census of Population: 1960*, Vol. 1, Table 202, pp. 528-533.)

the percentage of mathematicians who are women actually declined from 38 in 1950 to 26 per cent in 1960.

Table 1 presents the details on the percentage who are women in 1950 and in 1960 as well as the per cent increase for each sex, in the number employed in the scientific, professional, and technical occupations that concern us most directly. In 1960, only 7 per cent of the physicians and surgeons employed in the United States were women, as were 10 per cent of the natural scientists, and less than 1 per cent of the engineers. Within the natural sciences there is considerable variation: from a low of 2 per cent of earth scientists and 4 per cent of physicists to a high of 26 per cent of mathematicians and 27 per cent of biological scientists.[3]

Secondly, the pattern noted for mathematicians holds true to some degree in most of these fields, i.e., the number of women in various scientific and engineering fields has increased, but at a rate so much lower than that for men that the proportion of women in the fields is lower in 1960

than in 1950. Thus the percentage who are women has declined in engineering from 1.2 to .08 per cent, in the sciences from 11 to 9 per cent, among engineering and physical science technicians, from 18 to 12 per cent. In some fields, like chemistry, the earth sciences and chemical, metallurgical, mining, and civil engineering, there are actually fewer women in 1960 than in 1950. This appears to be compensated for in engineering by a marked increase in the number of women in industrial engineering: a 359 per cent increase compared to men's 140 per cent increase, with the result that the percentage who are women in this engineering field has increased from 1.2 to 2.1 per cent. I do not know enough about engineering specialties to interpret this in very specific terms, but the same phenomenon may be at work there that appears in other segments of the labor force: women replace men at lower levels of a broad occupational field as the upper reaches of the field expand and are filled by men.[4] Thus women have been slowly replacing men as bank tellers as men move up into the expanding

TABLE 2   Percentage Who Are Women in Selected
Scientific Fields, by Degree Earned in 1961-1962

	Bachelor's		Master's		Doctorate	
	Per cent	No.	Per cent	No.	Per cent	No.
Biology	34	(10,018)	29	(804)	15	(178)
Mathematics	29	(14,610)	19	(2,680)	6	(396)
Chemistry	21	(8,086)	17	(1,404)	6	(1,114)
Astronomy	17	(46)	17	(46)	4	(25)
Geology	5	(1,404)	3	(550)	1	(182)
Physics	4	(4,812)	4	(1,425)	2	(667)

(Source: Office of Education data cited in *Physics: Education, Employment, Financial Support, op. cit.*, Appendix B, pp. 80-81.)

TABLE 3   Median Salary of Employed Scientists and
Engineers, by Sex and Degree, 1962

		Men	Women
Engineering			
	Bachelor's	$ 10,019	$ 7,576
	Master's	11,033	7,886
	Doctorate	13,635	10,295
Physics			
	Bachelor's	8,549	6,744
	Master's	9,503	6,633
	Doctorate	12,276	8,452
Biology			
	Bachelor's	7,211	5,845
	Master's	7,663	6,324
	Doctorate	9,881	8,291
Mathematics-statistics			
	Bachelor's	8,516	7,160
	Master's	9,220	6,702
	Doctorate	11,404	9,273

(Source: Unpublished data from a post-censal survey of professional and technical occupations, presently under analysis by Seymour Warkov, National Opinion Research Center, University of Chicago.)

categories of higher status managerial jobs in banking and business corporations. So in many of the jobs included in industrial engineering, women may be filling the vacancies left by men in industrial firms that produce consumer products as these men move into more complex and expanding engineering specialties, such as nuclear engineering.

Income, type of employer, and hours worked weekly

It is a simple matter to establish the fact that there is a decided difference between men and women in the income they earn in the scientific and engineering fields, but it is a complex matter to interpret with any satisfaction what accounts for this income difference. It is a fact that the median salary of men is between $2,500 and $3,000 higher than that of women in the scientific fields. One cannot simply conclude, however, that women are underpaid compared to men, for there are a number of reasons why women cannot be expected to earn as large an income as men. One reason, as we have noted before, is that women do not go on for advanced degrees to the same extent that men in these fields do. There is a steady decline in the percentage who are women in all scientific fields as you move from the bachelor's to the master's and the doctor's degree level, as shown in Table 2.[5]

However, the fact that there is a higher proportion of advanced degrees in the scientific and technical fields among men than among women does not account for very much of the income discrepancy between men and women. As seen in Table 3, at each level of educational attainment, and in each field, the median salary of men is considerably higher than that of women.

Another source of income difference between men and women is the type of employer they have. Using data from the 1962 National Register of Scientific and Technical Personnel, Table 4 shows that, although the men and women scientists in this register do not differ markedly in educational attainment,[6] they differ strikingly in the type of employer they have. Almost half the women but only a quarter of the men work in educational institutions; just the reverse holds for industrial and self-employment, where almost half the men, but only a fifth of the women, are located. This does not mean that half these women are teaching, for many are on research staffs in colleges and universities, as can be seen in the lower half of the table. Since men are four times more likely to be in management than women, and women twice as likely to be teaching as men, here is part of the reason for the income difference between the sexes.[7]

Women college graduates, class of 1961: marriage and career types

My own current research is based on a sample of women college graduates of the class that was graduated in June 1961. They have been sent four questionnaires during the period from the spring of 1961 when they were college seniors to the summer of 1964 when they had been out of college for three years. One major focus of this research is on career choice and the implementation of career plans, but the women in the sample were also questioned in considerable detail in the 1964 questionnaire concerning their actual experiences in and expectations of their domestic and family roles. At this writing, final results are only now becoming available for detailed analysis, but several preliminary excursions[8] have been made into these data which are of relevance to many aspects of the problem of why so few American women are found in the scientific and top professional fields.

One such excursion was to examine the differences among three types of women, classified by the extremely different career goals they had, as follows:

1. *Homemakers:* These are women who reported in 1964 that they had no career goal other than being "housewives."[9]

TABLE 4   Type of Employer and Work Activity of Men and Women Scientists (in per cent)

	Men	Women
Type of employer		
Education	27	48
Government	17	16
Nonprofit	4	8
Industry and self-employed	46	20
Other	4	2
No report	2	6
Work activity		
Research, development, and design	35	37
Management	24	6
Teaching	15	29
Other	25	23
N =	(200,362)	(14,578)

(Source: 1962 National Register of Scientific and Technical Personnel, cited in *Physics: Education, Employment, Financial Support, op. cit.,* Table 32, p. 60.)

2. *Traditionals:* Women whose long-range career goals are in fields in which women predominate: elementary and secondary school teachers (excluding mathematics and science teachers), social workers, nurses, librarians, secretaries, and home economists.

3. *Pioneers:* Women whose long-range career goals are in predominantly masculine fields: the natural sciences, business management, public and educational administration, medicine, law engineering, dentistry, architecture, economics.

The homemakers represent one-fifth of the sample of these women college graduates, and almost 90 per cent of them are married. The traditionals represent not quite half the women, and about two-thirds of them are married. The pioneers are only 7 per cent of the women, and half of them are married at this point in their lives.

There are interesting differences between single and married women in these three career types. Although the details of this analysis will be presented elsewhere, there is one striking impression that warrants presentation and discussion here. Among the pioneers, marriage appears to have the effect of restricting their expectations concerning the place of work and career in their lives, whereas for homemakers and traditionals, marriage has the effect of restricting their expectations concerning the place of family roles in their lives. It is almost as though the pioneers had romantic notions concerning careers and work which the reality of advanced study and employment temper, and homemakers had romantic notions concerning marriage and family roles which the reality of marriage and motherhood tempers.[10]

How does this pattern show itself? The majority of the women (and a sizable proportion of the men) expect "family relationships" to be the primary source of satisfaction in their lives, but among the single pioneers a large minority (some 40 per cent) expect "career" to be the primary source of life satisfaction. Less than 10 per cent of the married pioneers share this expectation. That pioneers in some sense expect this to happen is suggested by the fact that two-thirds of both the single and the married pioneers agree with the view that "it is more important for a woman to help her husband's career than to have one herself," implying as this does that marriage leads to putting her own career in second place. The pioneer in no sense regrets the choice of her field, agreeing to a large extent that more women should be encouraged to enter the "masculine" occupations and claiming that they would personally encourage any young woman with the interest and ability to enter such fields. On family-related items, the single and married pioneers do not differ: very few want to have large families, and the majority of both single and married pioneers approve of a woman's taking a part-time job when her child is a preschooler. Of special sociological interest is the further finding that few pioneers express any special enjoyment in "being with young children" or "visiting with relatives."

Marital status makes a decided difference among homemakers on these family-related items. Single homemakers want large families to a significantly greater extent than do married homemakers. (Only 7 per cent of both single and married pioneers want 5 or more children, but 22 per cent of the single homemakers to 10 per cent of the married homemakers want families of this size.) Of even greater interest is the difference between single and married homemakers on the age they believe a child should be before the mother takes a part-time job: only 16 per cent of the single homemakers say "under five years of age," but fully 35 per cent of the married homemakers approve maternal employment when a child is still a preschooler.[11]

The pattern of response to the activities that these women now "very much enjoy" has several points of interest. Certain things seem to decline in interest as a woman shifts from a single to a married state, while others increase in interest. Single women are more apt than married women to enjoy very much "active sports," "being with male friends," and "art and music"—one gets the image of the dating and courting couple at sports and cultural events. Married women are more apt than single women to enjoy the domestic activities of sewing and cooking. These are all predictably related to marital status. That marital status does *not* relate to "visiting with relatives" and "being with young children" is more surprising. Yet these two items are strongly related to career types: only one-third of both single and married pioneers very much enjoy being with young children, something that two-thirds of both single and married homemakers enjoy. Similarly only one-quarter of the pioneers, as compared to half of the homemakers, enjoy "visiting relatives."

What does this pattern mean? I believe the major part of the answer lies in the different meaning close interpersonal ties have for the homemaker, as compared with the pioneer, and represents part of the source of the very different paths these women are following in their adult lives. Women whose childhood was characterized by intense and extensive relationships with their families, with relatives as well as members of their immediate nuclear family, are far more apt to grow up with a very conservative image of appropriate roles for women: these are the women with both strongly nurturant and strongly dependent tendencies, nurturant toward those younger and frailer than themselves, dependent toward those older, stronger, or more authoritative than themselves.[12] Family and social life represent the major arenas in the lives of these homemakers, and, like the pattern of fifty years ago, the turning point in their lives is marriage rather than parenthood, following a very short period of time between school and marriage. They are fully socialized—indeed one might say overly socialized—for the assumption of marital and maternal roles. One suspects that these are the women occasionally overheard addressing their husbands as "Papa" and "Dad."

Pioneers, in contrast, have had looser ties with family and kin, have been oriented to the world of ideas and able to sustain less intense interpersonal relationships, have been free of the need to be dependent on others or nurturant of others. Their lower predisposition to nurturing is perhaps the reason they are less apt to enjoy being with young children. Being less predisposed to dependence, they are prepared to establish more egalitarian relationships with men, people older than themselves, or those in a position of greater authority than their own. Since their own needs to nurture are less strong, their own personal expectations are for fewer children, with a greater willingness to sever kin ties and participate in the job world despite the responsibilities of home management and child rearing. Consequently the more crucial event in their lives is childbearing rather than marriage. This suggestion is supported by the profile of what the married pioneers were doing in 1964: 70 per cent of them were working, 25 per cent were going to school. Among married homemakers, in contrast, only a third were working and 2 per cent going to school of some sort.

Further support for the general interpretation offered can be seen in the contrast between the pioneers and the homemakers when they were asked to rate themselves in comparison with "other women of your age" on a number of personality characteristics. Pioneers are strikingly more apt than the homemakers to characterize themselves as "dominant" and "occupationally competitive," and homemakers take the lead in characterizing themselves as "dependent" and "socially competitive." But on only one of these self-descriptions is there a strong contrast between the single and married pioneer: the single pioneer is twice as likely as the married pioneer to say she is "occupationally competitive." One of the effects of marriage for pioneer women may be the blunting of their career strivings.

There are two other ways in which the general interpretation of the differential effect of marriage on pioneers and homemakers can be shown. One item in the questionnaire permits a classification of the women in terms of their general ideological position on sex roles, from a feminist position of more equality and similarity in the roles of men and women, to a traditional position stressing the differences between the roles of the sexes.[13] About one-fifth of the total sample took the feminist position, slightly less than a third took the traditional position, and not quite half took a more moderate position combining features of both points of view. This ideological item strongly differen-

tiates the pioneers (half of whom subscribe to the feminist position) from the homemakers (40 per cent of whom subscribe to the traditional ideology). But when single women were compared with married women in each of these two career types, an interesting difference emerged: single homemakers are far more strongly traditional than married homemakers, whereas married pioneers are more inclined to take a "mixed" position than single pioneers. Once again, this suggests that marriage and family roles are less fully satisfying to the homemakers than they expected them to be, and that pioneers have found their career pursuits and living with a real husband rather than an idealized one a more difficult combination than they expected it to be. It suggests, further, that situational factors play an important role in the ideological values women hold concerning the social role of their own sex.[14]

SEX DIFFERENCES IN VIEWS REGARDING WOMEN'S ROLES

One last strategy can be employed to illuminate the probable effects of marriage upon the life patterns and expectations of the pioneers and homemakers. It will be recalled that, in the Michigan State study, college men were more traditional and conservative than women. The NORC college graduate study gathered the responses of men as well as women to a number of items concerning women's roles in American society and the combination of work and marriage.

These data also show that men are more conservative concerning women's role than women themselves are. Since marriage probably involves more adjustment of the woman to the man's views than vice versa, here then is evidence supporting the general interpretation. On an item reading "Even if a woman has the ability and interest, she should not choose a career field that will be difficult to combine with child rearing," half of the women but two-thirds of the men agree. Again, although half the women thought it appropriate for a woman to take a part-time job if a child was a preschooler, only one-third of the men approved. A quarter of the men, but only 14 per cent of the women, thought a full-time job should not be taken until the children were "all grown up."

In another section of the questionnaire, the college graduates were asked to check how much need they thought there was in American society for certain social and political changes concerning women, recommendations stemming from the report of the President's Commission on the Status of Women, though they were not labeled as such in the questionnaire. On each count, men were between two and three times more likely than women to state that there was "no need" at all for the recommended changes: 23 per cent of the men, but only 8 per cent of the women, thought there was "no need" to make available "professionally supervised child care facilities for children of working mothers at all economic levels"; 36 per cent of the men compared to 18 per cent of the women thought there was "no need" to urge "qualified girls to train for occupations which are now held mainly by men"; 32 per cent of the men to 14 per cent of the women believed there was "no need" to encourage women to "seek elective and appointive

TABLE 5   *Perceived Reasons for Low Representation of Women in Medicine, Engineering, and Science (in per cent)*

	Doctor	Engineer	Research Scientist
A job in this field is too demanding for a woman to combine with family responsibilities	80	38	54
Women today want to work only occasionally and on a part-time basis, which they can seldom do in this field	48	34	38
Most parents discourage their daughters from training for such a field	33	57	33
Men in this field resent women colleagues	38	56	23
To enter this field before marriage restricts a woman's chance to marry	25	14	20
Women are afraid they will be considered unfeminine if they enter this field	12	61	23
Such a job requires skills and characteristics women do not have	4	24	6
Other	8	7	9
N	(14,356)	(14,500)	(12,393)
No Answer	1,307	1,163	3,270
Total N, weighted sample	(15,663)	(15,663)	(15,663)

posts at local, state and national levels of government." Here is indirect evidence not only for the direction of the effect marriage may have upon women's views, but for the likely reception women may experience as these young men move into policy positions in the occupational world as employers, educators, and colleagues of women.

PERCEIVED REASONS FOR SMALL NUMBER OF WOMEN DOCTORS, ENGINEERS, AND RESEARCH SCIENTISTS

The women college graduates in the NORC study were asked why they thought few American women enter medicine, engineering, or the sciences. Their answers suggest that quite different obstacles are at work in restricting women's choice of engineering as a career goal from those militating against the choice of a career in medicine or science. With three professional fields and seven specified reasons for women's not choosing them as career goals, the data require a detailed analysis, but a few of the major highlights can be briefly described here, with the details shown in Table 5.

The ranking of these reasons is roughly the same for medicine and science. The two reasons the women college graduates cited most frequently involve the difficulty of managing demanding professional work with home and child responsibilities, and the desire on the part of women for occasional and part-time work rather than a full-time persistent commitment to a professional career. This is particularly the case with medicine, slightly less so for research in science. There is very little tendency to associate either medicine or science with inadequacy of skills on the part of women, or with an image of these professions as so dominantly masculine that a woman who entered them would be considered "unfeminine."

Engineering shows a rather different profile of perceived reasons. The major reason women see as accounting for the low representation of their sex in engineering is that women are afraid they would be considered unfeminine if they entered it, and perhaps for much the same reason, the second reason frequently endorsed is that parents discourage their daughters from training for such a field. In short, engineering is viewed as a thoroughly masculine field, which parents do not want their daughters to enter, and a field in

which men engineers resent the presence of women engineer colleagues. Unlike medicine and science, women also tend to believe that engineering requires skills and characteristics women do not have.

The "obstacles" women perceive concerning a choice of engineering as a career goal are thus factors operating much earlier in the life span than those concerning a choice of medicine or science. Parents discourage in their daughters while they encourage in their sons the interests and hobbies that precede, by many years, a choice of engineering as a career goal. A long childhood of learning "appropriate" sex role behavior militates against American girls' acquiring the interests and skills that might start them on a path leading to careers in engineering. In contrast, the barriers to a choice of medicine and science operate at a somewhat later point in the life span. These are fields rejected by young women because they believe they would conflict with family obligations, not that they are in conflict with feminine skills and interests.

A significantly large proportion of the women college graduates endorsed the view that women do not choose medicine, engineering, and science because they cannot get part-time or intermittent work in these fields. This is only one of several points in the study at which women show their reliance on part-time work as a solution to the dilemma of combining career and child-rearing responsibilities. Where the field permits it and the woman really needs it, part-time employment may indeed be a good solution for tiding a woman over the very early years of child rearing. But there is an unfortunate tendency in the past few years to overstress part-time work as "the" solution to the contemporary woman's need for both personal fulfillment and societal contribution. Almost half the women in the college graduate study tell us they think it all right for a woman to take a part-time job when a child is under five years of age, but only 18 per cent approve full-time employment when a child is a preschooler. Even the small minority of pioneers who are training for careers in the more demanding professions show this marked discrepancy in approval of maternal employment: one-quarter of the pioneers approve full-time employment when a woman has a preschooler, but fully 60 per cent approve part-time employment at this early stage of child rearing. If our general proposition is correct, that the experience of marriage and family roles leads to a reduction in the career focus of the pioneers, then as more of these young women actually have young children of their own, we may predict a very much lower endorsement of even part-time employment a few years from now.

There is a more fundamental question to be raised that is far more critical than the question of the availability of part-time jobs in the present labor market. What is the effect of withdrawal from her field for any significant number of years upon the creativity we may expect from a woman in the scientific and technical professions? That she will need some retraining and "rust removal" has been much stressed in recent years, and these are the functions fulfilled by programs and centers for continuing education for women. I think there is a danger that such centers institutionalize and lend further social pressure to the acceptance of the woman's withdrawal for a number of years, a pattern that should not be widely or uncritically accepted until we have better answers to the question concerning the effect this withdrawal has upon the contributions we may expect from her.

Lehman[15] investigated the relationship between age and creative achievement in such diverse fields as mathematics, opera composition, chemistry, philosophy, creative writing, and astronomy, to name only some of the many fields he has inquired into. His data include measures on the sheer quantity of published work produced by hundreds of men in these fields, as well as measures of the quality of their work as judged by experts in their fields. Both the quantity and the quality of these published works were then related to the age of the individual scholars when they completed such work. Lehman's over-all conclusions are that the quantity of output is sustained quite well throughout the life span of these men, but the quality of output is strongly related to age: the peak of creative work varies among the fields he studied from the late twenties and early thirties for the sciences, to the late thirties for such fields as music and philosophy.[16] Though his task of trying to do the same analysis for women that he did for men was complicated by the fact that so few women have contributed greatly to the sciences (and the fact that a large proportion of the women listed in biographical dictionaries failed to reveal their birth dates), what analysis he could attempt showed that women's most creative years in science do not differ greatly from the creative years of men.[17] The most creative work women and men have done in science was completed during the very years contemporary women are urged to remain at home rearing their families.

Consequently, we must seriously raise the question whether women with the greatest potential for significant contributions to their fields will have lost the primary chance to achieve such creativity if they withdraw from their professional work for any prolonged time during their youthful years. This is not to suggest that no woman can make outstanding creative contributions at a later stage of life, for we all know exceptions to this, but merely to stress that the probability of doing so is reduced. I think this is a point well worth bearing in mind in a period when women are enticed to believe that withdrawal from the labor force in their twenties, followed by part-time employment in their forties is their modern panacea to the conflict in women's roles.

There is one last point I should like to make in connection with the arguments for and against part-time employment as a solution to the woman's problem. If we take an historical perspective on the changes that have taken place in the relationship between the sexes, I think we can detect a natural sequence of change from a traditional to an egalitarian relationship which follows the human life span. It is difficult to imagine an egalitarian relationship between husband and wife after twenty years of marriage unless there was an egalitarian flavor to their marrige during the first twenty years of their life together.

My main point here is simply this: the five, ten, or fifteen years during which the woman is at home rearing her children are years during which the marital relationship is being stabilized. When she seeks to return to professional life, neither she nor her husband will be the same two people they were before the arrival of children. The children's expectations of their mother and the husband's expectations of his wife have jelled during those years. When the woman seeks a return to professional life, it then requires far more reorientation on the part of all members of the family, including the woman, than would be involved if she remained an independent and active professional while her combined wife-mother role was in the making. In light of these factors, and the findings of Lehman, older women who return to the labor force are an important reservoir for assistants and technicians and the less demanding professions, but only rarely for creative and original contributors to the more demanding professional fields.

CHARACTERISTICS OF THE SCIENTIST AND IMPLICATIONS FOR WOMEN'S CAREER CHOICES

Four factors have been found to be particularly characteristic of the scientist of note:[18]

1. *High intellectual ability*, with particularly high scores on tests of spatial and mathematical ability.

2. *Intense channeling of energy in one direction:* strikingly high persistence in the pursuit of work tasks, to the point that most are happiest when working.

3. *Extreme independence*, showing itself in childhood as a preference for a few close friends rather than extensive or organized group membership, and preference for working on his own; in adulthood as a marked independence of relations with parents and a preference for being free of all supervision, roaming in work where his interests dictate.

4. *Apartness from others*, with extremely low interest in social activities, showing neither preference for an active social life nor guilt concerning his socially withdrawn tendencies.

Let us now go back over these characteristics and examine them with an eye to the likelihood, or actuality where known, that women will have these characteristics as frequently as men. Since all these characteristics have their roots in childhood relationships and experiences, this procedure comes close to the basic sources of sex differences in early experiences that predispose one to scientific interest and its cultivation later in adolescence and early adulthood.

High Intellectual Ability[19] *and Independence.* For a considerable number of years it was assumed that there were no sex differences in intelligence, for, in study after study that relied on the Stanford-Binet intelligence test, practically no differences were found between boys and girls. An important point had somehow been lost to sight among psychologists, i.e., that in standardizing this test, items that revealed consistent sex differences were discarded because the test constructors were trying to create a test on which the scores of both boys and girls could be evaluated against the same norms.[20] Secondly, the Stanford-Binet is a test of general intelligence with a high stress on verbal ability. During more recent years, as specific tests have been constructed to tap different dimensions of intellectual and creative ability, consistent sex differences have begun to emerge.

From the results of these more highly specified tests, the following picture emerges. Perhaps because the developmental timetable is faster for girls than boys during childhood, girls do seem to be slightly ahead of boys: they talk at slightly younger ages, put words together into sentences somewhat sooner, count accurately sooner than boys; in school, learning to read seems to be easier for girls than boys, and fewer girls have reading problems requiring remedial help. This edge enjoyed by the girls disappears rather quickly: after the fifth or sixth grade, studies show boys doing as well as girls in reading comprehension, though girls show somewhat greater verbal fluency.

In mathematical skills, there are no sex differences during the early school years, but during high school, boys begin to excel girls, and, by the time they take the Scholastic Aptitude Tests as applicants for admission to college, the boys score an average of 50 points higher on the mathematical portions of the tests, and girls score only 8 to 10 points higher on the verbal portion of the test. Whether this reflects the fact that girls less often elect advanced mathematics courses than boys, or that girls lack certain abstract qualities of intellective ability that are required in these mathematical tests, is difficult to tell. Maccoby concludes that the evidence leans toward the second alternative, since throughout grade school boys excel in "spatial" tests—e.g. detecting a simple figure embedded in a more complex one, or telling how many surfaces there are on the side of a pile of cubes which the viewer cannot see, findings which suggest that "boys perceive more analytically, while the girls are more global, more influenced by all the elements of the field together."[21]

These results suggest that, on the average, girls develop cognitive abilities along somewhat different lines from boys, and that they enter early adolescence with a style of thinking less appropriate to scientific work than that of boys. Although the final interpretation of this sex difference awaits further research, what is known is that the key to the difference between boys and girls lies in the kind and degree of independence training the child receives in childhood. If a girl is encouraged to assume initiative, to solve problems for herself, she tends to develop the same analytic abilities as the boy typically does.

Maccoby cites one last convincing set of data on this point: pointing out that some children's scores on standard intelligence tests become higher over the years of formative development whereas the scores of others remain constant or decline, she draws a general picture of the child at age six who is among those whose IQ will increase by the time they are ten: "Competitive, self-assertive, independent and dominant in interaction with other children. The children who show declining IQs during the next four years are children who are passive, shy and dependent."[22] These two sets of characteristics also tend to differentiate girls from boys, women from men, and among women, the homemakers from the pioneers.

Some of these sex differences persist even among men and women who have chosen the same occupational field in adulthood. That women are more often found teaching science than doing science may in part reflect this. In fact, studies of college teachers have shown that what women mention as satisfying them most about their campus jobs are "good students" and "desirable colleagues," whereas men teachers stress "opportunity to do research" and "freedom and independence."[23] In stressing the interpersonal side of campus teaching, the women reflect not only less independence of thought but their psychological dependence on comfortable relations with other people, both peers and the young. In a recent article in *Science* by a chairman of a biophysics department, the author generalizes his observations of the differences between male and female graduate students in his field. One of the strategies he has found successful in combining the roles of laboratory scientist and department chairman is to keep a laboratory assistant, because the sheer fact of having such an assistant means he will feel internal pressure to remain in close daily touch with the progress of research in the laboratory. He urges, however, that such an assistant be a woman, explaining his reason in these terms:

The purpose of this assistant is to require daily instruction about what to do. Thus you are inescapably forced to plan for the operation of another pair of hands. *A female is better because she will not operate quite so readily on her own, and this is exactly what you want*[24] [italics mine].

The inference is strong, therefore, that behind the fact that few women are represented in science is the difference in cognitive style of male and female, which is in turn the result of differences in the ways girls are brought up compared to boys. If we want more women to enter science, not only as teachers of science but as scientists, we must encourage the cultivation of the analytic and mathematical abilities science requires. To achieve this means encouraging independence and self-reliance instead of pleasing feminine submission in the young girl, stimulating and rewarding her efforts to satisfy her curiosity about the world to the same extent her brothers' efforts are, cultivating a probing intelligence that asks why and rejects the easy answers instead of urging her to please others and conform unthinkingly to social rules. A childhood model of the quiet "good" sweet girl will not produce many women scientists or scholars, doctors or engineers. It may produce the competent meticulous laboratory assistant "who will not operate so readily on her own" as Pollard describes her, but not the creative scientist as Anne Roe has described him, for whom nothing else matters once intellectual independence is really tasted.

These are rather sober conclusions, for the problem of increasing the proportion of women in the sciences appears far less easily solved if one must change the social climate surrounding the young child than it does if one could merely rely on such institutional levers as increasing stipends and child-care facilities, retraining older women, changing our tax laws, or making symbolic appointments to high offices in the federal government.[25] How much hope is there, one may ask, for efforts directed at changing the ways in which parents rear their sons and daughters, or the ways teachers deal with boys and girls? Can one reach parents and teachers and change their view that science is for boys and not for girls? That sensitivity and independence are the necessary ingredients of creativity in both boys and girls? That sensitivity in sons should be encouraged and no longer considered unmasculine, and independence should be encouraged in girls and no longer considered unfeminine?

One experimental study by E. Paul Torrance[26] offers some encouragement in this regard. One of his researches into creativity involved assigning tasks to small groups of fourth, fifth, and sixth graders, to figure out the principles underlying a set of science toys. Many girls were reluctant even to work with the science toys, protesting that they "were not supposed to know anything about things like that." As a result, the boys demonstrated and explained about twice as many ideas as the girls did in experiments involving these toys. The research did not stop here, however, for Torrance initiated a series of conferences with the teachers in the school, and the parents of the children, explaining the results and pointing out the way in which girls are cheated of an important opportunity to learn and understand science, something desirable in itself in the complex technological world they will be part of as adults. The experiment was repeated the next year, after these conferences, and the results were quite promising. This time, there was no reluctance on the part of the girls to become engaged in the tasks, nor were they different from the boys in the enjoyment they expressed in the task, nor in their scientific knowledge. The mean performance of the boys and girls was almost identical. In only one respect did the differences between the sexes remain unchanged. Both boys and girls thought the contributions the boys made were better than the contributions the girls made. Pleasure and knowledge were positively affected; apparently group evaluation of the latter is harder to change. In any event, an experiment of this sort, which combined research and social action, is extremely encouraging to those concerned with changing the social climate surrounding the young girl.

Work Persistence and Apartness from Others. Prominent among the conclusions Anne Roe has drawn from her studies of eminent scientists, as it was from Cox's much earlier study of geniuses,[27] is the following: one of the hallmarks of the eminent men is high but not necessarily the highest intelligence, combined with the greatest degree of persistence and intense channeling of the individual's energies in his work. High intelligence is a necessary but scarcely a sufficient condition for a career in research science, for a great degree of persistence must be coupled with that intelligence.

That women with advanced degrees have sufficient intelligence to equip them for significant contributions to the fields in which they have worked is scarcely open to question. Self-selection works so much more strongly among women that, at each higher level of education, women probably have a greater potential for significant achievement than men. Since many more men than women go on for the Ph.D., one thing this implies is that the woman with an M.A. probably represents better potential than the male with an M.A.; yet women at this level still do not advance as far, earn as much, or achieve as much as men at their educational level. Studies of women with the Ph.D., like that on some 400 Radcliffe Ph.D.'s,[28] show that women publish substantially less than men of comparable jobs and rank. That this is not attributable just to the greater home responsibilities of the women is supported by the finding that married women had published as much as the single Radcliffe Ph.D.'s.

I believe that a major clue lies in the differences between the sexes in the two further characteristics of work persistence and apartness from others. Both these characteristics mark the eminent scientist, and both involve factors which women are not encouraged to have in our society. It is a much rarer social phenomenon to find women than to find men with either extreme persistence and intense channeling of energy in professional work, or tolerance of and preference for social isolation. The one is related to the other, for persistence in work can scarcely combine easily with a high need for interaction with others, or with a social world in which others make high demands for interaction.

To suggest that girls should be encouraged to be less dependent on others and to feel less need than they do for close ties with other people is sure to be met with considerable resistance and skepticism in many quarters. It is a recommendation made in a time when the tenor of our society is rather strongly in the direction of "social adjustment," smooth relationships with others, responsiveness to the opinions of others. Whether described in terms of the dominance of other-directedness by David Riesman, or in the more recent language of a shift from traditional to emergent values, as Spindler, Getzels, and Bidwell have described it,[29] recent studies have shown an increasing acceptance among young people of the stress on sociability, the relativist quality of morality and values generally, an excessive readiness to take on the coloration of the social environment and the views of others.[30] Some tendency toward social chameleonism may be the price we pay for the burgeoning of bureaucracy in our society. But the intellectual minority of the society who carry the burden and pleasure of creativity in the sciences as in the arts must work hard to resist this trend. When one reads in science education journals that many young people with scientific interests tend to be one-sided in their interests at the expense of all-round interests and social adjustment,[31] one worries that the educator or the psychologist who tries to help these young people become better adjusted may, in so doing, rob them of what would otherwise feed into persistence in scientific work and the willingness to run counter to public and scientific opinion, which is precisely what the creative person must do if he or she is to stretch and expand the walls of our knowledge.

Success as a woman: a concluding note of encouragement

I should like to conclude with one last result from the NORC study of women college graduates, for it may help to dispel the somewhat pessimistic note inevitable in any coming to grips with the basic sources of women's low representation in the sciences and professions.

There are a number of different paths that women can pursue toward "success" as a woman in American society. Women may be noted for their figure and dress, the décor of their homes, the prominence of their husbands, and the accomplishments of their children, as well as through achievements of their own by winning awards for artistic, scientific, or scholarly merit, or by successful election or appointment to important positions in voluntary or political organizations.

If we ask, which of these different kinds of success do college-educated women admire the most, and which would they like to have for themselves, an answer can be given, for these questions were asked of the women college graduates in the NORC study. For themselves, the picture is clear: it is to live in the shadow of the accomplishments of their husbands and children. The kind of success most often desired for themselves is to be the "mother of several highly accomplished children" and the "wife whose husband becomes very prominent." On the other hand, very few women college graduates chose such body-focused success as "Miss or Mrs. America contest winner," "outstanding film, stage, or TV star," or "one of ten best-dressed women in America." Nor do these women show much interest in becoming prominent for their volunteer or political participation, despite the pleas of their educators that these are spheres of activities important for women to work in and easy to combine with home duties. Fewer than 5 per cent showed any interest in success as a prominent leader of a voluntary organization or as a national figure holding an elective or appointive political office. When it is remembered that these are responses to a question asking not what they realistically expect, but what kind of success they would most like for themselves, it throws into sharp focus the tendency of women to define themselves in terms of their intimate affiliation with other people rather than in terms of their own unique abilities.

But what is of extreme interest are their responses to the kinds of successful women they most admire. The kinds of successful women that these college alumnae admire most of all are women who receive scientific or scholarly awards, followed closely by women who receive literary or artistic awards. Close to four out of five women college graduates admire women with these particular accomplishments. The majority of the college-educated women in the United States may have opted against the serious pursuit of a demanding professional life for themselves, but they represent a sympathetic, admiring audience for the small minor-

ity of women who enter the now masculine fields and win acclaim for their accomplishments.

NOTES

1. In the next decade, a shift is expected in the sex composition of labor-force growth. From the 65 per cent that women constituted of the increase to the labor force between 1950 and 1960, a decline to 43 per cent of total growth between 1960 and 1975 is the present expectation. The reason lies in the very large increase in young people who will enter the labor force in the decade ahead; since women in this age group work only a short time before withdrawing from the labor market, men will comprise more than half the net increase in the labor force. Cf. *A Report on Manpower Requirements, op. cit.,* pp. 36-37.

2. U.S. Bureau of the Census, *Census of Population: 1960*, Vol. 1, Table 202, pp. 528-533.

3. The Committee on Federal Employment of the President's Commission on the Status of Women gathered data on the distribution of women compared to men in various fields and civil service grade levels among federal employees. These data show less variation between physical and biological sciences than the census data do, women being only 4 per cent of the federally employed persons in biological sciences, 8 per cent in physical sciences, and 1 per cent in engineering. Cf. The President's Commission on the Status of Women, *Report of the Committee on Federal Employment,* Appendix D. *Grade and Occupational Distribution of Men and Women in White Collar Jobs.* October 1963.

4. In an analysis of the position of minorities in the labor force from 1900 to 1960, Dale Hiestand points out that white women have been of diminishing importance in the growth of the professional and related occupations as the over-all growth rates in these fields have accelerated. This occurs because the growth pattern of the majority group (white males) defines the rapidly growing fields; since minorities in the labor force like white women or Negro males and females constitute a small proportion of the total labor force by definition, they can usually provide only a small proportion of the added manpower in rapidly growing fields. Cf. Dale L. Hiestand, *Economic Growth and Employment Opportunities for Minorities.* New York: Columbia University Press, 1964.

5. Comparable data from the Office of Education for the distribution of earned degrees during the years 1949-1950 to 1961-1962 show an increase in the proportion who are women only among bachelor's degree holders in biology and chemistry, and master's degree holders in biology.

6. The same proportion of women as of men scientists in the 1962 Register hold doctorate degrees (31 per cent). Women scientists more often have master's degrees than men (39 per cent compared to 25 per cent), less often just the bachelor's degree or less educational attainment (27 per cent compared to 40 per cent).

7. Data from the post-censal survey provide further detail on the contrast between physical and biological sciences. In the physical sciences, women at both the master's and the doctorate level are more apt to be employed by colleges and universities than are men, who are predominantly in business and industry. In contrast, there are no major sex differences at any educational level in the biological sciences. Biologists with relatively low levels of advanced education are more apt to be employed in government and at the higher levels of educational attainment by educational institutions than is the case for physical scientists.

8. The data from the most recent questionnaire in this longitudinal study of college graduates only became available for final analysis in the spring of 1965, several months after the first draft of this paper was written. The presymposium version of the paper was therefore based on data from a nonrandom subsample of the first questionnaire returns. Whenever possible this final version of the paper has revised the figures to accord with patterns shown in the final total sample. This does not apply, however, to any figures given in the comparison of pioneers and homemakers, which are exclusively based on the nonrandom subsample. Results are therefore not presented in tabular form unless they stem from the final results of the total sample. There is little reason to expect major shifts in any of the patterns reported, however, since the preliminary analysis was based on 3,500 of the approximately 8,000 women who responded to this wave of the study. For a description of the study and the results from the questionnaires administered before college graduation, cf. James A. Davis, *Great Aspirations.* Chicago: Aldine Publishing Company, 1964.

9. The question on which the typology is based was: "Which field from the list in the cover letter best describes your anticipated long run career field? If you are a woman: if you plan to combine marriage and work, code the field of employment, not housewife. Use the code number for 'housewife' ONLY if you do not expect to work at all."

10. To simplify presentation of results, I shall exclude the traditional women from most of the discussion, comparing instead just the pioneers and the homemakers. On all the variables discussed, unless otherwise noted, the traditionals fall between the pioneers and the homemakers in their response profile, though much closer in most cases to the homemakers than to the pioneers.

11. The fact that differences of this magnitude differentiate between single and married homemakers should alert the social scientist against putting too much credence in the future expectations of young women when they are in college. One could readily predict far more conservatism concerning maternal employment than actually exists once these women are older and have such responsibilities in the home. One study, which shows perhaps the most conservative attitudes toward working wives of any study I have seen, should perhaps be viewed with this in mind. This study of college freshmen showed that the majority of the men and the women rejected the view that work to fulfill the self is appropriate for married women, though they accepted such employment when it stemmed from selfless motivation on the part of women. Thus they reject the view that women should work in order to have a life of their own and to use their abilities and training, and feel that this is the way women should feel. Yet the majority approve motivation such as "so their husband can complete his education" or to meet financial responsibilities, or to buy things for the home and family. College freshmen are still far enough from the reality of marriage to believe that it will or should fulfill women completely, a view that will be modified as they experience marriage and parenthood. It may also be that a generation of permissive childbearing has produced young adult women far less selfless than their mothers and grandmothers, women who feel they should serve their children and husbands but are not psychologically capable of such devotion to others. Cf. Vivian H. Hewer and Gerhard Neubeck, *College Freshmen's Attitudes toward Working Wives*, University of Minnesota Research Bulletin of the Office of the Dean of Students, February 1964 (mimeograph).

12. It would be interesting to know if this generation's suburban homemakers experience a lack of social rootedness because they lack the extensive familial ties women of this type had for emotional sustenance in the more stable communities of previous generations. Contemporary young women have been reared with a high need for the continuation of close familial ties, but the increased geographic mobility of their husbands in this generation cuts them off from the people they have emotional need for. If their need for interpersonal ties stems from such dependent motivations, it is little wonder that volunteer activities, political participation, or PTA meetings fail to fulfill them.

13. This item read: "Women vary a great deal among themselves on what they consider the most desirable pattern of life for women. Indicate the extent to which your own views approximate the "A" or "B" viewpoint:

"A. A *feminist* viewpoint, stressing greater equality and similarity in the roles of men and women than now exist, with greater participation of women in leadership positions in politics, the professions and business.

"B. A *traditional* viewpoint, stressing the differences between the roles of men and women, in which women's lives center on home and family and their job participation is in such fields as teaching, social work, nursing and secretarial service."

14. It must be stressed that these are suggested rather than final interpretations of the research data, which may be modified or nullified by more detailed analysis. Undoubtedly some part of the pattern shown in the text to differentiate single from married pioneers is not the "effect" of marriage, but a reflection of the fact that the most ambitious of the pioneers simply do not marry at as early an age as the less ambitious within their career type; and of course some portion of these single pioneers may not marry at all.

15. Harvey C. Lehman, *Age and Achievement*. Princeton, N.J.: Princeton University Press, 1953.

16. A more precise formulation of his findings, illustrated for chemistry, is as follows: "In proportion to the number of chemists that were alive at each successive age level, very superior contributions to the field of chemistry were made at the greatest average rate when the chemists were not more than 26-30" (Lehman, *ibid.*, p. 324).

17. *Ibid.*, pp. 97-99.

18. This brief profile is drawn primarily from the work of Anne Roe on eminent biologists and physicists, whom she compared with eminent psychologists and anthropologists. Cf. Anne Roe, "A Psychological Study of Eminent Biologists," *Psychological Monographs*, 65, No. 331, 1951; "A Psychological Study of Physical Scientists," *Genetic Psychology Monographs*, 43, May 1951; "Psychological Study of Research Scientists," *Psychological Monographs*, 67, No. 2, 1953; "Crucial Life Experiences in the Development of Scien-

tists," in E. P. Torrance (ed.), *Talent and Education*. Minneapolis: University of Minnesota Press, 1960; "Personal Problems and Science," in C. W. Taylor (ed.), *The Third University of Utah Research Conference on the Identification of Creative Scientific Talent*. Salt Lake City: University of Utah Press, 1959, pp. 202-212; and *The Making of a Scientist*. New York Dodd, Mead, 1953.

19. This brief description of sex differences in intellectual ability relies heavily on the work of Eleanor E. Maccoby, "Woman's Intellect," in Seymour M. Farber and Roger H. L. Wilson (eds.), *The Potential of Woman*. New York: McGraw-Hill, 1963; and the bibliographic review of sex differences prepared for the Social Science Research Council: Robert Oetzel, *Selected Bibliography on Sex Differences*, Stanford University, 1962 (mimeograph).

20. Quinn McNemar, *The Revision of the Stanford-Binet Scale: An Analysis of the Standardization Data*. Boston: Houghton Mifflin, 1942.

21. Maccoby, *op. cit.*, p. 29. Dyer also presents evidence from College Entrance Examination Board test result analyses, suggesting that even among the science-oriented students, who presumably have all taken considerable mathematics and science in high school, the boys still show higher scores in the mathematics test than the girls. Cf. Henry S. Dyer and Richard G. King, *College Board Scores: Their Use and Interpretation*, No. 2, College Entrance Examination Board, 1955.

22. Maccoby, *op. cit.*, p. 33.

23. Ruth E. Eckert and John E. Stecklein, *Job Motivations and Satisfactions of College-Teachers*, U.S. Department of Health, Education and Welfare, Office of Education, Cooperative Research Monograph No. 7, 1961.

24. E. C. Pollard, "How to Remain in the Laboratory though Head of a Department," *Science*, 145, September 4, 1964, 1018-1021.

25. This decade is one in which many doors are opening to bright and ambitious professional women, often with the support and by the politics of top governmental agencies, universities, and major industrial employers. But it must be realized that many of the present opportunities for adult women can only aid in implementing their choice of science as a career, not in helping greatly increased numbers of girls and young women to make the choices in the first place. Unless this is realized, many quarters of policymaking a decade from now may conclude that women do not want, or are not able to, become professionals and intellectuals in large enough numbers to warrant continued special opportunities for them. See the examples of exclusive stress on broad institutional levers affecting adult women's participation in the labor force in recent editorials on women in science and engineering, which appeared in *Science*: 145, No. 3628, July 10, 1964, and 145, No. 3639, September 25, 1964.

26. Cf. E. Paul Torrance, "Changing Reactions of Preadolescent Girls to Task Requiring Creative Scientific Thinking during a Thirteen-Month Period," *New Educational Ideas*, Proceedings of the Third Minnesota Conference on Gifted Children, 1960; and E. P. Torrance, *Guiding Creative Talent*. Englewood Cliffs, N.J.: Prentice-Hall, 1962, pp. 111-113.

27. C. S. Cox, *Genetic Studies of Genius*. Vol. II. *Early Mental Traits of Three Hundred Geniuses*. Stanford: Stanford University Press, 1926.

28. Radcliffe Committee on Graduate Education for Women, *Graduate Education for Women*. Cambridge, Mass.: Harvard University Press, 1956.

29. George D. Spindler, "Education in a Transforming American Culture," *Harvard Educational Review*, 23, Spring 1955, 145-153; Jacob W. Getzels, "Changing Values Challenge the Schools," *School Review*, 45, Spring 1957, 92-102; Charles E. Bidwell et al., "Undergraduate Careers: Alternatives and Determinants," *School Review*, 71, No. 3, 1963, 299-316.

30. A very good illustration of this shift was shown in the longitudinal study of college students at Michigan State University; one effect of four years of college education is a reduction of traditional beliefs and an increase in emergence values. Cf. Dorothy Robinson Ross, *The Story of the Top 1% of the Women at Michigan State University*, 1963 (mimeograph).

31. Thus one reads comments like the following: "The science-oriented pupil, whose voluntary work in microscopy, chemistry, radio or geology occupies much of his free time, may cut himself off socially from his age group and not receive the maximum educational advantages that the school can offer. Guidance must take into account social, emotional and intellectual growth of the potential scientist. It must consider him as a person as well as a potential technician." From Herbert S. Zim, "Opportunities for Pupils with Unusual Science Talent," *Bulletin of the National Association of Secondary School Principals*, 37, January 1953, 156-165.

13 The woman Ph.D.: a recent profile

Rita James Simon
Shirley Merritt Clark
Kathleen Galway

This paper assesses the professional characteristics and contributions of the woman Ph.D. who is primarily employed full-time, although not exclusively, by academic institutions. In recent years there have been a considerable number of articles and much research describing the social origins and professional qualifications of college and university professors, the responses of faculties to questions of loyalty, political allegiance and academic freedom, and the communication process by which jobs are secured or changed.[1] In concentrating as we do on the characteristics of one category of professional personnel employed by colleges and universities, we also compare that category to the dominant group, the male doctorates. This provides additional information about the professional characteristics of all members of university faculties, as well as essential data on the status and accomplishments of women in comparison to men with Ph.D.s.

Our study was directed toward answering the following questions. 1) Are women who have doctorates as productive as men with Ph.D.s (holding year and field constant); 2) are married women (with and without children) as productive as unmarried women; and 3) do anti-nepotism regulations seriously hinder married women from finding employment comparable to their training and experience. Since question 3 was the subject of a previous article, the present paper focuses on questions one and two.[2] The characteristics of the woman Ph.D. to be described are:

1) Employment situation (type, place, length of employment, income, and rank).
2) Productivity (number of articles, books, research grants, and consulting work).
3) Professional recognition (honorary societies, fellowships, and travel grants).
4) Professional identification (membership in professional organizations, offices, committees, and subscription to journals).

Method and description of respondents

Working from the universe of women who received their doctorates between 1958 and 1963 in the physical and natural sciences, the social sciences, the humanities and education, we obtained the names of 5370 women and were able to contact 93 percent of them through the mail. About sixty percent of the women who received a questionnaire filled it out and returned it. In order to be able to compare women Ph.D.s with men holding doctorates over the same time period, we drew a sample of male Ph.D.s that was one third the size of the female list and that maintained the same proportions by academic field. From a sample of 1787 men we were able to mail questionnaires to 1700 (95 percent of the sample) and received returns from about 60 percent.

Findings

Women with doctorates are different from men who have doctorates in one very basic respect. Over 95 percent of the men are married, in contrast to only 50 percent of the women. For respondents with degrees in education, the difference between men and women is even greater since only 35 percent of the women are married. Men are also more likely to have gotten married before they received their doctorates than women.

The Ph.D. places greater restrictions on the woman's choice of a spouse than it does on the man's. In our society a man is more likely to marry a person of lower social status than is a woman. We note in Table 2 that among those women who are married, about 80 percent have husbands who have professional positions. When years and fields were examined separately, the proportions were about the same for each category except that women in education were more likely to marry men in business (24 percent compared to 6, 10, and 9 percent for women in

Reprinted from Rita James Simon, Shirley Merritt Clark, and Kathleen Galway, "The Woman Ph.D.: A Recent Profile," Social Problems, 15:2, Fall 1967, pp. 221-236, by permission of The Society for the Study of Social Problems. Funds for the research on the "Productivity and Professional Contributions of the Woman Ph.D." came from the U.S. Office of Education Cooperative Research Project S-049.

TABLE 1   Marital Status of Women Ph.D.s by Field

Marital Status	Sciences	Social Sciences	Humanities	Education	Combined
			(in percent)		
Unmarried*	38.0	42.6	53.4	65.4	50.2 (886)
Married**	20.5	15.0	12.5	11.4	14.6 (259)
Married with children	41.5	42.4	34.1	23.2	35.0 (619)
Total N	381	554	311	518	100 (1764)

* This category describes respondents who have never been married.
** This category describes women who are married but who have no children.

TABLE 2   Husbands' Occupations by Field

Husbands' occupations	Sciences	Social Sciences	Humanities	Education	Combined
			(in percent)		
Professional	88.9	84.4	83.8	65.3	80.5 (707)
Proprietors, managers	6.4	10.2	8.5	23.9	11.5 (101)
Clerical and sales	.4	2.2	2.1	2.8	1.8 (16)
Skilled workers	1.3	.6	2.8	4.0	1.8 (16)
Retired, not employed	3.0	2.6	2.8	4.0	4.3 (38)
Total N	237	317	145	179	100 (878)

TABLE 3   Amount of Employment by Sex and Marital Status

Sex and marital status	Full time	Part-time	Not employed	Combined
		(in percent)		
Women				
Unmarried	96.3	—	3.7	100 (886)
Married	87.2	3.5	9.3	100 (259)
Married with children	59.3	24.5	16.2	100 (619)
Men	99.2	—	.8	100 (492)

other fields.) About 60 percent of the husbands had Ph.D.s (except among women in education where the figures dropped to 45 percent) and about 20 percent had master's degrees.

Seventy percent of the married women had at least one child. Again, this percentage is lower than it is for men. Over 90 percent of the men who were married had children.

Employment characteristics

The first interesting finding is the high proportion of women with doctorates who "practice their trade." As the figures in Table 3 demonstrate, practically all the unmarried women and 87 percent of the married women without children work full time. Even among the married women with children, 60 percent work full time and 25 percent work part time.

When questioned about why they were not employed, two-thirds of the married women explained that they were rearing their children, while only 6 percent said they could not find work. Almost all the women who work part rather than full time, indicated that they preferred it that way. It

gave them more time to look after their children and homes. Since such a high proportion of the respondents are employed full time, all of our subsequent tables describe only the responses of those subjects. The professional characteristics of the 25 percent who work part time are not reported in this paper.

Previous studies reported that women are less likely to be employed at universities (state or private) than are men, and that they are more likely to act as, and be cast in the role of, teachers rather than professors,[3] the crucial distinction being that a teacher is one who passes on an intellectual heritage and a professor is one who helps create the heritage.

Our findings partially support the first thesis. As the figures in Table 4 demonstrate, among those respondents who work in academic institutions,[4] the proportion of unmarried women compared to men who are employed at colleges rather than universities (state or private) is higher in the sciences and social sciences. In the humanities and education, there is little difference by sex. There is also some tendency for married women to be employed at private rather than public universities.

TABLE 4   Place of Employment by Field, Sex, and Marital Status*

Field, sex and marital status	Colleges	State university	Private university	Total N
			(in percent)	
Sciences				
Women				
Unmarried	24.8	50.5	24.8	105
Married	21.3	51.1	27.6	47
Married w/children	9.1	47.7	43.2	44
Men	13.6	61.0	25.4	59
Social Sciences				
Women				
Unmarried	26.8	54.1	19.1	157
Married	17.1	53.6	29.3	41
Married w/children	25.3	45.1	29.6	71
Men	18.2	57.3	24.5	110
Humanities				
Women				
Unmarried	32.0	54.7	13.3	150
Married	31.0	41.4	27.6	29
Married w/children	29.0	56.5	14.5	62
Men	31.9	44.4	23.6	72
Education				
Women				
Unmarried	17.4	71.3	11.2	258
Married	32.3	51.6	16.1	31
Married w/children	28.1	64.9	7.0	57
Men	16.8	74.3	8.8	113
Combined				
Women				
Unmarried	24.0	60.3	15.7	100 (670)
Married	24.3	50.0	25.7	100 (148)
Married w/children	23.9	53.4	22.6	100 (234)
Men	19.8	60.7	19.5	100 (354)

*The percentages in this table are based on the number of respondents employed at academic institutions.

When the respondents were asked to describe the work they do and were given choices of "teaching," "research," "both" or "other," we found that while there was considerable variation by field there was no consistent pattern between the sexes.[5]

The figures in Table 5 show that in the natural sciences and education the expectation concerning the higher proportion of women in teaching receives some support. In the sciences, however, only the unmarried women are more likely to be engaged in teaching; and in education the lower proportion of men in teaching does not mean they are more likely to be engaged in research. It means that a higher proportion have administrative or executive positions.

At a symposium on "Staff Needs and Opportunities in Higher Education," Gladys Borchers quoted salary figures reported by the National Education Association which indicate that "in 1959-1960 men on the faculties of colleges and universities received on the average $1041 more than women" and that in 1961-1962 this difference had risen to $1289.[6] Jessie Bernard reported that in 1959-1960 the median salary for women professors was about a thousand

dollars less than the median salary for men professors. But she noted that the differential was smaller in the lower professional ranks and predicted that the difference in income between men and women would be less among more recent Ph.D.s.[7]

We were able to make several comparisons between income and sex. First, we examined mean incomes among men, and married and unmarried women for each year from 1958 through 1963. In the 1958-1959 cohort the salary differences by sex or marital status are negligible. In the remaining years, the differences among the female categories are negligible, but between the unmarried women and the men there is a steady decrease in the size of the difference from 1959 through 1963, thereby supporting Bernard's expectations.[8]

We also compared mean incomes by field and sex and found that men earn noticeably more than women in only one field—education. In the other areas, the differences ranged from about $800 in the sciences to less than $400 in the humanities.

Our data are not completely comparable with the figures

TABLE 5   Type of Employment by Field, Sex, and Marital Status

Field, sex and marital status	Teaching	Research	Both	Other	Total N
			(in percent)		
Sciences					
Women					
Unmarried	31.7	35.2	28.9	4.2	141
Married	18.5	47.7	33.8	—	66
Married w/children	13.5	48.6	36.5	1.4	72
Men	15.5	38.1	39.2	7.2	97
Social Sciences					
Women					
Unmarried	38.7	11.6	23.1	26.7	215
Married	33.3	10.6	30.3	25.8	66
Married w/children	28.4	18.3	22.0	31.2	115
Men	46.3	8.8	23.1	21.8	147
Humanities					
Women					
Unmarried	79.6	—	14.2	6.2	158
Married	85.7	5.7	5.7	2.9	33
Married w/children	78.7	1.6	13.1	6.6	67
Men	75.6	—	9.8	14.6	82
Education					
Women					
Unmarried	56.2	2.2	15.7	25.9	325
Married	56.9	2.0	7.8	33.3	46
Married w/children	54.2	2.1	8.3	35.4	95
Men	38.3	3.1	13.6	45.1	162
Combined					
Women					
Unmarried	51.9	9.7	19.6	18.8	100 (839)
Married	42.9	18.9	22.1	16.1	100 (211)
Married w/children	41.5	17.4	19.7	21.5	100 (349)
Men	42.4	11.3	20.9	25.4	100 (488)

TABLE 6A   Mean Annual Income by Year, Sex, and Marital Status

	Year Ph.D. was received				
Sex and marital status	1958-59	1959-60	1960-61	1961-62	1962-63
Women					
Unmarried	9,960	9,600	9,410	9,210	8,900
Married	10,600	10,020	9,800	9,640	8,470
Married w/children	10,090	9,750	9,910	8,980	9,030
Men	10,030	10,920	10,640	10,380	9,690

reported by either Borchers or Bernard because not all of the salaries included in our mean are based on income from academic positions; salaries from private industry and government jobs are also included. But we noted earlier that in two of the fields (the natural sciences and the humanities) at least 85 percent of the respondents are employed by academic institutions. As a matter of fact, it is among the Ph.D.s in education, a field in which about 30 percent of the women and 45 percent of the men are *not* employed in academic institutions, that the differences between men and women are the greatest. Thus our data indicate that the differences of $1289 or $1000 between the salaries of men

TABLE 6B   *Mean Annual Income by Field, Sex, and Marital Status*

Sex and marital status	Field			
	Sciences	Social sciences	Humanities	Education
Women				
Unmarried	9,130	9,420	8,390	9,980
Married	9,090	10,110	7,871	10,470
Married w/children	9,000	10,200	8,152	9,980
Men	9,830	10,260	8,650	11,490

TABLE 6C

	Single Women	Married Women	Men
Assistant Professors			
Natural and biological sciences	9,277 (56)	9,039 (45)	9,188 (36)
Social sciences	9,334 (83)	9,060 (67)	9,336 (35)
Humanities	8,263 (80)	7,988 (62)	8,615 (37)
Education	9,131 (65)	8,859 (40)	10,007 (35)
Associate Professors			
Natural and biological sciences	8,990 (24)	8,292 (6)	10,381 (21)
Social sciences	10,006 (43)	10,184 (19)	10,712 (59)
Humanities	9,384 (43)	8,838 (20)	9,903 (36)
Education	10,244 (127)	9,998 (41)	10,888 (58)

and women in academia are exaggerated. Men probably earn about $700 a year more than women—a difference, nevertheless.

Concerning the distribution of professional ranks, our data show that among the unmarried women there are almost *five times* as many professors as there are instructors. Among the men the ratio is only slightly higher; there are more than *seven times* as many professors as there are instructors. It is among the married women that a reversal occurs. There is a higher proportion of instructors as compared to professors for both categories of married women.

As Table 7 indicates, when all ranks are compared within each field, the biggest difference between men and women occurs at the "associate professor" level. Married women are less likely than unmarried women to have been promoted to the rank of associate professor (in all fields except education, where there is little difference) and in the sciences (natural and social) married women are more likely to hold a non-professional position such as research associate.

The responses to the item asking about tenure are consistent with the findings about rank. Sex explains some of the differences, but marital status is the more crucial variable. Married women are less likely to have tenure than unmarried women.

When the proportion of men and women who have received tenure are compared by year of degree, we note that between unmarried women and men the male advantage decreases over time and that indeed by 1962-63 there is a reversal such that a higher proportion of women have tenure. The reversal comes about because of the greater likelihood of women in education receiving tenure early.

On the whole, the findings about tenure are consistent with the findings about income. On both measures, there appears to be a decrease in differential behavior between men and unmarried women Ph.D.s.

In summary, this analysis of the employment characteristics of the recent woman Ph.D. shows that in two of the fields she is employed at the same kinds of academic institutions as her male colleagues and in most instances she divides her duties between teaching and research in the same way that men do. Women with degrees in education are less likely than men to have administrative posts. However, they earn about $700 less a year than their male colleagues and they are less likely to be promoted or given tenure, especially if they are married. But there are signs that the income differential as well as the slower promotion rate and lack of tenure are decreasing among respondents who received their degrees more recently.

Relative productivity

Our two most direct measures of productivity are number of articles and number of books published as sole or senior author. Unfortunately, we have no measure of the quality or importance of the work done. In a survey of this type that kind of qualitative evaluation is difficult to obtain. Two additional measures of productivity are the numbers who have received research grants in their own name and those who do consulting work. Table 9 summarizes the findings pertaining to all the productivity measures. The first and third columns describe the percent who have not

TABLE 7　Professional Rank by Field, Sex, and Marital Status*

Field, sex, and marital status	Instructor	Assistant Professor	Associate Professor	Professor	Research Associate	Lecturer	Total N
				(in percent)			
Sciences							
Women							
Unmarried	4.6	38.9	17.6	8.3	27.9	2.8	105
Married	13.6	40.7	1.7	3.4	39.0	1.7	47
Married w/children	11.4	31.6	5.1	3.8	43.0	5.1	44
Men	——	52.6	26.3	7.0	10.5	3.5	59
Social Sciences							
Women							
Unmarried	2.1	51.0	25.2	13.3	7.7	.7	157
Married	10.9	52.2	10.9	6.5	15.2	4.3	41
Married w/children	9.6	39.5	14.9	6.1	18.4	11.4	71
Men	1.0	46.6	34.0	14.6	2.9	1.0	110
Humanities							
Women							
Unmarried	7.3	54.0	21.3	15.3	——	2.0	150
Married	10.3	62.1	24.1	3.4	——	——	29
Married w/children	24.3	45.7	8.6	7.1	——	14.3	62
Men	7.0	35.2	39.4	18.3	——	——	72
Education							
Women							
Unmarried	2.5	26.4	40.5	28.1	1.2	1.2	258
Married	——	40.0	40.0	20.0	——	——	31
Married w/children	10.9	32.9	30.1	16.4	1.4	8.2	57
Men	1.0	30.6	50.0	18.4	——	——	113
Combined							
Women							
Unmarried	3.9	40.4	28.8	18.5	6.8	1.6	100 (670)
Married	9.5	47.3	16.0	7.7	17.8	1.8	100 (148)
Married w/children	13.4	37.5	14.6	8.0	16.7	9.8	100 (234)
Men	2.1	40.3	38.6	15.2	2.7	.9	100 (354)

*The percentages in this table are based on the number of respondents employed at academic institutions.

published at all and the second and fourth columns give mean number of publications among those who have published.

Respondents in the natural and physical sciences are more likely to have published than respondents in other fields, but between men and women or between married and unmarried women the differences are negligible. Concerning the mean number of articles published, the differences between men and women were slight (men are a little higher in the social sciences, humanities, and education, and about the same in the natural sciences). It is interesting, however, that in every field married women publish more than unmarried women.

Book publication follows the same pattern except that a smaller percentage have had a book or monograph published. Among those who have, men publish slightly more than unmarried women. But, again, married women do better than either men or unmarried women. Bernard mentions a woman's emotional involvement and time spent with children as one explanation for her lower productivity. Sensible as that explanation sounds, it does not appear to be consistent with the results in Table 9 which show that married women with and without children do better or at least as well as unmarried women.

Men are more likely to receive research grants than women (married and unmarried) in the social sciences and the humanities. In education there is no difference among any of the categories and in the natural sciences the proportions are about the same for unmarried women and men. Married women are less likely to receive grants. We have no measure of the proportions of men and women who applied for research grants so we cannot say whether the lower percentage of women who received grants in the social sciences and humanities is due to a higher rate of turn down than their male colleagues or to a lower productivity.

Neither sex nor marital status turned out to be a significant variable in explaining the likelihood of working as a consultant except in the humanities where men do better.

TABLE 8A   Tenure by Field, Sex, and Marital Status*

Sex and marital status	Sciences	Social sciences	Humanities	Education	Combined
			(in percent)		
Women					
Unmarried	28.3	34.0	36.5	61.1	42.2 (670)
Married	1.9	12.2	26.7	57.9	21.8 (148)
Married w/children	16.3	19.5	46.7	25.6	25.6 (234)
Men	31.5	46.8	45.6	53.9	46.3 (354)

TABLE 8B   Tenure by Year, Sex, and Marital Status*

| Sex and marital status | Year Ph.D. was received | | | | | Combined |
	1958-59	1959-60	1960-61	1961-62	1962-63	
			(in percent)			
Women						
Unmarried	58.5	52.3	47.6	34.0	30.4	44.2 (670)
Married	33.3	27.8	23.1	20.8	12.3	21.8 (148)
Married w/children	28.4	42.6	16.7	17.8	28.6	25.6 (234)
Men	69.2	60.8	44.6	33.8	23.2	46.3 (354)

*The percentages in Tables 8A and 8B are based on the numbers of respondents who are employed at academic institutions.

The main finding is that respondents in education are more likely to serve as consultants than respondents in other fields.

To summarize, of the four measures of productivity, the two most direct ones, numbers of articles and books published, married women publish as much or more than men, and unmarried women publish slightly less than men. The differences on the whole are not great. Of the proportion receiving research grants, men in two out of four disciplines are more likely to have received a grant. The likelihood of doing consulting work does not appear to be affected by sex except among respondents in the humanities.

Professional recognition

We used three measures of professional recognition, none of which are unambiguous: post-doctoral fellowships, memberships in honorary societies, and travel grants. Receiving a fellowship, for example,[9] is in one sense a sign of recognition. There are more applicants than recipients of fellowships and distribution is generally based on prior achievement, recommendations, expectations concerning future work and the like. But it is quite likely that in many instances a woman, especially a married woman with a husband on a university faculty, would be more likely to apply for a post-doctoral fellowship than a man. A married woman who is having difficulty finding employment because her husband is on the faculty of the only college or university in town, where there is a formal or informal anti-nepotism rule, would find a post-doctoral fellowship an extremely convenient way to pursue her professional career while waiting for or negotiating some more permanent position.

The figures in Table 10 partly confirm our guess. Women are more likely to be awarded fellowships than men. But the small portion of respondents in all categories who report receiving fellowships, and the fact that the married women are no more likely to receive fellowships than unmarried women suggest that fellowships are "purer" signs of recognition than we had thought originally and, therefore, strengthen our belief in their validity as an index of recognition or reward. This finding about the higher proportion of women who receive fellowships is consistent with results (about pre- and post-doctoral fellowships) reported by Knapp and Greenbaum in their study of "The Younger American Scholar: His Collegiate Origins."[10] They found that women receive university fellowships somewhat more frequently than men. Jessie Bernard reports that the National Science Foundation awards in 1959 "were given to women in about the same proportion as men."

The second measure of recognition, also reported in Table 10, is membership in an honorary society. The ambiguity in this measure is that in most instances membership is bestowed when the respondent is still a student and therefore it is not directly a sign of professional recognition. Also, among women, membership in an honorary society as an undergraduate might be more of an incentive to go on and do graduate work than it is for male undergraduates. Thus, membership in an honorary society might be best used as an indication of which females are likely to seek the Ph.D. rather than as a sign of excellence or professional competence. The figures in Table 10 confirm our expectations, but do not resolve the ambiguity. Women in all fields are more likely to have been elected to honorary societies than men.

The third measure, "Travel Grants," not only had the same doubtful validity that the fellowship measure had, but

TABLE 9   *Productivity Measures: Article and Book Publication, Research Grant and Consulting, by Field, Sex, and Marital Status*

Field, sex, and marital status	Percent published at least one article (1)	Mean number of articles (2)	Percent published at least one book (3)	Mean number of books (4)	Percent received at least one grant (5)	Percent consult (6)
Sciences						
Women						
Unmarried	83.3	5.8	10.1	1.1	35.9	14.2
Married	75.4	6.3	6.2	2.6	30.4	7.8
Married w/children	91.9	7.8	9.5	1.7	25.6	7.9
Men	88.8	6.1	10.2	1.5	36.7	15.5
Social Sciences						
Women						
Unmarried	59.3	4.0	23.1	1.8	23.4	34.1
Married	61.5	4.2	20.9	2.1	22.2	27.2
Married w/children	66.9	3.9	19.9	1.5	24.9	33.6
Men	55.9	4.6	30.3	1.8	35.4	31.5
Humanities						
Women						
Unmarried	47.0	2.8	22.6	1.3	21.0	15.2
Married	69.7	3.7	22.9	1.6	28.2	10.3
Married w/children	69.7	3.4	32.8	1.6	18.6	14.4
Men	50.0	4.3	27.7	1.6	32.9	26.8
Education						
Women						
Unmarried	51.2	3.5	23.5	1.6	15.3	42.6
Married	57.4	5.4	35.3	1.7	15.3	50.9
Married w/children	39.6	3.9	26.0	2.0	14.2	41.5
Men	44.2	5.1	22.2	1.8	14.2	44.4
Combined						
Women						
Unmarried	57.9	4.1	21.1	1.6	21.9	30.6
Married	66.2	5.3	20.2	1.9	24.0	24.0
Married w/children	63.9	4.3	21.8	1.7	21.9	27.7
Men	57.5	5.2	23.1	1.7	28.2	32.2

in addition, less than 5 percent of all the respondents reported receiving travel grants. With such a small overall proportion, there is little to be said about the differences by sex or marital status and we did not bother to report the figures.

In summary, of the three rather vague measures of professional recognition, we found that for two of them, fellowships and election to honorary societies, women did proportionately better than men. The third measure, travel grants, yielded too small a return to make any comparisons worth while.

Professional identification

The last measure of the professional characteristics of the woman Ph.D. concerns her identification with her field. Professional identification should provide some measure of involvement or commitment to one's career suggesting at least a partial answer to the question of how seriously the woman Ph.D. takes her career. The implication would be that the greater her commitment, the harder she works, and the more she produces.

We used four indices of professional identification; subscription to at least one professional journal; membership in the professional organization representative of the discipline; membership on a committee in a professional organization; and office holding in a professional organization. The last two might also be considered as signs of professional recognition. We found that almost everyone (that is over 90 percent of the respondents in each category) is a member of at least one professional organization and a subscriber to at least one professional journal, women (married and unmarried) no less than men. Table 11 describes only the findings pertaining to the last two measures: committee

TABLE 10   *Professional Recognition: Fellowship and Honorary Society Membership by Field, Sex and Marital Status*

Field, sex and marital status	Received at least one fellowship (1)	Member of an honorary society (2)
	(in percent)	
Sciences		
Women		
Unmarried	22.6	56.3
Married	16.7	55.1
Married w/children	16.8	44.2
Men	11.3	43.3
Social sciences		
Women		
Unmarried	7.6	36.7
Married	7.5	34.6
Married w/children	8.8	33.2
Men	4.3	14.0
Humanities		
Women		
Unmarried	7.9	26.5
Married	—	40.5
Married w/children	2.0	20.0
Men	2.6	6.6
Education		
Women		
Unmarried	2.8	48.0
Married	1.8	44.8
Married w/children	3.6	40.7
Men	2.6	15.4
Combined		
Women		
Unmarried	8.2	42.5
Married	7.9	44.2
Married w/children	8.8	35.2
Men	4.9	19.4

membership and office holding in a professional organization.

We note first that a higher proportion of respondents (men and women) in education are likely to be involved in the activities of their professional organization than respondents in other fields. (There are probably more organizations, more committees, and more offices to be filled in education than in other fields.) But in education, as well as in the other fields, unmarried women are more likely to serve on committees and to hold offices in professional organizations than either men or married women. While none of our data explains the greater propensity for unmarried women to participate in committee and organizational work, it seems reasonable to look to the fewer demands

that are made on their time as compared to married women who have homes, husbands, and children to whom they are responsible. A full time job for most married women includes teaching, research, and writing. Most of them probably regard committee work as the most expendable part of their professional roles. Men, on the other hand, probably give greater priority to committee work than do married women, and such work competes not too successfully against time that can be devoted to research and writing. Thus, the unmarried woman who generally is more people-orientated than her male colleague and who has greater social needs than married women or men (almost all of them are married) turns to committees and organizations to help fill her social needs as well as to derive a sense of integration with her professional role. We do have responses to one additional item that support this explanation. We found that unmarried women are also more active in com-

TABLE 11   *Professional Identification: Member of a Committee and Office Holder in a Professional Organization by Field, Sex, and Marital Status*

Field, sex and marital status	Committee member (1)	Office holder (2)
Sciences		
Women		
Unmarried	14.4	19.8
Married	11.3	11.3
Married w/children	5.5	6.9
Men	15.5	15.7
Social Sciences		
Women		
Unmarried	27.5	31.2
Married	28.6	24.4
Married w/children	17.8	16.0
Men	17.9	17.5
Humanities		
Women		
Unmarried	27.0	33.3
Married	18.4	26.3
Married w/children	29.0	26.6
Men	18.1	27.7
Education		
Women		
Unmarried	58.0	57.2
Married	56.4	61.8
Married w/children	42.6	45.1
Men	38.3	42.9
Combined		
Women		
Unmarried	37.1	39.9
Married	28.2	29.2
Married w/children	21.6	21.2
Men	24.2	27.8

munity and fraternal organizations than either married women or men.

Concluding remarks

Our findings on such basic issues as the type of work the woman Ph.D. is engaged in, the institutions she is likely to be employed by, the salary and professional rank she achieves indicate that while there are some differences between her and her male colleagues, they are relatively small and they are decreasing. In so far as "formal rights" and objective measures of equality are concerned, the woman Ph.D. appears to be an accepted professional colleague.

Perhaps one explanation for her having achieved "formal equality" is her productivity and commitment to the profession. By various quantitative measures of productivity, the woman Ph.D. publishes as much as her male colleagues (married women, slightly more), she is involved in the activities of her professional organization, she is sought out as a consultant and she is more likely to be awarded fellowships and accepted in honorary societies.

A question that remains is: do women with doctorates on the faculties of colleges and universities have any legitimate basis for complaint? Can they make any reasonable case which would support a charge of discrimination? In their study of the *Academic Market Place* made ten years ago, Caplow and McGee claim that women scholars are not taken seriously and cannot look forward to a normal professional career. When they are hired, they are hired as teachers. They remain outside the prestige system entirely.

While these data do not support the specific factors mentioned by Caplow and McGee, the authors may have touched a crucial issue: namely the "atmosphere" in which she works, her colleagues' perceptions of her intrinsic as well as her exchange value, and her acceptance into the "club." Perhaps it is among these factors that there is a basis for complaint and indignation. From comments that respondents have written on their questionnaires and from conversations with women faculty members, we suggest that the "problem" which bothers the woman Ph.D. who is a full time contributor to her profession is that she is denied many of the informal signs of belonging and recogni-

tion. These women report that even on such simple daily activities as finding someone to have lunch or take a coffee break with, or finding someone with whom she can chew over an idea, or on larger issues such as finding a partner with whom she can share a research interest, the woman Ph.D. has a special and lower status. Perhaps, then, it is in matters such as these that she has achieved less than full membership in the "club," and she is left with a feeling that she belongs to a minority groups which has not gained full acceptance.

NOTES

1. Paul Lazarsfeld and Wagner Thielens, *The Academic Mind*, New York: The Free Press, 1958; Theodore Caplow and Reece J. McGee, *The Academic Market Place*, New York: Basic Books, Inc., 1958; Robert H. Knapp and Joseph J. Greenbaum, *The Younger American Scholar: His Collegiate Origins*, Chicago: University of Chicago Press, 1953; Bernard Berelson, *Graduate Education in the United States.* New York: McGraw-Hill Book Co., 1960; Mabel Newcomer, *A Century of Higher Education for American Women*, New York: Harper Bros., Inc., 1959; Jessie Bernard, *Academic Women*, University Park: Pennsylvania University Press, 1964; Warren Hagstrom, *The Scientific Community*, New York, Basic Books, 1965.
2. Rita James Simon, Shirley M. Clark, Larry I. Tifft, "Of Nepotism, Marriage, and the Pursuit of an Academic Career," *Sociology of Education*, 39 (Fall, 1966), pp. 344-358.
3. Stanley Budner and John Meyer, "Women Professors," unpublished manuscript; and Nicholas Babchuk and Alan P. Bates, "Professor or Producer: The Two Faces of Academic Man," *Social Forces*, 40 (May, 1962), pp. 341-348.
4. About 30 percent of the respondents are employed in non-academic institutions (government agencies, private industries, hospitals, welfare institutions, etc.)
5. The "other" was most often checked by respondents who were not employed at academic institutions. It is usually indicative of some type of administrative work.
6. Gladys L. Borchers, "Some Investigations Concerning the Status of Faculty Women in America," V. Totaro, School of Education, University of Wisconsin, 1963, pp. 5-19, in *Women in College and University Teaching*.
7. Jessie Bernard, *op. cit.*, p. 180.
8. We also tested this hypothesis concerning the decreasing differential by comparing mean income by rank and fields among those in academic positions. In two of the fields the data supported the hypothesis. In the natural and social sciences, men with the rank of associate professor earned more than women of the same rank; but on the assistant professor level, the differences by sex were negligible. In the humanities and education, however, the differential enjoyed by men among the associate professors continued down to the level of assistant professor.
9. These are fellowships that have been awarded after the respondent has received his doctorate.
10. Knapp and Greenbaum, *op. cit.*, p. 72.

14 Women mathematicians and the creative personality

Ravenna Helson [1]

Women mathematicians are rare. It has been suggested by both mathematicians and psychologists, informally, that a *creative* woman mathematician would have a brain different from that of other women. A normal woman, others say, could not so reject the life of feeling and concreteness without stifling her originality in the process.

Yet creative women mathematicians do exist. It seemed possible that these women, if they were not "mutants," might show conspicuously the essential traits of the creative personality, without which they would not have overcome whatever barriers make their numbers so small. A study of these Ss, then, might contribute to our understanding of creativity, regardless of sex, and certainly to the appraisal of creativity in women, and women's potential for scientific accomplishment (Mattfeld & Van Aken, 1965).

This paper describes the personality, research style, and background of some 45 women mathematicians, a sample from an estimated 300 in the United States at the time of the study (Albert, 1957). Of the 45, 18 included virtually all creative women mathematicians in the United States.

The study is one of several which have been conducted by the Institute of Personality Assessment and Research in the area of the creative personality. Particular reference will be made to a companion study of creativity in male mathematicians (Helson, 1967; Helson & Crutchfield, 1970).

Method

SELECTION OF SAMPLE

Names of women, who had attended graduate school and obtained the PhD in mathematics between 1950 and 1960, were furnished by the following institutions: Bryn Mawr College, Cornell University, Stanford University, Yale University, University of California (Berkeley and Los Angeles), University of Oregon, University of Texas, and University of Washington. Mathematicians at these and other institutions also provided additional names, particularly of women they considered creative. Columbia University, Massachusetts Institute of Technology, New York University, Radcliffe, University of Chicago, University of Illinois, and University of Pennsylvania each produced at least two of these Ss.

The Ss were invited to participate by means of a letter which explained the long-term interest of the Institute in studying soundness, achievement, creativity, and other forms of high-level functioning, and its present interest in conducting studies of professional women. A small honorarium was offered. Of 53 invitations extended, 44 (83%) were accepted. Three of these Ss were tested later than the others, and their data are not included in all analyses. Three additional mathematicians, being wives of faculty members at the University of California (Berkeley), were asked to provide data only about their research style. The number of Ss thus varies between 41 and 47.

The creativity of each S was rated by mathematicians in her field of specialization. A 7-point scale was used, a rating of 4.0 signifying that S was about as creative as the author of an average research paper in a mathematical journal. An average of three ratings was obtained for each S. Fewer than three were obtained for several older women who had not published beyond their dissertation. Ratings were highly reliable. More than half of the Ss received ratings with a range of less than two, and only two Ss received ratings with a range of more than three. The distribution of ratings was as follows: 8 Ss received average ratings of 3.0 or below, 8 were rated between 3.0 and 4.0, 12 between 4.0 and 5.0, 8 between 5.0 and 6.0, and 8 above 6.0. The Ss rated above 5.0 were classified as "creative." The creative group thus consisted of women rated as clearly more creative than the author of an average research contribution in mathematics. Subsequent comments from mathematicians lead us to believe that there were no important omissions from the creative group.

In age, Ss ranged from 24 to 64, the average age being 41. Two-thirds were married. One-third had Jewish parents, and most of the rest were from Protestant backgrounds. Creative and comparison women did not differ in these respects, nor in quality of graduate school. As in the sample of male mathematicians (Helson & Crutchfield, 1970), foreign cultural influence was strong. Half of the creative Ss were born in Europe or Canada, and almost half of the Ss born in the United States had at least one parent born in Europe. The difference between creative and comparison Ss in foreign birth is significant at the .10 level. However,

Reprinted from Ravenna Helson, "Women Mathematicians and the Creative Personality," Journal of Consulting and Clinical Psychology, 36:2, 1971, pp. 210-220. This study was supported by a grant from the Carnegie Corporation of New York.

TABLE 1   *Professional Achievement of Creative and Comparison Women Mathematicians*

Achievement	Creative Ss	Comparison Ss	$\chi^{2\,a}$
Age first published paper submitted			
Under 25	10	2	13.06*
25 or older	6	26	
Number of research papers			
5 or more	12	3	15.98*
Fewer than 5	4	25	

[a] Yates' correction embodied.
* $p < .001$.

foreign-born and native-born creatives differ not at all in any of the characteristics that we shall report as significantly differentiating the creative from comparison Ss. The personality of the creative mathematician, among women, seems to cut across national boundaries.

PROCEDURE

Two weekend assessments were held at the Institute of Personality Assessment and Research, and two others in the East, at Bryn Mawr and Swarthmore Colleges. Staff observers and interviewers did not know which Ss were creative, and indeed the criterion judgments had not yet been obtained. The assessment included a great variety of tests and measures, and the following have been selected for range of coverage and to demonstrate the consistency with which some of the salient findings recur:

1. Intelligence: Concept Mastery Test (Terman, 1956) and Mechanical Comprehension Test (Bennett, 1951); the Wechsler Intelligence Scale was administered after the assessments as part of a larger study by MacKinnon and Hall (1968) of the relation between intelligence and creativity.
2. Overall personality characteristics: California Psychological Inventory (Gough, 1964); Minnesota Multiphasic Personality Inventory (Hathaway & McKinley, 1951); Type Indicator (Myers, 1962); staff observations recorded by means of the 100-item Clinical Q Sort (Block, 1961); Adjective Check List (Gough & Heilbrun, 1965).
3. Interests: Strong Vocational Interest Blank (Male Form) (Strong, 1959); Activities Check List (Gough & Hall, 1957).
4. Cognitive and aesthetic tests: Gottschaldt Figures, Street Gestalt, Insight Puzzles, and Masked Word Tests as adapted by Crutchfield (MacKinnon, Crutchfield, Barron, Block, Gough, & Harris, 1958); Unusual Uses and Match Problems Tests (Guilford, Wilson, Christensen, & Lewis, 1951); Art Scale (Barron & Welsh, 1952); Mosaic Construction Test (Hall, 1958).
5. Mathematical style: Mathematicians Q Sort (Helson, 1967).
6. Personal history: Personal history questionnaire and interview.[2]

7. Professional history: Professional history questionnaire.

Results

VALIDATION OF CRITERION

Several findings support the criterion in showing that the women classified as creative were indeed performing at a level superior to that of the comparison Ss and had done so in the past. The creatives received the PhD at an average age of 26.0, the comparison Ss at an average age of 28.5 ($p < .05$). The creatives submitted their first paper for publication at an earlier age (before the PhD rather than after), had published more papers, and had received more grants and fellowships since graduate school ($p < .01$). Some of these findings are illustrated in Table 1.

INTELLIGENCE

According to data obtained for a partial sample of the women mathematicians by MacKinnon and Hall (1968), the group had an average IQ on the Wechsler Adult Intelligence Scale of 131. Creative and comparison Ss did not differ significantly, but only seven creatives were tested. On the Concept Mastery Test, developed to measure the utilization and enrichment of high intelligence in adult cultural experience, the creatives had a mean score of 144, and the comparison women a mean of 126. By t test, the difference is significant at the .10 level (Table 2), and the correlation with criterion ratings of creativity (.31) reaches the .05 level. Since the average score for the Stanford gifted S was 137, for industrial research scientists, 118, and for military officers, 60, one may judge that the mathematicians' scores are high. The creative male mathematicians had a mean score of 148, which is very similar to that of the creative women.

The Bennett Mechanical Comprehension Test has repeatedly shown large sex differences in the ability to understand physical and mechanical relationships (Bennett & Cruikshank, 1942), and it has been supposed that sex differences in this ability contribute to the disinclination of women for the abstract sciences. The women mathematicians did well ($M = 32.7$) as compared with most women, although less well than a sample of about 90 men, most in middle management but some in research supervision ($M = 41.5$).[3] Military officers, whose low Concept Mastery scores were previously reported, had a mean on this test of 35.0. The creative and comparison women mathematicians did not differ (Table 2).

PERSONALITY CHARACTERISTICS

Inventories. On the California Psychological Inventory, the women mathematicians score slightly below the mean on measures of social poise and assurance, and have peak standard scores of about 65 on Psychological Mindedness and Achievement by Independence. The creative Ss show these characteristics somewhat more markedly than the comparison Ss.

As shown in Table 2, the creatives have higher scores than

TABLE 2   *Differences in Intelligence and Personality between Creative and Comparison Subjects*

Measure	Creative Ss		Comparison Ss		t	df
	M	SD	M	SD		
Intelligence						
Wechsler adult intelligence scale	128.3	7.5	132.6	9.2	—	25
Concept mastery	143.6	30.1	125.6	33.5	1.75	42
Mechanical comprehension	31.0	10.0	33.7	9.2	—	39
Personality						
California psychological inventory						
Flexibility	15.3	3.5	11.0	4.6	3.09**	39
Achievement via conformance	26.2	3.4	29.7	3.4	−3.16**	39
Communality	24.1	1.7	25.4	1.9	−2.28*	39
Minnesota multiphasic personality inventory						
Mean level	56.6	6.3	53.1	5.0	1.96*	41
Validity (F)	59.0	6.1	54.0	6.0	2.52*	41
Hypochondriasis	56.1	9.8	49.4	6.6	2.58*	41
Depression	60.0	9.9	51.1	9.7	2.76**	41
Masculinity-femininity	48.5	5.1	45.0	10.0	—[a]	41
Psychasthenia	58.4	9.3	51.2	6.8	2.84**	41
Schizophrenia	60.6	9.0	54.9	6.8	2.26*	41
Hypomania	48.8	11.6	54.9	7.5	−2.02*	41
Social introversion	63.9	10.8	56.6	9.9	2.20*	41
Repression (Welsh)	22.5	3.7	18.2	3.5	3.70***	41
Aesthetic measures						
Mosaic construction: artistic merit	54.0	12.5	39.9	17.1	2.06*	27
Art scale	28.1	12.5	26.9	15.4	—	41

[a] $F = 3.76$; $p < .01$
* $p < .05$ (two-tailed).
** $p < .01$.
*** $p < .001$.

comparison women on the Flexibility scale ($p < .01$) and lower scores on Achievement via Conformance ($p < .01$) and Communality ($p < .05$). On all three of these scales, their mean standard scores—69, 45, and 41, respectively—are the most extreme of any creative or comparison group studied at the Institute of Personality Assessment and Research. Though strongly motivated to create their own form and to express and validate their own ideas, then, the creative Ss do not like to perform routine duties, nor can they work well within a highly structured framework. They are not bound by, do not recognize, and perhaps somewhat stubbornly resist, conventional patterns.

On the Minnesota Multiphasic Personality Inventory, the profiles for creative and comparison Ss show little similarity. Although the comparison women have higher scores on the Hypomania scale ($p < .05$), the creatives have a higher "mean level" on the eight clinical scales (Table 2). On individual scales, they score higher on Validity (F), Hypochondriasis, Depression, Psychasthenia, Schizophrenia, and Social Introversion. Barron (1968) and MacKinnon (1962) have reported a similar elevated mean level for creative writers and architects. Since the women mathematicians, like the writers and architects, do not score low on measures of ego strength, the interpretations offered by Barron and MacKinnon seem to apply in this sample as well. To

some extent, the elevated scores may be taken to reflect complexity of personality and lack of defensiveness. However, as both of these authors go on to say, the creative Ss seem really to have more psychological difficulties than the comparison Ss, though they differ from most neurotic or psychotic patients in also having excellent resources for dealing with their troubles. It may be relevant to the apparent maladjustment of the creative women mathematicians and male writers and architects that all these Ss are in "cross-sex" fields (Roe & Siegelman, 1964). Creative male mathematicians had higher scores than comparison Ss only on the Hypochondriasis scale.

Creative men usually score high on the Masculinity-Femininity scale of the Minnesota Multiphasic Personality Inventory. The creative women are significantly less variable on this scale than the comparison Ss, and they are (insignificantly) more feminine (Table 2). The creatives have higher scores on the Repression factor (Welsh, 1956). The combination of high Repression and high Flexibility, as manifested on the California Psychological Inventory, is unusual. In this context, the high Repression would seem to reflect a rather rigid rejection of outside influences and attractions.

The Myers-Briggs Type Indicator shows the women mathematicians to be strongly introverted and intuitive, in the

TABLE 3   Clinical Q-Sort Items Correlated with Creativity Ratings

Q-sort item	Creativity*
Thinks and associates to ideas in unusual ways; has unconventional thought processes	.64
Judges self and others in conventional terms like "popularity," "the correct thing to do," social pressures, etc.	—.62
Is an interesting, arresting person	.55
Tends to be rebellious and nonconforming	.51
Genuinely values intellectual and cognitive matters	.49
Appears to have a high degree of intellectual capacity	.46
Is a genuinely dependable and responsible person	—.45
Behaves in a sympathetic or considerate manner	—.43
Is self-dramatizing; histrionic	.42
Has fluctuating moods	.40
Favors conservative values in a variety of areas	—.40
Is moralistic	—.40

* $p < .01$.

Jungian sense of these terms. The preference for thinking over feeling is very slight, particularly for the creatives. No differences between creative and comparison Ss on the scales of the Type Indicator reached the .05 level.

Staff observations. After the assessment weekend was over, at least five psychologist-observers performed a clinical Q sort for each S. Reliability was satisfactory. Of 100 items, the following had the highest average placements for the entire sample: Genuinely values intellectual and cognitive matters; Appears to have a high degree of intellectual capacity; Values own independence and autonomy; Is a genuinely dependable and responsible person; and Prides self on being objective and rational. Items correlated with the creativity criterion (Table 3) show the creatives to be more original, intellectual, narcissistic, and unconventional.

Ten psychologists described each S on the Adjective Check List. The creatives were described more frequently as individualistic, original, preoccupied, artistic, complicated, courageous, emotional, imaginative, and self-centered. Comparison Ss were described more frequently as cheerful, active, appreciative, considerate, conventional, cooperative, helpful, organized, realistic, reliable, and sympathetic ($p < .05$).

INTERESTS

On the Strong Vocational Interest Blank, the women mathematicians as a group had seven average scores in the A range, all in Groups I, II, VI, and X. Scales significantly correlated with the criterion ratings of creativity at the .01 level were Artist, Psychologist, Physicist, Author-Journalist, and (negatively) Mortician. The entire group was thus characterized by strong symbolic interests, and the creatives especially so.

On the Activities Check List, creatives and comparison Ss expressed *strong* interest in about the same number of leisure activities, but the comparison Ss indicated a *moderate* interest in many more activities than the creatives ($p < .01$). Creatives were more homogeneous than comparison Ss in their strong interests, which were mostly intellectual in nature. More than half of the creatives checked Attending concerts, Listening to classical records, Going to

plays, Reading the classics, Other reading, and Hiking. The only activity in which half of the comparison group expressed strong interest was Going to plays.

Other measures of interests on the professional history questionnaire seem to show that the creatives had simplified their lives to a few things about which they cared very much. They spent most of their time in research and homemaking; they spent less time than comparison Ss in teaching, administration, community activities, and politics ($p < .05$).

COGNITIVE AND AESTHETIC MEASURES

Although the creatives showed a slight superiority on most of the cognitive tests (see Procedure section), few differences reached even the .10 level of significance. However, mosaic designs made by the creatives were judged as having more artistic merit and as more pleasing than those by comparison women (Table 2). Judges were faculty members from the University of California departments of art and of design. The creative and comparison Ss did not differ significantly on the Art Scale. Both groups scored about the same as creative men mathematicians, higher than the comparison men, and lower than creative writers and architects.

MATHEMATICAL STYLE

In performing the Mathematicians Q Sort, S placed 56 items about professional interests and attitudes according to a forced normal distribution, judging how characteristic each statement was of her own orientation. Items placed highest by 18 creatives and 28 comparison Ss show little overlap. The creatives seem to show a greater involvement in research, more participation of the unconscious in the research process, less interest in interpersonal communication, and less orderliness (Table 4).

PERSONAL HISTORY

The personal history findings have been evaluated by χ^2. Results significant at the .10 level of confidence are included, since most of them deal with important variables for which precise and differentiated measures are not avail-

TABLE 4   Items from Mathematicians' Q Sort Differentiating Creative and Comparison Women

Q-sort items	t
Items placed higher by creative Ss (N = 18)	
Subordinates other things to research goals; puts these values above all others	3.24**
Is thorough and patient in approach to research issues; does not get upset if progress is slow	2.86**
Research interests lie within a rather narrow range	2.70**
Must exert effort to express a mathematical train of thought in words	2.67**
Work is characterized by inventiveness and ingenuity	2.55*
Solution to a problem often comes from an unexpected direction	2.11*
Items placed higher by comparison Ss (N = 28)	
Has a need to teach; enjoys instructing and working with students	3.34**
Grasps other people's ideas quickly	3.05**
Desire for a salary increase is an important motivating factor	2.98**
Interested in philosophical problems which arise in mathematics	2.71**
Has an active, efficient, well-organized mind	2.58**
Has an interest and talents appropriate for writing on mathematics for intelligent laymen	2.38*
Is neat and orderly in habits and manner of work	2.18*

* $p < .05$ (two-tailed).
** $p < .01$.

able. Answers to open-ended questions were rendered anonymous and evaluated independently by two raters.

Two-thirds of the fathers of the creative women were professional men, whereas most of the fathers of comparison women were businessmen or skilled workers ($p < .01$). However, the creatives frequently described their family's socioeconomic position as having been poor or insecure. The lawyer could not collect his fees, the engineer was unemployed, the professor died, etc. (Table 5).

The fathers of the creatives tended to have received more education than the fathers of comparison Ss ($p < .10$), and a disparity in education between father and mother was more frequent in the creative group ($p < .05$). In the sample of male mathematicians, both fathers and mothers of creative Ss were more highly educated than the parents of comparison Ss.

Whereas more creative than comparison men mathematicians had been eldest children, what tended to distinguish the creative women in sibling relationships was that very few of them had a brother. In families of fewer than five children, even the exceptions are interesting. One creative had an elder brother but no father, one had a brother 10 years younger, and one had a brother 2 years younger.

The personal history interviewers used checklists to describe the salient features of the home background of the Ss. Although the home backgrounds had in common an almost universal emphasis on intellectual and cultural values, the pattern was a little different for the two groups. Items checked for more than one-third of the creatives were, in order of frequency, as follows: father had strong intellectual and cultural values; father was dominant in the family; and mother had strong intellectual and cultural values. The items checked for more than one-third of the comparison Ss were these: mother had strong intellectual and cultural values; father had strong intellectual and cultural values; father was a warm person; and mother was dominant in the family. The interviewers judged more creative than comparison women to have identified primarily with the father ($p < .05$).

Asked to evaluate factors in the origin of the Ss interest in mathematics, the interviewers more frequently checked for creatives "sublimation of curiosity about the body and its functions" or "satisfaction of need for autonomy in fantasy," whereas for comparison Ss, they more frequently checked "reaction formation to primitive expressiveness" or "withdrawal" (Table 5).

Most of the Ss did well in school, and many of them had been regarded as precocious children. During adolescence and in college, the creatives had a stronger intellectual orientation than the comparison Ss, more of whom were concerned with physical appearance or social relationships (Table 5). However, the years in graduate school were described as a period of social expansion by more creative than comparison Ss.

PROFESSIONAL ACHIEVEMENT OF CREATIVE MEN AND WOMEN

In age at PhD and age of submitting the first published paper (Table 1), the creative women did not differ from the 34 creative men studied by Helson and Crutchfield (1970b). However, at the time of the study, the creative men had published more papers ($p < .01$). They also held important positions at prestigeful universities. Only two or three of the creative women taught graduate students, and one-third, including some of the highest rated, had no regular position at all. Several had young children. Most of those married were married to mathematicians, so that nepotism was a frequent problem.

Marriage would thus seem to have been a handicap to the careers of the creative women. However, 6 of 11 creatives (and 4 of 19 comparison Ss) named their husband as the greatest asset in their work lives. He provided intellectual or mathematical companionship, they said, or a circle of mathematical friends.

On the California Psychological Inventory, the creative men and women have similar profiles, except that the men are higher on measures of social poise and assurance—on Dominance, Sociability, Social Presence ($p < .05$), and Self-acceptance ($p < .01$). The men also have higher scores on Intellectual Efficiency ($p < .05$) and lower scores, of course, on Femininity ($p < .001$). On the Strong Vocational Interest Blank, the creative men have higher scores on the scales for YMCA Physical Director, YMCA Secretary, Office Man, Mortician, and Sales Manager. The women have higher scores on scales for Artist, Architect, Mathematician, Physicist, and Chemist ($p < .01$).

On the Mathematicians' Q Sort, creative men placed the following items higher ($p < .01$): Has interests and talents for writing on mathematics for intelligent laymen; Desire for a salary increase is an important motivating factor; Has an earnest desire to "make a mark" in mathematics; and Is flexible and adaptable in his thinking, able to shift and restructure easily. Creative women placed higher ($p < .01$) the following items: Is somewhat deficient in command of basic sources and technical literature; Research interests lie within a rather narrow range; Does not enjoy collaboration; Must exert effort to express a mathematical train of thought in words; Is more interested in discrete problems than in continuous ones and Lacks confidence, is afraid to strike out in new directions.

These findings reflect the differences in professional status between the two groups, but other factors may be involved also. Support has been demonstrated elsewhere for the hypothesis that the creative men and women mathematicians have distinctive research styles which differ in level of ego control and degree of unconscious participation in the research process (Helson, 1967).

Discussion

First, the findings offer no support for the idea that creative women mathematicians are "mutants" with cognitive abilities different from those of other women PhDs in mathematics. Neither do the findings show the creative women to be more masculine, if one means by this that they might have been expected to score higher on measures of masculinity-femininity, or dominance, assertiveness, or analytical ability. We cannot evaluate the hypothesis that the creative Ss may have had some greater specific talent for higher mathematics (Revész, 1940) which was only slightly reflected in intelligence measures. However, the many large differences between the creative and comparison Ss in background and personality would seem to indicate that personality characteristics are powerful determinants of creativity in women mathematicians.

The traits most characteristic of the creative women would seem to be these (a) rebellious independence, narcissism, introversion, and a rejection of outside influence; (b) strong symbolic interests and a marked ability to find self-expression and self-gratification in directed research activity; (c) flexibility, or lack of constriction, both in general attitudes and in mathematical work.

These traits have all been ascribed to the creative person, regardless of sex, but they appear more clearly in creative women mathematicians than they do in creative men mathematicians (Helson & Crutchfield, 1970a, 1970b). Among the creative men, some were original, flexible, ambitious, but essentially conventional individuals. One may suppose

TABLE 5   Personal History: Creative and Comparison Women

Personal history	Creative Ss	Comparison Ss	χ^2 [a]
Place of birth			
United States	8	23	3.63
Other	8	5	
Occupation of father			
Professional	12	7	8.44**
Other	4	21	
Economic position of family			
Poor or insecure	8	5	3.63
Other	8	23	
$\phi = .79$			
Education of parents			
Father more educated than mother	11	7	5.84*
Other	5	20	
Sex of siblings (small families)			
Brother	3	14	2.92
No siblings or sister(s) only	10	10	
Father was warm person			
Checked	3	14	2.98
Not checked	13	14	
Identification with parents			
Primarily with father	10	7	4.80*
Other	5	19	
Origin of interest in mathematics			
Sublimation or satisfaction of need for autonomy in fantasy	10	8	4.14*
Other	4	17	
Most important aspect of college			
Intellectual growth or discovery	12	7	8.44**
Other	4	21	
$\phi = .84$			
Development in graduate school			
Expansion of social interests stressed	11	8	5.16*
Not stressed	5	20	
$\phi = .65$			

[a] Yates' correction embodied.
* $p < .05$.
** $p < .01$.

that a conventional woman would never develop the concentration, the "purity of motive" (Ghiselin, 1952), which seems to be necessary for a new symbolic structure to emerge. A rejection of outside influence and a cathexis of symbolic activity would seem to support, or constitute, purity of motive. Although one would expect to find this complex of traits in creative persons of either sex, it shows more clearly—being more necessary—in the creative women. The third characteristic, flexibility, may be interpreted as a lack of conflict in the person's basic goals. There is cooperation between the ego and the life of impulse; the individual has his own will, and his conditions of life harmonize with his work. That the creative women sought and to a considerable degree attained an integration and simplification of life, despite obstacles, would appear to be one of the important findings of the study. The fact that the creative person can attain a high degree of integration while also manifesting a high level of pathology may perhaps be related to the extreme concentration on the world of symbols. There is a rapproachement between conscious and unconscious, but the separation from people or from society is not overcome, and indeed it may maintain the creative motivation.

It could be argued that the creative women mathematicians manifest the essential characteristics of the creative person. Do their life histories also show us the essential conditions which mold the creative personality? Let us keep this question in mind as we review the main findings about background factors and personal history.

Almost all of the women mathematicians grew up in homes with strong respect for learning and cultural values. Most of them, as little girls, must have been rewarded for intellectual successes. That many *Ss* grew up outside the United States, or had at least one parent who was European, suggests that they were able to avoid some anti-intellectual influences of the mainstream of American culture.

The comparison *Ss* grew up in homes they considered secure. Their fathers, described as warm in about half the cases, were usually businessmen or skilled workers. The mothers were as well educated as the fathers, and the *Ss* identified primarily with their mothers. In some cases, a shy, intelligent girl found that mathematics was a subject in which she could excel, and the standards of her family—sometimes the rather narrow standards of the immigrant trying to make good—encouraged her to pursue scholastic excellence in a conventional way. In other cases, the child seemed concerned to defend herself against impulse, and to use mathematics for this purpose. There were, of course, other patterns which attained less statistical prominence.

The background of the creative *Ss* was different in a number of respects. Financial insecurity was common. The father was a professional man. He was seldom a warm person, and there was a differential in intellectual status between the father and mother. Except in large families, there was usually no brother. The interviewer judged that *S* identified more with the father than with the mother, and that in coping with her problems she used sublimation and a search for autonomy in fantasy rather than repressive techniques.

One forms the picture of a very intelligent child who was attracted by her father's intellectual status, felt alienated from her mother, adopted her father's attitudes toward work and achievement but received relatively little attention or affection from him. Isolated from both parents, she developed the strategy of making herself autonomous by nurturing, gratifying, and "growing" herself in symbolic activity. Though such a scheme describes a few creatives well, in many cases it seems to omit important special factors—that this girl had bouts of deafness, that this father was psychotic, that this motherless child resented the fact that she and her sister had to do all the housework while her brothers were a privileged elite.

Nevertheless, the personality and background characteristics reported in this study are similar to those obtained for a very different sample of creative women—college seniors, most of whom were interested in the arts and social sciences (Helson, 1966, 1968). In these studies, data were available from parents and siblings as well as from the creative and comparison women themselves. Ambivalence toward the mother, the need for autonomy, and the development of strong symbolic interests, a father who seems to have modeled the use of intellectual activity for self-expression and for purpose in life—this constellation recurs. Several parts of this pattern of findings have also been reported by Anastasi and Schaefer (1969) in a study of creative adolescent women. The importance of the father, as revealed in autobiographies of several outstanding women mathematicians of the past, has been emphasized by Plank and Plank (1954).

Most boys, of course, undergo an estrangement from the mother as a part of acquiring a masculine identity. This estrangement, termed independence, is eased by considerable social support, and the main obstacle to the development of a creative personality in men seems to be that what the mother represents will be devalued and repressed too much, so that pleasure in imaginative play or attention to feeling is rejected as feminine. Thus one finds among the men mathematicians that the mother is described with more respect and warmth by the creative men than by the comparison *Ss*. In a sense, it would seem that respect for the mother encourages a cathexis of symbolic activity in the boy, whereas a lack of respect may engender it in the girl. This statement contains some suggestive implications, but it is an oversimplification; a responsible comparison of the development of the creative personality in boys and girls would require a more extended discussion than the scope of the present paper allows. It shall be left as a hypothesis (which owes much to Rank, 1945) that the creative boy or girl experiences an estrangement in the primary milieu, a disadvantageous position from which he (or she) makes an adjustment away from people, seeking to have his own will and provide his own security and emotional satisfaction in intellectual activity, and retaining the hope of bringing about a reconciliation in the symbolic medium.

In the introduction, the question was raised as to how a woman could so suppress her feminine nature to be a mathematician without suppressing her originality also. Part of the answer seems to be that the women mathematicians are introverts, whose "natures" are not the modal American type. Beyond this, the creative women differed from the comparison *Ss* in their ability to express themselves rather fully and freely in creative activity, with emotional involvement, rather than emotional restriction, and with considerable participation from the unconscious.

The present study does not clarify why so few women in this country go into higher mathematics. The reasons may be deep seated and perhaps innate. However, the extent of foreign birth and parentage in the whole sample, and the degree to which the creative women were found to be rejecting of outside influence—these findings suggest that countervailing social pressures are strong.

Pribram (1963) seems to conceive the question of how women could be creative as that of how women could be made into men "in the best sense of the word." He fears the process would be agonizing if not impossible. However, this difficult approach does not seem necessary. Creative men and women show many similarities in basic personality. It is true that each group has characteristics of its own. Creative men mathematicians are more outgoing, self-accepting, and masterful. It seems very likely that these traits interact with strong symbolic interests, independence, etc., to bring about forceful direct assaults on difficult problems, critical breadth, a high level of productivity, etc. Even under optimal circumstances, creative women might be expected to make a contribution different in type from that of creative men. Of course, it should be noted that among creative men mathematicians, the most creative were not the most outgoing, self-accepting, and efficient. In any event, confidence and effectiveness would seem to be enhanced by success and cultural support. The striking differences between creative men and women in professional status and in productivity after graduate school seem to reflect social roles and institutional arrangements more than fundamental creative traits.

NOTES

1. Requests for reprints should be sent to Ravenna Heson, Institute of Personality Assessment and Research, University of California, Berkeley, California 94720.
2. Interviewers were Frank Barron, John D. Black, Peter Madison, Harold R. Renaud, Silvan S. Tompkins, George S. Welsh, and Charles Wenar.
3. The author is grateful to Harrison G. Gough for access to data for this comparison group.

REFERENCES

Albert, A. A. (Chm.) A survey of research potention and training in the mathematical sciences. Final report of the Committee on the Survey, Part I. Chicago: University of Chicago, 1957.

Anastasi, A. & Schaefer, C. E. Biographical correlates of artistic and literary creativity in adolescent girls. *Journal of Applied Psychology*, 1969, 53, 267-273.

Barron, F. *Psychology and personal freedom.* Princeton, N.J.: Van Nostrand, 1968.

Barron, F., & Welsh, G. S. Artistic perception as a possible factor in personality style: Its measurement by a figure preference test. *Journal of Psychology*, 1952, 33, 199-203.

Bennett, G. K. *Mechanical Comprehension Test Form BB.* (Rev. ed.) New York: Psychological Corporation, 1951.

Bennett, G. K., & Cruikshank, R. Sex differences in the understanding of mechanical problems. *Journal of Applied Psychology*, 1942, 26, 121-127.

Block, J. *The Q-sort method in personality assessment and psychiatric research.* Springfield, Ill.: Charles C. Thomas, 1961.

Ghiselin, B. (Ed.) *The creative process.* Los Angeles: University of California Press, 1952.

Gough, H. G. *Manual for the California Psychological Inventory.* (Rev. ed.) Palo Alto: Consulting Psychologists Press, 1964.

Gough, H. G., & Hall, W. B. *The Activities Check List.* Berkeley: University of California, Institute of Personality Assessment and Research, 1957.

Gough, H. G., & Heilbrun, A. B., Jr. *The Adjective Check List manual.* Palo Alto, Calif.: Consulting Psychologists Press, 1965.

Guilford, J. P., Wilson, R. S., Christensen, P. R., & Lewis, D. J. A factor-analytic study of creative thinking: Hypotheses and descriptions of tests. In *Reports from the Psychological Laboratory, No. 4.* Los Angeles: University of Southern California, April 1951.

Hall, W. B. The development of a technique for assessing aesthetic predispositions and its application to a sample of professional research scientists. Paper presented at the meeting of the Western Psychological Association, Monterey, Calif., April 1958.

Hathaway, S. R., & McKinley, J. C. *Minnesota Multiphasic Personality Inventory manual.* New York: Psychological Corporation, 1951.

Helson, R. Personality of women with imaginative and artistic interests: The role of masculinity, originality, and other characteristics in their creativity. *Journal of Personality*, 1966, 34, 1-25.

Helson, R. Sex differences in creative style. *Journal of Personality*, 1967, 35, 214-233.

Helson, R. Effects of sibling characteristics and parental values on creative interests and achievement. *Journal of Personality*, 1968, 36, 589-607.

Helson, R., & Crutchfield, R. S. Creative types in mathematics. *Journal of Personality*, 1970, 38, 177-197. (a)

Helson, R., & Crutchfield, R. S. Mathematicians: The creative researcher and the average PhD. *Journal of Consulting and Clinical Psychology*, 1970, 34, 250-257. (b)

MacKinnon, D. W. The personality correlates of creativity: A Study of American architects. In G. S. Nielsen (Ed.), *Proceedings of the XIV International Congress of Applied Psychology, Copenhagen, 1961.* Vol. 2. Copenhagen: Munksgaard, 1962.

MacKinnon, D. W., Crutchfield, R. S., Barron, F., Block, J., Gough, H. G., & Harris, R. E. *An assessment study of Air Force Officers: Part I. Design of the study and description of the variables.* (Tech. Rep. WADC-TR-58-91 (I), ASTIA Document No. AD 151 040) Lackland Air Force Base, Tex.: Wright Air Development Center, Personnel Laboratory, April 1958.

MacKinnon, D. W., & Hall, W. B. Intelligence and creativity. In D. W. MacKinnon (Ed.), *A study of three aspects of creativity, IPAR report to the Carnegie Corporation of New York.* Berkeley, Calif.: Institute of Personality Assessment and Research, 1968.

Mattfeld, J. A., & Van Aken, C. G. *Women and the scientific professions.* Cambridge: M.I.T. Press, 1965.

Myers, I. B. *Manual (1962) for the Myers-Briggs Type Indicator.* Princeton, N.J.: Educational Testing service, 1962.

Plank, E. H., & Plank, R. Emotional components in arithmetic learning, as seen through autobiographies. *The Psychoanalytic Study of the Child*, 1954, 9, 274-296.

Pribram, K. H. What is a woman. In S. M. Farber & R. H. L. Wilson (Eds.), *The potential of women.* New York: McGraw-Hill, 1963.

Rank, O. *Will therapy and truth and reality.* (Trans. by J. Taft) New York: Knopf, 1945.

Revész, G. The indivisibility of mathematical talent. *Acta Psychologica*, 1940, 5,(2-3), 1-21.

Roe, A., & Siegelman, M. *The origin of interests.* Washington, D.C.: American Personnel & Guidance Association, 1964.

Strong, E. K., Jr. *Manual for Strong Vocational Interest Blanks for men and women, revised blanks (Forms M and W.)* Palo Alto: Consulting Psychologists Press, 1959.

Terman, L. M. *Concept Mastery Test, manual, Form T.* New York: Psychological Corporation, 1956.

Wechsler, D. *Manual for the Wechsler Adult Intelligence Scale.* New York: Psychological Corporation, 1955.

Welsh, G. S. Factor dimensions A and B. In G. S. Welsh & W. G. Dahlstrom (Eds.), *Basic readings on the MMPI in psychology and medicine.* Minneapolis: University of Minnesota Press, 1956.

15 *The study of sex roles*

Shirley S. Angrist

For some years, behavioral scientists have played an ambivalent love affair with role theories. As a way of describing patterned behavior, they find role concepts relevant, useful, and handy—but also inadequate, muddled and overly simple. As Levinson (1959) said: "The concept of role remains one of the most overworked and underdeveloped in the social sciences." Discussions of this ambivalence about role theories are well documented in the literature and I will not dwell on them here. The key dilemmas in role analysis research could be summarized as follows:

. . . The terminology is various, inconsistent and only partly overlapping in usage. It is true that the core ideas have involved three elements: (a) role behavior based on role expectations of relevant others; (b) expectations keyed to a specific role; (c) a social location or interaction system for role expectations and behavior (Gross, 1958). However, the term role itself has been taken to mean different things: observable behavior, expectations for behavior (typically required behavior for the role incumbent), norms for behavior (what incumbent's behavior ought to be), or even some combinations of these.

. . . The context in which roles can be located ranges widely from the whole society to the narrowly dyadic group. Models of actors in their social location as role incumbents typically indicate reciprocity of the structural relationship between: man-woman, mother-child, teacher-pupil. In so doing, the interaction and influence between sets of role actors and their reciprocals is assumed to occur in a shared arena for the relationship. Thus, research has tended to concentrate on roles easily locatable, e.g., within the nuclear family or work settings. The society-wide role types, such as "male," "adult," "intellectual," have been notably more difficult to study in role theory terms.

Definitions of sex role

It has been proposed that role has three separate foci according to the main fields utilizing the construct. Gordon (1966) suggests that the anthropological, psychological, and sociological core meanings are respectively: position, behavior, and relationship. Supposing we take this three-pronged look beyond generic role to ask: what is meant by sex role?

The prime conclusions which emerge from such an inquiry are that sex role is rarely defined, the attempted definitions vary widely, the construct lacks clarity, and the three fields reveal overlap in usage. Still there is some differential emphasis as suggested in Table 1.

When sex role refers to a position, it *de facto* stresses the position's location in a highly structural social context. Indeed, strongly tied to Linton's (1945) classical definitive formulation, and utilized widely in anthropological field studies, the positional meaning dwells on sex as ascribed and tied to age groups. The ascriptive quality is elaborated in definitions of sex roles as "recruitment roles" and "non-relational" (Nadel, 1957; Banton, 1965). The prescriptions for appropriate behavior are assumed to be widely held and agreed upon. Further, the whole society is used for locating sex role; this jibes with the gestalt-type descriptive analyses of primitive societies. The main content thrust of this approach is the division of labor in society, with standards of appropriateness for the apportioning and fulfillment of tasks by sex and age (Mead, 1935; Murdock, 1966; Southall, 1959).

The overlap is evident

However, the aforementioned overlap in utilization of the sex role construct is also evident. Thus, in sociological studies, the positional meaning of sex role is apparent in groups smaller than whole societies: e.g., in small groups, involving study of the sorting out of tasks and special behaviors (Bales, 1958), in large-scale organizations, like legislatures and school systems (Gehlen, 1967; Gross, 1958), and in the American nuclear family division of tasks between husband and wife (Blood, 1960; Nye, 1963). It may be concluded that the sex role-as-position meaning is difficult to apply, if not irrelevant, to less structured settings where expectations are not largely consensual and organized, and behavior is not normatively based (Gross, 1958; Newcomb, 1950).

The view common in social psychological approaches assumes the universality of sex differences—their respective biological characteristics, however culturally elaborated, are the basis for polar behavior and attribute models. Stress is on behavior as measured by variables like school achieve-

Edited from Shirley Angrist, "The Study of Sex Roles," Journal of Social Issues, 25*:1, 1969, pp. 215-232.*

TABLE 1   Meanings and Usage of Sex Role

Meaning of sex role	Core definition	Emphasis	Social location
Position	Normatively appropriate expectations for M & F	Division of labor of group or societal tasks	Structured settings
Behavior	What M and F do and are like	Personality, abilities, preferences	Setting need not be relevant
Relationship	The process of role taking	Socialization and interaction	Dyad or larger groups with varying structure

ment, occupational choices, play object preferences, and on behavior-related attributes of the individual—personality, adjustment, need achievement, aspirations. Girls perform better on verbal tests, achieve higher grades; boys excel in science, mathematics and mechanical ability. Girls are more fearful and nervous, while boys have greater achievement needs and higher aspirations (See Brown, 1965, and Wigney, 1965, for summaries of relevant research). The behavioral focus is operationally tidy. The resultant dichotomies seem to reinforce the clusters of sex-related characteristics: women are women and men are men wherever they may live, eat, play, work or interact. However, developmental features of sex-related behaviors are accounted for as some researches emphasize age or stage as a factor (Emmerich, 1961; Wallace, 1966). The issue raised then is the validity of universal sex role behavior measures without regard to the delineations of other impinging characteristics or to the pertinent social location.

For sociology role theory is relevant

For the sociological approach, the setting for role-taking is indeed relevant and specified. Sex role grows out of self-development during the socialization process. The individual interacting with others learns his own and others' roles. He discovers and interprets behavior, revising temporarily fixed roles (Cottrell, 1942; Parsons, 1955; Mead, 1934; Sarbin, 1954; Turner, 1962). The difficulty lies in defining all the features pertinent to comprehension of the relationship between the role-taker and the others in the context. Group size and degree of structure immediately must be considered. Theoretically, any group can be studied, ranging from dyad to whole society. In practice, research on relationships has been most feasible in highly defined social locations (Angrist, 1968; Farber, 1959; Stryker, 1962). As Stryker pointed out, one cannot assume as Mead did that all social groups have rational orientations, utilitarian goals and highly organized structure. To specify daughter-in-law or ex-patient wife seems sufficiently concrete indication of the role-taker and the relevant others. But perhaps it is more accurate to zero in on the social specifics: e.g., a Polish Catholic first generation urban American young newly married couple as the nuclear family type in which the wife is being studied.

Thus, the deficiencies of role theories burden the sex role construct no less. Indeed, sex role epitomizes some difficulties: the many definitional stances, fuzzy empirical referents, and over-emphasis on delimited social arenas for studying roles. Sex role singularly suffers from absence of specific definition—its meaning is connotative instead of denotative. As several observers note concerning American society, there exists little consensus on the content of sex roles, especially for women (Goode, 1960a; Gross, 1958; Parsons, 1942). The definitional weakness may mirror the hardship of specifying and studying that which is rapidly changing, blurred and highly variant in form. In that sense, the social location problem is tied to the definitional one: how to pinpoint what is vaguely describable? How to describe what is vaguely locatable?

To deal with such variability, sex role may be seen as involving four elements: label, behavior, expectations and location. The label "male" or "female" refers to the biologically-determined phenomenological fact that the labeled individual probably has or probably will enact organized sets of behaviors open to persons with that label. He (or she) will probably himself expect to evidence, or others will expect him to evidence, what are sex-related attributes and behaviors. The expectations may be generically normative—what men-in-general should be or do, or concretely normative—what you, Man X, with your special characteristics in this particular situation, should be or do. The closer the relationship between actor and relevant other, the less generic and the more specific the norms that apply. No priority is given to expectations as evocative or determinative of behavior. Although that may be the case, equally likely is the evocation of expectations on the basis of specific behaviors or cues (Angrist, 1968). The label itself can activate both behaviors and expectations from others, but always in relation to a social location.

Sex role involves multiple roles

To delineate the exact context for sex role is to encompass the whole set of roles an actor is heir to. Reference here is to a role constellation: the combination of roles one individual can play at a given stage in his life vis-a-vis other individuals and groups (Angrist, 1967). The point has to be underscored that no single role is feasibly isolated except conceptually. In reality, individuals judge and are judged by multiple criteria. They react and are reacted to as complex bundles of characteristics. Even in the encounter between strangers, the "personal front" is conveyed through vehicles such as clothing, age, sex, racial features, size, looks, posture, bodily gestures (Goffman, 1959). No single such label or vehicle, but their combination, composes the front. Students of role behavior have amply documented the idea that a person participates in a complex society as a many-faceted actor, an incumbent of many roles, carrier of many labels, performer of different sets of behaviors, subject to multiple kinds of expectations.

How is role enacted?

How then is a given role enacted? Both from the actor's viewpoint (and usually the relevant others') and from the observer's view, the individual, through group- or self-determined priorities features one role above his other ones. Bates (1956) described this as a "dominant role," which temporarily and in appropriate context supercedes "latent roles." In this framework, age and sex-roles are dominant ones. Thus, father in the family is husband, sex partner, son-in-law, worker; influencing all these is his dominant role of male.

Life cycle aspects of sex role

While these conceptions deal with multiple roles, they stress the temporal, contextual or structural dominance of one role over others. Another kind of view is embodied in the life-cycle concept. Perhaps the strongest embodiment of the role constellation idea appears in the life-cycle framework of some family studies (Glick, 1965; Hill, 1964). The individual is seen in a natural history of social development through life stages from child-in-the-family to single adult, to husband, father, grandfather; or to wife, mother, grandmother. The stages comprise elements of sex and age, marital, familial, school and work roles so that, actually, some roles overlap others (e.g., child, schoolgirl, teenager), some endure (e.g., female, even "mother" is relatively long term), others change (e.g., college student). A given individual's life-cycle may be cut into, so to speak, in order to observe the combination of roles in that stage or time slice (Angrist, 1967; Axelson, 1960). Or the family as a group may be studied in terms of its stage, whose definition stems from such matters as the length of time the couple is married, the presence or absence of children, and school stages and ages of children, husband's work status, health of family members (Farber, 1961; Motz, 1950).

The life cycle time slice . . .

Implicit use of the life cycle time slice in family literature has led to the elision of sex role into family role: female, then, means wife-and-mother; male means husband-and-father. Although this seems a logical emphasis in the family field, some consequences derive from this highlighting: (a) the study of sex role has tended to concentrate on conjugal or marital roles especially for women; (b) the family is seen primarily in the stage of *procreation* rather than at *orientation*, thus families with adult children, especially unmarried ones, are rarely studied; (c) role constellations of the unmarried do not fit the familial life cycle model and tend to be either ignored—e.g., working divorcee with young children, single career girl, wealthy bachelor business executive—or defined as deviant. However, it is true that recently

the divorced have come in for scientific study and with some life-cycle analysis. See, for example, Hunt (1966).

The life-cycle approach assumes progression or development so that in the family, any one stage has a high probability of being followed by others in a predictable order. Each stage has its developmental tasks (Kenkel, 1960), and individual family members have careers, that is, they progress through a series of roles; in this sense the family is a system of careers (Farber, 1961). Further, adult roles are said to have a cycle with stages, each with unique tasks and adjustment problems. This role-cycling analysis provides a kind of microscopic look at the structure, content and continuity of a given role (Rossi, 1968).

It can be seen from the preceding illustrations that the features of role constellation (the natural history of the life span, the time slice, the role multiplicity of any single individual at any time in a given location) are already an explicit part of family studies.

Sex role constellation

What value has the role constellation approach to studying sex role?

First, it provides a workable solution to the location problem in studying sex roles. By close delineation of the several labels operative at a given time, relatively precise measurement of behavior and expectations vis-a-vis relevant others within the exact location becomes manageable and meaningful. The social location may be the household (composed of wife, husband, three children, maid) or the nuclear family (composed of wife, husband, three children).

Second, the normalcy of dealing with numerous and changing demands, expectations, and performing a wide repertoire of behaviors becomes apparent. The individual family member or school teacher is "many things to many people" as the colloquialism goes. Instead of struggling to unravel the threads of role conflict, the research task becomes to analyze the methods for meshing sets of individual behaviors and expectations. The idea that people manage to juggle, avoid, manipulate, interpret, the scope of their roles seems closer to empirical reality than that individuals act in terms of a single role blueprint at any given time or place. In fact, some mechanisms for behavior under potentially conflict-ridden conditions have been described as "role-segregation," the scheduling of role enactments so that their audiences are segregated (Goffman, 1961), and ordinary role relations as a sequence of "role bargains" in which each individual seeks to reduce his role strain (or felt difficulty) in fulfilling his role (Goode, 1960b).

To summarize, the utility of a role constellation approach to the study of sex roles rests on the fact that the individual rarely, if ever, behaves just as a man or woman. Rather sex modifies, sometimes weakly, whatever social interactions or relationships he is engaged in.

Role flexibility

The vagueness of indeterminacy of sex role expectations is well documented as evidence that men's and women's dress, family and work lives are increasingly less dichotomous in industrialized urban societies, and even polar personality differences hold less consistently (Silverman, 1967; Vincent, 1966). In marital roles this vagueness has been considered responsible for conflict—for example, women more often prefer a companionate-type marital role, while their husbands expect them to perform in more traditional domestic patterns (Rodgers, 1959). Women, in one study, emphasized an "ideal self" as modern but a "real self" as traditional female sex role (McKee, 1959). And young girls held quite traditional concepts of sex roles although these differ from what characterizes their own primary social groups (Hartley, 1959). This kind of discrepancy between sets of women's role expectations, or between male and female expectations for women, may be interpreted as evidence of confusion about sex roles—indeed, most observers have done so. But it also represents a range of maneuverability—as some students of role conflict suggest, the very multiplicity of choices coupled with absence of sharply defined expectations can foster flexibility for the actor (Parsons, 1942).

It is important to underscore this oft-observed phenomenon that all roles or realms of behavior have a stretch about them, or flexibility allowance.

Contingency orientation

The learning of adult sex roles, as indicated earlier, is seen primarily as occupation-directed for males and family-directed for females. While man's strait jacket during socialization is occupational choice and achievement, woman's straight jacket is marriage. This bifurcated picture is accurate in the sense of separate key goals for each sex, but it is inadequate to describe the flexibility phenomenon in sex role behavior. At this point, I am unprepared to substantiate such a hypothesis for males (although I submit that male role flexibility exists also) but the picture for females should emerge firmly.

My hypothesis is that flexibility in future fulfillment of women's roles is built into socialization both early and late as contingency training. In other words, woman lives by adjusting to and preparing for contingencies. The degree varies by social class, so that the lower the class the higher the contingency orientation. Indeed, women in lower socioeconomic groups have characteristically faced greater unpredictability in life style and greater acceptance of life's hazards as inevitable than higher class women (Rainwater, 1960). Lower class women may not only be more practical in this respect, but also more realistic (Lefton, 1962). The present discussion centers on middle and upper class college-educated women. This contingency orientation is reflected in personality development, in belief systems and in choices.

The girl learns to be "feminine"

The girl learns to be "feminine"—with all the adjectival subscales that term connotes—relative passivity, deference, low intellectuality, cooperativeness. That is to say, she learns to fit in, "to know her place," to take cues from authoritative males (Bem, in press). Catering to people's palates, to their moods, to their needs—these are feminine skills considered necessary to being wife and mother.

Beliefs and expectations about suitable behavior for a girl dwell primarily on the domestic realm of adult women's roles. Given that central theme for girls, an elaborate set of "ifs" surrounds it. For example:

(a) Douvan (1960) refers to the fact that a girl cannot commit herself to anything but marriage; she must remain malleable enough to fit the value system of her potential future spouse. One contingency element, then, is preparation to fit an unknown spousal relationship.

(b) A second contingency is lack of guarantee that she will marry. Although all but a few women hope and plan to marry, remaining single is both a fear and a possibility—ability to be financially self-supporting is a motivation for vocational training in case one does not marry.

(c) The economic necessity to work is considered a likely eventuality at some time in the woman's life. She may need to support herself and husband while he completes his education, she may have to supplement or temporarily supply the family income, or earn money for special purposes—a car, vacation, or college costs for children.

(d) After marriage, temporary or permanent childlessness becomes a possibility, whether by accident or design. Leisure activities or gainful employment, either to fill free time or to provide content to life, may be viewed as resources for filling such a gap.

(e) When children grow up and leave home, the woman faces a drastic decline, even elimination, of her mothering functions. The need or freedom to fill this void may re-open work or leisure pursuits as realistic options.

(f) Exmarriage like nonmarriage is a contingency to be prepared for with "security" or "insurance." Divorce or widowhood can require the woman to become a breadwinner. Hence, a common rationale among girls is to be able to work, "just in case."

The contingencies are real

Obviously, the contingencies are real. This does not mean that all growing girls perceive and deliberately plan for them. The research task would be to determine how much rational accounting and preparation for the adult woman's contingencies occurs, how categories of women differ in degree of preparation, and whether some contingencies are more directly prepared for than others.

Not all the possible contingencies are given equal weight. In fact, one contingency takes priority during late adolescence and early adulthood rendering others subordinate. It is preparation for, even overstress on, marriage and the marital role. Epitomizing as it does the essence of American conceptions of femininity, this marital role emphasis masks the multiplicity of functions which family life entails for the woman. As the key contingency, preparation to fit the unknown spouse leads girls to tailor their behavior for maximum eligibility. This means acting feminine (passive, cooperative, non-intellectual), in dating situations (Komarovsky, 1946) and high school girls' acceptance of traditional but disliked domestic responsibilities for their married lives (Hartley, 1959). It means perception of limited options in the occupational world. The inability of occupational choice theories to handle women's patterns reflects women's contingency orientations (Psathas, 1968). Women's expectations for adult roles have been dubbed unrealistic (Rose, 1951); on the contrary, one could argue that they are concretely realistic. While a boy enters college considering types and conditions of work, the girl's primary focus is on marriage. Work is peripheral. College then becomes important—as broadening social experience, for self-development, for mate-finding. Whereas during the preteen years boys and girls tentatively consider occupations, only boys consistently pass into the reality stages of exploring, crystallizing and specifying an occupation. Ginzberg (1963) notes that "... major adjustments must be made in the general (occupational) theory before it can be applied to girls. . . ."

Longitudinal research on role aspirations

In my current longitudinal research on college women's role aspirations, there is evidence for the extent to which a contingency orientation operates. Study subjects initially consisted of the 188 freshmen entering the women's college of a larger coeducational university. Students were asked to complete a questionnaire each fall and to be interviewed twice during the four years. Attrition over four years left 108 seniors; complete questionnaire data were obtained for 87 of this cohort.

Occupational preferences during freshman and sophomore years show extensive shifting: 37% shifted preferences within the first month of freshman year, fully 70% had changed by September of sophomore year (Cf. Davis, 1965, and Wallace, 1966).[1] Not only did choices change, but early in sophomore year 42% still reported feeling undecided about their occupational choice compared with 58% who had said so as freshmen. Indecision about or disinterest in occupation is reflected in the low proportion of the cohort of 87 who as freshmen were career salient—30%.[2] This percentage is especially noteworthy since the college in which the research was done is reputed as vocationally-professionally oriented. Indeed, by senior year, 43% were career salient, perhaps suggestive of the school's influence. But panel analysis of the choice patterns shows radical vacillation between career and non-career interests. Of the 37 who were career salient seniors, only 6 had been so consistently over the four years. The others had arrived there via one or more changes in salience. By contrast, girls who are not career salient predominated in all four years and showed considerably less shifting.

Marriage is the key contingency

The extent to which marriage is a key contingency is suggested from my analysis of single women's responses to questions about home versus career preferences. In a study of educated women's life styles, five and fifteen year alumnae of the women's college referred to above completed questionnaires on their leisure and work activities. Details on the sample and procedures are in Searls (1966) and Angrist (1967). Of the 318 respondents, 85% were married and mainly homemakers. Of 90 women employed at least part-time, roughly one-third each were single, married with-

out children, or married with children. For the single working women (average age of 27 years) 48% said they would most want to concentrate on home and family if they were to marry; only 24% and 12% of childless working women and working mothers, respectively, picked that option.[3] However, when preferred occupations are compared with actual ones, there is some indication that they now realistically confront the non-marriage contingency—compared with married working women, the single ones prefer substantially higher level occupations than those they have: 47% had professional jobs but 65% desired them. This discrepancy was highest for the single women.

Among the small group of 34 alumnae with a median age of 36, who were mothers and working part-time, only 44% reported working in fields which they preferred. The actual jobs held were generally related to their college major, but often unrelated to jobs they desired. In answer to the question: "What one occupation or field would you most like to work in if you had the necessary training?"—only one person preferred a sales, secretarial or clerical job, but 5 held such jobs, 7 preferred semiprofessional jobs but only 3 had chosen such. In general, the older the woman, the less likely her preferred job resembled her actual one. Thus, while marriage was an explicitly anticipated contingency, work appears to have been only vaguely prepared for. Although college major is reflected in later work choices, the major itself was probably chosen with the criteria reported by contemporary women in the same college: "to be practical," "to be able to work in case I ever have to."[4]

And after marriage

After marriage the contingency orientation shows up in new ways. While marriage was an explicit contingency one prepared for, others remained only implicit. Again, drawing on the alumnae data mentioned, one sees the married women's accommodation to stages and features of family life. For example, among full-time homemakers the type of leisure activities pursued varies according to ages of children—women with preschoolers tended to follow recreational and self-enrichment activities which are largely home-centered; women with school age children pursued predominantly community activities (Angrist, 1967). Similarly, the older homemakers found less enjoyment and mastery in homemaking than the younger women—perhaps they reflected boredom with domesticity, or else their late-found option to like homemaking less as it is less needed by older children (Searls, 1966).

Statistics on women in the labor force also show this contingency orientation. A pattern of phasing in and out of the work world represents married women's reactions to the family life cycle. Women's lowest participation in the labor force is between the ages of 25 to 34 when family responsibilities are greatest. The peak comes at 45 to 54 years of age when 42% of the married woman population is in the labor force. Whereas one quarter of women workers in 1940 came from the 45-54 age group, 50% did so in 1962; for the 35-44 age group, the figure rose from 29% in 1940 to 45% in 1962. These new peaks reflect younger ages at which women complete child-bearing and become freer of family responsibilities (U.S. Dept. of Labor, 1963).

Concern over women's work force trends and the compressed parental years, manifests itself in the "re-tread" phenomenon. Continuing education programs have arisen to deal explicitly with the presumed crisis of the later years, to help women take a kind of second look at life (Center for Continuing Education, 1965). Marriage becomes a past or minor contingency and others like filling time, or economic sufficiency loom large.

In conclusion

In this paper, several themes were discussed. (a) Sex role definitions and usage were reviewed in terms of their predominant meaning of role either as position, behavior, or relationship. Each meaning tends to be associated with a topical emphasis and social location assumptions. Sex role as positional usually involves the division of labor by sex in structured groups; as behavior, sex role tends to be defined in terms of personality, abilities, preferences without regard to context; as relationship sex role learning in socialization is the focus in varied social settings. Each meaning of sex role contributes something to another conception suggested in this paper of sex role as having four elements: label, behavior, expectations, and social location.

(b) The special vagueness of changing sex role norms in contemporary society justifies looking at the multiplicity of actual role involvement by actors, rather than isolating single roles. Study of role constellations is suggested as a way of dealing with the time-tried nature of roles based on characteristics such as age, stage in the life cycle, familial and occupational status. This approach de-emphasizes role conflict and implies the normalcy of multiple relationships with differing temporal and spatial priorities.

(c) The extent of role flexibility is illustrated from studies of women's roles. To some degree women perceive themselves and are seen as having options in their adult roles. These options are considered as contingencies around which women's sex role learning occurs. Socialization for contingencies is hypothesized to be a key theme in women's lives and manifest both in early and adult socialization. The primary contingency is marriage, but several others impinge on women and either implicitly or overtly influence their role constellations.

NOTES

1. These percentages are based on 125 freshmen of the 143 who became sophomores and for whom complete questionnaire data were obtained.
2. Career salient is defined in terms of answers to two questions about adult roles. Career salient are girls who 15 years from now would like to be career women (either single, married or with children) and who would work full-time or part-time even if their husbands earned enough so that they would never have to work.
3. The question was: assume that you are trained for the occupation of your choice, that you are married and have children, and that your husband earns enough so that you will never have to work unless you want to. Under these conditions, which of the following would you prefer? (Check one) (1) to participate in clubs or volunteer work, (2) to spend time on hobbies, sports or other activities, (3) to work part-time in your chosen occupation, (4) to work full-time in your chosen occupation, (5) to concentrate on home and family, (6) other (explain briefly).
4. Lotte Bailyn (1964) describes women's occupational choice process as revokable, irrational and discontinued. Of course, the ideas and data reported above need to be tempered with the work world conditions impinging on women's occupational choice, for example, the difficulties of finding high level part-time work.

REFERENCES

Angrist, Shirley S. Role constellation as a variable in women's leisure activities. *Social Forces*, 1967, 45, 423-431.

Angrist, Shirley S., Lefton, Mark, Dinitz, Simon and Pasmanick, Benjamin. *Women after treatment.* New York: Appleton-Century-Crofts, 1968, ch. 8.

Axelson, L. J. Personal adjustments in the postparental period. *Marriage and Family Living,* 1960, 22, 66-68.

Bailyn, Lotte. Notes on the role of choice in the psychology of professional women. *Daedalus,* 1964, 93, 700-710.

Bales, R. F. Task roles and social roles in problem-solving groups. In E. E. Maccoby, T. M. Newcomb and E. L. Hartley (Eds.) *Readings in social psychology.* New York: Holt, 1958, 437-447.

Banton, Michael. *Roles: an introduction to the study of social relations.* New York: Basic Books, 1965.

Bates, Frederick L. Position, role, and status: a reformulation of concepts. *Social Forces,* 1956, 34, 313-321.

Bem, Daryl J. and Bem, Sandra L. Training the woman to know her place. In Daryl Bem, *The psychological foundation of beliefs and attitudes.* In press.

Blood, Robert O., Jr. and Wolfe, Donald M. *Husbands and wives.* New York: Free Press, 1960.

Brown, Roger. *Social psychology.* New York: Free Press, 1965, 161-172.

Center for Continuing Education. *Opportunities for women through education.* Ann Arbor: University of Michigan, 1965.

Cottrell, L. S. The adjustment of the individual to his age and sex roles. *American Sociological Review,* 1942, 7, 617-620.

Davis, James A. *Undergraduate career decisions.* Chicago: Aldine, 1965.

Douvan, Elizabeth. Sex differences in adolescent character process. *Merrill-Palmer Quarterly,* 1960, 6, 203-211.

Emmerich, Walter. Family role concepts of children ages six to ten. *Child Development,* 1961, 32, 609-624.

Farber, Bernard. Effects of a severely mentally retarded child on family integration. *Monographs of Society for Research in Child Development,* 1959, 24, No. 2.

Farber, Bernard. The family as a set of mutually contingent careers. In Nelson N. Foote (Ed.) *Household decision-making.* New York: New York University Press, 1961, 276-297.

Gehlen, Frieda Foote. *Women members of the U.S. House of Representatives and role expectations.* Paper presented at Ohio Valley Sociological Society Annual Meeting, South Bend, Indiana, April 1967.

Getzels, J. W. and Guba, E. G. Role, role conflict, and effectiveness: an empirical study. *American Sociological Review,* 1954, 19, 164-175.

Ginzberg, Eli, Ginsburg, Sol W., Axelrad, Sidney and Herma, John L. *Occupational choice: an approach to a general theory.* New York: Columbia University Press, 1963, 160-176.

Glick, Paul C. and Parke, Robert. New approaches in studying the life cycle of the family. *Demography,* 1965, 2, 187-202.

Goffman, Erving. *The presentation of self in everyday life.* New York: Doubleday, 1959, ch. 1.

Goffman, Erving. Role distance. In *Encounters.* Indianapolis: Bobbs-Merrill, 1961, 85-152.

Goode, William J. Norm commitment and conformity to role-status obligations. *American Journal of Sociology,* 1960, 66, 246-258. (a)

Goode, William J. A theory of role strain. *American Sociological Review,* 1960, 25, 383-396. (b)

Gordon, Gerald. *Role theory and illness.* New Haven: College and University Press, 1966, ch. 1.

Gross, Neal, Mason, Ward S. and McEachern, Alexander W. *Explorations in role analysis.* New York: Wiley, 1958, ch. 1-5.

Hartley, Ruth E. and Klein, Armin. Sex role concepts among elementary-school girls. *Marriage and Family Living,* 1959, 21, 59-64.

Hill, Reuben and Rodgers, Roy H. The developmental approach. In Harold T. Christensen (Ed.) *Handbook of marriage and the family.* Chicago: Rand McNally, 1964, 171-211.

Hunt, M. M. *World of the formerly married.* New York: McGraw-Hill, 1966.

Kenkel, William F. *The family in perspective.* New York: Appleton-Century-Crofts, 1960, ch. 14.

Komarovsky, Mirra. Cultural contradictions and sex roles. *American Journal of Sociology,* 1946, 52, 184-189.

Lefton, Mark, Angrist, Shirley, Dinitz, Simon and Pasamanick, Benjamin. The social class, expectations, and performance of mental patients. *American Journal of Sociology,* 1962, 68, 79-87.

Levinson, Daniel J. Role, personality, and social structure in the organizational setting. *Journal of Abnormal and Social Psychology,* 1959, 58, 170-180.

Linton, Ralph. *The cultural background of personality.* New York: Appleton-Century-Crofts, 1945.

McKee, John P. and Sherriffs, Alex C. Men's and women's beliefs, ideals, and self-concepts. *American Journal of Sociology,* 1959, 54, 356-363.

Mead, George H. *Mind, self and society.* Chicago: University of Chicago Press, 1934, 354-378.

Mead, Margaret. *Sex and temperament in three primitive societies.* New York: William Morrow, 1935.

Mechanic, David. Some factors in identifying and defining mental illness. *Mental Hygiene,* 1962, 46, 66-74.

Merton, Robert K. *Social theory and social structure.* Glencoe, Illinois: Free Press, 1957, 368-379.

Motz, Annabelle Bender. Concepts of marital roles by status groups. *Marriage and Family Living,* 1950, 12, 136 and 162.

Murdock, George P. Comparative data on the division of labor by sex. In Bruce J. Biddle and Edwin J. Thomas (Eds.) *Role theory.* New York: Wiley, 1966, 263-264.

Nadel, S. F. *The theory of social structure.* Glencoe, Illinois: Free Press, 1957.

Newcomb, T. M. *Social psychology.* New York: Dryden Press, 1950.

Nye, F. Ivan and Hoffman, Lois. *The employed mother in America.* Chicago: Rand McNally, 1963, ch. 27.

Parsons, Talcott. Age and sex in the social structure of the United States. *American Sociological Review,* 1942, 7, 604-616.

Parsons, Talcott and Bales, R. F. *Family, socialization, and interaction process.* Glencoe, Illinois: Free Press, 1955.

Phillips, Derek L. Rejection of the mentally ill. *American Sociological Review,* 1964, 29, 679-687.

Preiss, Jack J. and Ehrlich, Howard J. *An examination of role theory.* Nebraska: University of Nebraska Press, 1966.

Psathas, George. Toward a theory of occupational choice for women. *Sociology and Social Research,* 1968, 52, 253-268.

Rainwater, Lee. *And the poor get children.* Chicago: Quadrangle Books, 1960.

Rodgers, David A. Spontaneity and specificity in social role relationships. *Journal of Personality,* 1959, 27, 300-310.

Rose, Arnold. The adequacy of women's expectations for adult roles. *Social Forces,* 1951, 30, 69-77.

Rossi, Alice S. Transition to parenthood. *Journal of Marriage and the Family* 1968, 30, 26-39.

Sarbin, Theodore R. Role theory. In Gardner Lindzey (Ed.) *Handbook of social psychology.* Cambridge: Addison-Wesley, 1954, 1, 223-258.

Schwartz, Charlotte. Perspectives on deviance—wives' definitions of their husbands' mental illness. *Psychiatry,* 1957, 20, 275-291.

Searls, Laura. College major and the tasks of homemaking. *Journal of Home Economics,* 1966, 58, 708-714.

Silverman, William and Hill, Reuben. Task allocation in marriage in the United States and Belgium. *Journal of Marriage and the Family,* 1967, 29, 353-359.

Southall, A. An operational theory of role. *Human Relations,* 1959, 12, 17-34.

Stryker, Sheldon. Conditions of accurate role-taking: a test of Mead's theory. In Arnold M. Rose (Ed.) *Human behavior and social processes.* Boston: Houghton-Mifflin, 1962, 41-62.

Turner, Ralph. Role taking: process versus conformity. In Arnold M. Rose (Ed.) *Human behavior and social processes.* Boston: Houghton-Mifflin, 1962, 20-40.

U.S. Department of Labor. *Handbook on Women Workers.* Washington, D.C.: Women's Bureau Bulletin No. 285, 1963.

Vincent, Clark. Implications of changes in male-female role expectations for interpreting M-F scores. *Journal of Marriage and the Family,* 1966, 28, 196-199.

Wallace, Walter L. *Student culture.* Chicago: Aldine, 1966.

Wigney, Trevor. *The education of women and girls.* Toronto: University of Toronto, 1965.

16 Career and family orientations of husbands and wives in relation to marital happiness

Lotte Bailyn

The role of the educated married woman has been the subject of much debate in the past few decades. People concerned with the economy and the professions have urged trained women with families to enter the labor market—and women have responded, though their participation in the highest job levels is still limited (Fogarty, Rapoport, 1967; Rendel, 1968). Some family experts, on the other hand, have warned about the possible disintegration of the family that would result if women forsook their traditional roles, though research findings, on the whole, have not supported this fear (Goode, 1963; Nye & Hoffman, 1963).

Both research and ideological pronouncements, however, have dealt almost exclusively with the life situation of the woman: with the complications and rewards she faces in trying to combine family and work. And though the importance of the husband is always assumed, little systematic

Reprinted from Lotte Bailyn, "Career and Family Orientations of Husbands and Wives in Relation to Marital Happiness," Human Relations, 23:2, 1970, pp. 97-114. This paper is part of a larger study of highly qualified women and their careers sponsored by The Leverhulme Trust in a grant to Political and Economic Planning (P.E.P.) under the direction of Michael Fogarty and Rhona Rapoport (P.E.P.) and Robert Rapoport (Tavistock Institute) London. The author worked with the Rapoports on their 'couples' data in 1969. The report on the overall study will appear in Fogarty, Rapoport & Rapoport (1970). The data on which the present paper on couples is based come from a sample of British university graduates questioned in 1968, eight years after finishing university. The sampling frame was provided by Professor R. Kelsall from a National Survey of 1960 Graduates directed by R. K. Kelsall, A. Poole and A. Moore. The data were collected by Research Services Ltd., and some of the analysis was done with the assistance of L. Hawkins of Survey Analysis Ltd., London, using his newly developed Conversational Mode Survey Analysis Program. Some of the items in the survey, upon which this paper is based, are drawn from a questionnaire designed by Alice Rossi in her study of university graduates (which was associated with James Davis' survey of graduates) conducted by The National Opinion Research Center, Chicago, Illinois. Thanks are due to all of the above mentioned, but the author is particularly grateful to the Rapoports for their help at all stages of the work for this paper.

attention has been given to the interplay between the chosen life style of an educated woman and that of her husband. Only recently have some writers begun to analyze the process by which men achieve an integration of family and their own work, and there has virtually been no study relating to married women's work patterns that deals simultaneously with husbands and wives.[1]

The hypothesis under investigation in this paper is that an educated, married woman's resolution of the 'career-family' dilemma cannot be adequately evaluated without knowledge of her husband's resolution—of the way he fits his work and his family into his life. In particular, it deals with the patterns that result when husbands with varying orientations to their families and their careers are combined with wives who also differ on this dimension, and it evaluates the different combinations by the degree of marital happiness associated with each.[2] The investigation is based on data from some two hundred British women, all university graduates of the year 1960, and from their husbands.[3]

Husband's orientation

It is assumed in our society that every man will spend a major portion of his time and energy on his work; and, indeed, every husband in the sample does so.[4] Yet the degree of men's involvement with their occupation varies greatly. Moore (1969) distinguishes between two approaches to work: '*conditioning* (implying a reluctant adjustment to a harsh reality) or *commitment* (enthusiastic acceptance of pleasurable duties)' (p. 868). Masih (1967) identifies career-saliency as a dimension along which people vary and defines it as consisting of three elements: 'a) the degree to which a person is career motivated, b) the degree to which an occupation is important as a source of satisfaction, and c) the degree of priority ascribed to occupation among other sources of satisfaction' (pp. 653-4). Similar distinctions exist in the extent to which a married man's satisfactions are determined by his family, and it is the relative weight of these two potential sources of satisfaction—career and family—that is used to differentiate the husbands in the sample.

The specific measure is based on the following questions:

(a) Which of the following gives you the most satisfaction in your life?
(b) Which gives you the next greatest satisfaction?

Your career or occupation
Family relationships
Leisure time recreational activities
Religious beliefs or activities
Participation as a citizen in affairs of your community
Participation in activities directed towards national or
    international betterment
Running a home
Other

Over half of the husbands (58 percent) indicated that they derived most satisfaction from their families; a little over one fourth (27 percent) said their careers were most satisfying; only 14 men, a mere 6 percent of the sample, checked the third most frequent choice—leisure time recreational activities. Further, over two thirds (69 percent) of

TABLE 1   Husbands' Sources of Satisfaction

Mentioned as source of satisfaction:		No.	%	
Only family		51	23	
				Family-oriented
1st choice		40	18	
2nd choice	140	11	5	
Both family and career				
Family first		89	41	
Career first		50	23	
				Career-oriented
Only career		20	9	
1st choice	70	11	5	
2nd choice		9	4	
Neither career nor family		7	3	
Total		217[a]	99	

[a]6 men who did not answer this question at all were eliminated from the analysis.

those whose greatest satisfaction comes from their families gave career as the source of their next greatest satisfaction, and over four fifths (82 percent) of those listing career first chose family as second. All in all, as may be seen in *Table 1*, only seven men did not mention either career or family as a source of great satisfaction for them.[5]

The 210 men who did mention career or family or both as sources of satisfaction in their lives, may be divided according to their primary emphasis, as indicated in *Table 1*. The 140 whose family relationships are the sole or greatest source of satisfaction comprise the group that is family-oriented; the 70 whose satisfactions stem more from their careers are considered career-oriented, a ratio of 2:1 in favor of the family.

The group of husbands as a whole, then, has a strong family emphasis. All are married and 88 percent either had children or were expecting their first child at the time they filled in their questionnaires, and both marriage and children increase the likelihood of men listing family relationships as their main source of satisfaction in life [Fogarty, Rapoport, & Rapoport, 1970 (in press), ch. V]. Further, this group of men all became part of the sample by being willing to answer a 'spouse questionnaire' for a study in which their wives, as 1960 university graduates, were the primary targets. This means that their family relations were close enough for them to cooperate with their wives in a joint venture, which, in itself, probably preselects those who are more oriented to their families. Also, not all of these men are university graduates themselves; on the contrary, almost one fourth of these husbands of university graduates had themselves not graduated from university and these tend to emphasize family more than do their counterparts who did graduate from university and who show a greater commitment to occupation.[6]

Still, both orientations are present in the sample: there are those whose primary emphasis is on their careers and those who emphasize their families more. The distinction is embedded in many aspects of a man's life; it cannot be isolated from his other attitudes or life experiences. Masih (1967) found that one of the main differences between male students whose careers were very salient for them and those for whom this was not the case, was the former group's lesser interest in interaction with the opposite sex and greater desire for 'enduring' long periods of work. In relation to a job, the 'high-saliency' group showed less concern about the security of steady work than did the group whose careers were less salient. In the present sample, too, such distinctions exist. The man whose primary emphasis is on his family is more concerned with human contact in the realm of work; the career-oriented men, in contrast, emphasize intellectual fulfillment more.[7] The latter group is more ambitious: 63 percent of the men whose primary emphasis is on their careers, as opposed to 49 percent of those more oriented to their families, fall into the ambitious category.[8]

These, then, are some of the characteristics that differentiate career-oriented from family-oriented men. They are obviously relevant to what happens when these men marry wives who differ in the degree to which they incorporate work into their lives.

Wife's orientation

The diversity of educated women's lives makes it particularly difficult to find a meaningful way of describing their career orientation at an early stage in their family life.[9] For the men in the sample, all of whom are married and working and, presumably, expecting to continue this double pattern, the relative contribution of these two realms to their satisfactions in life is a meaningful way of assessing career-family orientation. But these conditions do not hold for the women.[10] As has already been indicated, 88 percent of the wives in the sample either had children or were expecting their first child. And, only eight years after their graduation, the children were young: 83 percent of the families with children had at least one child under three. Thus, the pull of the traditional expectation that mothers of small children stay home must have been quite strong for these women.

Nonetheless, at the time of filling in the questionnaire, 46 percent of the wives were engaged in work for which they were paid, though only 15 percent were working more than 30 hours per week, and most of these (73 percent) were recruited from the small group without children. But, by itself, the fact of working is not a good indicator of career orientation. At any given moment in their lives, some wives who are working are doing so only out of necessity, waiting perhaps for circumstances to arise that would allow them to stop, and, conversely, some who are not working wish they could. In our sample, 45 percent of the non-working wives are not satisfied with their 'unemployed' state; and, among the sub-sample who are engaged in gainful work, fully 40 percent say specifically that they are *not* in favor of married women engaging in a career—of having any long-range occupational commitments.[11]

And even anticipated future work patterns—though not subject to these forces of the immediate situation—are not

TABLE 2   Wives' Career Orientations

Sources of major satisfaction:[b]	Attitude to married women having a career:[a]	
	In favor	Not in favor
Career mentioned	Integrated N = 45	Mixed (work-oriented) N = 22
Career not mentioned	Mixed (ideologically committed) N = 56	Traditional N = 99

	N	%
Integrated	45	20
Mixed	78	35
Traditional	99	45
Total	222	100

[a]3 wives who did not answer this question are classified as 'not in favor.'
[b]1 woman who did not answer this question is eliminated from the table.

as good a measure of career commitment as one might wish. In the present state of flux in women's roles, the difficulties involved in any chosen style—and all paths have their difficulties—may lead one to view an opposing style as unrealistically attractive.[12] There is evidence, for instance, for the existence of what might be called the 'traditional dream'—an expectation on the part of married women that having children will make family life all-fulfilling for them. That this anticipation is not always met in reality is attested to by the fact that over one third (36 percent) of the wives with children expect to be working more or less continuously, even when their youngest child is under three, as contrasted with only 19 percent of the married women who have not yet had their first child.

If, then, one is interested in a women's career commitment at an early stage in her family life, it is necessary to find a way of gauging it that is as little contaminated as possible by the specific circumstances she finds herself in at that time, or by unrealistic expectations of the future— whether these take the form of a traditional or of a 'pioneering' dream.

The measure chosen, which seems to meet these requirements, is based on two elements: whether or not a woman is generally—abstractly—in favor of married women having a career, and whether or not she herself gets personal satisfaction from her career or occupation. The first element is measured by a question that asked everyone in the sample to give his attitude 'to married women engaging in a career (i.e. in which there is a long-term occupational commitment).' Forty-five percent (N = 101) of the wives indicated they were 'in favor'; 29 percent (N = 64) were 'mixed or neutral'; and 26 percent (N = 58) were 'against' married women engaging in a career. The second element—the satisfaction a woman derives from pursuing such an activity—is based on the same question that was used to determine the men's career orientation. But because of the preponderance of family and other home-oriented responses among the women, the answers were categorized differently. All the women who mentioned career as either their first (only 15 did so) or next greatest source of satisfaction in life were considered career-satisfied: 30 percent of the sample (67 people) fell into this group.

The measure of career orientation among the wives is derived from the relation between these two elements, as indicated in *Table 2*. Those 45 women (20 percent of the sample), who are in favor of married women pursuing careers and who themselves get satisfaction from their own career activities, we have called *integrated*, to indicate a predisposition to integrate a career with their family life. Those 99 women, on the other hand—almost half of the sample—who are not in favor of married women engaging in occupations requiring a long-term commitment and whose satisfactions do not depend on work outside the family, comprise the *traditional* group, the group subscribing to the conventional pattern for women. In between is a mixed group, consisting mainly of wives who favor women having careers but for whom a career or occupation is not personally a major source of satisfaction, as well as a small group (10 percent of the sample) who do get satisfaction from work even though ideologically they are not in favor of married women pursuing careers.

Thus there is a similar tendency among the women to that of the men: the ratio of traditional to career-integrated wives is just about the same (2:1) as the ratio of family-oriented men to career-oriented men. It is important, however, not to equate traditional wives with family-oriented men. Rather, by the definition of our measures as well as by the forces working in society today, it is the wives who integrate a career with their family responsibilities, whose style of life is more analogous to that of family-oriented men, i.e., those men who add to their traditional concerns with a career, a primary emphasis on their families. Both career-integrated wives and family-oriented husbands have forsaken the expected concentration of their sex on only one of these two realms; both have added to their traditional concerns an emphasis on the realm most commonly associated with the other sex.

These analogies are based, of course, on the presumption that a woman's career orientation will bear some relation to the actual career pattern she will follow in her life. There is evidence that indicates this to be likely: nearly all (88 percent) of the wives in the career-integrated group were working at the time of the questionnaire; and, over three fifths (61 percent) were planning to work more or less continuously, even when their youngest child was under three (a plan held by only a quarter of the other wives in the sample). The career-integrated wives, thus, are recruited primarily from those who are now working and are satisfied with this work, who feel it is proper for married women to have a career, and who themselves plan to continue to include work as part of their life styles. And this work is an addition to, not a substitute for, a family. These wives are already married and only two do not plan to have any children (out of a total of five in the whole sample). But they do seem more likely to limit the size of their families: only 32 percent plan to have more than two children; more than half of the other wives have this plan (61 percent of

TABLE 3 *Distribution of Couple Patterns (Number of People in Each Combination)*

Wife's career orientation:	Husband's career-family orientation	
	Emphasis on family	Emphasis on career
Traditional	60 [64]ᵃ (29%)	35 [31] (17%)
Mixed	53 [48] (25%)	19 [24] (9%)
Integrated	27 [28] (13%)	15 [14] (7%)
	N = 209ᵇ (100%)	

ᵃNumbers in brackets indicate the frequencies expected in each cell if the two orientations are independent of each other: $x^2 = 2.75$, P=.25.

ᵇThis numer represents the number of men who could be classified by their career-family orientation (210, see Table 1) minus the one wife whose orientation to her career is unknown.

the traditionally oriented wives hope for three or more children).

Couples' patterns

When, now, the orientations of husbands are combined with those of their wives, 209 couples emerge whose distribution among the various patterns is given in *Table 3*. As the table shows, there is hardly any relation between husbands' and wives' orientations: career-oriented men are no more likely to marry traditional wives than are those whose emphasis is more on their families; nor do women who hope to integrate a career with their family lives show any preference for either family or career orientation in the men they marry. Clearly, career-family orientation is not a salient dimension when marriage decisions are made. Though such a state of affairs may not be optimal from the point of view of the individual marriage (and it sometimes is not, as will be seen), from the point of view of this study it is very useful since it permits one to investigate the different combinations of career orientations without too much concern for the possible effect of other related factors.

As we mentioned at the start, this paper is concerned with the extent of marital happiness associated with these different patterns. The following question, which was asked of every person in the sample, is used as the basis for classifying couples according to marital happiness:[13]

Taking things together, how do you really feel about your marriage?

Very happy
Pretty happy
Sometimes happy, sometimes unhappy
Not very happy
Unhappy

Sixty-one percent of the wives and 61 percent of the husbands stated that they were 'very happy' with their marriages; 25 percent and 28 percent, respectively, indicated that their marriages were 'pretty happy'; no wife said that her marriage was less than 'sometimes happy, sometimes unhappy,' though four husbands did. Not all couples agreed on the degree of their marital satisfaction: 13 percent of the husbands indicated a greater degree of happiness than did their wives; 12 percent of the wives rated themselves happier. Since consensus is a better way of characterizing a couple than is one partner's perception alone, only marriages in which *both* partners said that they were 'very happy' are classified as happy.[14] Fifty-five percent of the couples fall into this category.

It is obvious from *Table 4*—which indicates the marital happiness associated with each of the various combinations of career orientation—that one pattern stands out from all the others: marriages of men whose exclusive or primary emphasis is on their careers to women who themselves place store on integrating a career with their family lives are not very happy. As a matter of fact, the number of couples in this group who describe their marriages as 'very happy' is so low that it is not possible, with the present sample, to investigate the conditions that contribute to or might ease the strains of this pattern. It should be mentioned, however, that neither of the two couples of this pattern whose marriages are very happy has children; it should also be said that both husbands are in favor of married women having a career,[15] and both are very satisfied with their own work. It seems, then, that under special conditions this pattern can be accompanied by a happy marriage, but the conditions are rare in this sample.

All the other combinations in *Table 4* seem to be associated with about the same degree of marital happiness: between one half and two thirds of the marriages in each group are very satisfactory to both partners. In discussing the conditions that facilitate these successes, we shall emphasize two patterns: the conventional pattern (upper right cell of *Table 4*) and the co-ordinate pattern (lower left). Traditional wives married to career-oriented husbands represent the pattern, here called conventional, in which family roles are probably most differentiated by sex, with the man primarily oriented to his career and his wife primarily to the home. In contrast, it seems likely that the least differentiation of roles along traditionally accepted sex-linked lines occurs in the marriages of career-integrated wives to men who, though involved in a career, place primary emphasis on their families—the couples of the co-ordinate pattern.[16]

Table 5, which gives the basic data for this discussion, also includes information on the upper left cell of *Table 4*, in which traditional wives are paired with family-oriented husbands. This combination has the wife's orientation in common with the conventional pattern and the husband's orientation in common with the co-ordinate one. It thus allows one to make inferences as to the relative influence of each partner's orientation on the success of the contrasting family styles.

Conventional pattern

According to prevailing social expectations, the conventional pattern would not seem to require any particular justification. But when one considers the separation of interests it implies, with the husband primarily concerned

TABLE 4   *Couple Patterns and Marital Happiness (% of Couples with Very Happy Marriages)*

	Husband's career-family orientation	
	Emphasis on family	Emphasis on career
Wife's orientation:		
		Conventional pattern
Traditional	62% (N = 60)	54% (N = 35)
Mixed	62% (N = 53)	53% (N = 19)
Integrated	56% (N = 27)	13% (N = 15)
	Co-ordinate pattern	

with his work and the wife with the house and family, it becomes less obvious why such a pattern is assumed to be such a satisfactory one. It is not altogether surprising, therefore, that marital happiness is increased under conditions that minimize the built-in separation of interests of this pattern. A look at the first column of *Table 5*[17] shows that the more children conventional couples have, the less likely they are to have very happy marriages (item 1). More children, by increasing the care and time necessary to meet the needs of the family, would seem to exaggerate the differentiation of roles in a pattern in which the family is the more or less exclusive concern of one partner. Moreover, item 2 shows that the proportion of happy marriages declines the more satisfied the husband in this pattern is with his present work situation. Such an increase in satisfaction, by adding strong motivational support to the husband's primary concern with his work, would also seem to exaggerate the differentiation of roles implicit in the pattern. Finally, the conventional pattern is the only one in which marital satisfaction is greater when the fields of husband and wife overlap (item 3). Such a common interest seems particularly important for the success of a pattern based on rather strict differentiation of roles.

Table 5 also shows that the conventional pattern is the only one in which marital happiness is negatively associated with income—in which there is a larger percentage of happy marriages when income is low than when it is high (item 4). Further analysis shows this to be particularly true when the husband's ambition is low. Under this condition, only 17 percent of those with high incomes have very happy marriages, as compared with 71 percent of those whose incomes are low. In other words, marital happiness is very low indeed if the husband in a conventional couple combines low ambition with high income. In this situation he has, perhaps, the least justification for his primary emphasis on career, since it is based neither on his ambition nor on the need to make money.[18] Both of these—career ambition and need for family income—are traditionally accepted reasons for a husband's one-sided emphasis on his work; when neither is in force, the conventional pattern is not very successful.

That the conventional pattern is not automatically satisfactory but needs some justification is shown also by one other item in *Table 5*. Item 6 shows that a greater proportion of conventional marriages are happy if the husband's mother worked while he was growing up than if she did not work. That is, the pattern seems to be *less* satisfactory if it is 'conventional' as far as the husband's personal experience

TABLE 5   *Factors Associated with Marital Happiness for Different Couple Patterns (% of Couples with Very Happy Marriages)*

	Couple patterns		
	Conventional		Co-ordinate
Husband's primary emphasis: *Wife's career orientation:*	*Career traditional (N = 35)*	*Family traditional (N = 60)*	*Family integrated (N = 27)*
	%	%	%
1. Number of children:			
none (N = 33)[a]	67 (N = 9)	[100 (N = 3)][b]	50 (N = 6)
one (N = 41)	63 (N = 8)	64 (N = 14)	[75 (N = 4)]
two (N = 101)	47 (N = 15)	52 (N = 29)	53 (N = 15)
three or more (N = 34)	[33 (N = 3)]	71 (N = 14)	[50 (N = 2)]
2. Husband's feelings about his present work situation:[c]			
extremely satisfied (N = 51)	43 (N = 7)	78 (N = 18)	[100 (N = 4)]
somewhat satisfied (N = 115)	55 (N = 22)	65 (N = 31)	53 (N = 15)
neutral or dissatisfied (N = 39)	67 (N = 6)	22 (N = 9)	29 (N = 7)
3. Relation of own and spouse's field of work:[d]			
overlapping (N = 97)	67 (N = 18)	53 (N = 30)	57 (N = 14)
distinct (N = 100)	41 (N = 17)	69 (N = 29)	58 (N = 12)
4. Husband's income:			
high (>£2000/year) (N = 75)	36 (N = 14)	77 (N = 22)	70 (N = 10)
low (≤£2000/year) (N = 128)	67 (N = 21)	57 (N = 35)	44 (N = 16)
Mother's work status while growing up:			
5. wife's mother did not work (N = 93)	62 (N = 16)	71 (N = 31)	62 (N = 8)
wife's mother did work (N = 114)	47 (N = 19)	56 (N = 27)	53 (N = 19)
6. husband's mother did not work (N = 85)	33 (N = 12)	62 (N = 32)	83 (N = 6)
husband's mother did work (N = 124)	65 (N = 23)	61 (N = 28)	48 (N = 21)
7. Dominant values of social circle:[e]			
intellectual, academic (N = 95)	71 (N = 14)	67 (N = 21)	58 (N = 19)
suburban (N = 110)	46 (N = 24)	65 (N = 40)	62 (N = 8)
8. Attitude of social circle to women working:[f]			
same opportunities as men (N = 46)	[25 (N = 4)]	58 (N = 12)	56 (N = 9)
women's work secondary to home and family obligations (N = 111)	50 (N = 24)	70 (N = 30)	58 (N = 12)
very mixed feelings (N = 44)	83 (N = 6)	53 (N = 15)	50 (N = 6)
9. Division of labor in household (supervision and care of children; shopping for food):[g]			
only wife usually does it (N = 102)	61 (N = 18)	55 (N = 29)	43 (N = 14)
wife has some help (N = 104)	44 (N = 16)	67 (N = 30)	69 (N = 13)

[a]Numbers in parentheses indicate the number in the given category in the sample. They do not always add up to 209 because No Answers have been eliminated.

[b]Percentages in brackets are based on very small N's.

[c]In general, how do you feel about your present work situation? (If you are not working, indicate your feelings about being unemployed.)
Extremely satisfied
Somewhat satisfied
Neutral
Somewhat dissatisfied
Extremely dissatisfied
The last 3 categories are combined.

[d]Do you consider that your own field of work and your spouse's field of work outside the home are:
Very close and similar to one another
Overlapping to some extent, but with major areas of difference
Quite distinct from one another
The first 2 categories are combined. Couples are classified on the basis of information from the wife.

[e]Looking at your social circle as a whole, how would you characterize their main values or interests?
a. Suburban (emphasis on home, garden, kids, community etc.)
b. Intellectual, academic
A dominant value or characteristic
A secondary characteristic
Not a characteristic

TABLE 5   (Continued)

N's represent the number of people who said the given factor was 'a dominant value or characteristic.' Some may have given this response to both of the listed factors. Couples are classified on the basis of information from the wife.
   [f] Looking at your social circle as a whole, how would you describe their attitude to women working?
      i. Most people feel that women ought to have same opportunity to pursue an important career as men
      ii. Most feel that women ought to be able to work a bit but not so as to allow it to interfere with home and family obligations
      iii. Women ought not to work outside the home
      Very mixed feelings (some feel like i, some feel like ii, some like iii)
Categories ii and iii have been combined. Couples are classified on the basis of information from the wife.
   [g] Who usually does each of these things in your household?
      a. Supervision and care of children
      b. Shopping for food
         Husband
         Wife
         Both
         Domestic help
         No one in household
Those who responded 'wife' to *both* of these areas are compared to all the rest. Couples are classified on the basis of information from the wife.

is concerned—if, that is, it is merely a continuation in his adult life of the traditional pattern in which he grew up; it is *more* satisfactory if it represents a new family style in the husband's experience and is not merely fulfilling a social and personal expectation.

Thus it seems that the conventional pattern, if it is to be associated with marital happiness, requires support from a number of directions: some common focus or justification seems to be necessary. Items 7 and 8 of *Table 5* show, further, that its success is also dependent on support from the social circle in which it functions. The proportion of happy, conventional marriages decreases when a dominant value of the couple's social circle is the suburban one with emphasis on home, garden, kids, community, etc. (item 7)—a value more in line with a family-centered pattern—and when 'most people [in the couple's social circle] feel that women ought to have the same opportunity to pursue an important career as men' (item 8)—an attitude more consistent with a less differentiated pattern of family life.

Co-ordinate pattern

The kind of support necessary for the success of the co-ordinate pattern is quite different from that required by the conventional one. As items 7 and 8 of the last column in *Table 5* indicate, the attitudes and values of the couple's social circle are not associated with marital happiness in this case (though it is of interest that, compared to the sample as a whole, a large proportion of couples in this group describe their social circles as predominantly intellectual and as having an equalitarian attitude to women's careers). Nor does the community of interest represented by overlapping fields (item 3) relate to marital happiness of co-ordinate couples. Rather, the factors associated with happy co-ordinate marriages are more managerial ones, those that ease the physical burdens of integrating the realms of family and work. The proportion of happy marriages in this pattern is greater when the wife is not alone responsible for the care of the house and the children (item 9) and, perhaps not unrelated, when income is high (item 4).

It has previously been hypothesized that family-oriented men, like career-integrated women, are oriented to both work and family and seek satisfaction in both spheres, a

similarity that should make the differentiation of roles in the co-ordinate pattern more dependent on the particular personal characteristics of the partners than on those prescribed by social expectations. It was suggested, in other words, that the co-ordinate pattern represents a true integration of the realms of family and work for both husband and wife and is in no way a mere reversal of traditional family roles. Evidence from *Table 5* supports this line of reasoning. In contrast to the conventional pattern, happiness of co-ordinate marriages increases as the husband's work satisfaction increases (item 2). Also, further analysis shows that the proportion of happy co-ordinate marriages is particularly great when high income is combined with high ambition of the husband: 83 percent of these couples have very happy marriages. Thus, the family-orientation of the husband whose co-ordinate marriage is successful is not a substitute for work; on the contrary, work is both important and satisfactory to such a man and his family emphasis is based on choice, not on default.[19]

In one respect, the conditions associated with marital happiness of the co-ordinate pattern are similar to those of the conventional one: in both cases, marital happiness is greater if the life style of the family is different from the one in which the husband grew up. Item 6 of *Table 5* shows that co-ordinate marriages are happier if the husband's mother did not work while he was growing up than if she did. Couple patterns that represent a personally new style for the husband are thus more likely to be happy, no matter what that style may be.

The fact that the wife's mother plays no such differentiating role[20] is a first indication, perhaps, of the relative importance of the husband's orientation as compared to that of his wife in determining the personal satisfaction associated with a particular family pattern. Further corroboration comes from a look at the second column of *Table 5*. Couples in this column, as was previously stated, share the wife's traditional orientation with conventional couples and the husband's family emphasis with co-ordinate ones. For almost every item in *Table 5*, the distribution of happy marriages in this middle column matches that of the third column—the co-ordinate pattern—more closely than it does the first one—the conventional pattern. It is the husband's orientation, therefore—which the middle and co-ordinate columns have in common—more than that of the wife, that is crucial for the effects we have discussed.

The data of this study thus corroborate the hypothesis, stated at the start, that a husband's mode of integrating family and work in his own life is crucial for the success—at least in terms of marital satisfaction—of any attempt of his wife to include a career in her life. There is evidence, as a matter of fact, that identifying the conditions under which men find it possible to give primary emphasis to their families while at the same time functioning satisfactorily in their own careers may be even more relevant to the problem of careers for married women than the continued emphasis on the difficulties women face in integrating family and work.

NOTES

1. For an analysis of the problems confronting the professional woman who tries to combine career and family see Bailyn (1965). Writers who have concerned themselves with the relation of family and work in men as well as women include Brim (1968), who feels that one focus in the study of adult socialization should be on 'the two-way process of influence between the world of work and the world of the family in their varying demands upon the adult' (p. 203); Alice Rossi (1965a), whose emphasis on 'the development of a more androgynous conception of sex role' (p. 130) underlies all her work in this field; and Rapoport & Rapoport (1965), who emphasize the integration of the two realms at various periods of transition in the life cycle, an emphasis that has guided much of their research, including the study on which this paper is based. Their investigation of the 'dual-career family' (Rapoport & Rapoport, 1969)—an arrangement 'in which both husband and wife pursue careers (i.e. jobs which are highly salient personally, have a developmental sequence and require a high degree of commitment) and at the same time establish a family life with at least one child' (p. 3)—is one of the few that analyzes the work and family roles of husbands and wives simultaneously. See also Blood & Wolfe (1960) for a discussion of the effects of the comparative work participation of husband and wife on various aspects of the husband-wife relationship, though, not untypically, this information comes from interviews with wives only.

2. Other terms of evaluation are also possible: in particular, one would want to know about the consequences of the various combinations for the character of work produced by the couple, whether by one or both partners. It is entirely possible that a combination that is fully satisfactory to the individual couple may not be the most creative in its contribution to society. An evaluation in terms of work would be related to such questions as the distribution of talent and the special needs of the most creative minds. In this paper, we limit the context of our evaluation to the family.

3. Full details of the total sample (which includes men and women graduates, both married and single) are available in Fogarty, Rapoport & Rapoport (1970, in press). Here it is only necessary to say that each of 449 married women in the sample who had to agree to cooperate with the survey received two lengthy identical questionnaires through the mail: one for themselves and one for their husbands. Of these 348 (78 percent) returned their own questionnaires; 223 (64 percent) of the husbands of this group of respondents also returned questionnaires. These 446 questionnaires (223 filled in by the women, 223 by their husbands) comprise the data on which this paper is based. The 223 married women whose husbands also responded, were compared on a number of items to those who only returned their own questionnaires. The only differences found were in the small group without children. In that group, the wives in the 'couples' sample show somewhat greater marital happiness, are somewhat more likely to be working at the present time, and also hope for somewhat fewer children. Thus the 'couples' wives—as compared to the total sample of married women—slightly overrepresent the group of childless, working, happily married wives, who are not planning on large families. By far the larger proportion of the couples, however, already had children; and in this group the relevant distributions are very similar to the sample of married women as a whole. More differences, as will be seen below exist between the spouses of these wives and the sample of married men university graduates.

4. The few characteristics of husbands that have been studied in relation to married women's careers include occupation and income, attitude to women's work, willingness to help with household tasks (e.g. Mulvey, 1963; Weil, 1961). But there has been no effort to explore the relevance of men's attitudes to their own work and the part played in their lives by career and family.

5. This response may reflect a transient family-work situation: four of these seven have no children, the husbands in these couples are generally not very satisfied with their present work situation, and a disproportionate number of wives in this group did not answer questions relating to their anticipated future work patterns.

6. 74 percent of the husbands who did not graduate from university are family-oriented as opposed to 64 percent of the university graduates. When compared to the married men in the target sample of university graduates, husbands in the 'couples' group are also somewhat more likely to have working wives and to approve of this arrangement.

7. Each person was asked to indicate which of a number of 'factors which contribute to their personal ideals for a career' he personally considered most important:

	% giving each response:	
	career-oriented (N = 70)	family-oriented (N = 140)
Two factors concerned people:		
an opportunity to work with people rather than exclusively with things and ideas	13%	19%
an opportunity to be helpful to other people	4%	8%
Total People Responses	17%	27%
Three factors concerned intellectual fulfillment:		
a chance to use intellectual problem solving abilities	24%	19%
an opportunity to show what I can accomplish	17%	7%
an opportunity to be creative	11%	8%
Total Intellectual Responses	52%	34%

8. Included in the ambitious category are those men who, when asked to 'characterize your level of ambition' at the present time, said they wanted 'to get to the top'; as well as those who wanted only 'to hold a high position' but who, on another question, rated themselves as 'very' or 'somewhat ambitious'; and, finally, five who did not answer the main question but who rated themselves as 'very ambitious.' It should be noted that this difference in ambition is limited to husbands whose incomes are rated low (≤ £2000/year). The group that combines low income with low ambition—of which 74 percent is family-oriented—stands out in a number of ways: it contains more non-graduates than any other, and the men in this group who did graduate from university received less good degrees: they rated themselves as less assertive (based on self-ratings on three interrelated characteristics: 'competitive occupationally,' 'competitive socially,' and 'dominant') and were less satisfied with their intellectual abilities; they gave the fewest work-oriented responses when considering their ideal jobs and were least satisfied with their present work situations. Their family orientation is a part of this syndrome.

9. Obviously this is not true if one can study women at a stage of their lives late enough to allow classification according to the actual work patterns they have followed. The problem here is to get a measure that can be presumed to be a fairly good predictor of these patterns.

10. Masih (1967), for instance, found that judges had much more trouble classifying female students according to the degree of their career-saliency than they had with men.

11. Not all of these 40 percent, of course, actually dislike working. We shall see later that some wives are ideologically against married women having long-range career plans but actually get a great deal of satisfaction from their own work. Orden & Bradburn (1969), who asked their married women respondents whether they would work if they didn't need the money, found that only 23 percent of their college graduates answered negatively (*Table 3*, p. 398).

12. Alice Rossi (1965b) indicates the way experience tempers the expectations of the woman college graduates she studied: "... the pioneers [women whose long-range goals are in heavily masculine fields such as natural sciences, medicine, economics] had romantic notions concerning careers and work which the reality of advanced study and employment temper, and the homemakers [women with no career goals other than being 'housewives'] had romantic notions concerning marriage and family roles which the reality of marriage and motherhood tempers (p. 81)."

13. Obviously we are not suggesting that all the meaningful aspects of a marriage can be represented by a global question on professed marital happiness. Yet, there is evidence that such a question correlates sufficiently well with more refined ways of measuring success in marriage to make it a useful indicator for our purposes. In the present questionnaire the global question followed two others concerning the marital relationship: how well the respondent felt he was doing as a husband or wife and whether he ever felt he had married the wrong kind of person. Andrew Bebbington developed an index of marital satisfaction based on all three questions as well as on a measure of conflict based on the number of disagreements the couples had on a variety of subjects. Of all the items involved, the question used here had the highest correlation with the resulting index. Similarly, in a study of married women, Nye & MacDougall (1959, as presented in Nye & Hoffman, 1963, pp. 270-1) found that a global question on marital happiness along with questions on arguments and quarrels and on actual or contemplated separation met the Guttman criteria of scalability, hence, presumably, they all reflect a single dimension of marital success. In a more refined analysis of marriage happiness, based on data from married men and women (though not on couples), Orden & Bradburn (1968) develop a two-dimensional model of marriage adjustment: one dimension is positive, relating to the satisfactions—both the sociability and the companionship that husbands and wives share—of marriage; the other is negative, and concerns the tensions in marriage. The two aspects are independent of each other, yet they relate in the expected direction to a person's self-rating of marital happiness. In comparing their Marriage Adjustment Balance Scale, which is based on the difference of the scores on the two dimensions, to self-ratings of marital happiness, they conclude that there is little to choose between the two approaches if one's interest is in a summary measure of marital happiness, though the MABS has the advantage of allowing one to consider its components separately.

14. These distributions are very close to those of a number of other surveys which have asked for self-ratings on marital happiness, ratings which have been found to be very stable over time; further, other studies have found that the validity of self-ratings is increased when they are checked by those of the spouse (Orden & Bradburn, 1968).

15. It is of interest that this is the *only* pattern whose success is at all dependent on the husband's attitude toward careers for married women. Most of the studies that have shown this factor to be important were based on a woman's assessment of her husband's attitude (e.g. Weil, 1961). In our sample, where we know the wife's perception of her husband's attitude as well as his actual views, we find that 69 percent of the wives gauge their husbands accurately—match, on a three-point scale, his stated view. With a 30 percent error of assessment, it is possible that the correlations found in previous studies reflect a woman's rationalization and justification of her behavior as much as they do the actual influence of her husband's attitude.

16. Rapoport & Rapoport (1969) in their investigation of the 'dual-career family' chose couples in which both partners had a career—couples who, in our terms, could fit into either of the bottom two cells of *Table 4*. Yet, 'with the exception of one of the couples studied, family life in general and children in particular were highly salient' (p. 9). Thus, their couples seem to represent the pattern we have called co-ordinate. Other people have also investigated the marital adjustment of employed married women (see e.g. Orden & Bradburn, 1969). But the large difference between the degree of marital happiness associated with the bottom two cells of *Table 4* makes it difficult to compare their results with ours.

17. In this discussion, we shall only refer to factors that make at least a 25 percent difference in marital happiness. The proportion of happy marriages is about .5 in the groups under consideration. Under this condition, the probability of getting as large a difference as .25 or more is approximately .05 for equal samples of n = 30.

18. The direction of causality here is by no means clear. It is entirely possible that such a person emphasizes his career as a response to an unhappy marriage. In general, we view the association between a person's career-family orientation and his marital happiness as the result of a process of reciprocal influence—a process that can, however, be affected by other aspects of the person's temperament or experience at any point. We do not view marital happiness, therefore, as a direct consequence of a given pattern of career-family orientations, but see it, rather, as one of a number of factors that seem to go together under certain conditions.

19. It should be noted, however, that such an integration can result in a serious problem of physical and psychological overload (Rapoport & Rapoport, 1969) and is probably not compatible with the super-involvement with career that has been expected in some professions.

20. We are talking here about a differentiating role in relation to marital happiness. There is a slight tendency (as shown by the N's in parentheses) for wives whose mothers worked to be somewhat more frequently in the integrated group than there is for those whose mothers did not work.

REFERENCES

Bailyn, L. (1965). Notes on the role of choice in the psychology of professional women. In: R. J. Lifton (ed.), *The woman in America*. Boston: Houghton Mifflin.

Blood, R. O., Jr. & Wolfe, D. M. (1960). *Husbands and wives: the dynamics of married living.* Glencoe, Ill.: Free Press.

Brim, O. (1968). Adult socialization. In: J. Clausen (ed.) *Socialization and society.* Boston: Little Brown.

Fogarty, M., Rapoport, R. & Rapoport, R. N., (1967). *Women and top jobs.* London: Political and Economic Planning (P.E.P.).

Fogarty, M., Rapoport, R. & Rapoport, R. N. (1970). *Careers and families: sex roles and achievements.* London: Allen & Unwin.

Goode, W. J. (1963). *World revolution and family patterns.* Glencoe, Ill.: Free Press; London: Collier-Macmillan.

Masih, L. K. (1967) Career saliency and its relation to certain needs, interests, and job values. *Personnel & guidance j.* 45, 653-8.

Moore, W. E. (1969). Occupational socialization. In: D. A. Goslin (ed.) *Handbook of socialization theory and research.* Chicago: Rand McNally.

Mulvey, M. C. (1963). Psychological and sociological factors in prediction of career patterns of women. *Genetic psych. mon.* 68, 309-86.

Nye, F. I. & Hoffman, L. W. (1963). *The employed mother in America.* Chicago: Rand McNally.

Nye, F. I. & MacDougall, E. (1959). The dependent variable in marital research. *Pacific sociol. rev.* 2, 67-70.

Orden, S. R. & Bradburn, N. M. (1968). Dimensions of marriage happiness. *Am. j. sociol.* 73 , 715-31.

Orden, S. R. & Bradburn, N. M. (1969). Working wives and marriage happiness. *Am. j. sociol.,* 74, 392-407.

Rapoport, R. N. & Rapoport, R. (1965). Work and family in contemporary society. *Am. sociol. rev.* 30, 381-394.

Rapoport, R. & Rapoport, R. N. (1969). The dual-career family; a variant pattern and social change. *Hum. relat.* 22, 3-30.

Rendel, M. *et al.* (1968). *Equality for women.* London: Fabian Society.

Rossi, A. S. (1965a). Equality between the sexes: an immodest proposal. In: R. J. Lifton (ed.). *The woman in America.* Boston: Houghton Mifflin.

Rossi, A. S. (1965b). Barriers to the career choices of engineering, medicine, or science among American women. In: J. A. Mattfield & C. G. Van Aken (eds.) *Women and the scientific professions: the M.I.T. Symposium on American women in science and engineering.* Cambridge, Mass.: M.I.T. Press.

Weil, M. W. (1961). An analysis of the factors influencing married women's actual or planned work participation. *Am. sociol. rev.,* 26, 91-6.

Part III

The traditional role: gratifications, frustrations, and stresses

As new criteria for fulfillment become important, old assumptions are challenged. Now "femininity" is becoming difficult to achieve, just as "masculinity" has always been a characteristic earned rather than attributed. Once women could love, marry, have children and grandchildren, and then sit, head high, in a rocking chair, looking back with satisfaction on a fulfilling life that was well spent.

As traditional values coexist with new ones, and as different alternatives become possible, routes to identity become uncertain and one aspect of success endangers others. Conflicting roles compete for priority. As men adopt new criteria, valuing the goals of the humanists, the mark of health and maturity includes a capacity for openness, interpersonal trust, spontaneity, and an honest capacity to love. As men experience personal growth and value interpersonal esteem they will experience gratification and vulnerability in ways that have been traditionally feminine. Similarly, as women participate in visible and competitive positions and derive esteem from real achievements they will, like men, increase the possibility of real failure in real work. There are no role opportunities without obligations. Traditional roles offer fulfillment as well as frustration, and emerging life styles, though relieving people of stereotyped constrictions, will too. In this section we will review gratifications derived from the traditional family and analyze stresses inherent in the contemporary nuclear family.

In a paper published in 1960, Hartley points out that though we assume there has been widespread change in sex role patterns, especially because we believe that a significantly greater number of women are employed, we really cannot assess such change without good base data, and we don't have any. Hartley perceives less change than is common assumed. She presents a view of women working, where work is not an expansion of their own capabilities, interests, and goals, but is an extension of traditional responsibilities, another way of nurturing the family. The fact that women work does not provide any clear indication of the motives gratified by work. Thus the assumption that widespread female employment is evidence of a significant psychological or sociological change, is still presumption. We may wonder whether papers describing female motives written in 1960, or now, or 5 years hence, would differ. Actually, recent statistics describing female employment—the continued small number of professionals, managers, or entrepreneurs—support a rather conservative picture, not different from Hartley's 1960 statement that "we are not witnessing an elimination of differences—only an amelioration."

A role is idealized whenever one wants to participate in it and is for some reason thwarted. Rossi reminds us that there are no unambivalent roles but the hostility intrinsic to ambivalence can be expressed more readily when a role is optional. When there is no choice, and to the extent the role is critical, ambivalence is covert. The danger to the overburdened nuclear family seems clear: when mothers do not feel free to express small resentments, hidden rage corrodes the maternal relationship. Because the role is both critical and not optional, women cannot express their ambivalence about family relationships the way they can about work. (Men can express resentments about a particular job, but not about work itself.)

Our cultural values and style make maternity a consuming task in which love is central and ambivalence is inevitable. Rossi points out that basic to our model of child-rearing and a primary reason it is so demanding, is our focus on individuality. Each child is reared by itself by someone whose task is to cultivate every unique potential. The extension of the responsibility for the care of children to people and institutions beyond the mother can only occur if there is an enormous shift in our values about individualism and competition because it is in the way that we rear children that we prepare individuals to compete and work.

Contrasting the Soviet Union and the United States, Cox analyzes the family within the context of societies that value individualism versus those that give priority to the social organization. The closely knit family unit characteristic of Western society maximizes individuality with far less attention paid to the welfare of the state. In the rebellion of American youth, especially in the communes, we see a rejection of the egocentricism, isolation, and competitiveness of the nuclear family. Yet an inspection of the data from the Soviet Union or the kibbutzim of Israel show that although the nuclear family may be modified, it persists in some form though some of its responsibilities are taken over or shared with other institutions. In spite of the pains that result from the emotional intertwining of the family, and in spite of the cruelties members can impose upon each other, Cox suggests that the family survives as a social unit because it is the most effective way yet evolved to meet our human needs for permanence and commitment in relationships. Efforts might best be directed to relieving the nuclear family from some of its obligations, not to dissolve this form, but to reduce stresses and thus make it stronger.

When there are children, the permanence of, the commitment to, the gratifications from, and the stresses upon, the relationship between husband and wife increase enormously, especially in this child-centered culture. Why do people have children? Sometimes one can imagine that having children is the only real and important thing that some people do, the only irreversible commitment they make, the harshest task. Creating and raising children invokes the peak of fulfillment and the sharpest fears—the phylogenetic reality of living things.

Clark's paper is a very personal vignette of what it is like to be poor, black, and a mother. The logic of the welfare system coupled with the assumption that children need mothers—maternity is irreversible but not paternity—results in a desperate, bitter, funny, Kafka-esque dance of insanity. As far as the system is concerned, its mothers and children last. When neither the father nor any government institution provides realistic assistance to the mother for child-care, then care of the children becomes the inescapable responsibility that effectively prohibits mothers from earning a living, leaving them mired in a welfare system that holds them in contempt.

We have alluded to this culture as child-centered and in some of the papers we have, with academic calm, raised the question of what women are supposed to do when their children are in school or grown. If your existence has centered about your children, what is your role and what is your identity when you are no longer a mother? According to Bart's study, if you were a Supermother, especially a Jewish-Mother, and circumstances made it hard to be an active mother any more, you are a good candidate for a tail-spin depression.

When middle-aged women who were overcommitted to the maternal role cannot mother, they are existentially no-thing, without existence. In depression, anger is turned against the self, but much of it is displaced from unexpressed rage against ungrateful children. Supermothers produce guilty children because those children can never love their mothers enough. Of course, the most traditional women, whose sense of worth comes only from others, can never be loved enough.

In the next two papers we will be concerned with the end of marriage through either divorce or death. (We may ask what values are reflected when we note that there are almost no papers in the professional literature concerned with the effects upon the adults involved in these quite widespread occurrences.) For women, presumably more than for men, divorce or widowhood can be the loss of identity. For some, who have followed tradition entirely, who went from the role of daughter to the role of wife, that may be the first time that "I," shorn of relationships is questioned. One would expect that in this case those whose identity included, "mother of ———," would not be so bereft. Like the advent of the empty-nest syndrome of middle age, divorce and death are crises in part because old identities are jeopardized and new roles and identities must evolve.

As Bohannan notes in describing phases of divorce, the last and most difficult phase to be resolved is the psychic divorce, the perception of oneself as an autonomous individual. Divorce, like death, involves grief because of the loss of the loved partner, but divorce is guiltier because it involves either actively and deliberately rejecting someone you loved or being, yourself, actively and deliberately rejected. Unlike bereavement, in which there are social rites of mourning, in divorce one is alone, without even the comfort of shared ritual.

In Parkes' paper we study the process of grief during the first year of widowhood. Interestingly, most of the women were told that their husbands had a terminal illness at least a month before their deaths, but by using the defense of denial they were able to interact with them normally. The extent of the trauma is attested to by the fact that no matter what the external adjustment, some form of denial of the death usually persisted, and half of the widows still had trouble accepting their husbands' deaths a year later. Mourning was a long-term process in which the widows were preoccupied with thoughts of their husbands. Parkes believes this preoccupation is the core of grief and he describes these memories as so intense that they are experienced as perceptions. Preoccupation with memories of the dead husband, clear visual memories, illusions or hallucinations during the first month, and an enduring sense of the presence of the dead man, all seem to be part of a process reflecting the urge to look for and find the person they lost. In some form most of the widows "found" their husbands by identifying with them; "finding" them allowed them to retain a kind of stable reality that included their old identities. This seems to be a precondition for the development of the necessary new, more autonomous, identity.

17 Some implications of current changes in sex role patterns

Ruth E. Hartley

In recent times it has been the fashion to cry havoc and sound the alarm when discussing alleged changes in sex role patterns. The topic itself has had a certain bandwagon effect so that one could scarcely open a Sunday supplement without being faced with scare headlines about women in pants and the dire consequences of contact with dishwater to the male psyche.[1] All sorts of "experts" have had a heyday with "mannish" women and "emasculated" men, on the basis of very little evidence for the existence of either in unusual proportions. In view of undisputed interest in this topic, it seems desirable to take a sober look at the facts and make a considered assessment of the changes that actually have taken place, or are taking place, on the basis of systematically collected empirical evidence.

When we make such evidence the criterion for our evaluations, we find there is surprisingly little to go on. For one thing, to talk of change in sex role patterns implies comparison with some state before the change took place. In this case, it demands that we establish some temporal baseline, i.e., we must answer the question: change since when? An examination of the popular press seems to indicate that much of the recent and current hysteria had its beginning in conditions at the close of World War II, when some of the women who had been lured out of

Reprinted from Ruth E. Hartley, "Some Implications of Current Changes in Sex Role Patterns," Merrill-Palmer Quarterly, 3:6 April 1960, pp. 153-164. This paper is based on an address delivered at the annual meeting of the New York Society of Clinical Psychologists, May 23, 1959. The data reported here were collected as part of a project supported by Research Grant M-959 (C, C-1, C-2, C-3) from the National Institute of Mental Health, Public Health Service. The author wishes to thank Dr. Frank Hardesty, Research Associate on the project, for his skill in collecting a large portion of the data reported here and for his cooperation in handling the analysis.

private life for service in wartime industries and as substitutes for men withdrawn from essential public services refused to be pushed back again. The cries of anguish of the would-be persuaders are preserved in most of the post-1945 issues of the "slick" magazines addressed to homemakers. Our assumption, therefore, is that the change we are assessing must have taken place roughly within the last twenty years, between the beginning of World War II and now. If this is the case, we must look for reliable empirical material, preferably in quantitative form, depicting sex role patterns around 1940 and a set of similar measurements of current patterns, and compare them, before we can really know what, if anything, has happened to sex role patterns within the last two decades.

Anyone who has tried to find sets of validly comparable sex role data gathered over a twenty-year interval will acknowledge that the pickings are rather sparse. We have some statistics for who-does-what in limited samples of current families,[2] but with what shall we compare them? This just does not seem to have been a burning question in 1940—certainly not important enough for any systematic records to have been made.

The best evidence we have deals with only a small segment of sex role activities in adulthood and derives from census data. I refer, of course, to the figures depicting the striking rise in the number of women in the labor force during the last twenty years. Before we consider this evidence as a definitive criterion of change, however, I would like to quote a few words of caution by Smuts, who has been intimately involved in the intensive study of human resources conducted by the Conservation of Human Resources Project.[3] He writes:

The only source of comprehensive data on the number of working women and their occupations is the U.S. Census. Before 1940 the Census counted these persons, aged ten years and over, who were "gainfully occupied." A gainfully occupied person was defined, essentially, as one who pursued with some regularity an activity which produced money income. Since 1940 the Census has counted persons in the "labor force," which is a much more precise approach. The labor force includes all persons aged fourteen and over who work for pay or profit for any length of time during a given week or who seek such work; and those who work for fifteen hours a week or more in a profit-making family enterprise, even if not paid. . . .

Comparison of Census data on women's employment in different years must be undertaken with extreme caution. The definition of a gainfully occupied person was much narrower in 1890 than in later years. The 1890 Census counted a person as gainfully occupied only if he reported an occupation "upon which he chiefly depends for support, and in which he would ordinarily be engaged during the larger part of the year." This definition excluded most of the large number of women who earned money through homework and many of those who worked irregularly away from home. In addition, a great many who qualified under the definition were not counted. Because most women did not work regularly for pay, and because the Census instructions emphasized the circumstances under which women should not be counted as gainfully occupied, Census takers were likely to be careless in recording women's work. This tendency was reinforced by the *ad hoc* character of the Census organization and by the tendency of the respon-

dents to reflect the prevailing views of women's proper role by concealing the employment of female members of the family. As a result of all these circumstances, any woman who was both a housekeeper and a paid worker, or a student and a paid worker, was likely to be recorded only as a housekeeper or student.

It is particularly important to keep this in mind when evaluating analyses of long-term trends in women's work. The increasing employment of women shown by the Census data reflects not only the growing employment of women for pay, but also the growing willingness of respondents to report women's work, the broadening of Census definitions, improvement of the Census organization and procedures, and the decline of homework, which could be more easily overlooked than work away from home (20, pp. 157-159).

It seems clear from the above that even Census data are not a reliable indicator of the extent of social changes. Granting the validity of these qualifications, however, it still seems evident that there are more women in the labor force than ever before, and of these a larger proportion are wives and mothers than ever before. This is one definite change in sex role activity for which we have evidence and we might start our search for implications by asking what impact this change has had. First, however, it would be well to again attend to some admonitions from Smuts:

Emphasis on the new work of women, however should not be allowed to obscure an equally important fact. Today, as always, most of the time and effort of American wives is devoted to their responsibilities within the home and family circle. This is true even of those who are in the labor force. Since 1890 the demands of paid work have become much lighter. The normal work week has decreased from sixty to forty hours; paid holidays and vacations have become universal; and most of the hard, physical labor that work once required has been eliminated. Because of these developments, many women can work outside the home and still have time and energy left for home and family. Moreover, most working mothers do not assume the burdens of a full schedule of paid work. Among employed mothers of preschool children, four out of five worked only part time or less than half the year in 1956. Among those whose children were in school, three out of five followed the same curtailed work schedule. And even among working wives who had no children at home, only a little more than half were year-round, full-time members of the labor force (20, pp. 36-37).

As the last quotation suggests, this change in feminine roles apparently does not mean that women are abandoning their traditional family responsibilities to seek personal glory in the market place. It does not even seem to mean that women are particularly intent on competing with men, contrary to the accusations that have been frequently hurled at them. On this point, Smuts remarks:

Today, as in 1890, the great majority of working women have little interest in achieving success in a career. . . .
In recent years employers have been able to attract millions of additional women into the labor force without changing the relative levels of men's and women's pay, or greatly expanding women's opportunities for advancement. The decade between 1945 and 1955 was one of booming prosperity, labor shortages, unprecedented peacetime demand for women workers, and unprecedented increase in the number of women working. Yet, in 1955, the median

wage and salary income of women who worked full time was still less than two-thirds that of men—almost exactly the same as it was in 1945. This suggests that it is not particularly important to a great many working women whether or not they earn as much as men, or have equal opportunities for training and promotion. What they seek first in work is an agreeable job that makes limited demands. Since they have little desire for a successful career in paid work, they are likely to drift into the traditional women's occupations. They are willing to become teachers, though they could earn more as engineers; willing to take factory and service and clerical jobs that hold little hope of substantial advancement (20, p. 108).

These observations by Smuts have been supported by many studies of adolescent girls and young women in high schools and colleges distributed widely over the country (3, 4, 18, 19). We might legitimately ask if there are implications we can validly derive from this particular change in the role patterns of one sex. Below, we will consider the data we have as they apply to the women themselves, to their husbands, and to their children, as far as it is possible and valid to separate the three.

From lengthy interviews with about forty working mothers,[4] divided almost equally between professional and nonprofessional levels, the implication emerges that this change in sex role pattern is more a matter of form than function. Most of the working mothers we interviewed consider their work as an aspect of their nurturant function. It is another way in which they can serve their families. They do not substitute work for family obligations—they *add* it to the traditional roster of womanly duties and see it as another way of helping their husbands and providing for the needs of their children. Their husbands are still seen as the major and responsible bread-winners—the mothers consider themselves merely as "helping" persons in this area.

The opportunity to help in this way has happy consequences for many. They feel a greater sense of freedom of choice, less coercion by blind fate, more integrity as persons, less frustration and less harrassment by economic problems. The stimulation they receive from contact with others on the job and the change in physical surroundings between home and work even seem to make housework more satisfying and less like drudgery. The really bitter complaints about the hatefulness of household tasks tend to come from the nonworking women we interviewed rather than from those who worked at an outside job. That these salutary effects of the freedom to work may not be confined to our small sample is suggested by the findings of Hoffman, who in a study of 89 working mothers and 89 nonworking mothers, matched in pertinent variables, found that working mothers, in comparison to nonworking mothers, are warm, helpful, supportive and mild in their discipline, suggesting more relaxed and satisfied persons (9).

The freedom to work has, however, not been achieved without psychic penalty. The guilt some working mothers feel about their "self-indulgence" in going to work is marked and may have negative consequences to their daughters and to society at large. Typically, these "guilty" mothers do not work out of dire necessity; they enjoy their work and provide well for their absence from the household. Yet they seem to feel that there is something not

quite legitimate about their preference for working and almost invariably give their children the impression that they work only because they need the money. "What other excuse would I have for working?" one such mother asked the interviewer. It seems to us that this situation reveals a questionable state of social values which induces women to feel that they have not a natural right to work at something congenial to them, which makes a positive contribution to the community, and which need not deprive their school-age children to any significant degree. That this anxiety is a socially induced one is suggested by Williams,[5] who found that working mothers whose social contacts were mainly with others in a similar situation did not suffer these difficulties, while working mothers whose contacts were mainly with more traditionally oriented families experienced great discomfort. Perhaps as more and more mothers work, the social climate inducing these feelings will dissipate. Meanwhile, however, these attitudes are resulting in a strongly negative perception of the work situation in general on the part of many children (it is something one does only out of necessity) and a damaging lack of candor between parent and child. It is also, we feel, producing an ego-crippling effect on the female children involved, since it exerts a necessarily restrictive influence on the development of the child's self-concept (6, 7, 24).

Perhaps the most widely discussed area of concern related to this change in women's roles deals with its effect on men. The more sensational statements have implied the immediate emasculation of any male whose wife spends some time at money-earning. What does sober fact reveal? One traditional element of masculinity in our society is the dominance of the male in his family. Dominance implies control over other persons as well as control over possessions. Hoffman (9) suggests that control in the family situation might function in two ways: as *activity-control*, referring to control a person has over a given area of activities, regardless of whether or not this control has an important effect on others, and as *power*, defined as the degree to which one person makes decisions which control another person's behavior or makes decisions about object which affect another person in an important way. In relation to activity-control, Hoffman found that working wives had less control and their husbands more than in families where wives did not work. In relation to the power component, no difference was found between working women and matched nonworking women. Although the husbands of the working wives may have participated more in household tasks after the women went to work than they had before, this apparently did not perceptibly affect the quality of their status in the family group.[6]

Actually, we still have very little reliable information concerning the effect of the woman's work role on the man's domestic role. Blood and Hamblin report that the husbands of working women participate in domestic activities to a greater extent than the husbands of nonworking women (1). Our own data, coming from children's perceptions rather than adult reports, suggest that the class variable is more significant in relation to male participation in traditionally female household tasks than the work status of the wife.[7] Boys with working mothers assign domestic tasks to men more frequently than do boys with non-working mothers (p = .05), it is true, but boys from working-class and lower-middle-class homes exceed boys from upper-middle-class homes by an even greater margin in making such assignment of roles (p < .01). This finding might suggest that assumption of the work role by women of lower economic strata might have more impact on traditional male roles than the same phenomenon at higher economic levels, where outside persons substitute for the wife in domestic tasks more frequently. Careful examination of our data, however, reveals that in the class comparison boys from homes with nonworking mothers contributed the bulk of the male domestic role assignments!

It is interesting to note, in passing, that the boys in our sample were more prone to assign traditionally feminine domestic tasks to men than were the girls (.2 < p < .1). This may mean that these tasks are gradually being incorporated into the male self-concept, so that we may expect acceptance of an increasingly egalitarian division of all life tasks and a parallel diminution of rigid judgmental evaluations about the "manly" or "unmanly" nature of specific activities. A bit of clarification is necessary here, however. Male domestic involvement is regarded by our subjects as a "helping" role, with the major responsibility for household management and child care still unquestionably the woman's job. This feeling about male domestic participation echoes the feeling we have noted about the woman's participation in the work world: the activity is subordinate in importance both to the major responsibility of the sex involved and to the weight of the responsibility borne in the given area by the opposite sex. We are not witnessing an elimination of differences—only an amelioration.[8]

A few more items from the data collected in our study of the development of concepts of women's social roles might be of interest here. These deal with the apparent connections between a mother's work status and her children's concepts of the future roles of themselves and others. We found, for example, that the presence of a working mother made no difference in the assignment of nondomestic work roles to women by girls but was a significant variable (at the .05 level) with the boys. When we asked our female subjects about their own future plans, however, the work status of the mother was an important differentiating variable. Significantly more daughters of nonworking mothers mentioned housewife as their first choice of future occupation than did daughters of working mothers (p < .05). Significantly more daughters of working mothers said they thought they would work after they had children than did the others (p < .05). Similarly more daughters of working mothers tended to choose nontraditional vocations (among choices other than housewife) than did the daughters of nonworking mothers.

Despite the effect of working mothers on boys' assignment of work roles to women, significantly more girls indicated plans to work after marriage than there were boys who said they expected their wives to work (p < .01). This disparity echoes a common finding (15) and indicates a force which we believe serves to slow the movement of women into the work world.[9]

Differences in plans for the future expressed by daughters of working mothers as compared with daughters of non-working mothers may be explained in part by differences in their perception of the work role as such. This is suggested by the comparative proportions of children of working and nonworking mothers who made relatively positive and relatively negative interpretations of a pictured situation in which a woman was leaving her child to go to work.[10] Although about 64% of our subjects (N = 108) sensed some discomfort in this situation for the woman in the picture, only 37% of the children of working mothers interpreted her attitude as negative toward the work itself. In contrast, approximately 54% of the children of nonworking mothers thought that the woman must feel negative toward her work. These findings, combined with the others already described, suggest that the changes that have already taken place in sex role patterning will inevitably lead to extension of themselves, provided their orderly development is not interrupted by widespread social or economic crises.

The desirability of such extension may be a moot point. Some preliminary findings reported by Bromfenbrenner[11] from a study of family structure and personality development seem to be relevant here.

Studying the effects on children of parental absence, he gathered data from 450 students in the tenth grade of a small city and from the teachers. Parental absence was defined by a variable called "saliency" or the general extent to which a particular parent appears to be actively present in the child's world.

Bronfenbrenner found that the effect of parental absence on the child seems to depend on whether the missing parent is of the same or opposite sex and how much time the remaining parent spends in the home. The crucial person seems to be the parent of the same sex.

In relation to responsibility, for example, so long as the same-sex parent was present a good deal of the time, the child of either sex was rated as above average. If the same parent was in the high-absence group, and the opposite-sex parent was also absent a great deal, the responsibility rating dropped drastically. Similarly, if the remaining parent was in the high-presence category, the subject received a low rating. But if the same-sex parent was absent a great deal, and the opposite-sex parent present only an intermediate amount, the child received the highest mean rating on responsibility in the sample. Thus, if a boy's father was away from home a good deal, and his mother was either away excessively or present excessively, he tended to be rated low in responsibility. If the mother avoided either extreme, the son tended to be rated exceptionally high. Similarly for girls: if the mother was excessively absent, the relative presence or absence of the father seemed to determine the responsibility rating.

The implications of this study for our topic are intriguing. For one thing, it suggests that, in the traditional family set-up where the father is usually absent a great deal of the time, the continuous availability of the mother may be detrimental to her sons; they may be better served were the mother to be legitimately involved away from the home on a part-time basis. For girls, on the other hand, an optimal pattern would seem to be one in which the father is home somewhat more than ordinarily obtains, if the mother carries full-time responsibilities outside the home. The sex role pattern which seems to be currently increasing, with fathers fully employed and mothers employed part time, would seem to promise more for the development of boys than of girls. However, since the same-sex parent is still present a good deal of the time for girls, the latter seem not likely to be penalized.

Effects of parental presence and absence seem to differ markedly with differences in the socioeconomic status of the family, the father's level of education, and his work orientation (whether quality oriented or not). The differential impacts of such variables as these may account for apparent inconsistencies in findings presented by studies focusing on different respective segments of the population. Thus we find many apparent contradictions between findings reported by the Gluecks (5) who studied mainly families of low socioeconomic status and those reported by Hoffman, Blood and Hamblin, and Bronfenbrenner, who either concentrated on middle- and upper-middle-class subjects or included a significant number of such subjects in their samples. Recognizing this state of affairs, we must limit any implications drawn from the data we have discussed to the type of population from which the data were collected. With this qualification in mind, a few general observations seem to be warranted.

The direction of current sex role change seems to be toward consistently greater egalitarianism, with leadership centered in families of higher educational levels. As the tendency toward the spread of higher education continues, we can expect more and more families to share this pattern. If psychologists are correct in assuming that one can give to others only what one has as part of the self, increased feelings of self-fulfillment and freedom of action which seem to accompany current developments in women's roles should lead to a lessening of crippling maternal possessiveness and a diminution of "momism."

The implications for men are less clear. It is unfortunately evident that current socialization techniques used with boys continue to saddle many of them with irrational and damaging anxieties about their ability to implement the male role (8, 11, 12). These anxieties are frequently accompanied, as one might expect, by extreme conceptual rigidities and limitations in self-definition and by a tendency toward defensive hostility. It is obvious that any change in the *status quo* would cause discomfort to such anxious individuals, and an increase in the apparent capability of females, whom they are taught at all cost to avoid emulating and whom they are pressured to best in order to validate their masculinity, would be particularly threatening. Perhaps we are approaching an era of more confident women and more anxious men. Frankly, this is pure specualtion. It might be instructive to keep an eye on the sex ratio of male and female psychiatric referrals. At present they show a complete reversal between childhood and adulthood, with males far in the lead before adolescence and females coming out way ahead after adolescence (2, 14, 17, 21, 23). If significant changes in the relative proportions of satisfaction and

threat impinging on each sex accompany changes in sex role patterns, the gap between female and male referrals should lessen.

There is one possibility of more generalized male difficulty which relates to ego-development in childhood rather than functioning in adulthood. Current socialization practices in relation to male children can create even greater difficulties than they do at present as the permissible role activities of girls widen. It is conceivable that the widespread use of negative sanctions, generally phrased in the unspecific and semantically confusing adjuration not to be a "sissy," may be responsible for more and more limitation in permissible activity for boys as girls enter into more and more formerly exclusively masculine activities (10, 16). There is some indication that in certain localities this is happening (22). However, this suggestion may be borrowing trouble. There is no indication at present that activities cease to be regarded as suitably masculine just because girls also engage in them, if they have been considered acceptable before girls joined the fun.

In conclusion, I should like to emphasize the following five points:

1. Concern about a possible increase in children's confusion about sex roles because of alleged changes seems to be without foundation. For one thing, children are not aware of the changes since they do not have the time perspective for this. They react to the picture as they perceive it at any given moment, and changes in social roles are not so precipitous as to create contradictions from moment to moment. Let us beware of projecting our adult confusions on the children, and try to profit from them to create child-handling techniques that will ensure the necessary psychic flexibility that future developments will require.

2. Whatever changes have taken place seem to be mainly new means of fulfilling established and accepted functions and to imply no radical reversals of these.

3. There seems to be no realistic basis for the guilt many working mothers of school-age children feel about their work. Some of the evidence available at present suggests that it might, in fact, be desirable for some mothers to take part-time jobs.

4. There is no necessary implication of threat or damage in any perceptible current change in sex role activity. The real problem of adjustment to sex roles seems to be rooted in the differential pressures associated with respective developmental stages in each sex. Among males the pressures seem to be more exigent before adulthood; among females, during and after adolescence. In each case, special pressure toward limitation and restriction is identifiable during the periods for which comparative rates of breakdown are greatest for each sex.

5. In view of the above, current trends toward greater freedom of action for women would seem to be positive in implication, if the implied evaluative egalitarianism is also extended to the male sex. This seems to be taking place only in a very limited fashion, with the leadership centered in families of upper educational levels. Ego-strengthening socialization processes applied to male children seem to be

of central importance for the smooth synchronization of change in sex role activity patterns.

NOTES

1. See, for example, these articles: Ward Cannel, "Is the American Male Man or Mouse?" *Washington Daily News*, Dec. 11, 1958; Bruno Bettelheim, "Fathers Shouldn't Be Mothers!" *This Week Magazine*, Apr. 20, 1958; Jean Libman Black, "Husbands Shouldn't Do Housework!" *This Week Magazine*, Sept. 8, 1957; Dorothy Barclay, "Trousered Mothers and Dishwashing Dads," *New York Times Magazine*, Apr. 28, 1957; Mike Wallace and John A. Schindler, "Are the Two Sexes Merging?" *New York Post*, Oct. 17, 1957.

2. One source is an unpublished study by Lois W. Hoffman, Ronald Lippitt, and others, at the Research Center for Group Dynamics, University of Michigan, in which 450 middle-class families in Detroit were surveyed. The study was reported by John Sembower in *The New York Journal*, November 12, 1957, under the headline "Hear Ye, O Husbands, Dusting's Not Thy Destiny. . . ." References to the results of this survey can also be found elsewhere (1, 9, 13).

3. Established at Columbia University in 1950 as a cooperative research undertaking, the Project has led to major publications concerning the uneducated, the Negro potential, the effective soldier, and women as workers.

4. These interviews took place as part of a study of children's concepts of women's social roles and were used to gather data concerning the background of the children who were subjects as well as to assess the attitudes of the interviewees concerning the satisfactions and frustrations of woman's role from the adult's point of view. Each interview took from 1½ to 2½ hours to administer.

5. From a preliminary statement of findings by Dr. Robin Williams in correspondence with the author.

6. This opinion is also supported in the paper by Blood and Hamblin (1).

7. The raw data yielding these comparisons came from the responses of approximately 150 boys and girls, 5, 8, and 11 years of age, to the following statement: "Suppose you met a person from Mars and he knew nothing about the way we live here, and he asked you to tell him about girls (your age) in this world; what would you tell him girls need to know or be able to do?" These same questions were asked in relation to boys, women, and men.

8. This amelioration is not characteristic of sex role patterns only—it is only one aspect of a pervasive social trend. Turning again to *Women and Work in America*, we find Smuts pointing out: "The increasing employment of middle-class, middle-aged wives is but one aspect of a series of developments that have tended to eliminate sharp differences in American society. . . .

"Rural and urban ways of life have come closer together. Many local and regional pecularities have been all but erased as a result of increased industrialization. The vast gulf between the very rich and the very poor has been narrowed. Status distinctions among occupations have been blurred as the wages of manual labor have risen, and the brutalizing aspects of manual work in the last century have been abolished. The spread of free public education has reduced the cultural and economic advantages of the well-born. For present purposes, at least, the most important of the fading contrasts in American life is the contrast between the activities of men and women" (20, pp. 66-67).

9. This opinion was supported by materials collected from parents of our subjects. From interviews with 90 mothers, divided approximately equally among working and nonworking, we got the impression that the husband's attitude toward his wife's working often served as the deciding factor when neither economic necessity nor preschool children were involved—and some of the unhappiest women we talked with were among those who were prevented from working because there was no economic necessity for them to do so and their husbands could not conceive of any other valid reason. The unhappiest husbands we interviewed were those who aspired to upper-middle-class status, whose wives were compelled to work for economic reasons; their wives were not particularly unhappy about working.

10. The materials from which these data were derived were elicited in the following way. A picture showing a woman with a briefcase leaving the half-open door of a house through which a small child watched was presented to each subject. The interviewer said, "This little girl is at home and her mother is going to work. How does the mother feel about going to work? What makes you think so?" Other questions elicited reasons for the mother's working, alternatives to her working, and feelings of the child.

11. Personal communication from Dr. Urie Bonfenbrenner giving a preliminary report of findings.

REFERENCES

1. Blood, R. O., and Hamblin, R. L. The effect of the wife's employment on the family power structure. *Soc. Forces*, 1958, 36, 347-352.
2. *Department of Mental Hygiene, annual report for 1956.* Albany: Dept. Ment. Hyg., 1957.
3. Douvan, Elizabeth M., and Kaye, Carol. *Adolescent girls.* Mimeographed paper, University of Michigan.
4. Empey, L. T. Role expectations of young women regarding marriage and a career. *Marriage and Family Living*, 1958, 20, 152-155.
5. Gleuck, S. and Eleanor. Working mothers and delinquency. *Ment. Hyg., N.Y.*, 1957, 41, 327-352.
6. Harte, Joan B. *Modern attitudes toward women.* Issued as a separate by the Auxiliary Council to the Association for the Advancement of Psychoanalysis, 220 W. 98th St., New York 25, N.Y., 1950.
7. Harte, Joan B. *Women in our culture.* Issued as a separate by the Auxiliary Council to the Association for the Advancement of Psychoanalysis, 1953.
8. Hartley, Ruth E. Sex role pressures and the socialization of the male child. *Psychol. Rep.*, in press.
9. Hoffman, Lois W. Effects of the employment of mothers on parental power relations and the division of household tasks. *Marriage and Family Living*, 1960, 22, 27-35.
10. Jones, Mary C. A comparison of the attitudes and interests of ninth graders. Paper read at Society for Research in Child Development, Bethesda, Md., March, 1959.
11. Lynn, D. B. A note on sex differences in the development of masculine and feminine identification. *Psychol. Rev.*, 1959, 66, 126-135.
12. Lynn, D. B. Sex differences in identification-development. *Child Develpm.*, in press.
13. Miller, D. R., and Swanson, G. E. *The changing American parent: a study in the Detroit area.* New York: John Wiley & Sons, 1958.
14. *Patients in mental institutions 1955. part II. Public hospitals for the mentally ill.* Publ. Hlth. Serv. publication, no. 574. Washington, D.C.: Govt. Printing Office.
15. Payne, R. Adolescents' attitudes toward the working wife. *Marriage and Family Living*, 1956, 18, 345-348.
16. Rosenberg, B. G., and Sutton-Smith, B. A revised conception of masculine-feminine differences in play activities. *J. genet. Psychol.*, in press.
17. Schwartz, E. F. Statistics of juvenile delinquency in the United States. *Ann. Amer. Acad. polit. soc. Sci.*, 1949, 261, 9-20.
18. Slocum, W. L. *Occupational planning by undergraduates at the State College of Washington.* Pullman, Wash.: State College of Washington, 1954.
19. Slocum, W. L., and Empey, L. T. *Occupational planning by young women.* Pullman, Wash.: State College of Washington, 1956.
20. Smuts, R. W. *Women and work in America.* New York: Columbia University Press, 1959.
21. *Statistical report for the year ending June 30, 1955.* Sacramento: Department of Mental Hygene, 1955.
22. Sutton-Smith, B. *The games of New Zealand children.* Berkeley: University of California Press, in press.
23. Ullman, C. A. Identification of maladjusted school children. Publ. Hlth. Monogr., no 7. Washington, D.C.: Govt. Printing Office.
24. Wenkart, Antonia. *The career mother.* Issued as a separate by the Auxiliary Council to the Association for the Advancement of Psychoanalysis, 1947.

18 The roots of ambivalence in American women

Alice S. Rossi

The major focus of this paper is on the social and cultural roots of ambivalence among American women toward family and work roles or combinations of these primary social roles. My procedure will be to state a few general sociological propositions about ambivalence and social roles, and then analyze the implications of these propositions for the differences between men and women in their orientation to their major adult roles in the family and the occupational systems.

Social roles and ambivalence

1. There is no social role toward which there is no ambivalence. Whether the role is something anticipated in the future, or one currently held, there are negative as well as positive feelings toward every role. It follows from this that one can anticipate some ambivalence among men and women toward both family and work roles.

2. Roles vary in the extent to which it is culturally and psychologically permissible to express ambivalence, to discuss or admit to negative feelings toward them.

3. Ambivalence can be admitted most readily toward those roles which are optional. The more it is possible to either assume or reject a given role, the more likely it is that ambivalence will be overt. Where there is very little choice, ambivalence will operate covertly, often through the psychological mechanism of displacement.

4. The more critical the role is for the maintenance and survival of a society, the greater the likelihood that the negative side of ambivalence will be repressed, and negative sanctions applied to their expression.

Men and work

Let us now apply these propositions to the primary roles of men and women. The primary role for American men has been their occupational role, and for women, their family roles. Men have no choice of whether to work or not, hence whatever negative feelings they have will be covert and probably often displaced onto other areas of life. The majority of women do have a choice to work or not to work, hence their ambivalence can be openly shown. In fact, it is permissible for a woman to show the negative side of her feelings toward work and careers to a much greater extent than it is permissible for her to express a strong positive attraction to careers.

Not only are men lacking in any choice where work is concerned, but our society further expects men to aspire to jobs of the highest occupational prestige consistent with their abilities; indeed, his job should tax and stretch his ability or it will not be "challenging" enough. If they do not, if a man settles for a job below his abilities, we tend to consider this a "social problem," a "talent loss" in the current lingo. We do not even consider the possibility that such a gap between ability and job task might have some positive consequences for the man involved; that, for example, such a gap might release energies and time for creative contributions in other social roles, for more involvement in family life, community, politics or art. By sharp contrast, we not only tolerate but encourage women to work in jobs which are below their abilities, precisely because this *does* release energies for their central roles in the family.

It is as a result of this basic lack of option and the social expectation that occupational choice will be keyed to a job at least equal to the talent of the man, if not slightly above that talent, that we find the negative side of men's ambivalence toward work in disguised forms: somatic disorders of heart and stomach and varying degrees of hypertension are not a surprising toll. Furthermore, the stresses engendered by this lack of choice are generally absorbed by the family. It is assumed that job-generated tensions will be released at home, not on the job, a displacement which women are charged with the responsibility of managing and relieving, for their husbands.

These are important and fundamental structural factors which underlie the great concern expressed in recent years about the unrest and alienation of many of our brightest undergraduates. Parents, educators, government and business officials are all concerned to notice any tendency among undergraduates to question the high primacy of achievement and the work ethic, to complain about or reject impersonal bureaucracy, or to turn away from upper middle class professional and business occupations. This is deemed a serious social problem only because *male* undergraduates are involved. Few would be very deeply bothered if this unrest were confined to *women* undergraduates, for the simple reason that it is only the college men who are supposed to aspire for the most prestigeful occupations their skills equip them to hold, and clearly they should not question the primacy of work as the fundamental social role of an American male.

Edited from Alice S. Rossi, "The Roots of Ambivalence in American Women" (1966), unpublished paper.

Note, too, that this fundamental lack of choice dictates the design of sociological inquiries concerning men and their work. We ask women why they work, what they like and dislike about working per se, because they are presumed to have an option in this area. But we do not ask men what they like or dislike about working, only what they like and dislike about a particular job in a particular field.

Women and family

An analogous portrait can be drawn in the case of women where family roles are concerned, though here, unlike work roles, neither sex has any real choice. Neither men nor women are free to openly reject marriage and parenthood. The pressures are of course particularly strong upon the girl, but both sexes are socialized to accept the view that marriage is essential to achieve personal satisfaction and happiness in adulthood. A girl grows up with the knowledge that her fundamental social status will be determined by the occupational success of the man she marries. It takes no detailed inquiry into census data for a young woman to realize that no matter how well trained or competent she may be in her own field, most of her homemaker friends will enjoy a higher social status than she is likely to achieve by her own efforts.

So invariant is this pressure to marry, that even those who do not marry are apt to claim that they "never met the right man" or have carried the torch for a long lost love, in either case keeping intact the high desirability of marriage rather than saying anything about the reasons many single women have had for rejecting marriage. It is only married people who may joke about marriage.

If the pressure is strong to accept marriage, it is even stronger to accept maternity. Women (and men too, for that matter) are not free to say they do not want children, or after they have them, to indicate that they do not enjoy many aspects of their care. Thus we hear about the absence of adult stimulation from the young homemaker rather than the irritation of constant demands of young children upon her; or complaints about the tasks associated with her housewife role, often a displacement for complaints that stem from the maternal role. Just as sociological researchers do not ask men about their negative feelings toward work per se, so too they do not ask women about their negative feelings toward marriage or maternity per se. We have studies by the dozen about marital happiness and marital problems but not about the negative and positive feelings toward marriage itself, and certainly not to maternity itself. It is satisfaction with a particular spouse, or problems with a particular child that we study, not what do you like and dislike about being married or being a mother.

I noted earlier that it is because *male* undergraduates are involved that educators and parents have expressed acute concern about the questioning of primacy of work. For the counterpart to occur where women are concerned, one would have to find unrest and questioning on the part of women undergraduates concerning the primacy of marriage and maternity. Precisely because the family roles are considered to be the basic anchor points in women's lives, I would predict a widespread concern among parents and most educators, were college women to initiate any lively dialogue or questioning of the desirability of marriage and maternity.

And yet it is imperative that we begin an open discussion about precisely these aspects of women's lives, to question the cultural assumption that marriage and parenthood should be desired and attained by all men and women. We are not a rural society of small entrepreneurial units of farmer, wife and children with land to till. It may have been functional in such a society to exert strong social pressure on all to marry, have many children and work extremely hard, for the basic human needs of food and shelter could not be fulfilled otherwise. Nor could any line be drawn between procreative and recreative sex, as we can now do. It is ironic that in our urban technological society, when there is less social and economic necessity for a high proportion of the population being married, and clearly only dysfunctional for couples to have large numbers of children, that the marriage rate, and until very recently, the birth rate, have gone up rather than down.

There are several specific reasons for encouraging an open discussion about negative feelings toward the roles of spouse and parent. For one, a lot of the guilt women express about the effect of their working upon their children is a displacement of guilt which they really feel in departing from the cultural expectation that they should only experience positive feelings toward the maternal role. Thus I have found in discussion groups with women that the studies of maternal employment, which show no consistent pattern of any negative effect on children, do not really answer the unspoken sources of concern and guilt among the women. Women who work because they want to and not simply because they have to, are emotionally released only when someone speaks directly to the question of their underlying feelings toward child care. Laughter is often a good index of the points in such discussions was there as much release as when someone said in effect, "I just don't like the noise and constant demands for attention that children require of me. I am working because I like my work and I don't like full time motherhood. I think my kids would be a mess if I were with them all the time." This does not mean these women do not enjoy many aspects of maternity, but only to indicate that as with all social roles, there is a negative side as well as a positive. To be free to express the ambivalence they really feel toward the maternal role is a release all too many women are blocked from expressing.

A second reason to encourage an airing of ambivalence toward maternity, is out of concern for the children or potential children a woman may bear. For every child born to a woman who consciously did not want that pregnancy, there are many more born to women who are not even aware of the ambivalence they feel toward maternity and who are unconsciously prone to maternal rejection if not maternal destructiveness. Women may be an easy prey to self-deception in this area, but children are not. Witness only the extent to which children respond to fantasies about godmothers and bad witches, good fairies and bad stepmothers, and one can see that the child is aware of ambivalence in the mother toward the maternal role even is she is not. The babies many people in medicine and social work are currently concerned for—the "battered babies" brought to doctors and hospitals with undiagnosed "accidents"—are another indication of such underlying rejection of mothering and fathering. The invariance with which disturbance in the mother or father is found in case histories of the mentally ill, is further evidence of latent rejection of parenthood. These are but the tip of the iceberg and mask the vast unknown areas of parental role rejection that we know relatively little about outside the clinical literature. If we judge by the incidence of unsuccessful parenthood, it is clear that parenthood is *not* for everybody, men or women, and it is long overdue that we recognize this.

There has been considerable discussion about the fact that the overwhelming majority of Soviet physicians are women, a dramatic contrast to the small seven per cent that women represent among American physicians. Less well known is the fact that women are at least three times as well represented among physicians in other communist countries such as Yugoslavia and Hungary, in socialist countries like England, and in underdeveloped countries like India, Chile and Thailand as they are in the United States. Dissimilar as these countries are in their politics, culture and state of industrial development, they share a common characteristic that sets them in distinct opposition to the United States: they have not had a long historical tradition of very high value stress on individualism.

How this value contrast affects the ambivalence of women toward highly demanding professions can be seen in the cultural expectations concerning the rearing of children. In India a woman is not expected to rear her children by herself, but to let a number of other people, servants and relatives, care for and supervise them. Affective neutrality rather than intensity characterized both the Indian marital and parental relationship, since it was not the individual, but a kinship and caste group to whom primary allegiance had to be developed in the younger generation. The same expectation is found in the extended family system of many Latin American societies.

In the Soviet Union, societal values have been focussed far more on the collective group than on the individual, a pattern that did not suddenly emerge after the revolution, but had been a basic Russian characteristic in religion and social order of Czarist days. If societal values stress the submission of an individual to the group and team cooperation rather than individual competition, there is a cultural context congenial to leaving the socialization of youngsters to group control by agencies outside the nuclear family. What the extended kin group did before industrialization, the schools and creche systems did after industrialization. A school system that runs from 8 in the morning to 6 at night, and in which teachers go off with their students to summer camps, in which child-care creches and nurseries are taken for granted as services due any citizen in need of them, is thus consistent with the fundamental values of a society which values a collective and cooperative orientation.

By contrast, President Kennedy's plea to Americans—"ask not what you can get but what you can give"—struck a new and novel note because our society has always been focussed on the fulfillment and achievement of the individual in competition with others around him, rather than cooperation, dedication and service to others. Americans must first be true to themselves, and only then seek to be of service to others. Many societies reverse this, and believe that only by being of service to others, whether a kin group, a religious group or the nation at large, can there be fulfillment for the individual.

I think it is the fundamental focus on individuality which roots American women firmly in the maternal role to such an excessive degree, and which accounts for both the total lack of any community facilities to ease home and child care, and the very low representation of women in the ranks of the major professions. If each child must be reared in a very special way, accenting his development to his full unique potential and in competition with his peers, then he is best reared in a highly individuated manner by the person who most appreciates his uniqueness, his mother. Only such uniqueness and a self-conception rooted in it is considered appropriate to develop a competitve, go-getting, work-focused new generation.

It follows from this very high valuation of individuality that it will be a very difficult task to gain any acceptance in the United States of something like a national network of child care centers. This will be difficult even in those cases where children are reared in families in which the 21 hours they are *not* in headstart programs may undo any benefit they derive from three hours at a pre-school center, or for the children of women heads of households who must work. It is highly probable that the more fortunate American middle class families will accept and support day care for the children of working class families long before they will use them for their own children. In an ironic way, it may be by rearing young boys in such intimate association with their mothers during their younger years that American society produces in each generation men who suppress the tender, expressive side of themselves to guard the shaky sense of identity that follows from too much intimacy with mother, and thereby perpetuates the masculine quality of American life, and the supremacy of technology and science over the arts, culture and people-caring occupations. It is little wonder that sex in America tends to be gymnastic, non-verbal and narrowly genital, rather than subtle, verbal and inclusive of all the senses, nor that sex instruction, where it is offered at all, is likely to be given by a school nurse or a member of the physical education department!

19 *Marriage and the family*

Rachel Dunaway Cox

Reports coming out of Russia about recent developments in patterns of family living are stimulating, interesting, and, to some observers, alarming. Yet we should not make overly hasty judgments as to the value of these new modes of satisfying the basic needs of the human organism for shelter, food, sex, and the care of the young. What we know from experience too often seems the *only* way to satisfy both elemental and superficial needs. The satisfactions human beings derive from family, home, and the various modes of living by which members of the two sexes elaborate and extend their biological relationship are no doubt in part a function of what they are accustomed to.

And yet change of some sort—even though minor—is going on all the time. There is a body of evidence from anthropology, sociology, and social psychology that suggests that changes in basic institutions such as the market, the church, the family, and marriage are responses to historic, geographic, demographic, and economic changes, in short, responses to ecological alterations. Institutions are most likely to fit human need neatly and comfortably if they are true reflections of ecological factors. Not the least of these factors are intangible ones that are ideological—even philosophical—in nature. Thus any discussion as to whether a given form of marriage and the family is a good one must take into account, at the very outset, a value judgment. It must without apology or equivocation make some answer to the questions: What is the central value for which the society strives? What do persons in the society want out of life?

The individual versus the group

Only when some formulation—either explicit or implicit—is made in answer to those questions can an evaluation of institutions be made. If, then, one society places the fullest and highest development of the individual at the apex of the growth process whereas another society places the health, strength, and vigor of the social organization at the apex, then it may happen that the kind of family that will be meat for the first society will be poison for the second, and vice versa. In the first—the one that values the individual—the institution should maximize individuality. In the second, the institution should minimize the equity of the individual in the interests of the state. It is quite obvious that a society does not serve any individual well if it assumes no curbs on individual appetites and impulses. It is equally obvious that no society, however ideally organized, could long brush aside fundamental individual needs. Nevertheless there is a difference in orientation—and the difference may well determine what is "right" at a given time for a given society.

Let me turn for a moment to a consideration of the family as we know it in American society, with its avowed aim to nurture the individual and to cultivate his powers to the greatest extent within the limits of not hurting other persons or the social group. Part of our American assumption includes, to be sure, the idea that the *individual* grows through some sacrifice, that the flowering of the individual can come about only when he himself makes a considerable effort; that there are some things one will not do in order to advance himself, and that the crucial issue is not so much the welfare of the state but rather the moral growth of the individual. It is this ideology that has been built into much of the institutionalized life of the United States. Maximum freedom to pursue human happiness within the framework of a closely knit family unit is the pattern not only in the United States but in most of Western society.

Yet as reports have been coming out of the USSR about far-reaching revisions of family living, we find ourselves asking whether the tried and true family unit we know really does meet the needs of the individual best. Are we clinging to an outmoded pattern simply because we are unwilling to try anything else? Do we confuse ways of meeting needs with the needs themselves? Why have human beings clung so tenaciously to the unit of the father-mother-child living together with mutual responsibility over the life span? Is the persistence of this form of social organization merely a matter of convenience arising out of the fact that it has been the least annoying way to discharge the details of living? Or is it related to inalienable longings that are best met in this pattern?

That the need for shelter, food, and sexual release can be met in a greatly revised family setup seems indisputable. The pleasure we derive from our own vine and fig tree, shared with a few significant others, probably can be met in some degree by the revised family system. In any case, Americans move so frequently now that the notion of the old home place is for many of us only a lovely myth of the olden time. Yet without anchorage in place, or in the specified roles of baking the bread or harvesting the corn, there remains an essentially unchanged core which I would suggest *is* the family—this core is the relationship of persons to each other. It is this core that, it seems to me, is being impinged upon by the revision of the family now being undertaken in Russia.

The western core unit

Within the family persons have great freedom to be themselves. In this intimate and revealing relationship the worst as well as the best emerges—partly because of the minimum of social regulation and oversight that obtains. Parents can perpetrate many overt outrages against their children before the law steps in; similarly spouses can commit atrocities against each other—from neglect to mayhem—while authority is reluctant to intervene. As for the more subtle cruelties between parents and children, practiced within the bonds of matrimony, only the divorce lawyer and his clients can give an account. In a word, the very privacy, the institutionalized immunity to outside interference, lays the family and all its relationships open to some of the gravest evils that human society tolerates.

The family as an institution is vulnerable not only because of the weaknesses of its members and because of its relative freedom from outside interference, but because of its very nature there is implicit within it the potentiality for deep suffering. Hearing Mr. Bronfenbrenner's account of the socialization of Russian children, with their loyalty and their dependency upon the group felt as an abstraction—a whole platoon of nurses, doctors, teachers—one is led to the thought that attachments are likely to remain distant because there are so many persons and, as in any employment situation, the persons are bound to be more or less transient. Belongingness to a group, though perhaps a strong attachment, is likely to be somewhat impersonal. Not so the family in practically every known context. The engagements of child with mother and wife with husband are intense.

At the beginning young persons are called upon to rise to the challenge of becoming unstinting givers to their helpless young. This is no abstract notion; it is a physical, though sleep-sodden, response to an imperious cry at two o'clock in the morning. It is the mother's wearing the dress from year-before-last so a new pair of small shoes can be bought for the first day of school. It is the giving up of an evening of pleasure because the baby has a fever. All this—and much more—calls for a revamping of one's life style, indeed for a revamping of one's inner self. There are often growing pains in the process. How very different and less beset adult years would be if all the rigors of child nurture were by-passed by simply turning the newborn over to a state agency that would organize all this effort and spread it out over a team of trained personnel—much more painless and no doubt more efficient into the bargain.

Further, implicit in the family are the deep distresses that all too often accompany family living. We see much of this in the clinic. The pain of disappointment over what the child is, or is not. Mothers and fathers in the traditional family feel their child's misfortunes and failures keenly: his rejections by peers, the unfairness at the hands of callous adults, his young awkwardness, and his miscalculations. There is the wounded pride, the astonished unbelief when the bright promise of the toddler fades into the ordinariness of the school child. If the relationship of parent to child were a more superficial one—as might well be the case when the child becomes the ward of the state—if the parent knew less of the day-to-day vicissitudes of the children's lives, there would be less involvement. Pain would be diluted to concern, and concern would be shared with the conscientious and efficient agents of the state. Nor would the child feel the prick of necessity to live up to parental hopes.

In the traditional family the young adult struggles to shake off the bonds of parental love that expresses itself in solicitude and supervision. And for the parent whose child has made the necessary leap to freedom, there is the pain of letting go, of turning back to the silent house, the untenanted bed, the abandoned books and baseball bats. This emptiness, this loneliness and longing for the warmth, the clutter, the presence of the now grown-up family could occur only where one has experienced the closeness of family living. And finally the family cycle is marked by the distress of seeing the aging parent lose his powers and become, in truth, the child of the child. In this there lies the pain of loss, and the half-accepted anger that those once so strong, so full of grace, should be brought to weakness and dependency.

Viewing the cycle of family living thus, one wonders why we clasp to ourselves this thorny set of relationships. When some alternative arrangement such as the Russian state plan for child rearing is devised, why do we not jump at it?

On casual inspection, at least, it would seem that a plan that relieves a couple of the care of their young and discourages their too-close involvement would lead to relationships that are, on the whole, fairly pleasant, bland, and constructive. Relieved of intensity, the relationship would not bind; stripped of privacy, it could less readily be abused; curtailed in time, it would have lesser importance. With the responsibility for the child lessened and parcelled out over many persons and agencies, parents would feel less committed and children would have fewer obligations, felt or otherwise. Thus with lesser equity in the parent-child relation, everybody has less to lose or to gain; and although there may be less joy, we could certainly expect less pain.

It would be hazardous to say that human beings *cannot* be shaped to get considerable satisfaction in these diluted relationships. Human beings are very flexible. We accept what we know. But since we are thinking not of what is possible but what is desirable—what human beings really want out of their life span—we are free to explore what people desire, not just what they can learn to put up with. What *do* persons want?

What I shall say about this grows out of random reflections on the history of the family, as I know it, and on what I as clinician, teacher, and citizen have heard people say about their satisfactions and sorrows, their desires for themselves, and their hopes for their children. At this point one could relate reflections about the family to personality theory, for theory on this point is particularly rich. I have chosen, however, to discuss the future of the family in terms of values—goals that seem to have bearing upon the kinds of revision of family living that will take root in the modern world.

The needs of children

First, let me suggest that the picture of the family I first presented, with its recurrent episodes of cruelty, disappointment, and pain, is one side of the coin. Turn it over and you will discover tender devotion, the deepest pride, and the most exultant joy—all to be experienced in the bonds of permanent marriage and in the relationship of parent and child. While the intimacy and privacy of the family permits the greatest inhumanity of person to person, it provides also the richest soil for satisfactions in mutual giving. If our goal were bland, relatively affectless, human relations, the family is surely the wrong way to go about it. But if we seek the most profound feeling, then the family can scarcely be improved upon. I could tell you a story, many stories, of maternal and parental love within the family that fly in the face of reasonableness. But I do not need to do so. You know the stories as well as I. And in the only moral and aesthetic terms we know anything about they rank high in nobility and beauty.

Second, there appears to be something in people that calls for permanence. Permanence in place, in ways of doing things—but most of all for permanence in human relationships. Changes in the nature of the external world have snatched away much of the permanence of place and ways of living that people used to be able to count on, but there remains to us the possibility of enduring interpersonal relationships. Is this weakness? Are we, like Linus, clutching our security blankets? Or would it be truer to say that both Linus and we, in our longing for lasting relationships, have got hold of a fundamental from which we ought not to be parted? It seems probable that the family—the relationship among husband, wife, and their children—is a more effective way to meet the need for permanence in human relationships than any other as yet devised.

Another need that we see in children and parents alike is the need for commitment. It does not matter whether our child is brilliant or deficient, beautiful or homely, perfect or deformed, good or bad—he is ours. We are committed to him lastingly. Whether we rear our children on the right side of the tracks or the wrong, whether we are dunderheaded in politics or forward-looking enough to

please our adventurous offspring, we are theirs; they are committed to us. We may need to earn each other's respect—and I think we do—but we cannot earn commitment. It is a given—a condition of being a member of a family—and this we feel is a desirable thing, though this, like permanence, may have a high price tag in suffering as well as in satisfaction. Perhaps the same kind of commitment to the relationships in a state nursery can grow; we do not know. That it does to some extent is suggested by children reared in group situations, but much evidence indicates that these relationships are less permanent.

A fourth characteristic that flourishes within the family and that persons in Western society value highly is the uniqueness of the individual. Is this a vanity—a luxury that twentieth-century man on a crowded planet cannot afford? In countless ways we have given way to standardization and regimentation, and there is no doubt but that this move toward erasing individuality in clothing, food, furniture, and housing has raised the general level of living. This duplication of trappings, however, has to do with externals and may, by releasing energy, have made it more possible than before to give attention to the unique human being who is now more easily clothed, fed, and housed. I would like to suggest that the concept of the experience of individuality is of central significance in human existence. It is one of the things life is all about. Any institutional arrangement that tends to blur the uniqueness of each separate "I" is not in the interests of human dignity or happiness.

Much more could be said, both pro and con. As we see Russian women at work in callings that use all their gifts, we believe it is very likely that the full usefulness of human life is not being realized in Western society and that the particular way the family now operates tends to stifle some gifts and powers—especially those of the educated woman. Much talent is lying fallow. Much energy is going down the drain when it might be poured into socially useful channels. One reason this is so is that our concepts of the family routines and, perhaps, roles need some alteration to bring them into line with a technological age. Another reason is that the society itself needs to make this channeling more possible by opening wide some doors that are now only ajar, and by extending some institutionalized help. Yet in our particular society at least, the family—at its core—still serves our dearest needs and will, we hope, continue to endure, father-mother-children under one roof—each a unique person permanently committed to all of the others.

20 *Motherhood*

Joanna Clark

My first words as I came from under the ether after I had my son were, "I think I made a mistake." Unfortunately, since then, and one more child later, I've had very little reason to change my mind. This is not to say that children cannot be lovable. It's not them, it's all the foolishness that goes on in the name of them. From the beginning, motherhood took on the complexion of a farce.

To begin with, aside from the indignity of being trussed up like some sort of sacrificial pig in order to be delivered, there was the matter of nursing. I chose to brew my own rather than to spend the next few months encumbered by a slew of rattling bottles. At first the hospital staff was rather sweet and condescending about it. They'd bring me the baby, say something like, "Aren't you a good little mother," and then whip those bed curtains around to screen me from my roommate as if a little infant fellatio was the very least that was going to happen inside my hutch.

After the first day, however, someone decided that there was something strange about the color of my child's stool. The pediatrician came in to talk to me. The import of his conversation was that, while it was very rare, occasionally babies were allergic to their mother's milk and he wanted my permission to put the child on a formula. I said if he was allergic to anything it was probably the four-a.m. feeding they slipped him in the nursery. He turned and stomped out and I thought that was that, but the next time I took a walk down the hall to have a look in the nursery, I saw that my baby was in isolation. Since I had never heard of anyone having a contagious allergy, the only reason I could think of was that they felt there must be something inherently wrong with anyone who had a mother freaky enough to breast-feed. But, I must tell the truth, he wasn't just breast-fed—he was also uncircumcised.

I wasn't trying to prove anything. I had thought about it and it seemed to me that I had perfectly good reasons for having an uncircumcised son. I had read somewhere that circumcision lessened sexual pleasure. No one knows exactly how much, but it didn't seem to me that I had the right to start meddling in his sexual life before he could say a word about it. Then, I knew me, and I knew that the last thing I wanted to do was to take him home and have to deal with a gauze-wrapped, bloody, infection-prone little ding-a-ling. Besides soap and water are plentiful enough in this society so that no one need ever lose a penis to smegma.

When I refused to sign a release for the operation, I was visited by a platoon of doctors. They kept saying it would be cleaner and "How will he feel when he grows up and everybody's circumcised but him?" If he wanted to have it done when he was older that would be his business, but for the time being, I said no. One of the doctors snatched up the release and said huffily, "Well, never mind. We'll get your husband to sign it." Sure enough one of them laid in wait during visiting hours and proceeded to harass my husband. My son kept his foreskin and I received my first lesson in motherhood. You are everybody's whipping boy.

I may be more upsettable than most, but during the years I was involved with carriages and strollers and wagons and tricycles, I was always getting bugged. Why wasn't there, even in the children's section of a department store, a high chair so you could deposit your child and spend your money in some sort of comfort? Why did it have to be a major struggle to get a stroller or a shopping cart across a street; would it cost so much to rake the curbs? And why did the entrance to the playground offer the steepest curb of all? Small enough problems, but enough to clue you in to the fact that the last people anyone in charge of planning the city are concerned with are mothers and children.

So I should have been forewarned when I finally locked out my charming, but philandering and non-supporting Peter Pan of a husband. I was working (selling honeymoons in the Poconos and feeling like a hypocrite) when I turned the bolt. But if I didn't get sick, one of the children would, and if the three of us stayed on our feet, the baby sitter was sure to keel over with a gallbladder attack. I finally came up with a really simple solution. I would put the children in one of the city's day-care centers. It would certainly be more reliable and I'd probably save enough money to hire someone to stay with them while I finished my last semester at City College.

I called the Day Care Council to find where the nearest school was. The woman on the other end of the line wanted to know why I needed a nursery. I told her that I had to work. She seemed insulted. "What do you mean, you have to work? In New York City there's no such thing as a mother having to work. You can go on welfare!" I told her that I didn't want to go on welfare. The last thing I wanted to do was sit around all day in my Lower East Side hovel. I wanted to do something to get out of it. I didn't get the address of the nursery, but she did tell me where my nearest friendly welfare office was. On my own I found several nurseries and tried to register my children. If what those schools say about their waiting lists is true, three-quarters of their prospective clients will be through graduate school before there is an opening for them in the four-year-old-group.

I hung in there for a while longer, but, besides being sporadic, I have to admit that I wasn't selling honeymoons with total dedication. So I got fired. For a very short while I depended upon Peter Pan, but the next time the rent was due, there I was sitting in the welfare office. I had talked Peter into saying, if anyone asked, that he couldn't support us. It was the truth, but I wasn't sure that he knew it.

Despite what they say, I don't think the welfare department checks too deeply into eligibility. They use a cheaper system. They just keep putting you off and telling you to come back the next day. After a few days of that, if you can scrounge up money anywhere else, you will. On my third day I threw a fit that outdid every crotchety baby in the center. Within fifteen minutes I was a bonafide welfare recipient with a yellow card to prove it.

Anyone who can live on welfare should be courted by Wall Street. He is a financial genius. I paid $40 a month rent and received $69 every 15 days. That included an extra amount for electricity since I lived in a dark apartment. I guess I could have started having more babies and parlayed my allotment into something really terrific, but I didn't and I wasn't a financial genius so I depended upon the occasional kindness of my husband.

I had as an investigator a man extremely gung-ho about filling out forms. He had gold teeth and a glint in his eyes behind his gold-trimmed glasses that made me believe that within a few years he'd probably have a whole section of the welfare office under his supervision. He was on my doorstep so often that I assumed he must have been as tired of looking at me as I was of him. I made him an offer: if he arranged for the city to supply me with a homemaker and carfare for me to finish my last semester of college, within a few months a family of three would be off the welfare rolls at, in the long run, a considerable saving to the city. He almost had apoplexy on my living-room floor. The City of New York does not send mothers to school, and if I came up with the money to do it on my own, I must report it to him immediately so he could throw me off welfare. So much for being aboveboard.

Shortly after this I got a part-time job and found a woman in Queens who would keep the children from Monday morning until Friday night for only a few dollars a week more than the welfare department gave me. I even got a student loan.

I had just about made it. I had spent all my money and I was half dead, but school had ended and I had the promise of a job in a month. I could live on the welfare checks until then. But I hadn't reckoned on the men in my life. The investigator, in the interest of nice up-to-date records, paid a visit to Peter Pan. During the time I was married to the man I could never analyze his rationale so I won't try in retrospect. Whatever his reasoning, he decided to say that he didn't see why his family was on welfare since he was able to care for it.

The first I knew of his new capacity for caring was when I got a letter from the welfare department saying that I was no longer eligible. I was not too happy. I asked Peter Pan for money. He said that he didn't have any at the moment but he was sure he could borrow a couple of dollars for me if I really needed it. I ran to the welfare office and screamed that I didn't care what my husband had said, he wasn't giving me any money and if he was, let him show the receipts to prove it. It doesn't work like that. If he said yes and I said no, even if he couldn't substantiate his claim, the burden of proof was on me. The only thing I could do at this point was to take him to court.

The Support Court does not offer the most cheerful surroundings in which to while away a morning, especially if you are sitting there most nonchalantly ignoring your husband on the opposite bench, fighting a strong desire to hit him over the head with your copy of *Dr. Spock* as he pores soulfully over his collected John Donne. Nor is the urge to mayhem alleviated when a woman steps out of her office and says, "How do you do? I am your probation officer." Apparently, trying to collect money from a recalcitrant husband is a really antisocial act entitling you to parole without benefit of trial.

We went into her office, where, while I sat on my hands, swallowed my spume, counted to ten, and in general saw red, they dickered over what he could afford to pay. No one asked me what I needed to live on. After a while they turned to me and said that my spouse felt that he could, with great difficulty, eke out fifteen dollars a week. I suppose it was then that I began to nut out. "What the hell," I wanted to know, "am I supposed to do with fifteen dollars a week? Move into the Waldorf?" That probation officer interjected with the idea that I did not seem to have the proper attitude. "What attitude am I supposed to have?" I screamed. "I didn't mess up his life by running around telling people that I could support him. Well, I can't take care of two children on fifteen dollars a week. Let him do it. He can have them right now." That really brought the probation officer to her feet. "You can't desert your children. That's against the law."

"How can I be deserting them? I'm giving them to their father."

"But you can't do that! You're their mother." People, especially those without children, sometimes have a way of saying "mother" that I find incredible. They manage to pronounce a halo around it. I suppose if you're in the mood you feel like the Virgin Mary. I wasn't in the mood. "Suppose I offer to give him fifteen dollars a week along with the children. Would that be better?" It would not. Apparently if I tried to leave the building without two children she had the right to call the police. I was squelched for the moment. However my avarice got the better of me. If I was supposed to get fifteen dollars a week, where was my fifteen dollars? Peter explained that in a couple of weeks he would be able to make the first payment.

I held myself together long enough to collect the children from the court's nursery. And then, as I pushed them down the street in their stroller, I began to think over my alternatives. I refused to go sit in the welfare office again. I had no intention of just going home when there was no relief in sight. The only really definitive thing I could think of to do under the circumstances was to nut out. I hurried over to

St. Vincent's Hospital, which seemed a pleasant enough place as hospitals went to collapse upon.

I must have made quite a racket, which wasn't too difficult considering the mood I was in. All I knew was that I wanted someone to take care of those children while I went off and slept for a couple of weeks. Someone patted me on the back and maneuvered the three of us into a room to wait for a doctor. After a short while, in walked a young, blond, well-raised, right-thinking, white-clad paragon. "What seems to be the trouble?" he said. "I can't go on," I wept. "I'm married to this man who thinks that all you need to live on is a tiny bit of money and love will take care of the rest." He pulled up a chair. "What's wrong with that?" he wanted to know. "Love" is another one of those words like "mother." When my husband said "love," he meant whatever emotion he could generate in you that would sustain you enough to put up for and with him. It was too complicated and paranoid to try to explain, especially to anyone who wore white bucks. I decided to stick to the "I can't go on" thesis. He explained that St. Vincent's just didn't take in people from off the street, but that if I really couldn't go on, Bellevue was the place to go. Anyone can tell from just looking at that hospital that that is no place to go for a nice, peaceful, recuperative nervous breakdown. The drabness alone would finish off your mind. When I shook my head no to that, he told me to wait a minute, left the room, and reappeared shortly bearing aloft a mammoth hypodermic needle. "This is Librium," he said, "It will make you feel better." He gave me a shot in the behind and shoulder-patted me out of the room. Under the soothing effects of Librium, I began to nurture a sincere distrust in the judgment of doctors, and the nearest thing to hallucinations that I have ever known resulted.

After I left the hospital, I passed a waist-high iron fence and I kept seeing myself grabbing my daughter out of the stroller, holding her by the legs, and rattling her against the fence the way you would a baseball bat. I saw a police station ahead and I suppose it brought to mind ice cream cones and wearing the captain's cap. I staggered in and announced that I wanted to leave my children on the desk sergeant's blotter. They didn't take children accompanied by adults, but they did pat me on the shoulder and tell me about the Department of Welfare. Then, from my dealings with the nursery schools, I remembered the Department of Child Welfare. I didn't know what they were good for, but I looked them up in a telephone book and off I careened with my stroller thrust rakishly before me.

Between the tears and the Librium, I never saw a single streetlight. By rights, I should have been hit by a good fifty cars, in addition to being arrested for jaywalking and endangering the life of a minor at least two dozen times. To add to the joy of my escapade, some wizened old man followed me for a few blocks muttering about coming up to see his apartment. I'm not sure if he was after me or the children.

At the Department of Child Welfare, I wasted no time on pleasantries. I parked my stroller in front of the receptionist's desk and screamed at the absolute top of my lungs, "SOMEBODY'S GOT TO TAKE THESE GODDAM CHILDREN!" They believed me. All they wanted to know was if the children had a father, if so, were we married, and then

his telephone number so he could come in and sign his consent.

Good old Peter showed up in less than half an hour. But, once the pen was in his hand, he could not bear to dismiss himself of his responsibilities so summarily. The social worker brightened. Perhaps he was willing to help with some money. Unfortunately, at the moment he had only a token with which to get home, and, while under other circumstances he would be more willing to take the children himself, he happened to be living for the time being in diggings to which it would be grossly unfair to expose them. The social worker asked him what his wife was supposed to do at this point. "She's an intelligent woman," he said, "I'm sure she'll think of something."

I remember once a girl friend of mine was found wandering around the streets of Harlem trying to sell subscriptions to the *Jewish Daily Forward*, or if that didn't appeal, a visit to an orgone box she knew about. After she was tucked into Bellevue, I bumped into her husband, from whom she was separated, and asked him what he intended to do about their two children. He had decided that as soon as Karen was released she could have the children back because, no matter what, he still had faith in her as a mother. She got out, got the children back, and lasted two months, which was long enough for him to disappear. The children have spent the last five years in a foster home. But he's kept the faith.

Anyway, I was intelligent enough to tell my husband that I would have to defer for a while the pleasure of raising his children. That they were his children as well as mine and therefore I had just as much right to cop out as he did.

When a marriage is breaking up there is a tendency for onlookers and agency types to behave as if the mother in the case went out behind a barn somewhere and knocked herself up with the nearest twig. A divorced man may be grieved over leaving his children, but he manages to bear up and no one thinks of condemning him unless she's his bitchy ex-wife. Mothers may die, or occasionally run away, but if the father is adamant about keeping his family together, the city will supply him with a homemaker whom he pays on a sliding scale and who stays with him for years if necessary. There are a few ways of prying a homemaker loose from the city if you are a woman. The most effective one is to have a husband living in the home, ten children, and a terminal case of cancer. Where is the equity?

I had received the same education as my husband and the same amount of it. I hadn't even tried to excuse myself from gym classes on "those days." All right, I'd been foolish enough to have two children, but then, so had he. So now what kind of a job was I supposed to do on my head so that I could accept doing very little else in the next few years except raising children on the lowest possible terms?

There was nothing to do but go to court the next morning and swear out a deposition stating neither my husband nor I was mentally or financially capable of caring for our children. It was all simple enough after that, if you call never being able to take your children off someone else's property, or never seeing them naked, and having them smell like somebody else, simple.

After my children were in a foster home, I became aware of another inequity. Not only is the city willing to pay a couple to take care of other people's children, but it is willing to foot the bill for private doctors, dentists, and clothes. And the clothes, they encourage, should not be the cheapest, for the foster children should not be stigmatized in any way. You get the feeling that the mortgage on every other house in St. Albans is being paid for by foster children, and that the powers that be think that to provide the same assistance to the blood mothers would break the back of the free-enterprise system.

It's over now, and I have my children back. They have a new father who works. And while we haven't come along so far as to get out there into the park every Sunday with a baseball and bat, we do have a go at it with the frisbee every now and then. It's still very clean living and all-American. But I learned a lot. . . . A friend of mine not too long ago had a vaginal infection and took herself off to a gynecologist. He was good, but he was German. And the lady trembled lest Herr Doktor take one look at her little brown face and decide to practice a bit of "genocide." Black ladies, the last thing we have to worry about is genocide. In fact, we could use a little. Look at what's happened to us in the last hundred years; we've been bravely propagating and all we've gotten are a lot of lumps and a bad name. On the other hand, there are people like Glazer and Moynihan carrying on about our matriarchy and inferring that we've botched up the job long enough and that if we insist on doing something, confine ourselves to standing behind the man of the family and bringing him up to par. On the other hand, there are the brothers (from mother and son to brother and sister—what's so hard about being man and woman?). Anyway, there's the brother nattering away about how we've been lopping off balls long enough, it's time to stand aside. So you stand there looking as pink and white and helpless as is possible under the circumstances and he wants to know what's wrong with you, do you have at least the excuse of being sick or are you just going to stand there like some cow spending up his money?

We don't need it. If we've got to turn our eyes eastward and rediscover our heritage, let's not get hung up on the hairdos and the dashikis. There are more salient aspects of that culture to adopt. No self-respecting African woman would ever get married without a dowry, without something to back her up if the marriage ran into trouble. Admittedly, dowries are not too easy to come by, but the pill is. Let's not worry about what we think the white man thinks about his generosity with his contraceptives. The Jews have never been noted for their sprawling, epic-type families, yet they've managed to make themselves a race to be reckoned with. And they didn't do it by Soul.

I realize, or at least I think, that most women have had experiences in childrearing less picaresque than mine. I know some have had more gothic ones—but I relate mine to show what authority I hold for having the opinions I do. I have had a rare opportunity to see husband at bay and the legal system when it pertains to a man and wife. Once, when I was safely remarried and could afford to spend a day in court fighting for my rights, I had a set-to with my first husband over the amount he was in arrears with his child support. He owed something like a third of the amount he was supposed to pay. The judge (a man) looked me in the eye and said, "Well, Madam, he isn't doing too badly." Jesus Christ, let me try walking up to the man from Consolidated Edison busily turning off my service because I only paid one-eighth of the bill and saying, "Well, I'm not doing too badly."

As mothers, we are worse off than we think we are. In this age of the sit-in and the be-in, it is time for a sit-down. And let's not get up off of it until there's at least social security and unemployment insurance for every mother.

21 Depression in middle-aged women

Pauline B. Bart

A young man begs his mother for her heart, which a betrothed of his has demanded as a gift; having torn it out of his mother's proferred breast he races away with it; and as he stumbles, the heart falls to the ground, and he hears it question protectively, "Did you hurt yourself, my son?"—JEWISH FOLK TALE

I'm glad that God gave me . . . the privilege of being a mother . . . and I loved them. In fact, I wrapped my love so much around them . . . I'm grateful to my husband since if it wasn't for him, there wouldn't be the children. They were my whole life. . . . My whole life was that because I had no life with my husband, the children should make me happy . . . but it never worked out.—DEPRESSED MIDDLE-AGED WOMAN

We have all read numerous case histories in which a child's neurosis or psychosis was attributed to the mother's behav-

Chapter 6 of Woman in Sexist Society, *edited by Vivian Gornick and Barbara K. Moran,* © *1971 by Basic Books, Inc., Publishers, New York.*

ior. Only recently has the schizophrenogenic family replaced the demon double-binding schizophrenogenic mother in theories about the causes of schizophrenia. This inquiry deals with the reverse situation—how, given the traditional female role, the children's actions can result in the mother's neurosis or psychosis. This is a study of depressed middle-aged women in mental hospitals. The story of one such woman follows.

Mrs. Gold is a youthful Jewish housewife in her forties. Her daughter is married and lives about twenty miles away; her hyperactive brain-damaged thirteen-year-old son has been placed in a special school even farther away. After his departure she became suicidally depressed and was admitted to a mental hospital.

I asked her how her life was different now and she responded:

It's a very lonely life, and this is when I became ill, and, I think I'm facing problems now that I did not face before because I was so involved especially having a sick child at home. I didn't think of myself at all. I was just someone that was there to take care of the needs of my family, my husband and children, especially my sick child. But now I find that I—I want something for myself too. I'm a human being and I'm thinking about myself.

She was dissatisfied with her marriage; their mutual concern for their son held the couple together, but when their son entered an institution, this bond was loosened, although they visited him every Sunday. "My husband is primarily concerned with only one thing, and that is making a living. But there's more to marriage than just that [pause] you don't live by bread alone." Mrs. Gold states that she is not like other women for whom divorce is simple, but she is considering divorcing her husband if their relationship does not improve. Yet, another patient I interviewed later told me Mrs. Gold had cried all the previous night after her husband came to the hospital to tell her he was divorcing her.

Although she believes her life was "fuller, much fuller, yes much fuller" before her children left, she used to have crying spells:

... but in the morning I would get up and I knew that there was so much dependent on me, and I didn't want my daughter to become depressed about it or neurotic in any way which could have easily happened because I had been that way. So I'm strong minded and strong willed, so I would pull myself out of it. It's just recently that I couldn't pull myself out of it. I think that if there was—if I was needed maybe I would have, but I feel that there's really no one that needs me now.

She is unable to admit anger toward her children and makes perfectionist demands on herself. "It was extremely hard on me, and I think it has come out now. Very hard. I never knew I had the amount of patience. *That child never heard a raised voice.*"

While she is proud of her daughter and likes her son-in-law, an element of ambivalence is apparent in her remarks. "Naturally as a mother you hate to have your daughter leave home. I mean it was a void there, but, uh, I know she's happy ... I'm happy for my daughter because she's happy." Since she had used her daughter as a confidant when the daughter was a teenager, a pattern also present

among other women I interviewed, she lost a friend as well as a child with her daughter's departure. Mrs. Gold said she did not want to burden her daughter with her own problems because her daughter was student teaching. The closeness they had now was "different" since her daughter's life "revolved around her husband and her teaching and that's the way it should be." They phone each other every day and see each other about once a week.

Like most depressives she feels inadequate: "I don't feel like I'm very much." Since her son's departure she spent most of her time in bed and neglected her household, in marked contrast to her former behavior. "I was such an energetic woman. I had a big house, and I had my family. My daughter said, 'Mother didn't serve eight courses. She served ten.' My cooking—I took a lot of pride in my cooking and in my home. And very, very clean. I think almost fanatic." She considers herself more serious than other women and could not lead a "worthless existence" playing cards as other women do. She was active in fund-raising for her son's institution, but apparently without the maternal role, the role that gave her her sense of worth, fundraising was not enough. Formerly, her son "took every minute of our lives" so that she "did none of the things normal women did, nothing." "I can pardon myself for the fact [that he was placed in a school] that I did take care of him for twelve years and he was hyperactive. It was extremely hard on me ... I never knew I had that amount of patience."

Like most of the women I interviewed, Mrs. Gold is puritanical and embarrassed about sex.

I think anything that gives you pleasure or enjoyment, oh, is good as long as it's, uh, decent, and, uh, not with us [slight embarrassment] some women I imagine do things that they shouldn't do, but I'm not referring to anything like that. It's just that I'm not that kind of woman.

Where she is at psychologically and sociologically is dramatically apparent in her response to the question in which she had to rank the seven roles available to middle-aged women in order of importance. She listed *only one role:* "Right now I think *helping my children*, not that they really need my help, but if they did I would really try very hard." Thus, she can no longer enact the role that had given her life meaning, the only role she considered important for her. Her psychiatrist had told her, and she agreed, that a paying job would boost her self-esteem. But what jobs are available for a forty-year-old woman with no special training, who has not worked for over twenty years?

Mrs. Gold combines most of the elements present in the depressed women I interviewed, elements considered by clinicians to make up the pre-illness personality of involutional depressives: a history of martyrdom with no payoff (and martyrs always expect a payoff at some time) to make up for the years of sacrifice; inability to handle aggressive feelings, rigidity; a need to be useful in order to feel worthwhile; obsessive, compulsive supermother and superhousewife behavior; and generally conventional attitudes.

Why study Mrs. Portnoy and her complaints

Some of my hip friends ask, "Pauline Bart, what are *you* doing studying depressed middle-aged women?" The question itself, implying that the subject is too uninteresting and unimportant to be worth studying, indicates the unfortunate situation in which these women find themselves. But a nation's humanity may be measured by how it treats its women and its aged as well as how it treats its racial and religious minorities. This is not a good society in which to grow old or to be a woman, and the combination of the two makes for a poignant situation. In addition, there are practical and theoretical reasons why such a study is important. Women today live longer and end their childbearing sooner than they did in the last century. In other words women are more likely now to reach the "empty-nest" or postparental stage (a term used by those investigators who do not consider this life-cycle stage especially difficult). Depression is the most common psychiatric symptom of adulthood, but, like middle age, it too has been generally ignored by sociologists.[1]

Such a study is theoretically important for several reasons. First, it can illuminate that important sociological concept, role—the concept that links the individual to society—because at this stage a woman loses certain roles and gains others; some roles contract, others expand. Moreover, there is contradictory evidence as to whether middle age *is* a problem for women. Knowing the conditions under which these women become depressed helps us explain these contradictory theories. Why is it that one woman whose son has been "launched" says, "I don't feel as if I've lost a son; I feel as if I've gained a den," while another thinks the worst thing that ever happened to her was

when I had to break up and be by myself, and be alone, and I'm just—I really feel that I'm not only not loved but not even liked sometimes by my own children. . . . they could respect me. If—if they can't say good things why should they, why should they feel better when they hurt my feelings, and make me cry, and then call me a crybaby, or tell me that I—I ought to know better or something like that. My worst thing is that I'm alone, I'm not wanted, nobody interests themselves in me . . . nobody cares.

The *best* times of her life were when she was pregnant and when her children were babies.

One clue to the differing views of middle age is that many of the problem-oriented studies are written by clinicians who are generalizing from their patients, while the studies showing that the postparental stage is no more difficult for most people than any other life-cycle stage, that many people like "disengaging," come from surveys and interviews conducted by behavioral scientists. The patients clinicians see are not a random sample of the population; they are more likely to be middle class and Jewish. This is precisely the group in which I would expect the departure of children to cause stress because the departure of children is more difficult for women whose primary role is maternal—the situation in the traditional Jewish family. If this hypothesis is correct, the difference between the two approaches to middle age may result from clinicians' generalizations about a population that is more susceptible to the stresses of middle age—the Jewish mother.

There is no Bar Mitzvah for menopause

Émile Durkheim sheds light on the stresses that a mother may feel when her children leave. His concepts of both

egoistic and *anomic* suicide are relevant to the problems of "the empty nest." According to Durkheim, marriage does not protect women from egoistic suicide, as it does men; rather, the birth of children reduces the suicide rate for women, and immunity to suicide increases with the "density" of the family. "Density" diminishes as the children mature and leave. Few clear norms govern the relationship between a woman and her adult children; consequently, when her children leave the woman's situation is normless or anomic. This normless state is apparent in the responses to my question, "What do people expect a woman to do after her children are grown?" Mrs. West said that while a married woman is supposed to make a home for her husband, she did not know what was expected from a divorced woman like her. "I don't think they expect anything special . . . you just mind your own business. Let them mind theirs . . ." Another woman said, "My mission in life is completed. I have no place to go." All women verbally denied the obligations of adult children toward their parents. When asked what their children owed them, all the women say "nothing," even though, in fact, they are apparently dissatisfied with their present situation and want more from their children. Much as some of the mothers want to live with their children, they cannot openly state this as a *legitimate* demand.

As financial crises lead to anomic suicides because individuals must change their expectations, women whose children leave must also change their expectations. But not only have these expectations been given legitimacy through years of interaction, there are no guidelines, no *rites de passage* for the mother herself to guide her through this transaction. *There is no bar mitzvah for menopause.*

David Riesman, following the Durkheimian tradition, notes that autonomous persons have no problems when they age, but both the "adjusted," who find meaning in their lives by carrying out culturally defined tasks, and the anomic, whom the culture has been "carrying" but then drops, have difficulties as they grow older and these external "props" are no longer available. Thus, the woman's position dramatically changes; from being overintegrated into society through the props of domestic and maternal roles, she becomes unintegrated or anomic. It is true, as Marvine Sussman claims, that urban kin networks do exist, and that the concept of the isolated nuclear family is false, since kin are turned to in time of trouble.[2] But it is precisely *because* kin, that is, children, can be called upon in time of trouble that secondary gain is possible from depression. When a woman becomes depressed, once again she gets the attention, sympathy, and control over her children she had before they left.

Durkheim constructed a theory of social control and the pathological effects of its breakdown. The basis of social control is norms, the factors that control and constrain. However, Durkheim lacked an explicit social psychology, failing to posit any mechanism that could account for the manner in which these constraints are internalized. Role theory furnishes us with such a mechanism.

Role

The most important roles for women in our society are wife and mother. For example, one woman stated that getting married was the only thing she ever did that made her parents think she was worthwhile, compared to her younger brother, a doctor. The wife role may be lost at any time during the adult life cycle through separation, divorce, or widowhood, although the last is most common during old age. However, during the years between forty and fifty-nine, the maternal role is the one most frequently lost.

Two postulates from Ralph Turner's monograph, "Role Theory—A Series of Propositions," are illuminating. "Almost any stabilized role expectation contains some elements of latent feeling that the other ought to continue the same role and role behavior as before. . . . There is a tendency for stabilized roles to be assigned the character of *legitimate expectations.*"[3] While ideally a mother should be flexible and change her expectations of her children as they mature, if a woman's personality is rigid, as these women's personalities are, she may expect adult children, even if married, to act largely as they did when they were children and dependent on her. To the extent that they no longer act this way, she is likely to feel resentful; since, as Yehudi Cohen suggests, a woman is not "allowed" to be hostile toward her children, she may turn the resentment inward and become depressed.[4] Turner's second postulate states: "The degree to which ego can legitimately claim the privileges of his role tends to be a function of his degree of role adequacy" since "the actor who performs his role more adequately than could be legitimately expected raises thereby the legitimate expectations of other actors. The mother, for example, by being more patient or working harder than could reasonably be expected, places a moral debt on husband and children which is not satisfied by normal adequacy."[5]

Klayne kinder, klayne tsurus; grayse kinder, grayse tsurus[6]

Since the women that I predict will be most affected by the departure of their children are the supermothers, the martyrs, the self-sacrificing women who have devoted their lives to their children, they can legitimately expect their children to be more devoted to them, more considerate of them, bring them more satisfaction, than would otherwise be the case. The literature on the Jewish mother quite clearly portrays her as this type of supermother, this supermother is especially likely to be severely affected if her children fail to meet her needs, either by not making what she considers "good" marriages, or by not achieving the career aspirations she has for them, or even by not phoning her every day. The moral debt Turner refers to results in the child's feeling guilty. Therefore, if his mother does become depressed, he is particularly vulnerable, and he may expiate his guilt by becoming the "good" child again. Greenberg's best-selling satire, *How to Be a Jewish Mother,* refers to guilt as the mother's main method of social control;[7] it is no accident that his second book, *How to Make Yourself Miserable,* begins with the sentence: "You, we can safely assume, are guilty."

Not only is the traditional Jewish mother overinvolved with or overidentified with her children, obtaining narcissistic gratification from them, but the children are viewed as simultaneously *helpless* without the mother's directives and *powerful*—able to kill the mother with "aggravation."

As one depressed empty-nest woman says, "My children have taken and drained me." In a sentence completion test, she filled in the blank after the words "I suffer" with "from my children."

Overprotection and overidentification is apparent in the case of another depressed Jewish woman, Mrs. Berg, who moved from Chicago to Los Angeles with her husband four months after her daughter, son-in-law, and granddaughter did "because my daughter and only child moved here, and it was lonesome for her, you know. And I figured we had nobody," except a brother, and "you know how it is. My granddaughter was in Los Angeles. I missed them all." Mrs. Berg and her daughter are "inseparable." "She wouldn't buy a pair of stockings without me." However, the daughter had written to the hospital; in her letter she stated that much as she loved her mother, her need to be kept continually busy was destroying the daughter's own private life, and she had to enter psychotherapy herself.

Mrs. Berg thought that the worst thing that could happen to a woman of her age was for her children to leave home. "Children leaving home to me is a terrible thing, but mine didn't. She waited until she got married." When her daughter did not have a date, this supermother would say to her husband, "Oh, I don't feel so good tonight," so that she and her husband would stay home in case her daughter was lonesome.

I was one of those old-fashioned mothers. I thought that you have to stay home and take care of your child, or when she has a date see what kinda fellow she's going out with. . . . Today the mothers are a little bit different. We manage a building now and we could write a story—write a book about our life there. The way twenty, twenty-one and twenty-two year olds leave home. Even younger, and share an apartment in Hollywood. I—I oughta write a book on that, when I get the time and the health back.

She thought the best time for a mother was from infancy till the child was eleven or twelve "because after that they become a little self-centered . . . they think about good times and go bowling, go this and that, you know." The best thing for a woman after her children are raised is working. "Keep your hands occupied. Don't think too much. Just be occupied." Her greatest concern is her granddaughter. "It will be the greatest joy of my life when my granddaughter meets somebody and she'll get married."

Role and self

Role and self-concept are intimately interconnected. When people are given the "Who Are You" test to get at their self-concept, they usually respond in terms of their various roles—wife, doctor, mother, teacher, daughter, and so forth. As a person moves from one life-cycle stage to another, or from one step in a career to another, he or she must change their self-concept because the relevant or significant others, the people with whom they interact, change. A loss of significant others can result in what Arnold Rose called a "mutilated self."[8] Some roles are more central for one's self-image than others; self-esteem comes from role adequacy in these more salient roles. For most people, the social structure determines which roles these are. Because the most important roles for women in our society are the roles of wife and mother, the loss of either of these roles might result in a loss of self-esteem—in the feeling of worthlessness and uselessness that characterizes depressives. For example, one woman said:

I don't. I don't, I don't feel liked. I don't feel that I'm wanted. I don't feel at all that I'm wanted. I just feel like nothing. I don't feel anybody cares, and nobody's interested, and they don't care whether I do feel good or I don't feel good. I'm pretty useless. . . . I feel like I want somebody to feel for me but nobody does.

Another woman stated: "I don't feel like I'm doing anything. I feel just like I'm standing still, not getting anywhere."

Since mental health or a feeling of well-being is dependent on a positive self-concept, it is therefore dependent on the roles felt to be available to the individual. Women whose identity, whose sense of self, is derived mainly from their role as mothers rather than their role as wives and workers, women whose "significant others" are limited to their children, are in a difficult situation when their children leave. These women's self-conceptions must change; some of these women cannot make this change. They are overcommitted to the maternal role and in middle age suffer the "unintended consequences" of this commitment.

Integration of psychiatric and sociological theory

Psychiatric as well as sociological theory is relevant to a discussion of depression. Depression is usually considered a response to loss, loss of an ambivalently loved person or object by the psychoanalytically oriented, loss of a goal or self-esteem by ego psychologists, and loss of meaning by existentialists such as Ernst Becker.[9] Role loss is consistent with all of these approaches.

One possible way of combining the Freudian position which considers depression anger directed inward, the existential position concerning loss of meaning, and the sociological theory I am presenting may be the following. People who are intrapunitive, who turn anger inward against themselves rather than express it, are conforming to the cultural norms, especially if they are women. Since they have been "good" they expect to be rewarded. Therefore, when their husbands or children leave them their lives may seem meaningless; their world may no longer "make sense." Thus, introjected anger leads to "proper" behavior which in turn leads to expectations of reward; when this reward does not materialize, but in fact tragedy strikes, they suffer from a loss of meaning and become depressed.

Clinicians use the term "defense mechanism" to describe the way an individual characteristically copes with the problems of living. This construct can be refined by the addition of sociocultural factors. There is a relationship between the utility of a defense and the person's stage in the life cycle. Withdrawal as a defense in a society valuing instrumental activism is likely to cause problems early in life. However, if one *defends by doing*, one can manage very well in our society, barring physical illness, until retirement for men or the departure of children for women. My interview data and certain comments on the hospital charts, for example, "She needed to keep busy all the time,"

indicated that many of the women had such defense systems. This system had been rewarded by the society at earlier stages in the woman's life cycle; however, later when many women were physically ill, and there was little for them to do, this life style was no longer effective.

Methods: cross cultural, epidemiological, and interview

I used three kinds of data in this study: anthropological, epidemiological, and interviews with projective tests. First, in order to test the hypothesis that depression in middle-aged women was the result of the hormonal changes of menopause, I conducted a cross-cultural study of thirty societies, using the Human Relations Area Files, and intensively studied six cultures, using the original anthropological monographs (becoming the Margaret Mead of menopause).

After I completed this cross-cultural study of the roles available to women after childbearing ceased, I examined the records of 533 women between the ages of forty and fifty-nine who had had no previous hospitalization for mental illness. I used five hospitals, ranging from an upper-class private hospital to the two state hospitals that served people from Los Angeles County. I compared women who had been diagnosed "depressed" (using the following diagnoses: involutional depression, psychotic depression, neurotic depression, manic depressive depressed) with women who had other functional (nonorganic) diagnoses.

Five methods were used to overcome diagnostic biases. First, the sample was drawn from *five* hospitals. Second, "neurotic depressives" were merged with the "involutional," "psychotic," and "manic depressives" since I suspected that patients who would be called "neurotic depressed" at an upper-class hospital would be called "involutional depressed" at a lower-middle-class hospital, a suspicion that was borne out. Third, a symptom check list was used in the analysis of data, and I found that depressed patients differed significantly from those given other diagnoses for almost all symptoms. Fourth, a case history of a woman with both depressive and paranoid features was distributed to the psychiatric residents at the teaching hospital for "blind" diagnosis. The woman was called Jewish in half the cases and Presbyterian in the other half. The results showed no differences between the "Jews" and "Presbyterians" in number of stigmatic diagnoses since the most and least stigmatic diagnoses (schizophrenia and neurotic depression) were given to "Presbyterians." Fifth, thirty-nine M.M.P.I. profiles were obtained at one hospital and given to a psychologist to diagnose "blind." He rated them on an impairment continuum. The results supported the decision to combine psychotic, involutional, and neurotic depressives, because the ratio of mild and moderate to serious and very serious was the same for all these groups. But all the schizophrenics were rated serious to very serious.

Next, I conducted twenty intensive interviews at two hospitals to obtain information unavailable from the patients' records, to give the women questionnaires used in studies with "normal" middle-aged women, and to administer the projective biography test—a test consisting of sixteen pictures showing women at different stages in their life cycle and in different roles. These interviews provided an especially rich source of information. I did not read their charts until *after* the interviews so as not to have my perception affected by psychiatrists' or social workers' evaluations.

Maternal role loss was recorded when at least one child was not living at home. I considered an overprotective or overinvolved relationship present when a statement such as "my whole life was my husband and my daughter" was written on the woman's record, or if the woman entered the hospital following her child's engagement or marriage. Ratings of role loss and relationship with children and husbands were made from a case history that omitted references to symptomatology, ethnicity, or diagnosis; high intercoder reliability was obtained for these variables (an interesting serendipitous finding was that the Jewish coders were more likely to call parent-child relationship unsatisfactory than non-Jewish coders. The categories were refined so that this difference no longer occurred.) A woman was considered Jewish whether or not she was religious if she had a Jewish mother. The attitudes and values I am discussing need not come from religious behavior. For example, Mrs. Gold did not attend religious services and was unsure of her belief in God, but she taught her daughter that "we just don't date Gentile boys," and considered herself very Jewish, "all the way through, to the core."

Results: you do not have to be Jewish to be a Jewish mother, but it helps

Before embarking on the cross-cultural and epidemiological studies and the interviews and projective tests, I had made a number of hypothesis; some were confirmed and others were refuted.

Depressions in middle-aged women are due to their lack of important roles and subsequent loss of self-esteem, rather than the hormonal changes of the menopause. The cross-cultural studies indicated that women's status frequently rose at this life-cycle stage, that the two societies in which women's status decreased were similar to our own, and that, since middle age was not usually considered an especially stressful period for women, explanations of such stress based on the biological changes of menopause could be rejected.[10]

Role loss *is* associated with depression; middle-aged depressed women are more likely to have suffered maternal role loss than nondepressed women. Because we are symbolic creatures in which the past and future are ever present, even impending role loss can bring on depression.

I had hypothesized that certain factors—intrinsically satisfying occupations; satisfactory marriages; some children still at home; and children's residence near the mother—would make it easier for the mother when her children left. I had also felt that women who suffered other role loss in addition to maternal role loss and women who had unsatisfactory relationships with the departing children would find role loss much harder to bear. However, neither of these hypotheses was confirmed. Role loss is apparently an all or nothing phenomenon since predictions based on the as-

sumption that such loss is a matter of degree and can be compensated for by the expansion of other roles were not supported.[11]

Certain roles appear to be structurally conducive to increasing the effect of the loss of other roles (see Table 6-1). Women who have overprotective or overinvolved relationships with their children are more likely to suffer depression in their postparental period than women who do not have such relationships (see Table 6-2). Housewives have a higher rate of depression than working women since being a housewife is really, as Parsons put it, a "pseudo occupation."[12] Not only do housewives have more opportunity than working women to invest themselves completely in their children, but the housewife role is cut down once there are fewer people for whom to shop, cook, and clean. Middle-class housewives have a higher rate of depression than working-class housewives, and those housewives who have overprotective relationships with their children suffer the highest rate of depression of all when the children leave home.

Depression among middle-aged women with maternal loss is related to the family structure and typical interactive patterns of the ethnic groups to which they belong. When ethnic groups are compared, Jews have the highest rate of depression, Anglos an intermediate rate, and blacks the lowest rate. Since in the traditional Jewish family the most important tie is between the mother and the children and the mother identifies very closely with her children, the higher rate of depression among Jewish women in middle age when their children leave is not surprising. Table 6-3 shows that Jewish women are roughly twice as likely to be diagnosed depressed than non-Jewish women; in addition

TABLE 6—1 Conditions under Which Role Loss Is Increasingly Associated with Depression

Condition	Percent depressed	Total N (base)
Role loss	62.0	369
Maternal role loss	63.0	245
Housewives with maternal role loss	69.0	124
Middle-class housewives with maternal role loss	74.0	69
Women with maternal role loss who had overprotective or overinvolved relationships with their children	76.0	72
Housewives with maternal role loss who have overprotective or overinvolved relationships with their children	82.0	44

TABLE 6—2 Effects of Overprotective or Overinvolved Relationships with Their Children on Depression for Women with Maternal Role Loss

Relationship	Percent depressed	Total N (base)
Overprotective	76.0	72
Not overprotective	58.0	88

NOTE: No information on 83, of whom 47 were depressed.

there was a higher ratio of depression to other mental illness among Jewish women than among non-Jews.

However, when family interactive patterns are controlled, the difference between Jews and non-Jews sharply diminishes (Table 6-4). Although vertical frequencies show that overprotection or overinvolvement with children is much more common among Jews than among non-Jews, it is clear that *you don't have to be Jewish to be a Jewish mother.* For example, one divorced black woman, who had a hysterectomy, went into a depression when her daughter, her only child, moved to Oregon; the depression lifted when she visited her and recurred when she returned to Los Angeles.

The very small group of Jewish women whose mothers were born in the United States had a depression rate midway between that of Jewish women with mothers born in Europe and Anglo women. One of my hypotheses, that the departure of a son would be more closely associated with depression than the departure of a daughter, could not be tested because in every case when the Jewish women had sons who were only children, the sons still lived with their mothers. As one such woman told me, "My son is my husband, and my husband is my son." Such was not the case for Jewish only daughters or for sons or daughters in non-Jewish families. (The hypothesis had to be tested with only children because of the way the cards had been punched.)

Black women had a lower rate of depression than white women. The patterns of black female-role behavior rarely result in depression in middle-age. Often, the "granny" or "aunty" lives with the family and cares for the children while the children's mother works; thus, the older woman suffers no maternal role loss. Second, since black women traditionally work, they are less likely to develop the extreme identification, the vicarious living through their children, that is characteristic of Jewish mothers. In addition, there is no puritanical idea in black culture equivalent to that in Anglo and Jewish cultures, that sex is evil and

primarily for reproductive purposes or that older women are inappropriate sex objects. The famous black blues singers—women such as Bessie Smith—reached the height of their popularity when they were middle-aged.

Of course, one cannot entirely overlook the possibility that the low black depression rate simply reflects the black community's greater unwillingness to hospitalize depressed black women. Depressives are not likely to come to the attention of the police unless they attempt suicide. Therefore, if the woman or her family do not define her condition as psychiatric, she will remain at home. Only a prevalence study can fully test any hypothesis about the black family.

There were too few Mexican families in the sample to test my hypothesis that Mexican women would have a lower depression rate because Mexican women have larger families and the extended family is very much in operation; in addition, there is a shift in actual, though not in formal, power to the mother from the father as they become middle-aged.

Interviews

The interviews dispelled any of my doubts about the validity of inferences from the hospital charts that these women were overprotective, conventional, martyrs. Even though they were patients and I was an interviewer and a stranger, one Jewish woman forced me to eat candy, saying, "Don't say no to me." Another gave me unsolicited advice on whether I should remarry and to whom, and a third said she would make me a party when she left the hospital. Another example of the extreme nurturant patterns was a fourth patient who insisted on caring for another patient who had just returned from shock while I was interviewing her. She also attempted to find other women for me to interview. The vocabulary of motives invoked by the Jewish women generally attributed their illness to their children. They complained about not seeing their children often enough. The non-Jewish women were more restrained and said they wanted their children to be independent. All the women with children, when asked what they were most proud of, replied "my children"; occasionally, after this, they mentioned their husbands. None mentioned any accomplishment of their own, except being a good mother.

Two of the Jewish women had lived with their children and wanted to live with them again; their illness was precipitated when their children forced them to live alone. However, living with children was not a satisfactory arrangement for the women in the epidemiological sample, since the few women having this arrangement were all depressed. For example, one woman complained: "Why is my daughter so cold to me? Why does she exclude me? She turns to her husband . . . and leaves me out. I don't tell her what to do, but I like to feel my thoughts are wanted."

Table 6-5 shows the conventionality and the rigidity of the women interviewed. In middle age it is necessary to be flexible so that new roles can be assumed. The mother role, "helping my children," is most frequently ranked first or second, although only one of the seven women whose children were all home ranked it first, and one ranked it second. Since it is difficult to help children who are no

TABLE 6—3   *Relationships between Ethnicity and Depression*

Ethnicity	Percent depressed	Total N (base)
Jews	84.0	122
Non-Jews	47.0	383

TABLE 6—4   *Relationship between Depression and Overprotection or Overinvolvement with Children for Jewish and Non-Jewish Housewives with Maternal Role Loss*

Relationship	Jews		Non-Jews	
	Percent depressed	Total N (base)	Percent depressed	Total N (base)
Overprotective	86.0	21	78.0	23
Not overprotective	75.0	8	60.0	25

NOTE: No information for 8 Jews, of whom all were depressed and for 38 non-Jews, of whom 21 were depressed.

TABLE 6—5   Frequency of Ranked Choice

Role	1	2	3	4	5	6	7
Being a homemaker	5	-	3	2	2	-	-
Taking part in church, club, and community activities	-	1	3	4	1	-	-
Companion to husband[a]	2	2	1	-	1	-	1
Helping parents	1	1	-	1	1	-	-
Sexual partner	-	1	2	-	-	1	-
Paying job	1	3	-	-	-	1	-
Helping children	4	5	2	1	1	-	-

[a] Not including the two unmarried women who ranked this item first.

TABLE 6—6   Response to Old Age Picture

Response	In story	In inquiry
Positive	1	1
Negative	6	4
Denial	2	-
Neutral	2	1
Not used	9	-

longer home, women who value this behavior more than any other are in trouble; they are frustrated in behaving in the way that is most important to them. Items that were not chosen are as interesting as those that were; only one woman ranked "helping my parents" first. Her hospitalization followed her mother's move to Chicago after she had remodeled her apartment so that her mother could live with her. No woman listed "being a sexual partner to my husband" first, and only one woman listed it second. Three married women did not include it in their ranking, indicating its lack of importance or their embarrassment or rejection of this role. It is apparent that although eight of the women worked, the occupational role was not important to them; three did not even list it. In short, the women view as important precisely the roles of homemaker and mother that become contracted as the women age. Conversely, they do not consider as important the roles that could be expanded at this time: the sexual partner role, the occupational role, and the organizational role (taking part in church, club, and community activities).

The women interviewed were given the projective biography test—sixteen pictures showing women in different roles and at different stages in their life cycles. The clinical psychologist who devised the test analyzed the protocols "blind" without knowing my hypothesis. He said they were "complete mothers," showing total identification with the maternal role. I content analyzed the response to the sexy picture, the pregnancy picture, the old age picture, and the angry picture; Table 6-6 shows the responses to the old age picture.

The old age picture shows an old woman sitting in a rocking chair in front of a fireplace. The nine women who did not include this picture in their stories of a woman's life do not want to grow old and inactive. Only one woman used the picture in the story and responded positively to it. Two used it, but denied the aging aspects of it. An example of such denial is the following response: "Here she is over

here sitting in front of the fireplace, and she's got her figure back, and I suppose the baby's gone off to sleep and she's relaxing." This woman interpreted every picture with reference to a baby.

Six women did not like the picture (two responses were uncodeable). One woman who used the picture in the story said, "And this scene I can't stand. Just sitting alone in old age by just sitting there and by some fireplace all by herself [pause] turning into something like that. And to me this is too lonely. A person has to slow down sometime and just sit, but I would rather be active, and even if I would be elderly, I wouldn't want to live so long that I wouldn't have anything else in life but to just sit alone and you know, just in a rocking chair." Another woman who was divorced and had both her children away from home said, "This could look very much like me. I'm sitting, dreaming, feeling so blue." When she chose that as the picture not liked, she said, "Least of all, I don't like this one at all. That's too much like I was doing. Sitting and worrying and thinking . . ."

In the inquiry period, one more gave a positive response, four gave a negative response, and one response was uncodeable. One empty-nest woman who was divorced and living alone did not use the picture in her story. After listing eight other pictures which were like her life, she said, "I don't like to point to that one." One person liked this picture best, but did not perceive the woman as old, while six women included this picture among the ones they liked least.

How about men

Does this theory explain depression in men? I think it does. Men who have involutional psychosis are usually in their sixties, the retirement age; these are probably men whose occupational roles were "props." Men whose identity comes from their work role will also be depressed on retirement. For example, the director of admissions at the teaching hospital reported that it was not unusual for army officers to have involutional depressions on retirement. Rafael Moses and Debora Kleigler's study of involutional depression in Israel found loss of meaning a factor among old pioneers who believed "that the values so dear to them were rapidly disappearing. Current ideals and expectations were now alien to them and the sense of duty and sacrifice as they knew it seemed to exist no longer. They felt different, isolated and superfluous."[13]

What is to be done?

It is very easy to make fun of these women, to ridicule their pride in their children and concern for their well-being. But it is no mark of progress to substitute Mollie Goldberg for Stepin Fetchit as a stock comedy figure. These women are as much casualties of our culture as the children in Harlem whose I.Q.'s decline with each additional year they spend in school. They were doing what they were told to do, what was expected of them by their families, their friends, and the mass media; if they deviated from this role they would have been ridiculed (ask any professional woman). Our task is to make their sacrifices pay off, though in a different way from what they expected. As their stories are told, other women will learn the futility of this life style.

Two psychologists, Therese Benedek and Helene Deutsch, state that menopause is more difficult for "masculine" or "pseudo masculine" women. Benedek describes the "masculine" woman as one whose "psychic economy was dominated—much like that of man's—by strivings of the ego rather than by the primary emotional gratifications of motherliness."[14] Deutsch states that "feminine loving" women have an easier time during climacterium than do "masculine-agressive ones." While she believes in the desirability of "good sublimations" in addition to erotic and maternal qualities, "if their social and professional interests have taken excessive hold of them, these women are threatened in the climacterium by the danger that I call Pseudomasculinity."[15] However, my data show that it is the women who assume the traditional feminine role—who are housewives, who stay married to their husbands, who are not overtly aggressive, in short who "buy" the traditional norms—who respond with depression when their children leave. Even the M.M.P.I. masculine-feminine scores for women at one hospital were one-half a standard deviation *more* feminine than the mean. These findings are consistent with Cohen's theory of depression; he considers depression, in contrast to schizophrenia, an "illness" found among people too closely integrated into the culture.[16]

Ernest Becker's theory of existential depression among middle-aged women is borne out because these martyr mothers thought that by being "good" they would ultimately be rewarded. When there was no pot of gold at the end of the rainbow, their life pattern seemed meaningless. As one woman said:

I felt that I trusted and they—they took advantage of me. I'm very sincere, but I wasn't wise. I loved, and loved strongly and trusted, but I wasn't wise. I—I deserved something, but I thought if I give to others, they'll give to me. How could they be different, but you see, they be different, but you see those things hurted me very deeply and when I had to feel that I don't want to be alone, and I'm going to be alone, and my children will go their way and get married—of which I'm wishing for it and then I'll still be alone, and I got more and more alone, and more and more alone.

The norms of our society are such that a woman is not expected to "fulfill" herself through an occupation, but rather through the traditional feminine roles of wife and mother. More than that, she is not *allowed* to do so. The great discrimination against "uppity women"—women professionals—the cruel humor, not being taken seriously, the lower pay scale, the invisibility (literally and metaphorically), make it suicidal for a woman to attempt to give meaning to her life through her work. (We are told that women are not hired because they put their personal life first, and leave with the first available man. I think the sequence is reversed. It is only after she learns what her situation really is, after she has been treated as a nonperson, that she turns to a more traditional role. If she's lucky she still has that option.)

Until recent years, a common theme of inspirational literature for women, whether on soap operas or in women's magazines, was that they could only find "real happiness" by devoting themselves to their husbands and children, that is, by living vicariously through them. If one's satisfaction, one's sense of worth comes from other people rather than from one's own accomplishments, one is left with an empty shell in place of a self when such people depart. On the other hand, if a woman's sense of worth comes from her own accomplishments, she is not so vulnerable to breakdown when significant others leave. This point is obscured in much of the polemical literature on the allegedly castrating, dominant American female who is considered to have lost her femininity.

It is, after all, *feminine* women, the ones who play the traditional roles, not the career women, who are likely to dominate their husbands and children. This domination, however, may take more traditional female forms of subtle manipulation and invoking of guilt. If, however, a woman does *not* assume the traditional female role and does not expect her needs for achievement or her needs for "narcissistic gratification," as psychiatrists term it, to be met vicariously through the accomplishments of her husband and children, *then* she has no need to dominate them since her well-being does not depend on their accomplishments. In an achievement-oriented society it is unreasonable to expect one sex not to have these needs.

The women's liberation movement, by pointing out alternative life styles, by providing the emotional support necessary for deviating from the ascribed sex roles, and by emphasizing the importance of women actualizing their *own selves*, fulfilling their *own* potentials, can help in the development of personhood for both men and women.

NOTES

1. See my forthcoming chapter on "The Sociology of Depressive Disorders," in *Current Perspectives in Psychiatric Sociology* eds. Paul Roman and Harrison Trice (Science House, 1971) for a further discussion of this point.
2. Marvine B. Sussman, "Relationships of Adult Children with Their Parents in the United States," in Ethel Shanas and Gordon Streib, eds., *Social Structure and the Family: General Relations* (Englewood Cliffs, N.J.: Prentice-Hall, 1965).
3. Ralph Turner, "Role Theory—A Series of Propositions," *Encyclopedia of the Social Sciences* (New York: Macmillan and the Free Press, 1968). These ideas are incorporated in "Role: Sociological Aspects," *Encyclopedia of the Social Sciences*.
4. Yehudi A. Cohen, "The Sociological Relevance of Schizophrenia and Depression," in Cohen, ed., *Social Structure and Personality* (New York: Holt, Rinehart and Winston, 1961), pp. 477-485.
5. Turner, *op. cit.*
6. Small children, small troubles; big children, big troubles.
7. Dan Greenburg, *How to Be a Jewish Mother* (Los Angeles: Price, Stern, Sloan, 1964).
8. Arnold Rose, "A Social-Psychological Theory of Neurosis," in Rose, ed., *Human Behavior and Social Processes* (Boston: Houghton Mifflin, 1962), pp. 537-549.
9. Ernest Becker, *The Revolution in Psychiatry* (Glencoe: The Free Press, 1964).
10. These results are presented in greater detail in my "Why Women's Status Changes in Middle Age: The Turns of the Social Ferris Role," *Sociological Symposium* 1 (Fall 1969).
11. See *Society, Culture, and Depression* (Cambridge: Schenkman forthcoming) for elaboration of these and subsequent findings.
12. Talcott Parsons, "Age and Sex in the Social Structure of the United States," *American Sociological Review* 7 (1942): 604-606.
13. Rafael Moses and Debora S. Kleiger, "A Comparative Analysis of the Institutionalization of Mental Health Values: The United States and Israel," unpublished manuscript presented at the American Psychiatric Association meeting, New York, 1965.
14. Therese Benedek and Boris B. Rubenstein, "Psychosexual Functions in Women," in *Psychosomatic Medicine* (New York: Ronald Press, 1952).
15. Helene Deutsch, *The Psychology of Women: A Psychoanalytic Interpretation* (New York: Grune & Stratton, 1945), vol. 2.
16. Cohen, *op. cit.*

22 *The first year of bereavement*
A longitudinal study of the reaction of London widows to the death of their husbands

Colin Murray Parkes

Loss by death of a spouse has been shown to be associated with increased rates of physical and mental illness and even with an increase in the mortality rate.[1] Several studies have shown that psychological disturbances following bereavement commonly comprise atypical forms of grief (Lindemann, 1944; Parkes, 1965), but these studies have lacked a satisfactory reference group; the "typical" form taken by grief has seldom been adequately studied.

A number of accounts of the reaction to bereavement have been published in the scientific literature. One of the first was Lindemann's anecdotal account of the reaction of 101 subjects to the death of a close friend or relative (1944). His detailed observation and clarity of description have made this a classical contribution and the best-known paper on this subject.

Several others have described the reaction to bereavement in psychiatric and nonpsychiatric populations. The former are not the concern of this paper and have been summarized elsewhere (Parkes, 1965).

Taken together, these studies have given a fair picture of the overall reaction to bereavement, but they have left many questions unanswered and have necessarily failed to reveal the interrelationships between the features described and the variation of each feature over time. In particular they have not revealed clearly how long the various features of grief can be expected to last and what constitutes a pathological as opposed to a "normal" variant of grief.

Grief is a process not a state. It is necessary to view this process sequentially as it progresses if we are to see clearly its form and range of variation in an unselected population.

Method of investigation

This study was brought to the attention of general practitioners in the London area by the Socialist Medical Association and the College of General Practitioners. General practitioners who expressed an interest were asked to introduce the writer to any female patient registered with them[2] who lost a husband in the course of the study. The widow had to be under the age of 65 and willing to be interviewed. Widows over the age of 65 were not included in order to ensure a homogeneous sample. Previous work indicates that widows in the older age group show a different type of reaction to bereavement, with less overt emotional disturbance than in younger widows (Parkes, 1964b; Maddison and Walker).

As soon as we were notified of a death, a letter was sent to the widow explaining the purpose of the investigation and suggesting a time when the investigator would call.

Interviews were conducted by the writer with each widow—at 1, 3, 6, 9 and 13 months after bereavement—and in 7 cases additional interviews were thought necessary. The routine interviews were standardized to ensure that comparable information was obtained from each widow. At the start of each interview general questions were put to encourage the widow to describe her experiences. Only when she had finished, did the interviewer ask additional questions, to cover areas she had not mentioned, or to enable ratings to be made on the scales used. In this way an empathic relationship was established early, and a great deal of frank and affectively loaded information was obtained. Most widows regarded their participation in the project as helpful to themselves. Interviews lasted 1-4 hours, most were carried out in the respondent's home (3 widows were seen at the Tavistock Clinic), and with rare exceptions the interviewer and respondents were alone. Topics covered which are included in this report are:

Interview I (one month).—Terminal illness and reaction to it. Circumstances of death and reaction to it. Subsequent reaction. Life situation and family history.

Interviews II, III, IV, and V.—Events and reaction since previous interview. Check lists of psychological features.

Interview VI (13 months).—Ratings of psychological, social, and physical adjustment.

A questionnaire was sent to all G.P.'s who participated, approximately 9 months after the end of the study. They

Reprinted by special permission of The William Alanson White Psychiatric Foundation, Inc. Edited from Colin Murray Parkes, "The First Year of Bereavement," Psychiatry, 33:4, Nov. 1970, pp. 444-467. Thanks are due to Dr. John Bowlby and to the members of his research seminar at the Tavistock Institute of Human Relations for their helpful comments on the draft of this paper, to the Royal College of General Practitioners and the Socialist Medical Association for supporting the study and informing their members, to the 12 London General Practitioners who introduced me to widows, and most of all, to the widows themselves. The work was supported by a senior research fellowship from the Mental Health Research Fund and this article was completed during the tenure of grants from the Department of Health and Social Security for work arising out of this and other studies.

were asked to indicate the number of widows in their practice who fulfilled the requirements of the study but who had not been referred, and to state whether those not referred were more or less emotionally disturbed than those referred. They were also asked if the reaction to bereavement of those widows who were not referred seemed in any way atypical.

In the analysis of the data the rating scales were treated as scores. Wherever possible, ratings made at the time of the interview were used in preference to the retrospective ratings made by the widow.

Out of 110 possible interviews, 9 were not carried out at the expected time because the widow was not accessible. Usually missing information was obtained at a later interview but where this was not possible the missing scores were assumed to be the mean of all other scores of the same feature.

When an overall estimate of a particular feature taken over the whole year is reported, a "Mean Year Score" has been used, which is the mean of the five assessments.[3]

SAMPLE

Sampling.—Originally, 26 widows were referred, of whom 22 were included in the quantitative analysis of data. Of the 4 who were excluded one decided not to participate after the first interview and 3 were not available for the final interview.

On the whole these findings support the investigator's impression that the widows referred were fairly typical of London widows under 65 years of age. Nevertheless some reservations must be admitted in view of the fact that some of the widows would probably not have been referred if they had not visited their G.P. during their first month of bereavement.

Demographic characteristics of the sample.—All widows were living in London at the time of bereavement. Ten of the 22 had been born in London, 8 in other parts of the U.K., and 4 abroad (2 of the latter were negro). Their average age was 48.8 years with a range of 26-65 years. The average age of the husbands at death was 54.1 years with a range of 25-73. Husbands came from these occupational classes:[4] I(Professional) = 5, II(Intermediate) = 2, III-(Skilled) = 7, IV(Semiskilled) = 6, V(Unskilled) = 2.

Only 3 of the widows were childless; of the remainder, 3 had children under 5, 8 had school-age children, and 17 had children who had left school.

After bereavement 5 widows lived alone, 5 with children under 15 but no adults, 10 with adults only, and 2 with both children and adults.

The terminal illness.—The commonest cause of death of the spouse was cancer, which had occurred in 10 cases. Eight husbands had died from cardiovascular disease and 4 from other causes.

In all cases there had been some evidence of illness before death occurred although in one case this had only appeared an hour before death. Nineteen wives had been told of the seriousness of their husband's condition, 13 of them at least a month before the death. Only 6, however, felt that they had fully accepted what they were told and 8 were frankly disbelieving. Either they denied that the diagnosis was cor-

rect or they accepted the diagnosis but denied the prognosis. This denial of the seriousness of the situation enabled them, in most cases, to interact with the dying spouse without overtly breaking down. (Similar reactions have been described by Chodoff and his colleagues in the parents of children with neoplastic disease.) Fourteen nursed their husband at home during some part of his terminal illness but 11 had found this task a great strain. The terminal deterioration, when it occurred, was gradual (lasting more than 7 days) in 9 cases, rapid (lasting more than 2 hours) in 3 cases, and sudden in the remaining 10.

As in Gorer's study most of the husbands died in a hospital without their wife being present. Thus in 14 cases the death occurred in a hospital and in 8 at home. In 7 cases the wife was present, 2 wives found their husband dead, 6 were told the news by relatives, and 7 by hospital staff or others.

Results

THE IMMEDIATE REACTION TO THE DEATH

The most frequent reaction to the announcement of death was a state of numbness although this was sometimes preceded by an expression of great distress.

"I suddenly burst. I was aware of a horrible wailing and knew it was me. I was saying I loved him and all that. I knew he'd gone but I kept on talking to him." She went into the bathroom and retched. Then the feeling of numbness set in. "I felt numb and solid for a week. It's a blessing. ... Everything goes hard inside you ... like a heavy weight." She felt that the numbness enabled her to cope without weeping.

Numbness was described by 10 widows and lasted for 1-7 days in 5 cases and for more than a month in 2. "In a dream. ... I just couldn't take it all in. ... I couldn't believe it."

Sixteen of the widows, at this time, had difficulty in accepting the fact that their husband was really dead.

"There was so much to do but I didn't feel like I was doing it, for anyone—not for him, if you see. I couldn't take it in." "There must be a mistake." "I wouldn't believe it 'till I see him [dead] on the Monday [four days later]." "I didn't register at all. ... It didn't seem real."

Whilst the sense of numbness or stunning was a relatively transient phenomenon, some form of denial of the full reality of what had happened often persisted and a year later 13 widows said that there were still times when they had difficulty in believing their husband dead.

Outbursts of extreme behavior occurred briefly during the early period. Tearfulness was very common, being marked in 10 cases, but aggressive outbursts and even states of elation sometimes occurred.

One widow was quite calm at first. "I looked into his eyes and as he stared at me something happened to us. As if something had gone into me. I felt all warm inside. I'm not interested in this world any longer. It's a sort of religious feeling. ... I feel as big as a house. I fill the room." When "brought back to earth" she felt "distracted." She had several tearful outbursts, in one of which she made a half-hearted suicidal gesture.

Another felt stunned and angry, saying, "Why did he do this to me?" The next few days she kept herself very busy. Then, four days later, at dawn, "Something suddenly moved in on me—invaded me—a presence almost pushed me out of bed. It was my husband—terribly overwhelming. This was followed by a series of pictures like photographic plates, of faces." At the time she was uncertain if she might have been dreaming. The numbness persisted for two weeks.

In many cases there was an awareness of threat. "It's like walking on the edge of a black pit," said one widow who had "felt nothing at all" when told of her husband's death. She consciously avoided her feelings because she feared she would be "overcome" and become insane. She looked at the face of the corpse and felt "as if my inside had been torn out," but behaved in a controlled manner until three weeks later, when she broke down and wept in the street.

Panic attacks were commonest during the first month of bereavement but they also occurred at other times. They were described by 12 widows during the first month and 5 during the third to sixth month of the year.

Several times, in the course of her first month of bereavement, Mrs. Evans ran out of her flat and took refuge with friends next door. She described herself during this period as so fragile that "if somebody gave me a good tap I'd shatter into a thousand pieces." She was well aware that during the first few months she avoided thinking of her husband as dead. "If I let myself think Bob's dead I'd be overcome. I couldn't look at it and stay sane." Panic attacks occurred when, inadvertently, the real situation was brought home to her and denial was momentarily impossible—"I felt desperate." The frequency and intensity of these feelings diminished as the year passed although at the end of the year she admitted that she still felt panicky "from time to time."

There is thus considerable variation both within and between individuals in the immediate reaction to bereavement. Episodes of panic or distress alternate with longer periods of numbness or restless "busyness." Feelings are seldom admitted fully to consciousness but when they do "break through" they are experienced as overwhelming or as harming the widow herself. As described elsewhere (Parkes, 1969) the very fact of the loss is commonly avoided in one way or another.

These findings bear out the claims of Eliot and Tyhurst that the earliest reaction to bereavement (and to other major losses) is most commonly a phase of numbness, blunting, or shock. Bowlby has now revised his classification of the phases of mourning to introduce this "numbness" as the initial phase (Bowlby and Parkes).

OVERALL AFFECTIVE CHANGES

Whilst during the immediate reaction to bereavement those affects which were exhibited were often extreme, the overall level of affective disturbance was below its peak. When the period of numbness came to an end (5-7 days after bereavement in most cases) the overall level of affect rose sharply. This is seen in Figure 1, which is based upon

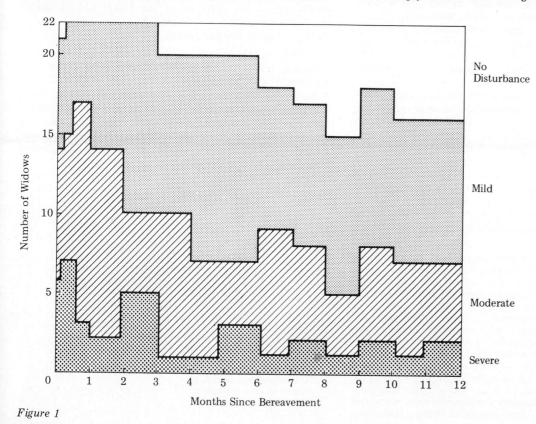

Figure 1

quantitative estimates of overall emotional disturbance made in consultation with the widow at each interview. (The scales upon which these and the other quantitative measures used in this study are based are described in the appendix.)

"Give sorrow words," writes Shakespeare, "the grief that does not speak knits up the o'erwrought heart and bids it break" (*Macbeth* IV.iii.208). Helene Deutsch, in more modern idiom, writes, "Unmanifested grief will be found expressed to the full in some way or other" (p. 13). The implication of these statements would seem to be that grief cannot be permanently postponed and that the longer and more complete the inhibition of feelings the more severe they will be when they finally emerge.

Support for this contention comes from an examination of the affective responses of 25 widows over the first three months. There were 9 widows who were each *severely disturbed during the first week* of bereavement. They remained disturbed during the first and second months but improved thereafter and by the third month only 3 of them were showing more than mild emotional disturbance. Nine other widows showed a *moderate amount of affect in the first week*, rather more in the second, but by the end of the month their affect was already in decline. At three months 3 of them still showed more than mild disturbance of affect. The most interesting group, however, consisted of 7 widows who expressed *little or no affect in the first week* and not much in the second but thereafter displayed a steady increase in affect; by the third month there was not one who was not moderately or severely disturbed.

As is to be expected from these findings, there is a significant negative correlation between overall affect in the first week after bereavement and that in the third month ($r = -.81$, chi square $= 5.96$, $p < .02$ using Yeates' correction).

During the remaining 9 months of the first year of bereavement the distinction between the three groups is less clear. The group with mild initial affect, which had been most disturbed in the third month, became indistinguishable from the other two groups during the sixth to ninth month. As the end of the year approached, however, they again became more disturbed and by the year's end 3 out of the 5 widows from this group remaining in the study were moderately or severely disturbed whereas only 1/8 of the moderate initial affect group and 3/9 of the severe initial affect group were similarly disturbed. An example follows:

"I've always been brought up to bottle up my feelings," said one 42-year-old widow who showed very little emotion after her husband's death. Coming from an unstable home background she had had a "marriage of companionship" which was unsatisfactory in many respects. Nevertheless the last four years she described as "terribly happy."

Her husband died, unexpectedly, on the day on which he was due to leave the hospital after recovering from a coronary thrombosis. She was unable to cry and for three weeks she "carried on as if nothing had happened."

During the fourth week "terrible feelings of desolation" began and she started sleeping badly and having vivid nightmares in which she tried to rouse her sleeping husband. During the day she had panicky feelings and vivid memories of her husband's corpse kept coming to mind. Headaches, from which she had suffered for years, became worse and she quarrelled with her mother and her employers.

Subsequently she remained depressed and restless. She emigrated to Australia nine months after bereavement, and wrote at length four months later describing herself as "very depressed" and "missing my husband dreadfully." She had no friends and felt insecure and worried about her future.

COMPONENTS OF THE SEARCH FOR THE LOST OBJECT

When the phase of numbness comes to an end, pangs of intense pining for the dead person (separation anxiety) begin. This has been called the phase of "Yearning" or "Protest" (Bowlby and Parkes). Bowlby believes that throughout this phase the bereaved person experiences a strong urge to recover the lost person. I have described elsewhere how this gives rise to a conflict between the desire to search and call for the lost person and a tendency to deny, inhibit, or avoid such useless and irrational behavior (Parkes, 1969, 1970). Whilst 3 of the widows interviewed in this study were able to recognize and comment on their impulse to search, in most cases searching was unconsciously revealed in the four components which go to make it up:

(1) Pining and preoccupation with thoughts of the deceased person.
(2) Direction of attention toward places and objects in the environment which are associated with the lost person.
(3) Development of a perceptual "set" for the deceased. A disposition to perceive or to pay attention to stimuli which suggest the presence of the object and to ignore those that are not relevant to this.
(4) Crying for the lost person.

In addition, there is "restlessness" which is a feature of searching, but it is also associated with anger and will be discussed in the section below on anger and guilt.

Each of these features was a common component of the reaction to bereavement of the sample of widows described here and the particular form they took supported the search hypothesis. The evidence will not be presented here. Instead the formal characteristics and changes with time of each feature will be described.

TABLE 1   *Cross-Correlation of Variables (r)*

Variable	Variable					
	1	2	3	4	5	6
1	1.00	0.73*	0.39	0.58†	0.54†	0.21
2	0.73†	1.00	0.38	0.56†	0.38	0.05
3	0.39	0.38	1.00	0.52*	0.37	0.07
4	0.58†	0.56†	0.52*	1.00	0.42*	0.17
5	0.54†	0.38	0.37	0.42*	1.00	0.37
6	0.21	0.05	0.07	0.17	0.37	1.00

1. Preoccupation with memories at interview.
2. Clear visual memory.
3. Illusions during first month.
4. Sense of presence of lost person at interview.
5. Tearfulness at interview.
6. Overall affective upset.
* $p < .02$.
† $p < .01$.

Thoughts of the deceased.—Preoccupation with thoughts of the deceased is mentioned by Lindemann (1944) but it has never been given the attention which it deserves. Along with its affective accompaniment, pining, I believe it to be the central and pathognomonic feature of grief. Without it grief cannot truly be said to have occurred and when present it is a sure sign that a person is grieving. Assessments by the interviewer of the degree of preoccupation with thoughts of the deceased were found to correlate highly with assessments by the widow of the clarity of her memories of the deceased (see Table 1).[5] Memories of the deceased were characteristically clear visualizations of the dead person as he was when alive. Usually he would be in his accustomed place in the room and the memory would be so intense as almost to amount to a perception. A similar clarity was often present in memories of his voice or touch, "I can almost feel his skin or touch his hands." At other times, and particularly at night or when attention was relaxed, the widow would go over in her mind events of the past in which her husband took part.

During the early months and again as the anniversary of the death approached, these were often haunting memories of the final illness or death of the husband. "I find myself going through it all over again." Alternatively, happy memories of the past would be recalled. Three widows described vivid recollections of events which had happened exactly a year previous to the interview. For example:

A year ago today was Princess Alexandra's Wedding Day. I said to him, "Don't forget the wedding." When I got in I said, "Did you watch the wedding?" and he said, "No, I forgot." We watched it together in the evening except he had his eyes shut. He wrote a card to his sister and I can see him so vividly I could tell you every mortal thing that was done on all those days. I said, "You haven't watched or anything." He said, "No, I haven't."

As the year passed the degree of preoccupation with memories of the husband declined (see Fig. 2) but the memories remained as clear as or clearer than they had been.

Direction of attention toward places and objects associated with the lost person.—Nearly half the widows (10) described feeling drawn toward places which they associated with their husbands. They visited old haunts or went to the cemetery or the hospital "to be near him." Thus one woman was unable to leave the house where her husband died for more than a short while without feeling a strong need to return. Nineteen treasured possessions which had previously belonged to their husbands although many of them also avoided intimate articles such as clothing or photographs which could evoke intense pining. The tendency to visit places and treasure objects associated with the husband showed no sign of abating as the year passed but the tendency to avoid reminders grew less marked. Some familiar objects and places which had seemed comforting during the early period gradually lost their hold so that a room which had had strong associations with the deceased could be redecorated and the furniture renewed. At the same time objects which had been put away shortly after the death because the pangs of grief which they evoked were so painful were gradually brought out again—

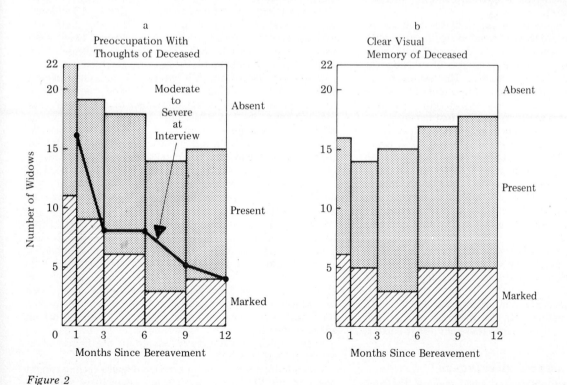

Figure 2

for example, photographs were rehung on the wall. Both of these actions involve a process of "distancing" which enables the bereaved person to accustom herself to her loss little by little.

Perceptual "set" for the lost person.—A perceptual "set" for the lost person is shown by the frequency with which he is misperceived to be present.

Hallucinations and illusions of the dead occupy a prominent place in folklore and legend. They were described in bereaved people in 1621 by Robert Burton, who quotes from several classical sources in *The Anatomy of Melancholy*, and more recently by Marris, who described the sense of the presence of the dead person in 36 of 72 widows whom he studied.

In the current study, 10 widows thought they heard or saw their husband at some time during the first month after his death (systematic assessments were not made of illusions and hallucinations in later months). Sometimes they would misinterpret small sounds about the house as indicating his presence, at other times they momentarily misidentified people in the street. These illusions rarely persisted for more than a few months before the widow would realize her mistake.

In several cases these amounted to transient hallucinations: one widow repeatedly "saw" her husband coming home through the door in the fence; another was upset by a hallucination of her husband sitting in a chair on Christmas Day. Nevertheless each of these widows recognized the experience as an hallucination.

Sixteen widows had a sense of the presence of their husband near them during the first month and this was still present in 12 a year later.

Quantitative assessments of the sense of the presence of the lost husband (see Table 1) correlated significantly with preoccupation with memories of the deceased, with clear visual memories, and with the presence of illusions or hallucinations during the first month. This seems to indicate that these features are each components of a single process and it is my contention that they all reflect the urge to look for and, in some sense, to find the lost person.

Crying.—Tearfulness is so much an expected feature of grief that it is likely to be taken for granted. It is mentioned here as a reminder of its function as a signal to promote reunion with a lost object or to obtain help. Sixteen widows cried during the first interview a month after bereavement. In subsequent interviews crying was much less frequent; thus at the end of the third month only 7 widows showed a tendency to cry and in only one case was this more than mild.

Although crying is associated with the "pangs" of grief, a widow may find it hard to say what the object of her cry is—what she is crying for. If she says anything it will be "my husband."

Assessments of tearfulness at interviews correlated significantly with preoccupation with the memory of the dead person, and with sense of presence. These and other correlations are shown in Table 1.

ANGER, GUILT, AND ASSOCIATED FEATURES

An assessment of irritability and anger made at the time of the interview correlated highly with restlessness ($r = .65$, $p < .01$), tension ($r = .58$, $p < .01$), and overall affect ($r = .54$, $p < .01$). This assessment did not correlate significantly with any of the searching features just described.

The Guttman scale shown in Table 2 emerged from consideration of a group of 17 psychological features not specifically associated with searching. After excluding the 5 "doubtful" cases shown as "?" in the table, $c = .97$. This means that those widows who expressed ideas of self-reproach during the first month were also found to be angry and socially withdrawn, but there were some who showed anger or social withdrawal who did not admit to ideas of guilt or self-reproach.

After the first month, anger and guilt were less closely associated, and taking the year as a whole the correlation between them was not statistically significant ($r = .28$). Despite this there are similarities in the form and character of the anger and guilt which justified studying them both in the same section.

Anger.—Anger was so prominent a feature of Robertson's studies of children separated from their mothers through admission to institutions that he christened the early phase of grief the phase of "Protest." Bowlby subsequently added "Yearning" to this as an alternative title and it is clear that both components belong to the same phase.

Anger, over and above trivial episodes, was described at some time in the year by all save 4 of the widows in this study. Nevertheless, at the time of the first interview only 7 widows showed anger rated as more than mild and thereafter the range was 2-4. Anger is therefore not usually a continuous state.

The most frequent form of anger, reported by 13 widows, was a general irritability or bitterness. This was commonly associated with a feeling that the world had become an insecure and potentially dangerous place, an attitude which persisted throughout the first year of bereavement.

When anger had an object it was most commonly directed against people whose actions had offended the widow in some way. In 5 cases it was a member of the family who had offended, in 3 it was clergy or doctors, in 2 it was officials in local government, and in 4 cases it was the spouse himself. ("Why did he do this to me?" "If he'd known what it was like you'd [*sic*] never have left me.") The failure of relatives to understand the widow's need to cry, aggressive behavior in children, quarrels with in-laws, and employers were commonly seen by the widows as reasons for their anger.

Less common but clearly present in 4 cases was anger toward other people whose actions were thought to have harmed the husband prior to his death. These included anger toward doctors who had failed to diagnose a husband's condition correctly at the time of his illness. "I still go over in my mind the way those doctors behaved," said one widow, and another expressed great bitterness toward a staff nurse who had hurt her husband by ripping off an adhesive dressing.

Anger which was indirectly related to the bereavement was expressed by 6 widows.

Taken individually these quarrels and angry feelings might occur in the life of any woman but when their frequency

TABLE 2   *Guttman Scale Showing Presence (Y) or Absence (N) of Anger, Guilt, and Social Withdrawal During First Month of Bereavement*

Case Number	Anger 1st mo.	Social withdrawal, 1st mo.	Anger, 1st interview	Guilt 1st mo.	Guilt, 1st interview
1	Y	Y	Y	Y	Y
16	Y	Y	N	Y	Y
4	Y	Y	Y	Y	N
20	Y	Y	Y	Y	N
13	Y	Y	Y	N	N
6	Y	Y	Y	N	N
21	Y	Y	?	N	?
3	Y	Y	?	N	N
7	Y	Y	?	N	N
10	Y	Y	N	N	N
17	Y	N	Y	N	N
11	Y	Y	N	N	N
14	Y	Y	N	N	N
22	N	Y	N	N	N
12	Y	N	N	N	?
18	N	?	N	N	N
2	N	N	N	N	N
19	N	N	N	N	N
9	N	N	N	N	N
15	N	N	N	N	N
5	N	N	N	N	N
8	N	N	N	N	N

and the atmosphere of bitterness and irritability in which they occur are taken into consideration one can only regard them as part of the typical reaction to bereavement. It is doubly unfortunate that the family members, who might have been able to help the widow to get things in perspective, were so often themselves affected by the bereavement that they were unable to be any more objective than the widow herself. Splits occurred, reputations were damaged, sources of help withdrawn, and the sense of insecurity increased as a result of these conflicts.

Most of the previous studies of bereaved individuals have drawn attention to the frequency with which irrational anger is expressed.[6] In this study two factors seemed to play a part in determining this response: (1) the sense of insecurity and frustration which resulted from the loss of a major source of support, (2) the wish to bring under control the impersonal destructive events of the bereavement—as Chodoff and his co-workers put it, a "search for meaning." Both of these factors explain aggressive behavior as somewhat desperate and belated striving for a mastery which cannot, of course, be obtained.

As time passed irrational anger became less marked; thus one widow who had been very angry with the hospital staff at the time of her bereavement, found her anger hard to sustain. Asked at the end of the year if she still felt angry she denied this but admitted, "I wish there was something I could blame."

Guilt.—Searching for meaning was also apparent in the self-reproachful ideas expressed by 13 of the widows. In its mildest form this was no more than a tendency to go over the events of the death in order, apparently to seek reassurance that all was done that could have been done. Typical comments were: "I think, 'What could I have done?'" "I think to myself, did I do right?"

Seven expressed self-reproachful ideas centered on some act or omission which might have harmed the dying spouse or in some way impaired his peace of mind. These were sometimes quite trivial matters: thus a year after bereavement one widow remarked that she felt guilty because she had never made her husband a bread pudding. More often the matter was a serious one but the attribution of blame dubious. Thus another widow kept regreting that she had supported her husband in his refusal to undergo a palliative operation. A third blamed herself for failing to encourage her husband's literary talents during his lifetime and endeavored to make restitution by getting his poems published after his death. Regarding their ambivalent relationship she said, "We were both always on the defensive. Now I can see how often he was right."

Several felt that they had failed their husband during the terminal phases of his illness. "I seemed to go away from him. He wasn't the person I'd been married to. When I tried to share his pain it was so terrible I couldn't." "I wish I could have done more. I don't think I could have done enough because he sat so helpless."

Five widows blamed themselves for the way they had behaved following bereavement. One blamed herself for her irritability: "I get furious with myself." Another reproached herself, "You tend to magnify, look for trouble."

Although self-reproachful ideas have been described in

several other studies,[7] they are not as prominent a symptom as anger and in this study they were not a major problem. At any given time after bereavement there were never more than two widows who expressed guilt rated as moderate to severe, and the guilt did not compare in intensity, frequency, or duration with the self-reproachful ideas reported to the writer by 22 bereaved patients who subsequently to their bereavement had developed a psychiatric illness (Parkes, 1965).

As stated above, guilt was significantly correlated with anger during the first month but not thereafter. The only other features which showed a significant correlation with self-reproach were identification features ($r = .49, p < .02$); these will be considered below.

Restlessness and tension.—Hyperactivity as a feature of the reaction to bereavement was first clearly established by Cobb and Lindemann using the "interaction chronograph" technique. In the current study, restlessness, tension, and anger as observed at interviews all correlated highly.

Restlessness was clearly manifest at the first interview in half the widows and nearly all of them (18) said that they had felt restless during the first month of bereavement. During succeeding periods the proportion fell gradually to a total of 9 at the end of the year.

Among these widows complaints of feeling "strung up" or "jumpy" were common. "I feel all in a turmoil inside," "I'm always on the go," "I'm at the end of my tether," "I can't pin myself down to anything," "Stupid little things upset me." Such remarks were made at times of moderate to severe restlessness and tension and indicate the general picture. When tension was severe an irregular fine tremor was often present and sometimes a stammer.

The general impression was of an intense impulse to action, generally aggressive, which was being rigidly controlled. Restless widows were likely to "flare up" from time to time or to fill their lives with activities.

Thus one described herself as "geared to a tremendous tempo" and driving herself to avoid depression. At the end of the year she was still very busy and seldom thinking of the past or the future. Instead she was living in a state of anxiety and tension which sometimes reached near-panic proportions. She was proud of the fact that she never broke down and had been taught always to control her feelings.

Another said, "I think if I didn't work all the time I'd have a nervous breakdown." Interviews were carried out "on the trot" as she passed from one household chore to another; she appeared at all times distraught, irritable, and tense. At the end of the year she could see "nothing to live for" and added bitterly, "It all seems to pointless."

Although these two widows claimed that they had deliberately filled their lives with activities with the purpose of avoiding depression, hyperactivity was not usually voluntary.

Retarded or anergic states are, as Lindemann (1944) has pointed out, excessively rare after bereavement and none was observed in this study.

METHODS OF MITIGATION OR DEFENSE

The distress engendered by bereavement is never continuous and each widow described times during which it was mitigated. Even when grief was at its most intense the "pangs" of grief were intermittent and a "pang" would be followed by a period of relative calm.[8]

The extent to which such mitigation of grief was under the control of the will varied considerably and in any given case it was often hard to determine the degree of voluntary "control" exerted. Thus there was a range of states between the involuntary "numbness" which has been described above as the most common immediate reaction to bereavement and the deliberate avoidance of people and places associated with the dead person and therefore likely to evoke painful pangs of grief.

Each widow seemed to have her own pattern of mitigation. These included: (1) *blacking out or denial of affect*, as seen most clearly as "numbness"; (2) *partial disbelief* in the reality of external events, "difficulty in accepting the fact of loss," "disbelief in the prognosis," and derealization (examples will be given below); (3) *inhibition of painful thoughts* by "avoidance of reminders," "selective forgetting," and idealization; and (4) *evocation of pleasant or neutral thoughts* as reflected in the "sense of presence of the lost person" and deliberate attempts to occupy the mind.

Measures of "numbness," "difficulty in accepting the fact of loss," "disbelief in the prognosis," the comforting "sense of the presence of the lost person," and deliberate attempts to keep occupied showed very little correlation with each other. Nor were they associated with "avoidance of reminders" or "idealization," which will now be described. This seems to suggest that if there is any general factor of "defensiveness" it does not play a very large part in determining the reaction to bereavement. Each widow adopted her own method of "distancing" which enabled her to tolerate the pain of grief with variable success.

Avoidance of reminders was clearly present from time to time in 14 widows during the first month of bereavement and was rated as "marked" in 8. During the rest of the year the number who said they were avoiding reminders dropped until at the final interview, "avoidance" was clearly present in 6 and marked in only one.

Avoidance was well illustrated by Mrs. Ellis, who had lost her husband suddenly and unexpectedly from a cerebral hemorrhage. She found it very difficult to believe that he was dead but kept breaking down and crying a great deal during the first week. Then she managed to stop crying by deliberately keeping her mind occupied with other things. She avoided going into her husband's room and persuaded her son to get rid of most of her husband's possessions. When first interviewed a month after bereavement she broke off several times, unable to talk for fear that she would cry. A year later her overall state was much calmer but she still avoided possessions which would remind her of her husband and disliked visiting his grave. "If he comes in me mind I try to get—to think of something else."

Two widows experienced *derealization* during the course of their grief.

"I feel I'm waiting for something to happen, for the unreal feeling to pass," said one. She spoke in a hushed voice and seemed "distant," often mishearing questions. "I feel this is a different life . . . as if there's another life going on somewhere else and I'll wake up." She admitted that in her "dream world" she imagined that her husband's death had not occurred. By the end of the year, however, the feeling of unreality had gone for the most part, with only occasional episodes when she was on her own. She no longer avoided people or things which reminded her of the past.

Another form of mitigation which has been described is *selective forgetting*. In a recent paper Lindemann (1960) notes how "The image of the deceased disappears from consciousness" (p. 14). This was described by one widow, who was unable to recall the face of her husband during the first month after his death. Thereafter she had a clear visual memory of him. More common than the total forgetting of the dead person's appearance was distortion of recollections of particular aspects of the person which were peculiarly disturbing.

It is the negative aspects of the relationship with the dead husband which are most easily forgotten and it seemed that *idealization of the dead* was very common although there were no objective criteria for establishing this in the current study.

Mrs. Harris was a woman of 59 who had quarreled frequently with her alcoholic husband. She had left him several times during their married life and at the time of the first interview she remarked, "I shouldn't really say so but it's more peaceful now that he's gone." In the course of her first year as a widow her two youngest daughters got married and left home, leaving her alone in the flat. She became very lonely and depressed and spoke nostalgically of the old days. At the final interview she had so far forgotten her antipathies that she said she would like to marry again—"To someone kind, like my husband."

IDENTIFICATION PHENOMENA

In his early formulation of the metaphychology of mourning in *The Ego and the Id*, Freud suggested that the withdrawal of libido which attaches one person to another can only take place when the lost object is "reinstated" in the ego—hence identification was the "sole condition under which the id can give up its objects" (p. 29). Subsequently he seems to have revised that view, and by 1933 he was saying, "If one has lost a love object or has to give it up, one *often* compensates oneself by identifying oneself with it . . ." (*New Intro. Lectures* . . . , my italics). Henceforth identification was seen as a mitigation of grief rather than an essential component of it.

Nevertheless the earlier view still reappears from time to time and recent writers, such as Krupp (1965) and Rochlin, continue to regard identification as the necessary condition without which grief cannot end.

Several types of identification phenomena have been described by psychoanalysts and all of them were found in the current study. They are included together here because of the traditional assumption that they have a common origin but the present writer has doubts regarding the homogeneity of this group.

Careful enquiry was made at each interview for symp-toms or behavior suggesting identification with the dead person but it was often hard to be sure whether a particular piece of behavior indicated identification or a chance resemblance. In all there were 5 widows who showed behavior which seemed clearly to indicate identification and a further 9 where the evidence was strongly suggestive. Five widows reported more than one type of identification.

(1) The commonest type, which was reported by 10 widows, was a tendency for the widow to *behave or think more like the spouse* than she had when he was alive. In two cases this was very clearly seen. For example:

"I enjoy the things my husband used to do. . . . It's like a thought in my head—what he would say or do," said Mrs. Baker, who cited watching the cup final and Goodwood Racing on television as examples of activities deriving from him. "I quite enjoy it because he liked it. It's a most queer feeling. . . . My young sister said, 'You're getting like Fred in all your ways.' . . . She said something about food—I said, 'I couldn't touch that,' and she said, 'Don't be stupid, you're getting just like Fred.' . . . There's lots of things I do that I wouldn't think of doing. . . . I suppose he's guiding me the whole of the time."

Eight examples of this type of behavior were reported in the final interview, with 3, 2, 4, and 4 examples occurring during the 1st, 2nd, 3rd, and 4th interviews.

(2) Less frequent but reported by 4 widows were *symptoms closely resembling the symptoms of the husband's last illness* (identification symptoms).

Mrs. Green had a succession of symptoms which, she claimed, resembled symptoms that her husband had suffered. He had had a cerebral vascular accident 5 years before his death which affected his left side. His death followed a coronary thrombosis which had given rise to chest pain and breathlessness for a week. Subsequently his wife had a series of fainting attacks, palpitations, and panics in which she gasped for breath and felt that her heart was bursting—"Just like my husband." Later in the year she developed uncontrollable spasms and pain in her left face and leg which her G.P. diagnosed as "mimicry of her husband's stroke." This was the only case in which the evidence was completely convincing.

(3) Three widows described feeling as if their dead husband were actually inside them.

Mrs. Baker, for instance, described a "pain going through my heart"—the pain was somehow "him inside me." "My husband's in me, right through and through. I've got like him. . . . I can feel him in me doing everything. He used to say, 'You'll do this when I'm gone won't you.' " "He's just guiding my life isn't it. I can feel his presence within me because of his talking and doing things." "My husband's a part of me, that's the trouble."

The resemblance of this feature to the "sense of presence" described above is worth noting, but the "sense of presence" was usually located as "nearby" rather than "inside."

"It's not a sense of his presence, he is *here* inside me. That's why I'm happy all the time. It's as if two people were one. . . . Although I'm alone we're, sort of, together if you see what I mean. . . . I don't think I've the will power to carry on on my own so he must be."

In 2 widows the sense of an internal presence was experienced dramatically as a welcome invasion shortly after bereavement, as described above in the section on immediate reactions.

(4) Another phenomenon is the *location of the dead husband within children*. There were 5 examples of this.

One widow spoke of her daughter: "Sometimes I feel as if D. is my husband. . . . She has his hands—it used to give me the creeps. . . . He always wanted a blonde girl." Another woman (not included in the statistical analysis), whose common-law husband had died, married and became pregnant within 9 months of bereavement. Of her unborn child she said, "Giving birth will be like getting Dick out of me . . . it's terribly important." To one widow it appeared that the daughter had attempted to become like her father; her mother found this most disturbing. "I feel she's trying to be him. . . . I said, 'You musn't become your father on me.' . . . At times I feel that she has taken his place, she resembles him . . . lives the life and does what he did. Dashed off to Paris with a boy, just like him."

Among the other psychological features studied, the only one which correlated significantly with my overall index of identification was "guilt or self-reproach" ($r = .49$, $p < .02$). This would seem to support Krupp's view (1965) that "symptomatic identifications" (identification symptoms) are conversion reactions in which the patient punishes himself for his ambivalence toward the other, and particularly for unconscious death wishes. Because of the small numbers involved in the current study it was not possible to undertake further analysis of these figures according to the type of identification phenomenon involved.

Possibly self-punitive identification and the forms of identification which seem to reflect attempts at finding the lost spouse and reenactment of reunion with him are two different phenomena but, as Krupp points out, it is possible for both to coexist. If we accept the view that some identification phenomena are means of psychological reunion with the lost person, then they are a form of mitigation or defense similar to the "sense of presence." Why some widows should locate the dead person in one place and some in another has not emerged from this study. Widows were not consistent in assigning their dead husbands to a particular locality. Mrs. Baker would sometimes describe her husband as inside her, at other times as occupying a particular chair or in the bed where he died. If she left the house she felt that she wanted to return quickly, to be near him, yet even at home she pined for him much of the time because he was not there. These varying locations of the husband seem to represent different forms of the phenomenon but they cannot all be regarded as indicating identification.

DREAMS

All widows were asked at each interview if they had dreamed of their husband during the preceding period. Eleven recalled dreams of their husband on one or more occasions and 2 had violent dreams in which someone was killed.

The striking feature of most of the dreams of the husband was their vivid and realistic quality. In this they resembled the clear visual memories of the dead person. Twelve such dreams were recalled by 8 widows. Most commonly these were happy dreams of interaction with the dead husband (7 single dreams, 2 recurrent). Less frequent were dreams of the husband dying or going away (6), coming to life again (2), or dead (1).

Characteristically these dreams ended with the dreamer's awakening with surprise and disappointment to find that the husband was not present after all. But as Waller has observed, even in dreams of happy interaction there was usually something to indicate that all was not well.

"He was trying to comfort me and put his arm round me. I kept turning away and crying and crying. Even in the dream I know he's dead. . . . But I felt so happy and I cried and he couldn't do anything about it. . . . When I touched his face it was as if he was really there—quite real and vivid." Another typical bereavement dream: "He was in the coffin with the lid off and all of a sudden he came to life and got out. . . . I looked at him and he opened his mouth—I said, 'He's alive. He's alive.' I thought, thank God, I'll have him to talk to."

These dreams illustrate, yet again, the effects of the urge to recover the lost object, which plays so large a part in grief. Each of them can be seen as an attempt to undo the painful reality of death, to recover the lost person and bring him back to life, but even in the dream this attempt is seldom completely successful and always there is, eventually, a "sad awakening."

INHIBITION OF OTHER APPETITES AND ACTIVITIES

While the widow is engaged in the painful and time-consuming process of grieving she pays little attention to less urgent matters. Sleeping, eating, and interest in day-to-day pursuits and relationships take second place, and although she may "keep busy" in an attempt to ward off distress there is little affect behind this behavior.

Insomnia was the rule during the first few weeks of bereavement. It was mentioned by 17 widows and was marked in 14. During the course of the first three months the severity of insomnia dropped off sharply, as shown in Figure 3, and was seldom a major problem thereafter. About half of the widows (12) took a sedative drug in the first month of bereavement and nearly a quarter (5) were taking them a year later.

The form of sleep disturbance varied. Approximately equal numbers complained of inability to get to sleep, tendency to wake during the night, and tendency to wake early. Five described more than one type of sleep disturbance. It was at night that widows were often most lonely; several of them were unable to sleep in the bed which they had shared with their husband and several lay awake thinking of him during much of the night.

Nineteen widows claimed that they lost their appetite during the first month of bereavement and in 15 this brought about recognized loss of weight. Six widows lost 14 pounds or more in the course of the first month and only one gained weight during this period. After the end of the first month, however, anorexia and weight loss were much less common and from the third month onwards it

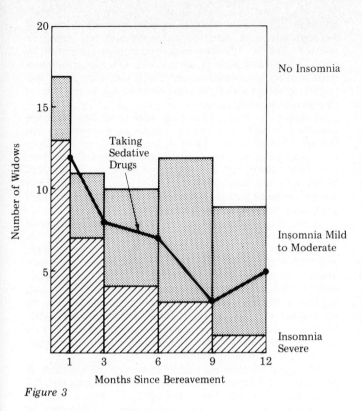

Figure 3

was weight gain that was more likely to be regarded as a problem.

These widows not only lost interest in food, but also lost interest in most of the other sources of gratification which were available to them.[9] In at least 4 cases this even included loss of affection for surviving children, and over half of the widows (13) cut themselves off from friends and shut themselves up at home. Those 7 who had jobs stayed away from work for an average of 12 days after bereavement. Nevertheless, in the long run, these widows found fresh interests and new friends earlier than the widows who had no job to take them out of the home.

No systematic assessment of sexual interests was attempted.

THE SITUATION THIRTEEN MONTHS AFTER BEREAVEMENT

Domestic, occupational and financial situation.—Nearly all widows (19) continued to live in the house which they had occupied during their husband's lifetime. Only 3 had moved (plus one who left the country and had to be excluded from the statistical analysis). On the whole, the widows seemed to like being in the house which they had shared with their husband although this was often too large for their requirements. Since most widows were statutory tenants who would have had to pay a higher rent if they had moved into smaller accommodations it is not surprising that all save one said they were satisfied with their present home and did not wish to change it.

Over half the widows (13) were financially poorer than

they had been before bereavement, 4 of them very much poorer. A third (7) stated that they were worried about money, and 2 had gotten into serious financial difficulties.

Fourteen widows were working outside the home and 2 of the 8 who were still at home were taking paying guests. Of the 14 who were working, 7 had worked in the same or similar jobs before bereavement but 7 had taken a job for the first time during the year. Working widows averaged 29 hours per week at work. Despite the fact that they had to look after the home as well as working they valued their work highly and enjoyed the social relationships which resulted from it.

Social relationships.—The widows spent an average four-fifths of their time at home and a third of them (7) now lived alone. Only 4 claimed that they now had more social contacts than before bereavement.

In each week the 7 widows who lived alone spent a mean of 130 hours inside and 38 hours outside the home. In this they did not differ from those who lived with others. Two of them frequently saw friends or relatives but the remaining 5 claimed that they had seen a mean of only 4 persons for more than 10 minutes during the week before the final interview. It is not surprising that loneliness was a common problem among these socially isolated widows.

Taking all factors into consideration overall social adjustment was rated by the interviewer as good in 5 cases, fair in 9, and poor in 8. In 6 cases social adjustment was definitely worse than it had been before bereavement.

Attitudes and plans.—It was postulated that a widow who had fully accepted bereavement and had made a good adjustment to her widowed state would be able to look back with pleasure and to the future with optimism. Only 3 widows satisfied both these criteria 13 months after bereavement. Six widows still found the past too painful to think of, but 9 asserted that they found it more pleasant than unpleasant and these widows tended to spend much of their time reminiscing. The remaining 7 had mixed feelings about the past and only thought about it intermittently. Five had an optimistic view of their future. The rest preferred not to think about it, and 5 were definitely pessimistic.

Four expressed a wish to remarry and one of these was already engaged. Of the remainder, 6 were quite clearly against remarriage and 12 denied that they had given the matter serious thought. This was probably a realistic attitude for the older widows, whose prospects of finding a suitable partner were remote. (According to Marris 17% of widows aged 20-24 remarry compared with 1% of those aged 50-59.)

On the whole newly bereaved widows seemed to view the world as an insecure and potentially hostile place. But there were several who had been surprised at their own capacity to make a successful adjustment. For instance one woman was proud of her new-found independence: "If I want to go a bit mad and buy something I can do it." She had taken up judo with the conscious intention of toughening herself up to face a hard world. At the same time she felt the need of a man to protect her.

Physical health.—There were 6 widows whose health was definitely worse than it had been before the illness and death of their husbands; none was now clearly healthier. Commonest complaints were headaches, digestive disturbances, and aching limbs. Self-assessments by the widows of their own general health were more closely correlated with measures of irritation and anger than they were with more objective assessments of ill health.

Psychological state.—Asked to rate their own level of contentment, 6 widows claimed that they were, on the whole, happy, 7 described themselves as sad, and 2 as neutral. Seven stated that their mood fluctuated a great deal between happiness and sadness and they could not make a general assessment.

The interviewer took the view that 3 were very poorly adjusted, depressed, and still grieving a great deal, 9 were intermittently disturbed and depressed, and 6 showed a tenuous adjustment which might easily be upset. Four had made a good adjustment and were not easily upset.

When compared to their psychological state before the terminal illness of the spouse, 9 widows were definitely in a worse state, 7 probably worse, 3 unchanged, and 3 better.

Two brief examples will be given to illustrate types of psychological outcome which occurred in this study.

Mrs. Green had an ambivalent relationship with her husband. During his terminal illness he had several times wished her dead and after his death had left his money tied up in such a way that she had very little of it. She denied all hostility for him but expressed considerable hostility toward the doctors and lawyers who refused to support her in her attempts to get the will set aside. A general attitude of bitterness and resentment persisted throughout the year and she had a series of panic attacks and identification symptoms which have been described above. Thirteen months after bereavement she thought that she was still as disturbed as she had been on the day he died. She felt that her husband had condemned her to death and she expressed suicidal ideas.

By contrast, Mrs. Smith made a good adjustment. She was a warm, affectionate woman who had had a close and unambivalent relationship with her husband. After his death she felt "numb" for several days, then became anxious and depressed, preoccupied with her husband's memory and retaining a strong sense of his presence. Her family rallied round and gave her a lot of support, and during the third and fourth months her grief began to diminish. During the seventh month she paid a visit to her sister in America. This confirmed her in her sense of being wanted and she returned confident and refreshed, prepared to care for an ailing relative and to be the center of a united family.

Most widows fell between these extremes. Thirteen months after bereavement a majority of the widows (15) claimed that they still spent much of their time thinking about their husband, and nearly all (18) had a clear visual memory of him in their minds. Over half (12) still had a sense of his presence nearby at times and the same proportion said that they found it hard to accept the fact that he was dead. Although headaches (complained of by 11) and painful limbs (10) were frequent, only 3 said their general health was bad and most (14) had a good appetite. About half said they were still restless (10) and this was evident at the time of the interview: the same proportion said they were irritable, and 9 still had occasional panicky feelings

although these were marked in only one case. Ideas of self-reproach were rare (4) and none still felt numb or blunted. Tearful episodes were exceptional (moderate in only 2 cases) and widows were able to talk about their loss with relative equanimity. Only 6 said that there were still people or things which they avoided because of the painful thoughts evoked by them.

It would be wrong to assume that what has just been described is the long-term outcome of widowhood. Although 13 months was fixed as the duration of the study on the assumption that most of the acute grief would by then have passed, this was not found to be so. The process of grieving was still going on and although the principal features were all past their peak there was no sense in which grief could be said to have finished.

In his classical account of his work with newly bereaved people, Lindemann (1944) claimed, "With eight to ten interviews in which the psychiatrist shares the grief work, and with a period of four to six weeks, it was ordinarily possible to settle uncomplicated and undistorted grief reactions." This statement has caused several workers, including the writer, to underestimate the probable duration of uncomplicated grief. Further studies are now being undertaken to follow widows and widowers two and three years after bereavement in order to ascertain what further decrement in the features of grief is to be expected.

Of course there is no simple answer to the question of how long grief lasts. In some senses it never ends and the writer has frequently been told by long-standing widows, "You never get over it." At anniversaries, for example, or when an old friend comes to call unexpectedly or when a forgotten photograph is discovered in a drawer all the feelings of acute pining and sadness return and the bereaved person goes through, in miniature, another bereavement.

But it does appear that, as time goes by, one after another of the features of grief becomes less frequently aroused and less intense than it was before. At the same time the interests and appetites which were lost at the time of the bereavement gradually return.

Discussion

This study has shown that the unselected London widows do have difficulty in accepting the fact of loss and do express irritability and anger with similar frequency to that expressed by bereaved psychiatric patients. In these respects they tend to resemble the Japanese widows studied by Yamamoto and the English Midland widows studied by Hobson rather than Marris's London widows.

In "Mourning and Melancholia" Freud has suggested that "ambivalence casts a pathological shade on the grief, forcing it to express itself in the form of self-reproaches" (p. 161). He attributes much melancholic illness to the "conflict of ambivalence." In the current studies, although the part played by guilt and ambivalence in much pathological grief has been evident, it should not be concluded that ambivalent relationships are the sole cause of these reactions. Research is currently being undertaken which should throw more light on the role of other important factors in determining outcome following bereavement.

THE PHASES OF GRIEF

In general this study has confirmed Bowlby's belief that grief is a phasic process although the transitions from one phase to another are seldom distinct and features from one phase of grief often persist into the next.

The most clear-cut transition is likely to be that between the first ("Numbness") phase and the second. This takes place a few hours to a few days after the bereavement. The second phase has two independent components, "Yearning" and "Protest." "Yearning" is characterized by pangs of intense yearning or pining which are thought to be the principal feature of the urge to reunite with the lost object. "Protest" is seen in restless irritability or bitterness toward others or the self. These components are at their peak during the second to fourth weeks of bereavement and then begin to decline. Tearfulness and the autonomic accompaniments of acute anxiety are the first features to decline; the degree of preoccupation with memories of the lost husband, the sense of his presence, the avoidance of reminders, irritability, and general restlessness and tension decline much more gradually throughout the whole of the first year. At the same time the tendency to treasure reminders and to cherish a clear visual memory of the deceased is growing.

As the intensity of yearning and protest diminishes, apathy and aimlessness are the rule and it is this disinclination to look to the future or to see any purpose in life which characterizes the third phase of grief, "Disorganization." Judged by their disinclination to look ahead, about two-thirds of the widows described here were still in this phase at the end of their first year of bereavement and it is not possible from this study to obtain a clear idea of its duration.

It is apparent, however, that all appetites and interests do not return at the same time. The appetite for food, for instance, perhaps as a consequence of partial starvation during the first month, is likely to have returned by the third. But interest in less essential objects takes a much greater time to return.

Conclusion

Grief, it seems, is a complex and time-consuming process in which a person gradually changes his view of the world and the places and habits by means of which he orientates and relates to it. It is a process of realization, of making psychologically real an external event which is not desired and for which coping plans do not exist.

In the course of grief it is to be expected that unrealistic attempts will be made to disbelieve the reality of what has happened, to call and to search for the lost person, and to achieve in dream and fantasy the reunion which cannot be achieved in fact. As repeated attempts fail, the griever experiences pangs of psychological pain, separation anxiety, and frustration, with intervening periods of depression and aimlessness.

A year after the death of her husband the young or middle-aged widow is still without plans and often depressed, but the intensity of her separation anxiety is diminishing and she is likely to be functioning effectively in most of her new roles.

APPENDIX

RESEARCH MEASURES AND OPERATIONAL DEFINITIONS

Two principal types of quantitative measures were used in this study, overall assessments and assessments at interview.

Overall assessments were based on the widow's account of her experiences between interviews. These were rated: (1) Not present, (2) Doubtful, (3) Present, (4) Marked. In practice very few "doubtful" ratings were made and in presenting the data, "Not present" and "Doubtful" have usually been amalgamated and labeled "Absent." The exception was "identification," which contained many "doubtful" examples.

Assessments at interview were made by the interviewer by combining information from the widow with his own direct observations. These were rated as: (1) Absent (denied at all times), (2) Mild (not clearly present at interview but mild at times), (3) Moderate (inconspicuous at interview but said to be pronounced at other times), (4) Marked (severe or pronounced during part of the interview), (5) Very marked (pronounced throughout interview).

In Figs. 2 and 3 the broken lines indicate numbers of widows rated 3-5 on this scale.

The meaning of most of the descriptive features is self-evident but some require more precise operational definition:

Overall affective disturbance.—General estimate of the amount of negative emotional upset, rated: (1) None—no more disturbed than usual, (2) Mild—only occasional disturbance, (3) Moderate—severe disturbance less than half the time, (4) Severe—severe disturbance most of the time, (5) Very severe—severe disturbance with serious thoughts of suicide.

Numbness.—Reports of feeling "numb," "blunted," or "cloudy."

Difficulty in accepting loss.—Difficulty in fully believing reality of husband's death; statements such as, "I still can't believe it's true."

Identification.—Adoption of traits, mannerisms, aims, occupation, or symptoms of the husband, or feeling of his presence within self.

Restlessness.—Observable hyperactivity.

Tension.—Observable muscle tension.

NOTES

1. See Parkes, 1964a, 1964b; Parkes et al., 1969; and Rees.
2. Under the National Health Service all members of the population are registered with a general practitioner, who keeps their medical records and is responsible for their day-to-day medical care. Since most husbands are registered with the same G.P. as their wives, the G.P.'s are likely to know whenever one of their patients becomes a widow.
3. Of the more important variables, 46, including all Mean Year Scores, were punched on IBM cards for statistical analysis at the Harvard Computing Center. This was carried out with the assistance of Dr. Kenneth Jones.
4. Social Class Groupings are those used in *General Register Office, Classification of Occupations*; London, H.M.S.O., 1960.
5. Unless otherwise stated, correlations are between Mean Year Scores.
6. See, for instance, Lindemann (1944); Marris; Hobson; Yamamoto et al.; and Stern, Williams, and Prados.
7. See Clayton et al.; Lindemann (1944); and Marris.
8. The search for the lost person seems to imply disregard for the permanence of the loss and could be regarded as itself a form of defense. But searching can hardly be said to mitigate anxiety and

bereaved persons often go to great lengths to avoid the pain of searching. See Parkes (1970) for a more detailed discussion of grief and defense.

9. There seems to be no good reason to attribute the anorexia which so often follows bereavement to defenses against oral-sadistic cravings as suggested in early psychoanalytic writings on mourning. Krupp's suggestion (1962) that it is more readily explained by generalized inhibition, as is seen in bereaved animals, is more in line with the view adopted here. Nevertheless the inhibition does not extend to the behavior described in connection with searching or anger.

REFERENCES

Bowlby, John, and Parkes, Colin Murray. "Separation and Loss," in E. J. Anthony and C. Koupernik (Eds.) *Internat. Yearbook for Child Psychiatry and Allied Disciplines*, Vol. 1, *The Child in His Family*; Wiley, 1970.

Chodoff, Paul, et al. "Stress, Defenses and Coping Behavior; Observations in Parents of Children with Malignant Disease," *Amer., J. Psychiatry* (1964) 120:743-749.

Clayton, Paula, et al. "A Study of Normal Bereavement," *Amer. J. Psychiatry* (1968) 125:168-178.

Cobb, Stanley, and Lindemann, Erich. "Neuro-psychiatric Observations after the Coconut Grove Fire," *Ann. Surg.* (1943) 117:84.

Deutsch, Helene. "Absence of Grief," *Psychoanal. Quart.* (1937) 6:12-22.

Eliot, Thomas D. ". . . Of the Shadow of Death," *Ann. Amer. Acad. Pol. & Soc. Sci.* (1943) 229:87-99.

Freud, Sigmund. "Mourning and Melancholia (1917)," *Collected Papers*, Vol. 4; Hogarth, 1959.

Freud, Sigmund. "The Ego and the Id (1923)," *Standard Edition of the Complete Psychological Works*, Vol. 19; Hogarth, 1961.

Freud, Sigmund. "New Introductory Lectures on Psycho-analysis (1933)," *Standard Edition of the Complete Psychological Works*, Vol. 22; Hogarth, 1964.

Gorer, Geoffrey. *Death, Grief and Mourning in Contemporary Britain*; London, Cresset, 1965.

Harvey, L. A., and Kistemaker, M. "The Resolution of Mourning Through Ego-Adaptive Mechanisms in Women Following Separation by Death of Their Husbands," M.S.W. thesis, Smith College School of Social Work, 1965.

Hobson, Celia, J. "Widows of Blackton," *New Society* (1964) 24:13.

Krupp, George R. "The Bereavement Reaction: A Special Case of Separation Anxiety," in W. Muensterberger and S. Axelrod (Eds.),

The Psychoanalytic Study of Society. Vol. 2; Internat. Univ. Press, 1962.

Krupp, George R. "Identification as a Defense Against Anxiety in Coping with Loss," *Internat. J. Psycho-Anal.* (1965) 46:303-314.

Lindemann, Erich. "Symptomatology and Management of Acute Grief," *Amer. J. Psychiatry* (1944) 101:141-148.

Lindemann, Erich. "Psychosocial Factors as Stress Agents," in J. M. Tanner (Ed.), *Stress and Psychiatric Disorders*; Oxford, Blackwell, 1960.

Maddison, David, and Walker, Wendy L. "Factors Affecting the Outcome of Conjugal Bereavement." *British J. Psychiatry* (1967) 113:1057-1067.

Marris, Peter. *Widows and Their Families*; London, Routledge & Kegan Paul, 1958.

Parkes, Colin Murray. "Recent Bereavement as a Cause of Mental Illness," *British J. Psychiatry* (1964) 110:198-204. (a)

Parkes, Colin Murray. "The Effects of Bereavement on Physical and Mental Health; A Study of the Case Records of Widows," *British Med. J.* (1964) 2:274-279. (b)

Parkes, Colin Murray. "Bereavement and Mental Illness. Part I: A Clinical Study of the Grief of Bereaved Psychiatric Patients. Part II. A Classification of Bereavement Reactions," *British J. Med. Psychology* (1965) 38:1-26.

Parkes, Colin Murray. "Separation Anxiety: An Aspect of the Search for a Lost Object," in M. H. Lader (Ed.) *Anxiety*; Oxford Univ. Press, 1969.

Parkes, Colin Murray. "The Search for a Lost Object: Evidence from Recent Studies of the Reaction to Bereavement," *Soc. Sci. and Med.*, in press.

Parkes, Colin Murray, et al. "Broken Heart: A Statistical Study of Increased Mortality Among Widowers," *British Med. J.* (1969) 1:740-743.

Rees, W. D., and Lutkins, S. G. "Mortality of Bereavement," *British Med. J.* (1967) 4:13-16.

Robertson, James. "Some Responses of Young Children to Loss of Maternal Care," *Nursing Times* (1953) 49:382-386.

Rochlin, Gregory. *Griefs and Discontents: The Forces of Change*; Little, Brown, 1966.

Stern, Karl, et al. "Grief Reactions in Later Life," *Amer. J. Psychiatry* (1951) 108:289-296.

Tyhurst, J. "The Role of Transitional States—Including Disasters—in Mental Illness," *Walter Reed Symposium on Preventive and Social Psychiatry*; Govt. Printing Office, 1958.

Waller, Willard, and Hill, Reuben. *The Family, Dynamic Interpretation*; Dryden, 1951.

Yamamoto, Joe, et al. "Mourning in Japan," *Amer. J. Psychiatry* (1969) 125:1660-1665.

23 *The six stations of divorce*

Paul Bohannan

Divorce is a complex social phenomenon as well as a complex personal experience. Because most of us are ignorant of what it requires of us, divorce is likely to be traumatic: emotional stimulation is so great that accustomed ways of acting are inadequate. The usual way for the healthy mind to deal with trauma is to block it out, then let it reappear slowly, so it is easier to manage. The blocking may appear as memory lapses or as general apathy.

On a social level we do something analogous, not allowing ourselves to think fully about divorce as a social problem. Our personal distrust of the emotions that surround it leads us to consider it only with traditional cultural defenses. Our ignorance masquerades as approval or disapproval, as enlightenment or moral conviction.[1]

The complexity of divorce arises because at least six things are happening at once. They may come in a different

Reprinted from Divorce and After, *by Paul Bohannan, pp. 29-55. Copyright © 1968, 1970 by Paul Bohannan, by permission of Doubleday & Company, Inc. The original paper discusses each of the six phases of divorce rather equally but I have edited so that sections discussing emotional processes are emphasized.*

order and with varying intensities, but there are at least these six different experiences of separation. They are the more painful and puzzling as personal experiences because society is not yet equipped to handle any of them well, and some of them we do not handle at all.

I have called these six overlapping experiences (1) the emotional divorce, which centers around the problem of the deteriorating marriage; (2) the legal divorce, based on grounds; (3) the economic divorce, which deals with money and property; (4) the coparental divorce, which deals with custody, single-parent homes, and visitation; (5) the community divorce, surrounding the changes of friends and community that every divorcee experiences; and (6) the psychic divorce, with the problem of regaining individual autonomy.

The first visible stage of a deteriorating marriage is likely to be what psychiatrists call emotional divorce. This occurs when the spouses withhold emotion from their relationship because they dislike the intensity or ambivalence of their feelings. They may continue to work together as a social team, but their attraction and trust for one another have disappeared. The self-regard of each is no longer reinforced by love for the other. The emotional divorce is experienced as an unsavory choice between giving in and hating oneself and domineering and hating one self. The natural and healthy "growing apart" of a married couple is very different. As marriages mature, the partners grow in new directions, but also establish bonds of ever greater interdependence. With emotional divorce, people do not grow together as they grow apart—they become, instead, mutually antagonistic and imprisoned, hating the vestiges of their dependence. Two people in emotional divorce grate on each other because each is disappointed.

In American society, we have turned over to the courts the responsibility for formalizing the dissolution of such a marriage. The legislature (which in early English law usurped the responsibility from the church, and then in the American colonies turned it over to the courts) makes the statutes and defines the categories into which every marital dispute must be thrust if legal divorce is possible. Divorce is not "legalized" in many societies but may be done by a church or even by contract. Even in our own society, there is only one thing that a divorce court can do that cannot be done more effectively some other way—establish the right to remarry.

The economic divorce must occur because in Western countries husband and wife are an economic unit. Their unity is recognized by the law. They can—and in some states must—own property as a single "legal person." While technically the couple is not a corporation, they certainly have many of the characteristics of a legal corporation. At the time the household is broken up by divorce, an economic settlement must be made, separating the assets of the "corporation" into two sets of assets, each belonging to one person. This is the property settlement.

All divorced persons suffer more or less because their community is altered. Friends necessarily take a different view of a person during and after divorce—he ceases to be a part of a couple. Their own inadequacies, therefore, will be projected in a new way. Their fantasies are likely to change

as they focus on the changing situation. In many cases, the change in community attitude—and perhaps people too—is experienced by a divorcee as ostracism and disapproval. For many divorcing people, the divorce from community may make it seem that nothing in the world is stable.

Finally comes the psychic divorce. It is almost always last, and always the most difficult. Indeed, I have not found a word strong or precise enough to describe the difficulty or the process. Each partner to the ex-marriage, either before or after the legal divorce—usually after, and sometimes years after—must turn himself or herself again into an autonomous social individual. People who have been long married tend to have become socially part of a couple or a family; they lose the habit of seeing themselves as individuals. This is worse for people who married in order to avoid becoming autonomous individuals in the first place.

To become an individual again, at the center of a new community, requires developing new facets of character. Some people have forgotten how to do it—some never learned. The most potent argument against teen-age marriages is that they are likely to occur between people who are searching for independence but avoiding autonomy. The most potent argument against hurried remarriage is the same: avoidance of the responsibilities of autonomy.

Divorce is an institution that nobody enters without great trepidation. In the emotional divorce, people are likely to feel hurt and angry. In the legal divorce, people often feel bewildered—they have lost control, and events sweep them along. In the economic divorce, the reassignment of property and the division of money (there is *never* enough) may make them feel cheated. In the parental divorce they worry about what is going to happen to the children; they feel guilty for what they have done. With the community divorce, they may get angry with their friends and perhaps suffer despair because there seems to be no fidelity in friendship. In the psychic divorce, in which they have to become autonomous again, they are probably afraid and are certainly lonely. However, the resolution of any or all of these various six divorces may provide an elation of victory that comes from having accomplished something that had to be done and having done it well. There may be ultimate satisfactions in it.

The emotional divorce and the problem of grief

One of the reasons it feels so good to be engaged and newly married is the rewarding sensation that, out of the whole world, you have been selected. One of the reasons that divorce feels so awful is that you have been de-selected. It punishes almost as much as the engagement and the wedding are rewarding.

The chain of events and feelings that lead up to divorce are as long and as varied as the chain of events that lead up to being selected for marriage. The difference is that the feelings are concentrated in the area of the weak points in the personality rather than the growing points of the personality.

Almost no two people who have been married, even for a short time, can help knowing where to hit each other if they want to wound. On the other hand, any two people—

no matter who they are—who are locked together in conflict have to be very perceptive to figure out what the strain is really all about. Marital fights occur in every healthy marriage. The fact of health is indicated when marital disputes lead to a clarification of issues and to successful extension of the relationship into new areas. Difficulties arise only when marital conflict is sidetracked to false issues (and sometimes the discovery of just what issue is at stake may be, in itself, an adequate conclusion to the conflict), or when the emotional pressures are shunted to other areas. When a couple are afraid to fight over the real issue, they fight over something else—and perhaps never discover what the real issue was.

Two of the areas of life that are most ready to accept such displacement are the areas of sex and money. Both sex and money are considered worthwhile fighting over in American culture. If it is impossible to know or admit what a fight is all about, then the embattled couple may cast about for areas of displacement, and they come up with money and sex, because both can be used as weapons. Often these are not the basis of the difficulties, which lie in unconscious or inadmissible areas.

These facts lead a lot of people to think that emotional divorce occurs over money or over sexual incompatibility just because that is where the overt strife is allowed to come out. Often, however, these are only camouflage.

MONEY AND THE EMOTIONAL DIVORCE

One of the most tenacious ideas from our early training is "the value of a dollar." When in the larger society the self is reflected in possessions, and when money becomes one mode of enhancing the self—then we have difficulty with anybody who either spends it too lavishly or sits on it more tightly then we do.

Money is a subject about which talk is possible. Most middle-class couples do talk about money; most of them, in fact, make compromises more or less adequate to both. But in all cases, money management and budgeting are endlessly discussed in the American household. If communication becomes difficult, one of the first places that it shows up is in absence of knowledge about the other person's expenditures.

I interviewed one divorced woman who blamed her ex-husband's spending practices and attitude toward money as a major factor in their divorce. She said that he bought her an expensive car and asked her to leave it sitting outside the house when she was not driving it. *She* announced that *he* could not afford it. He asked her to join a golf club. She refused, although she was a good golfer and liked to play— because *she* told him *he* could not afford it. Whenever he wanted to use her considerable beauty and accomplishments to reflect a little credit on himself for being able to have captured and kept such a wife, she announced that he could not afford it. After the divorce, it continued. Then one day, in anger, she telephoned him to say that she was tired of making sacrifices—this year she was going to take the children on a transcontinental vacation and that he would simply have to pay for the trip. He did not explode; he only thought for a minute and said that he guessed that

would be all right, and that he would whittle down his plans for the children's vacation with him, so that it would come within the budget.

This woman told this story without realizing what she had revealed: that her husband was not going to push himself or them into bankruptcy; that he did indeed know how much things cost, and that he could either afford or otherwise manage what he wanted to give her. There was doubtless a difference of opinion about money—she, it appears, preferred to save and then spend; he preferred, perhaps, to spend and then pay. She, for reasons I cannot know from one extended interview, did not recognize his feelings. She *did* announce to him, every time that he wanted to spend money on her, that he was inadequate. I suspect it was her own fear that she would let him down. Without knowing it, she was attacking him where it hurt him and where her housewifely virtue could be kept intact, while she did not have to expose herself or take a chance.

I am not saying that there are not spendthrift husbands or wives. I am saying that if differences that lie beyond money cannot be discussed, then money is a likely battleground for the emotional divorce.

SEX AND THE EMOTIONAL DIVORCE

Among the hundreds of divorcees I have talked to, there is a wide range of sexual attitudes. There were marriages in which sexual symptoms were the first difficulties to be recognized by the couple. There were a few in which the sexual association seemed the only strong bond. I know of several instances in which the couple met for a ceremonial bout of sexual intercourse as the last legitimate act before their divorce. I have a newspaper clipping that tells of a man who, after such a "last legal assignation," murdered his wife before she became his ex-wife. And I know one divorce that was denied because, as the judge put it, he could not condone "litigation by day and copulation by night."

Usually, when communication between the spouses becomes strained, sexual rapport is the first thing to go. There are many aspects to this problem: sexual intercourse is the most intimate of social relationships, and reservations or ambivalences in the emotions are likely to show up there (with unconscious conflicts added to conscious ones). The conflicts may take the extreme form of frigidity in women, impotence in men. They may take the form of adultery, which may be an attempt to communicate something, an unconscious effort to improve the marriage itself. It may be an attempt to humiliate the spouse into leaving. Adultery cannot sensibly be judged without knowing what it means to a specific person and to his spouse in a specific situation. Adultery is a legal ground for divorce in every jurisdiction in the United States, and indeed in most of the record-keeping world.

Because sexuality is closely associated with integration of the personality, it is not surprising that disturbance in the relationship of the spouses may be exposed in sexual symptoms. Except in some cases in which the marriage breaks up within a few weeks or months, however, sexual difficulties are a mode of expression as often as they provide the basic difficulty.

GROWING APART

Married people, like any other people, must continue to grow as individuals if they are not to stagnate. Only by extending themselves to new experiences and overcoming new conflicts can they participate fully in new social relationships and learn new culture. That means that no one, at the time of marriage, can know what the spouse is going to become. Moreover, it means that he cannot know what he himself may become.

Some of this growth of individuals must necessarily take place outside of the marriage. If the two people are willing and able to perceive and tolerate the changes in one another, and overcome them by a growing relationship directly with the other person, then the mutual rewards are very great, and conflicts can be resolved.

Inability to tolerate change in the partner (or to see him as he is) always lies, I think, at the root of emotional divorce. All marriages become constantly more attenuated from the end of the honeymoon period probably until the retirement of the husband from the world of affairs. That is to say, the proportion of the total concern of one individual that can be given to the other individual in the marriage decreases, even though the precise quantity (supposing there were a way to measure it) might become greater. But the ties may become tougher, even as they become thinner.

When this growing apart and concomitant increase in the toughness of the bonds does *not* happen, then people feel the marriage bonds as fetters and become disappointed or angry with each other. They feel cramped by the marriage and cheated by their partner. A break may be the only salvation for some couples.

In America today, our emotional lives are made diffuse by the very nature of the culture with which we are surrounded. Family life, business or professional demands, community pressures—today all are in competition with one another for our time and energies. When that happens, the social stage is set for emotional divorce of individual couples, because the marriage relationship becomes just another competing institution. Sometimes emotional divorce seems scarcely more than another symptom of the diffuseness.

EMOTIONAL DIVORCE AND GRIEF

Emotional divorce results in the loss of a loved object just as fully—but by quite a different route of experience—as does the death of a spouse. Divorce is difficult because it involves a purposeful and active rejection by another person, who, merely by living, is a daily symbol of the rejection. It is also made difficult because the community helps even less in divorce than it does in bereavement.

The natural reaction to the loss of a loved object or person (and sometimes a hated one as well) is grief. The distribution of emotional energy is changed significantly; new frustration must be borne until new arrangements can be worked out. Human beings mourn every loss of meaningful relationship. The degree depends on the amount of emotional involvement. Mourning may be traumatic—and it may, like any other trauma, have to be blocked and only slowly allowed into awareness. Mourning may take several months or years.

Divorce is even more threatening than death to some people, because they have thought about it more, perhaps wished for it more consciously. But most importantly—there is no recognized way to mourn a divorce. The grief has to be worked out alone and without benefit of traditional rites, because few people recognize it for what it is.

When grief gets entangled with all the other emotions that are evoked in a divorce, the emotional working through becomes complicated—in a divorce one is very much on his own.

The legal divorce and the problem of grounds

Judicial divorce, as it is practiced in the United States today, is a legal post-mortem on the demise of an intimate relationship. It originated in Massachusetts in the early 1700s as a means for dealing with the problems that emotional divorce caused in families, at the same time that all going households could continue to be based on holy matrimony. Legal divorce has been discovered and used many times in the history of the world, but this particular institution has no precursors in European history. The historical period in which it developed is important. In those days it was considered necessary that the state could profess its interest in the marriage and the family only in the guise of punishing one of the spouses for misconduct. Thus, the divorce itself was proclaimed to be the punishment of the guilty party. Whether divorce as a punishment was ever a commonsensical idea is a moot point—certainly it is not so today. Yet, our law still reflects this idea.

Thus, if the state is to grant divorces to "innocent" spouses as punishment to offending spouses, it must legalize certain aspects of the family—must, in fact, establish minimal standards of performance in family roles. Marriages break down in all societies; we have come, by state intervention, to solve some of these breakdowns with the legal institution of divorce. Until very recently, no country granted its citizens the clear right to divorce, as they have the clear right to marry. The right is always conditional on acts of misbehavior of the spouse, as misbehavior has been legally defined and called "grounds." Whatever the spouse does must be thrust into the categories that the law recognizes before it can be grounds for divorce.

Divorce lawyers are forced, in the nature of the law, to put the "real situation," as they learn it from their clients, into language that the law will accept. If a divorce action is to go to court, it must first be couched in language that the courts are legally permitted to accept. Both marriage counselors and lawyers have assured me that reconciliation is always more difficult after grounds have been discussed and legal papers written than when it is still in the language of "reasons" and personal emotion. Legal language and choice of grounds are the first positive steps toward a new type of relationship with the person one of my informants called "my ex-to-be." Discussion of grounds often amounts, from the point of view of the divorcing person, to listing all the faults that the spouse ever committed, then picking one.

We all know that grounds and reasons may be quite different. The divorcing person usually feels that he should not "tattle" and selects the "mildest" ground. Yet, every person who institutes a suit for divorce must wonder whether to use "adultery" if in fact it occurred, or to settle for the more noncommittal "mental cruelty." Does one use drunkenness when divorcing an alcoholic? Or desertion? Or does one settle for "incompatibility"?

One of the reasons that the divorce institution is so hard on people is that the legal processes do not provide an orderly and socially approved discharge of emotions that are elicited during the emotional divorce and during the early parts of preparation for the legal processes. Divorces are "cranked out" but divorcees are not "cooled out."

The economic divorce and the problem of property

The family household is the unit of economic consumption in the United States. As such, middle-class households must have a certain amount of domestic-capital equipment besides personal property such as cars and television sets. In most households, these items "belong to the family," even though they may be legally owned in the name of one of the spouses.

Behind the idea of fair settlement of property at the time of divorce is the assumption that a man cannot earn money to support his family if he does not have the moral assistance and domestic services of his wife. The wife, if she works, does so in order to "enhance" the family income (no matter how much she makes or what the "psychic income" to her might be). Therefore, every salary dollar, every patent, every investment, is joint property.

In most states, the property settlement is not recorded in the public records of divorce, so precise information is lacking. However, in most settlements, the wife receives from one-third to one-half of the property.

Many wives voluntarily give up their rights to property at the time they become ex-wives. Some are quite irrational about it—"I won't take *anything* from *him*!" Sometimes they think (perhaps quite justly) that they have no moral right to it. Others, of course, attempt to use the property settlement as a means of retaliation. The comment from one of my informants was, "Boy, did I make that bastard pay." It seems to me that irrational motives such as revenge or self-abnegation are more often in evidence than the facts of relative need, in spite of all that judges and lawyers can do.

ALIMONY

The word "alimony" is derived from the Latin word for sustenance, and ultimately from the verb which means "to nourish" or "to give food to." The prevailing idea behind alimony in America is that the husband, as head of the family, has an obligation to support his wife and children, no matter how wealthy the wife and children may be independently.

At the time of divorce, the alimony rights of the wife are considered to be an extension of the husband's duty to support, undertaken at the time of marriage. Therefore, alimony means the money paid during and after the divorce by the ex-husband to the ex-wife (rarely the other way around).

There is, however, another basis on which some courts in some American jurisdictions have looked on alimony—it can be seen as punishment of the husband for his mistreatment of the wife. Where this idea is found, the wife cannot be entitled to alimony if she is the "guilty party" to the divorce. In most states, the amount of alimony is more or less directly dependent on whatever moral or immoral conduct of the wife may come to the attention of the court. A woman known to be guilty of anything the court considers to be moral misconduct is likely to be awarded less than an "innocent" wife. The law varies widely on these matters; practice varies even more.

The most important thing about the award and payment of alimony is that it is done on the basis of a court order. Therefore, if it is not paid, the offending husband is in contempt of court. The institution of divorce is provided, as we have seen before, with only one formal sanction to insure the compliance of its various parties. And that is the court.

CHILD SUPPORT

Courts and citizens are both much clearer about child support than they are about alimony. The principle is obvious to all; as long as he is able to do so, the responsibility for supporting children lies with their father. Whether a man is morally and legally obligated to support his children depends only on one factor: his ability to do so. In assessing child support payments, the court looks simply at his ability to pay, including his health, and to the needs of the child. The amount may be set by the court; it is always ratified by the court.

The coparental divorce and the problem of custody

The most enduring pain of divorce is likely to come from the coparental divorce. This odd word is useful because it indicates that the child's parents are divorced from each other—not from the child. Children do not always understand this: they may ask, "Can Father divorce *me*?" This is not a silly or naive question; from the standpoint of the child what was a failure in marriage to the parents is the shattering of his kinship circle.

The children have to go somewhere. And even when both parents share joint legal custody of the child, one parent or other gets "physical custody"—the right to have the child living with him.

The word "custody" is a double-edged sword. It means "responsibility for the care of" somebody. It also means "imprisonment." The child is in the custody of his parents—the criminal is in the custody of the law. When we deal with the custody of children in divorces, we must see to it that they are "in the care of" somebody, and that the care is adequate—we must also see that the custody is not punitive or restricting.

Legal custody of children entitles the custodial parent to make decisions about their life-styles and the things they can do which are developmentally important to them—educational and recreational and cultural choices. In the common law, the father had absolute property rights over the child—the mother had none, unless she inherited them at the death of the father. About the time judicial divorce was established in America, custody preferences shifted until the two parents were about equal. With the vast increase in the divorce rate in the early third of the twentieth century, the shift continued, giving the mother preference in both legal and physical custody. We rationalize this practices by such ideas as mother love, masculine nature, or the exigencies of making a living.

Custody of the children, once granted to the mother, will be taken away from her by the courts *only* if she can be shown to be seriously delinquent in her behavior *as a mother*. Her behavior *as a wife* may be at stake in granting the divorce or in fixing the amount of the alimony—but not in granting custody. A woman cannot be denied her rights as a mother on the basis of having performed badly as a wife, or even on the basis of her behavior as a divorcee if the children were not threatened physically or morally. Similarly, a man cannot be penalized as a father for his shortcomings as a husband.

The overriding consideration in all cases is that the court takes what action it considers to be "in the best interests of the child." The rights of children as human beings override, in our morality and hence in our law, all rights of the parents as parents, and certainly their rights as spouses. We have absolutely inverted the old common law.

A man is always, either by statute law or by common law, obliged to take financial responsibility for his minor children. If there are overriding circumstances that make it impossible for him to work, then that responsibility devolves on the mother. Sometimes a mother refuses her ex-husband the right to support his children as a means to deny him the right to see them—some men accept this, but few would be forced by a court to accept it if they chose to question its legality.

The rights of the parent who has neither legal nor physical custody of the child are generally limited to his right of visiting the child at reasonable times. This right stems from parenthood and is not dependent on decrees issued by a court. The court may, of course, condition the rights of visitation, again in the best interest of the child.

CHILDREN AND ONE-PARENT HOUSEHOLDS

Children grow up. The association between parent and child and the association between the parents change with each new attainment of the child. The child grows, parents respond—and their response has subtle overtones in their own relationship. In divorce, their responses must necessarily be of a different nature from what it is in marriage. In divorce, with communication reduced, the goals of the spouses are less likely to be congruent—the child is observed at different times and from different vantage points by the separated parents, each with his own set of concerns and worries.

Coparental divorce created lasting pain for many divorcees I interviewed—particularly if the ex-spouses differed greatly on what they wanted their children to become, morally, spiritually, professionally, even physically. This very difference of opinion about the goals of living may have lain behind the divorce. It continues through the children.

The good ex-husband/father feels, "My son is being brought up by his mother so that he is not my son." A divorced man almost always feels that his boy is being made into a different kind of man from what he himself is. Often, of course, he is right. The good ex-wife/mother may be tempted to refuse her ex-husband his visitation rights because, from her point of view, "He is bad for the children." This statement may mean no more than that the children are emotionally higher strung before and after a visit, and therefore upset her calm. But the mother may think the father wants something else for the children than she does, thus putting a strain on her own efforts to instill her own ideals and regulations.

It is difficult for a man to watch his children develop traits similar, if not identical, to those he found objectionable in their mother and which were among those qualities that led to the emotional divorce. The child becomes the living embodiment of the differences in basic values. A man may feel that "she" is bad for the children even when he has the objectivity to see also that the children will not necessarily develop unwholesome personalities, but only different personalities from those they might have developed through being with him.

The problem for the mother of the children is different—she has to deal with the single-parent household, making by herself decisions, which she almost surely feels should be shared. She does not want somebody to tell her what to do, as much as somebody to tell her she is right and make "sensible suggestions." Like most mothers, she wants support, not direction.

There is a traditional and popular belief that divorce is "bad for children." Actually, we do not know very much about it. Children in divorce must pick up by instruction what they would have learned by habituation or osmosis in an unbroken healthy home.

The children must learn how to deal with the "broken orbit" of models for the roles they will play in life. A boy cannot become fully a man—or a girl a woman—if they model themselves only on the cues they pick up from one sex alone. A woman cannot teach a boy to be a man, or a girl a woman, without the help of men. And a man cannot teach either a boy to be a man or a girl to be a woman without help of women.

All of us interact with members of both sexes. Our cues about the behavior of men come from the responses of women, as well as from the responses of men. Children—like the rest of us—must have significant members of both sexes around them.

Obviously, children of even the most successful homes do not model themselves solely on their parents, in spite of the importance parents have as models. There are television models (boys walk like athletes or crime busters); there are teachers, friends, storekeepers, bus drivers, and all the rest. But the child who lives in a one-parent home has to adjust to a different mixture of sex-role models. The big danger may be not so much that a boy has no father model in his home, but that his mother stops his walking like Willie

Mays or a television cowboy because she doesn't like it. And worst of all, she may, without knowing it, try to extinguish in him the very behavior patterns he has learned from his father: especially, if she does not want to be reminded of his father.

Children who live in one-parent homes must learn what a husband/father is and what he does in the home—and they have to learn it in a different context from children of replete homes. They must learn what a wife/mother is in such a home. Children are taught to be husbands and wives while they are still children. In the one-parent home the children have to be taught actively and realistically the companionship, sexual coparenting, and domestic aspects of marriage.

A noted psychoanalyst has told me that in her opinion there are only two things children learn in two-parent homes that cannot be taught in one-parent homes; one is the undertone of healthy sexuality that is present in a healthy home. Nothing appears on the surface save love—but the sexual tone of married love permeates everything. Even in the most loving one-parent home this is something that can, perhaps, be explained to children, but something that they will have trouble feeling unless they experience it elsewhere. The other thing that is difficult to teach, she says, is the ambivalence of the child toward both parents. When the relationship of father-child is none of the business of the child's mother, or the relationship of mother-child outside the ken and responsibility of the child's father, then the illusion can be maintained by the child that father is wholly right and mother wholly wrong, or father wholly unjustified and mother completely innocent. It is seldom true.

In short, the ex-family must do many of the things that the family ordinarily does, but it does them with even more difficulty than the family. It is in the coparental aspects of the divorce that the problems are so long-lasting—and so difficult. And the reason, as we have seen, is that a child's mother and father are, through the child, kinsmen to one another, but the scope of activities in their relationship has been vastly curtailed.

The community divorce and the problem of loneliness

Changes in civil status or "stages of life" almost invariably mark changes in friends and in significant communities. We go to school, and go away to college. We join special-interest groups. When we are married, we change communities—sometimes almost completely except for a few relatives and two or three faithful friends from childhood or from college.

When we divorce, we also change communities. Divorce means "forsaking all others" just as much as marriage does, and in about the same degree.

Many divorcees complain bitterly about their "ex-friends." "Friends?" one woman replied to my question during an interview, "They drop you like a hot potato. The exceptions are those real ones you made before marriage, those who are unmarried, and your husband's men friends who want to make a pass at you."

The biggest complaint is that divorcees are made to feel uncomfortable by their married friends.

Like newly marrieds, new divorcees have to find new communities. They tend to find them among the divorced. Morton Hunt's book, *The World of the Formerly Married*, provides a good concise report on these new communities. Divorcees find—if they will let themselves—that there is a group ready to welcome them as soon as they announce their separations. There are people to explain the lore that will help them in being a divorcee, people to support them emotionally, people to give them information, people to date and perhaps love as soon as they are able to love.

The community divorce is an almost universal experience of divorcees in America. And although there are many individuals who are puzzled and hurt until they find their way into it, it is probably the aspect of divorce that Americans handle best.

The psychic divorce and the problem of autonomy

Psychic divorce means the separation of self from the personality and the influence of the ex-spouse—to wash that man right out of your hair. To distance yourself from the loved portion that ultimately became disappointing, from the hated portion, from the baleful presence that led to depression and loss of self-esteem.

The most difficult of the six divorces is the psychic divorce, but it is also the one that can be personally most constructive. The psychic divorce involves becoming a whole, complete, and autonomous individual again—learning to live without somebody to lean on—but also without somebody to support. There is nobody on whom to blame one's difficulties (except oneself), nobody to shortstop one's growth, nobody to grow with.

Each must regain—if he ever had it—the dependence on self and faith in one's own capacity to cope with the environment, with people, with thoughts and emotions.

WHY DID I MARRY?

To learn anything from divorce, one must ask himself why he married. Marriage, it seems to me, should be an act of desperation—a last resort. It should not be used as a means of solving one's problems. Ultimately, of course, most people in our society can bring their lives to a high point of satisfaction and usefulness only through marriage. The more reason, indeed, we should not enter it unless it supplies the means for coping with our healthy needs and our desires to give and grow.

All too often, marriage is used as a shield against becoming whole or autonomous individuals. People too often marry to their weaknesses. We all carry the family of our youth within ourselves—our muscles, our emotions, our unconscious minds. And we all project it again into the families we form as adults. The path of every marriage is strewn with yesterday's unresolved conflicts, of both spouses. Every divorce is beset by yesterday's unresolved conflicts, compounded by today's.

So the question becomes: How do I resolve the conflicts that ruined my marriage? And what were the complementary conflicts in the spouse I married?

Probably all of us marry, at least in part, to defend old solutions to old conflicts. The difficulty comes when two people so interlock their old conflicts and solutions that they cannot become aware of them, and hence cannot solve them. Ironically, being a divorced person has built-in advantages in terms of working out these conflicts, making them conscious, and overcoming them.

WHY WAS I DIVORCED?

Presumably the fundamental cause of divorce is that people find themselves in situations in which they cannot become autonomous individuals and are unwilling to settle for a *folie à deux*. Divorcees are people who have not achieved a good marriage—they are also people who would not settle for a bad one.

A "successful" divorce begins with the realization by two people that they do not have any constructive future together. That decision itself is a recognition of the emotional divorce. It proceeds through the legal channels of undoing the wedding, through the economic division of property and arrangement for alimony and support. The successful divorce involves determining ways in which children can be informed, educated in their new roles, loved and provided for. It involves finding a new community. Finally, it involves finding your own autonomy as a person and as a personality.

AUTONOMY

The greatest difficulty comes from those people who cannot tell autonomy from independence. Nobody is independent in the sense that he does not depend on people. Life is with people. But if you wither and die without specific people doing specific things for you, then you have lost your autonomy. You enter into social relationships—and we are all more or less dependent in social relationships—in order to enhance your own freedom and growth, as well as to find somebody to provide for your needs and to provide good company in the process. Although, in a good marriage, you would never choose to do so, you *could* withdraw. You could grieve, and go on.

These are six of the stations of divorce. "The undivorced," as they are sometimes called in the circles of divorcees, almost never understand the great achievement that mastering them may represent.

NOTES

1. The parts of this book that were written by Paul Bohannan are based on research carried out between 1963 and 1966 under grants MH 06551-01A1 and MH 11544-01 of the National Institute of Mental Health, and grant No. GS-61 from the National Science Foundation.

Part IV

The women's liberation movement

Unlike other collections of papers about women that are currently in print, this was not intended as a book about Women's Lib. Several papers about the movement were selected for inclusion because they represent different perspectives or data. With the exception of the first paper these are characteristically more passionate—angry, critical, and sarcastic—than others in this collection. As I noted in the preface, in this politically sensitive and aware time, there are no papers about women, no matter how scientific, academic, or neutral, that are not related to the status of women and therefore to the movement.

The paper by Shomer and Centers is out of a classic social-psychological model: in this case, male chivalry and chauvinism received experimental treatment with some surprising results. The sex makeup of the group affected males but not females when they answered questions about women's rights, duties, and obligations. When the group was male and the experimenter was male, the mean score was 1.8. But when a single female was in the group, male chauvinism was crushed, chivalry reached its experimental peak, and the mean score was 32.1. Thus the highest pro-feminist score of any group, male or female, was obtained when there was a single girl surrounded by men! (Apparently two females do not arouse such solicitousness, especially if one is the experimenter.)

It is interesting to note that although scores on a measure of feminist attitudes divided, in the predictable direction, by sex, there were no significant sex differences on a scale of attitudes about child-rearing. Not only have women internalized the child-centered values, but the men with whom they are involved and upon whom they are dependent, have internalized them too. Apparently values about child-rearing are shared by all members of the culture with the probably result that it will be difficult to innovate and implement child-rearing techniques that are less individualistically child-centered.

One of the most interesting phenomena on the current Women's Lib scene is the use of a leaderless group technique in which participants exchange ideas, attitudes, interests, histories, hopes, fears, values, expectations, resentments, and insights. In Gornick's paper it is clear that this has become a way of sharing and raising awareness that the position of women is a function of the class values of society. Thus women's discord within the system is less attributable to individual pathology than to pathological values of an entire culture. Attribution of cause to societal structures can, of course, become exaggerated, enabling participants to avoid insight into their own, real psychopathology. But, overall, this group technique of consciousness-raising seems a markedly healthy development, especially when the dominant and classic theories of the psychology of women are increasingly regarded by women (and some men) as phallocentric, demeaning, and most basically, wrong.[1] In Gornick's paper we are struck by how self-awareness, the perception, the measure of oneself, is changed when consciousness is extended in an honest but supportive atmosphere.

Although they are at the very base of the economic pyramid and would seem a logical, enthusiastic participant in the Women's Lib movement, black women have generally not participated in what continues to be primarily a white, middle-class action. Black women do not participate in a movement that they experience as racist while the major alternatives in their lives contain intrinsically destructive aspects. This becomes clear in the Hares paper:

though the reality is that the grueling hard work of black women enabled families to survive, newly militant, self-conscious black men, supported by the insight of the social science Establishment, have found the goat for male failure in castrating, emasculating, matriarchal black women. To the extent that they accept the dominant norms of "masculinity" and "femininity," together with a piercing awareness of their responsibility to blacks, black women experience resentment, guilt, and an uncertainty of what is right. Are they not due praise for their accomplishments? And wouldn't it be nice to be bored at home waiting for the responsible father to come home with lots of money? To middle-class blacks enjoying new luxuries and to lower-class black women trying to make it through the week, sexism is much less important than class and racism, and the movement is somehow just not very relevant. (In the last paper in this section Dixon furiously castigates the movement for its middle-class racist character.)

Howe's critique of Millett's Sexual Politics highlights the egocentric tunnel-vision, the single-minded reductionism, of radical feminism. Are all social institutions the result of a masculine plot? Are all relations motivated by sexist power plays? Are men not "enslaved" by institutions, responsibilities, and by living itself? What complex of dynamics has allowed the patriarchal family to evolve as a basic form within almost all cultures? A plot throughout history? A simple political sexism resting upon a fundament of total environmental determinism seems unable to explain such extraordinary uniformity. Because acknowledgment of biological differences between the sexes has always resulted in a rationale that perpetuates traditional role divisions and thus female subordination, it is politically reasonable that the movement denies these differences. But the evidence of biology and the consistency of institutions combine to require a complex interactional model of sexual determinism and the origins of male dominance.

Pointedly, Howe asks what motivates the critic. What contempt for women underlies the assertion that that which is distinctly human is the work usually reserved for men? Insofar as women are arbitrarily and unjustly restricted within the world of competitive, "masculine," work, they are entitled to honest rage. Is that, though, the best, and only life style?

The intellectual simplification characteristic of much of the radical polemic distorts the complex truth. Though exhilarating to its adherents, false simplification provides no answers. Dixon's model combines sociology, psychology, and economics in an analysis and justification for political revolution. Dixon denounces not only female subordination but the presumptions of the movement itself.

Dixon's 1969 paper is a tightly reasoned argument for women's liberation and the end of male chauvinism; in 1971 the arguments have a familiarity about them because the movement came to dominate the media. Dixon's 1971 paper is very different. That paper puts the women's movement in a context less of male arrogance than of national imperialism, racism, and classism. That the movement deludes itself by not recognizing that it is characterized by its middle-class, white, liberal, American values and perpetuates the race and class destructiveness of the country, fills Dixon with contempt and fury. For Dixon, significant change in the position of women will require a supranational political revolution. It isn't, for Dixon, that women are not exploited—they are. But the enemy is less men than an imperialistic form of economic exploitation requiring subordination of races, women, and classes in order to prosper.

Dixon challenges what she sees as an existential insanity: the rejection and loathing of the privileged, white, educated, middle-class woman for her privileged life. It is a unique phenomenon, this vast unhappiness of those lucky enough not to confront a hollow-bellied, war-riven, poverty-dominated search for existence. Asking, "who am I?" or "what am I doing?" or "where is my identity?" is itself a symbol of the privileged. Those who struggle for survival do not ask these questions. Dixon's paper challenges not only familiar male chauvinistic ideas but hallowed litanies within the movement. Affluent, educated middle-class women have significant problems of their own. They do not need to justify them in terms of the problems of others.

In the next section we will examine the role and status of women in other cultures, some of which are revolutionary.

[1] See Judith M. Bardwick, Psychology of Women (Harper & Row, 1971), Chapter 1.

24 Differences in attitudinal responses under conditions of implicitly manipulated group salience

Robert W. Shomer
Richard Centers

Man as a social being is a member of many groups. In discussing the implications of this fact in relation to the psychological consequences of minority group membership, Kurt Lewin (1935) pointed out that the characteristics of a social situation might so enhance the feeling of membership in a given group that such a feeling would be dominant in the determination of responses in the situation.

Situations occur in everyday life in which information that could arouse the salience of group belongingness may be conveyed in an implicit manner. This may happen in a situation where sex, race, distinct dress, insignia, badges, or other such cues such as length of hair, hair style, presence of beard, and the style of beard may inform an individual of the composition of the aggregate of persons present. Casual observation leads us to the hypothesis that such cues can also arouse or make salient, consciously or unconsciously, group belongingness factors that may determine or mediate verbal and nonverbal responses. This would be most likely to the degree that stimuli were also present to point up or subtly remind the individual of defference, conflict, or controversy.

The present research sought to examine the implications of the foregoing thoughts and, simultaneously, by deliberate systematic variation of the composition of an aggregate of subjects, also to test a hypothesis of essentially methodological relevance; it was designed to take account of the possible effects of the characteristics of the experimenter as well as the effects of group composition.

The principal hypothesis of the present inquiry was that responses to a questionnaire involving issues relevant to the norms of the group members would be affected by the composition of the group in a direction conforming to, or congruent with, the norms of the group, whereas responses to a questionnaire lacking issues relevant to the norms of the group would not be so affected. More concretely, for example, in a situation in which males and females are represented in varying numbers and where two types of questionnaire items are used, some relevant to being either male or female and others unrelated to sex group, we would expect cues provided by the aggregate composition to make sex-group membership salient. This, in turn, would evoke and make salient the attitudinal norms of the respective sexes toward the sex-related issues and elicit motivation to

conform to the norms in the respective cases. On the basis of previous research (Centers, 1961), it was assumed that an attitudinal norm of male chauvinism repressive toward females would mediate the responses of male subjects, whereas females' responses would be activated (or mediated) by chauvinistic attitudes assertive and supportive for their sex group. On the other hand, although they may exist, no specific norms were known which might mediate differential responses by the two sexes to the questions on child rearing. A second hypothesis was that questionnaire responses of group members would be affected by the sex of the experimenter (or administrator), such that the bias in the direction of the group norm would be reinforced for males with a male experimenter and for females with a female experimenter.

Results

The predictions relative to the particular groups and attitude instruments employed were that first, subjects' responses to the Feminist scale would show a large sex difference (with females more pro-feminist than males), but responses to the Child-Rearing scale would not. Second, responses to the Feminist scale would vary over the three conditions of group composition, but responses to the Child-Rearing scale would not. More specifically, for reasons explained above, males' attitudes in groups composed of half of each sex should display the least antifeminism. Females' attitudes should show corresponding degrees of profeminism in analogous conditions. Third, subjects' responses to the Feminist scale would vary under all conditions of group composition in accordance with the sex of the experimenter, but responses to the Child-Rearing scale would not.

Group averages for both the Feminist and the Child-Rearing scales over the three conditions of group composition appear in Table 1. The means for the Feminist scale for both sexes for the three conditions of group composition obtained under experimenters of different sex are shown in Table 2.

In order to obtain proportional numbers of subjects for analysis, following the method of Lindquist (1953), additional scores based on the cell means were added to certain

TABLE 1   *Mean Profeminist and Child-Rearing Scores for Three Conditions of Group Composition*

Sex of S	Profeminist scores			M	Child-rearing scores			M
	LMOS[a]	Equal	All		LMOS[a]	Equal	All	
Male	23.0	18.0	5.5	15.1	4.3	5.7	2.1	3.7
n	38	21	38	97	38	21	38	97
Female	27.4	27.3	29.8	28.3	3.6	5.6	3.9	4.1
n	47	21	45	113	47	21	45	113

[a]Lone member of the opposite sex.

TABLE 2   *Mean Profeminist Scores for Three Conditions of Group Composition and Male and Female Experimenter*

Sex of S	Male E			M	Female E			M
	LMOS[a]	Equal	All		LMOS[a]	Equal	All	
Male	32.1	16.0	1.8	15.8	14.8	20.2	10.1	14.3
n	18	11	21	50	20	10	17	47
Female	23.9	30.4	28.5	26.9	30.8	24.9	31.4	29.8
n	23	9	24	56	24	12	21	57

[a]Lone member of the opposite sex.

TABLE 3   *Analysis of Variance of Profeminist Scores*

Source	SS	df	MS	F
Sex of S (A)	8,911.1	1	8,911.1	13.43**
Group com-position (B)	2,768.6	2	1,384.3	2.09
Sex of E (C)	13.0	1	13.0	<1
A × B	4,503.6	2	2,251.8	3.39*
A × C	602.0	1	602.0	<1
B × C	2,583.4	2	1,291.7	1.95
A × B × C	1,763.5	2	881.8	1.33
Error variance	124,774.0	188	663.7	

* $p < .05$.
** $p < .001$.

TABLE 4   *Analysis of Variance on Child-Rearing Scores*

Source	SS	df	MS	F
Sex of S (A)	8.8	1	8.8	<1
Group com-position (B)	203.8	2	101.9	1.46
Sex of E (C)	15.7	1	15.7	<1
A × B	69.6	2	34.8	<1
A × C	33.3	1	33.3	<1
B × C	130.0	2	65.0	<1
A × B × C	214.3	2	107.1	1.53
Error variance	13,134.1	188	70.0	

TABLE 5   *Analysis of Variance for Simple Effect of Group Composition*

Source	SS	df	MS	F
B (males)	7,135.6	2	3,567.8	5.58*
B (females)	108.5	2	54.3	<1
Error variance	124,744.0	195	639.9	

* $p < .01$.

cells and scores were randomly eliminated from other cells. Two hundred of the original 210 scores remained after this procedure. Separate three-way analyses of variance were carried out on the Feminist scores and on the Child-Rearing scores. The results in Table 3 indicate that for the feminist items there was a large sex difference ($F = 13.43$, $df = 1/188$, $p < .001$). Not suprisingly, females' average profeminist scores were higher than those for males. For the Child-Rearing scores (Table 4), on the other hand, as expected, the effect of sex of subject was nonsignificant ($F < 1$). Thus, in support of the first prediction, responses to the feminist items were systematically related to the sex of the subject but responses to the Child-Rearing scale were not.

With respect to the second prediction, the effect of group composition, the results indicate that as expected, for the Child-Rearing scale, the effect of group composition was not significant ($F < 1$) nor were any of the interactions. Also, contrary to the prediciton, for feminist items the group composition effect failed to reach an acceptable level of significance ($F = 2.09$, $df = 2/188$, $p < .10$). However, a significant Sex of Subject × Group Composition interaction was obtained ($F = 3.39$, $df = 2/188$, $p < .05$). Therefore, an analysis of the simple effect of group composition was carried out. The results of this analysis, shown in Table 5, indicate that the effect of group composition was significant for males ($F = 5.58$, $df = 2/195$, $p < .01$), but not for females ($F < 1$). Evidently, when responding to a questionnaire involving women's rights, duties, and responsibilities, males are influenced by the number of each sex present, but females are not.

As indicated in Tables 3 and 4, the third prediction was only partially confirmed. As expected, the sex of the experimenter had no effect on responses to the Child-Rearing scale. However, contrary to expectation, the influence of sex of experimenter on feminist attitudes also failed to reach significance. Although it has no significant overall effect (see Table 2), the sex of the experimenter does seem

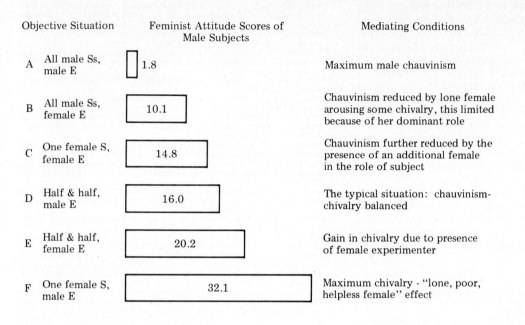

Objective Situation	Feminist Attitude Scores of Male Subjects	Mediating Conditions
A All male Ss, male E	1.8	Maximum male chauvinism
B All male Ss, female E	10.1	Chauvinism reduced by lone female arousing some chivalry, this limited because of her dominant role
C One female S, female E	14.8	Chauvinism further reduced by the presence of an additional female in the role of subject
D Half & half, male E	16.0	The typical situation: chauvinism-chivalry balanced
E Half & half, female E	20.2	Gain in chivalry due to presence of female experimenter
F One female S, male E	32.1	Maximum chivalry - "lone, poor, helpless female" effect

Figure 1. Chauvinism versus chivalry.

to relate in a complex way to specific conditions of group composition. The nature of this relationship will be discussed in the section to follow.

Discussion

As was indicated earlier, it was assumed that attitudes of sex group chauvinism were the mediating determinants of the differing responses of the respective sex groups. Although the data for females fail to show such an effect, those for males appear to bear out the assumption quite well. Yet there remain some quite puzzling questions when one examines Table 2, in which the mean scores for males are seen to vary quite markedly over the conditions of group composition as well as sex of experimenter. Attention is called especially to the mean scores obtained when there is a lone member of the female sex present in an otherwise all male group with a male experimenter. This score of 32.1 represents the highest mean profeminist score of any group, *male or female*, and contrasts sharply with the mean score of 1.8 obtained when the group is composed of males only with a male experimenter. The presence of a lone female in an otherwise all male group produces an almost astounding effect. It was initially supposed that the presence of a lone female would possibly make membership salience in the males of such a group even stronger than it would have been had no female been present. Obviously, the supposition was wrong, for the results do not sustain the assumption, at least not in terms of arousal of male chauvinistic norms.

But the hypothesis that the presence of a lone female would produce high group-membership salience in an otherwise all male aggregate is plausible if we suppose that the presence of the lone female arouses a conflicting male norm, that of *chivalry toward females*. This may appear lacking in credibility, however, when we look for a corresponding effect in the other condition where a lone female subject was present, for there, with a female experimenter, the profeminist score drops to only 14.8. It would be hasty to be thus convinced, however, for this drop becomes quite sensible if we assume conflicting male norms to be operating in this whole array of conditions, and that the interaction of cues arousing the conflicting norms accounts for the drop. The picture is a confusing one, but can be clarified by the aid of Figure 1, where the results for the several conditions are arrayed in a way ordered by the assumed arousal of conflicting norms of chauvinism versus chivalry.

Under the condition where maximum male sex-group chauvinism was believed to be aroused, in an all male group with a male experimenter (A), we find the lowest profeminist score of all. In the condition of a lone female subject in an otherwise male group with a male experimenter (F), where the greatest arousal of the male chivalry norm was believed to have occurred, we find the highest profeminist score of all. The conditions between these polar ones presumably reflect resolution of the conflicting norms aroused by the cues manipulated. In Condition B, where the group is all male but the experimenter is female, some chivalry is aroused, but so is some male chauvinism, for the female is now not a lone subject, but a lone female in a dominant, and characteristically male role. In Condition C, where there is also a female experimenter as well as a lone female subject, chivalry is augmented by the subject, increasing the effect as compared to Condition B, but probably dampened somewhat, because there are now two females, rather than one lone helpless one. In Condition D, there is the normal and usual situation of a male in a dominant role presiding over a group of mixed sex composition. Perhaps both male norms are aroused in such a situation, but if any condition could be said to consitute a base-line one, this is it. In Condition E, again with an equal sex mix, but with a female experimenter, chivalry arousal is present and produces a higher profeminist score for the group. In the case of females' attitudes toward feminist propositions, different group compositions had little if any effect. This result can be accounted for if we assume that due to their greater personal relevance, females' attitudes toward their own rights, duties, and obligations are held more strongly and are anchored more deeply than those of males toward these issues.

History itself attests to the emotionality and intensity of women in fighting for their rights, their militancy and determination in the face of the uncomprehending and often amused males, secure in their strength and established dominance (who gave in, incidentally, mostly out of feelings of chivalry).

REFERENCES

Bittner, A. C., & Shinedling, M. M. A Methodological investigation of Piaget's concept of conservation of substance. *Genetic Psychology Monographs*, 1968, 77, 135-165.
Blankenship, A. The effect of interviewer bias upon the response in a public opinion poll, *Journal of Consulting Psychology*, 1940, 4, 134-136.
Centers, R. Authoritarianism and misogymy. *Journal of Social Psychology*, 1961, 61, 81-85.
Charters. W. W., Jr., & Newcomb, T. M. Some attitudinal effects of experimentally increased salience of a membership group. In G. E. Swanson, T. M. Newcomb, & E. L. Hartley (Eds.), *Readings in social psychology*. (Rev. ed.) New York: Holt, 1952.
Festinger, L. The role of group belongingness in a voting situation. *Human Relations*, 1947, 1, 154-180.
Festinger, L. Laboratory experiments: The role of group belongingness. In J. G. Miller (Ed.), *Experiments in social process*. New York: McGraw-Hill, 1950.
Katz, D. Do interviewers bias poll results? *Public Opinion Quarterly*, 1942, 6, 248-268.
Kelley, H. H. Salience of membership and resistance to change of group-anchored attitudes. *Human Relations*, 1955, 8, 275-289.
Kirkpatrick, C. The construction of a belief-pattern scale for measuring attitudes toward feminism. *Journal of Social Psychology*, 1936, 7, 421-437. (a)
Kirkpatrick, C. An experimental study of the modification of social attitudes. *American Journal of Sociology*, 1936, 41, 649-656. (b)
Kirkpatrick, C. A comparison of generations in regard to attitudes toward feminism. *Journal of Genetic Psychology*, 1936, 49, 343-359. (c)
Lambert, W. E., Libman, E., & Poser, E. G. The effect of increased salience of a membership group on pain tolerance. *Journal of Personality*, 1960, 28, 350-357.
Lewin, K. Psycho-sociological problems of a minority group. *Character and Personality*, 1935, 3, 175-187.
Linquist, F. F. *Design and analysis of experiments in psychology and education*. Boston: Houghton-Mifflin, 1953.
Pedersen, D. M., Shinedling, M. M., & Johnson. D. L. Effects of sex of examiner and subject on children's quantitative test performance. *Journal of Personality and Social Psychology*, 1968, 10. 251-254.
Rosenthal, R. On the social psychology of the psychological experiment: The experimenter's hypothesis as unintended determinant of the experimental results. *American Scientist*, 1963, 51, 268-283.
Rosenthal, R. *Experimenter effects in behavioral research*. New York: Appleton-Century-Crofts, 1966.
Schaffer, E. S., & Bell, R. Q. Parental Attitude Research Instrument (PARI): Normative data. Unpublished manuscript. Library, National Institute of Mental Health, Bethesda, Maryland, 1955.

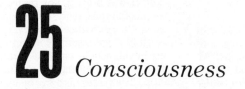

25 *Consciousness*

Vivian Gornick

In a lower Manhattan office a legal secretary returns from her lunch hour, sinks into her seat and says miserably to a secretary at the next desk: "I don't know what's happening to me. A perfectly nice construction worker whistled and said, 'My, isn't *that* nice,' as I passed him and suddenly I felt this terrific anger pushing up in me . . . I swear I wanted to *hit* him!"

At the same time, a thoughtful 40-year-old mother in a Maryland suburb is saying to a visiting relative over early afternoon coffee: "You know, I've been thinking lately, I'm every bit as smart as Harry, and yet he got the Ph.D. and I raised the girls. Mind you, I *wanted* to stay home. And yet, the thought of my two girls growing up and doing the same thing doesn't sit well with me at all. Not at all."

And in Toledo, Ohio, a factory worker turns to the next woman on the inspection belt and confides: "Last night I told Jim: 'I been working in the same factory as you 10 years now. We go in at the same time, come out the same time. But I do all the shopping, get the dinner, wash the dishes and on Sunday break my back down on the kitchen floor. I'm real tired of doin' all that. I want some help from you.' Well, he just laughed at me, see? Like he done every time I mentioned this before. But last night I wouldn't let up. I mean, I really *meant* it this time. And you know? I thought he was gonna let me have it. Looked mighty like he was gettin' ready to belt me one. But you know? I just didn't care! I wasn't gonna back down, come hell or high water. You'll just never believe it, he'd kill me if he knew I was tellin' you, he washed the dishes. First time in his entire life."

Reprinted from Vivian Gornick, "Consciousness and Raising," The New York Times Magazine, Jan. 10, 1971, pp. 22-23, 77-84. © 1971 by The New York Times Company. Reprinted by permission.

None of these women are feminists. None of them are members of the Women's Liberation Movement. None of them ever heard of consciousness-raising. And yet, each of them exhibits the symptomatic influence of this, the movement's most esoteric practice. Each of them, without specific awareness, is beginning to feel the effects of the consideration of woman's personal experience in a new light—a political light. Each of them is undergoing the mysterious behavioral twitches that indicate psychological alteration. Each of them is drawing on a linking network of feminist analysis and emotional upchucking that is beginning to suffuse the political-social air of American life today. Each of them, without ever having attended a consciousness-raising session, has had her consciousness raised.

Consciousness-raising is the name given to the feminist practice of examining one's personal experience in the light of sexism; i.e., that theory which explains woman's subordinate position in society as a result of a cultural decision to confer direct power on men and only indirect power on women. The term of description and the practice to which it alludes are derived from a number of sources—psychoanalysis, Marxist theory and American revivalism, mainly—and was born out of the earliest stages of feminist formulation begun about three years ago in such predictable liberationist nesting places as Cambridge, New York, Chicago and Berkeley. (The organization most prominently associated with the growth of consciousness-raising is the New York Redstockings.)

Perceiving that woman's position in our society does indeed constitute that of a political class, and, secondly, that woman's "natural" domain is her feelings, and, thirdly, that testifying in a friendly and supportive atmosphere enables people to see that their experiences are often duplicated (thereby reducing their sense of isolation and increasing the desire to theorize as well as to confess), the radical feminists sensed quickly that a group of women sitting in a circle discussing their emotional experiences as though they were material for cultural analysis was political dynamite. Hence, through personal testimony and emotional analysis could the class consciousness of *women* be raised. And thus the idea of the small "women's group"—or consciousness-raising group—was delivered into a cruel but exciting world.

Consciousness-raising is, at one and the same time, both the most celebrated and accessible introduction to the woman's movement as well as the most powerful technique for feminist conversion known to the liberationists. Women are *drawn*, out of a variety of discontents, by the idea of talking about themselves, but under the spell of a wholly new interpretation of their experience, they *remain*.

Coming together, as they do, week after week for many months, the women who are "in a group" begin to exchange an extraordinary sense of multiple identification that is encouraged by the technique's instruction to look for explanations for each part of one's history in terms of the social or cultural dynamic created by sexism—rather than in terms of the personal dynamic, as one would do in a psychotherapist's group session. (Although there are many differences between consciousness-raising and group therapy—e.g., the former involves no professional leader, no exchange of money—the fundamental difference lies in this fact: in consciousness-raising one looks not to one's personal emotional history for an explanation of behavioral problems but rather to the cultural fact of the patriarchy.)

Thus looking at one's history and experience in consciousness-raising sessions is rather like shaking a kaleidoscope and watching all the same pieces rearrange themselves into an altogether *other* picture, one that suddenly makes the color and shape of each piece appear startlingly new and alive, and full of unexpected meaning. (This is mainly why feminists often say that women are the most interesting people around these days, because they are experiencing a psychic invigoration of rediscovery.)

What *does* take place in a consciousness-raising group? How *do* the women see themselves? What *is* the thrust of the conversation at a typical session? Is it simply the man-hating, spleen-venting that is caricatured by the unsympathetic press? Or the unfocused and wrong-headed abstracting insisted upon by the insulated intellectuals? Or yet again, the self-indulgent contemplation of the navel that many tight-lipped radical activists see it as?

"In this room," says Roberta H., a Long Island housewife speaking euphemistically of her group's meetings, "we do not generalize. We do not speak of any experience except that of the women here. We follow the rules for consciousness-raising as set out by the New York Radical Feminists and we do not apply them to 'woman's experience'—whatever on earth that is—we apply them to ourselves. But, oh God! The samenesses we have found, and the way in which these meetings have changed our lives!"

The rules that Roberta H. is referring to are to be found in a mimeographed pamphlet, an introduction to the New York Radical Feminists organization, which explains the purpose and procedures of consciousness-raising. The sessions consist mainly of women gathering once a week, sitting in a circle and speaking in turn, addressing themselves—almost entirely out of personal experience—to a topic that has been preselected. The pamphlet sets forth the natural limitations of a group (10 to 15 women), advises women to start a group from among their friends and on a word-of-mouth basis, and suggests a list of useful topics for discussion. These topics include Love, Marriage, Sex, Work, Femininity, How I Came to Women's Liberation, Motherhood, Aging and Competition with Other Women. Additional subjects are developed as a particular group's specific interests and circumstances begin to surface.

When a group's discussions start to revolve more and more about apparently very individual circumstances, they often lead to startling similarities. For instance, a Westchester County group composed solely of housewives, who felt that each marriage represented a unique meaning in each of their lives, used the question, "Why did you marry the man you married?" as the subject for discussion one night. "We went around the room," says Joan S., one of the women present, "and while some of us seemed unable to answer that question without going back practically to the cradle, do you know?, the word love was never mentioned *once*."

On the Upper West Side of Manhattan, in the vicinity of

Columbia University, a group of women between the ages of 35 and 45 have been meeting regularly for six months. Emily R., an attractive 40-year-old divorcée in this group, says: "When I walked into the first meeting, and saw the *types* there, I said to myself: 'None of these broads have been through what I've been through. They couldn't possibly feel the way I feel.' Well, I'll tell you. None of them *have* been through what I've been through if you look at our experience superficially. But when you look a little *deeper*—the way we've been doing at these meetings—you see they've *all* been through what I've been through, and they all feel pretty much the way I feel. God, when I saw *that!* When I saw that what I always felt was my own personal hangup was as true for every other woman in that room as it was for me! Well, that's when *my* consciousness was raised."

What Emily R. speaks of is the phenomenon most often referred to in the movement, the flash of insight most directly responsible for the feminist leap in faith being made by hundreds of women everywhere—i.e., the intensely felt realization that what had always been taken for symptoms of personal unhappiness or dissatisfaction or frustration was so powerfully and so consistently duplicated among women that perhaps these symptoms could just as well be ascribed to *cultural* causes as to psychological ones.

In the feminist movement this kind of "breakthrough" can occur no place else than in a consciousness-raising group. It is only here, during many months of meetings, that a woman is able finally—if ever—to bring to the surface those tangled feelings of anger, bafflement and frustrated justice that have drawn her to the movement in the first place. It is only here that the dynamic of sexism will finally strike home, finally make itself felt in the living detail of her own life.

Claire K., a feminist activist in Cambridge, says of women's groups: "I've been working with women's groups for over two years now. The average life of a group is a year to 18 months, and believe me, I've watched a lot of them fold before they ever got off the ground. But, when they *work!* There is a rhythm to some of them that's like life itself. You watch a group expand and contract, and each time it does one or the other it never comes back together quite the same as when the action started. Something happens to each woman, and to the group itself. . . . But each time, if they survive, they have *grown*. You can see it, almost smell it and taste it."

I am one of those feminists who are always mourning after the coherent and high-minded leadership of the 19th century. Often, when I observe the fragmented, intellectually uneven, politically separated components of the woman's movement I experience dismay, and I find myself enviously imagining Elizabeth Cady Stanton and Lucretia Mott and Susan B. Anthony sitting and holding hands for 40 years, sustaining and offering succor to one another in religious and literary accents that make of their feminism a heroic act, an act that gave interwoven shape to their lives and their cause. And I think in a panic: "Where would we all be without them? Where would we be? They thought it

all out for us, and we've got not one inch beyond them." Lately, however, I have changed my mind about all that. . . .

I was on my way to a meeting one night not too long ago, a meeting meant to fashion a coalition group out of the movement's many organizations. I knew exactly what was ahead of me. I knew that a woman from NOW would rise and speak about our "image;" that a Third Worlder would announce loudly that she didn't give a good goddamn about anybody's orgasms, her women were starving, for chrissake; that a Radicalesbian would insist that the woman's movement must face the problem of sexism from within *right now;* and 10 women from the Socialist party would walk out in protest against middle-class "élitist" control in the movement. I knew there would be a great deal of emotional opinion delivered, a comparatively small amount of valuable observation made, and some action taken. Suddenly, as the bus I was on swung westward through Central Park, I realized that it didn't matter, that none of it mattered. I realized it was stupid and self-pitying to be wishing that the meeting was going to be chaired by Elizabeth Cady Stanton; what she had done and said had been profoundly in the idiom of her time, and in the idiom of *my* time no woman in the movement was her equal, but something else was: the consciousness-raising group.

I saw then that the small, anonymous consciousness-raising group was the heart and soul of the woman's movement, that it is not what happens at movement meetings in New York or Boston or Berkeley that counts, but the fact that hundreds of these groups are springing up daily—at universities in Kansas, in small towns in Oregon, in the suburbs of Detroit—out of a responsive need that has indeed been urged to the surface by modern radical feminism. It was here that the soul of a woman is genuinely searched and a new psychology of the self is forged. I saw then that the consciousness-raising group of today is the true Second Front of feminism; and as I thought all this I felt the ghost of Susan B. Anthony hovering over me, nodding vigorously, patting me on the shoulder and saying, "Well done, my dear, well done."

That ghost has accompanied me to every movement meeting I have attended since that night, but when I am at a consciousness-raising session that ghost disappears and I am on my own. Then, for better or worse, I am the full occupant of my feminist skin, engaged in the true business of modern feminism, reaching hard for self-possession.

And now let's go to a consciousness-raising session.

Early in the evening, on a crisp autumn night, a young woman in an apartment in the Gramercy Park section of Manhattan signed a letter, put it in an envelope, turned out the light over her desk, got her coat out of the hall closet, ran down two flights of stairs, hailed a taxi and headed west directly across the city. At the same time, on the Upper West Side, another woman, slightly older than the first, bent over a sleeping child, kissed his forehead, said goodnight to the babysitter, rode down 12 flights in an elevator, walked up to Broadway and disappeared into the downtown subway. Across town, on the Upper East Side, another woman tossed back a head of stylishly fixed hair, pulled on a beautiful pair of suede boots and left her tiny apartment, also heading down and across town. On the Lower East Side, in a fourth-floor tenement apartment, a woman five or six years younger than all the others combed out a tangled mop of black hair, clomped down the stairs in her Swedish clogs and started trudging west on St. Marks Place. In a number of other places all over Manhattan other women were also leaving their houses. When the last one finally walked into the Greenwich Village living room they were all headed for, there were 10 women in the room.

These women ranged in age from the late 20's to the middle 30's; in appearance, from attractive to very beautiful; in education, from bachelor's degrees to master's degrees; in marital status, from single to married to divorced to imminently separated; two were mothers. Their names were Veronica, Lucie, Diana, Marie, Laura, Jen, Sheila, Dolores, Marilyn and Claire. Their occupations, respectively, were assistant television producer, graduate student, housewife, copywriter, journalist, unemployed actress, legal secretary, unemployed college dropout, schoolteacher and computer programmer.

They were not movement women; neither were they committed feminists; nor were they marked by an especial sense of social development or by personal neurosis. They were simply a rather ordinary group of women who were drawn out of some unresolved, barely articulated need to form a "woman's group." They were in their third month of meetings; they were now at Marie's house (next week they would meet at Laura's, and after that at Jen's, and so on down the line); the subject for discussion tonight was "Work."

The room was large, softly lit, comfortably furnished. After 10 or 15 minutes of laughing, chatting, note and book exchanging, the women arranged themselves in a circle, some on chairs, some on the couch, others on the floor. In the center of the circle was a low coffee table covered with a coffeepot, cups, sugar, milk, plates of cheese and bread, cookies and fruit. Marie suggested they begin, and turning to the woman on her right, who happened to be Dolores, asked if she would be the first.

Dolores (the unemployed college dropout): *I guess that's okay . . . I'd just as soon be the first . . . mainly because I hate to be the last. When I'm last, all I think about is, soon it will be* my *turn.* (She looked up nervously.) *You've no idea how I* hate *talking in public.* (There was a long pause; silence in the circle.) *. . . Work! God, what can I say? The whole question has always been absolute hell for me. . . . A lot of you have said your fathers ignored you when you were growing up and paid attention only to your brothers. Well, in my house it was just the opposite. I have two sisters, and my father always told me I was the smartest of all, that I was smarter than he was, and that I could do anything I wanted to do . . . but somehow, I don't really know why, everything I turned to came to nothing. After six years of analysis I still don't know why.* (She looked off into space for a moment and her eyes seemed to lose the train of her thought. Then she shook herself and went on.) *I've always drifted . . . just drifted. My parents never forced me to work. I needn't work even now. I had every opportunity to find out what I really wanted to do. But . . . nothing I did satisfied me, and I would just stop. . . . Or turn*

away. . . . Or go on a trip. I worked for a big company for a while . . . Then my parents went to Paris and I just went with them. . . . I came back . . . went to school . . . was a researcher at Time-Life . . . drifted . . . got married . . . divorced . . . drifted. (Her voice grew more halting.) *I feel my life is such* waste. *I'd like to write, I really would; but I don't know. I just can't get going. . . . My father is so disappointed in me. He keeps hoping I'll really do something. Soon.* (She shrugged her shoulders but her face was very quiet and pale, and her pain expressive. She happened to be one of the most beautiful women in the room.)

Diana (the housewife): *What do you think you* will *do?*

Dolores (in a defiant burst): *Try to get married!*

Jen (the unemployed actress) and Marie (the copywriter): *Oh, no!*

Claire (the computer programer): *After all that! Haven't you learned yet? What on earth is marriage going to do for you? Who on earth could you marry? Feeling* about your-*self as you do? Who could save you from yourself? Because that's what you* want.

Marilyn (the school teacher): *That's right. It sounds like "It's just all too much to think out so I might as well get married."*

Lucie (the graduate student): *Getting married like that is* bound *to be a disaster.*

Jen: *And when you get married like that it's always to some creep you've convinced yourself is wonderful. So un-·derstanding.* (Dolores grew very red and very quiet through all this.)

Sheila (the legal secretary): *Stop jumping on her like that! I know* just *how she feels. . . . I was* really *raised to be a wife and a mother, and yet my father wanted me to do something with my education after he sent me to one of the best girls' schools in the East. Well, I didn't get married when I got out of school like half the girls I graduated with, and now seven years later I'm still* not married. (She stopped talking abruptly and looked off into the space in the center of the circle, her attention wandering as though she'd suddenly lost her way.) *I don't know how to describe it exactly, but I know just how Dolores feels about drifting. I've always worked, and yet something was always sort of confused inside me. I never really knew which way I wanted to go on a job: up, down, sideways. . . . I always thought it would be the most marvelous thing in the world to work for a really brilliant and important man. I never have. But I've worked for some good men and I've learned a lot from them. But* (her dark head came up two or three inches and she looked hesitantly around) *I don't know about the rest of you, but I've always wound up being propositioned by my bosses. It's a funny thing. As soon as I'd begin doing really well, learning fast and taking on some genuine responsibility, like it would begin to excite them, and they'd make their move. When I refused, almost invariably they'd begin to* browbeat *me. I mean, they'd make my life miserable! And, of course, I'd retreat. . . . I'd get small and scared and take everything they were dishing out . . . and then I'd move on. I don't know, maybe something in my behavior was really asking for it, I honestly don't know anymore. . . .*

Marie: *There's a good chance you* were *asking for it.*

I work with a lot of men and I don't get propositioned every other day. I am so absolutely straight no one dares. . . . They all think I am a dike.

Sheila (plaintively): *Why is it like that, though? Why are men like that? Is it someting they have more of, this sexual need for ego gratification? Are they made differently from us?*

Jen (placing her coffee cup on the floor beside her): *No! You've just never learned to stand up for yourself! And goddammit, they* know *it, and they play on it. Look, you all know I've been an actress for years. Well, once, when I was pretty new in the business, I was playing opposite this guy. He used to feel me up on the stage. All the time. I was scared. I didn't know what to do. I'd say to the stage manager: That guy is feeling me up. The stage manager would look at me like I was crazy, and shrug his shoulders. Like: What can I do? Well, once I finally thought: I can't stand this. And I bit him. Yes, I bit the bastard, I bit his tongue while he was kissing me.*

A Chorus of Voices: *You* bit *him????*

Jen (with great dignity): *Yes, dammit, I bit him. And afterward he said to me, "Why the hell did you do that?" And do you know? He respected me after that.* (She laughed.) *Didn't* like *me very much. But he respected me.* (She looked distracted for a moment.) *. . . I guess that* is *pretty funny, I mean, biting someone's tongue during a love scene.*

Veronica (the assistant TV producer): *Yeah. Very funny.*

Laura (the journalist): *Listen, I've been thinking about something Sheila said. That as soon as she began to get really good at her job her boss would make a pass—and that would pretty much signal the end, right? She'd refuse, he'd become an S.O.B., and she'd eventually leave. It's almost as if sex were being used to cut her down, or back, or in some way stop her from rising. An instinct he, the boss, has—to sleep with her when he feels her becoming really independent.*

Lucie (excitedly): *I'll buy that! Look, it's like Samson and Delilah in reverse. She* knew *that sex would give her the opportunity to destroy his strength. Women are famous for wanting to sleep with men in order to enslave them, right? That's the great myth, right? He's all spirit and mind, she's all emotion and biological instinct. She uses this instinct with cunning to even out the score, to get some power, to bring him down—through sex. But, look at it another way. What are these guys always saying to us? What are they always saying about women's liberation?—"All she needs is a good ——." They say that* hopefully. Prayerfully. *They know. We all* know *what all that "All she needs is a good —— " stuff is all about.*

Claire: *This is ridiculous. Use your heads. Isn't a guy kind of super if he wants to sleep with a woman who's becoming independent?"*

Maire: *Yes, but not in business. There's something wrong every time, whenever sex is operating in a business. It's always like a secret weapon, something you hit your opponent below the belt with.*

Diana: *God, you're all crazy! Sex is fun. Wherever it exists. It's warm and nice and it makes people feel good.*

Dolores: *That's a favorite pipe dream of yours isn't it?*

Sheila: *It certainly doesn't seem like very much fun to me when I watch some secretary coming on to one of the lawyers when she wants a raise, then I see the expression on her face as she turns away.*

Marie: *God, that sounds like my mother when she wants something from my father!*

Veronica (feebly): *You people are beginning to make me feel awful!* (Everyone's head snapped in her direction.)

Marie: *Why?*

Veronica: *The way you're talking about using sex at work. As if it were so horrible. Well, I've always used a kind of sexy funniness to get what I want at work. What's wrong with that?*

Lucie: *What do you do?*

Veronica: *Well, if someone is being very stuffy and serious about business, I'll say something funny—I guess in a sexy way—to break up the atmosphere which sometimes gets so heavy. You know what I mean? Men can be so pretentious in business! And then, usually, I get what I want—while I'm being funny and cute, and they're laughing.*

Diana (heatedly): *Look, don't you see what you're doing?*

Veronica (testily): *No, I don't. What am I doing?*

Diana (her hands moving agitatedly through the air before her): *If there's some serious business going on you come in and say: Nothing to be afraid of, folks. Just frivolous, feminine little me. I'll tell a joke, wink my eye, do a little dance, and we'll all pretend nothing's really happening here.*

Veronica: *My God, I never thought of it like that.*

Laura: *It's like those apes. They did a study of apes in which they discovered that apes chatter and laugh and smile a lot to ward off aggression.*

Marilyn: *Just like women! Christ, aren't they always saying to us: Smile! Who tells a man to smile? And how often do you smile for no damned reason, right? It's so natural to start smiling as soon as you start talking to a man, isn't it?*

Lucie: *That's right! You're right! You know—God, it's amazing!—I began to think about this just the other day. I was walking down Fifth Avenue and a man in the doorway of a store said to me, "Whatsamatta, honey? Things can't be that bad." And I was startled because I wasn't feeling depressed or anything, and I couldn't figure out why he was saying that. So I looked, real fast, in the glass to see what my face looked like. And it didn't look like anything. It was just a face at rest. I had just an ordinary, sort of thoughtful expression on my face. And he thought I was depressed. And, I couldn't help it, I said to myself: "Would he have said that to you if you were a man?" And I answered myself immediately: "No!"*

Diana: *That's it. That's really what they want. To keep us barefoot, pregnant, and* smiling. *Always sort of begging, you know? Just a little supplicating—at all times. And they get anxious if you stop smiling. Not because you're depressed. Because you're* thinking!

Dolores: *Oh, come on now. Surely, there are lots of men who have very similar kinds of manners? What about all the life-of-the-party types? All those clowns and regular guys?*

Claire: *Yes, what about them? You* never *take those guys seriously. You never think of the men of real power, the guys with serious intentions and real strength, acting that* way, do you? And those are the ones with real responsibility. The others are the ones women laugh about in private, the ones who become our confidantes, not our lovers, the ones who are just like ourselves.

Sheila (quietly): *You're right.*

Lucie: *And it's true, it really does undercut your seriousness, all that smiling.*

Sheila (looking suddenly sad and very intent): *And underscore your weakness.*

Dolores: *Yes, exactly. We smile because we feel at a loss, because we feel vulnerable. We don't quite know how to accomplish what we want to accomplish or how to navigate through life, so we act feminine. That's really what this is all about, isn't it? To be masculine is to take action, to be feminine is to smile. Be coy and cute and sexy—and maybe you'll become the big man's assistant. God, it's all so sad. . . .*

Veronica (looking a bit dazed): *I never thought of any of it like this. But it's true, I guess, all of it. You know (and now her words came in a rush and her voice grew stronger), I've always been afraid of my job, I've always felt I was there by accident, and that any minute they were gonna find me out. Any minute, they'd know I was a fraud. I had the chance to become a producer recently, and I fudged it. I didn't realize for two weeks afterward that I'd done it deliberately, that I don't want to move up, that I'm afraid of the responsibility, that I'd rather stay where I am, making my little jokes and not drawing attention to myself . . .* (Veronica's voice faded away, but her face seemed full of struggle, and for a long moment no one spoke.)

Marilyn (her legs pulled up under her on the couch, running her hand distractedly through her short blond hair): *Lord, does that sound familiar. Do I know that feeling of being there by accident, any minute here comes the ax. I've never felt that anything I got—any honor—any prize, any decent job—was really legitimately mine. I always felt it was luck, that I happened to be in the right place at the right time and that I was able to put up a good front and people just didn't know . . . but if I stuck around long enough they would. . . . So, I guess I've drifted a lot, too. Being married, I took advantage of it. I remember when my husband was urging me to work, telling me I was a talented girl and that I shouldn't just be sitting around the house taking care of the baby. I wanted so to be persuaded by him, but I just couldn't do it. Every night I'd say: Tomorrow's the day and every morning I'd get up feeling like my head was full of molasses, so sluggish I couldn't move. By the time I'd finally get out of that damn bed it was too late to get a babysitter or too late to get to a job interview or too late to do anything, really.* (She turned toward Diana.) *You're a housewife, Diana. You must know what I mean.* (Diana nodded ruefully.) *I began concentrating on my sex life with my husband, which had never been any too good, and was now getting really bad. It's hard to explain. We'd always been very affectionate with one another, and we still were. But I began to crave . . . passion.* (She smiled, almost apologetically.) *What else can I call it? There was no passion between us, practically no intercourse. I began to demand it. My husband reacted very badly, accused me of—oh God, the most awful things! Then I had an affair. The sex was*

great, *the man was very tender with me for a long while. I felt* revived. *But then, a funny thing happened. I became almost hypnotized by the sex. I couldn't get enough, I couldn't stop thinking about it, it seemed to consume me; and yet, I became as sluggish now with sexual desire as I had been when I couldn't get up to go look for a job. Sometimes, I felt so sluggish I could hardly prepare myself to go meet my lover. And then . . .* (She stopped talking and looked down at the floor. Her forehead creased, her brows drew together, she seemed pierced suddenly by memory. Everyone remained quiet for a long moment.)

Diana (very gently): *And then?*

Marilyn (almost shaking herself awake): *And then the man told my husband of our affair.*

Jen: *Oh, Christ!*

Marilyn: *My husband went wild . . .* (her voice trailed off and again everyone remained silent, this time until she spoke again.) *He left me. We've been separated a year and a half now. So then I had to go to work. And I have, I have. But it remains a difficult, difficult thing. I do the most ordinary kind of work, afraid to strike out, afraid to try anything that involves real risk. It's almost as if there's some training necessary for taking risks, and I just don't have it . . . and my husband leaving me, and forcing me out to work, somehow didn't magically give me whatever it takes to get that training.*

Laura (harshly): *Maybe it's too late.*

Diana: *Well, that's a helluva thought.* (She crossed her legs and stared at the floor. Everyone looked toward her, but she said no more. Jen stretched, Claire bit into a cookie, Lucie poured coffee and everyone rearranged themselves in their seats.)

Marie (after a long pause): *It's your turn, Diana.*

Diana (turning in her chair and running thin hands nervously through her curly red hair): *It's been hard for me to concentrate on the subject. I went to see my mother in the hospital this afternoon, and I haven't been able to stop thinking about her all day long.*

Jen: *Is she very sick?*

Diana: *Well, yes, I think so. She underwent a serious operation yesterday—three hours on the operating table. For a while there it was touch and go. But today she seemed much better and I spoke to her. I stood by her bed and she took my hand and she said to me: "You need an enormous strength of will to live through this. Most people need only one reason to do it. I have three: you, your father and your grandmother." And suddenly I felt furious. I felt furious with her. God, she's always been so strong, the strongest person I know, and I've loved her for it. All of a sudden I felt tricked. I felt like saying to her: "Why don't you live for yourself?" I felt like saying: "I can't take this burden on me! What are you doing to me?" And now suddenly, I'm here, being asked to talk about work, and I have nothing to say. I haven't a goddamn thing to say! What do I do? After all, what do I do? Half my life is passed in a fantasy of desire that's focused on leaving my husband and finding some marvelous job. . . . At least, my mother worked hard all her life. She raised me when my real father walked out on her, she put me through school, she staked me to my first apartment, she never said no to me for any-*

thing. *And when I got married she felt she'd accomplished everything. That was the end of the rainbow. . . .*

Dolores (timidly): *What's so terrible, really, your mother saying she lived for all of you? God, that used to be considered a moral virtue. I'm sure lots of men feel the same way, that they live for their families. Most men* hate *their work. . . .*

Marilyn: *My husband used to say that all the time, that he lived only for me and the baby, that that was everything to him.*

Lucie: *How did you feel about that? What did you think of him when he said it?*

Marilyn (flushing): *It used to make me feel peculiar. As though something wasn't quite right with him.*

Lucie (to Diana): *Did you think something wasn't quite right, when your mother said what she said?*

Diana (thinking back): *No. It wasn't that something wasn't quite right. It seemed "right," if you know what I mean, for her to be saying that, but terribly wrong suddenly.*

Lucie: *That's odd, isn't it? When a man says he lives for his family it sounds positively unnatural to me. When a woman says it, it sounds so "right." So expected.*

Laura: *Exactly. What's pathology in a man seems normal in a woman.*

Claire: *It comes back, in a sense, to a woman always looking for her identity in her family and a man never, or rarely, really doing that.*

Marie: *God, this business of identity! Of wanting it from my work, and not looking for it in what my husband does. . . .*

Jen: *Tell me, do men ever look for their identities in their wives' work?*

Veronica: *Yes, and then we call them Mr. Streisand.* (Everybody breaks up, and suddenly cookies and fruit are being devoured. Everyone stretches and one or two women walk around the room. After 15 minutes . . .)

Marie (peeling an orange, sitting yogi-fashion on the floor): *I first went to work for a small publicity firm. They taught me to be a copywriter, and I loved it from the start. I never had any trouble with the people in that firm. It was like one big happy family there. We all worked well with each other and everyone knew a bit about everybody else's work. When the place folded and they let me go I was so depressed, and so lost. For the longest time I couldn't even go out looking for a job. I had no sense of how to go about it. I had no real sense of myself as having a transferable skill, somehow. I didn't seem to know how to deal with Madison Avenue. I realized then that I'd somehow never taken that job as a period of preparation for independence in the world. It was like a continuation of my family. As long as I was being taken care of I functioned, but when I was really on my own I folded up. I just didn't know how to operate. . . . And I still don't, really. It's never been the same, I've never had a job in which I felt I was really operating responsibly since that time.*

Sheila: *Do you think maybe you're just waiting around to get married?*

Marie: *No, I don't. I know I really want to work, no matter what. I know that I want some sense of myself that's not related to a husband, or to anyone but myself, for that matter. . . . But I feel so lost, I just don't know where it's all at, really.* (Five or six heads nodded sympathetically.)

Claire: *I don't feel like* any *of you. Not a single one.*

Dolores: *What do you mean?*

Claire: *Let me tell you something. I have two sisters and a brother. My father was a passionately competitive man. He loved sports and he taught us all how to play, and he treated us all exactly as though we were his equals at it. I mean, he competed with us exactly as though we were 25 when we were 8. Everything: sailing, checkers, baseball, there was nothing he wouldn't compete in. When I was a kid I saw him send a line drive ball right into my sister's stomach, for God's sake. Sounds terrible, right? We loved it. All of us. And we thrived on it. For me, work is like everything else. Competitive. I get in there, do the best I can, compete ferociously against man, woman or machine. And I use whatever I have in the way of equipment: sex, brains, endurance. You name it, I use it. And if I lose I lose, and if I win I win. It's just doing it as well as I can that counts. And if I come up against discrimination as a woman, I just reinforce my attack. But the name of the game is competition.*

(Everyone stared at her, openmouthed, and suddenly everyone was talking at once; over each other's voices; at each other; to themselves; laughing; interrupting; generally exploding.)

Laura (dryly): *The American dream. Right before our eyes.*

Diana (tearfully): *Good God, Claire, that sounds awful!*

Lucie (amazed): *That's the kind of thing that's killing our men. In a sense, it's really why we're here.*

Sheila (mad): *Oh, that love of competition!*

Marie (astonished): *The whole idea of just* being *is completely lost in all this.*

Jen (outraged): *And to* act *sexy in order to compete! You degrade every woman alive!*

Veronica (interested): *In other words, Claire, you imply that if they give you what you want they get you?*

Diana (wistfully): *That notion of competition is everything we hate most in men, isn't it? It's responsible for the most brutalizing version of masculinity. We're in here trying to be men, right? Do we want to be men at their worst?*

Lucie (angrily): *For God's sake! We're in here trying to be* ourselves. *Whatever that turns out to be.*

Marilyn (with sudden authority): *I think you're wrong, all of you. You don't understand what Claire's really saying.* (Everyone stopped talking and looked at Marilyn.) *What Claire is really telling you is that her father taught her not how to win but how to lose. He didn't teach her to ride roughshod over other people. He taught her how to get up and walk away intact when other people rode roughshod over her. And he so loved the idea of teaching* that *to his children that he ignored the fact that she and her sisters were girls, and he taught it to them, anyway.* (Everyone took a moment to digest this.)

Laura: *I think Marilyn has a very good point there. That's exactly what Claire has inside her. She's the strongest person in this room, and we've all known it for a long time.*

She has the most integrated and most separate sense of herself of anyone I know. And I can see now that that probably has developed from her competitiveness. It's almost as though it provided the proper relation to other people, rather than no relation.

Sheila: *Well, if that's true then her father performed a minor miracle.*

Jen: *You're not kidding. Knowing where you stand in relation to other people, what you're supposed to be doing, not because of what other people want of you but because of what you want for yourself . . . knowing what you want for yourself . . . that's everything, isn't it?*

Laura: *I think so. When I think of work, that's really what I think of most. And when I think of me and work, I swear I feel like Ulysses after 10 years at sea. I, unlike the rest of you, do not feel I am where I am because of luck or accident or through the natural striving caused by a healthy competitiveness. I feel I am like a half-maddened bull who keeps turning and turning and turning, trying to get the hell out of this maze he finds himself in. . . . I spent 10 years not knowing what the hell I wanted to do with myself. So I kept getting married and having children. I've had three children and as many husbands. All nice men, all good to me, all meaningless to me.* (She stopped short, and seemed to be groping for words . . .) *I wanted to do something. Something that was real, and serious, and would involve me in a struggle with myself. Every time I got married it was like applying Mercurochrome to a festering wound. I swear sometimes I think the thing I resent most is that women have always gotten married as a way out of the struggle. It's the thing we're encouraged to do, it's the thing we rush into with such relief, it's the thing we come absolutely to hate. Because marriage itself, for most women, is so full of self-hatred. A continual unconscious reminder of all our weakness, of the heavy price to be paid for taking the easy way out. Men talk about the power of a woman in the home. . . . That power has come to seem such a malevolent thing to me. What kind of nonsense is that, anyway, to divide up the influences on children's lives in that bizarre way? The mother takes care of the emotional life of a child? The vital requirement for nourishment? Out of what special resources does she do that? What the hell principle of growth is operating in her? What gives a woman who never tests herself against structured work the wisdom or the self-discipline to oversee a child's emotional development? The whole thing is crazy. Just crazy. And it nearly drove me crazy. . . . What can I say? For 10 years I felt as though I were continually vomiting up my life. . . . And now I work. I work hard and I work with great relish. I want to have a family, too. Love. Home. Husband. Father for the children. Of course, I do. God, the loneliness! The longing for connection! But work first. And family second.* (Her face split wide open in a big grin). *Just like a man.*

Lucie: *I guess I sort of feel like Laura. Only I'm not sure. I'm not sure of anything. I'm in school now. Or rather "again." Thirty years old and I'm a graduate student again,* starting out almost from scratch. . . . *The thing is I could never take what I was doing seriously. That is, not as seriously as my brother, or any of the boys I went to school with, did. Everything seemed too long, or too hard, or too something. Underneath it all, I felt sort of embarrassed to study seriously. It was as if I was really feeling: "That's something the grownups do. It's not something for me to do." I asked my brother about this feeling once, and he said most men felt the same way about themselves, only they fake it better than women do. I thought about that one for a long time, and I kept trying to say myself: What the hell, it's the same for them as it is for us. But . . .* (she looked swiftly around the circle) *it's not! Dammit, it's not. After all, style is content, right? And ours are worlds away. . . .*

Veronica: *Literally.*

Lucie: *I don't know. . . . I still don't know. It's a problem that nags and nags and nags at me. So often I wish some guy would just come along and I'd disappear into marriage. It's like this secret wish that I can just withdraw from it all, and then from my safe position look on and comment and laugh and say yes and no and encourage and generally play at being the judging mother, the "wise" lady of the household. . . . But then I know within six months I'd be miserable! I'd be climbing the walls and feeling guilty. . . .*

Marilyn: *Guilty! Guilty, guilty. Will we ever have a session in which the word guilty is not mentioned once?* (Outside, the bells in a nearby church tower struck midnight.)

Diana: *Let's wrap it up, okay?*

Veronica (reaching for her bag): *Where shall we meet next week?*

Marie: *Wait a minute! Aren't we going to sum up?* (Everyone stopped in mid-leaving, and sank wearily back into her seat.)

Lucie: *Well, one thing became very clear to me. Every one of us in some way has struggled with the idea of getting married in order to be relieved of the battle of finding and staying with good work.*

Diana: *And every one of us who's actually done it has made a mess of it!*

Jen: *And every one who hasn't has made a mess of it!*

Veronica: *But, look. The only one of us who's really worked well—with direction and purpose—is Claire. And we all jumped on her!* (Everyone was startled by this observation and no one spoke for a long moment.)

Marilyn (bitterly): *We can't do it, we can't admire anyone who does do it, and we can't let it alone. . . .*

Jen (softly): *That's not quite true. After all, we were able to see finally that there was virtue in Claire's position. And we are here, aren't we?*

Marie: *That's right. Don't be so down. We're not 102 years old, are we? We're caught in a mess, damned if we do and damned if we don't. All right. That's exactly why we're here. To break this bind.* (On this note everyone took heart, brightened up and trooped out into the darkened Manhattan streets. Proof enough of being ready to do battle.)

26 *Black women 1970*

Nathan and Julia Hare

Ever since she first stepped off the slave ship (at least one woman was among the earliest African slaves imported to Virginia around 1620), the black woman has occupied a peculiar position in American society. Not only did she play a leading part in helping her race survive slavery, she has had to be, under many circumstances and in many ways, both male and female in the socioeconomic arena. For her efforts to compensate for her predicament, she has been labeled "aggressive" or "matriarchal" by white scholars and "castrating female" by blacks.

Today, she experiences dual—in fact triple—exploitation (black, female and, in most cases, poor), and, as one black woman recently put it, she "must do more of everything for less of everything than any other sexual group." She lives largely isolated from whites except in her occupational life, and she is particularly subject to ambivalent relations with her mate. Before the black power movement, which had as a major goal the restoration of the supremacy of the black male at her expense, she played a salient role in the struggle for civil rights. Since then her role and position have been expressly subordinated, yet she almost unanimously shuns the Women's Liberation movement.

Black women/black men

What does the black woman think—and feel—about her general situation? What are her relationships and experiences with white women? What are her attitudes toward white men, toward black men, and why has she rejected collaboration in the Women's Liberation movement?

Though many black women reject the white sociologist's label of "matriarch," they nonetheless possess a keen sense of themselves as the backbone and major source of strength in the black family unit. Many feel cast into two roles, male by day and female after five, required to play the feminine role as prescribed by social custom yet driven to a masculine role by white society's harsher rejection of the black man occupationally. Thus even the positive virtues of being a black women—easier access to jobs and financial favors compared to black men—have negative consequences in that they deprecate the black male. The more she asserts herself, the more intense her conflict with him. Accordingly, even as she may despise and regret being forced into a "matriarchal" role, she boasts of her "mother wit," which she sees as compensating for her lack of formal education or real socioeconomic power to fulfill the role thrust upon her.

"Being a black woman is like being put by society into a bag. Nobody likes it. They feel that they are kind of trapped individuals." None of the women we talked with could name anything to like about the ordeal of being a black woman in the United States.

Toward the black man many black women must be deceptive. On the one hand these women must hide their conviction that black men have failed as liberators of the race, while on the other hand they are well aware of the necessity of being the backbone of the family without seeming to be so. They have mixed feelings about black men and speak of "hurting" experiences with them. They believe that they have been torn apart by whites and can't understand why black men do not, in their view, appreciate the way in which they, black women, have "helped the black race to survive."

They generally must take pains to avoid the appearance of posing a threat to black men as leaders or whatever and thus feel compelled to express positive attitudes toward them. At the same time, however, they have internalized white society's low regard for black men, but they are troubled by their appraisals of black men and their performance.

The way the system has crushed and dehumanized the black man I can never forgive them.

The black man spends too much time trying to prove that he is the great lover that he is accused of being by the white man.

I really dug a black man who loved me, and I was the one, but couldn't manage to find time to cut some of his screwing around, not all, just some. It was explained that 200 years of brainwashing forced him to prove he was "super dick."

Thus the burden of the family seems to fall upon the black woman, in her view, at the same time as she is told that the man should be superior and that she must "play second fiddle."

Still, many of her attitudes toward the black male merely echo the white feminist's attitudes toward white men.

Black men tend to take everything for granted—that you'll cook when they are hungry and screw when they want it. A "fox" is a sex machine, and that "ugly girl" sure can burn [cook].

They come home from work and have a beer while you finish dinner, then they sit down and watch the sports while you are washing the dinner dishes, fall asleep on the

Reprinted from Nathan and Julia Hare, "Black Women 1970," Transaction, Nov./Dec. 1970, pp. 65-90. © Nov. 1970 by Transaction, Inc., New Brunswick, New Jersey.

sofa while you get the children ready for bed and then turn around after you've done all this work and stick his mouth out as long as something else is sticking out—his privates—if you don't feel like screwing. They say that the white man is more affectionate. I don't know, but I do know that the black man jumps right up after screwing or turns over and snores. He never just holds you. I used to fret when he got mad if I didn't give him any, but now I don't care. If I'm tired, I'm tired.

In the case of the educated black woman, all too often she must marry beneath her station in life because this society has kept the black man in lowly occupations. Census data show that college-trained black women such as schoolteachers are more likely to marry than white women in that group yet are more subject to see their families broken up, partly due to conflicts resulting from their marrying down the socioeconomic scale. Too often the marriage of a black woman is confined to anyone she can find within the proximity of her movements.

Black women/white men

Although she longs for the financial security offered by the white male, she feels ethically obliged to reject his overtures on grounds of loyalty to her race and its suffering at the white man's hands. Besides she is aware and resentful of the fact that the white man marries only the more successful black woman whenever he does marry a black woman. As one woman put it, "It is almost an impossibility for a black woman who has not achieved some prominence or fame to attract a white man outside of some dark alley."

Another told us, "White men dig us but are too timid or weak to engage in an open affair. He wants the women of both races. His mouth waters when he sees all the beautiful flowers growing in pastures."

The relationships between most black women and white men are restricted and, usually, clandestine and sinister sexual arrangements or abuses. Black women complain of day-to-day rebuffs (white men letting doors slam or close in their faces after holding them open for white women) and sometimes more forthright insults. Many tell of being fired for failure to capitulate to white male overtures, but some see the withholding of sexual favors from white men as a last-ditch stronghold against white domination.

When I was 13, living in San Diego, a white man swerved his car to miss a white woman and killed my only brother. He said it was an accident, but he went all the way across the street, so I'll always believe he made some choice. They try to flirt with me sometimes now, but I shine them on because if the white woman is first in death she might as well be first—and last—in sex. They can kill my brother, but they can't screw me to boot.

However, some claim that their experiences with black men have been disastrous, though largely because of an alleged black male disrespect for black women and their inability to "stand up as a man." She regards their submission to the white man as in some ways excessive and regrets the all too prevalent compensatory projection of their failure on to the black woman. One woman commented, "Having been told by whites that the black women emasculated them, they tend to take out their frustration on black women, when in reality it was whites who emasculated them."

Black men are generally recognized by black women to have been on the rise in recent years, but many women also feel that black men believe they have failed their roles and need to be "helped along" toward full manhood. The black woman anticipates that her rejection of the traditional female role would be psychologically threatening to the black male. She must encourage him and lay as much groundwork for black liberation as he will let her. It is necessary to be patient with black men whenever they engage in symbolic assertions of manliness. She must not dominate but merely assist strongly.

At the same time, however, there are many black women who feel deeply that the black man must be urged to "be a man but not to rock the boat," as this may risk the loss of jobs or affluence for her family. He must stand up to the white man but be no Malcolm X.

The more militant women oppose the black man's new suppression of the black woman's role—in contrast to the historical record from Harriet Tubman and Sojourner Truth to Daisy Bates, Artherine Lucy and Gloria Richardson. These women are viewed as having assumed leadership, not as against black men but to help blacks as a whole. Some black women today condemn black men for shunting them into the background, especially since they lack complete confidence that black men will produce the necessary revolutionary results.

Black women/white women

Probably the most painful part of being a black woman, as she views it, is the rape of the short male supply by white women. "White women are using everything in the book to catch our man," said one. Black women already sense a shortage of black men, and it hurts to have to share them with white women (who get a whack at men from both races and whose motives are generally not thought to be trustworthy or commendable). What is worse, black women take it as a personal insult, a denunciation of their own black beauty. They express contempt for "black men who embrace the blue-eyed devils," for the "pain when they waltz around the white woman" and "white chicks who want to play the easy lay." Invariably, black women feel, the union is rooted in pathology and/or white subterfuge. Either the white woman is relieving guilt or the black man is compensating for his historical rejection ("lynched for touching white women") and chasing after forbidden fruit. White women are thought to exploit the myth of their superiority and the appeal of forbidden fruit to "take in" the black man and to aggravate the conflicts between black men and black women to their own advantage. The black man is merely a source of sexual gratification to the white woman, who is incapable of relating in genuine love relationships or otherwise across racial boundaries.

In defense of black men, some black women claim that the men are largely victims, that white women court them, lured by the myth of the black male animal, in compensation for the sexual failure of the white man. And in defense of black women it is sometimes argued that black women generally have been made more passive by their mothers who train them to defend themselves against anticipated sexual exploitation and thus make the white woman seem more forward by contrast. To many it is intolerable to see a black man with a white woman, and they grow furious over the sight of it. Only a minority are able to take a nonchalant approach to a union of white women and black men. In such cases, they accept it only philosophically as a necessary ideal. Reflecting this view, one woman said, "Love should be free. It is pathetic that races have to be considered at all. If race is considered before one loves, the relationship becomes a mission to find someone in a particular race to love. This infringes on the freedom to love."

The black woman's contacts with white women have hardly been more satisfactory than those with the white man. White women who are strangers, not personal friends, exhibit a "cool, indifferent attitude," as a black woman put it. Even when white women try to be friendly they may frequently be mistrusted: "They are so phony. As soon as they see you they say, 'Oh, let me make this little black woman my friend.' All the time they don't give a damn about you." Liberal or otherwise, the white woman is perceived by the black as finding "little nasty ways" to put her down. She says "you girls," or she assigns the black woman the dirty work on the job or in her kitchen. Many black women reserve a special contempt and resentment for those white women, often with rich husbands, who do volunteer work in community programs and then leapfrog over the paid (of necessity) black workers to high job positions. Some of these women belong to volunteer organizations such as the Junior League which, though not admitting blacks, may monopolize much of the work at a given institution. Then the white volunteer who rises to the highest paid and most powerful position will say: "I started as a volunteer."

The bitterness that black women often feel toward white stems also from the fact that the black woman is expected to compete with the white woman in the beauty parade but all too often cannot afford the frills, finery and cosmetics. On top of this, for years all of the cosmetics and skin preparations were geared to the white woman, even down to the hair dryers and the curlers. Even bell bottoms were made for white women. Many young black girls can get them on, but the black woman's hips typically grow too large with age, in contrast to the flatter-hipped norms of white women.

On another level, the black woman's resentment is sometimes triggered by being treated as a "mammy object" by white women. One black woman told us the following story:

They [white women] expect support and a great deal of candid understanding of their sexual problems. I roomed with a white girl once for four months when I first got out of college. It turned out that I was a social cover so she could have black men coming to see her. White men did not seem interested in her. She became bizarre. I moved out, and it became clear to everybody that she was seeing black men. Suddenly white men, even the janitor, began to hit on her. A black psychiatrist pointed out the homosexual motivation of these white men who found her a desirable vehicle for indirectly sharing a bed with black men.

Black women/women's lib

Many black women express the same notions of the Women's Lib movement as are common to the population at large. The movement, in this view, is flooded with lesbians, and we have heard black women boast of offers from white lesbians to "take me out of the ghetto if I would be her lover." At the same time, however, one often hears a kind of scornful understanding of what white Women's Lib people are doing. White women are said to be sexually inhibited and relatively more chained to girdles and corsets and artificiality and Emily Post and less free even in the way they serve their meals. It is thought to be understandable that they, white women, should rebel, and there is some wonder as to why they did not do so sooner, why in the South, for instance, they knowingly kept silent on the extramarital affairs their husbands were having with black mistresses who then gave birth to mulatto children "looking more like their husbands in some instances than their own." Another black woman spoke in the same tone: "Black women have not had the tradition of being bound down and girdled up in clothes. That's why we're burning buildings, not bras."

Still, no black woman could remain unaffected by the difference between her status as a woman and that of the white woman as a woman:

White women think they are God's gift to the world. Car doors opened for you. Holding your elbow when you step off the curb. Now white women are saying that they don't want that.

The white woman has been taught from the cradle that she is to receive special treatment.

The white man places white women on a pedestal while seeking black women as objects of sexual release in order to prevent an alliance of black and white women.

Even those black women who share the goals of the Women's Liberation movement are reluctant to participate, on the grounds that white women always dominate in coalitions and are always in charge. Most, however, do not feel that the movement as currently projected relates to their interests. On the contrary, it appears to some that white and black women are in a race to change places. The white woman is trying to escape the drudgery of the home for rewarding employment outside, while the black woman still longs to escape the labor force and to get into the home. Domestics, for instance, say that they would rather be at home doing their own dishes instead of out doing those of the white woman while she seeks liberation. There is agreement, however, that both white and black women need freedom from the white man since "he is the oppressor," but "let white women worry about their own sex hangups with white men."

Women in the growing black middle class just coming into a modicum of affluence and its household gadgetry such as blenders, washing machines and dryers want now to enjoy these things for a while. The lower-class black woman lacks the educational background to move into male positions and therefore does not see that as an immediate possibility. In any case, it is hard for a black woman to imagine liberating herself from the household when she already has been forced out to work. In the past she has long tried against great odds to adhere to society's concept of the woman's role and so now stands perplexed when she is suddenly told that the old ideals of marital and family life are no longer desirable.

The things white women are demanding liberation from are what we've never even experienced yet. How many black women stay home bored with kids while husband is off earning a lot of money? I'm sure many black women would love to stay home and be "housewives."

They mock white women who "like to feel that our problems as a woman are the same as theirs—you too have cramps, my husband loves his roast beef rare, and so does yours."

On a political level, the black woman is inclined to regard the Women's Liberation movement as potentially divisive of black men and women, as "a lot of trivia to get blacks off the main issue of racism." Some go so far as to suggest that it is deliberately so conspired and instigated, probably by some white men, to undercut the current black thrust. A black female college professor in New York City pointed out the striking historical parallel of the suffragettes coming into the limelight during the time of Marcus Garvey, just as today the Women's Liberation movement has blossomed in an era of rising black consciousness. Almost unanimously in the minds of black women, the Women's Liberation movement poses the danger of injecting a wedge between black men and black women at a time when black unity seems of paramount importance. Even those who foresee that they may someday have to fight the black man in the same way the white woman is fighting the white man now nevertheless believe that this is "putting the cart before the horse" and "we can cross that bridge when we get to it."

Meanwhile, racism is more oppressive, they feel, than sexism, and there is no justification for collaborating with the white woman at this time. A domestic worker explained: "You enter this life with one role assigned to you, and that is to make life pleasant for white people. But enough is enough." Besides, they fear that if Women's Liberation does succeed in obtaining access to better jobs and wages for black women, without at the same time raising the black man's lot, the problem of male-female relations among blacks will be deepened.

In addition, white women are regarded as "just as racist as the white man." "The white Lib movement is racist. They want to equate their oppression to that of black people. When has a white woman been lynched. Many of them are anti-men, don't want to have babies when that is one of the few things a black woman could ever say was hers." In many ways the movement is regarded as one of "crass insensitivity" to the cause of black freedom. White women want equal footing with white men (even at the expense of the black man) while black women want black men on the same base with white men. "The black woman's struggle is the black struggle."

Many black women are convinced that, before giving up his own, the white man would take the black man's jobs and give them to white women, pushing the black man still farther down. To this extent, the goals of Women's Liberation and black liberation are viewed as contradictory.

As one woman put it, "the black woman must take her place not behind or in front of the black man but beside him, and together they must strive for the freedom of the black race."

In other words, there can be no liberation of black women until black men—all black people—are free.

27 The middle-class mind of Kate Millett

Irving Howe

At the heart of *Sexual Politics*, in the key chapter, "Theory of Sexual Politics," lies a nightmare vision of endless female subordination to and suffering at the hands of men. "Sexual dominion [is] perhaps the most pervasive ideology of our culture and provides the most fundamental concept of power." The relations between the sexes are basically political, that is, relations of power. Everything else that happens to and between men and women—from sex to love to mutual responsibility in family life—is secondary. In these relationships the status of woman is that of a

"chattel" a status accorded legal sanction through marriage: "an exchange of the female's domestic service and (sexual) consortium in return for financial support." The woman is exploited for her labor and/or used as a sexual object; and the exploiters are men.

Since sexual dominion is the very fundament, as also the *raison d'être*, of the patriarchal family and can't, indeed, be eradicated short of destroying the patriarchal family, we soon arrive at a terrifying impasse: an all-but-timeless and all-but-indestructible system of oppression, one in which

Edited from Irving Howe, "The Middle-Class Mind of Kate Millett," Harper's, Dec. 1970, pp. 110-129.

"the entire culture supports masculine authority in all areas of life and—outside of the home—permits the female none at all." Why all-but-timeless and all-but-indestructible? Because the patriarchal family seems virtually coextensive with history itself; as Miss Millett must acknowledge, it has been "a basic form . . . within all societies."

This system of power, in which the woman "is customarily deprived of any but the most trivial sources of dignity or self-respect," rests primarily, in Miss Millett's judgment, on the social indoctrination of "sexual temperament," a learning process whereby little boys and girls are persuaded not merely of their differences but also of male superiority. Sometimes this process of indoctrination occurs through outright insistence upon male dominance, sometimes through brainwashing rationales for confining women to home and children, and sometimes through "the chivalrous stance . . . a game the master group plays in elevating its subject to pedestal level."

Now what needs first and foremost to be noted about this theory is that, in any precise sense of the term, it isn't a theory at all. It is a cry of woe, partly justified; and it offers a description of sexual relationships said to hold pretty much for all of human history. But a cry of woe isn't a theory, and neither is a description. For a group of statements to be given the status of a theory, good theory or bad, it must account for a complex of phenomena in respect to genesis, persistence, necessary characteristics, and relationships to other phenomena. With the possible exception of the third item in this list, Miss Millet satisfies none of these requirements. To say "man is a beast" is not a theory about the nature of humanity, it is at best a statement of description; but to say "man is a beast because he is fallen in nature, or because he fails to obey the injunctions of Christianity, or because he has been brutalized by capitalist society"—that is to *begin* developing a theory. Miss Millett, however, makes no effort to account for the origins of male "sexual dominion," and more important, the reasons for its remarkable persistence and prevalence. Given her approach, she really cannot do so. She has no theory.

Miss Millett is determined to resist the view that biological and physical differences between the sexes may have determined or may still crucially determine a sequence of secondary and social differences, for she fears, rather naively, that any concession to biology must mean to accept as forever fixed the traditional patterns of male domination. The result is that she must fall back upon an unarticulated but strongly felt vision of conspiracy. And also upon a mode of reasoning utterly circular. Why does the patriarchal family persist through all recorded history? Because the social learning process trains us to accept it as a necessary given. But why does this learning process itself persist through history? Because it is needed for sustaining the patriarchal family. And what does Miss Millett spinning in circles illuminate here? Very little. Worse still, she presents a vision, misnamed a theory, which if taken seriously offers little hope of change or relief, for she cannot specify any historical factors, other than the "altered consciousness" of a "revolutionary" intellectual elite, which might enable us to end the dominion of patriarchy.

Let us approach the problem from a slightly different angle. Miss Millett argues that there "is no biological reason why the two central functions of the family (socialization and reproduction) need be inseparable from or even take place within it"; further, that we shouldn't take seriously the view that male physical endowment has been or remains a crucial factor in male social ascendancy. One must consequently ask: how then has so "basic a form [as] patriarchy" managed to arise and survive in just about every civilized society? If this "basic" form isn't even needed for socialization and reproduction, what is the secret of its hold? In what way can it even be considered "basic"? These questions, which follow inexorable from her assertions, seem never to trouble Miss Millett, since she writes with the thrust of the polemicist rather than the curiosity of the historian; and the punishment she thereby suffers is to create a picture, all but unknowingly, of endless female subordination from which, analytically, there seem hardly an escape. The root premise of her work, which naturally she does not care to express openly, is that women have been kept down because men have chosen to keep them down—which seems a more terrible tribute to the masculine will than any of its celebrants have ever dreamt of proposing. As a key to "the most pervasive ideology of our culture and . . . the most fundamental concept of power," this view of the life of the sexes is, let us say, a little inadequate.

Now, there have been other theories positing the centrality of social oppression in history. Marxism, for one, sees history thus far as a sequence of class struggles, though with the nature and relationships of the contending classes in constant change. Whatever one may think of this theory, the Marxist approach has one overwhelming advantage over Miss Millett's: it provides a principle of causation and change within society. Far from looking upon man's physical setting and conditions as somehow an "enemy" of the hope for social change, as Miss Millett does, the Marxist view places social change within a natural context, or more precisely, it sees mankind as making its history through the materials and within the limits provided by nature. As men gain mastery over nature and thereby free themselves from the burdens of brute labor, the internal relationships of society are transformed and men begin *to be able* to determine their own destinies in a distinctly "human" way. (At the least, this avoids the simplistic either-or of biology/culture to which Miss Millet is addicted.) And while Marx believes all history to have been a history of class struggle, he is utterly scornful of those—precursors in economic terms of Miss Millett's sexual monism—who see history as a vista of undifferentiated oppression. He insists upon the crucial difference, say, between the master-slave relationship and the bourgeois-proletarian relationship: that is, he insists that historical change occurs and that historical change matters.

By contrast Miss Millett makes no concession to this central fact of history. Fixated upon the patriarchal family as if it were an all but supra-historical constant, and forced to acknowledge its omnipresence, she sketches out a grisly picture of the life of women. She makes no serious effort to differentiate among various kinds of patriarchal family (after all, there may have been and of course were enormous differences in its endless manifestations) or to differentiate among the life-styles by which women have tried to fulfill themselves at different points in history. Her method here is exactly that of "vulgar Marxism," that caricature of Marxist thought which insists that the only reality is the economic and all else, being "superstructural," must be insignificant. Thus, with a reckless thrust of the phrase, Miss Millett can dismiss chivalry as "a game the master group plays. . . ." But such "games" crucially affected the lives of millions of men and women during the Middle Ages when the cult of Mariolatry became so powerful in the Church that a symbolic struggle between Mother and Son, female and male principles, was enacted among the faithful. Can one really explain such complex events as "a game the master group plays"? Isn't such historical reductionism a sign of an impoverishment of sensibility? A crude simplification such as we have come to expect in the work of Stalinist historians? It is striking that for all her far-ranging ambition of reference and passion of female defense, Miss Millett does not even list in her index, and only mentions two or three times in trivial contexts, the single most important woman in all Western history: the Virgin Mary.

A host of other questions press for consideration. The woman who worked sixteen hours a day in the Midland mines during the Industrial Revolution—was she really a "sexual object" up for "barter" to the "master group" (the wretched men who also worked sixteen hours a day in the same mines) quite in the same way as the bourgeois ladies of, say, Matisse's Paris? Does the "passivity" Miss Millett says patriarchal society induces in women characterize the American pioneer wife staking out a homestead in Oklahoma? Was the Jewish immigrant mother working in a sweatshop, often shoulder to shoulder with her equally exploited husband, "customarily deprived of any but the most trivial sources of dignity or self-respect"? Are the ladies of the Upper East Side of Manhattan simply "chattels" in the way the wives of California grape pickers are, and if so, are they "chattels" held by the same kinds of masters? Has the fact of being female been more important in the social history of most women than whether they were rich or poor, black or white, Christian or Jewish? Has the condition of women since the rise of the patriarchal family been so unvarying, so essentially the same repeated and endless story of oppression, that it can really be summoned through Miss Millett's one simple model? Have not human beings, men and women, found some paths to fulfillment and fraternity, some side alleys to decency of relationship and respect for sexual difference, even under the patriarchal curse? In short, does Miss Millet have any sense at all of the range and variety and complexity—and yes, even once in a while the humane achievements—of our history?

For what I am trying to suggest through the questions I have just asked—the list should be extended for pages—is not only that Miss Millett flattens out all history into a tapestry of "sexual dominion," not only paints a picture of the past and present depriving women of any initiative, will, or capacity, but that she systematically ignores those cru-

cial factors of class position which have the most far-reaching impact on the life of women. Most of the time, when she speaks of women she really has in mind middle-class American women during the last thirty years. About the experience of working-class women she knows next to nothing, as in this comic-pathetic remark: "The invention of labor-saving devices has had no appreciable effect on the duration, even if it has affected the quality, of their drudgery." Only a Columbia Ph.D. who has never had to learn the difference between scrubbing the family laundry on a washboard and putting it into an electric washing machine can write such nonsense. As with most New Left ideologues, male or female, Miss Millett suffers from middle-class parochialism.

And more: she suffers from a social outlook which, despite its "revolutionary" claims, is finally bourgeois in character. She writes that "nearly all that can be described as distinctly human rather than animal activity (in their own way animals also give birth and care for their young) is largely reserved for the male." And again: "Even the modern nuclear family, with its unchanged and traditional division of roles, necessitates male supremacy by preserving specifically human endeavor for the male alone, while confining the female to menial labor and compulsory child care."

These sentences indicate that Miss Millett is at heart an old-fashioned bourgeois feminist who supposes the height of satisfaction is to work in an office or factory and not be burdened with those brutes called men and those slops called children. For one must ask: why is the male's enforced labor at some mindless task in a factory "distinctly human," while the woman bringing up her child is reduced to an "animal" level? Isn't the husband a "chattel" too? Hasn't Miss Millett ever been told by her New Left friends about the alienation of labor in an exploitative society? And is the poor bastard writing soap jingles in an ad agency performing a "human" task morally or psychologically superior to what his wife does at home, where she can at least reach toward an uncontaminated relationship with her own child? Why can't Miss Millett here remember the sentence, one of the best in her book, that appears in another context: "In conservative economies with an ethos of aggressive competition [and in other economies too!—I.H.], the 'home' seemed to offer the last vestiges of humane feeling, the only haven of communal emotion"? That animals also raise their young (in the same way? toward the same ends of socialization and ethical continuity?)—does this remarkable piece of information really deny the "distinctly human" character of women's experience in raising their children? In some remarks Miss Millett betrays a profound distortion of values, a deep if unconscious acquiescence not only to the corruptions of the bourgeois society against which she rails but to all those "masculine values" she supposes herself to be against.

What is lacking in Miss Millett's "theory of sexual politics," as throughout her book, is a felt sense of, a deep immersion in, the actualities of human experience which must always be the foundation of any useful theory. What is present in her "theory" is an imperious condescension toward all those complications of past and current experience that won't fit into her scheme, as toward all human beings who don't satisfy her categories. In a remark worthy of that other leftist snob, Herbert Marcuse, she tells us that "many women do not recognize themselves as discriminated against; no better proof could be found of the totality of their conditioning." And those women who *do* recognize themselves as discriminated against—would not Miss Millett leap to declare that "no better proof could be found of the acuteness with which they recognize the reality"? Against the imperviousness of circularity, reason is helpless.

Now, it is true that the lot of women has frequently been that of a subordinate group—though not that alone. The relationship between men and women, like other relationships in our society, does often have a strand of ugly commercialism—though not that alone and often not that predominantly. (How many of Miss Millett's readers or admirers, one wonders, would be ready to apply her categories—"chattel," "barter," "sexual object," etc.—to themselves? Women have been exploited throughout history, but most of the time in ways quite similar to those in which men have been, and more often than not, as members of oppressed or disadvantaged classes rather than as women alone. Yet it is also true that many women have suffered a kind of superexploitation, though this can't be understood in the gross terms of "sexual politics" but must be studied as an element in the tortuous development of mankind from the penalties of scarcity to the possibilities of plenty. And at the risk of being charged with "playing the game of the master group," let me add that even in their conditions of disadvantage women have also been able to gain for themselves significant privileges and powers. Males may have been "masters" and females "chattels," but this is perhaps the only such relationship in human history where the "masters" sent themselves and their sons to die in wars while trying to spare their "chattels" that fate.

That the relations between men and women have had and still have an element of "power" similar to that characterizing the relations between social classes is almost certainly true. But not the whole truth and very often not the most important truth. Indeed, the more closely one applies Miss Millett's "theory" to concrete instances both in history and immediate experience, the less adequate does it seem even as description. For the word "power" is very tricky in this context, and Miss Millett isn't the one to look carefully into its complexities. In any relationship of caring, people gain power over one another: the power to please, the power to hurt. Sexuality is a mode of power, and often, as history indicates (for Miss Millett, one gathers, no female face ever did launch a thousand ships . . .), sexual power has been of a magnitude to overcome the effects of economic power. Sexuality gives us power at varying times of our lives, and often with radical inequities for which there seems to be no solution or even solace. That men have held power over women, in both the desirable and deplorable senses, is a truth that was noticed before the appearance of Miss Millett's book. That women have held power over men, usually in the more desirable but often enough in quite deplorable ways, is a thought with which Miss Millett will have no commerce. And it is even possible—indeed, if one clings to some sort of tragic view of life, it is likely—that the powers we hold over one another are both of the desirable and the deplorable kinds, the two fatally and forever mixed.

Yet it would be a sad mistake, and for the women's movements a strategic folly, to suppose that the relations between men and women, so entwined with the deepest and most mysterious elements of our psychic life, can ever be understood by the sexual monism, the historical reductionism of Miss Millett.

Freud's "entire psychology of women," writes Miss Millett, "is built upon an original tragic experience—born female." This is true enough in a way, and there is also a simplified truth in the claim that Freud sees women as defining their existence through their relations to men (though to say that isn't necessarily to *convict* him of a falsehood or bias). Finally, however, this is not so devastating a charge as Miss Millett supposes. For it is Freud's judgment that the psychology of men rests also on an original tragic experience—born male. Miss Millett manages to neglect the fact that in the Freudian system the theory of penis envy finds a polar equivalent and necessary balance in the theory of castration anxiety. The male is seen as being quite as heavily burdened by nature and circumstance as the female, and perhaps less well equipped to cope. In Freud's view, nature lets no one off easily. If women feel it "unjust" to be told they are conditioned by residues of their childhood envy for that "novel article"—Miss Millet's high-ironic parlance for "penis"—then men may feel it quite as "unjust" that they must live out their lives in constant anxiety as to sexual performance. Freud does, however, envisage a possibility for at least a partial relief or transcendence of these troubles, and perhaps a shade more so for women than for men. Women are said by him to be able to emerge from the hold of penis envy, in part through a strong and positive identification with their mothers. Nor, by the way, are they the only ones in the Freudian outlook who experience envy; men are seen as at times quite envious of that very passivity which Miss Millett regards as so libelous an attribution to her sex.

Why should all this outrage Miss Millett so much? She really has, I would venture, only a slight intrinsic concern with Freudianism. A major reason for her passionate assault is that, by making a simplistic leap from one order of experience (psychological) to another (social policy), she sees the theory of penis envy as the basis for an alleged Freudian belief that "the intellectual superiority of the male, constitutionally linked with the penis, is close to an ascertainable fact. . . ." And again she provides a footnote from Freud supposedly buttressing this claim:

We often feel that when we have reached the penis wish and the masculine protest we have penetrated all the psychological strata and reached "bedrock" and that our task is completed. And this is probably correct, for in the psychic field the biological factor is really rock bottom. The repudiation of femininity must surely be biological fact, part of the great riddle of sex.

Whatever the truth or falsity of what Freud says here, he is clearly not saying what Miss Millett claims he is saying. She simply will not read with care.

Yet, once her ideological assaults and manipulations are put aside, there does remain the fact that Freud's view of women, his analysis of their sexual natures and roles, doesn't happen to lend itself to the more extreme visions of the Women's Liberationists. Freud tended to believe, as Philip Rieff says, that "women are erotic hoarders in the male economy of culture. In the strife between sensuality and culture, women represent the senses." To someone like Miss Millett this immediately seems an invidious distinction, for she is completely identified with the values of the bourgeois activist male, the one who performs (what she supposes to be) "distinctly human" work. But in Freud's canny and ambiguous view, those who "represent the senses" are at times far more "distinctly human." For even while regarding women as the agents of racial survival and men as the culture-creators, Freud also fears, like many other nineteenth-century European thinkers, the death of spontaneous life at the hands of an increasingly tyrannical culture, the nightmare of a rationalistic self-destruction as "the world of the senses becomes gradually mastered by spirituality." No one is obliged to accept these views, but anyone wishing to attack Freud in a serious way ought to be able, at the least, to report the complexities, the inner sequence of change and doubt, and the frequently problematic tone which characterize his work.

What shall we say, however, if we are committed to equality between the sexes and yet continue to believe that Freud remains one of the great minds of our age? It is the kind of question that divides those who want everything neatly aligned, slogan stacked against slogan, from those prepared to accept conflict and unresolved contradiction.

We can say of course that Freud was a product of his age, and that while he did more than anyone else to overcome its prejudices, inevitably he still shared some of them. If there is a streak of patriarchalism in his writing, as I suppose there is, we must recognize that fifty or sixty years ago people could not possibly see things as they are seen in 1970: that is known as historical perspective. In fairness, we must then add something Miss Millett fails to mention, that Freud greatly admired intellectual women and that the psychoanalytic movement was one of the first intellectual groups in this century to give a large number of gifted women the opportunity to fulfill themselves professionally. Still, to say this isn't enough.

We can add that Freud's views on women, especially those expressed in his more "philosophical" moments, must be separated from some clinically more cogent portions of his work. Freud would not be the first great thinker whose method can be used critically against portions of his writings. Still, to say that isn't enough.

We can then try to struggle with the fact that Freud advances conclusions as to the nature and consequence of sexual differences which rub against our progressive inclinations—but which can't, simply for that reason, be dismissed. For we must always recognize that analytically he may be right. Yet why should even this possibility create anxiety or anger? If the concepts of penis envy and castration anxiety prove, in some sense, to be valid for psychoanalysis, this surely doesn't at all affect the claims of women for socioeconomic justice—though it may affect

some of the more nightmarishly utopian fantasies of writers like Miss Millett.[1]

Freud believed that the process of maturation for women presented certain special difficulties, and perhaps these would persist in the best of societies—though to say that such difficulties seem to be rooted in biology isn't at all to say that they can't be eased by social policy and education. To persuade a woman to like herself and to accept herself sexually, which was one of Freud's aims, isn't necessarily to persuade her to stay in the kitchen—though it may well be to tell her, Miss Millett's arrogant ultimatism notwithstanding, that if she does prefer to stay at home, this doesn't stamp her as inferior or brainwashed or a "chattel" of the "master group."

Freud seemed also to believe that the biological differences, or if you prefer disadvantages, of women inclined them toward the sphere of private values and experience. Even if we suppose this to be true, why should it at all lessen our zeal—I mean the zeal of both women and men—for seeing to it that those women who enter upon careers be given every kind and equality of opportunity? I suspect, however, that what troubles Miss Millett is not merely the injustice of sexual discrimination but the very idea of sexual difference. For all that she is so passionate an advocate of the cause of women, she shows very little warmth of feeling toward actual women and very little awareness of their experience. Freud speaks in his essay on "Femininity" of the woman's "active pursuit of a passive function," and Miss Millett finds the phrase "somewhat paradoxical," thereby revealing a rather comic ignorance of essential experiences of her sex, such as the impulse toward the having of children. Indeed, the emotions of women toward children don't exactly form an overwhelming pre-occupation in Sexual Politics: there are times when one feels the book was written by a female impersonator.

For what seems to trouble Miss Millett isn't merely the injustices women have suffered or the discriminations to which they continue to be subject. What troubles her perhaps most of all—so one is inclined to say after immersing oneself in her book—is the sheer existence of women. Miss Millett dislikes the psycho-biological distinctiveness of women, and she will go no further than to recognize—what choice is there, alas?—the inescapable differences of anatomy. She hates the perverse refusal of most women to recognize the magnitude of their humiliation, the shameful dependence they show in regard to (not very independent) men, the maddening pleasures they even take in cooking dinners for "the master group" and wiping the noses of their snotty brats. Raging against the notion that such roles and attitudes are biologically determined, since the very thought of the biological seems to her a way of forever reducing women to subordinate status, she nevertheless attributes to "culture" so staggering a range of customs, outrages, and evils that this "culture" comes to seem a force more immovable and ominous than biology itself.

Miss Millett lashes out against the Freudians not merely because some of them indulge in male chauvinism, but because they persist in seeing, within the common fate of humanity, a distinctive nature and role for women. Insofar as Miss Millett assaults the notion that current styles of perceiving "masculine" and "feminine" must be taken as eternal verities, I don't see that she can be faulted. Who would care to deny the attractiveness of historical variability, or the hope that men and women will be able to define themselves with greater freedom than they have in the past? But Miss Millett will not let it go at that, for she is driven by some ideological demon—the world as commune? the end of the nuclear family? the triumph of unisex?—which undermines what is sound in the cause of women's protest. In a remarkable sentence she writes:

Removed from their contexts of social behavior, where they function to maintain an order not only of differentiation but of dominance and subordinance, the words "masculine" and "feminine" mean nothing at all and might well be replaced with what is biologically or naturally verifiable—male and female.

No longer is Miss Millett insisting on the probable truth that the claim for the biological determination of sexual roles has often been an excuse for reactionary laziness. She is now saying that the very idea of distinctive sexual psychologies, responses, and life patterns—in short, masculine and feminine as modes of behavior deriving from but more extensive in consequence than the elementary differences between male and female—means "nothing at all." And here she betrays a rashness such as one rarely finds in scholars who are genuinely committed to their subject.

For what is obvious to anyone who even glances at the literature on this matter—and that is all I claim to have done—is the agreement among scholars (who may agree on nothing else) that they don't yet know enough to make the kind of absolutist declaration I've just quoted from Miss Millett. There appear to be three *kinds* of difference between the sexes: the quite obvious physical and physiological ones; the more shadowy and ambiguous ones in role, attitude, and potential that are sometimes called "secondary"; and those that are culturally derived or imposed. Just as few scholars would now deny the last two in favor of the hegemony of the first, so few would deny the first two in favor of the hegemony of the third. The most problematic is of course the second, that is, those differences pertaining to behavior yet seeming to derive mainly from the physical and physiological.

Now there are moments when one is tempted to dismiss the whole matter by repeating Oscar Wilde's reply to a question about the differences between the sexes: "Madam, I can't conceive." For Wilde's remark points to a fundamental fact of our existence which ideologists forget at their peril and most other people, whatever their grave failings, do seem to remember. Together with the accumulated prejudice and mental junk of the centuries, there really is something we might call the experience, even the wisdom of the race, and it is not to be disposed of simply by fiat or will (as many revolutionists find out too late). It tells us, through the historical pattern of a sexual division of labor universal in form but sharply varying in content, that for good or ill our natures shape our conduct.

Now the real question is, why should any of this trouble Miss Millett? That there are sexual differences extending beyond anatomy and into behavior—why should this be supposed to endanger the case for equality, *unless Miss*

Millett tacitly or explicitly accepts the male chauvinist view that the mere evidence of difference is proof of superiority? Why cannot intelligent and humane people look upon sexual difference as a source of pleasure, one of the givens with which nature compensates us for the miseries of existence? Why must differences be seen as necessarily invidious? And even if these differences suggest the possibility that fewer women will reach "first-rate achievement" than men, why should that keep anyone from being responsive and responsible to those women who will do valuable work outside the home? Any more, say, than we should feel dismay at the possibility that an adjustment in sexual roles might decrease the number of men reaching "first-rate achievement"?

The dominating obsession of Miss Millet's book—which is to insist that all but rudimentary sexual differences are cultural rather than biological in origin—is a token of her lack of intellectual sophistication. If you insist, as she in effect does, that the biological be regarded as somehow untouched by cultural alloy, then it becomes virtually impossible to offer any biological evidence, if only because man is a creature that always exists in a culture, so that whatever we can learn about him must always be through the prism of cultural perspective. Culture is, at least in part, that which we make of our biology. If certain patterns of existence, such as the family, are invariable throughout the development of human culture, then it seems reasonable to suppose, even if it may be difficult to prove, that they satisfy requirements of our biology as these have manifested themselves through culture.

But as Miss Millett uses "biology" and "culture," they become absolutist polarities ranged in an endless battle against one another. She begins by noting quite properly that in the past the case for biological determinism has been overstated, especially in popular writings, and ends by doing pretty much the same thing for cultural determinism, though with not much more persuasive evidence. In her somewhat desperate reliance on the transforming powers of "culture," she reminds one of the thrust Morris Raphael Cohen once made against John Dewey's use of the term "experience": it was hard, said Cohen, to know what in Dewey's system was *not* experience.

To fail to see the improvement in large areas of (black) life in America isn't merely political obtuseness of the kind to which the New Left is pledged unto death, it is the snobbism of those who will have nothing to do with the small struggles and little victories of human beings unless these are patterned to their ideologies and slogans. This is the very opposite—in spirit, in feeling, in political consequence—of genuine radicalism. It is, instead, a symptom of the contempt that today rages among our intellectual and professional classes: contempt for ordinary life, contempt for ordinary people, contempt for the unwashed and unenlightened, contempt for the unschooled, contempt for blue-collar workers, contempt for those who find some gratification in family life, contempt for "the usual."

You would never know from Miss Millett's book that working-class life can be marked by that easy warmth and fraternal steadiness in the relations between sexes that Richard Hoggart has sketched in *The Uses of Literacy*. You would never know from Miss Millett's book that there are a great many middle-class Americans who have struggled to find and perhaps in part found, terms of personal respect through which to share their lives. You would never know from Miss Millett's book that there are families where men and women work together in a reasonable approximation of humanness, fraternity, and even equality—at least as reasonable as one can expect in an unjust society, in a bad time, and with all the difficulties that sheer existence imposes on us.

NOTES

1. The most egregious of these fantasies is Miss Millett's cavalier play with the notion of the abolition of the family. That the family,

at once the most conservative of human institutions and endlessly open to social and psychological changes, has been coextensive with human culture itself and may therefore be supposed to have certain powers of endurance and to yield certain profound satisfactions to human beings other than merely satisfying the dominating impulses of the "master group," hardly causes Miss Millett to skip a phrase. Nor does the thought that in at least some of its aspects the family has protected the interests of women as against those of men.

In any case, one might suppose that Miss Millett would cast a glance at one of the very few contemporary social institutions—the Israeli *kibbutz*—where a serious effort has been made, if not to abolish the family, then at least significantly to modify its nature. Had she troubled to do so, and read the reports of, say, Stanley Diamond, an anthropologist of radical inclination, she would have had to recognize that at least in terms of psychological consequences, that is, the kind of children it brings forth, the evidence from the *kibbutz* isn't likely to persuade one that abolishing the family will greatly enrich the human race.

28 The rise of women's liberation

Marlene Dixon

The old women's movement burned itself out in the frantic decade of the 1920s. After a hundred years of struggle, women won a battle, only to lose the campaign: the vote was obtained, but the new millennium did not arrive. Women got the vote and achieved a measure of legal emancipation, but the real social and cultural barriers to full equality for women remained untouched.

For over 30 years the movement remained buried in its own ashes. Women were born and grew to maturity virtually ignorant of their own history of rebellion, aware only of a caricature of blue stockings and suffragettes. Even as increasing numbers of women were being driven into the labor force by the brutal conditions of the 1930's and by the massive drain of men into the military in the 1940s, the old ideal remained: a woman's place was in the home and behind her man. As the war ended and men returned to resume their jobs in factories and offices, women were forced back to the kitchen and nursery with a vengeance. This story has been repeated after each war and the reason is clear: women form a flexible, cheap labor pool which is essential to a capitalist system. When labor is scarce, they are forced onto the labor market. When labor is plentiful, they are forced out. Women and blacks have provided a reserve army of unemployed workers, benefiting capitalists and the stable male white working class alike. Yet the system imposes untold suffering on the victims, blacks and women, through low wages and chronic unemployment.

With the end of the war the average age of marriage declined, the average size of families went up, and the suburban migration began in earnest. The political conservatism of the '50s was echoed in a social

conservatism which stressed a Victorian ideal of the woman's life: a full womb and selfless devotion to husband and children.

As the bleak decade played itself out, however, three important social developments emerged which were to make a rebirth of the women's struggle inevitable. First, women came to make up more than a third of the labor force, the number of working women being twice the prewar figure. Yet the marked increase in female employment did nothing to better the position of women, who were more occupationally disadvantaged in the 1960's than they had been 25 years earlier. Rather than moving equally into all sectors of the occupational structure, they were being forced into the low paying service, clerical and semi-skilled categories. In 1940, women had held 45 per cent of all professional and technical positions; in 1967, they held only 34 per cent. The proportion of women in service jobs meanwhile rose from 50 to 55 per cent.

Second, the intoxicating wine of marriage and suburban life was turning sour; a generation of women woke up to find their children grown and a life (roughly 30 more productive years) of housework and bridge parties stretching out before them like a wasteland. For many younger women, the empty drudgery they saw in the suburban life was a sobering contradiction to adolescent dreams of romantic love and the fulfilling role of women as wife and mother.

Third, a growing civil rights movement was sweeping thousands of young men and women into a moral crusade—a crusade which harsh political experience was to transmute into the New Left. The American Dream was riven and tattered in Mississippi and finally napalmed in Viet-Nam. Young Americans were drawn not to Levittown, but to Berkeley, the Haight-Ashbury and the East Village. Traditional political ideologies and cultural myths, sexual mores and sex roles with them, began to disintegrate in an explosion of rebellion and protest.

The three major groups which make up the new women's movement—working women, middle class married women and students—bring very different kinds of interests and objectives to women's liberation. Working women are most concerned with the economic issues of guaranteed employment, fair wages, job discrimination and child care. Their most immediate oppression is rooted in industrial capitalism and felt directly through the vicissitudes of an exploitative labor market.

Middle class women, oppressed by the psychological mutilation and injustice of institutionalized segregation, discrimination and imposed inferiority, are most sensitive to the dehumanizing consequences of severely limited lives. Usually well educated and capable, these women are rebelling against being forced to trivalize their lives, to live vicariously through husbands and children.

Students, as unmarried middle class girls, have been most sensitized to the sexual exploitation of women. They have experienced the frustration of one-way relationships in which the girl is forced into a "wife" and companion role with none of the supposed benefits of marriage. Young women have increasingly rebelled not only against passivity and dependency in their relationships but also against the notion that they must function as sexual objects, being defined in purely sexual rather than human terms, and being forced to package and sell themselves as commodities on the sex market.

Each group represents an independent aspect of the total institutionalized oppression of women. Yet, in varying degrees all women suffer from economic exploitation, from psychological deprivation, and from exploitive sexuality. Within women's liberation there is a growing understanding that the common oppression of women provides the basis for uniting to form a powerful and radical movement.

Racism and male supremacy

Clearly, for the liberation of women to become a reality it is necessary to destroy the ideology of male supremacy which asserts the biological and social inferiority of women in order to justify massive institutionalized oppression.

The ideology of male chauvinism can only be understood when it is perceived as a form of racism, based on stereotypes drawn from a deep belief in the biological inferiority of women. The very stereotypes that express the society's belief in the biological inferiority of women are images used to justify oppression. The nature of women is depicted as dependent, incapable of reasoned thought, childlike in its simplicity and warmth, martyred in the role of mother, and mystical in the role of sexual partner.

It has taken over 50 years to discredit the scientific and social "proof" which once gave legitimacy to the myths of black racial inferiority. Today most people can see that the theory of the genetic inferiority of blacks is absurd. Yet few are shocked by the fact that scientists are still busy "proving" the biological inferiority of women.

Yet one of the obstacles to organizing women remains women's belief in their own inferiority. This dilemma is not a fortuitous one, for the entire society is geared to socialize women to believe in and adopt as immutable necessity their traditional and inferior role. From earliest training to the grave, women are constrained and propagandized. Spend an evening at the movies or watching television, and you will see a grotesque figure called woman presented in a hundred variations upon the themes of "children, church, kitchen" or "the chick sex-pot."

Such contradictions as these show how pervasive and deep-rooted is the cultural contempt for women, how difficult it is to imagine a women as a serious human being, or conversely, how empty and degrading is the image of woman that floods the culture.

Countless studies have shown that black acceptance of white stereotypes leads to mutilated identity, to alienation, to rage and self-hatred. Human beings cannot bear in their own hearts the contradictions of those who hold them in contempt. The ideology of male supremacy creates self-contempt and psychic mutilation in women; it creates trained incapacities which put women at a disadvantage in all social relationships.

It is customary to shame those who would draw the parallel between women and blacks by a great show of concern over the suffering of black people. Yet this response itself reveals a refined combination of white middle class guilt and male chauvinism, for it overlooks several essential facts. For example, the most oppressed group within the feminine population is made up of black women, many of whom take a dim view of the black male intellectual's adoption of white male attitudes of sexual superiority. Neither are those who make this pious objection to the racial parallel addressing themselves very adequately to the millions of white working class women living at the poverty level, who are not likely to be moved by this middle class guilt-ridden one-upmanship while having to deal with the boss, the factory, or the welfare worker day after day. They are already dangerously resentful of the gains made by blacks, and much of their "racist backlash" stems from the fact that they have been forgotten in the push for social change. Emphasis on the real mechanisms of oppression—on the commonality of the process—is essential lest groups such as these, which should work in alliance, become divided against one another.

White middle class males already struggling with the acknowledgment of their own racism do not relish an added burden of recognition: that to white guilt must soon be added "male." It is therefore understandable that they should refuse to see the harshness of the lives of most women—to honestly face the facts of massive instutionalized discrimination against women.

We must never forget that the root of the ideology of male superiority, female inferiority and of white racism is a system of white male supremacy. White male supremacy is part of the ideology of imperialism, first European, then American. The European powers stripped India, China, Africa, and the new world of its wealth in raw materials, in gold, slaves, in cheap labor. Such brutal forms of exploitation required justification, and that justification was found in the doctrines of white racial superiority and the supremacy of European and American "civilization" over the "heathen" civilizations of Africa, Asia and Latin America. Even more, we must never forget that the doctrine of white supremacy included the *supremacy of white women* as well as of white men.

The rise of Capitalism in the west was based upon the wealth looted from other civilizations at the point of a gun: Imperialism was the root and branch of racism and genocide then as it is now. It is at the root of mass prostitution in Saigon, the torture and murder of innocent Vietnamese and Indochinese women and children, at the root of all the sufferings of war inflicted upon the innocent at home and in Indochina. White, American women must understand their oppression in its true context, and that context *is* a brutal, anti-human system of total exploitation having its corporate headquarters in New York and its political headquarters in Washington, D.C. And white women must understand that they are part of the system, benefitting from the loot secured through genocide.

This is why we must clearly understand that male chauvinism and racism *are not the same thing*—they are alike in that they oppress people and justify systems of exploitation—but in no way does a white woman suffer the exploitation and brutalization of women who are marked by both stigmata: female and non-white. It is only the racism of privileged white women, self-serving in their petty, personal interests, who can claim that they suffer *as much* (or must serve their own interests first) as black women, or Indochinese women, or any woman who experiences the cruelty of white racism or the ruthless genocide of American militarism.

The contradiction of racism distorts and contaminates every sector of American life, creeps into every white insurgent movement. Understanding their own oppression can and must help white women to confront and to repudiate their own racism, for otherwise, there will be no freedom, there will be no liberation.

Marriage: genesis of women's rebellion

The institution of marriage is the chief vehicle for the perpetuation of the oppression of women; it is through the role of wife that the subjugation of women is maintained. In a very real way the role of wife has been the genesis of women's rebellion throughout history.

Looking at marriage from a detached point of view one may well ask why anyone gets married, much less women. One answer lies in the economics of women's position, for women are so occupationally limited that drudgery in the home is considered to be infinitely superior to drudgery in the factory. Secondly, women themselves have no independent social status. Indeed, there is no clearer index of the social worth of a woman in this society than the fact that she has none in her own right. A woman is first defined by the man to whom she is attached, but more particularly by the man she marries, and secondly by the children she

bears and rears—hence the anxiety over sexual attractiveness, the frantic scramble for boyfriends and husbands. Having obtained and married a man the race is then on to have children, in order that their attractiveness and accomplishment may add more social worth. In a woman, not having children is seen as an incapacity somewhat akin to impotence in a man.

Beneath all of the pressures of the sexual marketplace and the marital status game, however, there is a far more sinister organization of economic exploitation and psychological mutilation. The housewife role, usually defined in terms of the biological duty of a woman to reproduce and her "innate" suitability for a nurturant and companionship role, is actually crucial to industrial capitalism in an advanced state of technological development. In fact, the housewife (some 44 million women of all classes, ethnic groups and races) provides, unpaid, absolutely essential services and labor. In turn, her assumption of all household duties makes it possible for the man to spend the majority of his time at the workplace.

It is important to understand the social and economic exploitation of the married woman, since the real productivity of her labor is denied by the commonly held assumption that she is dependent on her husband, exchanging her keep for emotional and nurturant services. Household labor, including child care, constitutes a huge amount of socially necessary labor. Nevertheless, in a society based on commodity production, it is not usually considered even as "real work" since it is outside of trade and the marketplace. In a society in which money determines value, women are a group who work outside the money economy. Their work is not worth money, is therefore valueless, is therefore not even real work. And women themselves, who do this valueless work, can hardly be expected to be worth as much as men, who work for money.

Women are essential to the economy not only as free labor, but also as consumers. The American system of capitalism depends for its survival on the consumption of vast amounts of socially wasteful goods, and a prime target for the unloading of this waste is the housewife. She is the purchasing agent for the family, but beyond that she is eager to buy because her own identity depends on her accomplishments as a consumer and her ability to satisfy the wants of her husband and children. This is not, of course, to say that she has any power in the economy. Although she spends the wealth, she does not own or control it—it simply passes through her hands.

In addition to their role as housewives and consumers, increasing numbers of women are taking outside employment. These women leave the home to join an exploited labor force, only to return at night to assume the double burden of housework on top of wage work—that is, they are forced to work at two full-time jobs. No man is required to expected to take on such a burden. The result: two workers from one household in the labor force with no cutback in essential female functions—three for the price of two, quite a bargain. Regardless of her status in the larger society, within the context of the family the woman's relationship to the man is one of proletariat to bourgeoisie.

One consequence of this class division in the family is to weaken the capacity of oppressed men and women to struggle together.

For third world people within the United States the oppressive nature of marriage is reflected negatively—for example, motherhood out of wedlock is punished, either through discriminatory welfare legislation or through thinly disguised, genocidal programs of enforced sterilization. This society punishes unmarried women even more than it punishes married women. As a result, many third world and poor white women want help with their families, and need a husband in the home. The destruction of families among poor people, as a result of economic exploitation and social oppression, results in deprivation in every facet of life for poor women and children. White middle class women, bound up with the psychological oppression of marriage, have often been blind to the extent of suffering—and the extent of the needs—brought by the deliberate destruction of the families of the poor. Unemployment and pauperization through welfare programs creates very different problems than does the experience of boredom in the suburb.

In all classes and groups, the institution of marriage nonetheless functions to a greater or lesser degree to oppress women; the unity of women of different classes hinges upon our understanding of that common oppression. The 19th century women's movement refused to deal with marriage and sexuality, and chose instead to fight for the vote and elevate the feminine mystique to a political ideology. That decision retarded the movement for decades. But 1969 is not 1889. For one thing, there exist alternatives to marriage. The cultural revolution—experimentation with life-styles, communal living, collective child-rearing—have all come from the rebellion against dehumanized sexual relationships, against the notion of women as sexual commodities, against the hardship, alienation and loneliness of American life.

Lessons must be learned from the failures of the earlier movement. The feminine mystique must not be mistaken for politics, nor legislative reform for winning human rights. Women are now at the bottom of their respective worlds and the basis exists for a common focus of struggle for women in American society. It remains for the movement to understand this, to avoid the mistakes of the past, to respond creatively to the possibilities of the present.

Economic exploitation

Women's oppression, although rooted in the institution of marriage, does not stop at the kitchen or the bedroom door. Indeed, the economic exploitation of women in the workplace is the most commonly recognized aspect of the oppression of women.

The rise of new agitation for the occupational equality of women also coincide with the re-entry of the "lost generation"—the housewives of the 1950s—into the job market. Women from middle class backgrounds, faced with an "empty nest" (children grown or in school) and a widowed or divorced rate of one-fourth to one-third of all marriages, returned to the workplace in large numbers. But once there they discovered that women, middle class or otherwise, are the last hired, the lowest paid, the least often promoted, and the first fired. Furthermore, women are more likely to suffer job discrimination on the basis of age, so the widowed and divorced suffer particularly, even though their economic need to work is often urgent. Age discrimination also means that the option of work after child-rearing is limited. Even highly qualified older women find themselves forced into low-paid, unskilled or semi-skilled work—if they are lucky enough to find a job in the first place.

Most women who enter the labor force do not work for "pin money" or "self-fulfillment." Sixty-two per cent of all women working in 1967 were doing so out of economic need (i.e., were either alone or with husbands earning less than $5000 a year). In 1963, 36 per cent of American families had an income of less than $5000 a year. Women from these families work because they must; they contribute 35 to 40 percent of the family's total income when working full-time, and 15 to 20 per cent when working part-time.

Despite their need, however, women have always represented the most exploited sector of the industrial labor force. Child and female labor were introduced during the early stages of industrial capitalism, at a time when most men were gainfully employed in crafts. As industrialization developed and craft jobs were eliminated, men entered the industrial labor force, driving women and children into the lowest categories of work and pay. Indeed, the position of women and children industrial workers was so pitiful, and their wages so small, that the craft unions refused to organize them. Even when women organized themselves and engaged in militant strikes and labor agitation—from the shoemakers of Lynn, Massachusetts, to the International Ladies' Garment Workers and their great strike of 1909—male unionists continued to ignore their needs. As a result of this male supremacy in the unions, women remain essentially unorganized, despite the fact that they are becoming an even larger part of the labor force.

The trend is clearly toward increasing numbers of women entering the work force: women represented 55 per cent of the growth of the total labor force in 1962, and the number of working women rose from 16.9 million in 1957 to 24 million in 1962. There is every indication that the number of women in the labor force will continue to grow as rapidly in the future.

Job discrimination against women exists in all sectors of work, even in occupations which are predominantly made up of women. This discrimination is reinforced in the field of education, where women are being short-changed at a time when the job market demands higher educational levels. In 1962, for example, while women constituted 53 per cent of the graduating high school class, only 42 per cent of the entering college class were women. Only one of three people who received a B.A. or M.A. in that year was a woman, and only one in ten who received a Ph.D. was a woman. These figures represent a decline in educational achievement for women since the 1930s, when women received two out of five of the B.A. and M.A. degrees given, and one out of seven of the Ph.Ds. While there has been a dramatic increase in the number of people, including women, who go to college, women have not kept pace with men in terms of educational achievement. Furthermore, women have lost ground in professional employment. In 1960 only 22 per cent of the faculty and other professional staff at colleges and universities were women—down from 28 per cent in 1949, 27 per cent in 1930, 26 per cent in 1920. 1960 does beat 1919 with only 20 per cent—"you've come a long way, baby"—right back to where you started! In other professional categories: 10 per cent of all scientists are women, 7 per cent of all physicians, 3 per cent of all lawyers, and 1 per cent of all engineers.

Even when women do obtain an education, in many cases it does them little good. Women, whatever their educational level, are concentrated in the lower paying occupations. The figures tell a story that most women know and few men will admit: most women are forced to work at clerical jobs, for which they are paid, on the average, $1600 less per year than men doing the same work. Working class women in the service and operative (semi-skilled) categories, making up 30 per cent of working women, are paid $1900 less per year on the average than are men. Of all working women, only 13 per cent are professionals (including low-pay and low-status work such as teaching, nursing and social work), and they earn $2600 less per year than do professional men. Household workers, the lowest category of all, are predominantly women (over 2 million) and predominantly black and third world, earning of their labor barely over $1000 per year.

Not only are women forced onto the lowest rungs of the occupational ladder, they are in the lowest income levels as well. The most constant and bitter injustice experienced by all women is the income differential. While women might passively accept low status jobs, limited opportunities for advancement, and discrimination in the factory, office and university, they choke finally on the daily fact that the male worker next to them earns more, and usually does less. In 1965 the median wage or salary income of year-round full-time women workers was only 60 per cent that of men, a 4 per cent loss since 1955. Twenty-nine per cent of working women earned less than $3000 a year as compared with 11 per cent of the men; 43 per cent of the women earned from $3000 to $5000 a year as compared with 19 per cent of the men; and 9 per cent of the women earned $7000 or more as compared with 43 per cent of the men.

What most people do not know is that in certain respects, women suffer more than do non-white men, and that black and third world women suffer most of all.

Women, regardless of race, are more disadvantaged than are men, including non-white men. White women earn $2600 less than white men and $1500 less than non-white men. The brunt of the inequality is carried by 2.5 million non-white women, 94 per cent of whom are black. They earn $3800 less than white men, $1900 less than non-white men, and $1200 less than white women.

There is no more bitter paradox in the racism of this country than that the white man, articulating the male supremacy of the white male middle class, should provide the rationale for the oppression of black women by black men. Black women constitute the largest minority in the United States, and they are the most disadvantaged group in the labor force. The further oppression of black women will not liberate black men, for black women were never the oppressors of their men—that is a myth of the liberal white man. The oppression of black men comes from institutionalized racism and economic exploitation: from the world of the white man. Consider the following facts and figures.

The percentage of black working women has always been proportionately greater than that of white women. In 1900, 41 per cent of black women were employed, as compared to 17 per cent for white women. In 1963, the proportion of black women employed was still a fourth greater than that of whites. In 1960, 44 per cent of black married women with children under six years were in the labor force, in contrast to 29 per cent of white women. While job competition requires even higher levels of education, the bulk of illiterate women are black. On the whole, black women—who often have the greatest need for employment—are the most discriminated against in terms of opportunity. Forced by an oppressive and racist society to carry unbelievably heavy economic and social burdens, black women stand at the bottom of that society, doubly marked by the caste signs of color and sex.

Faced with discrimination on the job—after being forced into the lower levels of the occupation structure—millions of women are inescapably presented with the fundamental contradictions in their unequal treatment and their massive exploitation. The rapid growth of women's liberation as a movement is related in part to the exploitation of working women in all occupational categories.

Part V

Intercultural comparisons

The papers in this section review the status of women in different societies. Some are revolutionary in ideology (Israel, the Soviet Union and China), one is evolutionary (Finland), one is cross-cultural, and one is a historical view of the position of women in Colonial America.

The paper by Lantz et al. is an analysis of the power patterns between husband and wife, the attitudes and behaviors toward premarital and extramarital sexual behaviors, and motives for marriage are seen in Colonial magazines published in the preindustrial era of 1741-1794. The data imply that power was normally vested in the male but that his authority was not always exercised. Using subtle power, women exerted considerable influence during courtship and may have shared equal influence in the areas of finance and morality. The pattern of romantic love as the basis for marriage, at least among upper status groups, was common as part of a general valuing of individualism. The data suggest that when someone deviated from the sexual norms, the attitude toward women was one of sympathy and toward the male, ostracism. But with respect to behavior, the women were physically punished or ostracized whereas the men were not! Some patterns within the American family, some aspects of the status of women, some moral distinctions, have origins predating our Industrial Revolution.

As we have seen, questions of the uniformity or diversity of social institutions and sex-role distinctions have become significant feminist issues. This is simultaneously an important theoretical question bearing upon the decisiveness of constitutional predisposition and human plasticity. Barry, Bacon, and Child reviewed the ethnographic reports on 110 cultures, most of them nonliterate. The response to very young children was dominated by their status as "baby": 92% of the 96 cultures for which ratings included the infancy period were judged to have no sex-linked differences in response to infants.

During childhood the overwhelming majority of cultures did make sex-linked distinctions. Girls were most often pressured to become nurturant and responsible (and less clearly, obedient), while boys were pushed to achieve and become self-reliant. There was very little overlap in diverse cultures on those variables. Sex differences seen in our society, like those of nonliterate people, are cultural adaptations to certain biological characteristics. But the variability between and within cultures attests to a relativity or a functionalism of sex differences. In this study, large sex differences were associated with economies that placed a premium on strength, and cultures where large cooperative families existed. Thus, isolated nuclear families (especially in industralized nations), are likely to be characterized by adults able to take over the responsibilities of the other partner. The socialization of middle-class American girls shows that to be largely true. But, as Bacon noted in the later paper, men and women must also be prepared to fulfill tasks specifically associated with their sex. Overall, then, socialization tendencies in this culture are complex and, since Colonial times, reflect both sex categorization and a premium placed upon individuality.

Scandinavian sex-roles are usually regarded as progressive. Women's participation in the labor force is common and child-care facilities and other helping institutions exist. In her paper, Haario-Mannila reports the results of interviews with women in Helsinki. In spite of egalitarian values, she found that within the home older divisions persist: women are responsible for *household tasks and equality between the sexes is far more of a reality at work than at home. Quite traditionally, the women interviewed considered marital fidelity the single most important role requirement within marriage, which they considered their primary role. In spite of similar education but dissimilar occupational ranking, the majority of women were satisfied with their occupational positions. Almost unanimous responses revealed two coexisting attitudes: the sexes are equal and are entitled to freedom of choice, but it is important for girls to be trained for their household tasks and it is the husband's duty to provide for his family.*

That conservative values coexist with more liberal ones, and that the bulk of contention relates to the allocation of household tasks seems logical. In Finland, as in the United States, attitudes about women's participation in the labor force are in transition, changing more slowly than the reality of the percentage of women working. As long as the nuclear family persists, so will household tasks. As long as women and men continue to perceive the main economic responsibility as the husband's, they will continue to perceive the main family responsibilities as the wife's. But as women work equally with men, this inequity is resented, and both partners are forced to reallocate their responsibilities to each other.

In the next three papers we will examine the role of status of women in cultures where equality of the sexes forms part of a revolutionary ideology. In the Marxist view, woman has been a member of an oppressed and exploited class and her liberation will occur with the advent of socialism as the first step to full communism. Only with this revolution in social structure can women cease being the chattel first of their fathers and then of their husbands. Essentially similar ideologies (though with differing social structures) characterize the kibbutz of Israel and postrevolutionary China. How have the women fared?

Field and Flynn explain that because of the population of men decimated during World War II the Soviet economy does not have the luxury of "permitting" women to work. That is, female labor is an intrinsic and absolutely necessary part of the labor force. Simultaneously, an increase in the population is necessary because of war-incurred deaths and birth losses. Thus, two esteemed goals for women coexist: good Soviet women work and good Soviet women have children. The ideology maintains that maternity is in the service of the state and it is, therefore, the responsibility of society to care for and educate its children. But the reality is that there are insufficient child-care facilities and women remain hampered by domestic duties, which deny them full participation in political, social, and economic activities.

Compared with women in Western countries, Soviet women enjoy a far greater proportional participation in political organizations and in professions. They are, however, infrequently found in the higher levels of political organization and they are overrepresented in subordinate and menial jobs. Currently there are efforts to increase the number of men in medicine and teaching, fields in which women are heavily represented. Although more Soviet women than men are channeled into the lower levels of the educational system, and the educational status of women is not quite equal with that of men, it surpasses most other countries, including the United States.

Soviet women continue to have sole responsibility for the domestic obligations. They are angered by the imposition of two full jobs, especially when housework is devalued and there is the implication that within the family the man automatically has higher status and prestige. Field and Flynn contend that along with an ideology of equality there is an important lack of respect for women, which is observable because women are considered the natural candidates for strenuous and dirty jobs. Thus, in housework and care of the children, equality of the sexes breaks down. Soviet men do not help at home; men have twice as much freedom as women. Even though the status of Soviet women has been significantly raised through education and occupation, dual roles still are assumed, required domestic contributions are not valued, and domestic labors are inefficiently time-consuming and energy-draining. (Is it a reflection of the status of women when the least-developed aspects of society relate to domestic tasks?)

In the Israeli kibbutz a commitment to a radical ideology of feminine equality led to the development of unique social institutions, including children's houses, communal dining halls, communal education, and clothes stores. These innovations were designed to free women from their restrictive traditional responsibilities. The views of the original settlers were extreme, leading them to deny differences in physical capacities because it was important for both sexes to share responsibilities and jobs. That original view has modified and Rosner asks what has replaced it.

In kibbutz interviews, Rosner found that the majority of his respondents had fairly egalitarian evaluations of intellectual capacities but that 90% felt that physical differences in strength limit the work women can do. Although the images of men and women are generally equal, the majority noted significant differences in ambitions and inclinations. In spite of the ideal, the majority felt that women give major consideration to their families and men to their work. Equality of the sexes is the prevailing and powerful ideology, but in reality there is a growing pattern of sex-role differentiation with the different roles evaluated unequally. In Rosners' sample, the attribution of sex-linked stereotyped characteristics became the explanation and justification for sex-role differentiation.

Similar to what Field and Flynn observed in the Soviet Union, Rosner feels that the kibbutz is changing to a society where the family is recognized as the basic social unit. When that happens, especially in a period of relative affluence, there seems to be a tendency for a return to more traditional role divisions. This means, especially, an increase in women's family participation. Increasingly, especially in light of developments within the kibbutz, there is increasing recognition that children may prosper more when they are reared in some extent by their mothers rather than by grandmothers or social institutions.

Quite familiarly, one of the problems in the kibbutz is the fact that productive work is given preference while the service sector has low prestige. As a result of sex-role differentiation, the service sector is the exclusive concern of women. We are familiar with the fact that service occupations such as nursing and teaching are dominated by women in the United States. In the Soviet Union medicine is dominated by women. Nursing and teaching in the United States, medicine in the USSR., and service occupations in the kibbutz, are all low-status occupations.

Nonetheless, and in spite of increasing differentiation, Rosner believes that an egalitarian relationship can be maintained. Buoyed by the evidence that even now kibbutz women do not generally feel discriminated against, Rosner calls for a general recognition that women have greater family responsibilities and simultaneously she calls for the deliberate encouragement of women's participation in important sectors in which they are underrepresented.

Rosner seems to feel that maintaining equalitarian relationships between the sexes will depend, in the long run, on recognizing and changing those conditions that limit women's participation in esteemed work—which is quite different from trying to change the evaluation of family activities and service contributions. As in many other cultures, whereas the ideology of sexual equality remains an important norm in the kibbutz, it is seriously jeopardized by increasing role differentiation and unequal value assigned to the differentiated roles.

A major social change in Communist China has been the effort to significantly elevate women, primarily through a change in loyalty from family to state. Loyalty to the state means a commitment to work and production. Participation in the labor force ends economic dependence and therefore ends the subordination of women to men. In Huang's paper it is clear that public opinion, like that in the Soviet Union, is hostile to women who elect to stay home. In the political ideology concern for one's own family is counterproductive to a more rewarding loyalty to one's larger family—the state. In spite of the pressure, some conflict between the two loyalties continues. But at least in this early phase of the revolution (in contrast to the more affluent Soviet Union and Israel), the status of women in China will continue to rise as they single-mindedly pursue work.

Consistently, equal status between the sexes is initially achieved through equality of education, employment, and productivity. In spite of any professional equality, it is in domestic obligations that status inequities persist. The core of the inequity is the higher value placed upon all nondomestic work and the assumption that women do it. Domestic (and traditionally feminine) achievements at least in industrialized countries, seem never to achieve the status of work done outside of the home for money. Are there feminine motives that preclude a single choice and an easy solution? Maternity jeopardizes equal status insofar as it removes women from productive labor. More important, women who have families seem to have strong and enduring motives to protect, nurture, and enhance them. (Obviously sustaining the family is not necessarily linked with washing dishes, but old role divisions, assumptions, and privileges paint them all with the same brush.) Perhaps the priority of the family originates in the relationship women have with their young children; in any event, it seems to have deeper origins than just the role expectations of other people.

This priority seems to continue in spite of work-oriented ideologies, public pressures, and institutions designed to relieve women of traditional responsibilities. Perhaps the realization of women's potential includes equality in education, work, the economy and politics—and an affirmation, a glorification, of that which has been characteristically feminine.

29 Pre-industrial patterns in the colonial family in America: a content analysis of colonial magazines

Herman R. Lantz
Margaret Britton
Raymond Schmitt
Eloise C. Snyder

It has been a widely accepted opinion that modern courtship and mate selection are products of urbanization and industralization. Freedom in mate choice and romantic love as bases for marriage are thought to have been made possible because family control and rules of enogamy had less impact in a individualistic milieu.

This essentially passive view of the family as a reacting agent has been criticized by Greenfield (1967:312-322) and Goode (1963:ch. 1) who question the assumed relationship between family change and industralization, and suggest that in reality some of the characteristics of the modern family may have been present prior to industrialization.

Furstenberg (1966:326-327) has been perhaps the most recent writer to cast doubt on the origin of modern courtship and mating practices (also Udry, 1966:19-22; Wilkinson, 1962:678-682; Mott, 1965:294-295). He points out that several of the characteristics of the modern family, such as freedom of choice, romantic love, and permissiveness in parent-child relations, were observed by European travelers in the United States during the first half of the nineteenth century.

Investigations of the emergence of particular family practices are helpful in coming to terms with history, but from a more strict sociological point of view, it is imperative that we understand what given developments in the social structure, such as industrialization, are related to what consequences in the institutional configuration.

The effort to explain contemporary social behavior presupposes a linkage between given forms of social behavior and different kinds of social structures. However, if given forms of social behavior or characterological types have always been in existence through varying social structures, the fact would raise questions about the usefulness of contemporary sociological explanations concerning many types of social behavior, and it would set a somewhat different course for the pursuit of sociological inquiry. Many issues regarding the evolution social change would be reopened, and a reexamination of the relationships between social structure, social behavior and social change would be necessitated.

The problem

Any sociological reinvestigation of history presents formidable problems with respect to available source materials and method. Travel accounts and diaries, though interesting and worthwhile, are still merely suggestive. There are difficulties in evaluating the bias of the reporter and the exent to which the contents are representative. Another troublesome but potentially significant *source of available data* are the newspaper and the magazine. In the present study, the investigation of family patterns in the pre-industrial period involved a systematic examination of colonial magazines, with a view to determining whether or

Reprinted from Herman R. Lantz, Margaret Britton, Raymond Schmitt, and Eloise C. Snyder, "Pre-Industrial Patterns in the Colonial Family in America: A Content Analysis of Colonial Magazines," American Sociological Review, 33:3, June 1968, pp. 413-426. The authors are indebted to the staff of the Morris Library, Southern Illinois University, for assistance in obtaining the source materials necessary for this project.

not particular characteristics of the modern family existed during this earlier era. Specifically, we examined the following features of the American colonial family structure: power patterns present in the man-woman relationship, types of attitudes and actions toward premarital and extramarital sexual involvement, and motivations for entering into the marital relationship. The research did not attempt to cover other important phases of the family and *is limited to these aspects.* These particular variables were selected because the traditional view of the relationship between industralization and the family structure posits that each of them was influenced considerably by the advent of industralization. Hence, we gathered evidence concerning these variables during the 1741-1794 period.

Source, method, and procedure

Our investigation of the American colonial period centered about a content analysis of fifteen magazines which were published during the years 1741-1794.[1] These time limits were based upon Mott's work (1930), *A History of American Magazines.* Mott, a leading authority on the history of journalism, divided his history into five periods: 1741-1794, 1794-1825, 1825-1850, 1850-1865, 1865-1885, and 1885-1905. Before 1741, Americans read British magazines rather than publishing their own. In fact, even during the period from 1741-1794, the British influence upon American magazines was great, with much material being reprinted directly from the British magazines. This period ended in 1794 with the Postal Act, which allowed magazines to be sent through the mails and thus increased circulation and influence. Mott's initial period included the Late Colonial Period, The Period of Revolution, and The Early Years of the New Nation; the period in which America was developing its own customs and traditions.

Mott's work also guided our decision to study the American colonial family structure on the basis of a content analysis of fifteen magazines. He indicated that the 1741-1795 period was characterized by a circulation of thirteen *important magazines.*[2] A magazine was defined by Mott (1930) as a bound pamphlet issued more or less regularly; it contained a variety of reading matter and possessed a connotation of entertainment. Magazines were judged important or unimportant by Mott (1930) on the basis of their literary worth, circulation, and influence upon the reading public. Six of these magazines were of particular interest to women, while the remaining seven were oriented toward the general public. Mott also listed two additional magazines which were of particular concern to women. Although he does not label them important, we have also included them in our study, since they were designed especially for women and contained references to the existing family structure of the period.[3]

Two characteristics of these fifteen magazines should be noted. (1) The magazines were primarily written for the middle and the upper classes. The data indicate that the typical subscriber to these magazines had servants, participated in leisurely recreation, entertained often, and was well-educated. Since the writers most likely wrote with these people in mind, the articles probably reflect the upper and middle class subcultures of the period more than the lower class subculture. (2) The magazines were all published in New England and were circulated primarily in the Northern section of America. Problems in distribution prevented extensive circulation of distant areas. Hence, conclusions of this study can *most legitimately be applied to New England's middle and upper classes during the period 1741-1794.*[4]

The universe comprised all issues of the fifteen magazines that were published during the years 1741-1794.[5] A total of 98 issues were published during the years 1741-1776, while 448 issues were published during the years 1776-1794. The entire 546 issues constituted our sample.[6]

Since it would have been extremely time consuming to read the 546 issues in their entirety, article titles were used as indicators of the relevance of the article. As the variables being coded were rarely explicitly mentioned in the titles, we considered an article to be relevant if the title indicated that it pertained to women.[7] Each of these articles was read for its general content and then reread in detail if it seemed pertinent.

The unit of analysis in content analysis may be words, themes, characters, items, etc. (Berelson, 1952:135-146), but the only unit of analysis used in this study was the *explicit discussion* of one of the variables being coded. Reliability was approached in a manner similar to that used by Sebald (1962:318-322) in his study of national character. Sebald suggests that reliability of content analysis may be approached by a consistent application of criteria for classification. This involves both specific statements and overall explicit meaning. He believes that a sufficient degree of objectivity and reproducibility may thus be achieved.[8]

A schedule was employed to examine each issue in the sample. This schedule was used to record the presence of a discussion, bibliographical data concerning each magazine, and known biases of the publishers or editors. In addition, distinctions were made between fiction and non-fiction and between an advocated pattern and existent pattern.

Once the data were tabulated, tests of significance were applied at various points in the analysis.[9] The formula for testing the difference between two proportions for uncorrelated data was used when comparisons *between* time periods were of interest.[10] The total number of issues in each of the two time periods were expressed as N_1 and N_2 in this formula.[11] The chi-square goodness-of-fit test with a correction for continuity was used for comparisons *within* time periods.[12] The assumption here, of course, was that if there is no difference between the number of discussions in the categories, the expected frequencies should equal the total number of discussions divided by the number of categories. In some instances, the latter test could not be applied because the total number of discussions was too small.

The results

POWER IN THE MAN-WOMAN RELATIONSHIP

Since the female has been traditionally viewed as occupying a subservient position relative to the male in the U.S. prior to industrialization, various aspects of the power relationships between male and female during the 1741-1794 period were investigated.

TABLE 1   Various Dimensions of Power in the Man-Woman Relationship and Source of Power by Character of Discussion (Fiction or Non-fiction), State of Power (Advocated or Existent) and Time Period (in Frequency of Discussions)

	Power in general												Power over morality											
	1741-1776						1777-1794						1741-1776						1777-1794					
	Advocated			exists			Advocated			exists			Advocated			exists			Advocated			exists		
Source of power	F[a]	N[b]	T[c]	F	N	T	F	N	T	F	N	T	F	N	T	F	N	T	F	N	T	F	N	T
Overtly by male	3	4	7	4	4	8	4	12	16	18	38	56	0	0	0	0	1	1	0	0	0	19	8	27
Overtly by female	0	0	0	1	3	4	2	0	2	2	6	8	0	0	0	0	0	0	0	0	0	0	2	2
Subtly by female	1	1	2	0	4	4	2	3	5	4	17	21	0	6	6	0	1	1	5	10	15	5	19	24
Mutual cooperation	0	3	3	0	0	0	2	10	12	1	3	4	0	0	0	0	0	0	0	0	0	0	0	0

	Power in courtship												Power over finances											
	1741-1776						1777-1794						1741-1776						1777-1794					
	Advocated			exists			Advocated			exists			Advocated			exists			Advocated			exists		
Source of power	F[a]	N[b]	T[c]	F	N	T	F	N	T	F	N	T	F	N	T	F	N	T	F	N	T	F	N	T
Overtly by male	0	0	0	0	1	1	0	0	0	1	5	6	0	0	0	0	0	0	0	0	0	1	5	6
Overtly by female	0	0	0	1	0	1	0	0	0	0	5	5	0	2	2	0	1	1	0	0	0	6	5	11
Subtly by female	0	2	2	1	2	3	0	2	2	2	12	14	0	0	0	0	0	0	0	1	1	0	0	0
Mutual cooperation	0	0	0	0	0	0	0	2	2	0	0	0	0	0	0	0	0	0	0	1	1	1	0	1

	Power in other areas												
	1741-1776						1777-1794						
	Advocated			exists			Advocated			exists			
Source of Power	F[a]	N[b]	T[c]	F	N	T	F	N	T	F	N	T	Row Sum
Overtly by male	0	0	0	0	0	0	0	0	0	0	8	8	136
Overtly by female	0	1	1	0	0	0	0	0	0	1	4	5	42
Subtly by female	0	0	0	0	0	0	0	1	1	1	3	4	105
Mutual cooperation	0	2	2	0	0	0	0	8	8	2	3	5	38

[a]F is fiction.
[b]N is non-fiction.
[c]T is total.

For our purposes, power was defined as the ability of one individual to dominate another or others, to coerce and control them, obtain obedience, interfere with their freedom, and compel their action in particular ways. The various categories of power were dictated by the magazine content. They included general discussions of power, i.e., explicit discussions of power that did not pertain to a particular form of behavior, power over morality, i.e., power over sexual, gambling, or drinking behaviors, power in the handling of finances, power in the courtship situation, and power in certain other situations, i.e., child rearing, minor decision making, etc.

As we were interested in male-female comparisons with respect to each of the power categories, the source of power was considered in all instances. Power was coded as being exerted overtly by the male, overtly by the female, subtly by the female, or by both cooperatively.[13] Subtle female power refers to situations where the female is in control but where the male may not be fully aware that he is being manipulated. These data are presented in Table 1.

Attention was first given to a comparison of those discussions wherein power was *exerted overtly* by the male and by the female. There were *136 such discussions* in the male category for the total period and *42 discussions* in the female category for the same period. The resultant p of the chi-square test was less than .001. When the male-female totals are examined in the ten *exists* columns of Table 1, it can be seen that there was significantly more discussions involving the male as the source of power in the general power category (p <.001) and in the morality category (p <.001) during the later time period. However, the differences between males and females in the finance, courtship, and other categories, during the later period were not significant at the .05 level. The difference between males and females in the general power category during the earlier period also was not significant at the .05 level. The remaining four totals could not be meaningfully tested.

The number of discussions *advocating* that overt power should be held by the male or the female were practically nil except for the general power category. For both time periods, there were more discussions involving the male: The difference for the latter period, which could be tested statistically, was significant below the .01 level.

This analysis lends considerable support to the traditional

view of the male-female power relationship before industrialization. In four instances, the male was involved in significantly more discussions than the female,[14] and in no instance was the female involved in significantly more discussions than the male. Nevertheless, it should be noted that in some power categories there was no evidence that the male possessed more overt power than the female.[15] It should also be emphasized that there were 42 discussions over the total period that either indicated that the female possessed overt power or advocated that she should possess it.

Attention was next given to those discussions that reflected subtle power on the part of the female. As we were essentially interested in the overall power position of the woman relative to the power position of the male, the discussions that indicated either *overt or subtle* female power were compared with those discussions that indicated overt male power.[16]

There were *136 discussions of male overt power* during the entire period and *147 discussions of female power* (overt and subtle) for the same period. The resultant p of the chi-square test was not significant at the .05 level. When the male-female totals are examined in the ten *exists* columns of Table 1, it is found that there were significantly more discussions involving the male *only* in the general power category during the later period (p <.01), and there were significantly more female discussions in the courtship category during the later period (p <.02). Also, there were no significant differences at the .05 level between males and females in the morality, finance, and other categories during the later period. Nor was there any difference at this level of significance in the general power category during the earlier period. The remaining four totals could not be meaningfully tested.[17]

With respect to the courtship category during the later period, the data suggest that the male had the power of choosing whom to court (or who was to court his daughter), but the female may have had control of the relationship through the threatened, or actual withholding of affection and through "playing the coquette." The data also suggest that the female controlled the courtship process, similar to Willard Waller's principle of least interest, by which the one with the least interest in the continuance of a relationship controls it.

The implications of our data are that authority was normatively vested in the male (the initial analysis of male and female overt power implies this), but that this authority was not *de facto* always exercised by the male. More often than by use of subtle power rather than by overt power, the female apparently was able to exercise influence in various areas (Becker and Hill, 1955:135). The data indicate that she exerted significantly greater influence than the male in the area of courtship during the later period, and that she may have had an equal influence in the finance, morality, and other categories during the later period. There were also significantly more discussions advocating that the female should have power rather than the male in the area of morality during the later period.[18]

The existence of subtle female power does not necessarily indicate that the family in this period was not male dominated. The pattern of subtle female power may be viewed as a reaction to or a way of dealing with male authority. Our findings do suggest areas of delineation in regard to how power may have been distributed and expressed by husband and wife. The data also raise relevant questions about the role subtle female power. If power represents the ability to move others, then obviously the female possessed power. The basic questions raised by our findings are as follows: How much subtle female power can be said to be present before power shifts from the man to the woman? Did subtle female power ever reach a point where the woman was, in fact, in control? Does the marked evidence for subtle female power suggest that the colonial family was in a period of dynamic change prior to industrialization?

Certainly it is true that the impact of industrialization was to enable subtle power to be supplanted by more open patterns of assertion and persuasion. Was this necessarily a change in actual power, or a change in the form in which power was expressed, or both? These are questions to be raised; our study provides no answers for them, however.

THE ROMANTIC LOVE COMPLEX

It is commonly believed that the romantic love complex which presently forms the basis for marriage in our society was essentially a consequence of industrialization (Goodsell, 1938:215-216; Furstenberg, 1936:326-327). We have already noted that Goode (1936) has raised doubts in this regard. Furstenberg (1966:330) notes in his study of European travelers to the United States during 1800-1850 that "most of the observers praised the American marriage system because it permitted young people to select mates whom they loved and with whom they could enjoy a happy marriage." Stewart (1954:182) has similarly stated, regarding the courtship process during the latter part of the colonial period, that "...in general, the attitude toward marriage might be termed 'moderately romantic.'" Our universe of magazines was examined for evidence concerning the romantic love complex. Romantic love has been defined in terms of five dimensions.

1. *Idealization of the Loved One* (Bell, 1963:107).
2. *The One and Only.*
3. *Love at First Sight.*
4. *Love Wins Out Over All.*
5. *Glorification of Personal Emotions.*

Examples of discussions depicting romantic love from the data are:

When I am not with her in the day, her enchanting image pursues me; and when I retire to sleep, she fills my every idea; I slumber . . . I wake, and starting up in agony, wander round my chamber maniac-like. . . .[19]
Here uncontroul'd foll'wing natures voice,
The happy lovers make the unchanging choice,
While mutual passions in their bosoms glow,
While soft confessions in their kisses flow,
While their free hands in plighted faith are given,
Their vows accordant reach approving Heaven.[20]

The frequency of discussions occurring in each of these categories is presented in Table 2. The character of the discussion (poetry, other fiction, and non-fiction) and the

TABLE 2   *Indicators of the Romantic Love Complex and Character of Discussion (Poetry, Other Fiction, and Non-fiction by Time Period in Number of Discussions)*

	1741-1776				1777-1794				
The indicator	*Poetry*	*Other fiction*	*Non-fiction*	*Total*	*Poetry*	*Other fiction*	*Non-fiction*	*Total*	*Summary*
Idealization of the loved one	2	1	6	9	24	52	17	93	102
The one and only	0	1	2	3	12	42	5	59	62
Love at first sight	0	1	2	3	2	21	3	26	29
Love wins out over all	2	1	7	10	12	46	17	75	85
Glorification of personal emotions	0	0	1	1	23	29	6	58	59
Total	4	4	18	26	73	190	48	311	337

TABLE 3   *Marital Motive and Holder of Motive by Character of Discussion (Fiction and Non-fiction) by Time Period (in Number of Discussions)*

	1741-1776							1777-1794							
	Fiction			*Non-fiction*				*Fiction*			*Non-fiction*				
The motive	*Parent*	*Ego*	*Not specified*	*Parent*	*Ego*	*Not specified*	*Total*	*Parent*	*Ego*	*Not specified*	*Parent*	*Ego*	*Not specified*	*Total*	*Row sum*
Happiness	0	0	1	0	6	3	10	13	40	5	4	11	14	87	97
Wealth	0	0	0	3	1	2	6	22	12	3	5	2	2	46	52
Status	0	0	0	0	0	0	0	11	2	0	1	1	0	15	15
Total	0	0	1	3	7	5	16	46	54	8	10	14	16	148	164

time period in which the indicator occurred are also shown in Table 2.

The most significant aspect of Table 2 is the unexpected number of discussions which portrayed the romantic love complex. There were *337 discussions* for the entire period.[21] Each of these discussions (poetry, other fiction, and non-fiction) described the romantic love complex as being in existence. There were only nine *other* discussions (not included in Table 2) wherein the authors indicated that romantic love did not exist. Eight *other* discussions advocated that the romantic love complex be made the basis for the man-woman relationship, while nine *other* discussions opposed romantic love as the basis for marriage. The majority of the 337 discussions occurred during the later period (p <.001). A significant number of these discussions occurred in fiction (poetry and other fiction) rather than in non-fiction (p <.001). The discussions during both periods were fairly evenly spread across the five categories in Table 2. However, the idealization category and the love-wins-out-over-all category contained the highest frequencies during both periods. The love-at-first-sight category during the later period had the lowest frequency.[22]

The data certainly indicate that the romantic love complex was known in colonial American society and that, indeed, it may have been a common pattern among large sections of the upper status groups. Thus, with regard to the impact of industrialization, it may well be that indus-

trialization *facilitated* the development of a romantic love complex already in *existence*. Finally, presence of the romantic love complex must be seen in the broader context of the emergence of individualism and the role of personal wishes as an important basis in mate choice.

Although the romantic love complex was often discussed, other motivations for marriage existed, and these were considered. It was found that only three motives of this type were discussed with any regularity in the magazines—*happiness, wealth,* and *status*. We noted whether these motives were held by the individuals entering into the marital relationship or by their parents. The motive of happiness was indicated when the person in courtship or the parents perceived enjoyment as a major reason for marrying a particular person. The motive of wealth was indicated if selection was based primarily on financial aspects. The motive of status was indicated if the end of marriage was primarily to acquire a mate from a family with an *equal* or *higher* social standing. Social status was indicated in the literature by such expressions as "from a good family," or "people of an equal rank and fortune," etc. The data are presented in Table 3.

Although the reader may wish to make a more detailed analysis of Table 3, the final row sums are of primary interest to us at this point. For the entire period, there were *ninety-seven discussions* that indicated that *happiness* was regarded as a motive for entering marriage; *fifty-two discussions* indicate that wealth was regarded as a motive for

TABLE 4   Attitudes that Sanctions Should Be Implemented toward Individuals Involved in Premarital or Extramarital Sexual Relations during the 1777-1794 Period by Character of Discussion and by Sex (in Frequency of Discussions)

Sanction (attitude)	Male			Female			
	Fiction	Non-fiction	Total	Fiction	Non-fiction	Total	
Punishment	0	1	1	0	0	0	1
Ostracism	14	19	33	2	0	2	35
Sympathy	0	0	0	23	16	39	39
Total	14	20	34	25	16	41	75

TABLE 5   Sanctions Implemented toward Individuals Involved in Premarital or Extramarital Sexual Relations during the 1777-1794 Period by Character of Discussion and by Sex (in Frequency of Discussions)

Sanction (behavior	Male			Female			Row sum
	Fiction	Non-fiction	Total	Fiction	Non-fiction	Total	
Punishment	1	0	1	4	5	9	10
Ostracism	0	0	0	26	18	44	44
Sympathy	1	2	3	3	1	4	7
Total	2	2	4	33	24	57	61

entering marriage, while only *fifteen discussions* gave any indication that social status was a motive for entering into the marital union. It should be observed that there were significantly more discussions of these three motives during the later period (p <.001), and a significantly greater number of these discussions occurred in fiction (p <.001).

The frequency with which personal happiness as motivation for marriage appears (a motivation compatible with the romantic love complex), adds weight to our previous conclusions with respect to the existence of the romantic love complex in America during the colonial period. Moreover, this result is in direct contrast to the traditional discussions of strong economic and utilitarian goals that were said to characterize the marital union in the pre-industrial period.

SEXUAL STANDARDS

The traditional view holds that industrialization tended to liberalize the sexual norms in the American social system. The belief is that the conservative sexual norms of the post-industrial period were modified by the industrial revolution *and* the corresponding movement towards urbanization. Reiss (1960:67), for example, in his consideration of premarital sexual standards in America, maintains this position:

Another consequence of city life was the lessening of social controls and resultant increases in indivergent viewpoints. In short, the city did not have the intimacy, the control by reputation and gossip which the farm or the small town had. People hardly knew their neighbors and were not as strongly concerned with their opinions. Then, too, in the small town, there was usually general agreement on what was proper; in the city, this agreement was often lacking, so that if one group of people criticized a person, it would not be difficult to find another group supporting

him in his position. Thus, individualization of behavior was encouraged. *This situation, of course, helped destroy many of the older sexual standards and made possible the growth of newer, more liberal and equalitarian standards.*[23]

Since there were few direct references to the actual sexual normative structure of the period, certain indirect indices of the prevailing sexual norms of the period had to be used. Consequently, we decided to analyze the content of the magazines in terms of the sanctions that were exhibited towards those individuals who deviated from the existing sexual mores of the period. Sanctions were selected as the indicator for two reasons: (1) They appeared to be a reasonable indicator of the existing sexual normative structure. (2) They were discussed in the magazine content.

There were three forms of sanctions that appeared with any regularity in the important magazine content of the period: (1) punishment, (2) ostracism, and (3) sympathy.[24] At times, these discussions indicated that the particular sanction *had been* implemented toward the person mentioned in the article, while in other instances, the writers indicated that the particular sanction *should* be implemented toward the person being discussed in the article. Hence, the three forms of sanctions were classified into one of two categories—*behavior or attitudes.* The data are presented in Tables 4 and 5.

These tables concern only the 1777-1794 period, since there were only three discussions of sanctions during the 1741-1776 period. Two of these indicated that the female had been ostracized for deviating from the sexual mores, and one advocated that the male should be ostracized for his deviation. Each of these discussions occurred in non-fiction.[25]

There were seventy-five discussions during the 1777-1794 period advocating that our three designated sanctions *ought to be implemented* towards the sexual deviator (see Table 4). Thirty-nine of these occurred in fiction, while thirty-six occurred in non-fiction. There was only one indication that physical punishment should be given to those involved in premarital and extramarital sexual affairs, and the indication was that the male should receive this punishment. There were, however, thirty-five instances in which it was proposed that the deviator should be ostracized. Interestingly, thirty-three of these discussions concerned the male, whereas only two concerned the female (p <.001). Fourteen of the discussions involving the male occurred in fiction, while nineteen appeared in non-fiction. On the other hand, there were no advocates of sympathy for the male offender, although sympathy was indicated for the female in thirty-nine instances (p <.001). Twenty-three of these discussions occurred in fiction and sixteen occurred in non-fiction. Thus, the data suggest that with respect to attitudes toward the sexual deviator, *the male was to be ostracized and the female was to receive sympathy.*

There were sixty-one discussions during the 1777-1794 period which indicated that our three designated sanctions had been implemented towards the sexual deviator (see Table 5). Thirty-five of these occurred in fiction, while twenty-six appeared in non-fiction. There was only one indication that physical punishment was inflicted upon the male, and this was a fictional episode that concerned self-inflicted punishment: suicide. There were nine instances, however, wherein physical punishment was inflicted upon the female (p <.05). Five of these negative sanctions were suicide and four were legal punishments, i.e., fines, jail sentences, or whippings. Similarly, there were forty-four discussions wherein the female was ostracized, but there was not a single discussion that indicated that the male was ostracized for his sexual deviation (p <.001). Seven discussions fell into the sympathy category, and these were divided approximately evenly between males and females. Thus, the data suggest that with respect to behavior toward the sexual deviator, *the female was physically punished or ostracized, while the male was not.*

Although one must exert caution in generalizing from the quantity and quality of these presentations to conclusions regarding the normative sexual structure of the period,[26] the evidence implies that the prevailing norm(s) of the period concerning premarital and extramarital sexual relationships were of the *ancient double standard type and/or of the formal standard of abstinence type* (Reiss, 1960:chs. 4 and 9). The following reasons are offered for this conclusion: (1) The only sanctions that were discussed with any regularity in the literature were negative ones. If a liberal or semiliberal normative structure had existed with regard to the behaviors under consideration, this *probably* would not have been the case. Physical punishment and ostracism were advocated for, and implemented against, the sexual deviator, and these sanctions are typically considered to be rather severe overt negative sanctions. Even sympathy cannot be viewed as a positive sanction since it was typically advocated or given only if the person had engaged in premarital or extramarital sexual relationships due to circumstances out of his control (force) or because he had become involved as a result of his sincerity and trust in

others. This implies that such behavior was culturally prohibited. It should also be noted that many of the discussions involving sanctions occurred in non-fiction. (2) The sanctions were differentially applied toward the male and the female. Although punishment was advocated for the male and sympathy for the female, the literature also indicates that the female was physically punished or ostracized, while the male was not. The following quote is indicative of a discussion reflecting the double standard which seemed to be well entrenched.

Nothing but an unjust custom has rendered vice in a man less odious than in a woman; and shall we smile upon, and approve of a custom that is so encouraging to them, and so destructive to us? Were those in particular, who glory in seducing, and betraying innocence, to meet with the contempt they deserve, and the neglect of every person of virtue, they would soon be ashamed of their practices, and reduced to the necessity of quitting their unlawful pursuits. But while they are caressed, and admitted into the best companies they find restraint unnecessary . . . women are said to be the weaker vessel; and but few men will allow them to be equal in strength of mind; yet is the uprightness and rectitude of angels expected from them: instead of imputing their errors to the defect of their judgment, and the inferiority of understanding they pretend to reduce them to, they view every failing in an aggravated light, and for one false step forever deprive them of all that renders life valuable, and, although (as is often the case) their mistake may be owing to ignorance, inexperience, or a credulity that results from an honest heart, their persons are despised, their company avoided and their characters sacrificed . . . while the base betrayer is suffered to triumph in the success of his unmanly arts, and to pass unpunished even by a frown . . . surely compassion is due to misfortune, even if it arises from misconduct.[27]

(3) There was no substantial evidence in the literature that the female was expected to be, or allowed to be, permissive in her sexual behavior before or outside of marriage.[28] There were no recurrent discussions of positive sanctions for such behavior, nor were there any indications that the female should have such rights.[29] This is particularly noteworthy because of the traditional view that industralization tended to liberalize the sexual norms of our society in that the female, more than the male, was accorded additional rights and privileges in the area of sex (Reiss, 1960:Chs. 2, 5, 6). Certain other evidence not presented in Tables 4 and 5 also lends support to this conclusion. There were, for example, fourteen discussions of illegitimacy. These were generally very sentimental and moralizing the great emphasis placed on the *dire* consequences of sexual deviance. Ten other discourses emphasized the dire alternatives that were open to the female who had engaged in premarital intercourse.[30]

Summary and implications

The primary goal of this research was to examine *selected* aspects of the colonial American family structure via the content analysis procedure in order to determine whether certain facets of current family structure which have been attributed largely to the effects of industrialization were in evidence earlier.

Some aspects of the American family structure usually attributed to the effects of industrialization were noted in the important magazine content of the pre-industrial period. This appears to be the case regarding the existence of the *romantic love complex*, and the influence which this may have had on personal freedom in mate selection. Although there was some evidence to support the traditional view that economic goals and parental control in mate selection were present in the colonial courtship process, there was a considerably greater number of discussions that involved a component of the *romantic love complex*. Similarly, the findings with respect to motive in mate choice indicate the importance placed on *personal happiness* in contrast to traditional economic concerns.

The results regarding power indicate a patriarchal pattern with considerable subtle female power. These findings raise interesting questions regarding the meaning and significance of subtle female power in the family. It seems important to understand more about the dimensions of power in the pre-industrial family: Was power a single or multi-faceted phenomenon? Under what conditions and in what manner was power, overt and subtle, *exercised* and *expressed*. Finally, was subtle female power ever developed to a point where control did, in fact, rest with the woman of the house?

Although the evidence dealing with romantic love raises important questions regarding some patterns of the pre-industrial family, the data on sex do not. The evidence here is consistent with the general view regarding the conservative nature of sexual norms, including some evidence for the existence of the double standard.[31]

To be sure, the results obtained in this report should be interpreted with caution for several reasons. In this regard, there is always the problem of the limitations. *Not all aspects of the colonial family were studied.* The peculiar strategical decisions of the study should be evaluated. The inherent restrictions of the content analysis procedure must be kept in mind. The use of literary documents presents limitations with regard to our ability to generalize about social behavior, but such difficulty, more pronounced in research of this type, is a general problem we confront in social research. All we may add is that the prevalence of particular points of view in magazines concerned with sex, marriage, and family behavior suggest a *concern for*, and *preoccupation with* these areas among a section of the populace. While one might expect occasional articles to appear on any subject, the *frequency of discussions*, as indicated in this paper, clearly suggests that some patterns consistent with the modern industrial family were present in the colonial period, although we recognize that frequency of themes may not always be a reliable indicator.[32]

In addition, while the class bias of the magazines must be recognized, it may be that the more privileged classes represented a model upon which other groups may have patterned their behavior. It may also be that the magazines studied that were published in England represented the views of a more highly industrialized society than was the case in the colonies at the time. Nevertheless, the problems presented by an empirical reexamination of the family in an earlier period are so formidable that the task is one of seeking out innovative ways of dealing with the data while making efforts to refine and improve such methods.

Why is history so relevant in this regard? As sociologists, we may be inclined to view the past, in this instance the colonial family social structure, as more homogeneous, integrated and consistent than it was in fact, forgetting, for example, even the significance of class differences. We are aided in this view by a rural myth of simplicity and homogeneity. Yet we also realize that *consensus, integration,* and *change* reveal themselves in varying ways, depending at what point in time the investigation is undertaken. The colonial family was undoubtedly a family in transition, perhaps in some areas a *more marked transition* than is commonly recognized.

Unless we can document the past with *base lines*, it becomes difficult to differentiate the dimensions and the extent of change. Such investigations might be especially helpful in refining our understanding of the relationship between industrialization and the family.

NOTES

1. The standard source with respect to this method is still Berelson (1952). For a more recent discussion of this method see De Sola Pool (1959).
We also divided this time period into two subperiods in order to examine any changes that might have occurred in the family structure during this critical period of history. The year 1776 was used as a breaking point due to its historical importance.
2. These thirteen magazines were: *The American Magazine,* December, 1787-November, 1788. *The American Magazine and Historical Chronicle.* September, 1743-December, 1746. *The American Magazine and Monthly Chronicle for the British Colonies.* October, 1757-October, 1758. *The American Magazine, or A Monthly View of the Political State of The British Colonies.* January, 1741-March, 1741. *The American Museum, or Repository of Ancient and Modern Fugitive Pieces, etc., Prose and Poetical (The American Museum, or Universal Magazine,* 1790-1792). January, 1787-December, 1792. *The Christian's, Scholar's and Farmer's Magazine.* April-May, 1789-February-March, 1791. *The Columbian Magazine, or Monthly Miscellany (The Universal Asylum and Columbia Magazine,* 1790-1792). September, 1786-December, 1792. *The General Magazine, and Historical Chronicle, For All the British Plantations in America.* January, 1741-June, 1741. *The Massachusetts Magazine or Monthly Museum of Knowledge and Rational Entertainment.* January, 1789-December, 1796. *The New York Magazine or Literary Repository.* January, 1790-December, 1797. *The Pennsylvania Magazine or American Monthly Museum.* January, 1775-July, 1776. *The Royal American Magazine, or Universal Repository of Instruction and Amusement,* January, 1774-March, 1775. *The Worcester Magazine Containing Politicks, Miscellanies, Poetry and News.* First week of April, 1786-Last week of March, 1787.
3. These two magazines were entitled *Boston Magazine,* and *Lady's Magazine and Repository of Entertaining Knowledge.*
4. However, this is a conservative position. The conclusions *may* also extend to the lower class of New England and/or to other regions of the United States.
5. Six of the magazines were published in the 1741-1776 period and nine in the 1777-1794 period.
6. We felt that this procedure would eliminate any sampling error with respect to the selection of issues.
7. This criterion was selected for two reasons: (1) The variables being coded, power patterns presented in the man-woman relationship, the presence of the romantic love complex in the man-woman relationship, types of attitudes and actions toward premarital and extramarital sexual involvement, and motivations for entering into the marital relationship, all involved women. (2) If authors were ignoring women during any part of this period of history, this criterion should offset this bias somewhat. Mott (1930:64-67) discusses this point.
8. However, a *blind reliability check* was undertaken on a random sample of the magazines previously examined with respect to *one* of the variables considered in the *initial* analysis, i.e., the romantic love complex. This check *suggested* that the initial results may have been *slightly conservative.* (A correlation coefficient was not calculated since we felt it might tend to *overemphasize* the *exactness* of the

check.) *If* this conservatism did tend generally to characterize our initial results, it would in fact strengthen our conclusions *in most instances*. The reader should, of course, evaluate each *specific* conclusion in light of this footnote.

9. As we had included the whole universe of issues in our sample, our data did not actually represent a random sample. Nevertheless, we felt it was legitimate to use tests of significance since this universe could realistically be viewed as a random sample from some *hypothetical* universe, i.e., the universe of all important published material during this period. Hagood (1941:ch. 17) discusses this. Two-tailed tests were used at all times.

10. Since many of our proportions were extreme, i.e., less than .10, we based the standard error of the difference on the proportion in the two groups combined. Downie and Heath (1965:148-151) discuss this.

11. Although this formula standardizes for the difference in the number of issues between the two periods, the possibility exists that the lengths of the issues may have varied.

12. Although at times several discussions occurred in a single article, the discussions generally represented independent events, i.e., the classification of the N + 1 discussions were not *systematically* dependent upon the classification of the initial discussions. However, independence of units has been a problem in content analysis studies (for example Osgood, 1959:65) and some readers may wish to view the statistical results only as benchmarks.

13. Instances of subtle male power were almost never discussed.

14. This includes the comparison that was made between male and female overt power for the entire period. It is also noteworthy that 63 percent of the discussions involving overt male power occurred in non-fiction.

15. The reader is cautioned to keep in mind the possibility of a Type II error.

16. These combined totals are not presented in Table 1. However, the reader can easily obtain these totals from the given data if he so desires. For example, there were 42 discussions over the total period that reflected overt female power, and there were 105 discussions for the same period that indicated subtle female power. Hence, there were 147 discussions of overt or subtle female power for the entire period.

17. Comparisons were also made between the male overt power totals and the combined female subtle and overt power tools in the ten *advocates* power columns in Table 1. Only two of these totals were large enough to test statistically. In these instances, it was found that (1) there were significantly more discussions advocating that the female have power rather than the male in the morality category during the latter period (p < .001), and (2) while there were more male discussions in the general power category during the later period, the difference was not significant at the .05 level.

18. The necessity of power in the hands of the widow hints at Lantz's (1958:ch. 5) hypothesis that "a mother-centered, or mother-dominated home, is believed to have developed out of situations in which the continuation of the father's role was in danger."

19. The Drone, XXI, *The New York Magazine*, April, 1794, p. 198.

20. "A Poem on the Happiness of America," *Boston Magazine*, August, 1786, p. 351.

21. It should also be noted that there were 57 discussions of individualism in marriage choice, i.e., the selection of the marriage partner by ego rather than by someone else, during the entire period. Although individualism is not a *sufficient* condition with respect to the existence of the romantic love complex, it is a *necessary* condition with respect to its existence. For this reason, we did not consider it to be an unquestionable indicator of the romantic love complex. However, the existence of the 57 discussions on individualism indicates that the romantic love complex *could have been* in existence.

22. Although it should be viewed only as a *posthoc* suggestion, the idea occurred to us that if one were to hypothesize concerning the *development* of the romantic love complex in a particular social system, it would be logical to suspect that various components of the *complex* might be likely to emerge before other components. Further, it might be argued that the emphasis on *love* and the emphasis on love *toward the loved one* would precede other indicators of love, such as love at first sight. In other words, one would not suspect the courtship system to be characterized by "love at first sight," *unless* love, and the loved one, were already emphasized as desirable in the culture. It so happens that our data fit this hypothesis.

23. Our italics.

24. A discussion which indicated that a person should or did receive understanding when premarital or extramarital sexual relations occurred because he was a victim of circumstances beyond his control (force) or because he became involved as a result of sincerity and trust in others was included in one of the sympathy categories.

25. This represents the same pattern that was observed during the later period (see below).

26. A twofold caution should be exercised at this point. We not only have the problem of making inferences from the magazine content to the real world but we also have to make inferences from our working definitions (sanctions) to our concept (sexual norms).

27. Letter to the Editor, *Boston Magazine,* August, 1784, p. 419-420.

28. Of course, the possibility of a Type II error exists.

29. Certain of the discussions, however, expressed dissatisfaction with the "extreme" rights of the male in the sexual area.

30. It should be noted that a majority of the discussions referred to under point four occurred in non-fiction.

31. It should be observed that with respect to differences in the proportion of discussions of various aspects of the family structure between the two periods—1741-1776 and 1777-1794—it was typically observed that more discussions occurred during the later period. However, we cannot be sure *why* this happened. It may be a function of the American Revolution, or of an increased interest in the family structure, or of certain other factors. Perhaps future research will illuminate this point.

32. Albrecht (1956:722-729), dealing with contemporary media, believes short stories in wide circulation reflect cultural norms and values (of family) but cautions against the frequency of themes as a reliable basis for such an assumption. Backman (1956:729-733) also discusses this.

REFERENCES

Albrecht, Milton C. 1956. "Does literature reflect common values?" American Sociological Review 21:722-729.

Backman, Carl W. 1956. "Sampling mass media content: the use of the cluster design." American Sociological Review 21:729-733.

Becker, Howard and Reuben Hill (eds.). 1955. Family, Marriage and Parenthood. 2nd Ed. Boston: D.C. Heath and Company.

Bell, Robert R. 1963. Marriage and Family Interaction. Homewood, Illinois: The Dorsey Press, Inc.

Berelson, Bernard. 1952. Content Analysis in Communication Research. New York: Free Press of Glencoe.

De Sola Pool, Ithiel (ed.). 1959. Trends in Content Analysis. Urbana, Illinois: University of Illinois Press.

Downie, N. M. and R. W. Heath, 1954. Basic Statistical Methods. 2nd Ed. New York: Harper and Row.

Furstenberg, Frank F., Jr. 1966. "Industrialization and the American family: a look backward." American Sociological Review 31 (June):326-337.

Goode, W. J. 1963. World Revolution and Family Patterns. New York: Free Press of Glencoe, Ch. 1.

Goodsell, Willystine. 1938, Pp. 215-216 in Bernhard J. Stein (ed.), The Family in the Nineteenth Century. New York: Appleton Century Crofts.

Greenfield, Sidney M., 1967. "Industrialization and the family in sociological theory." American Journal of Sociology 67:312-32.

Hagood, Margaret Jarman. 1941. Statistics for Sociologists. New York: Henry Holt and Company.

Lantz, Herman R. 1958. People of Coal Town. New York: Columbia University Press.

Mott, Frank Luther. 1930. A History of American Magazines: 1741-1850. Vol. 1. New York: D. Appleton and Company.

Mott, Paul E. 1965. The Organization of Society. Englewood Cliffs, New Jersey: Prentice-Hall.

Osgood, Charles E. 1959. "The representational model of relevant research methods." P. 65 in Ithiel De Sola Pool (ed.), Trends in Content Analysis. Urbana Illinois: University of Illinois Press.

Reiss, Ira L. 1960. Premarital Sexual Standards in America. Glencoe, Illinois: The Free Press.

Sebald, Hans. 1962. "Studying national character through comparative analysis." Social Forces 40 (May): 318-322.

Stewart, George R. 1954. American Ways of Life. New York: Country Life Press.

Udry, J. Richard. 1966. The Social Context of Marriage. New York: J. B. Lippincott.

Wilkinson, Thomas O. 1962. "Family structure and industrialization in Japan." American Sociological Review 27:678-682.

30 A cross-cultural survey of some sex differences in socialization

Herbert Barry III
Margaret K. Bacon
Irvin L. Child

In our society, certain differences may be observed between the typical personality characteristics of the two sexes. These sex differences in personality are generally believed to result in part from differences in the way boys and girls are reared. To the extent that personality differences between the sexes are thus of cultural rather than biological origin, they seem potentially susceptible to change. But how readily susceptible to change? In the differential rearing of the sexes does our society make an arbitrary imposition on an infinitely plastic biological base, or is this cultural imposition found uniformly in all societies as an adjustment to the real biological differences between the sexes? This paper reports one attempt to deal with this problem.

Data and procedures

The data used were ethnographic reports, available in the anthropological literature, about socialization practices of various cultures. One hundred and ten cultures, mostly nonliterate, were studied. They were selected primarily in terms of the existence of adequate ethnographic reports of socialization practices and secondarily so as to obtain a wide and reasonably balanced geographical distribution. Various aspects of socialization of infants and children were rated on a 7-point scale by two judges (Mrs. Bacon and Mr. Barry). Where the ethnographic reports permitted, separate ratings were made for the socialization of boys and girls. Each rating was indicated as either confident or doubtful; with still greater uncertainty, or with complete lack of evidence, the particular rating was of course not made at all. We shall restrict the report of sex difference ratings to cases in which both judges made a confident rating. Also omitted is the one instance where the two judges reported a sex difference in opposite directions, as it demonstrates only unreliability of judgment. The number of cultures that meet these criteria is much smaller than the total of 110; for the several variables to be considered, the number varies from 31 to 84.

The aspects of socialization on which ratings were made included:

1. Several criteria of attention and indulgence toward infants.

2. Strength of socialization from age 4 or 5 years until shortly before puberty, with respect to five systems of behavior; strength of socialization was defined as the combination of positive pressure (rewards for the behavior) plus negative pressure (punishments for lack of the behavior). The variables were:

(a) Responsibility or dutifulness training. (The data were such that training in the performance of chores in the productive or domestic economy was necessarily the principal source of information here; however, training in the performance of other duties was also taken into account when information was available.)

(b) Nurturance training, i.e., training the child to be nurturant or helpful toward younger siblings and other dependent people.

(c) Obedience training.

(d) Self-reliance training.

(e) Achievement training, i.e., training the child to orient his behavior toward standards of excellence in performance, and to seek to achieve as excellent a performance as possible.

Where the term "no sex difference" is used here, it may mean any of three things: (a) the judge found separate evidence about the training of boys and girls on this particular variable and judged it to be identical; (b) the judge found a difference between the training of boys and girls, but not great enough for the sexes to be rated a whole point apart on a 7-point scale; (c) the judge found evidence only about the training of "children" on this variable, the ethnographer not reporting separately about boys and girls.

Sex differences in socialization

On the various aspects of attention and indulgence toward infants, the judges almost always agreed in finding no

Reprinted from Herbert Barry III, Margaret K. Bacon, and Irvin L. Child, "A Cross-Cultural Survey of Some Sex Differences in Socialization," Journal of Abnormal and Social Psychology, 55:3, Nov. 1957, pp. 327-332. This research is part of a project for which financial support was provided by the Social Science Research Council and the Ford Foundation. We are greatly indebted to G. P. Murdock for supplying us with certain data, as indicated below, and to him and Thomas W. Maretzki for suggestions that have been used in this paper.

TABLE 1   *Ratings of Cultures for Sex Differences on Five Variables of Childhood Socialization Pressure*

Variable	Number of cultures	Both judges agree in rating the variable higher in		On judge rates no difference, one rates the variable higher in		Percentages of cultures with evidence of sex difference in direction		
		Girls	Boys	Girls	Boys	Girls	Boys	Neither
Nurturance	33	17	0	10	0	82%	0%	18%
Obedience	69	6	0	18	2	35%	3%	62%
Responsibility	84	25	2	26	7	61%	11%	28%
Achievement	31	0	17	1	10	3%	87%	10%
Self-reliance	82	0	64	0	6	0%	85%	15%

sex difference. Out of 96 cultures for which the ratings included the infancy period, 88 (92%) were rated with no sex difference by either judge for any of those variables. This result is consistent with the point sometimes made by anthropologists that "baby" generally is a single status undifferentiated by sex, even though "boy" and "girl" are distinct statuses.

On the variables of childhood socialization, on the other hand, a rating of no sex difference by both judges was much less common. This finding of no sex difference varied in frequency from 10% to the cultures for the achievement variable up to 62% of the cultures for the obedience variable, as shown in the last column of Table 1. Where a sex difference is reported, by either one or both judges, the difference tends strongly to be in a particular direction, as shown in the earlier columns of the same table. Pressure toward nurturance, obedience, and responsibility is most often stronger for girls, whereas pressure toward achievement and self-reliance is most often stronger for boys.

For nurturance and for self-reliance, all the sex differences are in the same direction. For achievement there is only one exception to the usual direction of difference, and for obedience only two; but for responsibility there are nine. What do these exceptions mean? We have reexamined all these cases. In most of them, only one judge had rated the sexes as differently treated (sometimes one judge, sometimes the other), and in the majority of these cases both judges were now inclined to agree that there was no convincing evidence of a real difference. There were exceptions, however, especially in cases where a more formal or systematic training of boys seemed to imply greater pressure on them toward responsibility. The most convincing cases were the Masai and Swazi, where both judges had originally agreed in rating responsibility pressures greater in boys than in girls. In comparing the five aspects of socialization we may conclude that responsibility shows by far the strongest evidence of real variation in the direction of sex difference, and obedience much the most frequently shows evidence of no sex difference at all.

In subsequent discussion we shall be assuming that the obtained sex differences in the socialization ratings reflect true sex differences in the cultural practices. We should consider here two other possible sources of these rated differences.

1. The ethnographers could have been biased in favor of seeing the same pattern of sex differences as in our culture.

However, most anthropologists readily perceive and eagerly report novel and startling cultural features, so we may expect them to have reported unusual sex differences where they existed. The distinction between matrilineal and patrilineal, and between matrilocal and patrilocal cultures, given prominence in many ethnographic reports, shows an awareness of possible variations in the significance of sex differences from culture to culture.

2. The two judges could have expected to find in other cultures the sex roles which are familiar in our culture and inferred them from the material on the cultures. However, we have reported only confident ratings, and such a bias seems less likely here than for doubtful ratings. It might be argued, moreover, that bias has more opportunity in the cases ambiguous enough so that only one judge reported a sex difference, and less opportunity in the cases where the evidence is so clear that both judges agree. Yet in general, as may be seen in Table 1, the deviant cases are somewhat more frequent among the cultures where only one judge reported a sex difference.

The observed differences in the socialization of boys and girls are consistent with certain universal tendencies in the differentiation of adult sex role. In the economic sphere, men are more frequently allotted tasks that involve leaving home and engaging in activities where a high level of skill yields important returns; hunting is a prime example. Emphasis on training in self-reliance and achievement for boys would function as preparation for such an economic role. Women, on the other hand, are more frequently allotted tasks at or near home that minister most immediately to the needs of others (such as cooking and water carrying); these activities have a nurturant character, and in their pursuit a responsible carrying out of established routines is likely to be more important than the development of an especially high order of skill. Thus training in nurturance, responsibility, and, less clearly, obedience, may contribute to preparation for this economic role. These consistencies with adult role go beyond the economic sphere, of course. Participation in warfare, as a male prerogative, calls for self-reliance and a high order of skill where survival or death is the immediate issue. The childbearing which is biologically assigned to women, and the child care which is socially assigned primarily to them, lead to nurturant behavior and often call for a more continuous responsibility than do the tasks carried out by men. Most of these distinctions in adult role are not inevitable, but the biological differences between the sexes strongly predispose the distinction of role, if made, to be in a uniform direction.[1]

The relevant biological sex differences are conspicuous in adulthood but generally not in childhood. If each generation were left entirely to its own devices, therefore, without even an older generation to copy, sex differences in role would presumably be almost absent in childhood and would have to be developed after puberty at the expense of considerable relearning on the part of one or both sexes. Hence, a pattern of child training which foreshadows adult differences can serve the useful function of minimizing what Benedict termed "discontinuities in cultural conditioning" (1).

The differences in socialization between the sexes in our society, then, are no arbitrary custom of our society, but a very widespread adaptation of culture to the biological substratum of human life.

Variations in degree of sex differentiation

While demonstrating near-universal tendencies in direction or difference between the socialization of boys and girls, our data do not show perfect uniformity. A study of the variations in our data may allow us to see some of the conditions which are associated with, and perhaps give rise to, a greater or smaller degree of this difference. For this purpose, we classified cultures as having relatively large or small sex difference by two different methods, one more inclusive and the other more selective. In both methods the ratings were at first considered separately for each of the five variables. A sex difference rating was made only if both judges made a rating of this variable and at least one judge's rating was confident.

In the more inclusive method the ratings were dichotomized, separately for each variable, as close as possible to the median into those showing a large and those showing a small sex difference. Thus, for each society a large or a small sex difference was recorded for each of the five variables on which a sex difference rating was available. A society was given an over-all classification of large or small sex difference if it had a sex difference rating on at least three variables and if a majority of these ratings agreed in being large, or agreed in being small. This method permitted classification of a large number of cultures, but the grounds for classification were capricious in many cases, as a difference of only one point in the rating of a single variable might change the over-all classification of sex difference for a culture from large to small.

In the more selective method, we again began by dichotomizing each variable as close as possible to the median; but a society was not classified as having a large or small sex difference on the variable only if it was at least one step away from the scores immediately adjacent to the median. Thus only the more decisive ratings of sex difference were used. A culture was classified as having an over-all large or small sex difference only if it was given a sex difference rating which met this criterion on at least two variables, and only if all such ratings agreed in being large, or agreed in being small.

TABLE 2   Cultural Variables Correlated with Large Sex Differences in Socialization, Separately for Two Types of Sample

Variable	More selective sample		More inclusive sample	
	ϕ	N	ϕ	N
Large animals are hunted	.48*	(34)	.28*	(72)
Grain rather than root crops are grown	.82**	(20)	.62**	(43)
Large or milking animals rather than small animals are kept	.65*	(19)	.43*	(35)
Fishing unimportant or absent	.42*	(31)	.19	(69)
Nomadic rather than sedentary residence	.61**	(34)	.15	(71)
Polygyny rather than monogamy	.51*	(28)	.38**	(64)

* $p < .05$.
** $p < .01$.
Note.—The variables have been so phrased that all correlations are positive. The phi coefficient is shown, and in parentheses, the number of cases on which the comparison was based. Significance level was determined by χ^2, or Fisher's exact test where applicable, using in all cases a two-tailed test.

We then tested the relation of each of these dichotomies to 24 aspects of culture on which Murdock has categorized the customs of most of these societies[2] and which seemed of possible significance for sex differentiation. The aspects of culture covered include type of economy, residence pattern, marriage and incest rules, political integration, and social organization. For each aspect of culture, we grouped Murdock's categories to make a dichotomous contrast (sometimes omitting certain categories as irrelevant to the contrast). In the case of some aspects of culture, two or more separate contrasts were made (e.g., under form of marriage we contrasted monogamy with polygyny, and also contrasted sororal with nonsororal polygyny). For each of 40 comparisons thus formed, we prepared a 2 × 2 frequency table to determine relation of each of our sex-difference dichotomies. A significant relation was found for six of these 40 aspects of culture with the more selective dichotomization of over-all sex difference. In four of these comparisons, the relation to the more inclusive dichotomization was also significant. These relationships are all given in Table 2, in the form of phi coefficients, along with the outcome of testing significance by the use of χ^2 or Fisher's exact test. In trying to interpret these findings, we have also considered the nonsignificant correlations with other variables, looking for consistency and inconsistency with the general implications of the significant findings. We have arrived at the following formulation of results:

1. Large sex difference in socialization is associated with an economy that places a high premium on the superior strength, and superior development of motor skills requiring strength, which characterize the male. Four of the correlations reported in Table 2 clearly point to this generalization: the correlations of large sex difference with the hunting of large animals, with grain rather than root crops,

with the keeping of large rather than small domestic animals, and with nomadic rather than sedentary residence. The correlation with the unimportance of fishing may also be consistent with this generalization, but the argument is not clear.[3] Other correlations consistent with the generalization, though not statistically significant, are with large game hunting rather than gathering, with the hunting of large game rather than small game, and with the general importance of all hunting and gathering.

2. Large sex difference in socialization appears to be correlated with customs that make for a large family group with high cooperative interaction. The only statistically significant correlation relevant here is that with polygyny rather than monogamy. This generalization is however, supported by several substantial correlations that fall only a little short of being statistically significant. One of these is a correlation with sororal rather than nonsororal polygyny; Murdock and Whiting (4) have presented indirect evidence that co-wives generally show smoother cooperative interaction if they are sisters. Correlations are also found with the presence of either an extended or a polygynous family rather than the nuclear family only; with the presence of an extended family; and with the extreme contrast between maximal extension and no extension of the family. The generalization is also to some extent supported by small correlations with wide extension of incest taboos, if we may presume that an incest taboo makes for effective unthreatening cooperation within the extended family. The only possible exception to this generalization, among substantial correlations, is a near-significant correlation with an extended or polygynous family's occupying a cluster of dwellings rather than a single dwelling.[4]

In seeking to understand this second generalization, we feel that the degree of social isolation of the nuclear family may perhaps be the crucial underlying variable. To the extent that the nuclear family must stand alone, the man must be prepared to take the woman's role when she is absent or incapacitated, and vice versa. Thus the sex differentiation cannot afford to be too great. But to the extent that the nuclear family is steadily interdependent with other nuclear families, the female role in the household economy can be temporarily taken over by another woman, or the male role by another man, so that sharp differentiation of sex role is no handicap.

The first generalization, which concerns the economy, cannot be viewed as dealing with material completely independent of the ratings of socialization. The training of children in their economic role was often an important part of the data used in rating socialization variables, and would naturally vary according to the general economy of the society. We would stress, however, that we were by no means using the identical data on the two sides of our comparison; we were on the one hand judging data on the socialization of children and on the other hand using Murdock's judgments on the economy of the adult culture. In the case of the second generalization, it seems to us that there was little opportunity for information on family and social structure to have influenced the judges in making the socialization ratings.

Both of these generalizations contribute to understanding the social background of the relatively small difference in socialization of boys and girls which we believe characterizes our society at the present time. Our mechanized economy is perhaps less dependent than any previous economy upon the superior average strength of the male. The nuclear family in our society is often so isolated that husband and wife must each be prepared at times to take over or help in the household tasks normally assigned to the other. It is also significant that the conditions favoring low sex differentiation appear to be more characteristic of the upper segments of our society, in socioeconomic and educational status, than of lower segments. This observation may be relevant to the tendency toward smaller sex differences in personality in higher status groups (cf. Terman and Miles, 8).

The increase in our society of conditions favoring small sex difference has led some people to advocate a virtual elimination of sex differences in socialization. This course seems likely to be dysfunctional even in our society. Parsons, Bales, *et al.* (5) argue that a differentiation of role similar to the universal pattern of sex difference is an important and perhaps inevitable development in any social group, such as the nuclear family. If we add to their argument the point that biological differences between the sexes make most appropriate the usual division of those roles between the sexes, we have compelling reasons to expect that the decrease in differentiation of adult sex role will not continue to the vanishing point. In our training of children, there may now be less differentiation in sex role than characterizes adult life—so little, indeed, as to provide inadequate preparation for adulthood. This state of affairs is likely to be especially true of formal education, which is more subject to conscious influence by an ideology than is informal socialization at home. With child training being more oriented toward the male than the female role in adulthood, many of the adjustment problems of women in our society today may be partly traced to conflicts growing out of inadequate childhood preparation for their adult role. This argument is nicely supported in extreme form by Spiro's analysis of sex roles in an Israeli kibbutz (7). The ideology of the founders of the kibbutz included the objective of greatly reducing differences in sex role. But the economy of the kibbutz is a largely nonmechanized one in which the superior average strength of men is badly needed in many jobs. The result is that, despite the ideology and many attempts to implement it, women continue to be assigned primarily to traditional "women's work," and the incompatibility between upbringing or ideology and adult role is an important source of conflict for women.

NOTE ON REGIONAL DISTRIBUTION

There is marked variation among regions of the world in typical size and sex difference in socialization. In our sample, societies in North America and Africa tend to have large sex difference, and societies in Oceania to have small sex difference. Less confidently, because of the smaller number of cases, we can report a tendency toward small sex differences in Asia and South America as well. Since most of the variables with which we find the sex difference to be significantly correlated have a similar regional distribution, the question arises whether the correlations might better be ascribed to some quite different source having to do with large regional similarities, rather than to the functional dependence we have suggested. As a partial check, we have tried to determine whether the correlations we report in Table 2 tend also to be found strictly within regions. For each of the three regions for which we have sizable samples (North America, Africa, and Oceania) we have separately plotted 2×2 tables corresponding to each of the 6 relationships reported in Table 2. (We did this only for the more inclusive sample, since for the more selective sample the number of cases within a region would have been extremely small.) Out of the 18 correlations thus determined, 11 are positive and only 3 are negative (the other 4 being exactly zero). This result clearly suggests a general tendency for these correlations to hold true within regions as well as between regions, and may lend further support to our functional interpretation.

Summary

A survey of certain aspects of socialization in 110 cultures shows that differentiation of the sexes is unimportant in infancy, but that in childhood there is, as in our society, a widespread pattern of greater pressure toward nurturance, obedience, and responsibility in girls, and toward self-reliance and achievement striving in boys. There are a few reversals of sex difference, and many instances of no detectable sex difference; these facts tend to confirm the cultural rather than directly biological nature of the differences. Cultures vary in the degree to which these differentiations are made; correlational analysis suggests some of the social conditions influencing these variations, and helps in understanding why our society has relatively small sex differentiation.

The following paragraph is edited from Herbert Barry III.

Cross-cultural perspectives on how to minimize the adverse effect of sex differentiation

(Presented as a symposium on Behavioral Sciences American Psychological Association, Washington, D.C. September 3, 1969 and originally published by KNOW, Inc. 726 St. James Street, Pittsburgh, Pennsylvania)

I suggest that individualism and freedom can best flourish in a society which is segmented into small nuclear families and with considerable autonomy not only for individuals but also for local political and economic units. The foregoing article showed that small sex differences in child training are characteristic of societies which have independent, nuclear families. At the time we assumed this was due to the necessity for the parents in a nuclear family to assume each other's role when the other became incapacitated. This theory assumed a universal cultural pressure toward a maximal differentiation between sexes, with the differentiation being counteracted by the need for flexibility in the husband and wife taking over or assisting in each

other's role when no other man or woman was readily available. However, the individualistic, segmented society also requires each woman to perform the feminine functions when no other man or woman was readily available. However, the individualistic, segmented society also requires each woman to perform the feminine functions and each man to perform the masculine functions when no other member of the same sex is readily available for this purpose. A society of this type makes it impossible to abolish or even minimize the differentiation in sex role. Therefore, I believe that the reason why this type of society is characterized by relatively small sex differentiation is because this type of society permits and encourages a greater degree of individuality for both men and women. This individuality, encouraged by society and expressed by the people, is the key to modifying the world so that women who want to participate meaningfully are not regarded as and are not in fact deviant.

NOTES

1. For data and interpretations supporting various arguments of this paragraph, see Mead (2), Murdock (3), and Scheinfeld (6).

2. These data were supplied to us directly by Professor Murdock.

3. Looking (with the more inclusive sample) into the possibility that this correlation might result from the correlation between fishing and sedentary residence, a complicated interaction between these variables was found. The correlation of sex differentiation with absence of fishing is found only in nomadic societies, where fishing is likely to involve cooperative activity of the two sexes, and its absence is likely to mean dependence upon the male for large game hunting or herding large animals (whereas in sedentary societies the alternatives to fishing do not so uniformly require special emphasis on male strength). The correlation of sex differentiation with nomadism is found only in nonfishing societies; here nomadism is likely to imply large game hunting or herding large animals, whereas in fishing societies nomadism evidently implies no such special dependence upon male strength. Maximum sex differentiation is found in nomadic nonfishing societies (15 with large difference and only 2 with small) and minimum sex differentiation in nomadic fishing societies (2 with large difference and 7 with small difference). These findings further strengthen the argument for a conspicuous influence of the economy upon sex differentiation.

4. We think the reverse of this correlation would be more consistent with our generalization here. But perhaps it may reasonably be argued that the various nuclear families composing an extended or polygynous family are less likely to develop antagonisms which hinder cooperation if they are able to maintain some physical separation. On the other hand, this variable may be more relevant to the first generalization than to the second. Occupation of a cluster of dwellings is highly correlated with presence of herding and with herding of large rather than small animals, and these economic variables in turn are correlated with large sex difference in socialization. Occupation of a cluster of dwellings is also correlated with polygyny rather than monogamy and shows no correlation with sororal vs. nonsororal polygyny.

REFERENCES

Benedict, Ruth. Continuities and discontinuities in cultural conditioning. *Psychiatry*, 1938, 1, 161-167.

Mead, Margaret. *Male and female.* New York: Morrow, 1949.

Murdock, G. P. Comparative data on the division of labor by sex. *Social Forces*, 1937, 15, 551-553.

Murdock, G. P., & Whiting, J. W. M. Cultural determination of parental attitudes: The relationship between the social structure, particularly family structure and parental behavior. In M. J. E. Senn (Ed.), *Problems of infancy and childhood: Transactions of the Fourth Conference*, March 6-7, 1950. New York: Josiah Macy, Jr. Foundation, 1951. Pp. 13-34.

Parsons, T., Bales, R. F., *et al. Family, socialization and interaction process.* Glencoe, Ill.: Free Press, 1955.

Scheinfeld, A. *Women and men.* New York: Harcourt, Brace, 1944.

Spiro, M. E. *Kibbutz: Venture in Utopia.* Cambridge Univer. Press, 1956.

Terman, L. M., & Miles, Catherine C. Sex and personality. New York: McGraw-Hill, 1936.

31 Sex differentiation in role expectations and performance

Elina Haavio-Mannila

In recent years sex roles have been the object of considerable public debate and also serious sociological research in Scandinavia. Many articles and popular books have been published, especially in Norway and Sweden. Sociologically most valuable is the Swedish-Norwegian collection of research conducted on the woman's life and work, which has now been published also in English.[1] Harriet Holter has written a thorough article for the *International Labour Review* about the woman's occupational situation in Scandinavia.[2] At the moment a considerable amount of research is being carried out on this topic in every Scandinavian country.[3] The researchers even have regular meetings twice a year to discuss common problems; this is just one example of the rather close Scandinavian cooperation in sociological research.[4]

Sex-role debate and research are related especially to the woman's changing role in home, work, and society at large. Full equality of the sexes in social life is the goal of the radicals. To attain this goal, changes in both attitudes and norms regulating role performance of the sexes and in the material conditions for equal participation, such as rearrangement of both men's and women's working time and an increase of collective services, are required and worked for.

This article is concerned, first, with the description of the role-sets of men and women in Helsinki, capital of Finland: How much do the expectations concerning the behavior of the sexes and the actual behavior of men and women differ from each other? Secondly, an analysis of the attitudes and behavior connected with the division of tasks, according to sex, at home and work and social participation in general is carried out on the basis of some background data. A purpose of this report is to show how many separate dimensions of attitudes and behavior are related to the woman's changing role in the family and the society at large.

The data

The results presented in this very preliminary report are mainly based on interviews conducted in Helsinki in the spring of 1966. The sample consisted of 378 Finnish-speaking and 66 Swedish-speaking persons[5] between the ages of 15 and 64 years, randomly selected from the address register of the Helsinki Police Office by the method of equal intervals. The distribution of the sample according to age and sex of respondents is shown in Table 1.[6] The total sample consisted of 550 persons of which 81 percent could be interviewed.

The interview dealt with data on (1) social background, (2) social participation like employment, association membership, political and cultural interests, (3) division of household tasks between husband and wife in the family (for married respondents only), (4) attitudes toward women's social participation and division of household tasks between men and women, and (5) satisfaction with different aspects of life and appearance of some neurotic symptoms.[7]

Some aspects of the role-sets of men and women outside the home

Norms prescribing the appropriate behavior for men and women, role expectations on a very general level, were measured by asking how important the respondent considered some kinds of social activities (1) for men and (2) for women. The items concern various kinds of behavior, mostly social participation. Two items—temperance and fidelity in marriage—are more related to moral issues than the others. They have been included as indicators of the persistence of "double standards." Items concerning household duties were omitted, because attitudes toward this division were measured in a number of other ways; although for comparisons it would have been useful to have them here too. The means are computed on the basis of a one-to-four point scale ranging from "very important" (one) to "not at all important" (four). Results can be seen in Table 2.

Temperance, church attendance, fidelity, and cultural interests are more often expected from women than from men. Education, work, and political and other organization-

TABLE 1   Age and Sex Distribution of the Sample

Age	Men	Women
15-29	72	85
30-49	97	69
50-64	60	61

Reprinted from Elina Haavio-Mannila, "Sex Differentiation in Role Expectations and Performance," Journal of Marriage and Family, 29:3, August 1967, pp. 568-578. Part of the research for this paper was supported by a grant from the Finnish Cultural Foundation (Suomen Kulttuurirahasto).

TABLE 2   *The Relative Importance of Selected Activities for Men and Women*

It is important to	Means		
	Men	Women	Differences
Most feminine activities			
be a teetotaller	1.84	1.48	+.36
attend church	2.79	2.58	+.21
be absolutely faithful in marriage	1.34	1.20	+.14
be interested in culture	2.10	2.00	+.12
get a good education	1.35	1.58	−.23
participate in voluntary associations	2.42	2.66	−.24
speak at meetings	2.18	2.45	−.27
have positions of trust	2.21	2.49	−.28
get ahead in one's career	1.63	1.94	−.31
be interested in politics	2.25	2.78	−.53
Most masculine activities			

TABLE 3   *The Relative Occurrence of Selected Activities among Men and Women*

Activity	Men		Women		Differences (in percent)
	%	(N)	%	(N)	
Attend church during the last year	40	229	62	215	−22
Attended theater, concert, or opera during the last year	59	229	67	215	−12
Passed matriculation examination	24	229	19	215	+ 5
Member in a voluntary association	68	229	47	215	+21
Spoke at a meeting during the last year (association members)	72	148	56	97	+18
Has an office of trust (association members)	28	148	25	97	+ 3
Belongs to highest status ranks (1-3)*	15	229	4	215	+11
Is very interested in politics	24	229	10	215	+14

*Based on Rauhala's occupational prestige scale (see footnote 8 to the text).

al activities belong to the man's role in society. Even if family responsibilities were not measured, one can notice that for a woman the marital role is considered very important: marital fidelity is the most important role requirement not nearly equalled by the others. For men good education is almost as important as fidelity. The family role is thus considered the *woman's* main role, but for the *man* education and career almost equal it. The most differentiating items between sexes are temperance and politics. The function of the norm for teetotalism for women may be connected with the—at least earlier—sexually unprotected position of women; these norms are perhaps meant to guard her against uninhibited sex life, which was traditionally connected with the use of alcohol and has deeper consequences for women than for men.

The distribution of items indicating actual behavior corresponding to these expectations is shown in Table 3. In general, expectations and actual behavior correspond to each other. The same items make the sex-role sets in both lists. The educational level of women in Helsinki is lower than that of men, if matriculation examination is used as a cutting point. The same holds true when academic rank is taken as a divider. But secondary-school education (middle school) is more common among women than among men. Among men, 58 percent have no secondary schooling;

among the women, 54 percent. The main difference between men and women is thus not so much in educational but in occupational status. Men and women with similar educational achievements fall in different occupational strata, as Table 4 shows.

The occupational ranking of women is about .7 points below that of the men, according to Rauhala's nine-point ranking scale of occupations.[8]

Women, however, have been socialized to this underdog situation and do not complain about it. About the same proportions of men (67 percent) and women (71 percent) think they have gotten ahead in their occupations according to their abilities and education. Two-thirds of both men

TABLE 4   *The Social Strata of Men and Women according to Educational Level*

Educational level	Mean social stratum			
	Men		Women	
		(N)		(N)
Elementary school only	6.0	(75)	6.7	(65)
Vocational or secondary school	5.3	(99)	5.9	(111)
Matriculation examination	3.8	(55)	4.6	(39)

TABLE 5   Expectations Concerning Women's Employment in Percent (N = 444)

	Absolutely agree	Partly agree	Partly disagree	Absolutely disagree	No answer	Total
A married woman ought to have an opportunity to stay at home while the children are under school age.	75	18	6	1	—	100
Education in home economics has to be improved and girls trained for the housewife's occupation.	68	24	5	2	1	100
A married woman ought to have a free choice between employment and staying at home.	62	27	8	2	1	100
It is mostly the duty of the man to be responsible for earning a living for the family.	64	23	9	4	0	100
There ought to be more day-care institutions for children so that women can participate in work and public activities.	43	36	14	5	2	100
Young girls ought to be encouraged to choose also technical and other traditionally male occupations according to their abilities.	35	38	18	8	1	100
A married woman as well as her husband has the duty of helping to earn a living for the family.	41	42	19	8	—	100
Education in home economics for boys ought to be increased as much as for girls.	34	34	20	11	1	100
The women ought to quit their jobs in order to take care of children and the home.	31	33	23	12	1	100
A man and his wife ought to have the same opportunities for part-time employment while the children are small.	24	25	25	21	5	100
Women ought to have obligatory military service or something comparable to it.	3	13	12	71	1	100

and women say that they have jobs which quite correspond to their education.

Expectations concerning the behavior of men and women as members of society were found to differ in the same direction as actual behavior. The lower pressure toward achievement in careers for women—even if high educational levels are expected and also exceptionally often achieved among the Finnish women[9]—is reflected by the fact that they do not attain the highest ranking position in society, but are nevertheless quite satisfied with their occupational positions.

The division of labor between the sexes

ROLE EXPECTATIONS

Dimensions of Expectations. A number of attitude questions were included in the interview concerning women's and men's duties and privileges at home, work, and in society. The distributions of the answers are presented in Tables 5 and 6. The majority of the items have been borrowed from the questionnaires used in studies of women's employment is Oslo, Gothenburg, and Copenhagen.

Some of the items yield very unanimous answers. These are mainly related to the general idea of equality of the sexes or to freedom of choice. Traditional opinions about the importance of household training for girls and the duty of the husband to provide for his family, in the majority of the interviews, also get total approval. The plans for wom-

en's military service are, on the contrary, clearly condemned.

In Table 6 the distribution of the respondents' conceptions of "other people's" opinions (unqualified) is presented. They were included in the questionnaire following the example of Harriet Holter's study in Norway.

In every case the respondent's own opinions are more modern or radical than his conceptions of the opinions of others. Is there a pluralistic ignorance of the liberal attitude towards the woman's role?

Correlations were computed between the attitude questions and some background data. They were computed separately for men, women, and both. Differences are minimal. Scale reliabilities are based on correlations computed from the total sample.

There appear some clear clusters of correlations among the attitude variables. Attitudes connected with women's activities outside the home—social participation, leadership, education, career, and employment—are more or less closely connected with each other. They are supposed to measure, in different ways, the egalitarian ideas of the woman's possibilities for full participation in social life. Four subscales were formed on the bases of the correlations between the items. Reliabilities of the scales were computed by the Spearman-Brown technique.

The subscales consisted of the following items:

1. Interest and participation in politics and associations

TABLE 6   Expectations Concerning Women's Participation in Society in Percent (N = 444)*

	Agree	Uncertain	Disagree	No Answer	Total
Girls ought to get as good an education as boys.	87	6	4	3	100
	71	18	9	2	100
In the family both of the spouses ought to have as much to say on important matters.	85	8	4	3	100
	65	20	12	3	100
Women ought to have as good possibilities for leading positions in work life as the men.	75	13	10	2	100
	48	31	19	2	100
Boys as well as girls ought to learn to take care of the home.	59	16	22	3	100
	42	27	8	3	100
In general women ought to stay at home and care for the children.	58	17	22	3	100
	52	29	17	2	100
In general men should leave the housework to women.	55	13	30	2	100
	53	25	20	2	100
The man has to decide on important matters concerning the family.	47	9	40	4	100
	49	23	24	4	100
It is the woman's duty as well as the man's to participate in leading and administering society.	45	26	26	3	100
	33	34	30	3	100
Women ought to keep themselves in the background when politics are discussed.	17	12	67	4	100
	21	35	40	4	100
Women in general should not have leading positions.	14	19	62	5	100
	20	35	40	5	100

*First row = own opinion, second row = opinion of "other people."

		Patriarchalism		
		Yes	No relationship	No
New arrangements of household duties	Yes	—	The woman's duty to go to work	The woman's full social participation
	No	The woman's place is at home	—	—

(reliability .84): It is important for women to be interested in politics, participate in voluntary associations, speak at meetings, and have positions of trust.

2. Leadership (.65): It is the woman's as well as the man's duty to participate in leading and taking care of things in society; women ought to have as good possibilities for leading positions in work life as men; and disapproval of the item "women in general should not have leading positions."

3. Education and career (.50): Girls ought to get as good an education as boys; young girls ought to be encouraged to choose technical and other traditionally male occupations according to their abilities; and it is important for women to get good educations and to get ahead in their careers.

4. Employment of married women (.40): A man and his wife ought to have the same opportunities for part-time employment while the children are small; a married woman, as well as her husband, has the duty of helping to earn a living for the family; and a married woman ought to have a free choice between being employed and staying at home. The reliability of this subscale is very low. The first two items have a correlation of .22; they have correlations of .17 and .15, respectively, with the last item.

The Pearson product-moment correlations between these subscales are as follows:

	(1)	(2)	(3)	(4)
1. Participation				
2. Leadership	.47			
3. Education and career	.31	.33		
4. Employment	.15	.20	.20	

The "married women's employment" scale does not correlate with the others very much. This could be seen from the preliminary item correlations too. Thus, a scale based on the 11 items in the three first subscales were combined to form a "women's social participation" scale which is very reliable (.78). Married women's *duty and right to work* shall be considered as a separate variable.

These modern, egalitarian attitudes towards the woman's role could be expected to conflict with the traditional idea of "the woman's place is at home." A scale measuring these attitudes has a reality of .62 and consists of the following items: A married woman ought to have an opportunity to stay at home while the children are below school age; women ought to quit their jobs in order to take care of children and the home; and, in general, women ought to stay at home and care for children.

TABLE 7   Scale Means for Attitude Clusters Concerning Sex Roles by Sex

	Scale means*	
	Men	Women
Attitude cluster	N = 229	N = 215
Social participation	3.2	2.9
Duty to work	1.8	1.6
Men's housework	2.0	1.5
Patriarchalism	2.1	2.4
Women should stay at home	1.2	1.4

*The lower the mean, the more participation is expected.

This orientation is, contrary to expectations, not clearly negatively correlated with the former dimensions: correlations remain very low (from -.02 to -.07) except in the case of the second subscale (2), women's possibilities for leadership. With this subscale the "women-should-stay-home" orientation has a correlation of -.14, which indicates that these ideas are the contrasting ones on the scale from conservatism to radicalism. There are, anyway, apparently three rather independent attitude clusters connected with the role of women. The connecting links in these three role-types recommended for women are the power relations between the sexes in the family and the arrangement for child care and housework.

Opinions concerning power relations in the family and the woman's participation in discussions about politics and public affairs were combined into a three-item scale. The husband's duty to decide on important matters in the family versus equal power in family decisions and expectations about women's silence in political discussions can be said to reflect *patriarchal* orientations.

In general there are two possibilities for lessening the burden of housework for the working wives: institutional home-help or men's participation in housework. Three items measuring expectations concerning men's participation in housework and increasing the teaching of home economics for boys were combined into a scale with a reliability of .63. The item "there ought to be more day-care institutions for children so that women can participate in work and public activities" is connected with these items, but the correlations are not higher than .17. It will thus be treated separately. Both these solutions—men's participation in housework and day-care institutions for children— represent *new kinds of household arrangements* compared with the traditional one of the wife taking care of everything at home.

These partly separate orientations in the attitude universe of the division of labor between the sexes are connected with each other as shown in the following sixfold table.

Patriarchalism is correlated negatively with the woman's social participation scale (r = -.26) but positively with the "woman's-place-is-at-home" scale (r = .24). Patriarchalism, on the other hand, has nothing to do with the cluster of the "woman's duty for employment" (r = -.04). "Duty to work" is not very much related to the radical attitudes toward equality of women nor at all to the conservative ones demanding that women stay at home (r = -.06). Atti-

TABLE 8   Agreement with the Item "Men Ought to Leave the Housework to Women" according to Sex and Age

	Percent agreeing			
Age	Men		Women	
15-24	57%	(40)	46%	(54)
25-34	71	(62)	34	(53)
35-44	70	(47)	46	(41)
45-64	62	(79)	54	(67)

TABLE 9   Expectations Concerning Women's Social Participation according to Sex and Education

	Scale means*	
Education	Men	Women
	(N)	(N)
Matriculation	3.2 (55)	3.4 (39)
Vocational or middle school	3.3 (99)	2.9 (111)
Elementary school	2.9 (75)	2.8 (65)

*The lower the mean, the more participation is expected.

TABLE 10   Employment of the Wife according to Husband's Social Stratum

Husband's social stratum	Wife is working
	% (N)
1-3	49 (47)
4	57 (42)
5	74 (81)
6	65 (68)
7-9	77 (30)
All	65 (268)

TABLE 11   Educational Level and Employment of Married Women

Educational level of the wife	Wife is working
	% (N)
Elementary school only	60 (116)
Vocational schooling	75 (44)
Middle school	65 (78)
Matriculation examination	71 (34)

TABLE 12   Employment of the Wife according to Education and Husband's Social Stratum

	Wife is working	
Wife's education	Husband's social stratum	
	1-4	5-9
	% (N)	% (N)
Elementary school only	48 (21)	63 (93)
More	54 (68)	79 (77)

TABLE 13   *Primary Reasons for Employment of Married Women according to Social Stratum of the Husband*

Primary reasons for employment outside the home	Social stratum of the husband			
	1-4	5	6-9	All
	(N = 20)	(N = 25)	(N = 22)	(N = 67)
Earning money	50%	84%	95%	78%
Satisfaction with work	61	68	50	60
Meeting people	58	56	44	54
Getting independence	28	38	33	33
Retaining connections to work-life and not losing social security allowances based on continued employment	21	35	33	30
Utilize the education attained	42	36	18	30
Not enough to do at home	17	36	18	25
Lack interest for home work	5	20	13	14

tudes toward women's work in Helsinki can reflect two kinds of thinking: (1) the woman's right for employment as an indicator of her equality or (2) the woman's duty to work because of economic necessity. The latter attitude reflects the actual situation of many families in Finland both in the agrarian society, where economic activity on the farm was expected from women as well as men, and in the industrializing society with a low standard of living.

The arrangement of household duties is the central issue in the question of division of labor between the spouses in the family. It is essential to make some changes in the traditional arrangements if the wife is supposed to participate in social life or be employed. Thus it is natural that requirements for men's participation in household tasks are connected with expectations about women's participation and their duty to work (r = .36 and .23), as is the demand for day nurseries. There is no need for such changes when one considers that the woman's place is at home.

Some Social Determinants of Expectations. A very rough preliminary analysis of the relationship of social characteristics of the respondents and their sex-role expectations will be presented here to give hints for further study.

The attitudes of men and women are compared in Table 7. The differences are not very great but are in the expected direction: women want more equality; men are more patriarchally oriented and want women to stay at home.

The relationship between age and role expectations is often curvilinear. The young and the old having the same opinions. Thus, the correlations remain low. Age has sometimes a different influence on the attitudes of men and women, as can be seen from the example in Table 8.

Men in the two middle categories (25 to 44 years) want to leave the housework to women, but women in the same age groups oppose it. At that age the question of how to divide the household tasks at home is very relevant: the children are small, and there is plenty of housework to be done. Men would like to leave it to the women, but women do not accept this solution. Especially the women who are 25 to 34 years of age disapprove being left alone with the housework.

Education and social stratum have rather high correlations with role-type expectations. Lower-class respondents expect the women to participate in earning a living for the family. At the same time, however, they also consider that

the woman's place is at home. Working out of economic necessity but against one's inner wishes has been and is—as will be shown—customary in the working class. People in the lower social strata favor new household arrangements but are, at the same time, patriarchal in their attitudes about the woman's participation in family decisions and political discussions. In any case, the lower educational and social groups, in spite of their patriarchal attitudes, are most in favor of the woman's social participation in general (see Table 9). The most conservative are the women in the highest educational level and the men in the middle educational groups. The relationship between sex-role expectations and social background needs further study before any conclusions can be made.

Comparisons between the two language groups in Helsinki show that the Swedish-speaking Finns have a more modern, radical attitude toward the woman's role in society. This is especially true of Swedish-speaking women. The Swedish-speaking men, more than the Finnish-speaking men, oppose the duty of women to work. Eighty-six percent of the Swedish-speaking, compared with 66 percent of the Finnish-speaking, men consider it mostly the duty of the man to be responsible for earning a living for the family. Free choice between employment and staying at home is the ideal for married women among the Swedish-speaking men. More than the Finnish-speaking men, they stress the importance of social participation of women.

ROLE PERFORMANCE

Role expectations concerning the woman's proper place vary somewhat according to social background. Variations in role performance at work, in social participation, and at home will be examined next.

Work. The attitudes toward the employment of married women are rather scattered and diverse. In Finland the proportion of married women working outside the home is, internationally compared, very high. This might be partly caused by the low degree of industrialization of the country if we compare Finland with, for instance, Sweden. As Harriet Holter has shown, the economical situation alone does not explain the differences among the Scandinavian countries in women's employment. In Norway, compared with Finland, women work very little outside the home in spite of the countries' rather similar economical struc-

TABLE 14   Membership in Organizations according to Sex and Education

Educational level*	Association members			
	Men		Women	
	%	(N)	%	(N)
1 (high)	77	(22)	70	(10)
2	78	(32)	69	(29)
3	78	(40)	57	(60)
4	52	(60)	43	(51)
5 (low)	68	(76)	28	(65)

*1 = academic examination, 2 = matriculation examination, 3 = middle school, 4 = vocational school, 5 = elementary school only.

TABLE 15   Membership in Associations according to Sex and Social Stratum

Social stratum	Association members			
	Men		Women	
	%	(N)	%	(N)
1-3 (high)	82	(33)	87	(8)
4	62	(34)	57	(23)
5	70	(69)	59	(54)
6	70	(57)	38	(63)
7-9 (low)	53	(34)	36	(66)
All	70	(228)	47	(214)

tures.[10] The study of cultural influences on the woman's role in society will be the focus of our future research.

According to the census of 1960, 53 percent of the married women in Helsinki were employed outside the home. The percentage was highest in the low social groups,[11] which points toward rather strong economic motives for married women's employment. In this sample the percentage also increases towards lower social strata (Table 10).

The relative educational levels of the husband and wife have an effect on the wife's employment, as Antti Eskola has shown in Helsinki.[12] According to present material, educated married women work outside the home somewhat more than non-educated women, but the differences are not very large (Table 11). In Table 12 the husband's social status and the wife's education are treated simultaneously. Especially the educated wives of lower-class husbands go to work outside the home: 79 percent of them are working. The opposite group of wives are those with elementary school only who are married to upper-class men: only 48 percent of them are employed.

Economic motives for employment predominate in the lower social strata as Table 13 shows. As could be expected, wives of lower-class husbands work more often than those of upper-class husbands for money, social security allowances based on long work relationships, and—as somewhat less expressed—get independence and because of lack of interest in housework. Among the upper-class wives, satisfaction with work, meeting people, and making use of education play a more dominant role than among the lower-class wives.

The statement that it is the wife's duty to work outside the home to help earn a living for the family was more often endorsed by lower- than upper-class respondents. The wives in fact do this, especially in the lower classes. The motivation of upper-class wives is different. It is understandable that upper-class respondents do not agree with statements like "women ought to quit their jobs in order to take care of the children and the home"; they identify themselves more with their work than those of the lower class.

Social Participation. Educational level has a very clear linear relationship with organizational membership among the women (see Table 14); 28 percent of women with elementary school only, but as many as 70 percent of women with academic degrees, are members of at least one organization. The differences among the men with different amounts of education are much smaller. Thus the differences between men and women are greatest among the non-educated.

In Table 15 social participation in associations has been cross-tabulated with social stratum. The results are similar to those in Table 14. An interesting difference is that men in the very lowest social strata do not belong to organizations as often as other men; whereas in Table 14 the participation of men is lowest in the group with vocational schooling. Age may account for this difference. Differences between men and women are greatest in the lower middle occupational stratum (6).

The Swedish-speaking people in Helsinki belong more often to organizations than the Finnish-speaking. This is particularly obvious among the women. Especially unmarried, widowed, and divorced Swedish-speaking women often hold offices or positions of trust in voluntary organizations.

The man's activity in voluntary associations increases with age; whereas the woman's does not (see Table 16). Older men also have more positions of trust in organizations than young men and women. It has been supposed that women have a good opportunity to engage in voluntary activities when their children grow older, that is, when the women are about 40 years old. That is not the case: women do not join organizations even after their child-care responsibilities have ended. The passivity of women compared to men is more marked in the older than the younger age groups.

Housework. A slight majority of the respondents, 55

TABLE 16   Membership in Associations according to Sex and Age

Age	Association members			
	Men		Women	
	%	(N)	%	(N)
15-24	52	(40)	39	(54)
25-34	63	(62)	51	(53)
35-44	77	(47)	51	(41)
45-64	75	(79)	48	(67)

TABLE 17   *Division of Some Household Tasks in the Family*

| Household task | Usually taken care of by | | | | |
	Wife	Husband and wife	Husband	Other person*	N
Preparing the dinner	85%	9%	2%	4%	271
Washing the man's shirts and socks	80	11	4	5	271
Buying the food	74	20	2	4	271
Feeding the children	74	20	—	6	128
Daily cleaning	73	18	1	8	271
Preparing the breakfast	72	16	8	3	271
Getting children dressed	70	24	1	5	139
Washing the dishes	70	20	4	6	271
Making the beds	67	25	3	5	271
Putting children to bed	54	41	1	4	137
Washing the windows	51	32	6	11	271

*Other persons represent relatives or household help employed in the family. The total proportion of households (married couples) with any help is 12 percent, and-one-half of these are part-time or occasional helpers.

percent, agree on the item "men should leave the housework to women." Thirty percent disagree, and the rest do not know. These expectations correspond to the actual diversion of labor in the family: various household tasks, in 10 to 40 percent of the families, are not done by women alone but by husbands as well, as Table 17 shows.

The division of household tasks in the family can be expected to vary according to the social status of the family. Families in different social strata have different possibilities for hiring household helpers, and the norms connected with sex-role performance can be expected to vary too. In Table 18 an average of five items concerning household tasks—who takes care of preparing the breakfast, buying the food, washing the dishes, daily cleaning, and making the beds—has been computed.

The husbands participate least in housework in the highest social strata,[13] where outside help is available and where the wives more often stay at home. A curvilinear relationship prevails in families with housewives: husband's participation is most frequent in the middle strata. The explanation for the differential participation may lie either in the time available for housework or sex-role norms. Upper-class husbands with working wives help a little less than those in the lower class, but if we omit families with outside helpers, the difference disappears. The husband's

TABLE 18   *Husband's Participation in Housework according to Social Stratum and Wife's Employment*

| Social stratum of the husband | Wife employed | | Wife at home | | All |
	%	(N)	%	(N)	%
1—3	25	(23)	8	(24)	17
4	25	(24)	16	(18)	21
5	30	(60)	16	(21)	27
6	31	(44)	17	(24)	27
7—9	30	(23)	11	(7)	27
All	29	(174)	14	(94)	24

lesser participation is thus explained by the possibility to hire outside helpers.

Men in the Swedish-speaking middle and lower classes are especially active housekeepers, but the upper-class Swedish-speaking men avoid household tasks more than the Finnish-speaking men in the same social strata.

The wives are not very happy and satisfied with this division of labor at home. Only 48 percent of the wives, compared with 81 percent of the husbands, are very satisfied with the amount of housework done by the spouse. The percentage of dissatisfied wives is eleven, for husbands two. The others are rather satisfied. It may be recalled also that women do not express their dissatisfaction with occupational advancement even if, from an objective point of view, there would be reason to do so.

Conclusion

On the basis of the above discussion, a few remarks concerning the sex-role differentiation and its more general implications may be in order. The traditional division of labor between the sexes still persists in most of the families, although two-thirds of the wives are working outside the home. This circumstance causes dissatisfaction: women are more often dissatisfied with their husbands' participation in household tasks than with their own statuses at work and social activities even if their formal positions in the latter are inferior to the men's positions. It may be, simply, that it is easier to complain about home matters than about one's position at work. But the explanation may also be that the official norms demanding equality of the sexes are better followed in public than in private life, where neither formal nor informal sanctions (except those of the family) can be applied.

The role-sets of men and women were found to differ from each other. The social role of the man is to get ahead in his career and to be interested in politics and public affairs; whereas the woman is expected to take care of the home, go to church, be interested in culture, and behave morally. These traditional roles, however, are undergoing change, which will be the subject of further research.

Three separate dimensions in expectations and performance related to the woman's role in the home, at work, and in society have to be taken into consideration when speaking about the role of women in Finland. The woman's full social participation in all areas of life, her duty to go to work, and the traditional view that "a woman's place is at home" are three aspects only partly connected with each other. These expectations and corresponding behavior patterns are related to social characteristics. In the further study an analysis of the congruence and discrepancy between expectations and behavior will be made. This preliminary report provides mainly descriptive information on the situation of women in Helsinki.

NOTES

1. *Kvinnors liv och arbete,* ed. by Edmund Dahlström, Stockholm; Studie-förbundet för Näringsliv och Samhälle, 1962.
2. Harriet Holter, "Women's Occupational Situation in Scandinavia," *International Labour Review,* 93:4 (April, 1966), pp. 383-400.
3. Part of this research has been reviewed in Swedish in a debate book *Kynne eller kön,* Om Könsrollerne i det moderne Samhället, En Debattskrift under medverkan av bl. a. Harriet Holter, Per Holmberg, Rita Liljeström och Elina Haavio-Mannila, Stockholm: Raben & Sjögren, 1966.
4. Erik Allardt, *Scandinavian Sociology,* Research Reports, Institute of Sociology, University of Helsinki, 77 (1966), pp. 24-26.
5. Helsinki has a 14-percent Swedish-speaking minority population (1960).
6. The sex ratio in the sample does not correspond to that in the population of Helsinki. The men are overrepresented. This has been taken into consideration in most of the calculations. For example, all the correlations have been computed separately for men, women, and the total sample. Only in Tables 2, 5, and 6, the replies of men and women have been presented together. The reader should bear in mind that the answers of the men there weigh more than in the total population.
7. Part of the questions have been derived from questionnaires of Harriet Holter in Oslo, Barbro Jansson in Gothenburg, and Johannes Noordhoek in Copenhagen. The writer is grateful for their cooperation.

8. A nine-point scale evaluation of the prestige of occupations made by Urho Rauhala, *Suomalaisen yhteiskunnan sosiaalinen kerrosiuneisuus* (Social Stratification of Finnish Society), Helsinki; WSOY, 1966. The method was approximately the same as in the North-Hatt study, but the list of occupations consisted of 1,293 occupations.
9. Anna-Liisa Sysiharju, *Equality, Home and Work,* Mikkeli, 1960; and "Mietteitä suomalaisnuogisosta opintiellä," *Sosiologia,* 3:4 (December, 1966), pp. 170-177.
10. Holter, *op. cit.,* pp. 389-391.
11. Elisabeth Elfvengren, "Gifta kvinnors yrkesverksamhet" (Employment of Married Women), *Statistiska manadsuppgifter för Helsingfors* (August, 1965), pp. 341-366.
12. Antti Eskola, "Aviopuolisoiden roolijakoon vaikuttavat tekijät" (Some Factors Influencing the Differentiation of the Roles of Spouses), in *Väestöntutkimuksen Vuosikirja* (Yearbook of Population Research in Finland), VI (1960), Vammala: Väestöpoliittinen Tutkimuslaitos, 1960, pp. 87-89.
13. Similar results have been obtained by Kalevi Heinilä, "Perhekumppanuus ja perheen kiinteys" (Family Companionship and Family Cohesion) in *Väestöntutkimuksen Vuosikirja* (Yearbook of Population Research in Finland), VII (1961-1962), Vammala: Väestöpolittinen Tutkimuslaitos, 1962, pp. 86-87.

REFERENCES

Relevant recent publications by Prof. Haavio-Mannila include:

Veronica Stolte Heiskanen and Elina Haavio-Mannila, The Position of Women in Society: Formal Ideology vs. Everyday Ethic, *Social Science Information,* Vol. VL, No. 6, 1967, 169-188.
Compensative Mechanisms among Women, *Research Reports, Institute of Sociology, University of Helsinki,* No. 109, 1968.
Suomalainen nainen ja mies (Finnish Woman and Man), Porvoo: Werner Söderström, 1968 (312 pages).
Some Consequences of Women's Emancipation, *Journal of Marriage and the Family,* Vol. XXXI, No. 1, 1969, 123-134.
The Position of Finnish Women: Regional and Cross-National Comparisons, *Journal of Marriage and the Family,* Vol. XXXI, No. 2, 1969, 339-347.
Sex Roles in Politics, *Scandinavian Political Studies,* Vol. 5, 1970, 209-239.
Convergences between East and West: Traditional and Modernity in Sex Roles in Sweden, Finland and the Soviet Union, *Acta Sociologica,* No. 1-2, 1971, 114-125.
Sex-Role Attitudes and Their Changes in Finland During 1966-70, *Research Reports, Institute of Sociology, University of Helsinki,* No. 162, 1971.

32 *Worker, mother, housewife: Soviet woman today*

Mark G. Field
Karin I. Flynn

The dictum attributed to Engels that the culture of a society reflects its attitudes toward women (Shim, 1967) has become firmly rooted in Soviet ideology, and each one of the great Soviet leaders of the past has found it necessary from time to time to reaffirm the complete equality of the sexes in Soviet Russia. In a strictly Marxist sense, woman is a member of the traditionally oppressed and exploited class, and her liberation and flowering can come only

Reprinted from Mark G. Field and Karin I. Flynn, "Worker, Mother, Housewife: Soviet Woman Today," with the permission of the publisher from Role and Status of Women in the Soviet Union, *Donald R. Brown, pp. 7-56. (New York: Teachers College Press, 1968; copyright by Teachers College, Columbia University.) This version is a revised and updated abridgment of the original paper and appeared in George H. Seward and Robert C. Williamson,* Sex Roles in Changing Society, *pp. 257-284, published by Random House. The first version of this paper was presented at the Mary Winsor Symposium, Bryn Mawr College, April 23-25, 1964. The assistance of the Russian Research Center at Harvard University in making this study possible is gratefully acknowledged.*

through a proletarian revolution, the abolition of the private ownership of the means of production, and the advent of socialism, the first stage on the road to full communism. To paraphrase countless Soviet broadsides, only under a Soviet type of social structure can a woman really be free, can she really be "human," can she fully realize her own potentials unfettered by the restrictions common under feudalism and capitalism where she is nothing but slave and chattel, the property first of her father and then of her husband.

Some ideological considerations

To start with the obvious, and in spite of all the brave talks of feminists, there is a "difference" between men and women, though not necessarily one that automatically implies "inferiority" of one sex to the other. Oscar Wilde, when asked by a lady to explain the nature of that difference, is supposed to have paused and replied: "Madam, I can't conceive." (Money, 1963, p. 63). Marxists, and particularly Engels, regarded the division of labor between man and woman for the procreation of children as the first division of labor. Later on he added that the first class antagonism in history was the development of tensions between man and woman in monogamy, and that the first oppression was that of the female by the male (Fréville, 1950). Seen through the prism of the Marxist optic, the battle of the sexes was the prototype of the class struggle—man appropriated and enslaved woman (or several women) as his private means for the production of children to whom his private property could be transmitted. To ensure that this property was passed on to his "real" children, man enforced strict monogamy on his wife (or wives), hence the strictures against the adulteress, while he himself enjoyed the double standard, philandered, and encouraged prostitution.

The introduction of industrialization, according to Marx and Engels, was accompanied in its early phases by the employment of women (and often children) in factories and plants, usually at the expense of their health and domestic functions as wives and particularly as mothers. It is enough to read certain passages from *Capital* (Marx, 1906) or from Engels' *The Condition of the Working Class in England* to realize that part of the reason for the seriousness of the Marxist indictment of industrial capitalism stemmed from the working conditions of factory women. Engels (1908), for example, wrote:

When women work in factories the most important result is the dissolution of family ties. If she works for 12 or 13 hours a day and her husband is employed . . . what is the fate of the children? . . . this can be seen by the increase in the number of accidents to little children which occur in the factory districts. . . . Many midwives and others who assist at childbirth state that female factory operatives experience more difficult labor in childbirth than other women, and that miscarriages are more frequent among them then is normal. . . . It is quite common for women to be working in the evening and for the child to be delivered the following morning, and it is by no means uncommon for babies to be born in the factory itself among the machinery [pp. 160-61].

The approach of Marx to this question, however, is a more dispassionate one. While he excoriates the ruling classes for their exploitation of women and children, he finds in a truly dialectic fashion that industrialization also has its positive aspects since, by providing employment opportunities to women *outside* of the home, it liberates them from the tutelage of their fathers and husbands. The disintegration of the traditional family thus leads to a higher stage of the history of mankind where women will truly achieve freedom and equality through their participation in the productive processes. In his words (1906):

However terrible and disgusting the dissolution, under the capitalist system, of the old family ties may appear, nevertheless, modern industry, by assigning as it does an important part in the process of production, outside the domestic sphere, to women, to young persons, and to children of both sexes, creates a new economical foundation for a higher form of the family and of the relations between the sexes. . . . Moreover, it is obvious that the fact of the collective working group being composed of individuals of both sexes and all ages must necessarily, under suitable conditions, become a source of humane development; although, in its spontaneously developed, brutal, capitalistic form, where the labourer exists for the process of production, and not the process of production for the labourer, that fact is a pestiferous source of corruption and slavery [p. 536].

The Bolshevik revolution was thus looked upon by its theoreticians as the opportunity to liberate woman from her servitude and to provide her with the same rights and opportunities granted men, particularly in the economy. Fannina Halle (1933), for example, pointed out that since the Soviets seized power, hardly anything had been written or said about the economic development of the new Russia without reference to the significance of the expanding growth of women's labor. Thus, the employment of women in Soviet Union was not only congruent with the economic needs of that society, but also with the basic tenets of its official ideology and practical policies. It is quite clear, for instance, that at least in its first years the regime looked upon the Soviet woman as one of its "natural" allies, for had it not liberated her and did she not owe her freedom and opportunities to the Soviet regime? It was forthermore assumed by the regime that even the obstacles to educational, occupational, and political opportunities caused by her biological role as mother could and would, insofar as possible, be removed (Massell, 1968). Maternity was to be recognized as a social function and society was to assume the care, education, and training of children and adolescents. The abolition of private property in the means of production was to have repercussions in the marriage relationship, which was to be based on truly monogamous love and founded on mutual attraction, equality, and dignity. When love ceased to exist, the marriage bonds would be automatically dissolved. Common-law marriages were to have the same validity as registered ones: no social stigma was going to be attached to unmarried mothers, nor would there be made any distinction between the child born in wedlock and the natural or illegitimate child.

The history and the vicissitudes of Soviet family law show the unrealistic nature of many of these ideas, given the realities and demands of Soviet society. Abortions, legalized in 1920, were made illegal in 1936, except for very specific and restricted medical cases. Divorces were made more difficult and costly and measures were taken to force fathers to support their children. In 1944, divorces were returned to the courts with no statutory ground being given for the dissolution of the marriage, this being left to the discretion of the superior court. Unregistered marriages lost their validity and equality with registered marriages; illegitimate children were from then on to carry their mother's name (the name of the father remaining a stigmatizing blank on the birth certificate); the mother could not sue for paternity nor could the child inherit any of his father's property (Inkeles, 1959).

Some measure of relaxation and liberalization was introduced in the wake of reforms following Stalin's death in 1953. For example, abortion on "social" grounds was relegalized on January 1, 1966, making divorces simpler and cheaper but still avoiding the issue of illegitimacy (Juvilier, 1967). It is likely that in the near future, illegitimate children will be able to use their father's name and that paternity suits will be allowed, therefore putting an end to their unfair stigmatization. However, this is only one more step toward, rather than the final realization of, the complete emancipation of the woman. Indeed, as long as it is not possible for society to undertake the complete care of the child for every woman who wishes to have it so, and as long as she is saddled with domestic duties, her equal participation in political, social, and economic activities will be hampered.

Demography and the economic role of Soviet women

In the area of demography and economics, some of the basic explanations of the role of Soviet women may be found. In the Soviet Union perhaps more than in most other industrial countries, women do not merely constitute a reserve labor force, nor do they constitute, as is often the case, an important but still a minority of the labor force; they are, in the Soviet Union, an integral and indispensable part of that force. Indeed, it may be fair to say that the Soviet economy and Soviet society, at least until now, could not operate, barring drastic structural changes, without the labor provided by women.

Throughout Soviet history, women have constituted a majority of the population, reflecting not only their greater life expectancy but also the selective male losses incurred by such events as World War I, the two revolutions of 1917, the civil war, foreign intervention, the epidemics and famine of the twenties, the industrialization drive, the forced collectivization of agriculture, the purges of the thirties, and finally, in the forties, the traumatizing effects of World War II. In 1926, according to the first census taken by the Soviet regime, women constituted 51.7 percent of the population; in 1939, that percentage rose to 52.1; in 1946, it was estimated at 57.4 percent, representing an excess of 25 million women in a total population of about 176 million.

In 1959, according to the first postwar census taken fourteen years after the end of hostilities, women still constituted 55 percent of the population. Population losses and deficits of births due to World War II and its immediate

aftermath have been very roughly estimated at about 45 million (20 million as birth deficits and 20 million men and 5 million women as excess mortality). There are, however, wide variations in the percentage of women to the total population in the several republics that constitute the Soviet Union, with those areas that were most exposed to the brunt of the German invasion showing the highest percentage, and those areas that were spared (Central Asia, for example) showing the lowest. Furthermore, the 20 million surplus of women noted in the 1959 census is not distrubuted evenly among all age groups of the population, but is concentrated primarily among those cohorts old enough at the beginning of the war to be selectively affected by hostilities. For example, in the age groups over thirty-five in 1959, the number of women per 100 of the population does not fall below the 600 mark. Statistically speaking, this indicates that one-third or more of these women had either no chance of finding a marriage partner or were widowed. Of the population aged sixteen to fifty-nine in 1946, it can be estimated that 60.3 percent were women and approximately *one-half* of all men alive in 1939 did not survive the war (Dodge, 1966).

These losses are also reflected in the 1959 statistics about marriages: more than 90 percent of the males between the ages of thirty and sixty-nine were married in 1959, but among women, only 72 percent in the thirty-five to thirty-nine group, 62 percent in the forty to forty-four group, 54 percent in the forty-five to fifty group, and less than half in all age groups older than fifty. The poignant loneliness of the Soviet woman has been expressed, better than statistics can ever do, by Vladimir Semenov (1959) in a poem addressed to a Soviet girl:

You tried to find him everywhere
He must exist
He is someplace.
You asked:
Where is he? Where?
There was no answer.
Your youth is gone.
You paled and withered.
You, whose beauty shone once,
You do not know the verity
That a wife to no one
You long since are
A widow . . .
You do not know that he was killed
in War
Before you met him.

At the same time, only an increasing birth rate could even begin to partly compensate for the losses and deficits caused by the war. As a result, women have been encouraged to increase the number of children they have while, at the same time, not withdrawing from the labor force. Thus, the decree of July 8, 1944 encouraged large families by establishing honorific titles for women who brought more than five children into the world. In addition, the 1944 decree seems to have had two other purposes: (1) it was an attempt, in line with other conservative measures adopted in family law since the mid-thirties, to imbue men with a more responsible attitude toward their family obligations; and (2) it was also a recognition that, as a result of the war,

TABLE 1   *Employed Women in the Soviet Union by Type of Employment, 1959*

	Women (000)	Percentages of Total
Women employed in sector of material production, including:	38,342	80.5
Industry, construction, transportation, and communications	14,152	29.7
Agriculture	20,764	43.6
Trade, public catering, procurement, material-technical supply and retail	3,178	6.8
Women employed in nonproductive sectors, including:	9,204	19.4
Housing, communal housing services, organs of administration and banking	2,276	4.9
Education, science, public health, and medicine	6,928	14.5
Not assigned to any sector, not giving or inaccurately giving place of work	59	0.1
Total, Women Employed*	47,605,000	100.0

*Excludes members of families of collective farmers, and of workers and employees engaged in subsidiary (private plot) agriculture.

many women would find it impossible (statistically speaking) to bear children in wedlock. It thus afforded unmarried women some financial provisions for the support of their children who were desperately needed by the regime to compensate for the war losses. As we have already seen, unmarried mothers were prohibited from suing for paternity or for alimony, a measure that was designed, as Juviler (1967) has suggested, ". . . to spare a man and his legal family the financial and emotional shocks that might arise from paternity and support suits, from his official acknowledgment of paternity, or from an extramarital child's bearing his name" (p. 52). In effect, the decree actually licensed men to increased irresponsibility toward their illegitimate children since it was aimed precisely at an increase of the fertility rate of both married *and* unmarried women.

While we may expect, in the not too distant future, a change in family law that would tighten the responsibilities of parents for their children, and while the drastic sex unbalance that characterized the Soviet population in the postwar period is gradually disappearing, some consequences of that war are still affecting Soviet society and provide additional background to an understanding of the role of women. For example, the excess mortality and the birth deficits of World War II have led to a very sharp reduction in the number of entrants into the labor force fifteen to twenty years after the end of the war (Feshbach, 1966). In 1959, when the number of new entrants into the labor force was at about its lowest ebb, M. Ya. Sonin (1959) wrote that ". . . it is more important than ever to free this small generation (or cohort) from being tied to household work—to ensure an even, 'natural' growth of the work force" (p. 88). At the same time, the smaller number of people who have, in recent years, entered adulthood and the child-begetting ages will also mean another potential drop in the labor force a generation from now.

The significance of women in the Soviet economy and particularly in industry was illustrated by the 1959 census and is summarized in Table 1 (*Zhenshchiny i deti v SSSR*, 1963, p. 79).

The table reveals that more than four-fifths of all employed women were occupied in production—industry, construction, transportation, agriculture, and so on—and less

than one-fifth in the occupations that might be called services, such as education, public health, science, and medicine. By 1965, the picture had not substantially changed. Figures on the number of women occupied in agriculture, that is, as farm hands on collective farms, are not available for the more recent years (collective farmers are not "employed" or salaried by the state), but in 1959 almost 30 million women as against 18,600,000 men comprised the labor force on the land (Karcz, 1967).

While women are engaged in practically all types of work, they are underrepresented in the occupations that embody directive, managerial, decision-making, and executive functions, and they tend to be overrepresented in the subordinate and junior positions and in the menial jobs. On the other hand, if one were to compare the Soviet figures for professions such as engineering and medicine with those of Western countries, one would see a far greater proportional participation of women in the Soviet Union. There are some indications, however, that the regime may not be completely satisfied with those professions having heavy female representation such as medicine and teaching. Indeed, in the last few years, the proportion of women in medicine has slightly decreased and will probably continue to do so as more and more of the entering classes are more evenly balanced as to sex, an indication that the highly skewed figures of the past were due primarily to a shortage of men and to their going into the more technical occupations (Parry, 1967).

As to teaching, the Minister of Education of the Russian Republic declared in 1966 that the overwhelming majority of school teachers and students in pedagogic institutes and academics were women, who do their job "with great tact and skill," and yet, the Minister continued, "There should be more men entering our . . . institutes and . . . academies" (Prokofev, 1966).

Women have thus become an integral part of the Soviet labor force, not so much because of ideology as because of manpower shortages and economic needs. There is still little likelihood that for the present time at least, the regime wants or can afford to release them from their occupational obligations, although it will continue, within its limitations and needs, to attempt to improve their working and living conditions. With time, it is also likely that a greater proportion of women will eventually be employed in white-collar, semiprofessional and professional occupations rather than manual and unskilled jobs, particularly as more mechanical power and automation become available to the economy and industry becomes less labor-intensive and more capital-intensive.

Recent literature indicates that part-time employment will be available for housewives within a year or two. This would both ease the workload of some women who are now working full time, and it would make it possible to employ others whose family commitments prevent tham from taking a full-time job. An article by Sonin and Savranskaia (1966) points out that this is done in Czechoslovakia for those (primarily women) who wish either a shortened workday or partial workweek with corresponding remuneration. The authors go on to say:

One cannot forget that, besides production work, a woman as a rule still manages the household and brings up the children; many of them like to change to shorter working hours. If such an order is introduced, then housewives who want to work but who cannot be away from home all day will go into social production (especially in ther service sphere). Investigations carried out in several districts and cities say that by this it is quite possible to draw approximately a quarter of the housewives to work. [p. 1].

This statement, interestingly enough, implies that women will be freed from their household drudgery only to be primarily employed in the servicing industry which, with its centralized facilities for washing, dry-cleaning, shoe repairing, and home delivery of products or mail order purchases, does not in essence distinguish itself from housework, nor is it held in any higher esteem. As a matter of fact, the authors point out that students graduating from secondary schools scrupulously avoid employment in this area and, if they accept such a job, frequently hold on to it for no longer than a year (Sonin and Savranskaia, 1966). And yet, it is likely that this kind of employment, given the gradual shift in the production of most household items of consumption to commercial enterprises, will become more available to women than the less suitable and more arduous occupations in agriculture, construction, and heavy industry. It is quite possible that the occupational distribution of women will, in time, tend to resemble that of other industrialized and urbanized societies.

Educational status of Soviet women

The indispensable underpinning for full participation of women in the life of a country is undoubtedly that of education. While in predominantly agricultural countries women can and do contribute significantly to the work force through farm work even though they may have little or no education, as soon as a society begins to industrialize, urbanize, and mechanize, the importance of literacy and education becomes overwhelming. While in the period between 1926 and 1959 the proportion of women in the agricultural labor force increased from 50 percent to 62 percent, the proportion of the total female labor force engaged in agricultural pursuits diminished from 91 percent

to 53 percent. This decrease was due to industrialization and the increased educational levels of women that enabled them either to specialize in some area of agriculture or to shift to more gratifying and less backbreaking jobs in other sectors of the economy (Karcz, 1967).

Before the Revolution, not more than 15 percent of the students in higher and secondary educational institutions were women (Beilin, 1935); by the school year 1927-28 the percentage had already climbed to 28 percent, and by 1940-41, to 58 percent. Since then, the percentage of women students in higher and secondary specialized schools has fluctuated, dropping to 53 percent in 1950-51, and to 42 percent in 1961-62, and then increasing again to 44 percent in 1965-66 (*Zhenshchiny i deti v SSSR*, 1963; *Vestnik Statistiki*, 1967). While there have been fluctuations in the percentage of women in educational institutions, the absolute number of such women keeps climbing.

An examination of levels of education by sex shows that in 1959 the men, though fewer in number, had somewhat higher rates of education than the women, and the rural population trailed behind the urban population, as the figures in Table 2 (Itogi Vsesoiuznoi, etc., 1962) will show. It can be surmised in the absence of precise statistics that the situation as of 1968 could not be radically different.

An examination of these figures reveals that residence (urban or rural) is probably one of the most important factors in determining access to education, particularly higher or university education. There are, of course, differences in the rates between the sexes, but these differences are not as marked as those due to residence. As might be expected, the largest discrepancy exists between urban men and rural women (7.5 times) in the realm of completed higher education. But in the urban population there were less than one-third more men then women with this level of education. In the rural areas, the rate was 50 percent higher for the males than for the females. The greatest equality (given the basic differences between urban and rural settings) was among those who had either an incomplete higher education or an incomplete intermediate education. There was more uniformity in the educational levels of the rural and urban populations among those who had only either an elementary or an incomplete seven-year school education. As a matter of fact, the rates of those with only this level of education for both sexes were higher in the rural than in the urban setting.

While the general level of education has risen considerably in the last two decades, the women's educational rate has risen faster than that of the men, if only because the women started from a more disadvantaged position. It seems, however, that women are channeled more frequently into the lower reaches of the educational system and that men still dominate the upper reaches. For example, women constituted exactly half of the students in semiprofessional schools in 1965-66, but only 44 percent in professional schools (*Vestnik Statistiki*, 1967). It is quite conceivable that cultural, economic, geographic, psychological, and social factors inhibit the full participation of women in education and this accounts for the rather large variations in the educational level of women in the different Soviet republics. Although women of the Central Asian Republics

TABLE 2   *Education of Population 10 Years and Older, 1959, by Sex and Residence*

	Higher Education Completed*	Incomplete Higher and Incomplete Secondary Education*		Elementary and Incomplete 7-Year Education
Urban and rural population				
Men and Women	23	338	310	162,464,288
Men	27	365	377	70,442,003
Women	20	318	258	92,022,285
Urban population				
Men and Women	40	429	298	80,282,263
Men	45	442	358	35,172,835
Women	35	420	252	45,109,428
Rural population				
Men and Women	7	249	321	82,182,025
Men	9	289	396	35,269,168
Women	6	219	264	46,912,857

*Expressed in rates per 1000 population.

have progressed faster between 1939 and 1959 than those in most of the other republics, they are still trailing considerably behind the more industrialized sections of the Soviet Union. As is the case in most societies, the very fact that education is available for all at low or no cost does not necessarily secure equal participation of all groups. It might be added that although the educational status of Soviet women is not quite at par with that of men, it is surpassed by very few other countries, the United States included.

THE POLITICAL ROLE OF THE SOVIET WOMAN

A brief review of the political role played by women in the Soviet Union seems to indicate that it falls somewhat short of the complete equality proclaimed by the Constitution and the ideologists. The most important political organization, the maker of policy and the wielder of power, is the Communist Party of the Soviet Union. In 1924, the Party was composed of 8.2 percent women; it doubled by 1932 to 15.9 percent, but declined by one point in 1941. The magnitude of the role played by women during World War II was reflected in the sizable increase in their proportion in the Party—17 percent by 1945, and about 20 percent by 1950. Since then, this proportion has remained more or less stationary. Three percent of the adult female population belongs to the Party as against five times as many among the corresponding males. The participation of women in leading Party organs has been rather trivial. In conclusion, the role of women in the Party is more than a token one, but it does not approach any degree of equality. In the *Komsomols* (Communist Youth League), the proportion of women members has always been higher than in the Party, a situation consistent with the observation that women are found in larger numbers in lower ranks and junior positions than in higher levels. At the present, between two-fifths and one-half of the *Komsomol* members are women. In the higher *Komsomol* organs, while women are better represented than in the Party, they are still in the minority. In the soviets, which are the formal governmental structure but not the real holders of political power, the

percentage of women is below their proportion in the adult population. Among Soviet leading organs such as the Supreme Soviet of the USSR, the proportion of women varies from less than one-third to about 43 percent in local soviets. This representation should not, however, be lightly dismissed: symbolically and visibly, the role of women in the soviets is an important one, and does represent a major advance over prerevolutionary days.

In the labor unions, state-controlled organs to ensure maximum productivity, women are fairly well represented, varying from 30.8 percent in top union organs to a high of 66.8 percent among labor organizers (*Zhenshchiny i deti v SSSR*, 1963).

In the period 1918-67, women have been awarded one-third of all awards, medals, decorations, and other signs of distinction, a most respectable performance.

In conclusion, women participate in the political life of the Soviet Union at a rather restrained and subdued level, particularly in the light of professed ideology. Time and again, the press has deplored the lack of greater participation of the distaff side in Party and other activities and has called for remedial action, but little has been accomplished. The regime, particularly the Party, is caught in a dilemma between the "inherited symbolism" of the working-class struggle and the formerly disinherited and dispossessed (including women), and the "logic of elitism" that requires it to lead and manage the society and thus take into its ranks those who can best further that leadership (Fainsod, 1963, p. 247). Somehow the woman, just like any worker or peasant, does not quite easily fit into that group.

The social roles of the Soviet woman

THE SOVIET HOUSEWIFE—A "DEPENDENT"?

One of the characteristics of the traditional, agrarian society was its "undifferentiated" nature: the family as a social unit was a kinship structure (a group of people related to each other by particularistic ties of descent and marriage) as well as an economic structure (a group of people working together in a common enterprise). In addition, it often was a religious group united by common symbols and an educational enterprise, since parents taught their children the skills necessary for adult life and work. The survival of the family over time depended on its ability to produce enough food and other implements, to bear children, and to socialize its young. The position of women as daughters, then wives, mothers, and grandmothers, was fairly clear and unambiguous and, given their limitations due to child-bearing and physical strength, they participated in the economic life of the group, often assuming a very important role in it.

One of the basic features of an industrialized society results from the shift of its locus of economic activities from the kinship group and the land to the factory, the plant, the mine, or the office. These require large concentrations of specialized manpower. People are brought together for the specific purpose of economic production and not related to each other by particularistic ties. The family, as such, has lost its major productive focus, and the members of the family who work must be able to leave their homes and "go to work." When both husband and wife work today, in most instances they do not work side by side. Indeed, the hiring of a spouse *qua* spouse would contravene the "achievement" or "universalistic" orientation of industrialized society. At the same time, as the family ceases to be a productive unit but continues as a consuming group, it must increasingly purchase commercially produced items, sometimes at a lower cost than an equivalent produced at home. This then requires additional cash income, and the commercial production of consumer goods and services opens employment opportunities for women who thus transfer their economically productive hours from the home to the plant, factory, or the office.

While the process of industrialization has had roughly similar effects on the role of women and the family wherever it has occurred, we suggest that there may be certain elements peculiar to the Soviet situation. The first, and perhaps the most significant, is the extraordinary loss of manpower suffered by the Soviet Union between 1917 and 1945. The second is the tempo of the industrialization and collectivization drive launched by Stalin in the late twenties, which required the fullest economic participation of the population. The third factor is the existence of an explicit ideology that encourages women to take part in the economic and social life of the country. Finally, equality of rights means, of course, equality of obligations in all activities.

The involvement of woman in economically productive processes outside the home has not, in any way, meant that she could leave the domestic sphere with impunity and concentrate exclusively on her job or her profession. Indeed, today's modern woman, including the Soviet woman, has one foot at home and one foot in industry, and maintains a precarious equilibrium between the two. Unable because of her domestic obligations to devote herself fully to a job or a career, she is often held down and stigmatized because of the "menial" nature of the functions she is called upon to perform as a housewife and mother. She resents her continued status as a "dependent," with the implications that in a family situation the man has the higher status and prestige. In the light of the critical role that Soviet women played during the war and in the postwar reconstruction, the calls on the part of the regime for her active participation in the "building of communism," and the official statements of her equality, it is humiliating for many a Soviet woman and housewife to have the word *izhdivenka* (dependent) entered in the blank calling for her occupation in her passport. Thus, the wife of a demobilized officer and the mother of two wrote:

Well, what kind of "dependents" are we? Even when we watch television we are knitting sweaters for the children. Our work is not easy; every woman, every real housekeeper knows this. We wash, scrub floors, clean, cook, sew, knit and mend; we alone raise our children—as a rule successfully—and help raise the children of others. We get neither vacation nor holidays. Then why aren't we respected; why are we treated so contemptuously? [Tatu, 1965, pp. 96-97].

This contempt seems to result, again, from the fact that the functions of the housewife, while "necessary," do not compare favorably with those required in the larger economic system. Furthermore, these functions contradict the claims of the equality of women, since men are not "stuck" with the same work.

One answer to the dilemma would be for the Soviet woman to establish and maintain her claim to equality through her employment in the society's economy, leaving behind once and for all the stigma of domestic functions. The theme that only through "hard" work on equality with man can the Soviet woman "earn" her respect and independence is sometimes sounded in the Soviet press by the more fundamentalist believers in female equality. Witness the following letter, printed in *Literaturnaia Gazeta* in 1967, entitled "Freedom for the kitchen?" (Lebedinskaia, 1967):

One often hears women who have devoted themselves entirely to housework in families where the fathers can afford everything needed complain bitterly that their husbands reproach them for their inability to save money. Any woman who has any self-respect at all would not only dig ditches but do the dirtiest work, if only to avoid hearing humiliating reproaches and to have the right to spend the money she has earned as she sees fit [p. 12].

In a later discussion in the same paper, Larisa Kuznetsova (1967) again formulated the dilemma faced by the Soviet woman. "It would be criminal," she writes, "even to look askance at those women who voluntarily choose the home and the family as their life's work and who are great in their world of selflessness and love." And yet, these women suffer from a lack of esteem in their society. The author continues:

Cooking, washing floors, and doing the laundry are the same sort of difficult and unskilled labor that we object to when done in industry by women. The entire difference, however, is that in industrial labor is of social importance and is paid for by the state, while housework is restricted to the private sphere and earns neither moral nor material rewards [p. 12].

There is little doubt, from a perusal of the Soviet sources, that the woman who deliberately chooses to become a housewife and mother and to restrict her activities to husband, children, and hearth is not considered a "complete" Soviet woman because she is not participating fully in the building of the new society and because her position and "dependence" are too strongly reminiscent of the bourgeois housewife of a former stigmatized past.

That some attention should be paid in the Soviet Union to the theme of the women who retreats voluntarily or under compulsion into domesticity and dependency is not, of course, accidental. It does reflect certain aspects of social reality and certain demands made upon the Soviet woman. The solution to this "problem" offered in fiction, the theater, and propaganda is her recognition, or the recognition on the part of those around her who would keep her in a dependent position, that not only does she have duties toward her state and fellow-man that transcend the narrow circle of her family, but that she could not be happy living as a "parasite" or "kept woman" because she would not be a "complete" or "real" person. The reality and the wholeness of her person can come only through her full participation in "life" and in the building of communism. That solution is, of course, well-suited to a society with a leadership that claims a feminist ideological heritage through Marx, Engels, Lenin, and the Russian revolutionary movement (Fréville, 1950). It is also convenient because of the Soviet Union's need to utilize female labor due to the manpower situation that makes the nonparticipation of women in the economy a problem probably more serious in the Soviet Union that in almost any other contemporary society.

The woman who chooses to participate and earn her independence on the basis of her occupational and other achievements is likely to be defined as exemplary, *provided* she does not totally neglect her other functions. We can thus delineate four general types of social roles of the woman in the Soviet Union based on her participation in the life of the country outside her home. Needless to say, these types are artifical constructs for the purpose of analysis. The first two types, the "strong" women, are positive heroines; the third and fourth types, the "weak" women, are considered socially regressed and thus negative representatives of their sex.

FOUR TYPES OF SOVIET WOMEN

Comrade Positive is the prototype of the *femme engagée*, the heroine of production who, in spite of tremendous obstacles, finds it possible to combine useful, productive work or study, with her family life and obligations. Like a tower of strength, she provides continuity and support to those around her and is able to transcend the narrow circle of her family. This positive, if somewhat manic and hyperactive, type of woman is endowed with endless energy and boundless devotion to the cause of building a communist society. She is the woman who is eager and ready to "prove herself" (*Slovo o nashikh zhenshchinakh* 1958). We find her, for example, described in *Pravada*, typified in six girls working at the foundry of the Likhachev Automobile Works in Moscow: "Their job is to pour hot mixtures into molds. Their work is strenuous, requiring no small exertion of muscles, eyes, and nerves." But mornings the girls walk to the foundry ". . . as though carried by the wind. One would imagine that they are hurrying to a ball, a date, a skiing party," so eager are they to pour "hot mixtures" into the molds (Hindus, 1961, pp. 279-80). But that is not all; they also decide to contribute a Sunday to work on the construction of a new stadium. One of them, however, a "frail, delicate, white-faced girl," failed to show up. "Neither her fragility, nor her pallor saved her from the sharp rebukes of her teammates."

These girls presumably find their ideal in someone like junior lieutenant Tereshenkova, the first woman cosmonaut, who proved the value of women in "building the glory of the state" (Topping, 1965):

To millions of Soviet women, junior lieutenant Tereshenkova is a promise of the future . . . [she] represents Soviet women as the Kremlin pictures them when an ideal Communist society, still a dream of the future, becomes a reality. She wears her hair in the latest, most popular, short, fluffy "kitten cut," but to Soviet propagandists, her space feat is proof that Soviet women are on "equal footing in work that calls for great courage, physical endurance, and much knowledge."

Comrade Positive is the one who will repay her debt to the society that gave her a free education and training, regardless of any obstacles that might confront her. If she cannot find employment in the foundry or the field, she at least will devote herself to social and community activities, for example, taking care of children whose mothers do work, setting up kindergartens in her building, or watching after the local authorities to see to it that they build the necessary facilities to take care of the children. At all times she wants to be prepared to have a good answer should her children or grandchildren ask her: "Mama (or Babushka), what did you do to help build communism?" (Chelovek i kollektiv, 1962)—a question aimed at mobilizing anticipatory anxiety, like the World War I poster depicting a deeply furrowed father being queried by his small son: "Daddy, what did *you* do during the war?"

Comrade Willing, But . . . is not less positive than the previous type, but some objective barriers keep her from fully participating in the building of communism. Her family situation, for example, prevents her from seeking employment; she is the "household prisoner" who is constantly trying to extricate herself from the "secondary" tasks of housework and childraising in order to go to work. She is ashamed of performing daily menial and unrewarding tasks and feels that, in the meanwhile, life outside is slipping by with real and important work waiting for her. It is, of course, primarily for her that the regime makes some special effort by investing in creches and kindergartens for the care of her young children, and since the building of a sufficient number of such institutions takes time and money, the waiting period for her liberation is sweetened by official attempts to raise her public image. *Pravda*, for example, has pointed out that housewives constitute a huge (labor reserve) army and they undoubtedly perform useful and needed work, but *Pravada* continues: "Ask these women, 'Are you satisfied with your position?' and the majority of them will answer this question in the negative. Only necessity has forced them to give up their occupations, and at the first opportunity, they will return to their beloved jobs" (January 6, 1962). Although the regime, understandably, does not blame her for her condition, there is an undertone in the comments about her type that implies that she is sometimes apt to give up too early and too easily in her efforts to find a solution to her dilemma.

In order for her to remain in this category and not to slide into the next, more opprobrious one, it must be shown that she is trying in every possible way to extricate herself from the secondary tasks of childrearing and housekeeping in order to go to work. Here again, one must not discount the influence of her environment, her friends, "the collective," the *Komsomols*, and the sympathetic husband who understands how much his wife suffers from having to stay home when excitement and joy await her outside of the confines of her home. Witness, for example, the anguished cry of the husband who writes: "I am very ashamed that I must maintain at home a young woman whose desire is to work" (*Chelovek i kollektiv*, 1962).

Comrade Reluctant is the negative type, as she is too easily inclined to slide into nonparticipation and lacks sufficient motivation or drive to involve fully herself in the life of the country. The dutiful and often spoiled and lazy daughter who awaits marriage in her parents' comfortable home, or the submissive wife who accepts the more traditional, i.e., "bourgeois" female roles centered around home, husband, and children, thus emerges as the standard "negative" person so dear to Soviet didactic literature (Dunham, 1960).

The temptation on the part of Soviet girls and women to remain in or backslide into dependency and domesticity might be called, to borrow from another context to be sure, "social regression" (Slater, 1963, pp. 339-64). Social regression may be defined as a tendency, either of individuals or of a group, to withdraw into largely self-sufficient roles leading to isolation from a larger network of social relationships and participation and the consequent failure to perform socially needed roles. The problem of social regression is particularly acute in a politically monolithic society such as the Soviet Union, which demands the full participation of *all* its members and their undivided loyalty to the regime. A case in point is Vera, the object of some attention on the part of *Pravda* (Mikhailova, 1962).

Vera completed a high school technical course on the assumption that she would later enter a higher institute or a university. In the meantime, she went to work in a plant as a lathe operator. There she met a nice fellow whom she soon married, although he had only seven years of education and certain old-fashioned ideas about the place of women. When he told her to stop working at the plant and to stay home and take care of their infant daughter, she passively acquiesced. Vera's mother, a good Soviet citizen, then wrote an anguished letter to *Pravda* and asked: "How did this happen? And am I the only one guilty of the fact that instead of a young specialist I raised an ordinary housewife?" *Pravda* did not quite think so and sent a correspondent to interview Vera and make a report. The fault, it asserted, lay in Vera's "collective," her school, her *Komsomal* comrades, and her coworkers at the plant who had forgotten her. Her husband must, of course, bear the

large share of the responsibility: the selfish oaf has a wife who takes good care of him, a nice little daughter, work he loves, and a good group at the plant. He has, meanwhile, imprisoned his wife within the four walls of dependent domesticity, and even Vera herself has forgotten that these four walls are her prison. The solution *Pravda* suggests is that the *Komsomols*, the collective, everyone is obligated to help Vera find her true happiness, which is in collectivism. Family life is nice, but, *Pravda* tells us, it always must be organically tied to creative work and education—to the life of the country. If one multiplies Vera by several million (about eleven million able-bodied women are neither working nor studying), and if one then juxtaposes this figure against the decreased number of new entrants into the labor force of the sixties, one realizes how critical Vera's attitude may be to the regime.

Comrade Parasitic is a more socially regressed type than Vera, who revealed to the correspondent from *Pravda* some degree of shame and discomfort at no longer working. Comrade Parasitic, on the other hand, does not work, does not want to work, and apparently does not feel that she ought to work if she has either parents or a husband to support her. Letters to *Pravda*, for example, all express the righteous indignation of women who have taken it upon themselves to blame their unemployed sisters and to support public morality. We are informed, for example, by the Moscow Comrade Z. Nemchinova that Ala, a young woman in her apartment, married a neighbor and the day after the marriage registration she did not return to work. Nemchinova and other neightbors,

. . . assured her [Ala] that one must work and study. But the young woman did not listen to . . . [their] advice. Soon Ala became pregnant and somehow she got a job only in order to receive compensation for the statutory leave. . . . . After the birth of the child she did not return to work. At home her mother does everything for her . . . one simply marvels at how a young, healthy woman can satisfy herself with such a life.

The tone of other letters to *Pravda* is more ominous: some of them even raise the question of *forcing* such women to work. Indeed, according to the 1961 Decree of the Presidium of the Supreme Soviet of the RSFSR, "On the strengthening of the struggle with persons who shirk socially useful labor and lead an anti-social, parasitic life" (*Sovetskaia Iustitsia*, 1961), Ala could technically be classified as a parasite and be subject to prosecution by a Comrades' Court, although there is not much evidence that women, by contrast to many men, have been convicted of "parasitism." But under present conditions, the official attitude seems to be that these women are considered as little more than deserters, kept women, and social prostitutes. If, in addition, they have received a specialized or technical education, they are considered to have accepted the training under false pretenses and to be swindling the state and *the people* in their refusal to work.

WORKING CONDITIONS

Granting that most women in the Soviet Union should and must work, the question that has been raised in the pages of *Literaturnaia Gazeta* is, "What kind of work

TABLE 3   Time Budgets, Nonworking Time, Men and Women*

	Men			Women		
	Hours	Minutes	Percent of total	Hours	Minutes	Percent of total
Free time	3	09	20.0	1	43	10.8
Housework and self-care	2	43	17.3	5	10	32.6
Time for sleep and meals	8	58	57.1	8	11	51.7
Expenditure of time connected with production work	0	53	5.6	0	47	4.9
Total nonworking time	15	43	100.0	15	51	100.0

*Based on a sample of 1,477 families, Moscow and Novosibirsk, 1959.

should women do?" In the past few years, two viewpoints have been expressed on the subject. One is that equality of the sexes means that women must undertake exactly the same kinds of jobs as men to justify that equality: any kind of differential or preferential treatment would smack of inequality and discrimination. The other viewpoint is that a woman, simply because she is a woman, is entitled to some respect and should be spared certain types of work—the heavy and dirty jobs, for example—which should be left to the men. In a review of the controversy perpared by Vera Bil'shaia for the *Literaturnaia Gazeta* (1959), the author quotes a woman reader named Nilova, who had written that "... only with sweat on her face can a woman compel respect for herself, not only as a mother but also as a human being." This is perhaps an extreme viewpoint. We have seen that there is specific labor legislation regulating the work of women and forbidding their employment in certain kinds of occupations—including underground mining. Yet there is plenty of evidence, some of it gathered by Nemtsov (1957; 1958) and published earlier in *Literaturnaia Gazeta*, that women are employed in the roughest, most difficult, and physically most strenuous occupations, including coal mining, asphalt paving, stevedoring, and foundry work. Nemtsov asks why women should perfom such jobs, particularly when men are available to do them, and why, in general, such jobs are not performed by machines now that the Soviet Union has a technology so advanced that it can put a manned satellite into space. He then suggests several explanations, the most important being a culturally ingrained lack of respect for the woman that leads to her being considered a natural candidate for the heaviest and dirtiest jobs. In others words, it does not shock Soviet people to see women used as beasts of burden. As a result, men will be appointed as foremen over women because of their sex and not on the basis of their qualifications.

The second factor is the usual one of bureaucratic inertia and costs: managers will not install labor-saving devices if they are not forced to do so. Nemtsov had complained to an engineer that in a certain plant men in one shop worked in almost surgical cleanliness making radio tubes, while the casting shop next door where most of the heavy work was performed by women was dirty and poorly ventilated. The engineer saw nothing anomalous in this situation, explain-

ing that "technology determines everything." When Nemtsov sked, "What about the people?" the engineer muttered something about an extra milk allocation to women doing arduous work.

Two more factors also help to determine the jobs available to women: one is that girls finishing the intermediate schools often do not have a specialized education and can work only in relatively unskilled jobs. The other is that in certain districts there are no alternate employment possibilities for women who are presently engaged in totally unskilled or rough occupations.

DOMESTIC WORK: "THE SQUIRREL IN THE CAGE"

The fate of the Soviet housewife is not, from what one can read and observe, a particularly happy one. Since the family today has become primarily a consuming unit, the purchase of the necessary items for the family's daily needs is a woman's job. With the poor development of shopping and retail facilities typical of the Soviet Union, it is likely to be the equivalent of a full-time occupation. Domestic duties are further complicated by the difficult housing conditions under which most urban families must live, in particular, the frequent necessity of sharing kitchen and bathing facilities with several other families in the same apartment.

In addition to her housework, the woman has to care for the children. The average housewife may spend as much as three hours a day shopping and as much time preparing food, cleaning, making beds, washing dishes, and doing the myriad other tasks that women, particularly when they have no labor-saving devices, must perform. Consequently, men, according to time-budget studies, have twice as much if not more free time at their disposal than women, as shown in Table 3 (Prudenski and Kolpakov, 1962). But women were running in their apartments like "squirrels in a cage" (Nemtsov, 1957). It is, of course, at that point that the vaunted equality guaranteed in the Constitution completely breaks down.

Women, like men, are expected to put in a full day's work at the office, in the plant, or in the field, but Soviet men, jealous of their masculinity and spoiled by their indulgent mothers and submissive sisters, refuse to help their wives in their household duties. What would the neighbors say if they saw him washing the dishes or making the beds? No wonder, then, that some Soviet women have taken to complaining in the newspapers that they are asked to work just as hard as their husbands on the job, but that at home their husbands will not lift a finger to help.

At this point, it may be of some interest briefly to summarize what remedial steps have been proposed in the Soviet press (Nemtsov, 1957):

1. Strict or stricter adherence to labor regulations on the work of women, and possibly reserving some of the "lighter" types of work for women.

2. Greater flexibility in the employment of married women with children: part-time work, elimination of night shifts, shortening of the work day, and work that can be done at home. These suggestions are being considered by the regime, but no major move has yet been made toward their implementation except, as noted earlier, part-time work.

3. Reducing the women's domestic load: more institutions for the care of children, better and more household appliances, and relief from some food preparation through more restaurants and better commercial processing and preparation of food, such as precooked meals by catering organizations.

4. General cultural reshaping of national attitudes by artists, writers, and film makers who should stop romanticising hard work by women, or even its routine acceptance. Youth should be inculcated with an attitude of greater respect for women so they will not find it "natural" to see girls employed as stevedores or coalminers.

CHILDBEARING, WORK, AND THE BIRTH RATE

We must raise another consideration: If woman plays a crucial role in the economic life of a society, she plays an even more indispensable role in the bearing and raising of children. To some irreducible degree these functions and regular employment in industry conflict, and too great an emphasis on woman as a worker might depress the birth rate below a desirable level. With better medical care and environmental conditions, a lower infant mortality rate and consequent longer life expectancies, a society can maintain itself with a proportionately much lower birth rate than it could in earlier times.

From the viewpoint of society, furthermore, the removal of an unskilled and easily replaceable woman from the work force so that she may bear a child or several children will be less costly than the removal of a woman who has had many years of costly professional training and education. Moreover, a professional woman who took five or ten years to complete her childbearing cycle would find that some of her skills had become obsolete by the time she returned to work, a situation not facing the unskilled person. There might, therefore, be more of a tendency for a professional woman to restrict her childbearing than for a nonprofessional, leading to a division of labor not only between the sexes, but also within the female sex according to sociooccupational levels. Soviet data, summarized in Table 4 (*Zhenshchiny i deti vSSSR*, 1963, p. 68), indicate that farm women have more children than women workers, and the latter have more children than women employees, a category that includes professionals. This may, of course,

TABLE 4   *Families according to Number of Children under 16 Years by Occupational Groups (Percentage of all families) 1962*

	Employees	Industrial Workers	Collective Farmers
With one child	50	46	40
With two children	41	39	32
With three children	8	12	19
With four or more children	1	3	9
Total	100	100	100

be partially the result of geographical factors and the supply of housing as well as of Soviet policy, which encourages large families among the lower-income population. We might further surmise that it is possible for a professional woman to find a career, a kind of interest and commitment similar to that found by a man, and that she might not be inclined to have a large family, if she chooses to have any children at all.

Research on displaced Soviet women indicated that professional women and specialists tended to be consistently more satisfied with their jobs than men, but that women responded to their work experience predominantly according to the occupational level and only incidentally according to sex; the higher their type of job, the greater their satisfaction with it. With mechanization and automation, unskilled women workers may well be gradually withdrawn from the labor force, not necessarily to go back to their homes, but perhaps to engage in social, welfare, and cultural work. Professional women will continue their full-time commitment to their work equally with men. From a functional viewpoint, the elimination of women from the pool of skilled and professional talent would be disastrous in terms of their contribution to society. By the same token, the elimination of the childraising role, or its toning down and replacement by other institutional arrangements, might present other problems we will briefly mention below.

MOTHERHOOD

What about the children? This question must be raised because the mere physical production of children is *never* enough to ensure the continuity of a society. They must be "socialized," i.e., transformed into reasonably well-behaving members of the adult world. Traditionally, socialization has been a family function, with the mother playing the most important role as an extension of her childbearing functions.

The logical application of Engels' scheme of the societal and public upbringing of children by agencies other than the family, toward which Soviet society on ideological grounds seems to be heading, raises the very critical question of maternal deprivation—the psychological correlates of institutional upbringing upon the personality of children brought up without a close relationship with the mother. It has been found that this does produce a deleterious effect on personality, on the intellectual level, and on social adjustment, that is for all practical purposes irreversible (Bowlby, 1952; World Health Organization, 1962). It is in this light that the Soviet scheme for the institutional upbringing of children, which is consonant with Marxist ideology, the belief in the plasticity of the individual and the importance of the milieu and economic needs, should be examined with critical interest. If the hypothesis of the effects of maternal deprivation is a valid one not only for Western cultures, then the Soviet scheme should be a source of important information for the planners for institutionalized societies. Some evidence has come to light that Soviet children raised in orphanages or children's homes, i.e., raised in a nonfamilial atmosphere, invariably perform more poorly in their school work than those who come from families, even though these families might be economically deprived. One of the main reasons for this is that the children in institutions do not have a single adult person with whom they can identify and establish a continuous relationship. In one Soviet school, for example, children could not recognize themselves in group pictures because someone had forgotten to hang mirrors. In another such institution, the personnel were so busy in routine tasks that they had hardly any time to converse with their charges (Field and Anderson, 1968).

There is also some indication that a great deal of the juvenile delinquency the increasingly seems to plague Soviet society may be due, among other things, to broken families and to families in which the mother, because she either has to work or wants to work, neglects her children. If she is lucky she has her own mother or a relative to cook and mind the children when she is at work (Fischer, 1961). However, most women have to cope alone with every aspect of their occupational and domestic life. Needless to say, not too much individual attention can be devoted to the upbringing of children if the mother works between forty and forty-five hours a week. Futhermore, the lack of day-nurseries, kindergartens, and boarding schools forces working mothers to leave their children alone as soon as they are old enough to care for themselves. And even a loving and doting grandmother is not always an ideal substitute for a mother: she is particularly prone to overindulge her grandchildren and thus is frequently blamed if the youngsters get into trouble (Parygina, 1968).

The mother's lot, at least from the evidence we have in the Soviet sources, seems to be a particularly difficult one. She is expected to work outside the home and often is blamed if, as a result, her children bear the familiar characteristics of parental, particularly maternal, neglect. If she stays at home to care for her children and household, she receives little recognition and is criticized for her withdrawal from the "real" life of building the new society. And if her children grow up into responsible adults, she will earn no particular credit.

It is possible that as Soviet society becomes more prosperous and the critical need for women in the economy recedes, the traditional role of motherhood will receive more unequivocal support. Indeed, the recognition of the critical role played by mothers was well-stated in an article by N. I. Pirogov (Garina, 1967), published in *Izvestiia* in 1967:

The upbringing of society must go hand in hand *with the upbringing of children* .... All who are preparing to be useful citizens must first learn to be people. ... Let women realize that by tending the cradle of a human being, by establishing the games of his childhood and teaching his lips to say his first words ... they become the chief architects of the society [p. 6].

The article further asks that the importance of the task of childraising be recognized on a par with that of giving birth and it argues that only a mother, and not a kindergarten or other similar institution, can give the child the individual attention he requires. The author then faults a society that esteems a woman who works in a factory more highly than one who stays at home supervising the growth and upbringing of her children. It is therefore quite possible that as the industrialization drive reaches a plateau in the Soviet Union and the demand for womanpower begins to decrease, greater official recognition will be accorded to the importance of motherhood for the emotional and intellectual balance of society and that this mechanism of socialization will be judged, after all, as more effective than the institutional arrangements of the type suggested by the more utopian Marxists.

"WOMANHOOD"—OR THE REDISCOVERY OF FEMININITY

The emphasis on equality and the large scale employment of women in the economy, the ideological rejection of the bourgeois-like qualities of the wife and daughter with their implication of parasitism, have all tended to play down, if not to eliminate from the Soviet scene, any of the accepted concerns with femininity that seem so commonplace in the West. And yet, this concern has not disappeared—indeed it seems to be reappearing with great vigor. What is it, then, that Soviet men expect from Soviet women and from which they find it so difficult to part? A survey conducted in different areas of the Soviet Union revealed that Soviet men want "... wives who are sincere, cultivated, loyal, who like family life, domestic comfort and children" (Kasiukov and Mendeleev, 1967, p. 18). These results seem to indicate that after fifty years of propaganda to emancipate Soviet women from the domestic and bourgeois virtues and to turn them into equal participants in the building of a new society, there is still a longing among Soviet men for "feminine" women and feminine qualities. The obvious lack of femininity so often observed by visitors to the Soviet Union and apparently a source of pride for those who believe in absolute equality, was publicly lamented in 1967 by an elder poet, Ilia Sel'vinskii in the *Literaturnaia Gazeta*, who called, among other things, for the idealization of "feminine charms":

Feminine beauty is not a bourgeois prejudice. Woman is the most perfect being that nature ever created. The esthetic of feminine beauty is vital to the whole country, to men, as well as women. Some of the greatest masterpieces of poetry, painting and sculpture have been dedicated to feminine charm [p. 12].

Sel'vinskii further complained about the apparent indifference of women and young girls to their appearance. According to him, even leading women in the professions do not concern themselves sufficiently with this.

There are, on the other hand, increased indications that Soviet women are just as interested in how they look as their counterpart in the West (Curtis, 1967), and that this concern with their appearance is not, as it formerly was under Stalin, interpreted by the moral censors as kowtowing to an ideologically alien and subversive culture. The young women of the Soviet Union, conscious of the fact that their mothers have aged and even died prematurely as a result of the heavy burden they carried, seem determined not to share their fate. Perhaps the remark of a Moscow girl to an American friend expresses this feeling (Frost, 1965):

Russian women work. A full week—that's tiring. They also run the house. Shop. Stand in line. Take care of the children. Do the wash. Stand in another line. After they are married, they haven't got five minutes to look in the mirror, let alone take care of what needs to be done. They get their work done somehow but simply have no energy left to look after themselves. So they deteriorate. But our generation will be different, I assure you. . . . Our generation is different! We know what the trouble is, and we *care* about our appearance [p. 17].

The Russian woman who "cares" spends her money on cosmetics and attractive clothes as far as they are available. She dyes her hair, demands more household appliances as well as more creches and kindergartens, and seems on the whole as anxious as any woman in any industrialized society to be recognized both as a person *and* as a woman.

Conclusions

An examination of the status and the role of woman in Soviet society may shed some light not only on the specifics of the Soviet situation but, in more general terms, on the fate of woman in the contemporary, large-scale industrialized or industrializing society. The Soviet case, though it has its unique cultural and structural features, may represent in an acute and concentrated form, the relatively new dilemmas and uncertainties of modern woman, torn between her blurred feminine identity and her role as a wife and mother with the economic trivialities of her domestic pursuits on the one hand, and the uncertainties, temptations, pitfalls, and opportunities of an occupational world that often needs her services and yet has looked with ambivalence on her equal participation and status in that world.

REFERENCES

Beilin, E. A. *Kadry spetsialistov SSSR [Specialized Personnel of the USSR].* Moscow, 1935, p. 348. Cited in Alex Inkeles and Raymond A. Bauer, *The Soviet Citizen.* Cambridge: Harvard University Press, 1959.

Bil'shaia-Pilopenko, Vera L'vovna. "Kto prav: Vl. Nemtsov ili E. Nilova?" ("Who is Right Vl. Nemtsov or E. Nilova?"). *Literaturnaia Gazeta,* January 10, 1959.

Bowlby, John *Maternal Czre and Mental Health,* 2nd ed. Geneva: World Health Organization, 1952.

"Chelovek i kollektiv" ("The Individual and the Group") *Pravda,* March 23, 1962.

Curtis, Charlotte. "Soviet Women Cherish Their Femininity." *New York Times,* October 9, 1967.

Dodge, Norton T. *Women in the Soviet Economy: Their Role in Economic, Scientific, and Technical Development.* Baltimore: Johns Hopkins Press, 1966.

Dunham, Vera Sandomirsky. "The Strong Woman Motif." *The Transformation of Russian Society.* Cyril E. Black, ed. Cambridge: Harvard University Press, 1960, pp. 459-83.

Engels, Friedrich. *The Condition of the Working Class in England in 1844.* W. O. Henderson and W. H. Chaloner, trans, and eds. New York: Macmillan, 1958.

Fainsod, Merle. *How Russia Is Ruled.* Cambridge: Harvard University Press, 1965.

Feshbach, Murray. "Manpower in the U.S.S.R.: A Survey of Recent Trends and Prospects," *New Directions in the Soviet Economy, Part III, The Human Resources.* Washington, D.C.: U. S. Government Printing Office, 1966.

Field, Mark G. "Re-legalization of Abortion in Soviet Russia." *New England Journal of Medicine,* 255 (August 30, 1956), 421-27.

_____ and David E. Anderson. "Family and Social Problems." *Prospects for Soviet Society* Allen Kassof, ed. New York: Praeger, 1968, pp. 386-417.

Fischer, Markoosha. "The Grandmothers." *Harper,* Special Supplement, May 1961.

Fréville, Jean, ed. *La Femme et le Communisme: Anthologie des Grands Textes de Marxisme.* Paris, 1950.

Frost, G. "What Russian Girls Are Like." *New York Times Magazine,* January 24, 19nn.

Garina, Ye. "Izvestiia v krugu sem'i: Y kolybeli chelovek" ("Izvestia with the Family Circle: At the Cradle of a Human Being"). *Izvestiia,* August 17, 1967. Also available in English, *Current Digest of the Soviet Press, CDSP,* 33.

Halle, Fannina. *Woman in Soviet Russia.* New York: Viking Press, 1933.

Hindus, Maurice. *House without a Roof.* Garden City, N.Y.: Doubleday, 1961.

Inkeles, Alex. "Family and Church in the Postwar USSR." *The Annals of The American Academy of Political and Social Sciences,* 263 (May 1949), 33-44.

Itogi Vsesoiuznoi Perepisi Naseleniia 1939 Joda 1962, Table 20, 74-79.

Juviler, Peter. "Family Reform on the Road to Communism." *Soviet Policy Making: Studies of Communism in Transition.* New York: Praeger, 1967.

Karcz, Jersy F., ed. *Soviet and East European Agriculture.* Los Angeles: University of California Press, 1967.

Kasiukov, I., and A. Mendeleev. "Mnenie sotsiologa: Nuzhni li talent sem'ia-ninu?" ("Sociologists Opinion: Must a Family Man Have Talent?"). *Nedelia,* 12 (March 12-18, 1967). Also available in English in *CDSP,* 19, 13.

Kuznetsova, Larisa. "Kak chei zhe udel' kukhnia?" (Whose Job Is in the Kitchen?"). *Literaturnaia Gazeta, CDSP,* 19, 33, (July 12, 1967).

Lebedinskaia, L. "Svoboda dlia Kukhni?" ("Freedom for the Kitchen?"). *Literaturnaia Gazeta,* February 22, 1967.

Marx, Karl. *Capital: A Critique of Political Economy.* Edited by Friedrich Engels, translated from Third German Edition by Samuel Moore and Edward Aveling, and revised and amplified according to the Fourth German Edition by Ernest Unterman. New York: Modern Library, 1906. First ed., Hamburg: Meissner, 1890-1894.

Massell, Gregory J. "Law as an Instrument of Revolutionary Change in a Traditional Milieu: The Case of Soviet Central Asia." *Law and Society Review,* 2, 2 (1968), 179-228.

Mikhailova, O. "Spravedlivaia obida" ("A Justified Vexation"). *Pravda,* January 6, 1962.

Money, John. "Development Differentiation of Femininity and Masculinity Compared." In *The Potential of Women,* Seymour M. Farber and Roger H. L. Wilson, eds. New York: McGraw-Hill, 1963.

Nemtsov, V. "Ob uvazhenii k zhenshchine" ("On Respect toward Women") *Literaturnaia Gazeta,* June 11, 1957.

_____."Eshche raz ob uvazhenii k zhenshchine" ("Once More on Respect toward Woman"). *Literaturnaia Gazeta,* April 12, 1958.

Parry, Albert. "Soviet Women Physicians: A New Numerical Balance?" *Review of Soviet Medical Sciences,* 4, 1 (1967), 13-21.

Parygina, Natalia. "Zhiteiskie besedy: Dobrota vo vred" ("Everyday Conversation: Kindness to a Fault"). *Pravda,* January 26, 1968; *CDSP,* 20, 4.

Prokofev, M. K. *Komsomoskaya Pravda,* May 20, 1966; *CDSP,* 18, 23 (1966).

Prudenski, G., and Kolpakov, B. "Questions concerning the Calculations of Non-working Time in Budget Statistics." *Problems of Economics,* 12 (1962), 31.

Sel'vinskii, Ilia. "Proza o prekrasnoi dame" ("Prose about the Beautiful Lady"). *Literaturnaia Gazeta,* April 12, 1967.

Semenov, Vladimir. "Dva stikhotvorenia" ("Two Poems"), *Novii Mir (New World),* Vera S. Dunham, trans. 7 (1958), 137-38.

Shim, Eduard, "A nu-ka, vziali!" ("Ready Heave!"). *Literaturnaia Gazeta,* (February 1, 1967), 12.

Slater, Philip E. "On Social Regression." 28 (June 1963), 339-64.
"Slovo o nashikh zhenshchinakh" ("A Word about Our Women").
   Literaturnaia Gazeta, October 7, 1958.
Sonin, M. Ya. *Vosproizvodstvo . . . rabochei sily v SSSR i balans
   truda (Productivity of the Work Force in the USSR and the
   Balance of Labor).* Moscow: Gosplanizdat, 1959. p. 88.
Sonin, M. Ya., and Savranskaia. "Sotsiologicheskie zametkicheloveki
   rabota" (Sociological Notes—Man and Work). *Literaturnaia
   Gazeta*, September 22, 1966.

Tatu, Michel. "Are Soviet Housewives Citizens?" *Atlas* (February
   1965), 96-97 (trans. from *Le Monde*, 1963).
Topping, Audrey R. "First in Space—But Not in Femininity." *New
   York Times Magazine*, June 30, 1965.
Vestnik Statistiki (Statistics Bulletin), 1, 1967.
World Health Organization. *Deprivation of Maternal Care: A Reas-
   sessment of Its Effects.* Geneva: Public Health Papers, 1962.
*Zhenshchiny i deti v SSSR: statisticheskii sbornik (Women and
   Children in the USSR).* Moscow: Gostatizdat. 1963.

33 A re-evaluation of the primary role of the Communist Chinese woman: the homemaker or the worker

Lucy Jen Huang

One of the major changes in Communist China since 1949 has been the shift in the status of women and a re-education of their new roles in and out of the family. This paper is a report on this change, especially the re-shaping and the re-evaluation of women's attitudes and values concerning their loyalty and devotion to the family and their attitude toward work. Data for this paper was drawn from the problem discussion column of *Women of China*, a major women's magazine covering issues from April to September 1960. The editors of the magazine, realizing that there was still much conflict in the minds of women concerning their loyalty to the family and to the state through work and production, published a letter concerning the attitude of a married worker, Liu Soo-wo (written by one of her co-workers) with regard to her preference of family happiness and well-being over that of devotion to work. They invited the readers to express their views concerning Liu's case in the problem discussion column. Ten letters from readers were published, nine of which were disapproving of Liu's placing family happiness before her service to the state. The concluding editorial of this discussion was also reproachful of her capitalistic ideology in her pursuit of individual and family happiness instead of her contribution to the state through labor.

It is to be borne in mind that women's participation under the present regime does not only mean their contribution to the state and Communist Party, but it also means the liberation of women from the confines of the home, the daily household chores, and their subordination to men through economic dependence. The regime has made continuous attempts to impress public opinion with regard to this latter significance: the elevation of the status of women for the first time in Chinese history. Aside from the new Marriage Laws under the present government, the effective literacy campaign and equal opportunity in education between the sexes, the participation of women in the labor force has been of primary importance in the struggle for sexual equality in China.

However, the strong push for women to work full time outside the home has been so emphatic during the regime's first decade that the public has begun to frown on those who remain at home. They are typed as the "family woman" and often find difficulty in justifying their position. Editors of the magazine have begun to publish articles defending the much maligned women who remained at home. Numerous articles in the mid-fifties were devoted to such topics as: "How Can Family Women Better Serve Socialism?" "Is Family Labor Unimportant?" "It is Glorious to Serve in the Family." "It is Wrong to Look Down on Family Women" and "Family Women Should Do Their Utmost to Participate in Active Service in Society." Many women, due to frequent pregnancies, ill health or large numbers of small children, found it necessary to return home, but were reluctant to resume the dependent role of a "family woman," and the target of social ostracism. A short quotation from an article entitled, "A Correct Approach to the Problem of Retirement of Women Cadres" will illustrate this point:

Some woman comrades erroneously think that returning home for household work would turn themselves into "parasites," fearing that they would be looked down upon when they are not economically independent. . . . It is essential that she be ideologically prepared, takes a firm stand and has a strong conviction. She must not heed any sarcasm or ridicule but feel convinced herself that to take up housework is a glory, is beneficial to the nation and the people and carries with it a bright future.[1]

It is understandable that under such social pressure to

Reprinted from Lucy Jen Huang, "A Re-evaluation of the Primary Role of the Communist Chinese Woman: The Homemaker or the Worker," Marriage and Family Living, May 1963, pp. 162-168, by permission of the National Council on Family Relations. This article was supported by a research grant from The Human Ecology Fund.

work outside the home, many women who have found full time work impractical, burdensome, or taxing, continue to work for fear of criticism and ridicule, or for the sake of patriotism. Raffaello Uboldi,[2] in his articles on his first-hand impressions of Red China today, described the case of a commune worker, Mrs. Ting, a doctor's wife, the mother of five children, who earned from 24 to 26 yuan a month. After paying for food at the collective mess hall, sending children to the nurseries, washing, ironing and mending clothes, for transportation and for house-cleaning, it was found that every month Mrs. Ting used up not only her 24 to 26 yuan but also the amount her husband would ordinarily spend if she remained at home to look after the children. When the reporter observed to the director of the commune that Mrs. Ting did not have a penny's profit left and that she was actually giving the state eight hours of gratuitous work every day, he replied that Mrs. Ting, however, escaped from being enslaved to her husband and children.

New conflict of roles:
the homemaker and the worker

The letter the editors chose to publish concerned Liu Soo-wo, the daughter of a farmer who went to the city to work in a factory. She was a good worker and sent all her wages home to her parents. She was said to have envied girls with beautiful clothes and husbands with higher earning power. In 1957 she was introduced to a skilled worker with a high wage and married him. She began to dress better and be more concerned about her personal appearance. They were very happy in their little new home. She often told her friends in the factory, "After getting back to my warm home and seeing my husband, I forget about everything else."

Her home was far from the factory. When there were meetings in the evening in the factory, she would not get home until after 10 p.m. She often negotiated with her superiors to assign her Sundays off so she could have the day home with her husband. She complained that she did not have much time with her husband as it was. Her first baby arrived in 1958. Due to lack of milk she put her baby in a nursery and visited him every two or three days. She was afraid he would be mistreated there, according to the letter. When factory superiors asked her to move closer to the factory, seeing that her work efficiency had gone down, she refused, saying that she would rather stay with her husband who had two rooms facing the sun. She was described as having rushed home as soon as the bell rang, and was not eager to participate in contests in work production and new innovations. When her husband was sick she wanted to take leave to stay home with him. Friends warned her that she would not be paid if she left to nurse her husband. She replied, "I don't care. I have plenty of rice to eat even if I just stay home to take care of my child. After all, once married, a woman hasn't got as much time and energy to work as single girls do." She was criticized for her preoccupation with her dress and appearance, and for devoting too much time to her small family. "Who

doesn't want to have a good husband and a happy home?" she retorted. "Work is important, but one cannot ignore her family either."

The response to the published letter was, in general, disapproving of Liu's attitude from the letters selected by the editors. The single sympathetic letter,[3] written by a salesgirl, is quoted in part in the following:

"Before marriage, I was very efficient in my work. At that time my work was at its best. But after marriage it was different. I was soon pregnant. The effect of pregnancy was hard to take. I could not eat. I could not sleep. I was weak. My spirit was low, not to speak of work. Sometimes I even had to take a few days' leave. Pregnancy left me heavier and clumsier. I was very lazy. After the birth of the child there were heaps of difficult problems, taking the child to the feeding room, to the nursery, taking care of his food, clothes, bottles, and diapers. When the baby was sick, my heart was in great anxiety. I could not work in peace. This is the natural reaction of a mother."

The sympathetic reader continued to agree with Liu that single girls could work better since they did not have any involvement with a family. She explained Liu's unwillingness to work overtime, her preoccupation with spending Sundays with her husband and her eagerness to get home after work, as the expression of her true love for her husband: not wanting him to be lonely at home. She agreed with the other readers that one should not let these things affect one's work, yet it was hard not to be distracted after marriage. She showed concern that if Liu spent too much time after eight hours' work with overtime, meetings, study groups and Sundays away from her husband, it might arouse his dissatisfaction and affect their love. Her final statement runs as follows:

"The Revolution's objective is to bring happiness to everyone. And the source of this happiness is family happiness, something that no one should be deprived of. This should be considered the most important part of all. Therefore, I consider work and family are equally important."[4]

New values and attitudes
for women in socialism

Even though the above-mentioned reader considered the family equally important with work, rather than more important than work, her letter was highly criticized. The nine letters and the editorial opinions of the journal took the opposite view concerning this case, claiming that working for socialism should be considered of primary importance, and that the family should take a secondary position. They considered Liu guilty of "middle class thinking," "individualistic" and "intoxicated" by the warmth of her little family. They continued that there would be no happiness away from the group. They described Liu as taking a "convenient boat" and a "dead-end street." They reasoned that without working toward a happy socialistic society the family would have no future. "If socialism is well established, then family life will become better," one of them said. "If there's no happy society, there will be no happy family." The following are the new symbols and slogans of the Communist woman:

A. HEDONISM AND INDIVIDUALISM ARE DETRIMENTAL TO SOCIALISM

One of Liu's major weaknesses pointed out by readers was her personal philosophy of individualism and hedonism. Considerable discussion was centered on her choice of a mate which was "contaminated by economic factors," referring to her envying girls with husbands with a high earning power and social position, and finally marrying a high income worker herself. This is a serious charge in present day China in which a new trend[5] has emerged with girls marrying individuals who are their social and educational inferiors in the name of patriotism and political compatibility. The supreme respect for semi-skilled and unskilled labor, agricultural as well as industrial, necessitates a change in the traditional attitude of marrying someone whose "front door faces that of yours," or marrying for the sake of social mobility. Furthermore, her concern for personal appearance and beautiful clothes aroused much dissension among her colleagues due to the Communist drive toward frugality and simplicity in the new regime, reminiscent of the early American Puritanical values. One reader revealed her capitalistic philosophy and hedonistic way of life before her "awakening" as follows:

"Later I married a middle school teacher. He was very good to me. We love each other warmly. Our life was different after marriage. I was concerned with dressing and eating better. I admired those who dressed beautifully (something I used to frown upon.) When I went to work, my heart was not there."[6]

Another reader related her unhappy estrangement and separation for three years from her husband due to her lack of progressive thinking. "Because both of us were working, life was good. Why should we progress anymore? I became very reactionary. My husband criticized me and I was most unhappy."[7] She was able to return to the socialist way before her husband carried out his threat of divorce. One reader, the wife of an engineer, admitted that she was capitalistic in her thinking even after receiving Party education. She confessed that after work she used to be concerned with trifles at home such as caring for children, picking flowers, growing fish, tidying up the house or going out to see movies, opera and eat in restaurants.

B. LOVE FOR THE FAMILY IS SECONDARY TO WORK FOR THE PEOPLE

Another of Liu's reactionary qualities was her preoccupation with her home and love for her family, instead of devotion to her work for the people. Her frank admission that when she got home and saw her husband she would forget everything else but her "small warm family" aroused much criticism among the readers. Her concern over the well-being of her baby in the nursery, her husband's health and her desire to be with him appeared to be an unnecessary "intoxication" with her little family. Married women, according to Liu's critics, did not have to lag behind single girls in work production if they placed labor for the welfare of the people in a more important position than family happiness. Several progressive women, newly converted from Liu's reactionary attitude, confessed that being "in-

toxicated" with the little family brought them contempt from husbands and colleagues. One said her husband described her as "backward to death." Not until she participated in wholehearted production did she recover her happy family again. She stated:

"Now we have a happy family. We not only have work, education and production experience, but also have love for each other. . . . It is only when one puts work first, with husband and wife joining in group production, compatible in political ideology that we can have lasting and beautiful happiness.[8]

Another converted socialist woman looked back at those days when she used to talk about trifles; children, clothes and other meaningless interests in the small family. Now conversations at home were enlivened with such mechanical subjects as automatic eye-washers, automatic urine indicators, automatic pain indicators and needle boilers. Her husband, instead of buying her gifts in clothes, now presented her with books in medicine and mechanics, encouraging her in further learning and working for Communism. She said though life was hectic, yet her health had improved and her life was meaningful and happy.[9] A high school teacher's wife tried to warn Liu against repeating her own past mistakes.

"In the midst of production I would be reminiscing walking down the street with my husband. I was intoxicated in my sweet married life. I often argued for time to be with (my husband) him. When I went to work Mondays I would wish it were Saturday again. Six days' parting was too long for me. I gradually felt that my work was standing in the way of my happiness."[10]

Her short sojourn at home did not prove to be as idealistic and happy as she had anticipated. She became bored, grouchy and envious of her working colleagues. Her husband began to look down on her for her "backwardness." The final happy ending came when her old factory leaders granted her request to return to labor for the people. She stated:

"After returning to the factory, I put the two children in the nursery. I saw them once a week. Everytime I saw them, I found them grown more in body and intelligence. . . . My husband no longer quarrels with me about the children. We live peacefully, we work together, we progress together and encourage each other. Our love grows deeper. . . . I would never be able to get such happiness if I locked myself in my small family."

C. THE IMAGE OF THE NEW HEROINE

The letters from critical leaders were not only disapproving of Liu's attitude and behavior, they were also full of citations of shining examples of the new socialist woman under Communism. These heroines were described as unselfish, hardworking, and progressive, thinking only of group welfare and contribution to the state instead of personal and family happiness. The image of such a heroine is seldom short of superhuman, performing Herculean tasks and endowed with saint-like qualities. A steel worker in an electrical machine factory, the mother of seven children, a delegate to the National Heroines Meeting, was described as follows:

"She was so interested in her work that she forgot food and sleep, increasing the electric fan button production up to 10 times the previous record. Last year she completed work of five workers. . . . On Sundays and holidays, after taking care of her seven children, she would visit 12 comrades. Under her persuasion the production in her small group continued to progress."[11]

Another delegate to the National Heroines Meeting, the mother of five children, admitted that she was so interested in her work that she had never been absent from work for five years. "When my two children had measles, the nurse asked me to take leave from work, but I refused to follow her suggestion . . . I'm the mother of five and thirty-six years old, but I am younger every year under wonderful socialism. Whatever single girls can do, I can do also. . . ."[12] When asked about the secret of her work spirit, she stated that if one understood the true meaning of work, then all the difficulties could be conquered. According to her, Liu's devotion to her small family would not bring her happiness or the correct upbringing of her children. The purpose of work to her was to build future welfare in the socialist society.

The image of the heroine is epitomized by another "patriotic pioneer" of communism. She married her husband in 1943 and had been active in underground work until 1949. Since liberation, she continued to work for the Party. Her six children were born in various wartime situations near the front where she served as a member of the medical corps following the movement of the troops. Her third child was born in a deserted mud hut; bleeding severely, she was carried by colleagues in a make-shift wooden frame immediately afterwards. The infant soon died of exposure and cold. Her husband, serving in the Army in different locations, had not seen their first child until he was nine years old. In the words of this heroic mother:

"Though we have five children, we never let them affect our work. We do not think family happiness is a matter of eating well and dressing well. We are still covered with a cloth quilt and an old army blanket from the war. . . . Many people think that everything ought to be perfect in our socialist society and that we should begin to be hedonistic. This is not at all realistic."[13]

D. DEVELOP COMMUNIST PHILOSOPHY: WORK FOR THE PEOPLE'S FAMILY

Ideological reform was recommended as the solution of Liu's problems. Her critics hoped that she would discard her middle class concept of a good wife and loving mother and her dependence on her husband, and contribute to the liberation of women. They felt that she should not consider her little family more important than anything else, and that she should not be "tied down by narrow, idiotic family affairs."

The editors of *Women of China*, summed up the problem discussion by suggesting that Liu should strive for the following goal:

"The Party has taught us a revolutionist ought to establish the philosophy of revolution. No matter when, he ought to put the career of revolution first and individual family matters second. . . . We must be concerned with the warmth of our people's large family. We must be concerned with the warmth of the whole world's people's family."[14]

Conclusions and interpretations

The large scale mobilization of women in the labor force in Communist China brought certain changes in the family. Working wives and mothers frequently found that their role of worker came into direct conflict with that of homemaker. Communist leaders in the role of magazine editors brought such a problem into open discussion. The case of Liu Soo-wo was introduced to stimulate discussion and to re-emphasize the new values and attitudes in the socialist society. The majority of the critics considered Liu's preoccupation with her family and marital life unbecoming a progressive Communist woman. They agreed, that in the socialist regime, working for the people and the state was more important than devotion to the family and individual members in it. A broader view of the family, according to the editors, was to serve the large family of the people.

It is to be expected that during the first few decades under the Communist regime, conflict in the values of the old and the new will continue to take place. Problems of the working wives and mothers are numerous and confusing, especially during the initial period of the socialist reconstruction.[15] Due to work assignments in different locations and to the care of the young children by nursery and school authorities, the family interactions of the husband and the wife and of parents and children differ greatly from that of pre-Communist China. The lack of consistent mother's care among young pre-school children and the minimum supervision of the school age children after school has created certain personality and behavior problems among the young, a phenomenon of great concern to both parents and teachers. Family stability, however, may not decrease for the Party's encouragement of compatibility in political ideology among spouses and their common conviction in building a socialist nation may counter-balance the limited family interaction brought about by women's labor participation. From the letters to the editors, spousal relationships have taken on a courtship flavor after their full time participation in work. Nurseries and collective mess halls have reduced the routine housekeeping and child-rearing duties to a minimum, and meetings at home at the end of the day or the week are therefore enlivened by reports of new experiences at work by spouses. There is no doubt that full time participation in labor will continue to raise the status of women in China today. For those women who require a greater challenge than the daily homemaker's duties, working for the common cause of socialist reconstruction may provide new incentives in their lives and contribute to greater loyalty toward the "people's large family," a concept not too remote from the traditional consanguineal family in pre--Communist China.

NOTES
1. *Women of China*, February 1958, No. 2.
2. Raffaello Uboldi, "A First Hand Impression of China Today," *Avanti*, July 24 to September 10, 1960.

3. *Women of China*, 9 (May, 1960), p. 28.
4. *Ibid.*, pp. 28-29.
5. Lucy Jen Huang, "Attitude of the Chinese Communists Toward Inter-Class Marriage," *Marriage and Family Living*, 4 (November, 1962).
6. *Women of China*, 10 (May, 1960), p. 23.
7. *Ibid.*, 11 (June, 1960), p. 28.
8. *Ibid.*

9. *Ibid.*, p. 29.
10. *Ibid.*, 10 (May, 1960), p. 23.
11. *Ibid.*, p. 22.
12. *Ibid.*, pp. 22-23.
13. *Ibid.*, (June, 1960), pp. 27-28.
14. *Ibid.*, 18 (September, 1960), pp. 29, 32.
15. Lucy Jen Huang, "Some Changing Patterns of the Communist Chinese Family," *Marriage and Family Living*, 2 (May, 1961).

34 Women in the kibbutz: changing status and concepts

In memory of Yonina Garber-Talmon   Menahem Rosner

It is the aim of this article to present an analysis of the changes that have occurred with respect to equality accorded women in the kibbutz. It features the conclusions reached by a wider research project carried out in 1965-6 which investigated the status of women in the kibbutz. This more general study was intended to examine the trend of kibbutz public opinion, especially among women members, on achievements attained and failures with regard to the status of women. It was our intention to examine the actual situation, in the light of the original aims which had been an integral part of the kibbutz ideology. We wished to determine how these attitudes are expressed today, more than fifty years after the establishment of the first kibbutz. The majority of the second generation has shown that it accepts the kibbutz framework and way of life, and there are already members of the third generation who have attained membership. Were the original ideals actually fulfilled or did they change in practice? Answers to these and many questions were sought, with the aid of intensive interviewing of 466 women members of twelve kibbutzim and some 86 men from 4 kibbutzim chosen as a 'control-group'.

A particular conception of the equality of women, and of their social role, serves as the justification, in principle, of a considerable part of organized kibbutz life, particularly with respect to co-operative consumption and communal education. The development of the communal dining-hall and clothes store, as well as the education system, was designed to free women from the restrictive roles of the house-wife and to allow them to participate fully in other social and work roles. This was a prime objective of the kibbutz, in conjunction with further principles of co-operation and equality and the realization of special educational aims.

Have, however, these principles been laid aside in the light of changing perceptions of the social roles of women? Are there features inherent in the kibbutz patterns of education and consumption which are detrimental to 'special feminine characteristics'? This claim has, in fact, been often expressed. This last question brings us to a consideration of the special nature or qualities of women. In this context we are not concerned with determining whether a special feminine nature does exist, in fact, but only with respondents' attitudes in this respect.

We presumed from the first that a change in the accepted ideals regarding the social equality of women has occurred among kibbutz members. We assumed that the original, more extreme views had been abandoned. These earlier ideals emphasized the need to ignore even the differences in the physical capacities of the sexes—women were encour-

Edited from Menahem Rosner, "Women in the Kibbutz: Changing Status and Concepts," Asian and African Studies, 3, 1967, pp. 35-68, by permission of the Israel Oriental Society. This study was carried out under the auspices of the Social Research Centre on the Kibbutz at Givat-Haviva. The project was planned by the author in conjunction with Mrs. Dorit Padan of the Hebrew University of Jerusalem. An advisory committee also participated in the planning of the project and included the following members: Sarah Michaeli, Sarah Braverman, Dr. Menachem Gerson, and Nenni Cohen. Interviews were carried out by a team of 30 women kibbutz members who devoted much of their time and energy to this project. Results were summarized and analysed by the staff of the Centre, namely, Beba Porter, Arela Shinwald and Alexander Abend. I extend my sincerest thanks to all of these for their assistance. The initial stages of the project were planned with the co-operation of Professor Yonina Garber-Talmon during the last days of her life. The research findings served as the basis for material presented to the Council of the Kibbutz Artzi devoted to problems of women in the kibbutz which met on 24-7 November 1966.

aged to take up hard physical activities, such as work in building construction and road-making. It should be pointed out that the 'Women Workers Movement', of which the kibbutz women were an active part, did not only emphasize the struggle for equal *rights*, as did the suffragettes, but stressed the equality in their pioneering *responsibilities*—full participation in all roles of construction and defence.

The question is, what is the dominant view today which has replaced the older, more extreme image of what might be called 'mechanical equality'. Has this in fact been replaced by a concept of 'qualitative equality', whereby the existing differences in biological nature and physical capacities between the sexes are taken into account, while recognizing the equal value of both?[1] This recognition of the equal value of the sexes should lead to complete equality between them with respect to their social roles and occupational activities. However, it may well be that the accepted orientation today is that there are basic differences between the sexes in abilities, characteristics, aspirations and social roles so that each should have its own particular and separate sphere of activity. Although even such an orientation implies equal evaluation of the separate areas of activity of the sexes, in practice it is usually found that inequality does in fact arise as a result of this differentiation.

We shall attempt to examine these three patterns of orientation as regards the question of the equality of women, as they are reflected in kibbutz public opinion.

(1) Is the opinion that there are natural differences between the sexes, with respect to their nature and capacities, widely held in the kibbutz?

(2) Are there feelings of discrimination and rivalry between the sexes—in spite of the accepted egalitarian values?

(3) The kibbutz has succeeded, to an outstanding degree, in freeing women from the more tedious burdens of their family roles. In spite of this—does a conflict between the two main roles of a woman continue to exist within the kibbutz?

Kibbutz opinion on the equality of women

The first question to be examined is the attitude that natural differences exist between the sexes and that these operate on four levels:

(a) abilities
(b) personality traits
(c) aspirations and inclinations
(d) social roles

(a) Four of our questions were designed to deal with the specific difference in abilities between the sexes. The approach was indirect as, for example, members were asked if a woman could fulfil managerial roles in the kibbutz. The replies received show that 51.7% were affirmative for all functions and 46.3% agreed with the reservation that women could fill managerial functions especially in the more traditional fields of women's activities.

A further example of the indirect approach adopted can be seen in the question as to whether the task of kibbutz secretary could be filled equally well by either of the sexes. The affirmative replies were 92% of the total. Other questions concerning the intellectual skills necessary for administrative work and co-ordinators indicate that at least 70% feel that these qualities are to be found equally among women and men. This finding illustrates the egalitarian attitude prevailing as regards intellectual capacities, and this is the opposite of that found concerning physical strength. Thus, only 6% replied that women are suited for work on a tractor, and other replies show that 90% feel that physical differences in strength do limit the range of work that women can adopt.

(b) Respondents were asked to evaluate whether 27 listed personality traits were characteristic of either or both of the sexes. In this way we felt that it would be possible to measure the kibbutz attitude towards the question of differences in traits between the sexes. The results show that, in the main, an egalitarian attitude does exist. Twenty-four of the traits were felt to be equally characteristic of both sexes. Only three traits were felt by the majority to be typically feminine, and these were the tendency to become emotional, a readiness to feel insulted, and shyness.

There is, however, certain evidence that some prejudices which find expression among kibbutz members reflect the generally accepted image. Men are seen to be active, as having initiative and as being both cruel and unsentimental. Women are seen as being passive, emotional, sensitive to insults, etc. It should, however, be emphasized that these replies reflect the opinion of only a minority of about 10% of the respondents, the majority showing strong egalitarian orientations.

(c) The third aspect examined related to whether different aspirations and inclinations are characteristic of each of the sexes. Some 75% of the respondents felt that such differences do, in fact, exist. Men show ambition in their desire to advance in political and economic affairs, while the ambition of women is felt to be expressed in family life, arts, belles-lettres and raising the standards of life and personal comfort. 79% of the respondents agreed that there were differences in the relative importance given by men, as compared to women, to work, family life and social activity. This difference is expressed in the primary consideration given by women members to family life, all other affairs remaining secondary. Men usually placed these activities in a reverse order. These replies reflect the situation as it actually exists and it is important to contrast this with what is felt to be desirable. The ideal is egalitarian—only a very small minority contended that such differences in orientation between the sexes is desirable. In practice, however, 79% claim that such differences do exist.

(d) The next area is that of social roles. Questions were framed so as to establish whether the sexes were thought to be equally suited for such roles as secretary, treasurer, committee co-ordinator, etc. No clear-cut picture emerged. Some 90% replied that either men or women could fill the role of work organizer. This was, however, felt to be applicable by only 24% as regards the role of economic co-ordinator and 44.1% in the case of the health committee co-ordinator. Work with poultry was thought by 94% of the respondents to be suitable for either sex, but only 47.4% were of this opinion as regards dairy work and 18% agreed in the case of vehicle driving.[2]

One could have assumed that there would be more differentiation concerning the perception of abilities, since these are less susceptible to change and are presumed to be inherent in the particular nature of either sex. On the other hand, egalitarianism could have been expected in the sphere of aspirations, inclinations and roles, since these are a result of socialization and are more determined by social structure and norms. In fact, the reverse seems to be the case. In general there is an egalitarian attitude with respect to skills and abilities and a differential one in the case of social roles and aspirations.

Not only does this differential attitude exist, but it is felt to be a deviation from the ideal attitude. We have mentioned this discrepancy between ideal and actual perceptions of the ordering of social role-areas for each of the sexes. A similar discrepancy was evident with respect to the differential allocation of roles between the sexes, in work and in social activities. A majority felt that such differential allocation does exist but only 26.2% of the respondents felt that this tendency should be encouraged.

In concluding this section it can be stated that the egalitarian social values are firmly entrenched and are held equally by both men and women in the kibbutz. However, in the light of the growing pattern of differentiation in practice strong feelings of deviation from the ideal are expressed by many members.

We shall now refer to the second type of attitude, that of competition and discrimination. In this regard questions were framed to examine whether men were seen as acting as obstacles to the advance of women. Such a feeling seems to be widely held in general society: a recent survey of women in management positions in Israel[3] shows that men refuse to fill positions subordinate to those held by women. Our research findings indicate that this is not usually the case in the kibbutz. About 31% of women members replied that they felt that men would object to having women as their supervisors at work. In reply to two other questions relating to feelings of competition the percentages were even smaller. Some 25% felt that men preferred to work in an all-male work group, and only 9% replied that they did know of actual cases where men did interfere and prevent women from making progress in responsible positions. Thus, it cannot be claimed that deeply antagonistic positions have developed between the sexes. But 10% to 30% of the women did express feelings of discrimination, and this is not a negligible proportion in a basically egalitarian society. It is, however, far less than what is known to exist in the society outside the kibbutz.

Special importance should be attached to the third attitude, namely that there is a contradiction in the roles held by women and that this affects her self-identity. In the context of the kibbutz this means a possible conflict between a woman's family roles and her work and social activities. These three spheres are interdependent, so that changes in work roles modify family activities and the possibility of taking part in other social functions. The problem whether there is only interdependence between the roles or a real conflict was the central question studied in our research project. At this point, however, we shall deal only with the changes which have occurred in the family roles of women in the kibbutz.[4]

The first change is demographic and reflects family size and other related aspects.[5] The second change is that of the educational role of the family, and the third involves the expansion of house-keeping activities and the division of labour within the family. A fourth change concerns the image of women in general, and such questions as concepts of beauty and life-style. The fifth element of change is related to questions of general family norms.

Our contention is that the kibbutz is changing from a society in which the family did not receive full legitimation as the basic social unit to a society placing more and more stress on the family group. This process has its source in (a) objective factors, such as the changes in age and family size; (b) social processes arising out of the changing social structure of the kibbutz and following general, external events. Thus, as social relationships between members in general become less intensive greater stress is placed on the family unit. In addition, there have been important changes in value-orientations: as the general collectivistic conception of life in the kibbutz tends to become weaker, more importance is given to the family unit.

Let us try to illustrate these tendencies by referring to our research findings. As regards demographic changes, various experts have contended that the 'return to the family', in American society for example, finds its expression in earlier age at marriage and an increasing number of children. To our question what the best age for marriage was, 34.5% of the women replied that the ideal age was shortly after the completion of military service.[6] An interesting point was that of the desired number of children. Some ten years ago the late Professor Yonina Garber-Talmon found that 40% of kibbutz members asked by her desired four children or more.[7] In our project this reply was received from 58.3% of the respondents. There is little doubt that the increase in respondents desiring a larger family indicates a tendency towards a more central evaluation of the family by women in the kibbutz. Concerning the allocation of parents' roles in the education of children we found a widely expressed feeling that the education of young children should primarily be the responsibility of the mother, during the period of the day when the child is with his parents (kibbutz children spend most of their time with their peer-group in the childrens' house). The father's role is felt to be important in the later, school-going age, and when the children enter secondary educational institutions both parents are felt to be jointly concerned with this task.

The division of labour within the family has undergone changes as well. Arranging and caring for the room is seen by 90% of the respondents as being a woman's role (but only 27% replied that women generally wash the dishes). Preparation of the four o'clock afternoon tea is seen by 58.6% of the women as being their responsibility. These findings should be evaluated in the light of the special kibbutz family arrangements. All meals, with the exception

TABLE 1   Reasons for Claim that Certain Work-roles and Social Activities Are Better Suited for Men or Women (opinions of women and men in percentages)*

Reason for attitude	Role in social activities—women		Role in social activities—men		Role in work —women		Role in work —men	
	Women	Men	Women	Men	Women	Men	Women	Men
Character, traits	49.8	34.5	30.0	15.3	61.5	57.3	23.5	19.5
Inclinations	27.6	32.0	28.8	25.6	38.1	48.7	30.0	28.0
Capacities	9.4	7.4	10.3	5.1	18.9	10.9	12.6	6.0
Physical ability	5.3	11.1	19.7	32.0	40.6	45.1	84.0	87.8
Previous experience	7.7	8.6	25.3	21.7	—	—	—	—

*All the percentages relate to the total of male or of female respondents. The number marks those who mentioned a specific reason. If a respondent gave two reasons of the same type, they are presented here as one. Since each respondent was allowed to mention a number of reasons, the total of percentages will usually exceed 100%.

TABLE 2   CHART A   Reasons for Advantages and Disadvantages in Work-differentiation (in percentages)

	Advantages		Disadvantages	
	Women	Men	Women	Men
Differentiation makes it possible to fit the work to biological-physical qualities	27.7	30.1	—	—
Differentiation enables each sex to contribute according to its ability	15.2	11.8	—	—
There are advantages only in those spheres where the work demands the labour of one sex (young children—women; field-crops—men)	11.2	5.9		
Differentiation makes it possible to adapt work-conditions to the traits and needs of each sex	4.3	12.9		
Differentiation harms the cooperation between the sexes	—	—	18.2	12.9
Differentiation harms social and human relations	—	—	15.9	16.5
Differentiation limits the possibilities of women in choosing an occupation	—	—	15.0	18.8
Differentiation limits interests to narrow spheres	—	—	10.1	12.9

of afternoon tea, are taken in the communal dining hall, and apartments consist of two rooms at the most. Children live in specially designed housing quarters. However, with a general rise in the standard of living there is a slow expansion of the 'family household'. It is because of this that questions raised in this sphere are of particular relevance. We also inquired whether women were interested in further expanding these types of activities. The result was negative: some 72% of our respondents did in fact some of their washing and ironing, but would prefer to use communal services if these were of wider scope. On the other hand, 70% of the women said that they occupied themselves with knitting because of personal interest and not because of lack of services.

We shall now take up the question of beauty-care. The earlier attitude of 'mechanical equality' rejected any claim for special consideration for beauty-care of women. Indicative of the change which has occurred is the fact that 96% of the women asked by us were in favour of the introduction of cosmetic treatment into the range of kibbutz services. There is, however, a significant division of opinion with regard to the attention to be given to a woman's external appearance. When asked whether the external appearance of a woman kibbutz member should be different from that of non-kibbutz women, two-thirds of the respondents said that kibbutz women should maintain a typical style of appearance. There has not emerged a definite style of this kind, but there is an emphasis on simplicity and naturalness. Cosmetic treatment is regarded as being necessary for women but not as being opposed to maintaining a distinct kibbutz style.

In the sphere of family norms questions were asked, but the findings do not indicate that distinct family norms have developed. Thus, when asked if they wore a wedding ring, 32.6% of replies were affirmative and 32.4 negative.[8] Analysis of the material indicates that here the two areas of kibbutz life-style and family norms are interrelated. But in general the tendency towards change in family life does not necessarily mean deviation from the accepted kibbutz pattern.

A further point in the sphere of family norms is the view that in marriage the man should be older than the wife. This is widely accepted and follows the traditional concepts of family structure. Other matters related to marriage do not, however, reflect the traditional attitude: only 1% of respondents agreed that following marriage between members of different kibbutzim the bride should join her husband's settlement. There would thus seem to be a degree of 'anomie' in this area of family norms, that is, no distinct norm-patterns have as yet emerged. However, in concluding this discussion of the question of family roles it can be said that emphasis on the family has definitely increased in the kibbutz.

Role-conflict or interaction between spheres?

While in the previous sections we presented the *attitudes* of the respondents we now turn to an analysis of the *reasons* underlying these attitudes. Examining the image of feminine 'nature' as reflected in the answers relating to the qualities, capacities and traits which characterize each sex, we found that the image of capacities and abilities was, in principle, egalitarian. However, considering the images relating to aspirations, interests and social roles, differentiation between the spheres and the roles characteristic for each sex increases. These differential images reflect the reality of the kibbutz and are not consistent with the egalitarian image concerning the capacities and abilities referred to previously.

We will attempt below to present the relationship between the general, more abstract image as regards the capacities and abilities and the specific, realistic conception of the appropriate social roles. If respondents indicated that certain work-roles and social activities are better suited for men or for women they were requested to explain these attitudes. Table 1 is a typology of these reasons for the various categories.

In examining Table 1 an interesting difference becomes apparent between the factors influencing the determination that a specific role in social activities or in work is fitting for women, and those mentioned as a reason for the determination that a role is fitting for men. With regard to the suitability for women the main factor is character or feminine traits (49.8% and 61.5%). The picture is more varied as regards suitability for men. For work the primary determining factor is physical strength (84%). For social activities character was also noted (30%), but considerable importance was also attached to inclinations (28.8%) and to previous experience in the role (25.3%). This distribution of the various factors is derived from the answers of the women in the sample; in the answers of the men these differences are still more apparent.

What are the 'feminine' traits which cause role-differentiation between the sexes? In the words of the respondents: 'a role requiring human relations and refinement is more suitable for women'; 'women have more patience with people'; 'they are sensitive to special problems'; 'women have intuition'; some even distinguished two types of the same quality in claiming that men are more suited for roles requiring 'masculine patience'.

Apparently, in determining which roles are suited for women qualities and traits for which there are no objective criteria have considerable importance. As against this, there are such criteria for the factors determining the roles suitable for men, especially physical ability and previous experience in the role. But it is still more interesting that the principal reasons given for characterizing work as suitable for women are the qualities which the vast majority of women interviewed designated as characterizing the two sexes to an *equal* extent.

The same reasoning may be further examined with regard to the question of differentiation between work and activities specific to men and those specific to women.

As against the findings of Table 1, the main reasons for the advantages and disadvantages of role-differentiation by sex in Table 2, Chart A, do not relate to the feminine character. Here the emphasis is placed on the biological-physical qualities. On the other hand, the danger that the differentiation will harm the co-operation between the sexes and social relations is stressed: 'It produces the lack of a common language between men and women'; 'it harms relations between workers'; 'it harms collective responsibility at all levels'. And, on the positive side: 'It is good to work in a variegated society, which makes for better social relations'. In order to emphasize the disadvantages of differ-

CHART B *If a Man and a Woman Are Work-co-ordinators, Is It Desirable That the Man Deals with the Productive Branches and the Woman with Services?* *

	Women	Men
No reply	4.2	5.8
Desirable	56.5	55.0
Not desirable	43.4	45.0

Reasons	% of all replying yes		% of all replying no	
	Women	Men	Women	Men
Women know more about the services	48.3	45.1	—	—
Men know more about the productive branches	38.8	39.4	—	—
There must be co-ordination between the work allocators	—	—	55.9	70.6
The woman should get to know the farm	—	—	14.7	2.9
The man should get to know the services	—	—	9.4	2.9
It is usual and has proven itself	—	—	6.5	8.8
A greater proportion of the problems of services devolves upon the woman	—	—	4.1	2.9
Other reasons	12.9	15.5	9.4	11.9
Total	100.0	100.0	100.0	100.0

*The role of work-allocator is central to the organizational structure of the kibbutz. It involves the directing of members to work in the various branches of the kibbutz economy. In many cases two members (often a man and a woman) fill this role in conjunction—but there are different ways in which the work is divided between them. In some instances all the work is carried out by both, in others the man deals with productive branches and the woman is responsible for services, where mainly women are employed.

CHART C   *Should the Trend of Differentiation between the Work of Men and Women Be Continued?*

	Men	Women
No reply	10.3	14.1
Yes	26.2	23.3
No	73.3	76.7
Don't know	0.5	—

entiation some reasons were mentioned which had a direct bearing on the situation of the woman in the work-sphere: 'Differentiation prevents women from participating in other types of work and from widening their horizons'; 'It limits the occupational possibilities of the woman.'

We may now try to explain the reasons for the inconsistency noted above with regard to the feminine character and qualities. First, it will be noted that in some spheres no attempt to abolish differentiation between the sexes has ever been made, for example, in the education of very young children. However, this has been justified in the past by reference to the biological qualities of women and their experience in this sphere. The situation is different with regard to other roles in which there exists differentiation in present-day reality (although to a different extent in different kibbutzim). The respondents attempted to explain this situation in their replies to the question according to which criteria they thought roles to be more suitable for either sex (Table 1). In this attempt to explain present-day reality (which emerged in contrast with the ideal conception which aspired to abolish role-differentiation by sex) the respondents used generally accepted stereotypes for the qualities and character of the sexes. The mentioning of these qualities represented, perhaps, not only an explanation of the existing situation but also provided a certain legitimation for it.

However, while the feminine character and qualities are very common reasons to explain the suitability of roles according to sex, they feature hardly at all in connection with the analysis of the advantages of differentiation, or in connection with the concrete question: if a man and a woman are work-co-ordinators, is it desirable that each should deal with a different sphere? In these cases different inclinations are mentioned, previous experience enabling the individual better to adapt himself in a given sphere, but not qualities and character. However, this reliance on spheres of interest, inclinations and previous experience which are to a large extent tied up with one another, also indicates the possible results of the existing process of differentiation. This process may lead to the growth of nonegalitarian images expressing legitimation of the existing situation, or to the emergence of a vicious circle, in which it is claimed that there is a difference in the inclinations and spheres of interest between the sexes, which strengthens the tendency for role-differentiation, and the differentiation itself leads to the development of inequality as regards experience and spheres of interest. There exists, therefore, the possibility of a self-confirming development in the direction of the continuation of the process of differentiation, in opposition to the desire expressed by the majority

of respondents. Thus, most of the respondents conformed with the existing situation in answering to the question whether it was desirable to separate the spheres dealt with by a man and a woman who are both work co-ordinators, while in answer to the more general question of principle, whether the trend of differentiation should be continued, the vast majority opposed the possible results of this situation.

The conception of the difference in the inclinations, spheres of interest and aspirations which exists today between men and women is demonstrated in Table 3.

It appears that the respondents made a clear distinction between the spheres in which women are more interested and those in which men are more interested. There are only two spheres, closely related to one another, with regard to which differences of opinion exist: the aspiration to advance and achieve satisfaction in work, and the aspiration to complete advanced studies. The majority, however, is convinced that men are more interested in them.

The interest and aspirations of the woman, according to the respondents, concentrate on the family in the wider sense of the word; this sphere is not mentioned at all for men, whose alleged spheres of interest are wider and more variegated. Culture, art and entertainment is mentioned as being more characteristic of women, but only by a small percentage of respondents.

TABLE 3   *Spheres in Which Men or Women Are More Interested, and to Which They Aspire to a Greater Extent (in Percentages)*

	Interest, aspirations —Women		Interest, aspirations —Men	
	Women	Men	Women	Men
Family life, herself, the closer environment	35.0	31.8	—	—
The household	18.7	12.9	—	—
Education	10.5	11.8	0.2	—
Entertainment and care of children	10.3	8.2	2.6	2.4
Advancement, satisfaction in work	8.4	7.1	31.5	33.0
Studies, advanced education	8.2	3.5	15.9	4.7
Comfort, quiet life, happiness	7.7	4.7	—	—
External appearance	7.3	10.6	—	—
Culture, art, entertainment	5.4	9.4	0.2	2.4
Social and public activities	0.6	3.5	12.2	12.9
Politics	0.4	—	11.2	10.6
Social status, personal advancement	1.9	2.4	10.3	10.6
The technical sphere	—	—	9.4	9.4
The farming-agricultural sphere	—	—	8.4	14.1

The table provides some additional support for the fact that the sphere of the family holds first place for women before work and social activities, and that these last two spheres are more important for men. Only 27% maintained that this is desirable. However, it is interesting to note that the vast majority of these 27% justify their attitude by 'natural' differences between the sexes; 'it is natural that the mother tends more towards the family and the man towards work'; 'in accordance with natural inclinations the woman identifies herself with her family and the man tends more towards the wider environment'; 'it is a part of nature and it is impossible to determine whether it is desirable or not'; 'the difference is connected with nature and it would be a bad thing if social activities would take precedence over the family for the woman too.' Most of the reasons are of this type (64.4% of the reasons given by women, 74.4% of the reasons given by men). It is significant that reasons of nature, character and various other qualities appear here not only as an explanation and legitimation of an existing situation but also as a basis for its desirability.

Within the large majority which sees the existing situation as not desirable there is a part which denies the existence of a natural difference in this respect: 'It is not related to sex but to the viewpoint of each individual'; 'the tendency is personal and the cause does not lie in sex'. Others, while admitting the existence of differences in inclinations, suggest the creation of conditions for their limitation: 'The kibbutz is based on equality between the sexes and the woman, too, should contribute her abilities in kibbutz activities'; 'it is desirable that the family should also occupy an important place in the life of the man'; 'by limiting the working-day of the woman she will be able to be as free as the man for social life and activities'. The desired tendency, as expressed by most of the respondents, is therefore the limitation of differences, not by neglecting one of the spheres but by the creation of such conditions that spheres which are neglected by one of the sexes (the family by the man, social activities by the woman) may receive more emphasis.

From the foregoing it is again clear that the family plays a major role in the differentiation process among inclinations, spheres of interest and the social roles of the sexes. It will, consequently, be necessary to clarify a number of questions:

(1) Does the considerable importance of the family sphere for the woman engender a feeling of *multiplicity of roles*, involving that by fulfilling the family role equal consideration cannot be given to the spheres of work and social activities, and is thereby a *conflict* between the spheres and the roles produced?

(2) Does the conflict between the family role and work and social activities produce a feeling of *inferiority* and *deprivation?*

(3) Does the process of differentiation between the masculine and the feminine spheres of work and social activities lead to the inferiority of the feminine spheres, and does a feeling of *deprivation* exist concerning them?

On the basis of our enquiry, the results of which have only partly been summarized in this article, we were able to conclude that the differentiation processes are stronger in the work sphere than in that of social activities. They are influenced by the differential images as regards character and particular feminine characteristics. Furthermore, the assertion concerning the particular feminine character is prevalent in justifying the existence of special feminine tasks and roles in work rather than in social activities (see Table 1). The conflict with 'familistic' trends is, by contrast, stronger in the sphere of social activities. However, while the smaller participation of women in the various spheres of social activity does not usually arouse feelings of inferiority and deprivation, such feelings exist in the work-sphere.

It is, however, difficult to determine whether the feelings of deprivation are a result of the differentiation process only. It seems that there is a combination of two factors at work here. First, the preference which was given to the productive sector as compared to services in the initial stages of the development of the kibbutz was the result of both ideological and practical considerations. Secondly the differentiation process which has made the service sector the exclusive concern of the women, has also resulted in a great extent of identity between the problems of the services and the problems of the work of the woman. The low prestige given to services produces a sense of deprivation in women active in this field. Thus deprivation has preceded differentiation between the sexes, and has not only been the result of differentiation.

While the feelings of deprivation are prevalent with regard to work in the service branch, they are not expressed in relation to the small participation of the woman in the various spheres of social activity. Here we find that it is claimed that not enough has been done to encourage the woman to participate in social activities, in order to create the conditions enabling her advancement by providing special training, etc. The prevalent feeling is that the woman occupies an inferior position in the sphere of social activities from the start because of traditional social practices. It is thus possible to attain equal status and position only by means of direct preference and encouragement.

This particular character of the feelings of deprivation in the spheres of work and social activity also explains the fact that we found only very few expressions of competition and rivalry between the sexes. Although 30% of the women interviewed claimed that in their opinion men opposed the management of a branch by a woman, we did not as a rule find crystallized opinions concerning competition between the sexes. To the extent that complaints against men or against the institutions exist, these do not usually refer to deprivation but rather to the lack of sufficient encouragement.

What is the basis of the feeling that from the beginning the women occupy an inferior position in the sphere of social activities so that special efforts are required in order to encourage their participation? Here too it appeared that two factors are at work: first, the fact that in society at large the status of women in the sphere of social activities is also relatively inferior (there has been less progress in this sphere than in the sphere of work); secondly, recognition of the fact that greater responsibility falls on the woman in the sphere of the family, in particular with regard to the education of very young children.

Must we then assume that in the kibbutz too there exists a conflict between the family role and the other roles of a woman, despite the efforts directed towards overcoming this problem by means of common organization of needs and common education? It appears that this is not the case today. In the work sphere the conflict is only marginal. In the sphere of social activities the conflict is more serious, although it is not impossible to overcome it. This is indicated by the fact that some kibbutzim constitute exceptions, in the positive sense, in this sphere, and respondents from these kibbutzim indicate that this achievement is due to the efforts which have been made to encourage the woman to participate in social activities.

It does not seem possible in the existing situation to avoid the increasing importance of the family unit in the social life of the kibbutz. It is, indeed, possible to moderate this process by strengthening the integrative factors within the kibbutz as a whole and within the framework of the social groups which constitute it. It is also possible to restrain the widening functions of the family in the consumer and educational spheres. However, the demographic processes and personal aspirations in this sphere should not be ignored. It is therefore necessary to search for ways to ensure maximum equality of women in the spheres of work and social activities on the basis of the growing importance of the family. The ways for achieving this are by increasing the contribution made by men in meeting family responsibilities; by creating conditions for the lightening of the special burden which falls on the woman; and by the development of special facilities for work-training and the creation of work-conditions and patterns of social activity that take into account the present family situation. It is to be hoped that by these means it will be possible to establish the equal standing and importance of the spheres of work, social activities and the family in the life of both men and women in the kibbutz, since this is felt to be essential by most of the women interviewed.

Changes in the spheres of public activity and work, so as to increase the representation of women in professional and administrative tasks, will serve to answer the demands expressed by women respondents. These expressed a desire for qualitative equality, that is, equal opportunities for men and women to gain the fullest measure of rewards available in the kibbutz. In the absence of material advantages to be obtained, these rewards are satisfaction in work and the sense of creativity while giving the fullest possible expression to all elements of the individual's personality.

NOTES

1. The concepts of 'mechanical equality' and 'qualitative equality' are widely used in kibbutzim to refer to various means of allocating common goods. 'Mechanical equality' involves the consideration of universal criteria only, while 'qualitative equality' takes particular factors into account. These may be such features as sex.

2. The differences in the way these roles are perceived reflect, to a considerable extent, the situation as it actually exists today. While women, in many kibbutzim, do act as work organizers, there are very few cases of women acting as economic co-ordinators. (The work organizer is concerned with routine allocation of workers to various economic branches; the economic co-ordinator, on the other hand, deals with the over-all administration of the entire economy of the kibbutz and regulates the interlocking operations of the different branches.) Differing situations exist in various kibbutzim with respect to the role of the health committee co-ordinator. Some kibbutzim see this as being a woman's role while others make no differentiation at all according to sex. The replies received also reflect the actual situation with respect to work-roles.

3. T. Weinshall and M. Bader, 'The Status of Women in Managerial Roles' (in Hebrew), *Netivey Irgun u-Minhal*, No. 4 (74).

4. An extensive discussion of the changes in the position of the family in the kibbutz is to be found in Y. Garber-Talmon, 'The family in collective settlements in Israel' in M. Nimkoff (ed.) *Comparative family systems*, New York, 1964.

5. The kibbutzim were established by groups of young people, and there were few families. Now there are many kibbutzim where the children or even grandchildren have attained full membership.

6. All girls in the kibbutz serve in the army and complete this service at 20 years of age. Therefore, respondents who did not accept this as the best age for marriage preferred an older age.

7. Y. Garber-Talmon, 'Social Structure and Family Size', *Human Relations*, vol. 12, No. 2, 1959, pp. 121-46. Also in: R. H. Coser, *Family, its structure and function* (forthcoming).

8. While the kibbutz founders did not attach any special importance to wedding ceremonies these have received full legitimation by now. This is not the case with respect to the wearing of wedding rings; this remains a purely personal decision and no clear social norm has as yet developed.

Part VI

Women in relationship to their bodies

The psychodynamics of people are ultimately psychobiological. That is clear, of course, when we observe such physiological processes as pregnancy, birth, nursing, menstruation, and sex. The psyche and the body are not divisible. The interaction between the physical and mental systems is discussed in the first paper in this section, by Benedek. Below immediate awareness, the endocrine levels in women seem to produce a general psychic state, mood, or tendency, upon which specific thoughts or acts are superimposed.

Benedek explains that the menstrual cycle phases are accompanied by predictable shifts in affect. The types of emotions experienced correlate significantly with hormone levels and much less with individual characteristics. The response to menstruation (a feeling of acceptance, repugnance, or relief) is more specifically linked to personal attitudes. Furthermore, motherhood is not a derivative motive, an attempt to compensate for a missing penis. The quality of motherliness—the receptive, retentive tendencies of women—arises from the mind's organization and response to the endocrine system. Of course, mothering behaviors become more understandable when one knows the personality characteristics of the mother, but to completely understand any of these reproductive events it is necessary to know the underlying hormone contributions to the psyche. That is, we must know the conscious and unconscious motives and anxieties both common to the condition and unique to the individual who is in this extraordinary crisis phase.

In Benedek's paper it is clear that specifically female motives have partial origins in the woman's body. This is in strong contrast to older theoretic models. Bosselman describes the evolution of the classical psychoanalytic theory that penis envy is at the root of female neurosis (and maternity and other normal motives). Because, for men, the penis is uniquely pleasurable and its loss a most threatening trauma, it follows, from the male viewpoint, that women must covet such an organ. The error is to generalize from the neurotic to the normal woman and to derive feminine motives from a phallocentric perspective.

Bosselman notes that penis envy in women is much less frequent in psychiatric patients than male castration anxiety. The male's masculinity is imperiled by his constant need to achieve it and to deny his profound dependency longings. This frequently takes the form of castration—that is, masculinity anxieties. That is common and possibly inevitable in contemporary reality. For Bosselman, penis envy is less prevalent because the feminine role is ultimately more gratifying. A redefinition and a new perspective about penis envy will be one of the consequences of awareness of widespread male phallocentric assumptions.

It is fashionable in some circles to minimize the importance of the physical differences between the sexes. Still, they exist and any theory of sex differences should acknowledge their consequences. Bermant has observed an interesting fact: men are much more likely than women to engage in deviant sexual behaviors. That is, they are more likely to masturbate, be homosexual, be fetishists, and so on. That is true in the United States, in Europe, and in less industrialized societies. Cross-culturally, this difference is a characteristic of people. It is also a characteristic of animals. Bermant feels that any tendency so universal must have some simple, universal origin. He believes the source of the difference in sexual behaviors lies in the location the clitoris and penis. Because the penis is more exposed than the clitoris, boys experience ...isurable genital stimulation more frequently. Because the experiences begin in infancy, boys ill tend to be in a state of relatively high sexual drive before they can cognitively discriminate and evaluate the appropriateness of a sexual object. Consequently, they are more likely than girls to choose biologically inappropriate objects.

It also seems that boys will comprehend sex initially and primarily as genital. In girls, the less frequent stimulation of the smaller, hooded, clitoris, the lack of exquisite sensitivity in the vagina, and the acquired cognitive distinctions and inhibitions will combine to make sex less genital and more cognitive, emotional, and inhibited. Sexual arousal in women is more variable, more closely linked to psychological factors, than it is in men. Both more complex and less well-known ideas about feminine sexuality—perceived in its own right rather than as a derivation from male sexuality—are just beginning to appear in the literature.

Most of the professional literature on sex seems never to talk of love. If love is too poetic perhaps we could discuss mutuality, commitment, and trust. Or we could discuss the different sentiments that result when women use sex in order to establish and maintain an uncertain relationship, thus reducing their own self-esteem. Bardwick's paper discusses the effects of the persistence of a conservative morality coexistent with an ethic where sexual liberation is a mark of psychological health. With contraception available, fear of pregnancy is no longer a usable excuse for nonparticipation by those who are frightened, hesitant, and anxious.

Bardwick and Zweben's data, which were taken from college students, suggest that girls still perceive the achievement of a successful heterosexual relationship as their essential task. As sexual participation has become assumed along with changes in contraception, classic psychological vulnerabilities are increased by uncertain moralities. Sexual anxiety and ambivalence characterized most of the sample and anxieties were exacerbated because girls feared abandonment in their uncertain relationships either because of sexual participation or abstinence.

The psychosomatic and psychological data converge in portraying vulnerability in interpersonal relationships and an inability (or unwillingness) to depsychologize sex. Whereas women may have unlimited sexual capacity, as Sherfey suggests, it also seems true that most women's sexual responsiveness tends to be bound up with feelings of affection, esteem, and commitment.

Most psychological data come from middle-class people. Often we simply do not know how justified we are in generalizing from those findings. In Rainwater's study, lower- as well as middle-class women were included and, again, women's sexual attitudes had to be understood within the context of a relationship.

Unlike the myth of unbridled and joyous passion among those who are fortunate enough (in this context) not *to be either white or middle class, Rainwater's interviews revealed a pleasureless, duty-bound vision of sex. This was especially true of lower-class women whose lives are essentially separate from their husbands'. Without a feeling of involvement and without a commitment by their partner to them, a very large percentage of women do not enjoy sex. Bardwick and Rainwater's papers attest to the idea that sexual attitudes and behaviors in women are most often extensions of more general psychological needs and interpersonal realities.*

Not just sex, but all of women's reproductive functions become psychologically important as they signify and affirm one's normal femininity. Maternity in particular has always been crucial in establishing an adult identity. The functions of the reproductive system can be a route to esteem and identity, but they bring stress upon the adapting ego and may be a source of fear, anxiety, or guilt. It is also true that women who are characteristically fearful, anxious, or guilty have a significant tendency to experience symptomatic problems in the reproductive system. The reproductive system may become involved in psychosomatic responses because pregnancy and babies effect real changes that threaten the status quo. Or, the reproductive system may be affected primarily because it is such an integral part of the self-concept of women that it is particularly vulnerable.

McDonald has reviewed the experimental literature on emotional factors effecting obstetric complications. A popular hypothesis is that obstetric complications often have psychogenic origins. An important problem, which becomes clear in the paper, is that different experimenters, using diverse techniques, looked for quite different variables, making it hard to generalize. Nonetheless, a survey of data concerning pseudocyesis, pernicious vomiting, habitual abortion, prolonged labor, and prematurity in the infant, reveals certain psychological consistencies. Compared with women with no symptoms, symptomatic patients fear pregnancy or the child, are markedly anxious in general and particularly about sex, are immature, dependent, over-compliant, and feel inadequate and uncertain of their husbands. Frequently they use the immature defense of denial. Causation cannot be established from these studies but the implications seem clear.

Anxious women, immature and unable to cope with real stress, dependent upon others for esteem, and uncertain within relationships, tend to be "good," conformist, conventional women who are afraid to act upon their hostilities or anxieties. Characteristically, their identity is traditional and motherhood is critical. But while they are motivated to be mothers, they are simultaneously fearful of body penetration, body changes in pregnancy, birth, and the responsibility of a child. The papers by Bardwick, McDonald, the Newtons, Melges, and Grimm demonstrate that, in general, these same basic personality variables recur in the psychosomatic literature.

In addition to personality characteristics, reproductive functions may also be affected by other variables. This is particularly true for breast feeding. Obviously one can be a mother and not nurse the baby. Nursing is the most intimate reproductive behavior in which there is real choice. The Newtons reviewed the variables affecting declining or increasing breast feeding rates, attitudes about nursing, and correlations with nursing success or failure. In addition to personality variables, rates of nursing are influenced by attitudes specific to it, historical trends in fashion, and women's roles and status. Societies vary in how difficult or easy it is for mothers to nurse. In addition to values held by the mother, nursing is affected by the baby's responses. The course of breast feeding is influenced by the mother's attitude toward her body and correlates with her feelings about sex, so the similarity in the sensations of nursing and sex is probably also a factor.

Though it is not common, it is also not unusual for women to experience severe depression after giving birth to a child. One contributing factor may be the radical postpartum decline in estrogen and progesterone levels. There is some evidence that a significant change in these levels, especially a decline, may correlate with increased depression, anxiety, and hostility. But all women who give birth experience reduced endocrines while only a small percentage experience significant psychiatric symptoms. It is possible that some women are more sensitive to endocrine change than most, and we would expect them to experience severe postpartum affect changes as well as during the menstrual cycle. Alternatively, or additionally, one can look for psychogenic factors that distinguish between women who suffer postpartum symptoms and those who don't. That is the subject of the paper by Melges.

The 100 postpartum patients making up Melges' sample experienced a syndrome of feelings of severe shame, helplessness, and confusion. The major psychological difficulties that they reported were conflicts over mothering (68%), the feeling that the baby trapped them into a situation they wanted to be free of (15.5%), and the loss, real or threatened, of the baby, their mothers, the pregnant state, or freedom of youth (10%). Overall, they identified inadequately with the mothering role, and the existence of the baby threatened their sense of identity. Feeling anxious and incompetent, they didn't know how to act. This feeling of incompetence is exacerbated because infants do not reinforce feelings of adequacy by responding accurately or affirmatively to the cues from the mother. Not identified with their own mothers, these patients lacked internal guidelines for mother, regressed, and with the symptoms of withdrawal, confusion, depression, and fear, psychologically removed themselves from a situation in which they could not cope. Their symptoms are also a cry for help and support from an environment perceived as nonsupportive.

Grimm found that habitual aborters, defined as women who had had four previous spontaneous abortions, were unable to plan and anticipate and had poor emotional control. This is the same quality of ego immaturity found in the other psychosomatic studies. Compared with women who had never had a spontaneous abortion, they were more conformist and

*conventional. Conventions provided external guides for acceptable behavior and "goodness."
Dependent, these women were prone to feeling guilty, and were very fearful of expressing
hostility.*

*With some variation according to the specific syndrome, the critical personality characteristics
distinguishing women with reproductive symptoms are significant feelings of hostility and
dependence in immature women with low self-esteem. Because of their dependence, low
self-esteem, and fears of being rejected and abandoned, they outwardly conform to stereotyped
concepts of femininity, inhibiting expressions of anger. Symptoms express fear, anger, and need
for love and support. Without guilt, without conscious awareness of motivation, the body is
altered in order to protect the vulnerable self. When femininity is threatening, the symptoms
are often (logically) in the reproductive system.*

35 The psychobiology of pregnancy

Therese Benedek

Pregnancy is a "critical phase" in the life of a woman. Using the term as ethologists use it, it implies that pregnancy, like puberty, is a biologically motivated step in the maturation of the individual which requires physiologic adjustments and psychologic adaptations to lead to a new level of integration that, normally, represents development. For a long time the significance of the psychobiologic processes of pregnancy was neglected by psychoanalysts. Freud, impressed by the emotional calmness of pregnant women, considered pregnancy as a period during which the woman lives in the bliss of her basic wish being gratified; therefore, he assumed that pregnant women are not in need of or accessible to psychoanalytic therapy. Since then psychoanalytic investigations have revealed the two opposing poles which account for pregnancy as a critical phase. One is rooted in the drive organization of the female procreative function, the other in the emotional disequilibrium caused by the stresses of pregnancy and the danger of parturition.

Recently, Rheingold collected into a large volume references regarding women's "fear of being a woman," with emphasis on the fear of death connected with childbearing [12]. This concept is so deeply ingrained in the human mind that even Freud failed to recognize the emotional manifestations of the instinctual tendency to bear children in the drive organization of women. Helene Deutsch, in her major work, attributes "the devoted patience which women of uncounted generations have shown in the service of the species" to the necessity of woman's socioeconomic dependence on man [9]. An ever-growing literature abounds in the discussion of this concept, drawing its arguments from

folklore, religion, mythology, and from the history of civilizations [8]. Against such telling evidence it may seem foolhardy to propose the results arrived at by psychoanalytic investigations. Yet it seems safe to do so since investigations have revealed the psychobiologic process of the female reproductive function without which mankind would not exist.

An investigation begun thirty years ago with the aim of discovering whether psychologic correlates of ovulation could be detected by psychoanalytic method fortunately directed my attention to the emotional accompaniments of the hormonal processes during the menstrual cycle [3]. Neither a description of that investigation nor the precise correlations of the emotional cycle with the cyclic changes of the gonadal hormones—the sexual cycle—are relevant here. However, a brief discussion of the psychologic processes corresponding to ovulation and the postovulative phase of the sexual cycle is unavoidable, since they, by elucidating the psychodynamic processes of the reproductive drive, facilitate our understanding of the well-being and also of the psychopathology of pregnant women. In the perspective of the psychobiologic processes of pregnancy, one can evaluate the clinical significance of the developmental conflicts and their constellation in the personality organization of women; these conflicts, revived during pregnancy, influence women's feelings about motherhood and their attitude toward their child and/or children. Psychoanalyses of pregnant women or women in the postpartum period thus provide clues to the interactions of three generations in the psychology of parenthood.

Reprinted from Therese Benedek, "The Psychobiology of Pregnancy," Chapter 5 of Parenthood: Its Psychology and Psychopathology, *pp. 137-151, edited by E. J. Anthony and Therese Benedek,* © 1970 by Little, Brown and Co., Publishers, Boston.

Growth, neurophysiologic maturation, and psychosexual development are intrinsically interwoven processes. The master gland, the anterior lobe of the pituitary, secretes the hormones which regulate metabolism, growth, and the propagative functions, including lactation and maternal behavior. In accordance with the two phases of the female reproductive function, copulation and childbearing, the ovaries produce two groups of gonadal hormones: estrogen, the follicle-ripening hormone, and lutein, the hormone of progestation; the latter is also termed progesterone, since it prepares the uterus for implantation of the fertilized ovum and helps to maintain pregnancy. Corresponding to the follicle-ripening phase, the prevalent emotions are motivated by an active, i.e., object-directed, heterosexual tendency, the biologic aim of which is to bring about copulation. With ovulation, the direction of the dominant sexual tendency changes and libido becomes directed toward the self.

The impact of ovulation is accompanied by systemic reactions. Among these the best known is the heightened basal body temperature by which ovulation is often diagnosed. On the psychologic side, a sense of relaxation and well-being seems to flood the woman with libido. As if the psychic apparatus has registered the somatic preparation for pregnancy, the emotional concern shifts to the body and its welfare. The manifestly narcissistic emotional response to ovulation corresponds with the peak of the hormonal cycle and expresses the psychobiologic readiness for conception.

On the basis of psychoanalytic observations Helene Deutsch generalized that a deep-rooted passivity and a specific tendency toward introversion are characteristic qualities of the female psyche [9]. Investigation of the sexual cycle has revealed that these propensities reappear in intensified form correlated with the specifically female gonadal hormone, lutein, during the postovulative phase of the cycle. Such observations justify the assumption that the emotional manifestations of the specific receptive tendency and the self-centered retentive tendency are the psychodynamic correlates of a biologic need for motherhood. Thus motherhood is not secondary, not a substitute for the missing penis, nor is it forced by men upon women "in the service of the species," but the manifestation of the all-pervading instinct for survival in the child that is the primary organizer of the woman's sexual drive, and by this also her personality. Thus the specific attributes of femininity originate in that indwelling quality of woman's psyche which is the manifestation and result of the central organization of receptive and retentive tendencies of the reproductive drive that becomes the source of motherliness.

The 4 to 6 days following ovulation—the lutein phase of the sexual cycle—represent a plateau of high hormone production, since both hormones, estrogen and progesterone, are produced. Yet in the psychoanalytic material, in dreams and fantasies—rarely, however, in behavior—the heterosexual tendency appears masked by psychologic expressions of the preparation for motherhood. Parallel with the preparation of the uterine mucosa for nidation, the emotional manifestations of intensified receptive-retentive tendencies represent the psychologic preparation for pregnancy. Correspondingly, the overt behavior as well as dreams and fantasies reveal the wish to receive and retain, or the defenses against that wish, if the woman is for any reason unconsciously or consciously afraid of pregnancy.

The comparative study of lutein phases in several women, through a number of cycles, affords evidence of the significance of lutein stimulation in the development toward motherhood. Introduced by an introversion of psychic energies at the time of ovulation, the receptive and retentive tendencies, characteristic of infancy, become intensified and recharge the memory traces introjected during infancy. These unconscious memories, interacting with the emotional reality of the individual, induce a great variety of phenomena. Most accessible to psychoanalytic observations are the repetitions of developmental identifications and conflicts with the mother. The psychoanalytic material reveals attempts at resolution of these conflicts as well as failures of such attempts. The latter eventuality is usually in the center of our attention since failures frequently motivate symptoms of "oral" origin. Psychoanalytic investigation of several consecutive cycles, or several cycles at greater intervals, reveals the factors upon which success or failure of attempts to resolve the developmental conflicts depend. From puberty to menopause, in monthly repetition, as her physiology prepares the woman for childbearing, her personality organization evolves that sublimation of psychic energies which we call motherliness.

It is a physiologic characteristic of woman that her reproductive function requires an increase of metabolic processes. Each phase directly connected with childbearing—the lutein phase of the cycle, pregnancy, and lactation—goes hand in hand with an increase of receptive and retentive tendencies; these phases are the psychic representations of the need for fuel to supply energy for growth. At the time of ovulation and during the lutein phrase, the actual increase in metabolic need must be minimal, yet the psychic responses are recognizable. This signifies that in the presence of signal stimulation the psychic apparatus sets in motion an innate pattern of responses which, if actually not needed, affords learning by repetition.[1]

When conception occurs, the cyclic function of the ovaries is interrupted and is not reestablished with regularity until after lactation is finished. Because of the uninterrupted and enhanced function of the corpus luteum, the psychobiology of pregnancy can be best understood as an immense intensification of the lutein phase of the cycle. While this seems to be an oversimplification of the complexity of the physiologic and psychologic processes of pregnancy, it refers to its foundation, namely, to the increased hormonal and metabolic processes and their psychologic manifestations motivated by intensified receptive and retentive tendencies.

Pregnancy is a biologically normal but exceptional period in the life of women. At conception a "biologic symbiosis" begins that steers the woman between the happy fulfillment of her biologic destiny and its menacing failures. The heightened hormonal and metabolic processes which are necessary to maintain the normal growth of the fetus augment the vital energies of the mother. It is the interlocking physiologic processes between mother and fetus that make the pregnant woman's body abound in libidinous feelings.

As metabolic and emotional processes replenish the libido reservoir of the pregnant woman, this supply of primary narcissism becomes a wellspring of her motherliness. Self-centered as it may appear, it increases her pleasure in bearing her child, stimulates her hopeful fantasies, diminishes her anxieties. One can, however, observe differences in women's reactions to this psychobiologic state. A woman whose personality organization makes her a natural mother enjoys the narcissistic state with vegetative calmness, while a less fortunate woman defends herself, often consciously, against that experience. As women succeed in adjusting to the hormonal influences of pregnancy, the initial fatigue, sleepiness, some of the physical reactions such as vertigo or morning sickness, diminish. Thus women are able to respond to their physical and emotional well-being by expanding and enjoying their activities. While the pregnant woman feels her growing capacity to love and to care for her child, she experiences a general improvement in her emotional state. Many neurotic women who suffer from severe anxiety states are free from them during pregnancy; others, in spite of morning sickness or in spite of realistic worries caused by the pregnancy, feel stable and have their best time while they are pregnant. Healthy women demonstrate during pregnancy just as during the high hormone phases of the cycle an increased integrative capacity of the ego.

Yet the drive organization which accounts for the gratifications of pregnancy harbors its inherent dangers. It tests the physiologic and psychologic reserves of women. Realistic fears, insecurities motivated by conception out of wedlock, economic worries, unhappy marriages make the test more arduous. Yet even such pregnancies usually have a normal course. We might assume that such pregnancies, in our age of relatively free use of contraceptives, are often deliberately or unconsciously chosen for their drive gratification and therefore have a curative effect. To this assumption one might object, since we all know that the hope for a change for the better in an interpersonal relationship or in an external situation may enhance the gratification of pregnancy. To this, however, I would answer that the increased libidinal state of pregnancy enhances hope and by this might favorably influence not only the pregnancy but also the realities of the environmental situation. Whether the hope will be fulfilled or disappointed, the fact is that hope arising from the libidinal state of pregnancy is often the motivation of motherhood. The point to be emphasized is: *only if the psychosexual organization of the woman is loaded with conflicts toward motherhood do actual conditions stir up deeper conflicts and disturb the psychophysiologic balance of pregnancy.*

Psychopathology of pregnancy

Since the complex steps toward maturity, motherhood, and motherliness begin with infancy, the psychodynamic processes of normal and pathologic pregnancy can be discussed in terms of the oral dependent phase of the mother's development. Receptive-dependent needs having been revived, pregnant women thrive on the solicitude of their environment and suffer, sometimes unduly, if such needs are frustrated. It seems that the exceptional condition brings about exceptional needs, which by requiring attention provide for emotional gratification. Well-known symptoms such as the perverse appetite of pregnant women, even nausea and morning sickness, might be so motivated, since such symptoms seem to diminish under the changing attitudes toward pregnancy. Yet the question remains—which changes in attitude affect the emotional health of pregnant women? Grete Bibring, in her preliminary publication of a large-scale investigation of the psychologic processes in pregnancy, assumes that much of the psychopathology of pregnancy in our current culture might be activated by our "scientific" approach to pregnancy, which does not pay enough attention to the emotional needs of pregnant women [7]. This scientific attitude communicates to women a scientific requirement, namely, to take a natural, i.e., an objective, attitude toward themselves, toward their condition during pregnancy. However, self-imposed frustration of needs and repression of fears might also be a factor in activating pathologic reactions.

The inner-directed psychologic state of pregnancy has a regressive pull which brings about mood swings from the calm elation of the narcissistic state to the anxious depressive mood of deep-seated insecurity. The intensification of receptive and retentive tendencies activated by the physiology of pregnancy brings about id regression in the service of the species, to paraphrase the felicitous formulation of Kris, which under certain circumstances might bring about a regression of the ego, hence the vulnerable ego state of pregnant women [11].

Whether the woman fully enjoys her pregnancy or is ambivalent toward her motherhood, in any case the integrative task of pregnancy and motherhood—biologically, psychologically, and realistically—is much greater than a woman has ever faced before. In some cases the adaptive task appears greater with the first child, when the woman experiences something completely new. The physiologic and emotional maturation of the first pregnancy usually makes motherhood easier with the second and third child. Yet it also happens that women, fatigued by the never-ceasing labor of motherhood, afraid of the burden of another child, experience pathogenic regression during later pregnancies. Yet the security of marriage, the considerate affection of a good husband, the pleasure in her children, and the support of her parental family supply the feedback which helps to keep in balance the emotional household of a pregnant woman. Actual deprivations, by increasing the integrative task, intensify the regression and stir up the basic instinctual conflict at the root of the procreative function of woman. Concern about her future increases her need, and by this the intensity of her frustration. Unrelieved frustration and the accompanying helpless, hopeless anger interrupt the well-being of the physiologic symbiosis. Then the pregnant woman, like an angry, frustrated infant, cannot find gratification in her pregnancy. Ungratified, the frustrated woman feels unable to love and satisfy her unborn child; this, in turn, activates her anxiety. The rejection of the pregnancy goes hand in hand with the hostility toward the self, with the rejection of the self.

It is known that extreme rage may lead to spontaneous

abortion, especially during the first trimester of pregnancy. In the less acute cases, anorexia, vomiting, and consequent severe metabolic disturbances may result from the woman's destructive tendencies toward herself and toward her unborn child. It is pertinent here to note that such symptoms appear even under the most satisfactory emotional and socioeconomic circumstances, and they occur often in women who as infants had severe anorexia and/or other psychosomatic illnesses of the gastrointestinal tract. This again demonstrates that as the psychodynamic processes inherent in pregnancy revive the infantile ambivalence toward mother and motherhood, they reactivate the anxieties, frustrations, and pains referable to the pregnant woman's infancy, her oral phase of development.

In 1911 Karl Abraham conceptualized the pathogenesis of depression [1]. Since then it has been a well-established concept of psychoanalysis that regression to the oral phase of development is the psychodynamic condition of depression. "Since such regression is inherent in the physiology of pregnancy and lactation—even in the lutein phase of the sexual cycle—depressions of varying severity and psychosomatic conditions of oral structure are the basic manifestations of the psychopathology of the female propagative function" [5].

The further elaboration and symptomatic manifestation of that regression depend on all the factors, constitutional and experiential (environmental), which account for the personality organization of the individual. Among the experiential factors, as emphasized earlier (Chap. 4), are the vicissitudes of the female child's identifications with her mother. If this is not charged with intense hostility, the woman accepts her heterosexual desires without anxiety and motherhood as a desired goal. At the other end of the innumerable solutions to the same infantile conflicts is the extreme fear of pregnancy and motherhood which, under certain conditions, might lead to infertility.

Infertility, if not caused by organic pathology, can be considered a defense against the dangers inherent in the procreative function [4]. The conflicts leading to infertility are usually so deeply repressed that such women, some time in their lives, becoming aware of their inability to bear children, clamor with an anxious desire for a cure. Then psychoanalysis discovers the conflicts and ego defenses which, by enabling them to avoid pregnancy, protect them from the anxiety [6], which could shatter their personality organization. Other women, having similar primary conflicts but a constitution which enables them to conceive easily, still might be protected from their anxiety through spontaneous abortions or by psychosomatic symptoms which, by the severity of the illness, direct the anxiety away from its source, the pregnancy, and away from its object, the fetus. In illness the anxiety can be concentrated upon the self, upon one's own survival. Even without illness the anxiety stirred up by the threat to the ego might remain concentrated on the pregnancy itself; then the woman might become hypochondriacal, afraid of dying during or as a result of delivery. In other cases the hostility toward the fetus is closer to consciousness as the cause of death; in these instances, women fantasy about harboring a cancerous growth, a gnawing animal, or even a monster. Such

fantasies, alien to the ego and often in traumatic contrast to the woman's wish for pregnancy and motherhood, activate grave anxiety frequently experienced as losing her mind. Whoever has observed a pregnant woman's ego struggling to master her panic knows that the biologically motivated introversion magnifies the psychologic and consequently also the realistic task of motherhood. Many women have enough ego resources to overcome the panic, but even if the panic lasts only a few minutes, the victory is paid for dearly. Having become painfully aware of her fear of and hostility toward her unborn child, the anxiety might lead to severe phobic defenses against the sense of inadequacy in her motherliness. This, in turn, might create a vicious circle in the transactional processes between mother and her infant. Thus the disturbance of the biologic symbiosis, although we generally assume that it is experienced by the mother only, might disturb the postpartum symbiosis and the ensuing developmental interactions between a mother and her child.

Derivatives of the Oedipus complex and other fantasies

Until now we have concentrated on those representations of the primary object relationships which have a deleterious effect upon the emotional course of pregnancy, but they are the exceptions representing variations of pathologic states. While we are impressed by and concerned with pathology, we should not forget that infants grow up with the ability for normal motherhood. What is evident in the population statistics is confirmed by psychoanalytic investigation of many women of childbearing age, i.e., the positive balance of introjects during infancy, in spite of its oscillations, increases the wish for motherhood and the gratifications of pregnancy.

However, not all the fantasies about childbearing originate in the oral phase of development. Since the psychic representation of the primary object relationships are in continual interaction with all later object relationships during the development of an individual, the later course of her development also bears upon the woman's attitude toward pregnancy and motherhood. Many fantasies originating in later developmental phases revived during pregnancy by well-tolerated physiologic regression add to the enjoyment of pregnancy and color the woman's anticipations of her motherhood. Many of these can be grouped under the heading, fantasies about the content of the womb. They have different but significant meanings in the psychic economy of pregnancy. Among these the most important regarding the psychology of pregnancy is Freud's assumption that the fantasied content of the womb is the incorporated penis of the father.

It is well established that the outcome of the girl's oedipal development, although dependent upon the vicissitudes of the preoedipal phases, influences the woman's attitude toward the other sex, her acceptance of her sexual role in coitus. As the father influences the girl's heterosexual maturation, he alleviates her fear of being a woman and of bearing children. The investigation of the sexual cycle confirmed these assumptions; it demonstrated that during the follicle-ripening, estrogen phase, the developmental wish to become equal to mother and to have a similar sexual role with father is repeated. Oedipal wishes reactivated during pregnancy might motivate the fantasy that the content of the womb is the representation of the received and retained penis of the father. Although this fantasy is not as ubiquitous as it is interpreted, it demonstrates the integration of the two phases of the female reproductive drive, the heterosexual drive and the tendency to receive and retain, i.e., conceive. Although this fantasy cannot carry the weight of the psychobiologic concept of woman's propagative function, psychoanalysis in many instances has demonstrated its motivational power in women's attitudes during pregnancy.

Effects of other (common) fantasies

There are many common infantile fantasies. One or the other of them might have greater significance in the girl's development toward motherhood. Rekindled by the regressive processes, such a fantasy might influence the emotional course of the pregnancy and by this the mother's attitude toward her child. Such influence might be beneficial or anxiety-provoking. The main and most natural source of her fantasies is the pregnant woman's body, abundant with libido. Since the fetus is a part of the woman's body, it is cathected with narcissistic libido. But there are many aspects of the self-image charged with ambivalence. Is the fetus identified with the loving and loved self? If so, this is fortunate for both mother and infant. Or does the fetus represent the "bad, aggressive-devouring self," engendering fear of carrying a monster, creating panic or depression, and by this devaluating mother and child. The fetus might also represent the once-admired beauty or the envied pregnancy of the pregnant woman's mother. Such fantasies express hope for fulfillment in the child, or they may revive the hostility once felt toward the envied mother or sibling. Or does the fetus represent the missing and wished-for penis, as Freud assumed? Even this would not always represent an object charged exclusively with positive feelings. More often and closer to consciousness are fantasies which identify the fetus with its begetter. In such fantasies the oneness of the pregnant woman with her mate encompasses their yet unborn child, creating the psychodynamic foundation of the triad: father-mother-child.

The fetus does not always represent a genital symbol, even in the happy pregnant woman's fantasies. Some women identify the content of the womb, the fetus, with the content of the bowels, with feces; by this they relive the mysteries of the infantile fantasy, the anal child. Such fantasies charged with the once strictly forbidden pleasure of anal eroticism allow parents to indulge each other in their shared regression and in this way anticipate their future communication with their child in the language of infancy.

It is noteworthy to add here that husbands can and often do share the libidinous, happy fantasies of their wives if the latter are not embarrassed to talk about them. Women, understandably, do not talk about their aggressive, hostile fantasies unless they cannot help it; because of their mounting anxiety, they have to ask for help, for reassurance, for love. If love is available and is enough to relieve their anxiety, pregnancy will continue without a renewed flare-up of unconscious conflicts. Such confirmation of their love—his power and her reception of it—deepens the bond between husband and wife; it gives another perspective to her pregnancy which then encompasses both of them and their unborn child. It is different if the hostility and anxiety cannot be alleviated. Whether it spills over to the husband or not, it alienates the marital partners. Since the husband does not experience a regression motivated by the state of pregnancy, he often cannot have deep-rooted empathy with the incomprehensible reaction of his wife to a normally healthy, happy condition. However considerate the husband tries to be regarding the suffering of his wife, sooner or later he begins to resent her pathologic state, since it deprives him of the gratification of his virility in having impregnated his wife. This plants dissension between them. The child born out of that pregnancy often remains the center of the disunity of the parents. Thus the primary ambivalence, the root of the mother's pathologic state, might bring to the fore the ambivalent attitude in the father toward the child. The disunity between the parents endangers the emotional development of the child, since the transactional processes in such triads are reciprocally affected by the ambivalence of each of its members.

Citing the most frequent (typical) fantasies of pregnant women has proved to be rewarding, since it illustrates different levels of ego operations in response to (or motivated by) the biologic regression inherent in the physiology of pregnancy. A microscopic analysis of any one of the examples is beyond the scope of this presentation, but altogether they illustrate the psychobiologic continuum.

The fetus and the mother

One participant of this continuum seems to have been left out—the fetus itself. Does the psychobiologic disequilibrium influence the intrauterine environment and by this the fetus itself? Folklore takes it for granted that acute anxiety, sorrow, or worry disturbs the fetus and causes physical harm.[2] There are obvious reasons why investigations of this far-reaching problem are relatively recent and far from conclusive. Yet a rapidly growing interest and promisingly developing methodology of investigations of the fetal environment and the response by its inhabitor—the fetus—might expand our knowledge of the psychobiologic continuum to include fetal-maternal and neonatal-maternal processes into the ontogenesis of individuals. That which has long been a part of mythology and folklore has been brought into the focus of scientific inquiry during the second quarter of this century. Beginning with investigations that proved an infectious disease of the mother, rubella, causes malformations and mental retardation in the child, Sontag expanded his research to include more subtle effects of differences in the fetal environment and its effect on fetal behavior and physiology [13, 14]. An even more courageous move in the same direction was presented by Green [10], whose investigation led him to the premise that some kinds of objects are perceived very early by the developing human organism, that objects perceived via somatic rather than psychologic processes afford the organism a degree of variation in tension which maintains communication between mother—fetal environment—fetus.

Psychoanalytic investigation of pregnancy as a psychobiologic process reveals its significance for the individual and for the three generations which pregnancy links in sequence. The psychosexual maturity of the individual woman is the result of the girl's introjected developmental experiences. These form the self-image of being a woman and her characteristic attitudes, her acceptance of, or her rebellion against, her sexual role in intercourse and in motherhood. As these psychic precursors of motherhood come to be influenced by the physiologic processes of pregnancy, they mature and expand to encompass the yet unborn child with anticipation of fulfillment. Normal mother-and-child relationships are a relatively unobtrusive evolution of the culturally accepted manifestations of motherly love and care. Deviation from the normal demands attention. Clinical observations of the postpartum and later interactions between mother and infant reveal that the mother's ambivalence toward her procreative function influences her motherliness; it inhibits and blocks the natural flow of her mothering behavior. Since the father's attitude toward the child might be influenced by the communicated experience of his wife, the emotional course of the pregnancy is largely responsible for the psychologic environment of the child; since it might confirm or undermine the meaning of the marriage, it may stabilize or disrupt the primary social unit, the family.

NOTES

1. The unconscious repetition of memory traces of early infancy under the stimulation of the hormones of the corpus luteum is a good example of "psychosomatic learning." These memory traces interacting with later levels of mother identifications influence the psychic representations of motherhood and modify the anticipations connected with it. Thus the monthly repetition of the intrapsychic processes of the sexual cycle illustrates that psychosomatic learning occurs not only in infancy but throughout life as a result of integration of maturational and developmental processes.

2. For example, it is a widespread belief that the fetus will be born with a birthmark (nevus flammeus) on the face if the pregnant woman in sudden anxiety covers her face with her hands.

REFERENCES

1. Abraham, K. Notes on the Psycho-Analytical Investigation and Treatment of Manic-Depressive Insanity and Allied Conditions. In K. Abraham (Ed.), *Selected Papers.* London: Hogarth, 1927. Pp. 137-156.
2. Alexander, F. *Psychosomatic Medicine.* New York: Norton, 1950.
3. Benedek, T., and Rubenstein, B. B. *The Sexual Cycle in Women.* Washington, D. C.: National Research Council, 1942.
4. Benedek, T. Infertility as a psychosomatic defense. *Fertil. Steril.* 3:527-537, 1952.
5. Benedek, T. *Psychosexual Functions in Women.* New York: Ronald, 1952.
6. Benedek, T., Ham, G. C., Robbins, F. P., and Rubenstein, B. B. Some emotional factors in infertility. *Psychosom. Med.* 15:485-498, 1953.
7. Bibring, G. L. Some considerations of the psychological processes of pregnancy. *Psychoanal. Stud. Child* 14:113-121, 1959.
8. de Beauvoir, S. *The Second Sex.* (Translated by H. M. Parshley.) New York: Knopf, 1953.
9. Deutsch, H. *The Psychology of Women.* New York: Grune & Stratton, Vol. I, 1944; Vol. II, 1945.
10. Green, W. A. Early object relations, somatic, affective and personal. *J. Nerv. Ment. Dis.,* 126:225-253, 1958.
11. Kris, E. *Psychoanalytic Explorations in Art.* New York: International Universities Press, 1952. Pp. 173-188.
12. Rheingold, J. C. *The Fear of Being a Woman.* New York: Grune & Stratton, 1964.
13. Sontag, L. W. The significance of fetal environmental differences. *Amer. J. Obstet. Gynec.* 42:996-1003, 1941.
14. Sontag, L. W. Differences in modifiability of fetal behavior and physiology. *Psychosom. Med.* 6:151-154, 1944.

36 *Castration anxiety and phallus envy: a reformulation*

Beulah Chamberlain Bosselman

Theoretical formulations have for the most part been originated by men. This fact may be relatively insignificant in the fields of impersonal science, but it must be taken into account in evaluating theories of human behavior, since interpretation of behavior cannot fail to be affected by the attitudes of the interpreter. His attitudes in turn are largely determined by the traditions of the culture in which he lives.

Therefore when Sigmund Freud, living in the patriarchal society of nineteenth-century Western Europe, explained most problems of personality development as due to castration anxiety in the male and phallus envy in the female, one must consider his theory against the background of his social milieu.

The Freudian theories are based on the assumption of male superiority. They imply that the most fear-provoking and disorganizing concept to the male concerns the possible loss of his masculinity; and that the female, likewise acknowledging the supremacy of the phallus, is beset by feelings of inadequacy and resentment.

Reprinted from Beulah Chamberlain Bosselman "Castration Anxiety and Phallus Envy: A Reformulation," Psychiatric Quarterly, 34, 1960, pp. 252-259.

Most superficial observations would seem to bear out this implication. The very fact that social theories are formulated by men is obviously in itself one indication of male dominance. The important work of the world in politics, business, the professions and the arts is directed by men. There have been some female gods in obscure times and places but for the most part Heaven—and shall one add Hell?—also are ruled by male deities!

There are, however, some facts that do not fit smoothly into the masculine-superiority theory. The death rate among males of all ages is higher than among females. This may be a matter of unexplained biologic organization but one cannot rule out a contributing psychologic factor. Especially striking is the fact that, in practically every society about which statistics have been gathered, more men than women commit suicide. The proportion is at least two to one and in most places much higher than that.

To anyone who is intrigued by the concepts of constructive (life-preserving) versus destructive (life-destroying) forces battling in every human being, these facts stimulate speculation. Is life basically more valuable to the female, less easily given up? Is the "life instinct" (variously described as Eros or as "elan vital") stronger in the woman, and if so does this indicate that femininity allows a more gratifying way of life than does masculinity? These are the questions that provide the background for re-examination of Freudian theory.

Most psychiatrists will agree that the great majority of men who present themselves for treatment prove to be primarily fearful about their capacity for maleness—as defined by our cultural traditions. Their protests, expressed in variable ways, indicate a wish to be strong, dominant, aggressive—associated with a doubt as to the existence of these qualities in themselves. They are afraid to be passive, yet afraid to compete with other men; resentful of strong women and equally resentful of clinging ones.

This monotonously repetitive personality problem may express itself in symptoms of anxiety, depression, over-compensatory aggressiveness (even delinquency) or a defeated withdrawal. It may result in somatic illness, which rationalizes escape, or alcoholism, which deadens conflict. It may be projected in a paranoid placing of blame upon circumstances outside the self. But as the basic structure of the difficulty is revealed, it takes the form, over and over again, of fear of passivity; and underlying this is a more or less strongly repressed longing to be dependent, to assume a more protected, less responsible role. This longing, however, arouses intense fear of aggression. The man must be strong, he must compete with the father and brother figures in his milieu, or he will be subject to scorn. His socially-prized gift of masculinity will be snatched from him and there will be no place for him in the world.

This is the "castration anxiety" so astutely observed by Freud. It is evident as soon as the little boy becomes aware of his sex and at the same time becomes aware that he can no longer remain in close uncontested relationship with his mother. During his prolonged infancy, all his reactions have been directed toward interaction with the mothering person. His sucking and grasping reflexes reach out to her; she is his comfort and security, the stable unchanging focus point in the "big buzzing blooming confusion" of his world. He cannot resolve the problem, as his sister is expected to do, by identification with the mother. Instead he must make the sharper break, identifying himself with the father and assuming toward the mother the kind of attitude which he observes in the father.

The "Oedipal conflict" which develops in the boy at the age of three to six has been described largely in terms of competitive striving with the father for the mother. The fact that the child's diffusely erotic infantile feelings are at this time becoming genitalized tends to symbolize the competition in sexual terms. The boy must be like father; he must feel as the father does about the mother; he must be masculine. But in competition with the father he is a small and vulnerable male, in danger of "castration."

This focus of interest on aggressive sexualized strivings with the father has tended to overshadow the fact that the boy, in identifying with the father, must accomplish a sharper removal from his intimate symbiosis with the mother than is expected of the girl at this age. Father is presumably strong and protective in his attitude toward mother—an attitude which contrasts strongly with the dependency of the baby. In other words, the male child must in his personality development deal with two demands: First, he must give up his passive dependent attachment to his mother. Second, he must, in substitution for this, work out a satisfactory identification-competition with the father. The strong ambivalent feelings aroused by the second problem tend, as has been mentioned, to obscure the persistence of the deep dependency longings. It is the persistence of these longings—so disapproved by our aggressive patriarchal mores—that in later life underlies much neurotic disturbance in the male.

Let us now turn to the developmental problems of the female. The little girl also must renounce her exclusive dependency on the mother, and she too becomes in a more specifically sexual way attached to the parent of opposite sex—her father. This stimulates the same competitive strivings with the mother that the boy experiences with the father. However, it is not necessary for the girl to change her attitudes so radically, because in identifying with the mother she still remains in a protected-dependent role. She is allowed, within the social pattern, to continue to be passive-receptive. Her brother is given guns and is expected to negate the infantile role with gestures of control and active manipulation, whereas the girl in her play with dolls still continues vicariously to fantasy the baby-mother relationship. Even as she matures, she is allowed many infantile prerogatives which are denied the boy. The family is more tolerant if she is fearful, if she weeps and runs away. Brother is expected to fight and hold his ground, and is told that big boys don't cry.

The price the female pays for this social tolerance of her persistence in infantile attitudes is, on the surface, a high price. The male, encouraged in his out-going active strivings, becomes socially dominant, and, at least theoretically, the head of the family. In some times and places he has used his strength and authority to browbeat the female into a state of humiliating subservience. It is this appearance of inequality that has led to the implication of masculine superiority which influences the Freudian theories of behavior.

The theory of phallus envy as the root of female neurosis is implicit in the Freudian interpretation of castration anxiety. If loss of maleness is the most fearful of all traumata, then envy of maleness might well be assumed in the female. Its existence is borne out by the protests of "feminist" groups, and it can also be demonstrated in some of the neurotic symptoms of women who come for psychiatric treatment. It may be expressed as frank resentment of the feminine role, with a good deal of competitiveness and need to control the male. It may lead to efforts for a "career" in fields dominated by men or may express itself mainly in tyrannical control of the family—a matriarchal kind of rule.

This phallus-envy motif is, however, by no means as consistently found in psychiatric studies of women as castration anxiety is found in men. The concept is in fact much less prevalent in present-day psychoanalytic literature than it is in the earlier papers. It is nevertheless a presenting symptom in a certain percentage of conflict-ridden women.

Women who are involved in "masculine protests" of this kind are frequently either unmarried or have husbands who are described as weak and ineffectual. The simplest interpretation would seem to be that such women envy the dominant male and, therefore, are likely, if they marry at all, to choose a passive partner with whom they can reverse the roles. This often seems to be the situation as such women present it originally to the psychiatrist. They protest that they are dissatisfied with their places in life, want to accomplish more important tasks, feel restless and confined. They insist that men have the more interesting position, and they may dwell at length on the injustices of the social system. These protests, however, have to do more with the outward superficialities than with the basic personality needs. As psychiatric exploration penetrates these outer layers, it reveals them as a brittle defensive veneer. Essentially, woman has built up this competitive controlling defense because the men in her life have not accepted her in a male-to-female relationship. They have not created a situation in which she dares to be passive-receptive. The rejection usually begins with the father and may be an outright disinterest on his part, or it may be an attitude that accepts her as a son rather than as a daughter. If the girl's mother is at the same time competitive rather than supportive, the child has no recourse but to assume an aggressive manipulative attitude toward the world. "If you won't take care of me I will fight you; I won't give you an opportunity to hurt me."

This kind of attitude makes it difficult for the girl to develop good love-relationships in later life. The secure men who are best capable of admiring and protecting a woman turn rather to those better oriented in the feminine role. Dependent, mother-seeking men, on the other hand, turn to her as a seemingly strong woman, and a frustrating relationship is thereby set up. Both want to be taken care of; both resent the need to be strong and responsible.

This brings us to what is really the core of the problem. Personality difficulties in both men and women have a common origin: the persistence of old, insufficiently gratified hungers for the exclusive love and protection of the parent. The male has been taught to overcome this by assuming an outgoing aggressive attitude toward the world, implying a denial of infantile wishes. The female is allowed to continue in a more passive role, insofar as she is able to attach herself to supportive masculine figures.

As has been observed, the male role implies a sharper break with the original receptive attitude and it becomes, therefore, reinforced by rigid codes. It wins rewards however in the position of social control which it favors. To the man who is able to renounce his infantile strivings, the world is full of challenge and he can relate to his wife with real admiration for her feminine prerogatives rather than with envy and resentment.

The female, in an accepting milieu, finds continuing satisfaction in the receptive, rather than manipulative, position, and as she develops, is able to give freely to her husband and children the mothering love which they need. Her participation is activities outside the home then becomes determined by her intellectual curiosity and social consciousness rather than by a need to prove her worth in the "man's world." On the whole this is a smoother, more gratifying situation, which may explain the lower deathrate, and particularly the lower suicide rate in women. More of the simple primitive satisfactions of the child persist; there is less socially-imposed stress and strain.

Regarded in this way, one sees the masculine and feminine roles, not in terms of superiority versus inferiority, but rather as patterns determined by the exigencies of maturation. The process of growing up, renouncing the satisfactions of one stage of life to substitute those of the next, is not an easy process. The tendency is to cling to the old ways or to regress to them when adaptations become difficult.

In such situations the male, longing for protection and dependence, finds his impulses at sharp variance with the codes of society. He must be aggressive, or he meets with intolerance, even contempt. He feels vulnerable to the world, as in early childhood he felt vulnerable to the greater strength of his father. His "castration anxiety" expresses this vulnerability. "I must be what the world demands or my masculinity will be taken from me and I shall be nothing."

Phallus envy in the female, as has been observed, is a less frequently occurring phenomenon because of the more basically gratifying nature of the feminine role. When it does occur, it indicates only superficially an envy of the masculine position; more essentially it is the woman's protest at not being allowed to be a woman.

The problem of residual infantile longings struggling within cultural patterns of masculinity and feminity which we observe in our patients is a problem characteristically underlying the neuroses of our day. We know that the meaning of the typical neurotic disturbances of any time and place highlights the prevalent cultural stresses and strains. It would seem then, considered from a prophylactic point of view, that our standards of masculinity tend to be too rigid, demanding too completely and too suddenly the establishment of an aggressive, independent, "mature" position.

The boy, forced by great social pressure into this role, experiences more or less insecurity. This may express itself frankly or may be overcompensated by overly aggressive attitudes. The persistence of conflict in the man complicates his relationship with women. Envying their more dependent state, he may overemphasize his superior social position and express dictatorial, even sadistic, attitudes. On the other hand by such devices as illness, alcoholism, or repeated failure, he may manage to shift his responsibilities to the women in his life, making them "parent figures." Or he may vacillate between these attitudes, exacting care from the woman, but meanwhile depreciating and rejecting her, to deny his dependency.

Women's difficulties are to a large extent secondary to those of men, resulting, as we have seen, from the fact that men who resent and compete with women cannot offer them a genuine appreciation and affection—cannot gladly let them fulfill their feminine role.

The number of men and women who present this problem to a psychiatrist represents obviously a very small percentage of the people who struggle with it alone. Their difficulties are manifested in a high divorce rate, marital infidelity, frigidity and impotence, inadequate parental attitudes, homosexuality. Over a wider social area these conflicts in self-identification contribute to delinquency, prostitution, alcoholism and drug addiction, homicide and suicide.

Prophylaxis lies largely in the direction of better family attitudes. The child must gradually substitute for his infantile "consuming" instincts a more outgoing, sharing point of view. His needs must be reasonably satisfied or he will be forever hungry; yet he must also be guided to consider the needs of others. The child who is loved and accepted can most freely give, but unless he is also led to see himself in an interacting role, a unit in a larger dynamic social unit, he may remain expectant of continuing infantile satisfactions and, therefore, may never fully accept the responsibilities of adult life.

This basic challenge is the same for the boy and the girl. For each, the establishment of a sense of worth as a person provides the best foundation for a satisfactory masculine or feminine identification.

Summary

The differing demands which our culture imposes on the male and on the female influences the prevalent psychopathology of men and women.

The more compelling early need of the male to renounce dependency may well be related to his higher death and suicide rates and his higher incidence of alcoholism and delinquency. The role of the female is a biologically easier one to attain.

Castration anxiety and phallus envy, as formulated by Freud, are re-evaluated as products of the more primary problem of renouncing infantile satisfactions in favor of maturity and responsibility. Symptoms of castration anxiety appear to be universal among disturbed men but phallic attitudes in the female are less common. When they occur, they are often found to represent not the female's envy of the male, but her protest at his denial of her feminine prerogatives.

37 Behavior therapy approaches to modification of sexual preferences: biological perspective and critique

Gordon Bermant

I have two tasks to perform for this symposium. First, I am to provide some sort of general biological perspective on the general area under consideration. And second, I am to present a critique of the two papers that have been presented today. I will begin with the biological perspective.

There are already several papers written by comparative and/or physiological psychologists with an eye toward providing relevant information to clinicians interested in sexual behavior. For example, there is the paper by Denniston in Marmor's book *Sexual Inversion* and the chapters by Tinbergen and Richard Michael in Rosen's *Pathology and Treatment of Sexual Deviation*. The chapter by Michael is particularly valuable because of its physiological sophistication and its treatment of the rapidly developing research area of the behavioral endocrinology of neonates.

I shall not go over the ground these authors have covered. I shall not review for you the literature on rats in which sexual behavior has been punished, nor will I provide background information on the effects of neonatal androgenization. I shall instead call, or recall, your attention to a very

Reprinted from Gordon Bermant, "Behavior Therapy Approaches to Modification of Sexual Preferences: Biological Perspective and Critique," paper presented at the California State Psychological Association.

obvious fact about sexual deviation. I will next document the generality of this fact with sufficient examples to, hopefully, convince you of it. Then I will provide a simple, some will say simple-minded, explanation of why this fact is a fact. And finally I will try to relate this fact and its explanation to the therapy of sexual deviation. In doing this I will refer to alternative explanations of why the fact is true. It is virtually impossible that this exercise will be of immediate benefit to clinicians practicing in the area. Although this disturbs me, I take comfort in the fact that similar inputs from other biologically-orientated commentators have not themselves been clinically very useful.

What is the fact which intrigues me? It is simply this: *men demonstrate a larger incidence and frequency of biologically inappropriate sexual behavior than women do.* Specifically, men are more likely than women to masturbate, engage in homosexual behavior, become sexually fetishistic, or engage in erotically gratifying exhibitionism or voyeurism. To put the matter slightly a different way, there is a marked sex difference in the incidence of sexual deviations.

This generalization holds across a wide variety of different populations. To begin with, it is surely true for our current American population. Here there are several sorts of documentation that can be provided. First we can consider the Kinsey reports, which reported greater incidences of masturbation and homosexual experience for males than for females. And this difference in the reasonably broadly sampled population is also mirrored in the relative numbers of males and females who present homosexuality as a primary complaint to psychotherapists. You will recall, for example, that Bieber and his colleagues were able to collect information from 106 male homosexuals in psychoanalysis. However, Kaye *et al.* (1967), who did the "sister study" on lesbians, were able to locate only 24 practicing females in psychoanalytic treatment. Along the same lines, until today's symposium I had not run across any mention of behavior therapy being applied to female sexual behavior. This may be in part because a good proportion of this literature deals with fetishism, which is, as has been known for some time, virtually totally a masculine practice.

One could marshall still more evidence, and provide adequate quantification, but I think the point is clear enough for our own society. What is the case for societies other than our own? Today I will take it for granted that the general picture found in the U.S. holds as well for England and continental Europe, and consider instead more remote societies. Ford & Beach's 1951 *Patterns of Sexual Behavior* is still an authoritative source for cross-cultural considerations. In summarizing their findings from seventy-five societies, these authors concluded that there were few if any groups in which the incidences and frequencies of homosexual behavior and masturbation were equal for the two sexes. I will quote the relevant sentences concerning homosexuality: "Some homosexual behavior occurs in a great many human societies. It tends to be more common in adolescents than in adulthood and appears to be practiced more frequently by men than by women." And speaking of masturbation, they say ". . . it appears universally true that men are more likely to practice self-stimulation than women."

If the information on our own society were considered alone, one might argue that the observed sex difference in sexual behavior was a product of cultural conditioning, and hence unique to our own history and traditions. The data from other cultures, in which attitudes about homosexuality and masturbation vary widely, but in which, nevertheless, the difference between men and women is maintained, suggest that this sociological interpretation is too narrow. It appears instead that this sex difference represents an invariant aspect of the human sexual condition. The difference is a characteristic of man as a species.

The generality of this sex difference across the diversity of human cultures makes it reasonable to compare man in this regard with other animal species. The comparison is appropriate precisely because we are dealing with a phenomenon of species-wide occurrence.

Let us look first at the non-human primates. Concerning masturbation, one can find evidence for masturbation in new world monkeys, old world monkeys, and apes. Before the recent tremendous increase in data collected under relatively natural conditions, it was believed by some workers that this sexual manifestation was a product of the constrained conditions of captivity. It is now known that this hypothesis was incorrect; monkeys in the wild may masturbate. However, it is clearly true that the incidence and frequency with which males are observed to masturbate is substantially greater than the incidence and frequency observed for females.

Judgments concerning the incidence and frequency of homosexual behavior in non-human primates is a little more difficult to assess because of the utilization in many species of sexual-like postures and gestures in the general system of communication. Thus, as Peter Marler has recently pointed out, the "presenting response," which is the typical sexual invitiation of the estrous female, is used as well by nonestrous females and by males as a general signal which has the effect of decreasing the physical distance between individuals in a single social group. The utilization of gestures and postures in this way, for general social purposes, is higly developed in Old World monkeys and apes, and represents what could be called "the social use of sex." It is this use for "nonsexual purposes" which is so highly developed in man, and which makes the complete analysis of human sexual responses in simplistic terms impossible.

Nevertheless, it appears true that frank homosexual behavior occurs more often among male nonhuman primates than among females. This was the conclusion reached by Ford and Beach in 1951, and there has been to my knowledge no substantive amount of data published subsequently to alter that conclusion.

When we turn our attention to mammals other than primates, we run into a new set of problems. To begin with, manual masturbation is rare, in part I suppose because the species have no hands with which to masturbate. However, the lack of manual dexterity has not hampered resourceful males in several species. To rely on Ford and Beach once again, a male porcupine has been observed to masturbate while straddling a broomstick, an elephant may fondle his penis with his trunk, and a male dolphin may appose his penis to the rapidly flowing stream of water entering his tank. In numerous instances of male masturbation in non-primate mammals, the practice has resulted in orgasm and ejaculation.

As rare and behaviorally bizarre as male masturbation may have to be in nonprimate mammals, it occurs more often than it does in females. Female autoerotic behavior occurs only at times of normal sexual receptivity. This means, for example, that it will be observed at the most only during one brief period per year in wild ungulates, twice a year in domestic dogs and cats, and so on. It appears that automanipulation of the genitals in female nonprimate mammals is primarily a scratching of the vulva which has become swollen and tender as a result of the hormonal conditions surrounding the initiation of ovulation and behavioral receptivity. The close dependence of sexual behavior on hormonal cycles in these species makes a comparison with primates in general, and man in particular, tenuous for current purposes. Nevertheless, to the extent that it matters, the sex differences observed in primate masturbation hold for nonprimate mammals as well.

To complete this brief review we should consider the homosexual behavior of nonprimate mammals. Both males and females of numerous species have been observed to mount, and to submit to mounting by, conspecifics of the same sex. Indeed in some species, for example the domestic cow, this behavior is reasonably frequent in females. However, as was the case for masturbation, feminine homosexual activity is closely tied to the period of normal sexual receptivity. This is an important finding because it shows that the male-like behavior of mounting exists, relatively untutored, in the repertoire of sexually aroused females. However, it does not in my opinion weaken the substantial generality of the finding that males are more likely than females to produce genital stimulation by other than heterosexual copulatory channels.

Now we have the fact and a sketch of its documentation. The next step is to ask why. Why is it that male mammals are more likely to masturbate than female mammals? Why is it that male primates are more prone to engage in homosexual stimulation than female primates are? Why is it that we find virtually no reversals of these sex differences in diverse human cultures? Why is it that fetishism is completely a masculine hang-up? And finally, as I suppose some of you are already beginning to ask yourselves, why is it I believe that these several questions have answers with a single, simple foundation?

I will answer this last question first. It strikes me that this fact about sex differences in sexual behavior or sexual deviation is a very general fact indeed. And I make the assumption, or have the faith, that anything so general will not have not have a terribly subtle or complicated root cause. There has to be something invariant over all the cultures and species involved which lies at the basis of this difference. Moreover, it seems very reasonable to me that this invariance will be found in some anatomical or physiological difference between males and females. Now there are many differences between males and females: in average body size and weight, patterns of fat deposit, and so on. More to the point, there are substantial differences in the secretions of the gonads. Interestingly enough, the master

endocrine gland, the pituitary, is not sexually dimorphic. But the agency which controls it, the hypothalamus, is decidedly either male or female. It becomes this way in the process of pre- and neonatal development and is influenced in its development by the presence or absence of androgen, the male sex hormone. Given that the hypothalamus becomes sexually differentiated in the course of development through hormonal influence, it might well be that other portions of the CNS are similarly affected. Indeed we now know that pre-natal and neonatal hormonal conditions do produce clear-cut sex differences in several forms of activity in young rhesus monkeys. These differences presumably reflect differences in the central nervous systems of these animals.

I will return to these kinds of differences, which might be called "central differences" between the sexes, a little later. But for now I want to concentrate on a much more obvious difference between the sexes. Moreover, I am going to argue that it is this obvious, peripheral difference which is the root cause for the general sex-behavior differences I have described.

I am referring to the difference between the locations of the penis and the clitoris. The penis is an exposed organ while the clitoris is a closeted organ. It is from this peripheral anatomical difference that subsequent sex differences in sexual behavior arise.

Having made this bald assertion, I must now justify for you my belief in its importance. At the present time it is impossible to provide a scholarly documentation for this idea similar to the job that can be done for the behavioral difference itself. Instead what I must do is to sketch briefly, for the human case only, the obvious ontogenetic consequences of the anatomical difference between the sexes, and then point out how these consequences, when considered in conjunction with other reasonably stable psychological ideas, lead to an appreciation of the inevitability of the differences in sexual behavior already discussed.

I begin with what is beyond reasonable doubt: male human infants and little boys receive more direct stimulation on their penises than female infants and little girls receive on their clitorises. I am speaking here primarily of the *inevitable* stimulation that arises through ordinary practices of bathing, dressing, powdering, diaper changing, holding, the friction received from clothing while walking, and so on. Infants and children in some human cultures may additionally receive *intentional* genital stimulation from their parents; it is reported, for example, that Hopi and Siriono parents masturbate their children. Time permitting, I would return to the cross-cultural differences in adult sexual behavior that this early intentional stimulation might be expected to produce. But for now I must restrict my attention to the general case.

Given this initial baseline difference in genital stimulation, we need only realize that, for both boys and girls, the genital stimulation they do receive *feels good*. I put the matter this simply because, fundamentally, it is this simple. But it is also of substantial evolutionary importance that this stimulation feels good. For in the course of mammalian evolution there has been a trade-off of fixed behavior patterns, controlled by relatively simple sign stimuli, for a behaviorally plastic condition in which particular responses become established as a result of their functional consequences. In other words, the biologically appropriate stimulus for sexual activity is not given to man innately; he must acquire this knowledge. And the intensely pleasant feedback from genital stimulation provides the reinforcement requisite to the task.

Along with the flexibility of this system come certain risks. One risk is that the individual will develop preferences for genitally stimulating circumstances that are biologically inappropriate. Different societies work in different ways to minimize this risk; they prescribe the nature and extent of legitimate genital stimulation for different age groups and for the two sexes, and they provide positive and negative incentives to encourage obedience to the prescriptions. But one crucial point about these social systems regarding sex is that they operate primarily at a verbal level. Understanding them depends upon understanding the language. What the system teaches, indirectly, are the proper circumstances for the achievement of genital stimulation. But by the time individuals are competent to understand these teachings they have already accumulated a background of experience, inchoate and inarticulate, involving genital stimulation. And, directly to my point, boys have accumulated more of this experience, on the average, than girls have, simply because the penis is more exposed than the clitoris.

I want to recapitulate the argument now in a form that will test its relevance as a heuristic for the therapy of socially inappropriate sexual preferences. In both males and females there is a level of generalized genital eroticism which precedes an understanding of its social significance. This level is substantially higher, on the average, for males than for females. For purposes of expositional clarity I will state the case in this way: males approach the socialization process already "turned on," so that appreciation of the social significance of genital stimulations *follows* substantial experience with that stimulation. Females, on the other hand, receive direct genital stimulation *during or after* the time that their cognitive appreciation of the social significance of that stimulation has been developed. Because the experience of the stimulation is more closely allied in time with the ability cognitively to deal with it, women are less likely to commit social errors in the selection of sexual objects. Males, being in a state of relatively high sexual drive at an earlier age, are more likely to establish genitally related, socially inappropriate predispositions which, if insufficiently corrected through social education, may become marked to the degree that they become prescriptively deviant. I mean by "prescriptively deviant" only that the behavior is generally disapproved; not that it is statistically rare.

There is hidden in this argument an important implication that I need to make explicit. It goes something like this: *There is an indefinitely large number of causal pathways for the development of prescriptive sexual deviation in males. The number of causal pathways that lead to feminine prescriptive deviation, while also indefinite, is smaller than the one for males.* This implication stems from the random nature of early genital stimulation and the relatively high degree of erotic sensitivity which exists prior to the inter-

nalization of sexual norms. And when I say "random nature of early genital stimulation" I mean to imply that the pathways that lead from early erotic sensitivity to adult prescriptive deviance are manifold and practically unpredictable.

Before I come to my conclusion about the relevance of this view for the therapy of sexual deviation, I should discuss briefly two other theories which can be used to account for sex differences in sexual deviation.

First, and historically foremost, is the Freudian account. Freud's developed theory of the differences between masculine and femine sexuality starts exactly where the present argument does, namely at the distinction between masculine and feminine genitalia. In fact his first explicit exposition of the view appeared in 1929 with the title "Some psychical consequences of the anatomical distiction between the sexes." (Subsequent developments were published in 1931, in the paper "Female Sexuality," and in 1933, in Chapter 33 of the *New Introductory Lectures,* with the title "Femininity.") Freud's view was that the differences in genitalia, specifically the absence of a penis in the girl, combined with a knowledge of that difference by both boys and girls, was the key to the distinction between masculine and feminine sexual development. In particular, these factors caused different relationships between the castration and Oedipus complexes to be set up in the two sexes. Here I quote Freud: "As regards the relation between the Oedipus and castration complexes there is a fundamental contrast between the two sexes. *Whereas in the boys Oedipus complex is destroyed by the castration complex, in girls it is made possible and led up to by the castration complex.*" From this position Freud and his followers were able to argue to at least some of the observed sex differences in adult deviations. Because, in boys, the castration complex follows the Oedipus complex, it may remain unresolved by the time of adolescence. Intense castration fear, triggered and heightened by the knowledge that girls have no penis, may lead to the connection between sexual aim and sexual object that is deviant. For example, the boy may become a fetishist; in this regard I quote Gillespie: "The fetish represents the female phallus in which (the boy) can still believe and which now absorbs all his erotic interest; nonetheless, he is aware of real female genitals and is left with a feeling of aversion to them. Such a dual attitude to unacceptable reality is what Freud called a split of the ego." This fate does not await girls because the Oedipus complex has been interposed between the castration complex and the social demand to choose an adult sexual object. As another example, the boy may become a genital exhibitionist, but the girl will not. Regarding this difference I quote Rosen: "The absence of the perversion of genital exposure in women has been explained by the difference in development in the two sexes with regard to the castration complex. Absence of the penis in the woman is felt as a narcissistic injury; the exhibitionism is displaced on the whole of the rest of the body, especially the breasts, and on to a show of attractiveness. Therefore, the showing of the genitals cannot have the reassuring effect it has in men." Finally, and perhaps of most practical importance, is the distinction between male and female homosexuality. Here again the theory relies heavily on the reversal of temporal relationships between castration and Oedipus complexes. But I must admit that the vicissitudes that this part of psychoanalytic theory show in the literature make it difficult for me to summarize for you briefly. So I will not try it. Instead I will make one point about all of this theory: It admits only of single causal pathway for the development of each kind of deviation. This presumed causal uniformity must then be placed in the context of the huge cross-cultural variance that exists in practices of family rearing, not to mention the inevitable variability that intentionally and accidentally arises within any society. At this state it strikes me as implausible that a single, structured process could be present in this diversity and lead to the universally observed sexual behavior differences. I believe that the same argument can be made against the more modern psychoanalytic arguments of Bieber and his collegues that specify certain family relations (that is, a close-binding-intimate mother and a hostile or detached father) as a substantially necessary and sufficient condition for the development of male homosexuality. In short, there is too much input variance, and not enough output variance, in the observed data, for the psychoanalytic models to handle.

As a second alternative account I return to the central physiological differences between males and females that I mentioned earlier. As I said then, we are certain that from a very early age the nervous systems of boys and girls are different in at least some ways. At the very least we know that their hypothalamuses are different. We can suspect that the general activity of little boys is higher than that of little girls. And we believe that these differences are due to the prenatal effects of male sex hormone on the developing masculine fetus. In fact, John Money has described some eight-year-old girls, whose mothers took relatively high doses of androgen like drugs during pregnancy, who are presently quite "tomboyish," to use Money's phrase. Now what does this mean? It *could* mean that boys are *centrally* more predisposed to achieve genital stimulation than girls are, that they are less capable of inhibiting their genital responsiveness, that they are *fundamentally* less able to control impulses, on so on. This viewpoint, like the peripherally oriented viewpoint I have expressed, would account for both cross-cultural and cross-specific invariance. On the other hand, this alternative strikes me presently as being too *general*, that is to say it doesn't deal specifically with sexual manifestations (cf. Ford and Beach, 1951). I certainly can't prove it is wrong, but I am currently inclined to favor the more obvious peripheral hypothesis.

I hope it is now clear how my views relate to the therapy of sexual deviation. Arguing from a simple anatomical dis-

tinction and an admission of the law of effect, I feel forced to believe that there is likely to be a lot of variance in the pathways by which individuals achieve sexually deviant status in any society. This means that any therapy which demands an historical approach, which assumes a single set of possible causal pathways, and which moreover demands that the patient have an emotional appreciation of the significance of those pathways, is likely to be unsuccessful for the simple reason that this pathway has only a small probability of relating to the facts of the matter. There is little sense in getting a man to understand that his mother was close-binding-intimate, and his father hostile or detached, when in fact neither his mother nor his father fit this description.

On the other hand, a therapeutic technique which admits at the outset that the pathways which led the patient to his deviation were not intrinsically related to his current practices, and hence which de-emphasizes historical factors and deals in the "here and now" with the behavior as it exists, given the assumption of high intentionality to change on the part of the patient, will on the basis of the current argument be more likely to succeed. And this, I suppose, puts me, at least in principle, in the behavior therapy camp.

REFERENCES

Bieber, I., *et al.* (1962) *Homosexuality.* New York: Basic Books.
Denniston, R. (1965) Ambisexuality in animals. In J. Marmor (Ed.), *Sexual Inversion.* New York: Basic Books. Pp. 27-43.
Ford, C., & Beach, F. (1951) *Patterns of Sexual Behavior.* New York: Harper & Bros.
Freud, S. (1929) Some psychical consequences of the anatomical distinction between the sexes. *Standard Edition,* vol. XIX. London: Hogarth Press.
Freud, S. (1931) Female sexuality. *Standard Edition,* vol. XXI. London: Hogarth Press.
Freud, S. (1933) *New Introductory Lectures on Psychoanalysis.* New York: Norton.
Gillespie, W. (1964) The psycho-analytic theory of sexual deviation with special reference to fetishism. In I. Rosen (Ed.), *The Pathology and Treatment of Sexual Deviation.* London: Oxford University Press. Pp. 123-145.
Kaye, H., *et al.* (1967) Homosexuality in women. *Arch. Gen. Psychiat.,* 17, 626-634.
Marler, P. (1968) Aggregation and dispersal: two functions in primate communication. In P. Jay (Ed.) *Primates: Studies in Adaptation and Variability.* New York: Holt, Rinehart, and Winston. Pp. 420-438.
Michael, R. (1964) Biological factors in the organization and expression of sexual behavior. In I. Rosen (Ed.), *The Pathology and Treatment of Sexual Deviation.* London: Oxford University Press. Pp. 24-56.
Rosen, I. (1964) Exhibitionism, scopophilia, and voyeurism. In I. Rosen (Ed.), *The Pathology and Treatment of Sexual Deviation.* London: Oxford University Press. Pp. 293-350.
Tinbergen, N. (1964) Aggression and fear in the normal sexual behavior of some animals. In I. Rosen (Ed.), *The Pathology and Treatment of Sexual Deviation.* London: Oxford University Press. Pp. 3-23.

38 A predictive study of psychological and psychosomatic responses to oral contraceptives

Judith M. Bardwick

In the years 1967-1969 Joan Zweben and I interviewed 107 women before they began using an oral contraceptive in an attempt to predict psychological and psychosomatic responses to pill use. Physicians' impressions that an easy tolerance of the pill or severe discomfort and rejection were essentially psychological phenomena seemed a logical hypothesis and we tried to explore these dynamics with measures that assessed variables which had been important in psychosomatic studies of the female reproductive system. The three most important variables seemed to be passivity, or the inability to directly express aggression; dependence or the need to perceive oneself as valued by others because that is the major source for feelings of self-esteem; and denial, which is a primitive psychological defense in which reality is simply not perceived. Women who cope with anxiety by expressing it in psychosomatic symptoms tend to be dependent upon others for feelings of esteem, are very vulnerable to being rejected by others, are fearful of expressing anger because it may alienate others who would then reject them, and are very likely to use the immature and vulnerable defense of denial.

This model, although logical, proved too simplistic; the coding of responses had to be more specific. Denial was important as a mechanism but it was really best understood as a defensive attempt at coping by an immature personality who does not have more adequate and sophisticated defenses. The best single predictor was the specific denial of sexual anxiety rather than a general use of denial. We had to distinguish between a feeling, a conflict, and the defense. Thus denial was important as it related specifically to a particular conflict, such as sex, anger, dependency, and guilt. Similarly, passivity, in general, was indicative of a psychological structure or a maturity level, but the association between passivity level and pill responses emerged when passivity was divided into an inability to overtly express anger, and an inability to assume responsibility. Similarly, we had to distinguish between a developmentally normal level of anxiety about sex and pregnancy, and a sex anxiety which was not developmentally appropriate and expressed fears about body integrity.

We tried to measure the woman's psychological relationship to her body, feelings of trust or mistrust toward her sexual partner, her goals, her self-perceptions, what made her happy, angry or depressed, attitudes about contraception in general and the pills in particular and her sexual experiences, responses and motives. Before the woman started to use the oral contraceptive she was seen for two hours by Joan Zweben or myself. We gave her the Franck Drawing Completion Test (a measure of unconscious body relationships), the Nichols Subtle Scale (a questionnaire that measures passivity), The Cornel Medical Index for Women (a detailed health questionnaire), and a standardized interview. Three months later, each woman received a 4-card Thematic Apperception Test (with cards selected to measure unconscious attitudes toward heterosexual relationships, sex, maternity, dependence and passivity), and a detailed questionnaire about her response to the pills. The Franck, the TAT, and the two questionnaires were coded and scored by two clinicians.

The subjects were volunteers from a Planned Parenthood clinic in Ann Arbor and University of Michigan students recruited through advertisements in local papers. While the age range was from 17 to 35, the mean age was 20. While only four girls did not feel some level of committment to their sexual partner, only 15 were married, 32 were engaged, and 55 had a regular boyfriend. Eighty of the subjects were undergraduate or graduate students; among those married, many were the wives of students. Thus almost all of this sample were extremely motivated to use the pills successfully because there was no choice about pregnancy in their lives. Only 10 per cent of this sample had previously assumed responsibility for contraception, having used a female contraceptive like the diaphragm, foam or IUD; while 7 per cent had used rhythm, and 28 per cent relied on condoms, 41 per cent of this educated group had used nothing. These data reinforce our observation that the assumption of responsibility for contraception by young women is an extraordinarily important decision.

Body changes

The follow-up questionnaire revealed that all of the women reported body changes as the result of pill use. What emerged as interesting was the type of body change reported and the psychological response to that reported physical state. We divided the body changes into normal, unusual, and beneficent.

Normal body changes are probably directly related to steroid levels, ratios, and changes in levels. These symptoms

This paper forms the last third of James T. Fawcett (ed.), Psychological Perspectives on Population © *1972 by Basic Books, Inc., Publishers, New York. This part of Fawcett's book contains articles on such topics as the value of children to parents and the psychodynamics of abortion. The reader is directed especially to the articles by Hoffman and Hoffman, and David.*

include breasts larger and tender, menstrual cycle shorter, more regular with reduced flow, cramps reduced, some breakthrough bleeding and vaginal discharge, weight gain and water retention, nausea, diarrhea, less acne or other skin changes, headaches, varicose veins, nose bleed, leg cramps, sweating,and some fatigue.

In general, girls who are not psychologically healthy do not report these body changes—they report others. These changes are reported by psychologically healthier girls and each girl reports a limited number of changes. Healthier women do not report *unusual* or *beneficent* body changes (which are discussed below). That is, when psychologically healthier women report body changes they cite those that are linked to the physiological changes caused by pill use and each woman does not report many of these changes. Acknowledgment of these changes is accompanied with non-pathological levels of anxiety or hostility and similarly, there is no attribution of a magical beneficence to the change. Those who are psychologically healthy are not generally passive, they do not externalize responsibility and can deal with anger, they are not anxious about sex, they do not use denial, they do not normally have gynecological symptoms, and they did not report psychosomatic or anxiety symptoms before they began using the pills.

Unusual body changes are characteristically antithetic to the pharmaceutical effects and, most important, they are not only distressing to the woman, they ought to be distressing to the partner too. These symptoms are: breasts smaller, cycle less regular, menstrual flow increased, cramps increased, and acne increased. The major characteristic of women who presented these symptoms was passivity in the sense of difficulty in expressing anger. The passivity variable was more important than the level of sex anxiety, but the anger in this context was about being "sexually used" in the relationship. It is as though the woman is expressing her anger somatically, in a way that may force her partner to become responsible for contraception because they are both unhappy about these changes and because he ought to care for her welfare. Not only is she likely to induce guilt in her partner, she has also "made" herself less sexually desirable and less sexually available (e.g., flow and cramps increased). A woman following this pattern is characteristically low in guilt and not only does she report unusual body changes, she will also report negative psychological changes. Women who were similarly highly passive but also high in guilt, did not report unusual body changes and negative psychological changes. Those who were high in guilt internalized their anger while those who didn't feel guilt externalized their anger and manipulated the relationship.

Beneficent body changes do not seem linked to steroid levels, are not normal statistically, and unlike unusual changes, are characterized by very beneficent results. These symptoms are: more energy, decreased appetite, and loss of weight. These women were not necessarily passive—the major characteristic of those subjects who reported beneficent body changes was their high level of dependency which, in this context, means dependence upon the heterosexual partner for feelings of self-esteem. The beneficent symptom assures the continued use of the contraceptive and the assumption of contraceptive responsibility because the pill has positive effects which enhance the value of the girl (i.e. loss of weight, increased energy).

Psychological changes

We also analyzed the follow-up questionnaires for self-reported psychological changes. Negative psychological changes include (but are not limited to): feeling less accepting of the menstrual cycle, reporting the body is less attractive, feeling less feminine, increased depression, increased anxiety, feeling moodier, having less energy, less ability to cope, increased premenstrual tension, less interest in ones' appearance, less enjoyment of sex, decreased sexual arousability, and decreased frequency of orgasm. We should note that these responses were generated by the subjects; we did not offer a checklist of symptoms.

Negative psychological changes were reported by a group of healthier subjects and a group who were less healthy. We suspect that the healthier girls are experiencing appropriate (i.e., normal) levels of sexual anxiety and anger because they are responsible for contraception, and their negative sentiments express these dynamics as well as a recognition of normal body changes. It is likely that these negative feelings will be verbally expressed, including to the heterosexual partner, because these women characteristically do not use denial, are not passive about expressing anger, can accept responsibility, are not generally guilty, and see words as a way of resolving conflict. That is, these women experience some appropriate level of anxiety or resentment which can be verbalized to the interviewer. The motives of the healthier girl to continue to use the contraceptive outweigh her irritation, but she expresses her negative feelings and acknowledges body changes that she does not like—but these are normal body changes, pharmacologically related. The psychological data supports the idea of frequent resentment or ambivalence within the sexual relationship for this population, and the healthier girl seems able to tolerate awareness of her ambivalence and vulnerability.

Negative psychological responses were also reported by those women who were passive in the sense of being unable to accept responsibility. These women often had experienced psychosomatic symptoms before pill use, use denial, are sex anxious (but characteristically report that their sex life is good), report unusual body changes, and characteristically do not see words as a medium for resolving conflicts. The women do not feel guilt because of their hostility and seem to project their negative feelings onto somatic changes, attributing the responsibility for the negative somatic or psychological changes to the pill, the doctor, or the partner. That is an indirect form of hostility with the cause attributed to someone or something other than the self. This is not a general use of denial but the specific denial of sexual responsibility and involvement. Although she also feels negatively within the situation, the healthier girl is able to accept her responsibility and involvement and ambivalence and may cope with reality in a more mature manner.

Positive psychological changes—which are the opposite of the negative changes—are often reported by women who have a history of body symptoms. They tend to be women who characteristically experience psychosomatic symptoms and who, at least for a short time, experience tremendous relief when pregnancy is not possible, because pregnancy is an enormous threat to their body integrity. The dynamics here involve denial and are not healthy. There are at least two general kinds of sex anxiety. One is an expression of a relatively mature conflict, sexual in content, often Oedipal in dynamics. The other kind of sex anxiety, and the one which is germane here, is a much more primitive anxiety which is related to the threat of body damage, boundary vulnerability, and a lack of a strong body image. In this case the threat is less sexual than it is the destruction of body integrity through penetration and mutilation. Like beneficent body changes, the citing of positive psychological changes is linked with high levels of dependency—as well as sex anxiety, passivity and denial. The dependence seems, in vulnerable women, to result in a transformation of what are normally ambivalent or somewhat negative experiences to extraordinarily positive ones, so that their responses cannot endanger the heterosexual relationship through unpleasant physical changes, or less pleasing personalities. These are the subjects who most often report high levels of self-esteem at the follow-up.

We really did not find a clear cluster of healthier subjects reporting only positive psychological changes, and we feel that this is because the expression of only positive changes is an expression of psychological defenses. The pill does affect the body and ambivalence about those changes, fear of possible physical damage due to pill use, and ambivalence about sexual participation and responsibility are normal. The absence of these normal ambivalences seems to be due to the use of denial and other defenses. Therefore a moderate number of negative responses is often associated with a healthier personality with more mature coping techniques and a perception of reality.

Implications of this study

This was a predictive study and in a general sense it was successful. The personality variables that we assumed to be the critical ones do seem to be associated in meaningful ways with the dependent variables, and the use of dynamic models, projective techniques and clinical judgments in addition to more conscious data was critical. But I would like to add a note of caution: In addition to the very real possibility that there are other very significant variables operating that we did not measure, the specific psychological or psychosomatic outcome seemed to be the result of the net balance of these psychological variables and the prediction of individual responses becomes very complicated.

While we had set out to study psychosomatic responses we found that we had also studied morals, ambivalence, anxiety, and motives. While sexual mores have been changing since the 1920's, liberal sexual mores co-exist with more traditional, conservative ones. Similarly, girls' traditional primary motive to achieve heterosexual success and marriage has been challenged by the women's liberation movement but data indicates that this traditional goal has not

really changed. Characteristically, during adolescence the pressure to attract boys becomes crucial to self-esteem, and academic achievements become less important as affiliation needs become pre-eminent. Our data are consistent with the traditional idea that girls achieve identity within the affiliative relationship, are anxious within the relationship, and this period of uncertain morality has increased their feelings of psychological vulnerability.

The most frequently cited reasons for choosing the pill as a contraceptive were its safety, convenience, low cost, and the fact that it seemed least mechanical. At another level, however, motives for using the pill revealed hopes and anxieties about sex. Among our subjects, 42 per cent hoped that the pill would reduce fears about pregnancy and that would therefore enable them to become sexually aroused.

This makes sex spontaneous. The other way it's too premeditated.
I find I don't resent taking the pill like I did having to use the diaphragm and am not put off so much as I don't feel like I'm preparing for sex when I take the pill.
I expect the pill to make me able to reach orgasm.
The pill will make sex spontaneous.

Before they started to use the pill, some subjects denied any fears at all and those who did express worries tended to list negative consequences which are widely publicized in the media. "I expect things like morning sickness"; "About blood clotting, the danger is less than pregnancy, both psychologically and physically"; "I'm afraid they won't work"; "I'm afraid I'll forget to take them."
Responses at the time of the follow-up tended to reveal higher levels of fear than had been expressed at the initial interview:

I refuse to be scared. I won't have to worry. It's too easy.
Sometimes when I take the pill in the evening, I think I'm doing something against my body which isn't natural—like I would take away something of my femininity.
Before I took the pills I was kind of scared that I couldn't have as much control over myself as before.
I feel that to males the pill is kind of mystical because it prevents pregnancy.
I dislike feeling that I cannot control my body but a pill can.
Premarital sex I can justify, but you take the pill when you're alone, not romantic—whether you like him today or not.
I have the feeling that the menstrual cycle is not mechanical, something I caused, not a part of me.
The pill is not a tangible contraceptive.

In answer to the question, "If there was a pill for men like the pill for women, who would you prefer to be responsible for contraception?" 72 per cent said they wanted control, 16 per cent preferred male responsibility, and 12 per cent said both should be responsible. Responses to this question tended to indicate levels of trust or mistrust in the relationship, some resentment and envy that the male can enjoy sex without feeling responsible, and the idea that contraception threatens the male ego.

It doesn't matter, but I'm so frightened of pregnancy, then let me know I've taken the pill.

I think I trust him better than myself. Maybe me—because if anything happens, it happens to me.

Me. Because the girl would take pregnancy more seriously than the boy.

Women, because the man is more excited and he'd be less responsible.

My boyfriend wants me to take the pill because he see it as a commitment to the relationship.

Men should. It's bad enough they . . . I feel funny—taking all the responsibility and he's not doing anything. They should.

Men. Women have enough problems. Women have to have kids, take care of it, stay home. Men want sex—women do it because they love him.

Theoretically him—but pills don't bother me. Men would be better, more successful—women have to take them continuously. Hits the source with men.

Him—because I'm more moral—It bothers me more than it would him. And it would give him more of a commitment than me.

Women—because it's her baby and it would take away the masculinity of the boy.

I'm afraid, psychologically, that a man would feel impotent if he took a pill—and I don't care for myself.

We asked our subjects, "Why do you make love?" The responses tended to be stereotyped, part of the cultural milieu, but not true for the individual. In this population probably the most frequent response was that sex was a way of communicating love in a relationship which they hoped was mutual—or the observation that if they didn't participate sexually, he would leave the relationship. For most, physical sex was important because the male made it important; for these women, sex tended not to be important in its own right. Thus sexual attitudes tended to reveal the dynamics of the heterosexual relationship.

Because it's a means of getting closer to him.

With him it's a giving, sharing, relaxing experience. If I say that I don't feel like it, he'll just hold me instead. The ultimate is being together.

The emotional commitment resulted in my having orgasm.

I enjoy it and it makes the other person happy.

Right now to please him.

A very social thing to do—a way of reaching people.

I don't know. I think it's really necessary as a symbol of the involvement.

It's pleasurable I guess. It's expected.

It seems natural and because at this point it would harm the relationship not to.

He demands it.

I hate to deny my husband although he's very good.

Very few of our subjects experienced orgasm and while they expressed some disappointment it really wasn't terribly important because their major gratification from sex was the enhancement of closeness in the relationship. But when one is not certain that the commitment to the relationship is mutual, when one participates in sex primarily to secure love or because of fear of losing love, the psychological vulnerability overburdens the sex act. The assumption of contraceptive responsibility adds to the psychological burden because it means that the woman has to acknowledge her sexual decision. Thus taking the pill, at least in this population, can arouse anxiety about morality, and this anxiety and guilt is strongly defended against. In spite of any "Sexual Revolution," sex (and therefore contraception) is emotionally threatening because this population of young women derives little physical pleasure from coitus and because they are afraid that they have degraded themselves and will be abandoned by their partners because they are immoral. These anxieties were clearest in the TAT themes which were collected at the time of the follow-up. The most frequent themes were:

Repetitive themes of men walking out.
Men are argumentative, even violent.
Fear of rejection by men; very mistrustful of men.
Guilt in sex and the need to expiate it.
Sees the male as using the woman uncaringly, for his own pleasure.
Denial of hostility to men.
Men leave her behind. Very afraid of being left alone and helpless.
A view of sex as guilt-ridden and illicit.
Prostitution fantasy with much shame and guilt.
Sees self as constantly rejected, perpetually two-timed, deceived by men whom she serves loyally and trustingly.
Guilt about premarital sex.

We were shocked by the extremely high levels of anxiety, hostility, and what looked like general pathology centering on sexual themes in the TAT protocols, and we tested an additional 100 young women, most of whom were students at the university. Their responses were basically identical to those of the first sample and these data reinforce the idea that sexual anxieties and ambivalence are generally characteristic of this population. The young women whom we saw were logically preoccupied with the achievement of important heterosexual relationships and with their identity within the relationship. Participation in sex as well as the assumption of contraceptive responsibility seemed to increase powerful, negative emotions.

While some girls could talk about guilt feelings or fears that men would leave the relationship if they refused intercourse, on an unconscious level prostitution anxieties and fears of abandonment were the consequences of sex. Without an independent identity and self-esteem, this becomes an unresolvable conflict. Women whose self-esteem is high are better able to participate in sex as free agents, less vulnerable to feelings of being used. But young women of the age and status of our sample are characteristically dependent upon others' acceptance, fearful of being rejected, defining themselves, esteeming themselves, in terms of the responses of others—especially their male partner.

Based upon the subjects we have seen we think that conflict about the sexual use of the body has not diminished in this college generation in spite of safe contraception and an evolving sexual freedom in the culture. The origin of the conflict lies in the girls' ambivalence toward her reproductive system, her vulnerability in interpersonal relationships, her difficulty in experiencing sex as a physical rather than a psychological involvement, and the residues of an older morality which are still powerful and which have been internalized as a standard of behavior.

39 Some aspects of lower class sexual behavior

Lee Rainwater

Introduction

The belief that the price of increasing affluence and sophistication (at least through the middle ranges) is loss of the ability to act and feel as a "natural man" has long been a part of the American cultural traditon. Confounded in the complex myths which express this belief are natural virtue, innocence, honesty, love, fun, sensuality and taking pleasure where and how one can find it. Natural man as hero can be constructed by any selection of these characteristics; some versions emphasize virtue and innocence, others emphasize fun, sensuality and pleasuring oneself. But to our Puritan minds natural man can also be evil; we have myths of naturalness that emphasize immorality, hatefulness, sexual avarice, promiscuity and sensual gluttony. Many of the images which Americans have, and historically have had, of the lower class can be subsumed under one or another version of natural man as good or evil. Whatever the evaluative overtones to a particular version of these myths, they add up to the fact that the lower classes (like racial and ethnic minorities, primitive peoples, Communists and others) are supposed to be gaining gratifications which more responsible middle class people give up or sharply limit to appropriate relationships (like marriage) and situations (like in bed and at night).[1] These contrasting themes of naturalness-as-good and naturalness-as-evil are really mutually reinforcing, since they support the view that "naturalness" exists and is defined by the common terms of the two themes-and *pari passu* that "unnaturalness" exists and is defined by the absence of these two themes.[2]

An article dealing with lower class sexual behavior would be expected, then, to describe a group of happy or God-forsaken sinners who derive a great deal more sexual gratification in their society than do middle class respectables in theirs. However, the little empirical research which examines lower class sexual behavior—and, more important, lower class subjective responses to sex—tends to support quite a different view.[3] Since we have fuller comparative information on sexual relations within marriage for lower, working and middle class couples, we will examine sex within the context of marriage first.

Marital sexuality in the lower class

At all class levels, marital sexual relations provide the major source of sexual outlet for most men and women during their sexual careers. In all social classes also, marital sexual relations are considered the preferable and most desirable outlet. Other sources of outlet are most often seen by their seekers as compensations or substitutes rather than really preferable alternatives. We start, then, with a comparison of the ways husbands and wives in the lower, working and middle classes evaluate marital sexuality, the attitudes they have toward sexual relations, and the gratifications and dissatisfactions they find in these.

The material which follows is drawn from a larger study (18, 20) which examines marital sexuality as part of the family context for family size decisions and family limitation behavior. The study is based on interviews with 409 individuals—152 couples, and 50 men and 55 women not married to each other. Thus 257 families are represented. The respondents lived in Chicago, Cincinnati or Oklahoma City and were chosen in such a way as to represent the social class range of whites from upper middle to lower-lower and Negroes at the upper-lower and lower-lower class levels.

Men and women were asked to discuss their feelings about their sexual relations in marriage, the gratifications they found, the dissatisfactions they had, the meaning of sex in their marriages and the importance it had to them and to their spouses.

One dimension emerging from the answers to all of these questions can be thought of as a continuum of interest and enjoyment in sexual relations, which ranges from very great interest and enjoyment to strong rejection. The range is most apparent among women, of course; men only rarely say they are indifferent to or uninterested in sexual relations, but women present the gamut of responses from "if God made anything better, He kept it to Himself," to "I would be happy if I never had to do that again; it's disgusting." On the basis of each individual's response to all of the questions about sexual relations he was classified as showing either great or mild interest and enjoyment in sex, slightly negative feelings about sex, or rejection of sexual relations. Table 1 presents the results on this variable by social class. (Since there were no differences between the upper and lower portion of the middle class, these groups were combined in the tables.) It is apparent that as one moves from higher to lower social status the proportion of men and women who show strong interest and enjoyment of sex declines. Among men the proportion showing only

Reprinted from Lee Rainwater, "Some Aspects of Lower Class Sexual Behavior," Journal of Social Issues, *22:2, April 1966, pp. 96-108.*

TABLE 1   *The Lower the Social Status, the Less Interest and Enjoyment Husbands and Wives Find in Marital Sexual Relations*

	Middle Class	Upper-Lower Class	Lower-Lower Class
Husbands			
Show great interest and enjoyment	78%	75%	44%
Mild interest and enjoyment	22%	25%	56%
No. of cases	(56)	(56)	(59)
Wives			
Great interest and enjoyment	50%	53%	20%
Mild interest and enjoyment	36%	16%	26%
Slightly negative toward sex	11%	27%	34%
Reject sexual relations	3%	4%	20%
No. of cases	(58)	(68)	(69)

mild interest and enjoyment increases as one moves to the lower-lower class level. Among women the proportion who are slightly negative or rejecting in their attitudes toward sexual relations increases systematically from the middle to the upper-lower to the lower-lower class. (There is a small but consistent tendency for Negroes in the lower-lower class to show somewhat more interest in sex than similarly situated whites.)[4]

It would seem, then, that social status has a great deal to do with the extent to which couples manage in marriage to find sexual relations a valued and meaningful activity. This result is consistent with the findings of the Kinsey studies (9, 14, 15). For women the Kinsey study reports that erotic arousal from any source is less common at the lower educational levels, that fewer of these women have ever reached orgasm and that the frequency for those who do is lower. For men, the pattern is less clear-cut as far as frequency goes, but it is apparent that fore-play techniques are less elaborate at the lower educational levels, most strikingly so with respect to oral techniques. In positional variations in intercourse, the lower educational levels show somewhat less versatility, but more interesting is the fact that the difference between lower and higher educational levels increases with age, because positional variations among lower status men drop away rapidly, while the decline among more educated men is much less. This same pattern characterizes nudity in marital coitus.

The lesser elaboration of the sexual relationship among lower class couples which this suggests is apparent in our qualitative data. The longer the lower class man is married, the more likely he is to express a reduced interest in an enjoyment of sexual relations with his wife, as well as indicating reduced frequency of intercourse. In the middle class, while reduced frequency is universally recognized, there is much more of a tendency to put this in the context of "the quantity has gone down, but the quality gets better and better." An examination of the very small body of literature dealing with attitudes toward and feelings about sexual relations in lower class populations in other countries suggest that this pattern is not confined to the United States (16, 19, 25, 26, 27).

Having observed that lower class husbands and wives are less likely than are middle class ones to find sexual relations gratifying, we become interested in why that should be. The major variable that seems related to this class difference concerns the quality of conjugal role relationships in the different classes. In this same study we found that middle class couples were much more likely to emphasize patterns of jointly organized activities around the home and joint activities outside the home, while working and lower class couples were much more likely to have patterns of role relationships in which there was greater emphasis on separate functioning and separate interests by husbands and wives. Following Bott (2) we have classified couples who show a fair degree of separateness in their conjugal role relationships as *highly segregated*, those who show a very strong degree of joint participation and joint involvement of each in the other's activities were characterized as *jointly organized*. Those couples who fall between these two extremes we have characterized as having *intermediate segregation* of conjugal role relationships. Very few working or lower class couples show the jointly organized pattern, but there is variation in the intermediate to the highly segregated range. When the influence of this variable on sexual enjoyment and interest is examined, we find a very strong relationship.

Table 2 indicates that it is primarily among couples in highly segregated conjugal role relationships that we find wives who reject or are somewhat negative towards sexual relations. Similarly, it is primarily among couples in less segregated conjugal role relationships that we find husbands and wives who express great interest and enjoyment in sexual relations.

These results suggest that the lower value placed on sexual relations by lower class wives, and to a lesser extent by lower class husbands, can be seen as an extension of the high degree of segregation in their conjugal role relationship more generally. The couple emphasize separateness in their other activities; therefore separateness comes to be the order of the day in their sexual relationship. Since the wife's interest in sex tends to be more heavily dependent upon a sense of interpersonal closeness and gratification in

TABLE 2   *Lower Class Couples in Highly Segregated Conjugal Role Relationships Find Less Enjoyment in Sexual Relations*

	White Couples		Negro Couples	
	Intermediate Segregation*	Highly Segregated	Intermediate Segregation*	Highly Segregated
Husbands				
Great interest and enjoyment	72%	55%	90%	56%
Mild interest and enjoyment	28%	45%	10%	44%
No. of cases	(21)	(20)	(21)	(25)
Wives				
Great interest and enjoyment	64%	18%	64%	8%
Mild interest and enjoyment	4%	14%	14%	40%
Slightly negative toward sex	32%	36%	18%	32%
Reject sexual relations	—	32%	4%	20%
No. of cases	(25)	(22)	(22)	(25)

*Includes the few jointly-organized couples.

her total relationship with her husband, it is very difficult for her to find gratification in sex in the context of a highly segregated role relationship.

Close and gratifying sexual relationships are difficult to achieve because the husband and wife are not accustomed to relating intimately to each other. It may well be that a close sexual relationship has no particular social function in such a system, since the role performances of husband and wife are organized on a separatist basis, and no great contribution is made by a relationship in which they might sharpen their ability for cooperation and mutual regulation. Examination of the six negative cases in our sample, that is, those in which despite a highly segregated role relationship the wife enjoys sex a great deal, indicates that this comes about when the wife is able to being to the relationship her own highly autonomous interest in sex. To the extent that she is dependent upon her husband for stimulation, encouragement and understanding on the other hand, she seems to find frustration in sex.

Husbands whose wives do not enjoy sexual relations are not particularly confortable about this fact and in various ways either express some guilt, or try to conceal the state of affairs from both themselves and the interviewers. However, they seem to do little to correct the situation. Husbands in segregated relationships consistently overestimate the degree of gratification that their wives find in sex. Thus, half of the men in highly segregated relationships indicated that their wives enjoyed sex more than the wives themselves indicated, compared to only twenty-one percent of the men in less segregated relationships.

Lower class men in highly segregated relationships seem to make few efforts to assist their wives in achieving sexual gratification, and place little emphasis on the important of mutual gratification in coitus. For example, while 74% of the lower and working class husbands with intermediate relationships give some spontaneous indication that they value mutual gratification in the sexual relationship, only 35% of the husbands in segregated relationships speak of mutual gratification. It is not surprising, then, that a considerable number of wives complain about their husbands' lack of consideration. Forty per cent of the wives in segregated relationships spontaneously indicate that their husbands are inconsiderate of them in connection with sexual relations, compared to only 7% of wives in intermediate relationships. Similarly, 38% of those in highly segregated relationships spontaneously indicate that they consider sex primarily as a duty, compared to only 14% of the wives in intermediate relationships.

These differences among classes, and within the lower class between couples in intermediate and highly segregated role relationships, continue to appear when the focus of inquiry is shifted from degree of enjoyment of sexual relations to the question of the psychosocial functions which people think sex serves for them. Two common themes stand out in the ways couples talk about what sex "does" for men and women. One is that sex provides "psychophysiological" relief—it gets rid of tensions, relaxes, gives physical relief ("It's like the back pressure on a car that you have to get rid of.") and provides sensual pleasure in the form of orgasm. The other theme emphasizes, instead, the social-emotional gratifications that come from closeness with the partner, a growth of love, a sense of oneness, of sharing, of giving and receiving. Almost all of the respondents who mentioned one or the other of these functions mentioned the physical aspect, but there is quite a bit of variation in whether this is mentioned by itself or in combination with social-emotional closeness. Table 3 provides distributions by class and role relationship of the relative emphasis on these two themes.

The findings emphasize further the fact that one of the main differences between the middle class and the lower class, and within the lower class between couples in intermediate and highly segregated role relationships, has to do with the extent to which the sexual relationship is assimilated with other aspects of the on-going relationship between husband and wife. It seems very clear that in the middle class, and among those lower class couples with conjugal role relationships of intermediate segregation, the

TABLE 3   *Lower Class Couples in Highly Segregated Conjugal Role Relationships See Only Psychophysiological Pleasure and Relief in Sexual Relations*

| | | Lower Class | |
Sexual relations provide:	Middle Class	Intermediate Segregation	Highly Segregated
Husbands			
Socio-emotional closeness and exchange	75%	52%	16%
Psychophysiological pleasure and relief only	25%	48%	84%
No. of cases	(56)	(40)	(31)
Wives			
Socio-emotional closeness and exchange	89%	73%	32%
Psychophysiological pleasure and relief only	11%	27%	68%
No. of cases	(46)	(33)	(22)

sexual relation is seen as an extension of an overall husband-wife relationship which emphasizes "togetherness," mutual involvement and give-and-take. In the lower class, among couples in highly segregated conjugal role relationships, on the other hand, the sexual relationship is isolated from aspects of the husband-wife relationship and stands in sharp contrast to these other aspects because it requires concerted cooperation on the part of the two partners. Other data showed that in a great many cases, the wife's response is to cooperate only passively, by making herself available when her husband "wants it." In a few cases the wife is able to bring her own autonomous psychophysiological needs to sexual relations and find enjoyment in them.

Lower class non-marital sexual relations

We have much less systematic knowledge of lower class attitudes and customary behaviors concerning non-marital sexual relations than for marital sexual relations. We do know, however, a fair amount about the incidence of non-marital sexual relations from the Kinsey studies as this varies by social status (educational level). The considerable literature dealing with lower class adolescent peer groups also provides some insight into the place of premarital sexual relations in the peer group activities of young lower class boys and girls.

From the Kinsey studies of white males and females it seems clear that before the age of twenty both lower class boys and lower class girls are much more likely to have premarital coitus than are middle class boys and girls. However, even lower class girls are not as likely to have premarital sexual relations as are middle class boys; the overall cultural double standard seems to operate at all class levels. Further, after the age of twenty, status seems to influence premarital coitus in opposite ways for men and women. After that age middle class girls are more likely than lower class girls to have premarital relations, perhaps because the lower class girls are so quickly siphoned off into marriage, while lower class boys continue more frequently to have premarital relations.

From the Kinsey studies, we know that there are very great differences between white and Negro females in the extent to which they engage in premarital coitus. While the social class influence is the same in both groups, in the teens the level of exposure to sexual relations is on the order of three to four times higher for Negro girls than for white girls. Thus, while at age twenty only 26% of white grammar school educated girls have had premarital sexual relationships, over 80% of comparable Negro girls have.

These findings concerning premarital coitus are consistent with the impressions one gains from literature which deals with the peer group systems of white and Negro lower class adolescents and young adults (3, 4, 8, 10, 11, 19, 21, 24, 29). In the white lower class there is a great deal of emphasis on the double standard, in that white lower class boys are expected to engage in sexual relations whenever they have an opportunity, and pride themselves on their ability to have intercourse with many different girls. Making out in this fashion is turned into valuable currency within the boys' peer groups; there is much bragging and competition (leading to not a little exaggeration) among white slum boys about their sexual conquests.

The girls' positon in this group is a much more complex one. White slum groups tend to grade girls rather finely according to the extent of their promiscuity, with virgins being highly valued and often protected, "one man girls" still able to retain some respect from those around them (particularly if in the end they marry the boy with whom they have had intercourse), and more promiscuous girls quickly put into the category of an "easy lay." In groups, then, although boys are constantly exposed to stimulation to engage in sexual relations, efforts are made to protect girls from such stimulation and even to conceal from them elementary facts about sex and about their future sexual roles. Mothers do not discuss sex with their daughters, and usually do not even discuss menstruation with them. The daughter is left very much on her own with only emergency attention from the mother—for example, when she is unable to cope with the trauma of onset of menses or seems to be getting too involved with boys. When women at this level assess their premarital knowledge of sex, they generally say that they were completely unprepared for sexual relations in marriage or for their first premarital experiences, that no one had ever told them much about sex and that they had only a vague idea of what was involved. There is little evidence that in this kind of white lower class subculture many girls find the idea of sexual relations particularly attractive. Although they may become involved with fantasies of romantic love, they seem to show little specific interest in sexual intercourse.

In the Negro lower class the clear-cut differences between the amount of sexual activity respectively permitted girls and boys (and men and women) that seem to obtain in the white lower class are absent. Indeed, at age fifteen, according to the Kinsey results, more grammar school educated Negro girls have experienced coitus than white boys; this is also true at the high school level. With over 60% of *grammar school* educated Negro girls having had intercourse by the age of 15, and over 80% by the age of twenty, it seems clear that within the Negro *slum* community, whatever the attitudes involved, lower class Negro girls are introduced to sexual relations early and, relative to white girls, engage much more frequently in sexual relations once they have started. There are well-established patterns of seduction within Negro slum communities which Negro boys employ. They are sharply judged by other boys and girls on their ability to employ these techniques, and boys show considerable anxiety lest they be rated low on these skills. As is well known, this higher degree of sexual activity leads to a high rate of illegitimacy.

These bare behavioral statistics might lead one to believe that among the lower class *Negroes*, at least, there is a happy acceptance of premarital sexual relations, somewhat along the line of the natural man myth discussed above. However, *close observation* of ghetto peer group activities of late adolescent and early adult Negro males and females indicates that such is not the case (4, 11). In the first place, attitudes toward sexual relations are highly competitive (among own sex peers), and heavily exploitative (toward opposite sex). Slum Negro boys typically refer to girls, including their own "girlfriends" as "that bitch" or "that whore" when they talk among themselves. Negro girls who do engage in sexual relations in response to the strong lines of the boys who "rap to" them often do not seem to find any particular gratification in sexual relations, but rather engage in sex as a test and symbol of their maturity and their ability to be in the swim of things. Over time a certain proportion of these girls do develop their own appreciation of sexual relations, and engage in them out of desire as well as for extrinsic reasons. However, it seems clear that the competitive and exploitative attitudes on both sides make sexual relations a tense and uncertain matter as far as gratification goes. In discussing marital sexuality we noted that the high degree of conjugal role segregation seems to interfere with achieving maximum gratification in sexual relations. A parallel fact seems to operate in connection with premarital relations. That is, because of the culturally defined and interpersonally sustained hostilities that exist between the sexes, it seems difficult for both boys and girls to develop a self-assured and open acceptance of sex for the pleasure it can provide, much less for a heightened sense of interpersonal closeness and mutuality. When one seeks to study the meaning and function of sexual relations in such a very complex situation as the Negro lower class community, one becomes aware of how much more subtle and ramified the issues are than can be captured in the traditional categories of sex research.

The future of sex in the lower class

As the working class has attained greater prosperity and a sense of greater economic stability since World War II, there seems to have been a shift from traditional working class patterns of a high degree of conjugal role segregation and reliance by husbands and wives on their same sex peer groups for emotional support and counsel. Elsewhere Handel and Rainwater (12, 13) have discussed the increasing importance of a modern working class life style which seems to be gradually replacing the traditional life style among those working class families who are in a position to partake of the "standard package" of material and social amenities which represent the common man's version of the "good American life." We have seen that among those couples who have a lesser degree of conjugal role segregation there is a much greater probability of a mutual strong interest in sexual relations and an emphasis on sexual relations as an extension of the socio-emotional closeness that is valued in husband-wife relationships. We can predict, then, that shifts in the direction of greater cooperation and solidarity based on interpenetration of family role activities in marriage will carry with them an increased intimacy in the sexual sphere. This greater mutuality is both an expression of and functional for the increased self-sufficiency of a nuclear family, in which working class husband and wife now rely less on outsiders for support and a sense of primary group membership and more on each other. In this sense a "good" sexual relation between husband and wife can be seen as one of the major strengths of the adaptable nuclear family which Clark Vincent has argued is necessary for our kind of industrial society (28).

But what of those members of the lower class who do not participate in the increasing prosperity and security which the great majority of the working class has known for the past twenty years? In recent years there has been mounting evidence that sex-related pathologies of the Negro slum ghetto community—for example, the rate of illegitimacy, venereal disease, drug encouraged prostitution (4, 17)—are increasing rather than decreasing. It seems clear that so long as the socio-economic circumstances of slum Negroes do not improve, we can expect only a worsening of a situation in which sexual relations are used for exploitative and competitive purposes. There is much less clear-cut evidence concerning white slum groups; it may well be that the rates for the same sex-related pathologies show lesser increases because the white poor are not confined to ghettos which serve to concentrate the destructive effects of poverty, but instead tend to be more widely dispersed in the interstices of more stable working class neighborhoods (24).

In short, though we see some evidence to support the notion of a "sexual renaissance" with respect to marital sexuality in the modern working class, we see no such evidence with respect to the less prosperous lower class.

Sex research in the light of lower class sex behavior

It is probably not unfair to say that efforts to study sexual behavior scientifically have been plagued by an obsessive preoccupation with the terms of the larger public dialogue on the subject, and with the value conflicts and contradictions evident in that dialogue. Thus researchers who investigate sexual behavior have often been motivated by an effort to determine whether sex under particular circumstances is good or bad, or whether particular customs interfere with pleasure or are conducive to it. While these are legitimate concerns, they have tended to distract social scientists from an effort simply to understand sexual practices in their full human context. We have suggested that a close examination of lower class sexual behavior tends to disprove certain widely-held stereotypes—themselves not unknown in social scientists' own attitudes. But more important, the study of lower class sexual behavior emphasizes the importance of trying to understand that behavior *both* in the immediate context of relevant interpersonal relations (marital relations, peer group relations, etc.), and in the context of the structural position of the actors, and the stresses and strains that position engenders. Such an understanding can only come about through careful empirical research which does not take for granted supposed "fact" about the actors involved, but rather explores these interrelations empirically.

Once we have an adequate picture of the sexual behavior of individuals in a particular situation, we can begin to ask questions about the role of this sexual behavior in connection with other aspects of the individual's interpersonal relations. We can ask what the functions of particular forms of sexual behavior are for the individual and for the groups to which he belongs. More psychologically, we can ask, and not assume in advance that we know, what goals the individual seeks to effect through particular kinds of sexual behavior. It seems to me that this is the real legacy of Freud for the study of sexual behavior. Freud sought to show that sex is not simply sex, but a complex form of behavior built out of elements which extend genetically back into dim childhood history, and cross-sectionally into other vital interests which the individual seeks to maximize and protect. Just as any other applied field of social science profits from a wide application of contending theoretical paradigms, so the study of sexual behavior would profit from a more liberal application of the diverse conceptual tools at our disposal.

NOTES

1 John Dollard has analyzed some of the attitudes that white Southerners have toward Negroes, which compound both the positive and negative views of lower status naturalness. In his analysis he perhaps took somewhat too seriously the notion that lower class Negroes gain from the greater sexual freedom allowed them by the caste system (6). Allison Davis, an insufficiently appreciated pioneer in the study of lower class cultures, seems to have been similarly taken in by the myth: "In the slum, one certainly does not have a sexual partner for as many days each month as do middle class married people, but one gets and gives more satisfaction over longer periods, when he does have a sexual partner." (5, p. 33)

2 Kai Erikson (7) in an analysis of the functions of deviance and its control in the establishment of social boundaries comments, "Every culture recognizes a certain vocabulary of contrasts which are meant to represent polar opposites on the scale of human behavior.... [but] when we look across the world to other cultures ... or behind us to the historical past, it often seems that these contrasting forms are little more than minor variations on a single cultural theme."

3 The shift to a more jaundiced view of the happy impulse-free version of lower class sexual life is paralleled by a similar shift in the understanding of lower class delinquency. Bordua, in comparing the work of Frederick Thrasher in the 1920's with that of Walter Miller, Albert Cohen, Richard Cloward and Lloyd Ohlin, comments, "All in all, though, it does not seem like much fun any more to be a gang delinquent. Thrasher's boys enjoyed themselves being chased by the

police, shooting dice, skipping school, rolling drunks. It was fun. Miller's boys do have a little fun, with their excitement focal concern, but it seems so desperate somehow. Cohen's boys and Cloward and Ohlin's boys are driven by grim economic and psychic necessity into rebellion. It seems peculiar that modern analysts have stopped assuming that 'evil' can be fun and see gang delinquency as arising only when boys are driven away from 'good.' " (1, p. 136)

4 It should be noted that the careful and detailed study of blue-collar marriages by Komarovsky (13) reports that there were no differences in sexual enjoyment between higher and lower status wives within the working class (status indicated by high school education or less than high school education). I have no explanation for this difference in findings between two studies which parallel each other in most other respects, but the readers should be aware of Komarovsky's contrary findings (see especially pp. 93-94). However, the less educated wives did view sex as more of a duty, and refused less often.

REFERENCES

1. Bordua, David J. "Delinquent Subcultures: Sociological Interpretations of Gang Delinquency." *The Annals of the American Academy of Political and Social Science*, 1961, 338, 120-136.
2. Bott, Elizabeth. *Family and Social Network.* London: Tavistock Publications, 1957.
3. Cayton, Horace R., and St. Clair Drake. *Black Metropolis.* New York: Harper & Row, 1962.
4. Clark, Kenneth. *The Dark Ghetto.* New York: Harper & Row, 1965.
5. Davis, Allison. *Social Class Influence on Learning.* Cambridge: Harvard University Press, 1952.
6. Dollard, John. *Caste and Class in a Southern Town.* New Haven: Yale University Press, 1937.
7. Erikson, Kai T. "Notes on the Sociology of Deviance." *Social Problems*, 1962, 9, 307-314.
8. Frazier, E. Franklin. *The Negro Family in the United States.* Chicago: University of Chicago Press, 1939.
9. Gebhard, Paul H., *et al. Pregnancy, Birth and Abortion.* New York: Harper and Brothers, 1958.
10. Green, Arnold W. "The Cult of Personality and Sexual Relations." *Psychiatry*, 1941, 4, 343-44.
11. Hammond, Boone. "The Contest System: A Survival Technique," Master's Honors Essay Series, Washington University, 1965.
12. Handel, Gerald, and Lee Rainwater. "Persistence and Change in Working Class Life Style." In Arthur B. Shostak and William Gomberg, (eds.), *Blue Collar Worlds.* Englewood Cliffs, New Jersey: Prentice-Hall, 1964, pp. 36-42.
13. Kinsey, Alfred C., *et al. Sexual Behavior in the Human Male.* Philadelphia: W. B. Saunders, 1948.
14. Kinsey, Alfred C., *et al. Sexual Behavior in the Human Female.* Philadelphia: W. B. Saunders, 1953.
15. Komarovsky, Mirra. *Blue Collar Marriage.* New York: Random House, 1964.
16. Lewis, Oscar. *Life in a Mexican Village: Tepoztlán Restudied.* Urbana, Illinois: University of Illinois Press, 1951.
17. Moynihan, Daniel P. "Employment, Income and the Ordeal of the Negro Family." *Daedalus*, 1965, 94 (no. 4), 745-770.
18. Rainwater, Lee. *And the Poor Get Children.* Chicago: Quadrangle Books, 1960.
19. Rainwater, Lee. "Marital Sexuality in Four Cultures of Poverty." *Journal of Marriage and the Family*, 1964, 26, 457-466.
20. Rainwater, Lee. *Family Design: Marital Sexuality, Family Planning and Family Limitation.* Chicago: Aldine, 1965.
21. Rainwater, Lee. "The Crucible of Identity: The Negro Lower Class Family." *Daedalus*, 1966, 95 (no. 1), 172-216.
22. Rainwater, Lee, Richard Coleman and Gerald Handel. *Workingman's Wife: Her Personality, World and Life Style.* New York: Oceana Publications, 1959.
23. Rainwater, Lee and Gerald Handel. "Changing Family Roles in the Working Class'" In Arthur B. Shostak and William Gomberg, *Blue Collar Worlds*, Englewood Cliffs, New Jersey: Prentice-Hall, 1964, pp. 70-76.
24. Short, J. F. and F. L. Strodbeck. *Group Process and Gang Delinquency.* Chicago: University of Chicago Press, 1965.
25. Slater, Eliot and Moya Woodside. *Patterns of Marriage.* London: Cassell and Co., 1951.
26. Spinley, B. M. *The Deprived and the Privileged.* London: Routledge and Kegan Paul, 1953.
27. Stycos, J. Mayone. *Family and Fertility in Puerto Rico.* New York: Columbia University Press, 1955.
28. Vincent, Clark. "Familia Spongia: The Adaptive Function." Presented at the Annual Meeting of the National Council on Family Relations at Toronto, 1965.
29. Whyte, William F. "A Slum Sex Code." *American Journal of Sociology*, 1943, 49, 24-31.

40 *The role of emotional factors in obstetric complications: a review*

Robert L. McDonald

Pregnancy is widely recognized by obstetricians (and husbands) as an event precipitating profound changes. Foremost and extensive among these changes are normal physiological adaptations: the numerous hormonal[1] changes triggered in response to the increasing maintenance demands of the rapidly developing fetus. Psychological adaptations are also apparent. There is general agreement that even a normal pregnancy constitutes a period of transient ego vulnerability marked by at least minimal regressive changes.[2-9] At another level are the anticipated changes in the family unit—a shift from the primary husband-wife dyad to a more complex system of dyadic and triadic relationships. Harmony between these changes, particularly the psychological and physiological ones, is regarded as propitious—a sign of normal pregnancy.

Growing evidence emphasizing the dismaying effectiveness of emotional factors in altering the outcome of and recovery from physical illness[10] has stimulated speculation that emotional factors may also adversely influence physiological changes during pregnancy. The recent increase of investigations focusing on the role of emotional factors in obstetric complications attests to a growing interest in possible causal relationships between emotional factors and obstetric complications. Preliminary reports have suggested emotional factors as a determinant in these complications, but due to the numerous complications, the diverse populations, and the heterogeneous methodology involved, definitive statements regarding the relationships are rendered difficult. A review of the current literature in this area, then, seems warranted, from a heuristic viewpoint, to establish base-line knowledge which will provide impetus and direction to future research. The ultimate goal would be increased predictive power, which could result in prevention of fetal loss—through early detection and intervention—in subjects predisposed to psychogenic obstetric complications. This paper purports to serve this purpose, concentrating primarily though not exclusively on those articles that have appeared during the last decade. Since research efforts thus far have proceeded from several divergent approaches, this paper will summarize results obtained through each of these approaches, and will conclude with a discussion attempting to integrate the results.

Single complications

One methodological approach involves the comparison of personality characteristics of women experiencing a single complication with those of women of normal pregnancies. Pseudocyesis, hyperemesis gravidarum, habitual abortion, labor difficulties (usually prolonged), prematurity, and toxemia are the complications on which sufficient attention has been focused to merit individual consideration.

PSEUDOCYESIS

Pseudocyesis, the forme fruste of pregnancy, simulates pregnancy in its many aspects: amenorrhea, abdominal enlargement, sensation of fetal movements, breast changes, and mild uterine changes. In 1937, Bivin and Klinger[11] summarized the 444 histories reported at that time. Although their study is primarily descriptive, the authors suggest that the dynamics involved in pseudocyesis are the simultaneous wish for and fear of pregnancy, which creates a conflict sometimes resolved in a hysterical fashion by a simulated pregnancy. Similarly, the majority of recent reports are also case studies using interviews, and lack controls of any kind. This lack may stem from the nature of the process itself. For example, Greaves *et al.*[12] related the pseudocyetic condition in a 27-year-old female to (1) the fear of being abandoned by her husband and (2) the wish for a child, to stablize the marital relationship. Pregnancy symbolized feminine fulfillment to this frigid, insecure patient. Steinberg *et al.*,[13] though not discussing personality factors extensively, also emphasized both the desire for and fear of children, in a small series (N = 3) of females with pseudocyesis. These authors reported the salutary effect of informing the patients of their nonpregnant states: prompt cessation of symptoms and reversion of elevated hormonal levels to normal range. Dunbar[14] contended that the development of pseudocyesis occurred classically in 2 groups: neurotic, childless, menopausal-age females who desired children, and young, unmarried females engaged in illicit relationships and fearful of pregnancy.

Kaplan and Schobpach,[15] summarizing interviews from 9 female patients (7 Negro and 2 white), reported the basic psychological mechanism to be a strong unconscious mater-

Reprinted from Robert L. McDonald, "The Role of Emotional Factors in Obstetric Complications: A Review," Psychosomatic Medicine 30:2, 1968, pp. 222-237. Hoeber Medical Division of Harper & Row, Publishers. © 1968 by American Psychosomatic Society, Inc.

nal wish. The intelligence levels of these women ranged from dull to above normal; the one common factor, apart from their married state, was insecurity. Contrary to Dunbar's contention, none of these patients was menopausal. In a predominantly childless Negro sample (N = 27). Fried et al.[16] corroborated the personality factors involved as the wish for and fear of pregnancy. The psychometric data (Rorschach, Szondi, and Wechsler-Bellevue intelligence tests) revealed a wide range of intelligence, low tolerance of frustration, pronounced insecurity, inability to resolve tensions, difficulties in interpersonal situations, and a distaste for pregnancy.

HYPEREMESIS GRAVIDARUM

Hyperemesis gravidarum, pernicious vomiting disproportionate to the normal hormonal changes of pregnancy, popularly symbolizes disgorgement of the pregnancy. In investigating this hypothesis however, neither Coopen[17] nor Bernstein[18] confirmed a relationship between vomiting and rejection of child or motherhood. Rosen[19] concluded, on the basis of interviews with 54 lower-social-class hyperemesis patients during the second and third trimesters, that "vomiting is a reliable indication that the patient is under a considerable amount of emotional stress and *may* be unconsciously rejecting pregnancy." Chertok et al.[20] conducted weekly interviews with 100 primiparous females (68 vomiters and 32 nonvomiters) from the third month of pregnancy until delivery. Contrary to popular opinion, these workers concluded that the vomiting was symptomatic not of marked rejection but of ambivalence toward the nascent pregnancy—a conflict between wanting and rejecting the unborn child. In a somewhat different vein, Harvey and Sherfey,[21] on the basis of interviews and Rorschachs, related vomiting to high anxiety levels. The subjects, 20 females (7 white primiparas, 9 white multiparas, and 4 Negro multiparas) hospitalized for vomiting, were compared with 14 unmatched normals (8 primiparas, race not specified) tested during the first trimester. The vomiters were characterized by frigidity, pervasive immaturity and dependency, guilt toward their mothers, and a consistent association of GI dysfunction with sexual disorders. The role of anxiety attributed to this condition by Harvey and Sherfey was also stressed by Caldwell.[22] Caldwell subjectively trichotomized 300 white, privately delivered cases as "emotional" (N = 27), "well-adjusted" (N = 232), or "unhappy" (N = 41). A significantly higher incidence of hyperemesis was found among the "emotional" group, who were characterized as domineering, aggressive anxious, striving females. This study's conclusions are weakened, however, by its retrospective nature. The relationship of extroversion to hyperemesis was also demonstrated by Brown[23] in a comparison of 35 hypermesis patients and 68 controls. The patients with hyperemesis gravidarum described a significantly greater number of bodily symptoms and pregnancy worries.

HABITUAL ABORTION

Habitual aborters are defined as those women in whom 3 consecutive spontaneous abortions occur. Javet et al.[24] further classified habitual aborters as primary and secondary, secondary aborters being those in whom the consecutive abortions were preceded by delivery of viable infants. In a case study based on unspecified psychological tests, Weil and Stewart[25] described a habitual aborter seen weekly in psychotherapy as an anxious, immature, dependent, depressed female living in an insecure home situation. A successful pregnancy following psychotherapy led Weil and Stewart (as did other clinical experience) to conclude that the majority of habitual aborters are dependent and immature. Additionally, they emphasized the inadequate emotional support received by these patients from their husbands (or social group). In a subsequent uncontrolled study, Weil and Tupper[26] interviewed and administered 2 psychological tests (Rorschach and Progressive Matrices) to 18 habitual aborters, prior to delivery. These patients were characterized by overwhelming dependency, compliance, and self-sacrifical attitudes, and viewed pregnancy as a duty to be performed for their husbands. There was a marked degree of sexual confusion and poor relationships with ineffectual fathers who were quite similar to the husbands.

Through interviews, Berle and Javert[27] assessed the effects of various stressors on 32 habitual aborters (21 primary and 11 secondary). These women ranged widely in age, intelligence, socioeconomic status, and mental health, 20% presenting marked personality disorders. Psychological tests administered to only half of the subjects revealed tendencies to obsessiveness, perfectionism, dependency, and hypersensitivity to criticism. Regarding stress, the authors concluded that "the threat of greatest significance in the majority of cases appeared to be uncertainty concerning the husband."

In 2 separate reports, Mann[28, 29] compared "successful" (N = 31) and "unsuccessful" (N = 47) habitual aborters. The dichotomous classification refers to the parturitional response of aborters to subsequent psychotherapeutic intervention. Those in the unsuccessful group were found, in interviews, to have an extremely dependent, near-symbiotic relationship with their parents, particularly the mother. Many cases were characterized by paternal absence or inadequacy. Mann emphasized the relationship between regressive emotional changes and abortigenic physiological processes, precipitated by stress situations. He particularly noted the lack of husband's support, i.e., through job loss, which supports Berle and Javert's[27] similar findings. Grimm,[30] in an extension of Mann's work, compared 71 habitual aborters (51 primary, 19 secondary) with a group of 35 heterogeneous controls composed of (1) "presumably normal" pregnant females tested in the second trimester and (2) nonpregnant females referred for gynecological problems. The Wechsler—Bellevue (W—B) tests indicated no significant differences in age, education, or intelligence. On the Rorschach and TAT tests however, the habitual aborters demonstrated poorer emotional controls and stronger dependency needs than the controls, as well as conventionality and overconformity, greater anxiety regarding hostility, and greater proneness to guilt feelings. Unless so designated, the authors of the studies reviewed did not further specify sample composition.

LABOR DIFFICULTIES

Although labor difficulties are of 2 types (precipitate delivery and prolonged labor), this review deals exclusively with the latter, and most studies ruled out cases attributable to such purely physical causes as cephalopelvic disproportion. Prolonged labor is defined as labor exceeding 24 hr. total duration, with 95% occurring in primigravidas. Stewart[31] reported no reliable relationship between prolonged or "difficult" labor and marital status. An empirical assumption has been that prolonged labor culminating in an uneventful pregnancy would be related specifically to a woman's anxiety about delivery pain or the obstetrician's competence. In support of this assumption, Klein et al.[32] related favorable attitudes toward delivery associated with normal labor in 27 primigravidas. McDonald et al.[33] found a positive correlation between anxiety and labor times in 86 indigent, white, married clinic patients of mixed gravidity. Jeffcoat[34] supported this finding and in addition found that females with this complication have predominantly covert anxiety. Similarly, Scott and Thomson[35] evaluated 276 primigravidas by means of the Maudsley Medical Questionnaire (MMQ) scores and interviews ("stability grades") and found a low incidence of prolonged labor in those subjects judged well-adjusted by both methods. A higher incidence was noted in the mixed-rankings group (unstable—low MMQ score) than in the unstable-high MMQ group, a finding interpreted by Scott and Thomson as meaning that: "uterine dysfunction tends to be associated with concealed anxiety." Baird,[36] related difficult labor to higher income in a large group of primigravidas. In addition, he emphasized the inconsistent relationship between *overt* anxiety and difficulties. Kennedy,[37] meanwhile, observed that his prolonged labor patients were introspective, sensitive, and apprehensive but "gave little overt sign of this." In the best controlled study, by Cramond,[38] the results supported the role of denial in preventing expression of overt anxiety. Here, MMPI's were administered to 50 married patients with difficult labor who were matched for age, height, socioeconomic class, marital status, and gravidity with a like number of normal patients. Those in the "labor" group showed little overt anxiety (it being covertly maintained by denial) while the controls expressed anxiety overtly by means of motor movements.

Investigations have also focused on other personality factors. Kapp et al.[39] studied (following delivery) 18 primigravidas who had experienced labor difficulties and found (1) that they experienced more anxiety and fear than did a control group matched for race and marital status, and (2) that their attitudes toward motherhood, and relationships with mothers, were significantly more negative than those of the control group. Watson,[40] in an uncontrolled study consisting of interviews with 25 married indigent Negro females, related prolonged labor to sexual and childbirth attitudes derived from developmental experiences, and to guilt related to child-destruction fantasies.

PREMATURITY

Prematurity here refers specifically to the infant's size; i.e., a birth weight of less than 5½ lb. (2500 gm.).

Gunter,[41] with TAT, the Cornell Medical Index (CMI), and interviews, compared 20 Negro patients who delivered premature infants, with 20 controls matched for age, race, and parity. The prematurity group obtained reliably higher CMI scores (anxiety, feelings of inadequacy) and recalled more life stresses, such as desertion. These women described themselves as being more dependent and helpless, and desirous of a protective-type male, they possessed more bodily concern and feelings of feminine inadequacy, accompanied by sex-associated guilt. The normal group received significantly more help and support from their husbands (see *Habitual Abortion*) than prematurity group patients.

Blau et al.,[42] in a study possibly contaminated by its retrospective nature, matched 30 mothers of premature infants with 30 mothers of normal infants for age, race, socioeconomic class, education, and parity. On the W-B intelligence scale, and the Rorschach, TAT, and Bender-Gestalt tests, the premature group described attitudes reliably more negative toward pregnancy, and related to their having become pregnant unwillingly. These women demonstrated emotional immaturity, narcissism, and unconscious feelings of hostility and rejection toward pregnancy. Despite its methodological shortcomings, this study is noteworthy, as it is the sole study specifically comparing clinic and private patients.

TOXEMIA

Toxemia is defined by the triad excessive weight gain, significant proteinuria, and hypertension (blood pressure exceeding 140/90 after 24 weeks of gestation). Ringrose[43],[44] reported that toxemia patients are symptomatically more disturbed than normal patients. This investigator found, in separate groups of 41 unmarried white and 41 indigent married Negro toxic patients, a significantly greater number of patients with MMPI scale scores greater than 70 in comparison with normal patients. While most subjects were tested prior to delivery, 28 of the toxic subjects were tested post partum. Caldwell[22] reported that more of his "unhappy" group (dependent somatizers) were hospitalized for toxemia than his "well-adjusted" or "emotional" groups (anxious, domineering strivers). Elsewhere, Salerno[45] related toxemia to a general stress syndrome, while Wiedorn[46] depicted toxemia as a physiological equivalent of a psychotic episode.

Comparison of complications

A second methodological approach has involved the comparing of several obstetric complications to determine possible personality characteristics specific to a particular clinical entity. In a poorly designed study, Brown[23] compared 2 complications, hyperemesis gravidarum (N = 64) and prolonged labor (N = 30), and found nonsignificant personality differences, except between vomiters and nonvomiters: he found a significantly greater incidence of stressful life experiences among vomiters. Hetzel et al.[47] retrospectively compared groups of prolonged-labor (N = 44), hyperemesis gravidarum (N = 30) and toxemia (N = 40) patients with 54 controls 5-10 days post partum.

The hyperemesis group contained more Roman Catholics than did the normal group and the toxemia patients' husbands were considered more inadequate providers. These patternless differences appear meaningless in terms of specificity; moreover, no differences resulted from intercomplication comparisons. In a controlled prospective study involving Florence Crittenton Home (FCH) patients (unwed white primigravidas), McDonald[48] compared premature rupture of the membranes (N = 23), excessive weight gain (N = 25), and toxemia (N = 21) patients with 100 randomly selected normal patients by means of MMPI's administered at the seventh month of gestation. The composite "complications" group (N = 69) obtained higher scores on anxiety, social introversion, and hypochondriasis than did the normal group. The only significant finding resulting from intercomplication comparisons, however, concerned the lower mean hysteria (tendency toward conversion of anxiety into somatic complaints) scores in the premature-membrane-rupture group.

Multiple complications

The methodological approach which has generally produced the best-controlled studies is derived from the conceptualization of all complications as derivatives of a single common process. Women who have experienced normal pregnancies, labors, and deliveries, and delivered normal infants, are compared on personality parameters with women who have undergone a heterogeneous variety of clinical complications, such as third trimester bleeding, toxemia, and prolonged labor. On this basis, McDonald and Christakos[49] compared psychometric data from a sample of white, indigent married patients (N = 86) who were tested at the seventh month of gestation and classified after delivery as abnormal or normal according to standard clinical criteria. No significant differences in age, parity, or intelligence were noted between the 2 groups. The abnormal group (N = 44) obtained significantly higher mean scores on the Manifest Anxiety Scale (MAS), as well as on a majority of the MMPI scales. For this abnormal group, McDonald et al.[33] also observed higher composite IPAT Anxiety Scale scores and less use of repressive-type defense mechanisms at the seventh month of gestation.

McDonald and Parham,[50] using the MMPI, MAS, and Kent EGY Intelligence Scales, found essentially the same results with an unwed group of 160 FCH primigravidas. In addition to the prenatal third-trimester testing, retesting was done 7-10 days post partum. The prenatal group differences—i.e., higher mean scores for the abnormal group (N = 81) than for the normal group (N = 79) on the majority of the MMPI scales and MAS, and no differences in age or intelligence—were consistent with the senior author's findings among indigent married patients.

Interpersonal Check Lists were also administered to 177 FCH patients prior to delivery (seventh month) and 7-10 days post partum, to determine differences in self- and parental ratings related to complications and the effects of pregnancy on these ratings.[51] The normal group (N = 89) was found to be more extraverted and impulsive, and able to discuss sexuality and aggressive feelings more openly, while the abnormal group (N = 88) used denial, rationalization, and sublimation defenses to deal with their feelings. After delivery, both groups' self-ratings shifted to "strong" descriptions, but the abnormal group emphasized strength through power and aggression while the normal group possessed more nurturant qualities. Differences in the fantasy life of 107 ECH patients[52] in the seventh month of gestation were determined by TAT's. The data yielded only 2 reliable differences: The normal group (N = 55) revealed a greater ability to use apparently repressive measures to prevent overt behavioral expression of their hostile fantasies, and perceived significantly fewer pregnant women on the TAT cards. These findings would seem to indicate that the repressive ability was also related to cognitive functions.

The findings related to anxiety were substantiated by Davids et al.,[53, 54] who observed personality differences in 48 indigent females tested in the seventh month of gestation and post partum; he classified the women as normal or abnormal following delivery. No significant differences were found in age or intelligence. The abnormal group (N = 23) obtained higher mean anxiety scores (MAS) than the normal group (N = 25). Although the anxiety scores for both groups decreased post partum, the group differences were maintained. The abnormal group was reliably differentiated from the normal group by a TAT-derived alienation syndrome characterized by egocentricity, pessimism, distrust, and resentment. Davids and DeValut,[55] in a second sample of 50 patients and similar methodology, also found higher anxiety scores for the abnormal group (N = 26) by means of the MAS, self-ratings, others' ratings, TAT, and sentence completions. Again, no reliable differences were found for age, intelligence, gravidity, or parity.

Zemlick and Watson,[56] evaluating 15 white, married, primiparous females, demonstrated a relationship between both emotional and psychosomatic complaints and delivery adjustment (defined subjectively by the attending obstetrician). These ratings, made at the second and eighth months of pregnancy and 6 weeks post partum by means of the TAT, the McFarland-Seitz Psychosomatic Inventory, and the ZAR Pregnancy Attitude Scale, also revealed a significant inverse relationship between anxiety and prenatal maternal adjustment. Psychosomatic symptoms and attitudes of rejection were negatively correlated with a postpartum criteria, maternal adjustment, which was defined in terms of overprotection of the infant in the mother-child relationship.

Destounis,[57] implying a relationship between emotional factors (those amenable to psychotherapy) and obstetric complications, found that in an experimental group (N = 10) chosen during the first trimester for weekly psychotherapy the incidence of complications during pregnancy and delivery was significantly lower than in a control group (N = 52) who received only regular obstetric care. The validity of these findings is weakened, however, by the failure to establish pretherapy personality differences which might predispose to complications. Further, the author does not provide the experimental group's selection criteria.

Lastly, Grimm[58] assessed the differences in psychological "tension" as a function of the time interval remaining to delivery (N = 200), and the relationship between psychological tension and complications (N = 227). For the first part, the subjects were divided into 5 equal groups (N = 40) matched for parity, previous complications, race, cultural background, marital status, age, and education. Five personality assessment periods were chosen, beginning with the last half of the first trimester and extending, at half-trimester intervals, through the last half of the third trimester. One group was tested at each time interval, with an abbreviated TAT (5 cards). For the second part, 227 subjects tested at various time intervals were divided, following delivery, into abnormal (N = 122) and normal (N = 105) groups, depending on the presence of complications. No relationship was observed between the index of tension and complications, but there was a reliable increase in the percentage of subjects obtaining a "high tension index" from the first to third trimesters. These findings are hard to evaluate because subjects were tested at various intervals rather than all at each interval. The validity of tension scores, as the author emphasized, is also unknown.

Instruments

The demonstration on standardized tests (MAS, Rorschach) of personality differences between women who experienced normal preganancies and women who experienced complicated pregnancies has led to the development of custom-made questionnaires designed specifically to predict onset of complications. Use of the better known tests—the Parental Attitude Research Instrument (PARI),[59],[60] the Pregnancy Research Questionnaire (PRQ),[61] the H.I.P. Pregnancy Questionnaire,[62] the Maternal Attitude to Pregnancy Instrument (MAPI)[63] and the ZAR Pregnancy Attitude Scale[64] —has resulted in satisfactory validity and reliability scores during standardization. These tests have differentiated significantly between groups with complications and women who experience normal parturition. The general format consists of objective, multiple-choice items drawn from selected areas ranging from attitudes toward dependency, acceptance of bodily functions, and feelings toward pregnancy, to attitudes toward sex, marriage, and mother. Although the content of each form is unique, the questionnaires overlap considerably. The composite scores, however, represent indices of anxiety either explicitly or implicitly, and many items are nearly identical with MAS items.

Discussion

The foregoing summary clearly demonstrates the numerous methodological shortcomings contained in the current literature. For example, case studies or random clinical observations, despite their clinical utility, lend themselves poorly to research purposes. In general, justifiable criticisms of the large bulk of the studies reviewed—small sample size, inadequate or total lack of controls, heterogeneous experimental samples, the basing of conclusions on retrospectively gathered data, and an even more fundamental failure to document sample characteristics and/or methodology—may be raised. Such limitations invalidate or at least seriously weaken the conclusions derived from these studies,

and stress the need for well-designed experiments, rigorous application of statistical techniques, and a systematic exploration of psychological, physiological, sociological, and epidemiological variables.

The variables which have been dealt with to varying degrees include age, intelligence, marital status, gravidity, social class, and race. Since most studies were restricted to indigent white patients, the role of social class and race in the development of psychogenic obstetric complications is yet indeterminate. Futhermore, marital status and gravidity have not been systematically investigated. Since significant age or intellectual differences were seldom found between control groups and patients with complications, one may conclude tentatively that these 2 factors play minimal roles, per se, in effecting complications. This is not to say, however, that the incidence of certain complications is not age-related, and perhaps demonstrates a summative effect of this, as well as other factors.

Methodologically, the point in time during pregnancy at which personality assessment is made has received only cursory attention. Grimm attended to this problem by testing groups of subjects at chosen time intervals during the course of pregnancy, but unfortunately tested different groups at each interval rather than *each* subject serially. The time at which measurements are made would seem, purely on an empirical basis, to be quite important. Most studies made personality assessments at only 1 arbitrarily chosen temporal point during pregnancy, often the seventh month, or at best, at two points (pre- and post-delivery). Particularly desirable in this vein would be serial assessments, including preconception base-line testing.

Another problem involves selection of parameters to be measured (fantasy, overt behavior, symptomatic description, etc.). McDonald[52] and Grimm[30] demonstrated the poor discriminative power of the TAT in differentiating between complication and noncomplication groups. The prediction of complications seems more directly related to behavioral measures other than fantasy, because of the effects of the various defense mechanisms that intervene between fantasy and "surface" behavior. The instruments most widely used are the MAS and similar questionnaires with derivative content. One might conclude that self-report of anxiety is, to date, the most discriminating behavioral measure for presaging complications.

In general, the literature reviewed supports the idea of a positive relationship between psychological and physiological functioning during pregnancy. This relationship should not be too surprising, since these functions are 2 aspects of the same process, adaptation, in a single individual. Correlation implies but does not prove causality, and although correlative relationships are often interpreted in this fashion, doing so excludes investigation of the possibility that other factors are systematically affecting the 2 primary factors. It behooves investigators, therefore, to design studies which do in fact demonstrate causality between these 2 functions.

However (to return to the present findings), what specific information do these data yield regarding this relationship? Restricting the remainder of the discussion to the better controlled studies, several facts emerge clearly. Psychological differences were consistently found between complication samples and normal samples, whether the complication sample entailed a specific complication or was a composite group of different complications. The common denominator which differentiated the complication groups from the normal groups was an increase in anxiety levels, regardless of the test instrument used. Correspondingly, the complication groups were characterized by less use of repressive-type defenses. While anxiety levels were significantly lower in both normal and complication groups after delivery, the greatest decreases were evident in the complication groups, with a concomitant increase in repression and similar avoidance-type defenses, such as denial. The data also suggest that high anxiety levels are associated with extreme dependence in sexually immature females who have various conflicts related to pregnancy. Although the majority of these results were obtained from investigations of primigravidas, (unwed primigravidas, moreover) the success of predictive devices (see *Instruments*) whose content is markedly similar to the MAS, when applied to diverse populations, support (at least indirectly) the increased generality of these findings.

The thesis explored in this paper is that emotional factors may causally effect complications through adverse physiological alterations. This position seems valid a priori. Furthermore, various functional pathways connecting the anatomical loci subsuming emotional behavior[65] and the humoral complex (the regulator of physiological functioning[66-68]), have been traced,[69-74] and the current surge of neurophysiological and allied research promises fuller understanding of the relationships in the near future. The present survey offers no conclusive proof of causal relationship; however, even though the results are meager, the present findings provide a logical departure for future research. Operationally, anxiety is suggested as a central factor in psychogenic obstetric complications. This paper, therefore, will conclude with the presentation of a framework describing the presumed causal role played by anxiety in complications.

Conclusion

Anxiety occupies a central position in contemporary learning and psychoanalytical theory. It is generally considered a subjectively experienced dysphoric state arising from an individual's awareness of a vaguely defined impending danger which he strives to avoid in a number of different ways. Recent research[74] differentiates between an anxiety *trait* (of a characterological nature), which presumably stems from frustrating experiences early in life, and an anxiety *state*, which is related more directly to transient changes in the physiological state. Individuals who score high on anxiety trait measures tolerate stress more poorly than those who score low.

Psychoanalytical theory predicates defenses (e.g., repression, denial, conversion) as mechanisms which protect a person from anxiety. The ability of these mechanisms to maintain this protection from anxiety in the face of stress is called "ego strength," and denotes adaptive success. Anxiety is not unidimensional but has as minimum characteristics both duration and intensity, and its effects are differentially determined by these. Within certain limits anxiety serves the salutary function of alerting and mobilizing the individual to deal with the stressor, be it an object loss, a learning task, or a pregnancy. The optimal limits, of course, differ for various individuals, being determined by each person's adaptive abilities. Anxiety so pervasive, by virtue either of its intensity or chronicity, as to exceed the person's adaptive capacities leads to adaptive failure with far-reaching consequences, particularly with regard to the endocrine system. Wolff et al.[75],[76] and Sachar et al.,[77] in investigating chronic stress, have demonstrated that adaptive success in the face of chronic stress correlates meaningfully with low levels of endocrine secretion, while failure to master stress coincides with high levels.

As has been previously mentioned, pregnancy is a physical stress triggering changes in numerous organ systems. As part of these physiological changes, prenatal regressive changes of a psychological nature are normally observed. Women with unresolved conflicts about pregnancy—which stem from a variety of reasons, including extreme dependency and psychosexual immaturity—have been observed clinically to become and remain markedly anxious during pregnancy. Our data indicate that women with complications experience higher levels of anxiety during pregnancy than women with uncomplicated pregnancies. Their anxiety levels show a significantly greater mean decrease after delivery than the anxiety scores of control groups. McDonald's[52] findings suggest that elevated anxiety levels are related to the relative breakdown of a person's ego defenses. This investigator found no reliable differences in hostility scores at the fantasy level between a complication and control group, but the complication group obtained significantly higher hostility scores at the overt level of behavior. The complications group's greater mean fantasy, overt-level-difference hostility scores were inversely related to their repressive and denial abilities.

These data are consistent with the schema of Shainess,[78] in which the individual's adaptive response to an unwanted pregnancy is dynamically illustrated. Shainess describes the characteristic means of adaptive response observed in each trimester. The denial seen primarily in the first trimester shifts to somatic complaints and complications in the second and third trimesters. In the first trimester, psychological defenses deal with the pregnancy by denying its existence. In the presence of ineffective defenses, adaptive failure ensues, accompanied by endocrinologic alterations and onset of complications. The occurrence of normal pregnancies and deliveries in anxious females emphasizes the inconsistent relationship between anxiety and complications, and raises for consideration the set of conditions which, when present, lead to obstetric complications. One might conceptualize necessary and sufficient conditions[79] as prerequisites for the development of complications. In this sense, the presence of anxiety would constitute the necessary condition, with overwhelming intensity or duration being the sufficient condition. The temporal point at which a complication occurs would be viewed as the point of the individual's adaptive failure.

The problem of specificity is yet unaccounted for. This

problem, in a general way, has both intrigued and perplexed psychosomatic investigators for some time. Earlier theorizing placed importance on constitutional differences (organ vulnerability) with no specific correlation between the nature of emotional stress and the organ affected. Dunbar's[14] position, the relating of certain diseases to personality types, has largely been discounted in favor of Alexander's[80] proposal that specific emotional states (i.e., anger) lead to disturbances in certain vegetative functions. One prime example of this specificity, following Alexander, is the correlation between chronically sustained hostile impulses and essential hypertension. In this vein, Shainess[78] related preeclamptic hypertensive vascular constriction to responses likely to be seen in the rejecting personality, whose philosophy is "I must grit my teeth and bear it, no matter how much this angers me."

Because of the present lack of experimental validation, it is still unclear whether certain vegetative disturbances (as reflected in clinical diagnoses) do in fact stem from specific emotional states. Converging lines of evidence, however, have clearly shown autonomic response specificity following autonomic arousal. That is, following experimental stimulation, each individual responds with his characteristic pattern of autonomic activation, whose maximal arousal is typically seen in a particular autonomic nervous system (ANS) concept, e.g., heart rate, despite the stimulus. This response stereotype, originally established with palmar conductance, heart rate, and heart-rate variability,[81,82] has been extended to include other autonomic parameters.[83-91] Moreover, many individuals respond with a fixed patterning, or hierarchy, of autonomic activation among the various components, which is constant over a wide range of stressor agents. It is postulated that this differential reactivity among various ANS components, extending to end-organs activated either neurally or neurohumorally by these components, derives from significant psychological trauma experienced during developmental stages. It is not generally agreed, however, that the reactivity is psychodynamically determined, existing evidence suggests that these differences in autonomic responsivity are constitutionaly determined and may be quantified shortly following birth.[92] In any event, awaiting further clarification, one might hypothesize that constitutional ANS differential reactivity ultimately becomes attached via an interpersonal matrix to certain emotion states during developmental sequences. An infant who constitutionally responds to stress primarily with increased heart rate and blood pressure elevation may, through repeated oral frustrations leading to anger, eventually respond to all later stressful situations evoking anger with the same ANS response pattern.

Regardless of the ultimate ontogeny of autonomic response specificity, it is quite evident that various physiological components assume differential importance in mediating obstetric complications: GI tract (hyperemesis gravidarum, pseudocyesis), smooth muscle contractility (habitual abortion), and arterial system (eclampsia), to name a few. Further, without regard for the artifactual nature of clinical diagnoses, complications can be classified in terms of systems dysfunction. Complication specificity

may be conceptualized in the following way: Stress (in the form of unresolved conflicts about pregnancy) causes anxiety, which results in adaptive attempts to cope with the stress. In the face of intense or prolonged anxiety, adaptive attempts fail, and ANS activation occurs; the complications are most likely to occur in the physiological function or system showing maximal activation. Specificity is determined further by the interaction of the primary locus of ANS activation with the differences in such factors as endocrine secretion, arterial friability, and hematologic response (e.g., immune bodies).

To recapitulate, anxiety and extremes in its duration and intensity are postulated as necessary and sufficient conditions, respectively, for the development of psychogenic obstetric complications. Mobilization of anxiety, the ANS activation which triggers a host of regulatory mechanisms, may result from a multiplicity of unresolved conflicts about pregnancy. Adaptive failure at a particular point underlies the timing of complications. Specificity is accounted for by the interaction of constitutional differences and autonomic response specificity with a host of other physiological parameters.

The studies most fruitful in confirming or refuting this explanation involve a combined approach in which multilevel functioning is assessed throughout the pregnancy and, optimally, even prior to conception, to avoid confounding effects. Although these studies necessitate expenditures of much time and money, the information derived, by preventing psychogenic complications, would seem to justify the expense.

Summary

This article reviewed the literature of the past 2 decades, which explored the relationships between emotional factors and obstetric complications. Many of the studies were case studies or poorly substantiated clinical observations, and the majority of the conclusions drawn were limited by these and other methodological shortcomings. The data supported the notion of a positive relationship between psychological and physiological functioning during pregnancy, but no causal relationships between emotional factors and obstetric complications were established.

The main findings were that patients with obstetric complications had higher anxiety levels than women with normal gestations and deliveries, and were less inclined to use repressive-type defenses. With these findings as a departure and anxiety as a central concept, a model was forwarded to account for the occurrence, timing, and specificity of psychogenic obstetric complications.

REFERENCES

1. Eastman, N. J., and Hellman, L. M. *Obstetrics.* Appleton, New York, 1962, p. 162.
2. McConnell, O. L., and Daston, P. G. Body image changes in pregnancy. *J Project Techn* 25:451, 1962.
3. Hooke, J. F., and Marks, P. A. MMPI characteristics of pregnancy. *J Clin Psychol* 18:316, 1962.
4. Blitzer, J. R. On the transformation of early narcissism during pregancy. *Int J Psychoanal* 45:89, 1962.
5. Kiernan, A. J. The psychology of pregnancy. *Irish J Med Sci* 6:43, 1964.

6. McDonald, R. L. Effects of stress on self attribution of hostility among ego control patterns. *J Personality 35*:234, 1967.
7. Bibring, G. L. Some considerations of the psychological processes in pregnancy. *Psychoanal Stud Child 14*:113, 1959.
8. Chapple, P. A. Changes of personality in pregnancy and labor. *Practitioner 192*:286, 1964.
9. Robin, A. A. The psychological changes of normal parturition. *Psychiat Quart 36*:129, 1962.
10. Calden, G., Dupertuis, C. W., Hokanson, J. E., and Lewis, W. C. Psychosomatic factors in the rate of recovery from tuberculosis. *Psychosom Med 22*:345, 1960.
11. Bivin, G. D., and Klinger, M. P. *Pseudocyesis.* Principia Press, Inc., Bloomington, Ind., 1937.
12. Greaves, D., Green, P. E., and West, L. J. Psychodynamic and psychophysiological aspects of pseudocyesis. *Psychosom Med 22*:24, 1960.
13. Steinberg, A., Pastor, N., Winheld, E. B., Segal, H. I., Shechter, F. R., and Colton, H. H. Psychoendocrine relationships in pseudocyesis. *Psychosom Med 8*:176, 1946.
14. Dunbar, H. F. *Emotions and Bodily Changes* (ed. 4). Columbia, New York, 1954.
15. Kaplan, A., and Schobpach, R. Pseudocyesis: A psychiatric study. *Arch Neurol Psychiat 65*:121, 1951.
16. Fried, P., Rakoff, A. E,, Schopbach, R. R., and Kaplan, A. J. Pseudocyesis: A psychosomatic study in gynecology. *JAMA 145*:1329, 1951.
17. Coppen, A. J. Vomiting of early pregnancy: Psychological factors and body build. *Lancet 24*:172, 1959.
18. Bernstein, I. C. An investigation into the etiology of nausea and vomiting of pregnancy. *Minnesota Med 5*:34, 1952.
19. Rosen, S. Emotional factors in nausea and vomiting of pregnancy. *Psychiat Quart 29*:621, 1955.
20. Chertok, L., Mondzain, M. L., and Bonnaud, M. Vomiting and the wish to have a child. *Psychosom Med 25*:13, 1963.
21. Harvey, W. A., and Sherfey, M. J. Vomiting in pregnancy: A psychiatric study. *Psychosom Med 16*:1, 1954.
22. Caldwell, J. Personality in pregnancy and labor. *Southern Med J 51*:1026, 1958.
23. Brown, L. Anxiety in pregnancy. *Brit J Med Psychol 37*:47, 1964.
24. Javert, C. T., Finn, W. F., and Stander, H. J. Primary and secondary spontaneous habitual abortion. *Amer J Obstet Gynec 57*:878, 1949.
25. Weil, R. J., and Stewart, L. C. The problem of spontaneous abortion. III. Psychosomatic and interpersonal aspects of habitual abortion. *Amer J Obstet Gynec 73*:322, 1957.
26. Weil, R. J., and Tupper, C. Personality, life situation, and communication: A study of habitual abortion. *Psychosom Med 22*:448, 1960.
27. Berle, B. B., and Javert, C. T. Stress and habitual abortion. *Obstet Gynec 3*:298, 1954.
28. Mann, E. C. Psychiatric investigation of habitual abortion, preliminary report. *Obstet Gynec 7*:589, 1956.
29. Mann, E. C. The role of emotional determinants in habitual abortion. *Surg Clin N Amer 37*:447, 1959.
30. Grimm, E. Psychological investigation of habitual abortion. *Psychosom Med 24*:369, 1962.
31. Stewart, D. B. Abnormal uterine action in labor. *J Obstet Gynaec Brit Emp 59*:641, 1952.
32. Klein, H. R., Potter, H. W., and Dyk, R. B. *Anxiety in Pregnancy and Childbirth.* Hoeber, New York, 1950.
33. McDonald, R. L., Gynther, M. D., and Christakos, A. C. Relations between maternal anxiety and obstetric complications. *Psychosom Med 25*:357, 1963.
34. Jeffcoat, T. N. A. "Obstetrics." In *Brittish Obstetrics and Gynecological Practice*, E. Holland, Ed., Heinemann, London, 1955, pp. 552-565.
35. Scott, E. M., and Thomson, A. M. A psychological investigation of primigravidae: IV. Psychological factors and the clinical phenomena of labor. *J Obstet Gynaec Brit Emp 63*:502, 1956.
36. Baird, D. The cause and prevention of difficult labor. *Amer J Obstet Gynec 63*:1200, 1952.
37. Kennedy, C. Incoordinate uterine action. *Edinburgh Med J 56*:445, 1949.
38. Cramond, W. A. Psychological aspects of uterine dysfunction. *Lancet 2*:1241, 1954.
39. Kapp, F. T., Horstein, S., and Graham, V. T. Some psychologic factors in prolonged labor due to inefficient uterine action. *Compr Psychiat 4*:9, 1963.
40. Watson, A. S. A psychiatric study of idiopathic prolonged labor. *Obstet Gynec 13*:598, 1959.
41. Gunter, L. Psychopathology and stress in the life experience of mothers of premature infants. *Amer J Obstet Gynec 86*333, 1963.
42. Blau, A., Slaff, B., Easton, K., Welkowitz, J., Springarn, J., and Cohen, J. The psychogenic etiology of premature births. *Psychosom Med 25*:201, 1963.
43. Ringrose, C. A. D. Psychosomatic influence in the genesis of toxemia of pregnancy. *Canad Med Ass J 84*:647, 1961.
44. Ringrose, C. A. D. Further observations on the psychosomatic character of toxemia of pregnancy. *Canad Med Ass J 84*:1064, 1961.
45. Salerno, L. J. Psychophysiologic aspects of toxemia of pregnancy. *Amer J Obstet Gynec 76*:1268, 1958.
46. Wiedorn, W. S. Toxemia of pregnancy and schizophrenia. *J Nerv Ment Dis 120*:1, 1954.
47. Hetzel, S. S., Bruer, B., and Poidevin, L. O. S. A survey of the relation between certain common antenatal complications in primiparae and stressful life situations during pregnancy. *J Psychosom Res 5*:175, 1961.
48. McDonald, R. L. Personality characteristics in patients with three obstetric complications. *Psychosom Med 27*:383, 1965.
49. McDonald, R. L., and Christakos, A. C. Relationship of emotional factors during pregnancy to obstetric complications. *Amer J Obstet Gynec 86*:341, 1963.
50. McDonald, R. L., and Parham, K. J. Relation of emotional changes during pregnancy to obstetric complications in unmarried primigravidae. *Amer J Obstet Gynec 90*:195, 1964.
51. McDonald, R. L., and Gynther, M. D. Relations between self and parental perceptions of unwed mothers and obstetric complications. *Psychosom Med 27*:31, 1965.
52. McDonald, R. L. Fantasy and the outcome of preganacy. *Arch Gen Psychiat (Chicago) 12*:602, 1965.
53. Davids, A., DeVault, S., and Talmadge, M. Anxiety, pregnancy, and childbirth abnormalities. *J Consult Psychol 25*:74, 1961.
54. Davids, A., DeVault, S., and Talmadge, M. Psychological study of emotional factors in pregnancy: A preliminary report. *Psychosom Med 23*:93, 1961.
55. Davids, A., and DeVault, S. Maternal anxiety during pregnancy and childbirth abnormalities. *Psychosom Med 24*:464, 1962.
56. Zemlick, M. J., and Watson, R. I. Maternal attitudes of acceptance and rejection during and after pregnancy. *Amer J. Orthopsychiat 23*:570, 1953
57. Destounis, N. Complications of pregnancy: A psychosomatic approach. *Canad Psychiat Ass J 7*:279, 1962.
58. Grimm, E. R. Psychological tension in pregnancy. *Psychosom Med 23*:520, 1961.
59. Schafer, E. S., and Bell, R. Q. Development of a parental attitude research instrument. *Child Develop 29*:339, 1958.
60. Schaefer, E. S., and Manheimer, H. Dimension of perinatal adjustment. Paper read at Eastern Psychological Association, New York, April 1960.
61. Clifford, E. Expressed attitudes in pregnancy of unwed women and married primigravida and multigravida. *Child Develop 33*:945, 1962.
62. Grimm, E., and Venet, W. R. The relationship of emotional adjustments and attitudes to the course and outcome of pregnancy. *Psychosom Med 28*:34, 1966.
63. Blau, A., Welkowitz, J., and Cohen, J. Maternal attitude to pregnancy instrument. *Arch Gen Psychiat 10*:324, 1964.
64. Zemlick, M. J., and Concilio, A. An item analysis and scoring of the ZAR Pregnancy Attitude Scale. Unpublished data, 1951.
65. MacLean, P. D. Psychosomatic disease and the "visceral brain." *Psychosom Med 11*:338, 1949.
66. Everett, J. W. "Pituitary-ovarian Relationships." In *Progress in Clinical Endocrinology*, S. Saskin, Ed. Grune, New York, 1950, pp. 319-326.
67. Kaiser, I. H., and Harris, J. S. The effect of adrenalin on the pregnant human uterus. *Amer J Obstet Gynec 59*:775, 1950.
68. Kaiser, I. H. The effect of epinephrine and norepinephrine on the contractions of the human uterus in labor. *Surg Gynec Obstet 90*:649, 1950.
69. Green, J. D., and Harris, G. W. Neurovascular link between neurohypophysis and adenohypophysis. *J Endocr 5*:136, 1947.
70. Friedgood, H. B Neuroendocrine and psychodynamic factors in sterility. *West J Surg 56*:391, 1948.
71. Selye, H. The alarm reaction and the diseases of adaptation. *Ann Intern Med 29*:403, 1948.
72. Harris, F. W. Neural control of the pituitary gland. *Psychol Rev 28*:139, 1948.
73. Theobald, G. W. Centers in the hypothalamus controlling menstruation, ovulation, pregnancy, and parturition. *Brit Med J 1*:1038, 1936.
74. Spielberger, C. D. "Theory and Research on Anxiety." In *Anxiety and Behavior*, C. D. Spielberger, Ed. Acad. Press, New York, 1966, pp. 1-20.
75. Wolff, C. T., Friedman, S. B., Hofer, M. A., and Mason, J. W. Relationship between psychological defenses and mean urinary 17-hydroxycorticosteroid excretion rates: I. A predictive study of parents of fatally ill children. *Psychosom Med 26*:572, 1964.

76. Wolff, C. T., Hoefer, M. A., and Mason, J. W. Relationship between psychological defenses and mean urinary 17-hydroxycorticosteroid excretion rates: II. Methodologic and theoretic considerations. *Psychosom Med* 26:592, 1964.
77. Sachar, E. J., Mason, J. W., Kolmer, H. S., and Artiss, K. L. Psychoendocrine aspects of acute schizophrenic reactions. *Psychosom Med* 25:510, 1963.
78. Shainess, N. "Psychological Problems Associated with Motherhood." In *Handbook of American Psychiatry* (Vol. 3), S. Arieti, Ed. Basic, New York, 1966, pp. 47-65.
79. Wender, P. H. On necessary and sufficient conditions in psychiatric explanation. *Arch Gen Psychiat (Chicago)* 16:41, 1967.
80. Alexander, F. *Psychosomatic medicine: Its Principles and Application.* Norton, New York, 1950, 0. 87.
81. Lacey, J. I., Batman, D. E., and Van Lehn, R. Autonomic response specificity: An experimental study. *Psychosom Med* 15:8, 1953.
82. Lacey, J. I., and Lacey, B. C. Verification and extension of the principle of autonomic response-stereotypy. *Amer J Psychol* 71:50, 1958.
83. Engel, B. T. Stimulus-response and individual response specificity. *Arch Gen Psychait (Chicago)* 2:305, 1960.
84. Wenger, M. A., Engel, B. T., and Clemens, T. L. Studies of autonomic response patterns: Rationale and methods. *Behav Sci* 2:216, 1957.
85. Malmo, R. B., and Shagass, C. Physiologic study of symptom mechanisms in psychiatric patients under stress. *Psychosom Med* 11:25, 1949.
86. Malmo, R. B., Shagass, C., and Davis, F. H. Sympton specificity and bodily reactions during psychiatric interviews. *Psychosom Med* 12:362, 1950.
87. Wenger, M. A., Clemens, T. L., Coleman, D. R., Cullen, T. D., and Engel, B. T. Autonomic response specificity. *Psychosom Med* 23:185, 1961.
88. David, R. C., and Buchwald, A. M. An exploration of somatic response patterns: Stimulus and sex differences. *J Comp Physiol Psychol* 50:44, 1957.
89. Davis, R. C. Response patterns. *Trans NY Acad Sci* 19:731, 1957.
90. Davis, R. C., Buchwald, A. M., and Frankmann, R. W. Autonomic and muscular responses and their relation to simple stimuli. *Psychol Monogr* 69:1, 1955.
91. Davis, R. C., Lunderwald, A., and Miller, J. D. The pattern of somatic response during a repetitive motor task and its modification by visual stimuli. *J Comp Physiol Psychol* 50:53, 1957.
92. Schachter, T. Reactivity in human neonates. Paper delivered at Emory University Medical School, Atlanta, Ga., Nov. 21, 1966.

41 Psychologic aspects of lactation

Niles Newton
Michael Newton

The rapidity with which lactation failure spreads through human groups suggests that it is triggered by psychologic factors. For instance, national surveys indicate that the neonatal breast-feeding rate in the United States fell by almost half during just ten years.[1] In the course of twenty years in Bristol, England, the number of three-month-old breast-fed infants dropped from 77 to 36 per cent.[2] In an obstetric clinic in France the proportion of babies getting no breast milk increased from 31 to 51 per cent in just five years.[3] This decrease is so rapid that hereditary factors could not be operative and major physiologic changes in function would be unlikely in the absence of radical stresses such as starvation or epidemic disease. Human emotions and behavior, however, may change rapidly in keeping with the rapid changes observed in rates of breast feeding.

Human lactation is sensitive to a wide variety of interrelated psychologic factors, which may be roughly grouped as follows: individual emotions and attitudes; group-derived emotions and attitudes; and psychophysiologic mediating mechanisms. These will be discussed in succession.

Individual emotions and attitudes

VERBALIZED ATTITUDE OF MOTHER

Breast-feeding performance is closely related to what the mother says about her attitudes toward breast feeding. Newton and Newton[4] interviewed 91 patients in the immediate post-partum period. Replies to questions were written down verbatim as nearly as possible and judged by 2 independent referees who did not know the patients or their breast-feeding history. Feeding procedures were the same for all mothers. Babies were brought out to the mothers six times a day, staying with the mother for forty-five minutes to an hour each time. This allowed the mother with favorable attitudes toward breast feeding to relax with her baby, cuddling it and suckling it, up to four or five hours a day. The mothers judged to have positive attitudes toward breast feeding gave more milk (p less than 0.01) and were more successful (p less than 0.01)than those judged to express negative feelings toward breast feeding, as shown in Table 1.

Reprinted from Niles Newton and Michael Newton, "Psychologic Aspects of Lactation," The New England Journal of Medicine, 277:22, 1967, pp. 1179-1188. Adapted from a working paper prepared for the World Health Organization Scientific Group Meeting on the Physiology of Lactation held in Geneva, Switzerland, December 2-7, 1963.

Four subsequent studies have confirmed the finding that breast-feeding performance is related to verbalized attitudes toward breast feeding.[3-8]

PHYSICAL RESPONSE OF MOTHER

The survival of the human race, long before the concept of "duty" evolved, depended upon the satisfactions gained from the two voluntary acts of reproduction—coitus and breast feeding. These had to be sufficiently pleasurable to ensure their frequent occurrence.

The physiologic responses in coitus and lactation are closely allied. Uterine contractions occur both during suckling[9] and during sexual excitement.[10] Nipple erection occurs during both.[11,12] Milk ejection has been observed to occur during sexual excitement in women.[13] Moreover, the degree of ejection appears to be related to the degree of sexual response.[13]

Extensive breast stimulation occurs during breast feeding. Breast stimulation alone can induce orgasm in some women.[10] Emotions aroused by sexual contact and breast-feeding contact both involve skin changes. Sexual excitement causes marked vascular changes in the skin.[11] The breast-feeding act raises body temperature as measured in the submammary and mammary skin area.[14]

Masters and Johnson[15] found that nursing women had a higher level of sexual interest than non-nursing post-partum women. Nursing mothers not only reported sexual stimulation from sucking but also, as a group, were interested in as rapid a return to active intercourse with their husbands as possible.

Feelings of aversion for the breast-feeding act appear to be related to dislike of nudity and sexuality. The Newsons,[16] after interviewing more than 700 English mothers, commented: "For many mothers, modesty and feeling of distaste form a major factor in their preference for the artificial methods." Salber and her associates,[17] working with American mothers who had never attempted to nurse, stated, "The idea of nursing repelled them. They were excessively embarrassed at the idea or too 'modest' to nurse." Adams[18] found that primiparas who stated a desire to bottle feed showed significantly more "psycho-sexual disturbances" in various measures collected in interviews and by tests (p values ranging from 0.05 to 0.001). Sears et al.[19] found that mothers who breast fed were also significantly (p less than 0.02) more tolerant in sexual matters such as masturbation and social sex play. Nor are these feelings limited to those of Anglo-Saxon culture. Upper-middle-class Ladinos of Guatemala are reported to "express notions of modesty, distaste and boredom in regard to breast feeding."[20]

Both psychologic feelings of frigidity toward the breast-feeding act and physiologic measures of response have been related to breast-feeding failure. Both Bloomfield[21] and Newson and Newson[16] found indications of a positive relation between enjoyment of breast feeding and duration of breast feeding. Newson and Newson,[16] using questions that probed beyond the conventional answers, found that 66 per cent of the mothers who breast fed for two weeks or more "actively enjoyed the experience," often describing the tenderness and closeness engendered by the breast-

TABLE 1   Relation of Attitudes toward Breast Feeding to Breast Feeding Performance

Verbalized Attitude Toward Breast Feeding	Mean Amount of Milk Obtained by Baby at 4th-Day Feedings	Successful Nursing by Mothers*
	(gm)	(%)
Positive	59	74
Ambivalent	42	35
Negative	35	26

*As judged by no need for bottle supplement after 4th hospital day.

feeding act. Hytten et al.,[8] however, report that none of 32 primigravidas who breast fed for three months "found it physically or emotionally pleasurable."

On the physiologic level the thermal skin response and the nipple-erection reflex appear to be related to milk production. Abolins[14] reported a "strong positive correlation" between milk supply and rise in temperature of mammary skin due to nursing. Gunther,[22] in a study of nipple protractility in breast-feeding mothers, found that those whose total nipple protractility was 2.5 cm usually experienced successful breast feeding, whereas those with just 0.25 to 0.50 cm less protractility were notably less successful in establishing breast feeding. Masters,[11] studying nipple erection as part of sexual excitement, observed an increase of 1 to 1.5 cm in nipple length that was due to stimulation. This suggests that the nipple-erection reflex may lead to more efficient nursing.

OTHER MATERNAL BEHAVIOR AND ATTITUDES

In many mammals motherly interest and care are almost synonymous with the course of lactation. There is also evidence that maternal behavior and maternal attitude may be related to breast-feeding behavior in women.

Potter and Klein[23] did a detailed study of 25 nursing couples in a Brooklyn, New York, hospital. A rating of the mother's "nursing behavior" was obtained by observation of the way she handled the baby at breast-feeding time. Each mother was also rated on "maternal interest" through a lengthy interview centering on such questions as doll play in childhood, interest in other people's babies, and number of children desired. As calculated from the tabular data presented by Potter and Klein, the high correlation of +0.618 (p less than 0.001) is found to exist between the nursing-behavior index and the maternal-interest index. Home visits[23] to 16 mothers indicated that all those who rated low on the maternal-interest scale had discontinued nursing immediately upon discharge from the hospital. Of those who had ranked high on the maternal-interest scale, all but 1 had continued to nurse.

Other studies indicate a relation between breast feeding and motherly interest. Both Brown et al.[24] and Adams[18] questioned nulliparas concerning feeding choice during pregnancy. Both found that bottle-feeding choice was significantly correlated with mother-centered reasons for feeding choice, whereas those planning to breast-feed tended to give reasons concerned with the welfare of the baby. We[25] observed a significant relation (p less than 0.05) between ratings of reactions of mothers to the first sight of their babies and ratings of attitudes toward breast feeding as expressed during a later interview to a different observer who did not know the first rating. Mothers judged to react to their babies with joy and delight more frequently expressed the desire to breast-feed them.

Three studies have concentrated on the behavior of mothers of *older* children with *past* attempts to breast-feed. Two studies[19,26] dealing with populations in which breast feeding was on the average so brief that it might be considered "problem lactation found no statistically significant relations between maternal behavior and duration of breast feeding except that Sears et al.[19] did report differences in the area of sexuality as previously mentioned. Freeman[27] worked with children from the Institute of Child Guidance, New York City, who constituted a population in which some well established lactation existed. She studied 100 cases randomly selected from those breast-fed for one year or more and 100 cases randomly selected from those breast-fed for one month or less. The former were more than twice as likely to have been rated as suffering from maternal "overprotection" than those receiving little or no breast feeding, who were more than twice as likely to be rated as "rejected."

A recent investigation of the relation of lactation to maternal behavior by Newton, Peeler and Rawlins[28] controlled some of the variables that have made previous research studies suggestive but not conclusive. Nursing and non-nursing post-parturient mice were paired and given adoptive litters. Nursing and non-nursing post-parturient human beings were matched for parity and educational status. No significant difference in maternal behavior between pair members were found on some items of maternal behavior. However, nursing and non-nursing mothers differed significantly in their willingness to have the baby in bed with them. Seventy-four per cent of the nursing and 29 per cent of tne non-nursing mothers did so. The nursing members of mouse pairs manifested a similar significantly heightened drive to be in close contact with the young.

LIFE EXPERIENCES OF THE MOTHER

Some life experiences of the mother appear to be related to breast-feeding success, especially labor and breast-feeding of previous children, although more remote experiences associated with the breast-feeding mother's own infancy may also play a part.

The importance of obstetric experience is suggested by N. Newton's[5] finding that primiparas who had slow labors were significantly (p less than 0.05) more likely to have negative attutides toward breast feeding. Jackson and her co-workers[29] length of labor and use of forceps. The more difficult the labor, as rated by this scale, the lower the rate of breast feeding.

Previous attempts to breast-feed may also determine attitudes. Bloomfield,[21] working with a sample in which only 16 per cent breast-fed for three months, found that 66 per cent of the mothers who had been this successful once repeated the performance. Robinson,[30] in a study of 3266 infants, gained the clinical impression that multiparas who

failed in previous lactations were likely to take the infants off the breast when they returned to household duties. They failed and "were quite sure they would fail again."

Recent research with other mammals suggests the possibility that mother-baby contact in the mother's own infancy is also related to the ability to breast-feed in adulthood. For instance, 4 female macaque monkeys raised in partial isolation in individual wire cages were finally impregnated in spite of the "inadequacy of their sexual behavior."[31] The maternal behavior of all 4 mothers was completely abnormal, ranging from indifference to abuse. Whereas the usual macaque mother requires the efforts of more than 1 human attendant to separate her from her baby, these mothers paid no attention when their infants were removed for feeding by hand, necessitated by the mother's refusal to nurse. Eventually, 2 of the mothers did permit fairly frequent nursing, but at the same time became more violently abusive toward their offspring.[31] Similar abnormal maternal behavior has been observed in ratand goat mothers that had been subjected to partial mother separation in their own infancy.[32,33]

PERSONALITY

Of 3 recent studies specifically concerned with the relation of personality to breast feeding, only Call's[34] inadequately controlled exploratory report deals with the most pertinent problem—the relation of personality to success in breast feeding among those who try. He found indications that women who continued to breast-feed after starting were likely to be more maternal and less conventional. Women who decided to bottle-feed appeared to be the least anxious; yet of those who actually put the baby to the breast, it seemed to be the calmer mother who was most likely to continue.

Plans to bottle-feed or breast-feed appear to be related to certain other personality characteristics measured in pregnancy, in women expecting their first babies. Adams[18] found that bottle-choice women responded to pregnancy with significantly (p less than 0.01) more dependency as measured during interview. They also showed significantly more disturbed behavior on 8 items of the Blackey test, as compared with 1 item for the breast-choice group. Brown et al.,[35] working with women of higher and lower social class, found a personality difference that crossed class lines. Both clinic and private patients showed significant (p less than 0.01) differences in the Fc response on the Rorschach test. This may be interpreted to mean that the breast-choice mothers placed more importance on the exchange of affection with other people than bottle-choice mothers.

INFANT'S BEHAVIOR AND EMOTIONS

Breast feeding is a co-operative process between 2 people; smooth function depends on the behavior of the baby as much as on the behavior of the mother. Behavior problems in the baby can occur at the level of inefficient sucking, dislike of the nursing situtation and lack of responsiveness.

Inefficient sucking by the baby is sometimes related to medical management technics. Brazelton[36] found a high relation between the ability to nurse effectively and the amount of barbiturate medication given to the mother during labor. On the first day only 30 per cent of the feedings of babies from heavily medicated mothers were rated as effective as compared to 65 per cent of those of babies from the lightly medicated (p equal to 0.03). The differences for the second day were 25 per cent vs. 65 per cent (p equal to 0.002), for the third day 35 per cent vs. 75 per cent (p equal to 0.001) and for the fourth day 55 per cent vs. 87 per cent (p equal to 0.001). Not until the fifth and sixth days were the babies of heavily medicated mothers as alert and effective in nursing situations as those of less heavily medicated mothers. This finding has now been confirmed and extended. The study by Kron et al.[37] indicates that newborn infants whose mothers had received a single dose of obstetric sedation during labor sucked at significantly lower rates and pressures and consumed less nutrient than those born to mothers who had received no obstetric sedation. Drug effects persisted at a significant level throughout the four-day period that the infants remained in the newborn nursery.

Another frequent way in which the baby comes to reject breast feeding is by being taught other technics of sucking that are not appropriate to the breast. Davis et al.[38] studied neonates fed by bottle, cup and breast for ten days. Interest in sucking continued to rise in those fed by breast. They showed a significantly (p less than 0.01) longer sucking response on a standard sucking test from the fourth to the tenth day as compared to those fed by bottle. This finding is in keeping with the observation that supplementary bottle feeding interferes with the milk supply.[39, 40] Gunther[22] has suggested that the rubber nipple acts as a supersign stimulus to the infant in the same way that an oyster catcher, presented with her own eggs and wooden ones of twice the size, will sit on the larger, artificial ones.

The pleasantness of the feeding situation may also influence the baby's attitude toward breast feeding. Robinson[30] observed that "many infants whose mothers fed them strictly by the clock, refused point-blank to take the breast after the age of three months and had to be bottle fed or starve. The breast was not refused if the mother was easygoing and fed her infant by instinct rather than by the clock." Scheduling of a few large feedings causes the breast to be overfull, so that when ejection occurs, the milk may spurt out, choking the infant. Cutting out the air supply, even temporarily, may be a quick way to instill fear or ambivalence. Ejection-reflex failures can also teach the baby to dislike the breast; it may be frustrating to have little milk available at some times and an abundance at others. Newton and Newton[4] found that breast feeding was significantly (p less than 0.01) more successful when there was less fluctuation in the amount of milk obtained from 1 feeding to the next.

Responsiveness may also influence the baby's enjoyment and co-operation with breast feeding. Middlemore, as quoted by Gunther,[22] accurately described responsive and frigid breast feeding on the part of the baby. She stated: "The active satisfied babies established the sucking reflex and rhythm quickly . . . and showed their pleasure by seeking the nipple when it was withdrawn." These are contrasted to the inert ones: "they did not move much or cry at the breast."

The reaction of older babies to breast feeding is even more clearly observable. The total body shows signs of eagerness—rhythmic motions of hands, feet, fingers and toes may occur along with the rhythm of sucking. Erection of the penis is common in male babies. After feeding, there is often a relaxation that is characteristic of the conclusion of satisfactory sexual response. The sensuous enjoyment of breast feeding is likely to increase the baby's desire to suckle his mother frequently and fully, thus stimulating the secretion of milk.

Group-derived emotions and attitudes

FEELINGS RELATED TO FEMALE STATUS

The impact of an industrial money economy—with the breaking up of the wider family unit as the main economic unit of society—has had far reaching effects on the role of women and the value placed on woman's unique biologic contributions.[3] When the wider family group stops co-operating in home manufacture and home production of food and material, women and children in the family become economic liabilities unless they go out to work and earn money. Children are no longer associated with rise in social status; large families may pull down the social standing of a family in industrial culture. If economic matters are related to man's emotions, children are no longer as desirable and beloved, and the status of women *as bearers of children* has *fallen*. Furthermore, women who stay home while more and more of the economic activity leaves the home are no longer contributing so much to society economically. Feelings of security may depend in part on the feeling of being needed and essential.

N. Newton[5] has emphasized the point that women's joy and acceptance of the female biologic role in life may be an important factor in their psychosexual behavior, which includes lactation. She found through interviewing women under controlled conditions in the post-partum period that women who desired to bottle-feed also were significantly (p less than 0.005) more likely to say that men have a more satisfying time in life. Adams[18] similarly found that nulliparas who planned to breast-feed significantly (p less than 0.05) more frequently stated their satisfaction in woman's role in life.

This line of thinking and evidence tends to fit in with historical attitudes toward breast feeding. Periods of great wealth and luxury in the Western world—the age of Imperial Rome, Athens in the time of Pericles, the era of Louis XIV in Paris,[42] early eighteenth-century England and Colonial America[42,43] were characterized by the rejection of breast feeding by large numbers of women who used wet nursing or artificial feeding in the form of pap to sustain infants. In these eras upper-class women may have tended to be objects of amusement rather than real contributors to the work of the societies. Thus, they may have tended to feel somewhat worthless and insecure. However, in what Toynbee calls "times of trouble" breast feeding has been popular.[44]

FEELINGS RELATED TO REGION, EDUCATION, SOCIAL CLASS AND WORK

Woman's role in life, as determined by her cultural locale, education, social class and work, has been repeatedly shown to be related to her breast-feeding hehavior. Breast-feeding rates differ with even slight variations in region or culture. Thus, Meyer's[1] 1956 survey indicated that more than half the babies discharged from hospitals in Arizona, Colorado, Georgia, Idaho, New Mexico, Oklahoma and Utah were still getting some breast milk, whereas only 20 per cent or less of those discharged from hospitals in Connecticut, Maine and Massachusetts were still wholly or partially breast fed. The effect of size of community was shown in an extensive California study, in which the duration of breast feeding was found to *decrease* with *increase* in size of community where the mother lived most of her life.[45] The effect of subcultural groupings can be seen in a study of women in Victoria, Australia, where Greek-speaking and Italian-speaking mothers had a lower artificial feeding rate than English-speaking mothers.[46] Marked national differences in breast feeding were found in a cross-cultural study involving London, Paris, Stockholm, Brussels, and Zurich. Not only was the overall incidence different, but significant differences in the type of weaning curves were observed.[17]

Breast-feeding rates are very sensitive to differences in education and social class in some cultures. American mothers with high-school education have a lower breast-feeding rate than those with college education.[6,16,48] Higher education may also favor breast feeding in the developing country of Uganda.[49] A cross-cultural study found higher breast-feeding rates associated with high social status in Zurich and Stockholm, but not in Brussels and Paris, where no hint of class differences in breast feeding were noted.[47] British and American studies found that the highest social status definitely favored breast feeding.[6,16,48,50,51]

However, the relation between social class and breast feeding appears sometimes to be bimodal. Those of the very lowest social groups, like those of the highest, are sometimes reported with higher breast-feeding rates than the middle groups,[6,45,48] but this is not always true.[16,56]

Woman's work load certainly influences breast feeding, but here, again, the situation is complex and depends not on the work alone but on *how* the work is carried out. Work itself interferes little with breast feeding in cultures that are accepting enough of the baby so that they permit the baby to accompany the woman as she works. Many non-Western cultures of both the simple and the complex types depend heavily on women's work contributions, yet breast feeding flourishes for two or more years with each baby because the work does not involve mother-baby separation.[53]

On the other hand even very simple cultures can manifest emotional indifference to breast feeding when the mother is the chief source of economic support and when her work requires her to be away from the baby for long periods. This is true of the women of Alor in the Lesser Sundas.[53] Jelliffe[54] emphasizes the need for tropical women to go out to work all day as a cause of increasingly early weaning in urban groups and more sophisticated rural groups as well.

EFFECT OF FEELINGS OF OTHERS

Many people working with mothers acquire a strong suspicion that the attitude of husband, family, and friends may have a real bearing on breast-feeding behavior. However, this is difficult to document. There does not appear to have been any statistical effort made to correlate fathers' attitudes toward nursing and its success. Grandmothers' ardor for breast feeding does not appear to be related to breast-feeding rates.[7] Bloomfield[21] noted that mothers acted more like their friends, 80 per cent of whom preferred bottle feeding, than like their own mothers, 75 per cent of whom approved of breast feeding.

The effect of medical personnel is more clearly delineated. The enthusiastic physician can develop a practice in which the breast-feeding rates of his patients are far above that usual in the rest of the society.[55-57]

Enthusiasm about lactation in cultures with declining lactation rates, however, is frequently considered improper: the physican may lose status because of it. Two recent studies in the United States[24] and England[59] have analyzed the feelings of medical personnel toward breast feeding, finding a general lack of strong enthusiasm of the type that appears to be associated with successful medical breast-feeding programs.

As early as 1920 Sedgwick and Fleischner[60] were dismayed because so much more time was being spent in American medical schools teaching about artificial feeding than about breast feeding. Rejective feelings have also made it necessary to hide the fact of breast feeding, thus impeding the flow of knowledge by observation. Just twenty years ago in rural Mississippi, breast feeding in church was acceptable; seventy-five years ago in Indiana upper-class women naturally took their babies to afternoon parties to nurse them as needed. Now in the United States there is a strong taboo on nursing in public or even showing photographs of nursing babies, whereas bottle feeding in public and pictures of bottle feeding babies are totally acceptable. Thus, a young girl often starts breast feeding without ever once having had a chance to observe another woman breast feeding. She is ignorant, even if she is interested.

Psychosomatic mediating mechanisms

The route by which emotional and psychosocial factors influence milk production is also of interest. Although some psychosomatic mechanisms are probably unknown, 3 different factors are presently recognized: the milk-ejection reflex, suckling stimulation; and other types of sensory contact between mother and baby.

THE MILK-EJECTION REFLEX

This is a neurohormonal mechanism, regulated in part by central-nervous-system factors. The primary stimulus is suckling applied to the nipple, which triggers the discharge of oxytocin from the posterior pituitary gland that is carried to the breast in the blood. The oxytocin acts on the myoepithelial cells around the alveoli, causing them to contract, and thus pushing out the milk into the larger ducts, where it is more easily available to the baby.[61]

The psychologic importance of the milk-ejection reflex in human beings was first emphasized by Waller[62] in his book, *Clinical Studies in Lactation.* He used case histories to illustrate the fact that milk ejection can be inhibited by embarrassment and can be conditioned so that it is set off by the mere thought of the baby far away.

TABLE 2   *Effect of Maternal Disturbance and Oxytocin on the Amount of Milk Obtained by the Baby*

Maternal Disturbance	Mean Amount of Milk Obtained by Infant During Standardized Feeding
	(gm)
No distractions—no injection	168
Distraction—saline injection	99
Distraction—oxytocin injection	153

Newton and Newton[63] inhibited the milk-ejection reflex experimentally in a mother through distractive technics that did not appear to disturb the baby. These consisted of placing the feet in ice water, painfully pulling the toes, and asking the solution of mathematical problems, punishing mistakes with electric shocks.

Table 2 shows how the amount of milk obtained by the baby varied. On control days when there was no disturbance, the baby obtained significantly (p less than 0.01) more milk than when the mother was subjected to disturbance. The amount of milk rose to near normal, however, when oxytocin was injected to set off the milk-ejection reflex artificially.

The relation of the reflex as set off by natural stimuli to the overall success of breast feeding was studied experimentally.[41] The baby was first allowed to nurse fully to set off the milk-ejection reflex. Then, the breasts were each pumped for five minutes. Finally, 3 units of oxytocin (Pitocin) was injected, and each breast was pumped again for five minutes. The unsuccessful breast-feeding mothers showed some failure in natural ejection since 47 per cent of the total milk obtained was available only after artificial ejection. The percentage of successful breast-feeding mothers was 27. The difference is statistically significant (p less than 0.01).

The milk-ejection reflex appears to be very sensitive to small differences in oxytocin level, suggesting that minor psychosomatic changes may influence the degree to which the milk is available to the baby.[64]

SUCKING STIMULATION

Possibly even more important than the ejection reflex to the success of breast feeding is the amount of sucking stimulation permitted. Far less sucking seems to be permitted in cultures where negative attitudes toward breast feeding are common than in those where breast feeding is almost universal. It may be a frequent human reaction to try to cut down and regulate the disliked stimulus, which in this case is sucking at the breast. Cultures that seem to emphasize breast feeding tend to encourage it for at least two years. Ford,[65] in his survey of 64 preliterate cultures, found records of weaning age in 46. None of these cultures normally weaned any baby before six months. One culture weaned between six months and a year. Fourteen weaned some or all babies between one and two years. In 31 cultures the *earliest* recorded age of weaning any infant from the breast was two or three years.

Regulated, restricted, short breast feeding, in the extreme form that is now occurring in some Western industrial countries, has developed only comparatively recently.

There is considerable evidence in human beings that the restriction of sucking actually inhibits lactation. Salber[68] assigned 1057 neonates to 1 of 3 feeding groups during their hospital stay. Those on true self-demand, after initial weight loss, showed the most rapid weight gain and were nearest their birth weight at one week as compared to the schedule-fed infants. Neonates on three-hour schedules gained faster and were nearer their birth weight at one week than infants on four-hour schedules.

Other studies on the effect of sucking on lactation are reviewed elsewhere.[40,61,57,69,70,71,72]

OTHER SENSORY CONTACT

The milk-ejection reflex and suckling stimulation depend primarily on sensory stimulation of the nipple, but other sensory contact, particularly auditory, visual, olfactory and tactile, may be important. Hartemann et al.,[73] in a study of mothers of premature babies, gained the clinical impression that the desire to nurse fades if the mothers do not have contact with their babies. They recommend letting mothers of premature babies have their babies as soon as possible to see and feel, to keep up their interest in nursing. McBryde[74] found that when Duke Hospital changed from routine separation of mother and baby to routine rooming-in of baby with mother, the breast feeding rate jumped from 35.0 to 58.5 per cent.

In human cultures where breast feeding is enjoyable enough to continue its full course, mother-baby separation is not easily tolerated by the mother or baby. Matthews[78] describes the mother-baby sensory contact among the Yorubas of Nigeria observed in 1948 to 1950, when the usual breast-feeding period was eighteen to twenty-two months, as follows:

A strict breast feeding routine would be difficult to attain because the mothers, determined and obstinate, are not easily separated from their babies for long. Cots and cradles are not welcomed. The baby will remain from birth until about the second year of life almost constantly in close physical contact with the mother who will feed it at irregular intervals usually determined by the onset of crying.

Similar descriptions come from anthropologic accounts from Asia, North America, South America, Africa and the Middle East.[53] Mother and baby very frequently stay in continuous close sensory contact with each other (even when not in the act of nursing) in cultures characterized by late weaning and few lactation difficulties.

In contrast to this, Western cultures raise many barriers against sensory contact between mother and baby. Modern Western styles of female dress make breast-baby contact difficult. Families no longer sleep all together in 1 room. Narrow beds built for 1 person only are fashionable, and the baby, especially, is expected to sleep alone. Many hospitals in the Western world now practice separation of mothers and babies at birth, except for brief feeding times, and when the baby and mother return home the ideal is a separate room where the baby spends much of his time. These customs are relatively new. For instance, housing the baby away from the mother started in American hospitals only about sixty years ago.

Summary and conclusions

The rapid decline in breast feeding as it is occurring in many parts of the world today[79] almost certainly is closely related to psychologic changes triggered by changes in group interaction and influenced by economic and historical trends. Breast-feeding behavior appears to be associated with the following variables in the mother: verbalized attitudes toward breast feeding; physical responsiveness; other types of maternal behavior; life experiences, particularly in connection with labor and previous lactation; and possibly certain other personality characteristics. However, breast feeding depends not only on the individual response of the individual mother but also on the reaction of the infant to the breast-feeding situation and on certain social variables such as definition of the female role in society, social class and educational status and attitudes fostered by interaction with others in modern industrial culture. These factors in turn may influence actual production of milk through the psychophysiologic mediating mechanisms of milk-ejection reflex, sucking stimulation and possibly also more generalized central-nervous-system effects resulting from auditory, visual, olfactory and tactile contact between mother and infant.

NOTES

1. Meyer, H. F. Breast feeding in United States: extent and possible trend. *Pediatrics* 22:116-121, 1958.
2. Ross, A. L. and Herdan, G. Breast-feeding in Bristol. *Lancet* 1:630-632, 1951.
3. Rouchy, R., Taureau, M., and Valmyre, M. J. Current trends in maternal breast feeding. *Bull. de Fed. Gynec. et obstet. franc.* 13:471-473, 1961
4. Newton, N., and Newton, M. Relationship of ability to breast feed and maternal attitudes toward breast feeding. *Pediatrics* 5:869-875, 1950.
5. Newton, N. *Maternal Emotions: A study of women's feelings toward menstruation, pregnancy, childbirth, breast feeding, infant care, and other aspects of their femininity.* 140 pp. New York: Hoeber, 1955.
6. Salber, E. J., Stitt, P. G., and Babott, J. G. Patterns of breast feeding. I. Factors affecting frequency of breast feeding in newborn period. *New Eng. J. Med.* 259:707-713, 1958.
7. Wickes, I. G., and Curwen, M. P. Lactation and heredity. *Brit. M. J.* 2:381-384, 1957.
8. Hytten, F. E., Yorston, J. E., and Thomson, A. M. Difficulties associated with breast feeding. *Brit. M. J.* 1310-315, 1958.
9. Moir, C. Recording the contractions of human pregnant and nonpregnant uterus. *Tr. Edinburgh Obst. Soc.* 54:93-120, 1934.
10. Kinsey, A. B., Pomeroy, W. B., Martin, C. E., and Gebhard, P. H. *Sexual Behavior in the Human Female: By staff of Institute for Sex Research, Indiana University.* 842 pp. Philadelphia: Saunders, 1953.
11. Masters, W. H. Sexual response cycle of human female. *West. J. Surg.* 68:57-75, 1960.
12. Newton, N. Influence of let-down reflex in breast feeding on mother-child relationship. *Marriage & Family Living.* 20:18-20, 1958.
13. Campbell, B., and Petersen, W. E. Milk let-down and orgasm in human female. *Human Biol.* 25165-168, 1953.
14. Abolins, J. A. Das Stillen und die Temperatur der Brust. *Acta obst. et Gynec. Scandinav.* 33:60-68, 1954.
15. Masters, W. H., and Johnson, V. E. *Human Sexual Response.* 366 pp. Boston: Little, Brown, 1966.
16. Newson, L. J., and Newson, E. Breast feeding in decline. *Brit M. J.* 2:1744, 1962.
17. Salber, F. J., Stitt, P. G., and Babbott, J. G. Patterns of breast feeding in family health clinic. II. Duration of feeding and reasons for weaning. *New Eng. J. Med.* 260:310-315, 1959.
18. Adams, A. B. Choice of infant feeding technique as function of maternal personality. *J. Consult. Psychol.* 23:143-146, 1959.
19. Sears, R. R., Maccoby, E. E., and Levin, H. *Patterns of Child Rearing.* 549 pp. Evanston: Row, Peterson, 1957.
20. Solien De Gonzales, N. L. Breast-feeding, weaning and acculturation. *J. Pediat.* 62:577-581, 1963.
21. Bloomfield, A. E. How many mothers breast feed? survey in general practice. *Practitioner* 188:393-396, 1962.
22. Gunther, M. Instinct and nursing couple. *Lancet* 1:575-578, 1955.
23. Potter, H. W., and Klein, H. R. On nursing behavior. *Psychiatry* 20:39-46, 1957.
24. Brown, F., Lieberman, J., Winston, J., and Pleshette, N. Studies in choice of infant feeding by primiparas. I. Attitudinal factors and extraneous influence. *Psychosom. Med.* 22:424-429, 1960.
25. Newton, N., and Newton M. Mothers' reactions to their newborn babies. *J.A.M.A.* 181:206-210, 1962.
26. Heinstein, M. I. Behavioral correlates of breast-bottle regimes under varying parent-infant relationships. *Monogr. Soc. Research Child Develop.* 28(4):1-61, 1963.
27. Freeman, M. Factors associated with length of breast feeding. *Smith College Studies in Social Work* 2:274-282, 1932.
28. Newton, N., Peeler, D., and Rawlins, C. Unpublished data.
29. Jackson, E. B., Wilkin, L. C., and Auerbach, H. Statistical report on incidence and duration of breast feeding in relation to personal-social and hospital maternity factors. *Pediatrics* 17:700-715, 1956.
30. Robinson, M. Infant morbidity and mortality: study of 3266 infants. *Lancet* 1:788-794, 1951.
31. Harlow, H. F., and Harlow, M. K. Social deprivation in monkeys. *Scient. Am.* 207:136-146, 1962.
32. Guze, H. Effects of pre-weaning nursing deprivation on later maternal, hoarding and sexual behavior in rat. *Dissertation Abstr.* 18(6):2227-2229, 1958.
33. Liddell, H. S. Contributions of conditioning sheep and goat to understanding of stress, anxiety and illness. In Conference on Experimental Psychiatry Western Psychiatric Institute and Clinic. 1959. *Lectures on Experimental Psychiatry: Pittsburgh Bicentennial Conference Mar. 5-7, 1959.* Edited by H. W. Brosin, 361 pp. Pittsburgh: Univ. of Pittsburgh Press, 1961. Pp. 227-255.
34. Call, J. D. Emotional factors favoring successful breast feeding of infants. *J. Pediat.* 55:485-496, 1959.
35. Brown, F., Chase, J., and Winson, J. Studies in infant feeding choice of primiparae. II. Comparison of rorschach determinants of accepters and rejecters of breast feeding. *J. Project. Techn.* 25:412-421, 1961.
36. Brazelton, T. B. Psychophysiologic reaction in neonate. II. Effect of maternal medication on neonate and his behavior. *J. Pediat.* 58:513-518, 1961.
37. Kron, R. E., Stein, M., and Goddard, K. E. Newborn sucking behavior affected by obstetric sedation. *Pediatrics* 37:1012-1016, 1966.
38. Davis, H. V., Sears, R. R., Miller, H. C., and Brodbeck, A. J. Effects of cup, bottle and breast feeding on oral activities of newborn infants. *Pediatrics* 2:549-558, 1948.
39. Grulee, C. G. Breast feeding. Presented at International Assembly of Inter-State Post Graduate Medical Association of North America, 1943. Pp. 135-137.
40. Newton, N., and Newton, M. Recent trends in breast feeding: review. *Am. J. M. Sc.* 221:691-698, 1951.
41. *Idem.* Relation of let-down reflex to ability to breast feed. *Pediatrics* 5:726-733, 1950.
42. Salber, E. J. Rejection of breast feeding. *M. Times* 88:430-433, 1960.
43. Bracken, F. J. Infant feeding in American colonies. *J. Am. Dietet. A.* 29:349-358, 1953.
44. Jelliffe, D. B. Breast feeding in technically developing regions. *Courrier* (Paris) 6:191-195, 1956.
45. Heinstein, M. *Child Rearing in California.* 98 pp. Berkeley, California: Bureau of Maternal and Child Health, Department of Health, 1965.
46. Newton, D. B. Breast feeding in Victoria, *M. J. Australia* 2:801-804, 1966.
47. Hindley, C. B., Filliozat, A. M. Klackenberg, G., Nicholet-Meister, D., and Sand, E. A. Some differences in infant feeding and elimination training in five European longitudinal samples. *J. Child Psychol.* 6:179-201, 1965.
48. Robertson, W. O. Breast feeding practices: some implications of regional variations. *Am. J. Pub. Health* 51:1035-1042, 1961.
49. Welbourn, H. F. Bottle feeding: problem of modern civilization. *J. Trop. Pediat.* 3:157-166, 1958.
50. Yankauer, A., Bock, W. E., Lawson, E. D., and Ianni. F. A. J. Social stratification and health practices in child bearing and child rearing. *Am. J. Publ. Health* 48:732-741, 1958.
51. Salber, E. J., and Feinleib, M. Breast feeding in Boston. *Pediatrics* 37:299-303, 1966.
52. Curtin, M. Failure to breast feed: review of feeding history of 1,007 infants. *Irish J. M. Sc.* 6:447-456. 1954.
53. Mead, M. and Newton, N. Cultural patterning in perinatal behavior. In *Childbearing: Its social and psychological aspects.* Edited by S. A. Richardson and A. F. Guttmacher. 334 pp. Baltimore: Williams and Wilkins, 1967. Pp. 142-244.

54. Jelliffe, D. B. Culture, social change and infant feeding, current trends in tropical regions. *Am. J. Clin. Nutrition* **10**:19-45, 1962.
55. Kimball, E. R. Breast feeding in private practice. *Quart. Bull. Northwest Univ. M. School* **25**:257-262, 1951.
56. Vermelin, H., and Ribon, M. Management and results of maternal breast feeding at maternity hospital of Nancy. *Rev. franc. de gynee. et d'obst.* **56**:119-129, 1961.
57. Waller, H. K. Early yield of human milk and its relation to security of lactation. *Lancet* 153-56, 1950.
58. Rawlins, C. Tested program for breast feeding success. Unpublished speech given at University Medical Center, Jackson, Mississippi, May, 1963.
59. Huntingfold, P. J. Attitude of doctors and midwives to breast feeding. *Develop. Med. & Child Neurol.* **4**:588-594, 1962.
60. Sedgwick, J. P., and Fleischner, E. C. Breast feeding in reduction of infant mortality. *Am. J. Pub. Health* **11**:153-157, 1921.
61. Newton, M., and Newton, N. Normal course and management of lactation. *Clin. Obstet. & Gynec.* **5**:44-63, 1962.
62. Waller, H. *Clinical Studies in Lactation.* 173 pp. London: Heinemann, n.d.
63. Newton, M., and Newton, N. Let-down reflex in human lactation. *J. Pediat.* **33**:698-704, 1948.
64. Weiderman, J., Freund, M., and Stone, M. I., Human breast and uterus comparison of sensitivity to oxytocin during gestation. *Obst. & Gynec.* **21**:272, 1963.
65. Ford, C. S. *A Comparative Study of Human Reproduction.* 111 pp. New Haven: Yale Univ. Press, 1945. (Publications in Anthropology No. 32.)
66. Waller, H. K. Reflex governing the outflow of milk from breast. *Lancet* **214**:69-72, 1943.
67. Southworth, R. S. Maternal feeding. In *Practice of Pediatrics.* Edited by W. L. Carr. 1014 pp. Philadelphia: Lea, 1906. Pp. 89-107.
68. Salber, E. J. Effect of different feeding schedules on growth of Bantu babies in first week of life. *J. Trop. Pediat.* **2**:97-102, 1956.
69. Richardson, F. H. Universalizing breast feeding in community. *J.A.M.A.* **85**:668-670, 1925.
70. Egli, G. E., Egli, N. S., and Newton, M. Influence of number of breast feedings on milk production. *Pediatrics* **27**314-317, 1961.
71. Hartemann, J., and Richon, J. Maternal nursing and reduction of number of infant feeding times. *Bull. de Fed. gynee. et obstet. franc.* **14**:773-775, 1962.
72. Illingworth, R. S., and Stone, D. G. H. Self-demand feeding in maternity unit. *Lancet* **1**:683-687, 1952.
73. Hartemann, J., Rebon, M., and Dellestable, P. Effects of attraction of mother and child on maintenance of nursing. *Bull. de Fed. gynee. et obstet. franc.* **14**:770-773, 1962.
74. McBryde, A. Compulsory rooming-in in ward and private newborn service at Duke hospital., *J.A.M.A.* **145**:625-627, 1951.
75. Hersher, L., Richmond, J. B., and Moore, A. U. Maternal behavior in sheep and goats. *Maternal Behavior in Mammals.* Edited by H. L. Rheingold, 349 pp. New York: Wiley, 1963. Pp. 203-232.
76. Moore, A. U. Maternal neonate bond in sheep and goat: its formation and significance for later life in herd. Presented at 1960 APA meeting Chicago, Ill., September 1-7 (mimeographed from author).
77. Hersher, L., Moore, A. U., and Richmond, J. B. Effect of post-partum separation of mother and kid on maternal care of domestic goat. *Science* **128**:1342, 1958.
78. Matthews, D. S. Ethnological and medical significance of breast feeding: with special reference to Yorubas of Nigeria. *J. Prop. Pediat.* **1**:9-25, 1955.
79. McGeorge, M. Current trends in breast feeding. *New Zealand M. J.* **59**:31-41, 1960.

42 *Postpartum psychiatric syndromes*

Frederick T. Melges

When an infant is born into a family, it is usually a time of rejoicing and happiness. Why is it, then, that some women become bewildered and even psychotic at this time? Why is it, as Pugh *et al.*[1] have shown, that there is a four- to fivefold increase in risk of mental illness (especially psychosis) for women during the first 3 months after delivery?

Out of a host of possible variables, our research focused on two key questions which might explain the increased vulnerability: (1) Do postpartum psychiatric syndromes represent a delirium? In the many studies reviewed by Hamilton,[2] a delirium frequently has been assumed on the basis of mental confusion, without supporting evidence from electroencephalographic and cognitive changes. (2) Is

there a conflict over mothering in these women and, if so, what are its determinants? Rejection of the infant has been noted in some studies,[3-5] but it has been most often considered as a consequence of other stresses and not as a central facet of puerperal illness. The term "mothering" is here restricted to refer to those activities and attitudes necessary for the care of an infant of 3 months or younger.

Methods

One-hundred patients were included in the sample, being selected according to two criteria: (1) the onset of psychiatric illness took place within 1 month prepartum to 3 months postpartum and (2) the psychiatrist in charge of the

Reprinted from Frederick T. Melges, "Postpartum Psychiatric Syndromes," Psychosomatic Medicine, 30:1, Jan.-Feb. 1968, pp. 95-108. Hoeber Medical Division of Harper & Row, Publishers. © 1968 by American Psychosomatic Society, Inc. From the Departments of Psychiatry, Strong Memorial Hospital and the University of Rochester School of Medicine and Dentistry, Rochester, N. Y. The author is grateful to Professor John Romano for supervision and substantial guidelines on this project. Thanks also go to Dr. Mary Ann Friederich for obstetrical consultation, Dr. Richard Satran for EEG assistance, and Dr. Howard Iker for statistical guidance. Dr. David A. Hamburg and Dr. Irvin D. Yalom aided in the preparation of the manuscript.

patient deemed childbearing to be a significant factor in the onset or exacerbation of mental illness.

The median age was 28.0 years (range: 17-46). Ninety-one patients received in-patient care; 9 had out-patient care. Sixty-two patients were division status (unable to afford private psychiatric care); 38 were private patients. The model education was that of a high school graduate; 21% were college graduates. The sex of the infant from the delivery under consideration was as follows: male 46; female 53. (One was a macerated stillborn whose sex could not be determined.) The median gravidity was 3.0, with a range of 1-11. The median parity was 3.0, with a range of 1-9. Two patients had twins. Three patients were included in the study because of the onset of psychiatric illness in relation to the adoption of an infant. As there were 3 unwed mothers in the sample, 3 babies were given up for adoption.

Since the study was essentially exploratory, the data are based primarily on psychiatric workups, including some EEG, PBI, and psychologic tests. For the span of 3 years, the writer interviewed 74 patients; of these, he was the responsible psychiatrist for 13 and was involved in the diagnostic workup and management of 27 other patients. Information on 26 patients who had been admitted prior to 1962 was gleaned solely from the hospital chart. These case histories, along with a review of the literature,[2-8] served as a guideline for the construction of a data sheet centering on items related to delirium and precipitating stress. Problems of mothering were paramount, as has also been observed by Romano.[9] The data sheet was then used for the analysis of the charts and conduct of the interviews, which began in an open-ended fashion and progressed toward greater structure until all categories had been covered. For those patients not treated or managed by the writer, time taken for interviews averaged 3 hr. (range: 1-7). Serial observations were made on all in-patients. The interview data were then collated with information in the hospital chart, from family interviews, from teaching conferences, and from talks with the attending psychiatrists, medical students, and nurses. Insofar as was possible, inferential material was avoided; the patient's verbalizations were taken at face value with regard to her puerperal experience, her past and present object relations, and what she deemed to be her major conflicts. Since the data therefore represent conscious reports and behavioral observations, the more elusive unconscious factors are not dealt with.

Although the literature[2,10] has repeatedly assumed that deliria stemming from postpartum endocrine and fluid-balance changes account for the prominent mental confusion in such syndromes, there have been no specific tests directed to this hypothesis. Slowing of the alpha rhythm of the EEG and impairment of cognitive tests of concentration and attention are specific deficits found in delirium.[11] Thus, the following procedures were directed to this question of delirium. (1) The serial subtraction of 7 from 100 and the digit span were the tests used for judging attention and concentration. Since the most rapid endocrine and metabolic changes take place within the first 2 weeks postpartum,[12] it was decided to compare those patients who were admitted within 2 weeks postpartum (N = 18) with those admitted beyond 2 weeks, then comparing both of these groups to another general psychiatric population of 50 patients (33 women; 17 men). The latter sample had no instances of organic brain disease. (2) Fifteen EEGs were obtained for those patients in whom delirium was being considered from a clinical standpoint. (3) Since hypothyroidism has been implicated as the cause of the confusion,[2] 14 PBI tests were obtained. (4) In light of the high recurrence rate of postpartum distress, 6 patients with a history of previous postpartum psychiatric reaction (5 schizophrenic and 1 depressive reactions) were tested within 1 month before delivery and at 3 days postpartum for a subsequent pregnancy, using EEG, serial-7, and digit-span tests. Nine multiparous women without such a history served as a control sample for pre- to postpartum changes, again having each subject also serve as her own control. During delivery and the first 2 days postpartum, all patients received the same drugs, including anesthetic preparations. Drugs were eliminated for at least 24 hr. prior to each testing period. The alpha rhythm of the EEGs was determined by Engel's method.[13] When serial EEG changes are reported as not significant, there was less than a 0.5-cps change in alpha frequency.

For all other comparisons, the student t test was the statistical method used. When a result is reported as not significant, it did not reach the .05 level. Since the descriptive data were incomplete or indefinite in some instances, the results are reported in terms of percentages. The latter pertains only when N is over 50; below that, actual numbers are given.

Results

Before dealing specifically with the issue of delirium and the nature of the precipitating stress, the characteristics and background features will be outlined.

CHARACTERISTICS OF THE SYNDROMES

As shown in Fig. 1, 64% of the postpartum psychiatric syndromes (PPS) experienced the onset of illness within the first 10 postpartum days. The median onset was 4 days postpartum (range: 10 days before delivery to 89 days postpartum). Of the 4 patients whose illness began before delivery, the symptoms did not become incapacitation until after delivery. Sixteen patients had the onset of distress on the *first* day postpartum. This finding militates against the so-called "latency period" of 3 days[14] as a supposed physiological protective period prior to the decrement of various hormones.

The diagnostic breakdown, which reflects the discharge diagnosis of the responsible psychiatrist, is given below.

Schizophrenic reaction	51
Neurotic depressive reaction	24
Personality disorder	11
Psychoneurotic reaction	4
Manic depressive reaction	4
Psychotic depressive reaction	2
Other	3

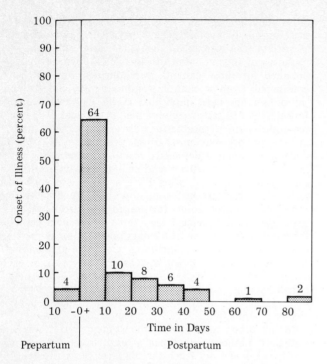

Figure 1.   Graph indicates time relationship of delivery to onset of illness.

No patient was diagnosed as having an acute brain syndrome or a delirium. Although there was a predominance of schizophrenic reactions, this label was often found wanting: (1) many psychiatrists preferred the terms "schizoaffective" or "atypical psychotic reaction," and (2) even though the official psychiatric nomenclature in the United States contains no term for PPS, such as "postpartum depression" or "postpartum psychosis," the description "postpartum" was nevertheless appended to the discharge diagnosis in 66 of the cases.

The following symptoms, centering around delirioid phenomena, were tabulated. Confusion, often marked by uncertainty and indecision, was present in 91.7% of the patients. Disorientation to time (more than 2 days off) was present in 19.1%, but only 2.2% were disoriented to place. Depersonalization, "dreamy" states, *deja vu*, misidentification, and distractability were common in those patients disoriented to time. Changes in time sense were prevalent in 89.7%. Both in perception of the passage of time and the orientation in time according to past, present, and future were often distorted, as has been noted.[15] As one patient stated, "I am going so far into the past that I cannot hold onto the present." Of the patients, 81% had insomnia; 63.4% were excited and restless. Irritability occurred in 94.6%, especially when the mothers were frustrated by their infants. Rapid changes in mood, fluctuating from tears to gaiety in matter of minutes, took place in 79.7%. Inexplicable crying occurred in 94.5%. Feelings of shame, helplessness, and depression were the most pervasive affects, often resulting from a feeling of inadequacy.

Thus, the essential characteristics consist of an early puerperal onset of a schizophreniform or depressive illness—marked by labile mood, shame, changes in time sense, and confusion (without disorientation) in the majority of cases.

PREDISPOSING AND BACKGROUND FACTORS

In considering predisposition, the most important finding was that of a high recurrence rate of postpartum distress. (1) Soon after their *first* delivery, 34 patients required psychiatric care; 30 experienced severe "postpartum blues" (lasting more than 2 weeks); 11, slight to moderate "postpartum blues" (lasting less than 2 weeks); 11, no reaction; and no data on 14 for the first puerperium. This degree of distress is in contrast to the Yalom *et al.*[16] study of 39 normal postpartum women in whom crying spells, though occurring in 67% of the women, were largely limited to less than 1-2 hr.; also, depression usually remitted within 24 hr. (2) The median duration of the previous "postpartum blues" (defined as distress precluding normal every-day activity) for the present sample was 30 days (range: 1-86), indicating quite a prolonged duration compared to the often-noted transitory reactions, which rarely last over 1-2 days.[16-18] (3) This tendency toward recurrent postpartum distress can best be seen in the high percentage of pregnancies resulting in either "postpartum blues" or PPS. Here, for each multigravidous woman, the percentage of pregnancies complicated by such reactions was calculated. Of a total of 313 pregnancies for 81 multigravidous women, the mean percentage of postpartum emotional disturbances ("post-partum blues" plus PPS) per individual was 76.1% (S.D. 29.9). The mean percentage of "postpartum blues," considered separately, was 31.8% (S.D. 25.6). The mean percentage of PPS per individual was 43.5% (S.D. 25.6), indicating roughly half of the pregnancies necessitated postpartum psychiatric care.

Other background features will be briefly mentioned: 51% of the women knew of severe emotional postpartum reactions among their relatives (23.3% for their mothers; 16.3% for their sisters). Further, 50% gave a history of severe premenstrual tension, i.e., anxiety, irritability, and depression that disrupted their every-day activities; 31% had moderate premenstrual tension. The position of the patient within the sibling order of her family paralleled Jansson's findings[10] of fewer eldest children: 41% came from the youngest third; 35% from the middle third; and 24% from the eldest third.

THE QUESTION OF DELIRIUM

In view of the prevalent but untested notion that PPs represent acute organic brain syndromes[2,10] secondary to puerperal metabolic abnormalities, the following negative results militate against this assumption. (1) Despite confusion and disorientation ($p < .01$) in the 18 patients admitted within 2 weeks after delivery (the period of rapid endocrine changes), there was no significant difference between the performance of these patients and the later admissions on the serial-7 and digit-span tests. Moreover, the performance of each group of PPS on these cognitive tests did not differ from 50 other psychiatric patients. (2) Of the 15 patients who had EEGs to rule out clinically

TABLE 1   *Classification of Postpartum Precipitating Stress*

	Major %	Moderate %	Slight %	None %
Conflict over mothering	68.0	26.0	4.0	2.0
Problems with identification				
Ambivalent identification with patient's own mother	49.0	39.0	4.0	8.0
Overidentification with baby	8.0	39.1	12.1	40.5
Difficulty with masculine-feminine identification	7.6	51.2	24.3	16.6
Distorted communication networks				
Conflicting messages	25.0	59.2	2.6	13.1
Lack of feedback from baby	6.8	50.0	1.7	41.3
Lack of rewards from husband	12.1	21.2	19.8	46.5
Difficulty in coping with task of mothering	30.0	58.0	3.0	9.0
Denial of mothering role	12.3	33.7	14.6	39.3
Hostility toward infant				
Primary*	2.4	14.6	13.4	69.5
Secondary	14.1	61.1	7.0	17.6
Object loss	10.0	24.0	22.0	43.0
Loss of baby	5.0	9.0	2.0	84.0
Loss of own mother or motherfigure	2.0	16.0	3.0	79.0
Loss of pregnant state	8.6	10.7	4.3	76.3
Other loss (includes change of plans)	13.0	16.0	3.0	68.0
Accentuation of "entrapment" feelings	15.3	48.3	10.9	27.4
Miscellaneous	6.6	43.3	33.3	46.6

*Hostility central in precipitating or maintaining illness.

suspected deliria, the mean frequency of alpha rhythm was 9.00 (S.D. 2.83). There was no instance of EEG slowing indicative of a delirium.[11] (3) For the 14 PBI determinations, the mean value was 5.5 μg. (S.D. 1.24), which is clearly within normal limits. (4) Finally, over the course of a subsequent partus, the 6 patients with a history of a previous PPS showed no significant pre- to postpartum differences on cognitive and EEF tests when compared to results in the 9 control subjects. Three of the 6 patients went on to require postpartum psychiatric treatment, but their EEDs, serial-7 and digit-span on the third day postpartum were not different from the prepartum-testing results. One patient developed an acute schizophrenic reaction on the fourth day postpartum—1 day after the second battery of tests, which showed no change from the prepartum exams. Three weeks postpartum, when the patient was still psychotic, she was given another EEG, which did not differ from her previous two.

Thus, there was no evidence for a classical delirium. It is still possible, however, that puerperal endocrine changes in these women may produce a syndrome similar to a "steroid psychosis," in which cognitive impairment and EEG slowing may not take place.[19] Future research should be directed to those hormones such as progesterone and prolactin which are known to influence maternal behavior in animals.[20] Along this line, there was evidence for symptomatologic changes in connection with the first puerperal menstrual period and with the ingestion of progestational agents for contraceptive purposes. Also, the median onset of illness at four days postpartum coincides with lactational changes.

NATURE OF THE PRECIPITATING STRESS

Table 1 delineates some of the most frequent psychological difficulties reported by the patients in this study. The percentages represent the totals within the categories of the data sheet. Each category was broken down into major, moderate, slight, and none in order to give a rough quantification of the degree of distress experienced. The classification is therefore primarily a convenient descriptive scheme which was found to be highly relevant to the patients' paramount concerns. The sub-categories overlap, but the "major" difficulties of the main headings are mutually exclusive: thus, 68% of the women had a major conflict with mothering, 10% with an object loss, 15.3% with "entrapment," and 6.6% with miscellaneous factors. These various categories will be illustrated by citing case histories and adding other supporting evidence.

Conflict Over Mothering was the area of greatest difficulty for the majority of women. Some of the most prominent features are exemplifed by the following case history.

A 17-year-old primiparous woman was admitted on the twelfth day postpartum in a confused, semicatatonic state. Pregnancy and delivery had been normal, except for some hyperemesis during the first trimester. Two days postpartum, the patient became irritable and was given to mood swings. Three days postpartum, when she was to leave the hospital with her baby, she had a 4-hr crying spell, feeling that she wanted to be "taken care of" and "didn't want to be a mother" because she felt "incapable." When home, her husband noted that she became nervous when the infant cried and would not feed it. She claimed that she herself could "feel" when the infant was hungry. Six days postpartum, the patient stated that the baby was dead and asserted that she and her own mother were the same person. Later, she felt that her mother was "coming to strangle" her, though she had not seen her mother since age 6, when her mother was committed to a state hospital. The patient talked of wanting to go back to her childhood and, in the emergency department, was observed in the fetal position, asking if she could go "pee-pee" and "poo-poo." She kept calling for her mother and repeatedly misidentified the nurse as "Mommy." History revealed that, after the commitment of her own mother, the patient had two step-mothers, both of whom rejected her. Her confusion of her own identity in relationship to these various maternal figures was a pervasive and recurrent theme.

This case portrays many of the sub-categories under the main heading of "conflict over mothering" in Table 1, which will be discussed separately.

Ambivalent Identification with the Patient's Own Mother: The re-activation of problems of maternal identification in the above case history is typical, and 88% of the women experienced major to moderate difficulties in this sphere. The evidence for this "ambivalent identification" was derived essentially from the following findings: (1) the patients' vociferous repudiation of their own mothers (or mother-substitutes) as adequate models, (2) their recognition of an increased tendency to behave similarly to their own mothers since their delivery, and (3) their dread of becoming like their own mothers. Since this category turned out to be the most important, it will be dealt with at some length.

The accentuation of identification during the puerperium was often portrayed by the patients taking on symptoms which their mothers had. For example, one patient felt she was a "dead mother" and that her nose, cheeks, and skin were being "eaten away"; her own mother had died of lupus erythematosus when the patient was 8 years old. Another patient developed "spells" and "jerks," even though her neurological and EEG exams were normal; her own mother had been incapacitated with epileptic attacks. The following case history exemplifies the re-enactment of a symbiotic, hostile tie between mother and child during the puerperium.

A 20-year-old primiparous woman was admitted on the seventh day postpartum after a serious suicidal attempt. Chief complaint: "I was afraid I would hurt the child." On the second day postpartum, the patient developed incapacitating anxiety about her ability to care for the infant, fear that her mother would usurp her role, and guilt over hostility toward the child. She openly denounced her own mother and refused all contact with her. She was confused and felt that her "mind had stopped—it was as if time did not exist."

History revealed that the patient had an interlocking relationship with a schizophrenic mother who was plagued with obsessions about being a "bad mother." The patient was an only child and, at that, an "accident." Ever since the patient was 6 years old, she had assumed the role of caring for her own mother. During the patient's pregnancy, the mother prophesied that her daughter's child would turn out to be a contorted animal, reflecting the mother's obsession with sodomy. After delivery, the daughter felt her mother's "thoughts had gotten to her." She, too, felt like a "bad mother," resembling not only her own mother, but also her

controlling, rigid maternal grandmother. About 1 month after the patient came into the hospital, the patient's mother had to be admitted because of obsessional guilt for having "caused" her daughter's illness.

This type of matriarchal line of controlling, rejecting mother (going back to the grandmother) was a definite finding in 7 other patients and suggestive in many others.

Using Schaefer's circumplex model for classifying maternal behavior,[21] 58.3% of the patients' mothers were described as concomitantly controlling and rejecting; 80.2% were rejecting; 70.0% were controlling. The breakdown, based on the patients' descriptions plus actual observations of many of the patients' mothers, is as follows: permissive-rejecting, 12; permissive-accepting, 3; controlling-rejecting, 56; controlling-accepting, 9; permissive, 1; controlling, 2; rejecting, 9; accepting, 4; insufficient data, 4.

Further data on the patients' mothers suggest that these women were inadequate models for mothering: 13% had been judged psychotic at one time; 30.4% received psychiatric care; 23.6% suffered a severe postpartum emotional disturbance; and 23% were either separated or divorced. Twenty-seven of the mothers had used symptoms of illness to control their families. Fourteen were dead at the time of their daughter's puerperal mental illness; 7 died before their daughters reached the age of 12.

Although control data are needed, developmental clues suggest that some patients may have repudiated the mothering role early in childhood. For example, 35% had played with dolls only slightly or not at all. One patient's favorite pastime was to stick pins in dolls and imagine them suffering. Another had a fetish for wax dolls, which she would melt on the radiator. Of the patients, 39% had served as baby-sitter only slightly or not at all. On the other hand, 8 patients had been forced to assume the role of "child mother" because of their own mothers' absence, death, or chronic illness.

Finally, 3 patients had a "postpartum equivalent reaction" secondary to the adoption of an infant. Each of these patients, within a few days after the arrival of the baby, became confused and conflicted about her capacity to mother, showing great lability of affect. Each had a controlling mother who had inhibited them from making decisions of their own. Curiously, all 3 patients were highly disorganized and perplexed, despite that fact that no puerperal physiological changes were taking place, suggesting that such confusion can have a nonorganic basis. The following case captures the essential features of these "postpartum equivalent reactions," which were remarkably similar to the other patients with an ambivalent identification with a controlling-rejecting mother.

A 41-year-old social worker, who had been childless for her 5 years of marriage, became giddy and confused upon the arrival of her adopted male infant—an event she had been anticipating for 18 months. Within 2 days, she was insomniac, garrulous, and felt inadequate as a mother, fearing that she might harm the child. She thought that her mother-in-law was trying to usurp her role as mother. On admission, she was unable to do serial-7 or digit-span tests and manifested flight of ideas, labile affect, and auditory hallucinations. Background history revealed that the patient had a domineering, cold mother who inhibited the patient from making any decisions of her own. The mother was described as a "large, dominant woman, a licensed real estate broker, the undisputed head of the household" who apparently dictated how the patient should look after her two younger sisters—a role that the patient resented. The patient's psychiatrist volunteered that the precipitating stress was the assumption of the mothering-feminine role which carried with it the identification with her own rejecting mother.

Overidentification with the Baby was a major problem for 8% of the patients and a moderate problem for another 39.1%. This difficulty largely revolved around changing from the role of being cared for to assuming the caretaking role. As one patient stated, "I would like to be a child again and start all over, but I'm not the baby . . . I'm the mother." Another patient mumbled that she was "way back in the past" and her behavior mimicked that of a baby: she could not hold her head up; she cried in a high-pitched breathless whine; she gurgled and patted herself on the chest while learning forward to induce burping.

Difficulty with Masculine-Feminine Identification: About 8% of the patients openly asserted that they would rather have been men, and another 51.2% stated that they were more like their fathers than their mothers. A severe tomboy phase, often extending into high school, was reported by 70.6%.

Turning now from identification problems to distorted communication networks, the pervasive theme was the lack of positive reinforcement in mothering the infant.

Conflicting messages was a severe problem for 25% and a moderate difficulty for another 59.2% of the patients. Here, conflicting and ambiguous communications came not only from the infant but also from other significant objects, such as the patient's mother, sisters, mother-in-law, and husband, who often gave insistent but discrepant advice as to how to care for the infant. Moreover, the new mother was often reluctant to take any advice or to give any hint of her inadequacy, for she felt that her conduct as a mother was a test for her worth and femininity.

Many mothers were perplexed also by the infant's crying, as portrayed by the following patient's statement: "When they cry, you don't know what they're crying for. . . . You do everything under the sun you can think of to do, and they still cry. . . . I get upset after a few minutes. . . . I feel that I am not being a good mother when I don't know what to do for him. I feel stupid, and it makes me mad to take care of him because I don't seem to be meeting his needs. I don't know what he wants half of the time, and I feel stupid when I hear other people tell me what it is."

Crying was often interpreted as angry rejection of the mother coupled with a desperate demand for help; this sometimes bordered on a classical "double-bind" situation in that the mother felt she had to respond despite the frequent possibility of failure to appease the infant.

Lack of Feedback from the Baby: Not only was interaction with the infant perplexing, but also it consisted of a rather global form of communication, punctuated by either gross distress and crying versus quiescence, with little positive reinforcement for the mother during the early puerperium. The infant's incapacity to give specific feedback and to signal for specific needs was a major difficulty for 6.8%

of the patients and a moderate difficulty for another 50%. Some mothers felt as if they were "talking to a dummy" or dealing with a "vegetable." There was not the "give-and-take" of adult interaction; rather the axis of reinforcing activity was from mother to infant, especially during the first month postpartum when the babies evinced little smiling and cooing.

Since the infants gave them little feedback on their mothering activities, the new mothers had to turn either to themselves or to others for guidance and rewards. Because many of the patients found little reward for mothering through identifying with their own mothers, they frequently became extremely dependent on the approval of other persons, especially the husband. If the latter remained detached or overly critical, the patient was left to herself again, puzzled by her lack of warmth and affection for her baby.

Lack of Rewards from Husband: Some of the husbands remained surprisingly uninvolved in their wives' struggle with mothering. It was rare for 12.1% of the husbands to give reinforcement for their wives' mothering duties, and another 21.2% were moderately disengaged. Five husbands increased their outside activities, such as taking on extra jobs, writing a book, etc., in order to get away from the home. This detachment is typified by one husband who nonchalantly left his wife off at the hospital before she delivered each of her 3 children, while he returned to work.

Difficulty in Coping with the Task of Mothering was a major problem for 30% and a moderate problem for 58% of the patients. Many patients felt overwhelmed by the demands placed upon them after the birth of the baby: not only did they have to care for the infant, but also they had to attend to their houses, meals, laundry, husbands, and interested guests and relatives. Moreover, if they had other children, the arrival of the infant often prompted regression and sibling rivalry in the older children, who then made even greater demands on the mother. A vicious circle frequently ensued, in which the mother's distress augmented the children's distress, and vice versa. Some patients felt unduly stressed by having too many young children to care for at one time.

Also included in this category are women who felt shamed because breast feeding was not adequate, guilty because of illness of the infant, hostile because they were not getting the help they expected from the husband, mother, etc. Of course, any fatigue or confusion—whether induced by physiological or psychological factors—aggravated this difficulty in coping.

Denial of Mothering Role: This was severe in 12.3% and moderate in another 33.7% of the patients. One patient was repulsed by the task of kissing her children good-night; her major concern was to "get away from the kids." Eleven patients attempted to get jobs outside the home within the first 2 months postpartum. When denial was prominent, these mothers responded to their infants mechanically, shunning emotional involvement and, consequently, getting little satisfaction from mothering. Since it was practically impossible to carry out this denial of mothering in the postpartum period, the use of this defense precipitated even more difficulty.

Hostility Toward the Infant: Only 2.4% of the patients had severe "primary" hostility toward their infants, i.e., overt fears of actively inflicting harm on them, which were central in precipitation of maintaining illness. Another 14.6% had fleeting thoughts of harming their infants. Such thoughts, especially that of infanticide, transfixed the patients with guilt; they frequently ruminated, "How could a mother have such thoughts? Why would a mother harm her helpless child?" Another 14.1% of the patients had major and 61.1% moderate "secondary" hostility toward their infants, i.e., anger stemming from a host of other conflicts and manifested as wishes and actions to leave the infant rather than actively to harm him. Along these lines, most of our postpartum patients had difficulty in tolerating and expressing their own aggressive ideas—for fear of rejection or disapproval of others. And for many, any anger toward the infant was unthinkable and shameful.

In summary, the conflict over mothering stemmed largely from an ambivalent identification with a controlling-rejecting mother which led to the repudiation of the mothering role, especially if the reinforcements from the concurrent environment were sparse and ambiguous.

Object Loss. The actual or threatened loss of a significant object constituted a major precipitating stress for 10% of the patients. Patients were included in this general category of precipitating stress if they had either an overwhelming object loss, or an incapacitating admixture of some of the below-listed types of object losses seen in the puerperium.

Loss of Baby was a major precipitating stress for 5% of the patients. Two infants died; 3 were given up for adoption. In another 9%, there was a threatened loss of the baby, through either infantile illness or intervention by a relative.

Loss of Own Mother or Mother-Figure constituted a major stress for 2% of the patients; another 16% experienced moderate difficulty because their mothers were no longer available, or because the birth of the infant reawakened memories of loss of their mothers.

Loss of Pregnant State: About 9% of the patients experienced this as a major stress. These patients stated that they wanted to be pregnant again, and that they missed the felicitous attention they received when they were pregnant. Included within this category are 5 patients who were upset by the change in "body image" upon delivery.

Other Loss: This residual category turned out to be quite important for 13% of the patients and moderately significant for another 16%. A frequent finding was the necessity of giving up some cherished and carefully laid out plans for the future after the arrival of the baby. For example, the care of the infant interfered with the pursuit of a career more than some mothers had anticipated. Or, a 43-year-old woman was preparing for travels and rest with her retired husband when another pregnancy appeared unexpectedly. Other factors consisted of the loss of freedom, loss of youth, and the necessity of moving from a familiar home to a new setting which would accommodate the infant.

There were no instances of the loss of the husband, either through death, separation, or divorce during the puerperium. But, as noted above, the husbands were frequently detached.

Accentuation of "Entrapment" Feelings. The feeling of "entrapment" was a major precipitating stress in 15.5% of the women and a moderate stress for another 48.3%. The arrival of the baby ensnared the mother in a marriage or other social situation from which she wanted to be free. In such instances there was often a more overt battle between husband and patient, as opposed to the above-mentioned aloofness and disengagement of the husband.

Miscellaneous. About 7% of the patients had major and 43.3% moderate difficulties which resided in conflicts other than those mentioned. Examples of this category are fearful states associated with physical illness of the patient (such as postpartum hemorrhage), competition with sisters and friends, financial difficulties, etc.

Comment

An adequate explanation of the postpartum psychiatric syndromes must account for the following essential features, found in this study and many others: the onset of illness soon after delivery, the high postpartum recurrence rate of mental illness in these women, and the marked confusion, shame, and labile affect. A metabolic derangement—recurring during rapid endocrine changes each puerperium and resulting in a delirium—could explain these findings.[2] But cognitive and EEG tests produced no evidence for a delirium.[11] Moreover, since 3 patients developed a similar syndrome in connection with the adoption of an infant, it is doubtful that organic factors alone explain the syndrome. Victoroff[5] reports 3 and Tetlow[4] describes 6 other postadoption psychoses, claiming that they were similar to those of their puerperal psychotic patients. While it is still possible that hormonal changes may make these women more vulnerable during the puerperium, it may prove fruitful to entertain a more *psychological* hypothesis. Briefly, the postulate is this: A conflict in assuming the mothering role, activated by caring for a helpless, relatively noncommunicative infant, led to *identity diffusion*[22] in these postpartum women. This factor may have accounted for the prominent confusion. The mothering of a noncommunicative infant hindered self-definition, for there was a relative lack of interpersonal feedback and less distinction between "self" and "other" in the early mother-child relationship. Moreover, identity as a mother was impaired because these women either lacked adequate maternal models or repudiated their own mothers as models.

Let us examine the postulate in terms of the basic findings. (1) The onset of illness took place within the first month postpartum for 82% of the PPS. This is the period when the infant is most noncommunicative. The median onset of 4 days postpartum coincides with the time most women were discharged from postnatal hospital care to assume major responsiblity for their infants. Thus, the onset of illness may not wholly relate to puerperal metabolic changes, but rather may stem from the conflicting messages and ambiguities surrounding the care of the infant. Over 75% of the patients stated that these factors were a major to moderate stress. In particular, they found infant crying perplexing in that it was interpreted as raging rejection as well as desperate need of the mother.

(2) The high recurrence rate may also relate to the ambiguities of communication and identification which reoccur postpartum in connection with mothering a neonate. For the sample of multiparous women as a whole, 43.5% of the pregnancies of each woman (expressed as an average) resulted in postpartum psychiatric care. This contrasts markedly with the low incidence of PPS in the general population, which is roughly 1 per 100 deliveries.[2]

(3) The prominent confusion, shame, and labile affect could also be explained on the basis of a conflict over mothering, resulting in identity diffusion. Confusion was found in 91.7%, but in contrast to the usual findings of an acute brain syndrome, disorientation to time was present in 19.1% and only 2.2% were disoriented to place. Carlson[23] has described an acute nonorganic confusional state in relatively healthy college students, usually arising at the time of psychosocial shifts and new commitments. Most of the students had previously formed a compliant, dependent relationship, largely through guilt and fear, with their unstable, rejecting, and controlling parents. When faced with an adult commitment, they found they had inadequate repertoires and personal identity to meet the task—resulting in feelings of failure, irritability, and confusion. Similar feelings of inadequacy, confusion, and dependency on domineering yet rejecting mothers were also noted in this and other postpartum samples,[4-6,24] but the possible interrelation of these factors have not been spelled out. Since 68% of the postpartum women gave evidence for a major conflict over mothering, it is possible that the ambivalent and vacillating commitment to mothering led to the acute confusional state. But why?

Essentially, by disavowing their own mothers, these women were bereft of a plan of action in a situation which demanded action, leading to untoward emotion and confusion.[25] Their sense of identity and feelings of competence became fragmented in that they were mothers without knowing how to act. The following postulates tie together the most prominent stresses found in this study (Table 1) into a process which may explain the onset of identity diffusion in these women. (1) Giving birth to a neonate who has extensive needs committed these women to mothering. (2) Since the young infant was incapable of specifying guidelines for his care, yielding little positive reinforcement, the new mothers became more dependent on the images and plans of action provided by significant maternal figures of her past and present. Her own mother was an important reference point. (3) This tendency to seek guidelines from maternal figures was further accentuated if: her own mother had been controlling, as 70% of them were, thereby inhibiting the patient from developing self-direction and repertoires of her own; when the concurrent environment offered little ongoing reinforcement for her mothering activities, as evidenced by the lack of rewards from the husband and the discrepant advice from many others; and when current stresses, resulting in object loss, frustration, and feelings of "entrapment," prompted the woman to recapture earlier periods of equilibrium, i.e., to regress—in this way, their own mothers' maternal behavior increasingly became a reference or model for their own program of action. (4) However, since their own mothers had often repudiated the mothering role, or were judged as inadequate maternal models, the increased identification entailed conflict—it was an ambivalent identification. Moreover, since 80% of their own mothers had rejected the patients, the identification often led to the new mothers' rejection of their own infants, despite conscious wishes to be unlike their own mothers. As Victoroff states, ". . . they . . . reject their children as they themselves were rejected."[5] The identity of the new mothers in this situation therefore vacillated: they felt helpless without the images of their mothers, yet ashamed when like their own mothers. Indecision, perplexity, and a loss of a sense of personal efficacy mounted. Uncertain in their role as mother and yet without a positive maternal model, these women felt lost and confused.

In essence, then, it is postulated that identity diffusion, stemming from identification and modeling problems in assuming the care of a relatively noncommunicative infant, may account for the early puerperal onset, the high recurrence rate, and the syndrome of labile affect, as well as feelings of shame and confusion in these postpartum women.

Conclusion: a note on treatment

Ideally, the patient should not be separated from her child, for this often confirms her suspicion that she is an inadequate mother. Useful tacks are getting family members to assist the patient with mothering, or, with hospitalized patients, allowing for frequent visits with the children and even admitting the infant with the mother. A number of institutions[26,27] have found the latter procedure to be of value and, of 16 joint mother-infant admissions to our hospital, it was found beneficial in 10 instances in that continual reinforcement and encouragement of mothering activities helped these patients find themselves as mothers. The staff's concern for the infant, rather than for the mother, occurred with 2 joint admissions and varied with 4 others, thereby aggravating the mother's shame and feeling of incompetence. Thus, careful attention should be directed to bringing the baby in at the proper time: when the mother, staff, and other patients are prepared to reinstate the patient as mother.

Summary

The study of 100 women, whose onset of psychiatric illness began from 1 month prepartum to 3 months postpartum, delineated the following features of "postpartum" psychiatric disorders. 1. The peak onset was close to the time of delivery (median onset, 4 days postpartum), indicating the psychiatric illness is not incidental to the puerperium. 2. The high recurrence rate of postpartum distress suggests that these women were vulnerable during most of their puerperal periods. 3. For the most part, the rapidly fluctuating affective and confusional symptoms were not adequately described by the usual nosological categories.[2,10] 4. Lack of difference between these patients and control subjects in performance on serial-7 subtractions and digit-span tests as well as in frequency analysis of the EEG militates against the existence of a toxic delirious state. 5. It is postulated that the high incidence of confusion most likely stems from identity diffusion, centering around a conflict in assuming the mothering role. 6. In the majority of patients, this conflict appeared to result from the patients' repudiation of their own mothers as adequate models. 7. Even though the patients' maternal identification was ambivalent, the puerperium intensified the need for maternal models as the infant was incapable of communicating guidelines for his care. 8. Hormonal changes may make some women more vulnerable, but since 3 patients became bewildered shortly after the adoption of an infant, it appears that the psychological conflict over mothering can precipitate a confusional syndrome in the absence of postpartum physiological changes.

REFERENCES

1. Pugh, T. F., Jerath, B. K., Schmidt, W. M., and Reed, R. B. Rates of mental disease related to childbearing. *New Eng J Med 268:*1224, 1963.
2. Hamilton, J. A. *Postpartum Psychiatric Problems.* Mosby, St. Louis, 1962.
3. Brew, M. F., and Seidenberg, R. Psychotic reactions associated with pregnancy and childbirth. *J Nerv Ment Dis 111:*408, 1950.
4. Tetlow, C. Psychoses of childbearing. *J Ment Sci 101:*629, 1955.
5. Victoroff, V. M. Dynamics and management of para partum neuropathic reactions. *Dis Nerv Syst 13:*291, 1952.
6. Benedek, T. *Psychosexual Functions in Women.* Ronald, New York, 1952.
7. Bibring, G. L., Dwyer, T. F., Huntington, D. S., and Valenstein, A. F. "A Study of the Psychological Processes in Pregnancy and of the Earliest Mother—Child Relationship." In *The Psychoanalytic Study of the Child.* International Universities Press, New York, 1961, vol. 16, p. 9.
8. Deutsch, H. "Motherhood." In *Psychology of Women.* Grune, New York, 1945, vol. 2.
9. Romano, J. Psychosocial aspects of obstetrical-gynecological practice: Implications for education and research. *Bull Sloane Hosp Wom 10:*267, 1964.
10. Jansson, B. Psychic insufficiencies associated with childbearing. *Acta Psychiat Scand (Suppl) 172:*1, 1964.
11. Engel, G. L., and Romano, J. Delirium, a syndrome of cerebral insufficiency. *J. Chronic Dis 9:*260, 1959.
12. Benson, R. B. Endocrinology of the puerperium. *Clin Obstet Gynec 5:*639, 1963.
13. Engel, G. L., Romano, J., Ferris, E. B., Webb, J. P., and Stevens, C. D. A simple method of determining frequency spectrums in the electroencephalogram. *Arch Neurol Psychiat 51:*134, 1944.
14. Karnosh, L. J., and Hope, J. M. Puerperal psychoses and their sequelae. *Amer J Psychiat 94:*537, 1937.
15. Melges, F. T., and Fougerousse, C. E., Jr. Time sense, emotions, and acute mental illness. *J Psychiat Res 4:*127, 1966.
16. Yalom, I. D., Moos, R. H., Lunde, D. T., and Hamburg, D. A. The "postpartum blues" syndrome: description and related variables. Unpublished data.
17. Pleshette, S., Asch, S. S., and Chase, J. A study of anxieties during pregnancy, labor, the early and late puerperium. *Bull NY Acad Med 32:*436, 1956.
18. Robin, A. A. The psychological changes of normal parturition. *Psychiat Quart 36:*129, 1962.
19. Glaser, G. H. EEG activity and adrenal cortical dysfunction. *Electroenceph Clin Neurophysiol 10:*366, 1958.
20. Riddle, O. Prolactin or progesterone as key to parental behavior: A review. *Anim Behav 11:*419, 1963.
21. Schaefer, E. S. A circumplex model for maternal behavior. *J Abnorm Psychol 59:*226, 1959.
22. Erikson, E. H. "Identity and the Life Cycle." In *Psychology Issues,* International Universities Press, New York, 1959, vol. 1.
23. Carlson, H. B. Characteristics of an acute confusional state in college students. *Amer J Psychiat 114:*900, 1958.
24. Ostwald, P. F., and Regan, P. F. Psychiatric disorders associated with childbirth. *J Nerv Ment Dis 125*153, 1957.
25. Pribram, K. H., and Melges, F. T. "Emotion: The Search for Control." In *Handbook of Clinical Neurology,* Vinken, P. J., and Bruyn, G. W., Eds. North-Holland Publishing Co., Amsterdam. (In Press.)
26. Grunebaum, H. U., and Weiss, J. L. Psychotic mothers and their children: Joint admission to an adult psychiatric hospital. *Amer J Psychiat 119:*927, 1963.
27. Baker, A. A., Morison, M., Game, J. A., and Thorpe, J. G. Admitting schizophrenic mothers with their babies. *Lancet 29:*237, 1961.

43 *Psychological investigation of habitual abortion*

Elaine R. Grimm

A single spontaneous abortion or miscarriage is usually caused by random factors operating only during that particular pregnancy, and according to Eastman, there are 87 chances in 100 that the next pregnancy will result in a term infant.[6] However, by the time a woman has had three successive miscarriages, a recurrent factor is suspected, and the chances of a succeeding term pregnancy are only 16 in 100. Virtually all authorities agree that after four miscarriages, the chances are less thatn 6 in 100. It has been estimated that the habitual-abortion syndrome, defined as the occurrence of three or more successive spontaneous abortions, is responsible for the loss of 50,000 fetal lives each year in the United States alone. In the majority of cases no abortigenic pathologic changes can

Reprinted from Elaine R. Grimm, "Psychological Investigation of Habitual Abortion," Psychosomatic Medicine 24:4, 1962, pp. 369-378. From the Department of Obstetrics and Gynecology, New York Hospital—Cornell Medical Center, New York, N. Y. The study reported in this article was supported by grants from the Commonwealth Fund and the Mental Health Study Section of the National Institutes of Health (M-2340).

be demonstrated, and obstetricians have become increasingly impressed by the importance of emotional factors as the recurrent theme in the development of this syndrome.[1,2,5,9,12,13,22,26]

As the first systematic interdisciplinary approach to the problem, a research program was initiated 6 years ago in the Psychosomatic Unit of the New York Lying-In Hospital to study the personality characteristics of women subject to habitual abortion and to determine the amenability of this syndrome to psychotherapy. The largest series of these patients ever studied has been and is currently under investigation. Their average number of previous spontaneous abortions is four. A consistent "success" rate, i.e., a term pregnancy, of 80 per cent following the use of psychotherapy alone is significantly higher than the rate of spontaneous cure and has already established the effectiveness of this form of treatment.[14-16]

In evaluating the patients to determine whether there are identifiable personality characteristics which distinguish habitual aborters from other women seen in obstetrical practice, psychological tests are but parallel to the clinical data of the psychiatrist obstetrician.[14-16] The specific aim of this paper will be to describe those characteristics, as reflected on psychological tests, which significantly discriminate between (1) habitual aborters and comparions patients, (2) habitual aborters with no known organic basis for their abortions and a small group having an organic basis, and (3) habitual aborters before and after successful therapy.

Subjects

The study group consists of the first 70 habitual aborters referred to the project. (Many more have been tested since that time and will be used in later cross-validation research.) Both the average and the median number of previous spontaneous abortions was 4. No known selection factor operated in the choice of patients for study, since all who presented themselves were accepted for evalutaion and treatment, provided that they could document at least three successive spontaneous abortions and that they were not pregnant at that time. Preconceptional evaluation was considered preferable to evaluation during a pregnancy, chiefly because it allowed time for the establishment of a therapeutic relationship before the period of stress. Fifty-one of the patients were classified as "primary aborters," indicating that they had not had a previous pregnancy resulting in the delivery of a viable infant, while the remaining 19 were classified as "secondary aborters," since the onset of the syndrome occurred after the term delivery of one or more viable infants.

The comparison group consists of the first 35 patients tested who had no history of spontaneous abortion. Of this number, 17 were presumably "normal" pregnant women who were tested before the fourth month of pregnancy, while 18 were nonpregnant women referred for some gynecological or obstetrical difficulty of possible psychosomatic origin. None of the analyses to follow showed difference even approaching significance between the two types of comparison patients.

Table 1 provides a description of the study and comparison groups with respect to several variables. There were no significant differences in average or range in respect to age at marriage, education, or I.Q., nor were there differences in distribution of socioeconomic status, cultural background, religion, or race.

The habitual-abortion group was, on the average, almost 4 years older. There was no way of equating this age difference without introducing a strong bias, for while the average age of women seen on the obstetrical service is approximately 25, the aborters would necessarily be somewhat older since the successive abortions have occurred over a period of time. From the fact that their average age at marriage was almost identical to that of the comparison group, it can be assumed that the aborter's age at childbearing would have been about the same, had they not encountered difficulties.

Nine of the 70 habitual aborters, or 13 per cent, were diagnosed, after initial evaluation, as having hypotonia or imparied sphincteric ability of the uterine isthmus.[17] Isthmic hypotonia was diagnosed preconceptionally by balloon studies, and cervical incompetence was confirmed by the observation of prolapsed membranes in the following pregnancy. The data obtained from these 9 patients have been treated separately, and hence the analyses of the group hereafter referred to as "habitual-abortion group" will be based on the remaining 61 cases.

Thus far, 18 patients have been retested after having had a successful pregnancy following psychotherapy. The treatment program, which consisted essentially of a brief and supportive type of psychotherapy before and during pregnancy, has been described in detail elsewhere.[14,15] The thirty-fifth week was chosen as the time for retesting because the fetus was almost certain to be viable from this time on, and the patient could be considered as having lost the original symptom of abortion proneness. It was thought that the results of tests given after delivery would be too contaminated by other factors, i.e., labor, delivery, the experience of taking care of a baby, and the like. In actuality, reaching the thirty-fifth week and delivering a normal, healthy, term baby were synonymous for this group of patients. Another 4 women in the group of 61 also delivered term infants, but because of various difficulties in scheduling, were not retested; these factors were in no way related to the cooperativeness of the patients. Of the origi-

TABLE 1   *Averages of the Habitual-abortion and Comparison Groups on Four Variables*

Group	N	Age	Age at marriage	Years of education	I.Q.
Habitual abortion	70	29.5	22.3	13.1	104.5
Comparison	35	25.9	22.6	13.0	106.9

nal group, 5 women failed to carry the first pregnancy after treatment to term and had spontaneous abortions. The results of the first pregnancy following psychotherapy are, therefore, known for almost half of the original group of habitual aborters, and for those who have become pregnant, the "success" rate was 22 of 27, or 81 per cent. Most of the remaining patients are either still being followed in psychotherapy or are in the early stages of pregnancy at present.

Procedure

All patients were given a battery of tests including the Wechsler-Bellevue, Rorschach, and TAT. Patients who were retested were given only the Rorschach and TAT again at a time 1-3 years after the initial evaluation.

Average total, verbal, and performance I.Q.'s on the Wechsler-Bellevue were computed, as well as average score, vocabulary scatter, and mean scatter for each of the 11 subtests.

The Rorschachs were scored according to the Klopfer method, and the usual percentages, frequencies, and ratios of formal scores were calculated.[10] In addition, the content of the Rorschach responses was analyzed in terms of affective symbolism according to the scoring system developed by De Vos.[3,4] Each response was classified as expressing affect subsumed under one of the following headings: hostility, anxiety, bodily preoccupation, dependency, positive feelings, miscellaneous, and neutral. Under each of these major categories, with the exception of neutral, are 6-14 subheadings describing the affect in finer detail.

Eighteen cards of the original Murray TAT set were used—1, 2, 3GF, 3BM, 4, 5, 6GF, 6BM, 7GF, 7BM, 8Gf, 8BM, 10, 12F, 12M, 13MF, 18GF, and 18BM.[19] The stories were coded according to the classification system devised by Eron.[7] Because of the large number of possible themes on each card, it was not sufficiently fruitful to deal with the frequency of occurrence of specific themes on each card. Two types of analysis were employed: (1) summation scores, or frequency of occurrence throughout the TAT of themes classifiable as hostility, helping, or guilt (for example, a score of 3 on helping themes would indicate that on three cards the patient referred to one person helping another, regardless of the relationship of the helper to the other people in the story or to the patient); (2) reaction time to each card, classified as longer or shorter than the patient's median RT to all the cards. Since the ease or difficulty of handling the cards varies greatly with the stimulus value of the cards themselves, the only meaningful measure is one which highlights the patient's own peculiar difficulties and the differential reactions in the two groups.

All responses were classified by the psychologist in such a way that at the time of scoring, the identity of the patient and the group to which she belonged were not known. When χ^2 values were computed according to the procedure recommended by Guilford (reference S, p. 234), Yates' correction was used whenever the expected frequency for any cell in a 2 × 2 table fell below 10.

Results and discussion

HABITUAL-ABORTION AND COMPARISON GROUPS

Table 2 presents the 10 test indicators which significantly discriminated between the habitual-abortion and comparion groups. The measure used was the number of patients in each of the two groups above and below the cut-off score. The two groups did not differ significantly in I.Q., number of Rorschach responses, length of TAT, or average reaction time to the TAT cards.

Despite the fact that there were no other differences in intellectual functioning, the two measures of scatter analysis and cut-off score used in Table 2 indicate that in general, the abortion-prone women performed more poorly on the picture arrangement test of the Wechsler-Bellevue. The function underlying effectiveness in this subtest has been described by Wechsler as the ability to "size up a total [social] situation"[24] and by Rapaport as the ability to "plan and anticipate" correctly.[20]

Two significant differences appeared in the analysis of the formal Rorschach scores. The habitual aborters gave a far greater number of color-form than form-color responses and a larger number of popular responses. Since the comparison group itself was at or above the expected norm in both respects, the aborters can be considered to have shown an extreme deviation. The first difference indicates lack of control of emotions, lability, and a tendency to act out conflicts.[11,21] The latter finding is characteristic of those who have a socially stereotyped course of associations and overcompliance with the conventional; not only did these patients have, on the whole, good reality testing, but they were geared to excessive conformity and social adaptability.[11,21] This has been described clinically[15] as the habitual aborters' quality of "self compromising compliance."

Analysis of Rorschach content in terms of affective symbolism resulted in significant differences in one major category and in two subcategories. By and large, the abortion-prone women had greater concern about dealing with hostile feelings. From inspection of the data, it became obvious that what was contributing to the aborters' high hostility percentage were *not* those responses indicative of feelings of direct, overt hostility usually given by individuals readily perceived as aggressive (Hor, Hempt, HH, Hdpr) but those indicating indirect hostility and tension concerning its expression (Ha, Hha, Hhat, Hhad, Hsm). Direct hostility responses include percepts in which teeth are used in an act of biting, figures are engaged in competition or in fighting, whether verbal or physical, or there is a depreciation of human figures (ridiculous old man, drunks, two old maids, relatives of Mickey Mouse, and the like). Indirect hostility responses include percepts in which an underlying concern with aggression or destruction is reflected, i.e., weapons, fires, claws, blood, eruptions or explosions, distorted or incomplete figures with parts missing or disunited, or violation of living tissue.[4] As shown by test indicator 5, a significantly greater number of aborters were found to have a preponderance of indirect, tension-laden responses over direct ones. An additional check showed that while there was no difference between the two groups in average percentage of direct, hostile responses, there was a difference, significant at the .05 level, in the average percentage of tension-laden hostility responses, indicating that the aborters showed much more anxiety and build-up of tension about such feelings.

Clinically, these women could not in any sense be des-

TABLE 2   *Test Indicators Discriminating between Habitual Abortion (HA) and Comparison (Comp.) Groups**

| Test indicator | Responses: cut-off score | No. patients | | x^2 | p |
		HA (N = 61)	Comp. (N = 35)		
Wechsler-Bellevue					
1. Picture arrangement	Pt's lowest or 2nd lowest subtest	20	4	4.43	< .05
	Higher performance	41	31		
Rorschach formal scores					
2. Color-form predominance	CF + C > 2FC	28	8	5.00	< .05
	CF + C ≤ 2FC	33	27		
3. Popular responses	P ≥ 6	35	10	7.39	< .01
	P ≤ 5	26	25		
Rorschach content scores					
4. Hostility %	H% ≥ 14%	36	12	5.44	< .02
	H% ≤ 13%	25	23		
5. Indirect vs. direct hostility	Hh + % > Hor + %	42	17	3.84	< .05
	Hh + % ≤ Hor + %	19	18		
6. Oral dependent symbolism	Dor present	26	7	4.99	<..05
	Dor absent	35	28		
TAT summation scores					
7. Helping themes	> 2	21	3	6.72	< .01
	≤ 2	40	32		
8. Guilt themes	> 1	30	9	5.04	< .05
	≤ 1	31	26		
TAT reaction times					
9. Card 8BM	> Pt's median RT	37	13	4.88	< .05
	< Pt's median RT	24	22		
10. Card 18GF	> Pt's median RT	43	17	4.61	< .05
	< Pt's median RT	18	18		
Total Score (10 indicators)	≥ 5	43	4	30.92	< .01
	≤ 4	18	31		

*A total of 109 test indicators or variables was used: 11 W-B subtests; 28 formal Rorschach scores: 7 major Rorschach content categories; 2 types of Rorschach hostility content; 55 minor Rorschach content categories; 3 TAT summation scores: 3 TAT RT's.

cribed as markedly either overtly or covertly hostile. When they did express such feelings, in keeping with the finding at every level that they were highly emotionally reactive, they were most likely to do so by acting out, sporadic explosions when frustrated, or dissolution into weeping. What did distinquish them from the Comparison Group was their greater build-up of tension in dealing with hostile feelings, and because of this, their impaired ability to make a direct, problem-solving attack.

The aborters tended to use oral dependent symbolism more frequently than did the comparison group, and presumably to be more dependent on others for gratification. This group of patients has been described clinically as being "addicted to dependency" on "an overly possessive and protective mother who virtually insisted upon dependent compliance."[16] Of interest is an additional finding concerned with the relationship between Dor scores (oral dependency) and Hor scores (oral aggressiveness). A greater number of habitual aborters than comparison patients had a preponderance of Dor over Hor scores; the difference between groups was significant at .05 level. The hypothesis is suggested that in the comparison group, oral needs and oral aggressiveness were fairly balanced, while in the case of the habitual aborters, oral needs outstripped the aggressiveness with which the satisfaction of such needs was pursued.

The TAT results parallel and add to the results obtained from the Rorschach. Of the three summation scores—aggression, helping, and guilt—the abortion-prone women showed significantly higher scores in two. They were more preoccupied than the comparison patients with helping themes, another indication of their more dependent inclinations, and with guilt themes. The area in which the guilt was focused varied but was often apt to be manifested in connection with sexual themes.

While there was close correspondence between Rorschach and TAT findings in regard to the strength of dependency needs, at first glance it seemed puzzling that the striking Rorschach finding of greater tension about hostility was not reflected in the more frequent occurrence of hostile themes in the TAT's of the habitual aborters. Since however, the Rorschach differentiation was not primarily one of greater amount of hostile affect but of greater anxiety and tension surrounding the presence of such feelings, it was hypothesized that this characteristic would be reflected on the TAT in differences in reaction times rather than in themes. It was predicted that Cards 3BM, 8BM, and 18GF would be most likely to produce such a differential disturbance, since their content so strongly suggests hostility in some form.[1] While the average reaction time was essentially the same for the two groups—21.6 sec. for the comparison, and 20.6 sec. for the habitual abortion group—the *only* two cards to which the aborters had significantly longer reaction times were SBM and 18GF. The comparison group had no significantly longer reaction times. Thus, the TAT results paralleled the Rorschach finding of greater tension about dealing with hostile feelings.

In order to summarize the pattern of scores, a total score was computed, consisting of one point for each of the 10 test indicators. When 5 was set as the critical score, 70 per cent of the aborters, as opposed to 11 per cent of the comparison patients, scored at or above this level. Of the total group of 96 patients, 77 per cent were classified correctly. Thus, approximately four times out of five, aborters could be discriminated from nonaborters on the basis of a pattern of psychological characteristics indicated by the total score.

To summarize, in contrast to the other patients, the abortion-prone women as a group could be characterized as demonstrating: an impairment of the ability to plan and anticipate (Indicator 1); poorer emotional control (Indicator 2); more emphasis on conformity and compliance with the conventional (Indicator 3); greater tension about hostile affect (Indicators 4, 5, 9, 10); stronger feelings of dependency (Indicators 6, 7); and greater proneness to guilt feelings (Indicator 8).

From these test scores, a synthesizing formulation can be offered. The habitual aborters are emotionally reactive, overly compliant women who, when they react with hostility to excessive demands and frustration, cannot openly and directly express the hostility in a way which would help alleviate the frustration, for fear of rejection and guilt. To avoid losing what dependent gratification they have learned to obtain through fulfilling the expectations of others, they continue to react compliantly at the price of an increasing build-up of tension and a subsequent psychosomatic reaction which, for the moment, serves to alleviate the aroused tension.

This formulation substantially agrees with that based on the clinical psychiatric findings reported of these same patients[14-16] and reported in another investigation of a smaller number of patients.[25,26] Three subgroups of these habitual aborters have been distinguished both clinically and psychometrically, as described elsewhere.[18] Suffice it to say that the personality characteristics of these three subgroups represent variations, with differing emphases, on the same basic dynamic theme formulated above. In one group the observed emphasis is on the strength of the dependent, compliant reaction engendered by a mother who demanded this as the condition for her love; in another, on the ease of arousal of guilt feelings fostered by a father who both encouraged and punished sexual acting-out; and in the third, on the degree of frustration and hostility directed at

TABLE 3   *Distribution of Total Scores of Three Groups of Patients*

Total score	Habitual abortion (N = 61)	Isthmic hypotonia (N = 9)	Comparison (N = 35)
≥ 5	43	1	4
≤ 4	18	8	31

the inadequacy of the husband as perceived by these patients. The total score developed from the tests represents a composite picture of the group of abortion-prone women as a whole, but the test indicators most likely to contribute to the total varied slightly from subgroup to subgroup.

RETEST OF HABITUAL-ABORTION GROUP

Table 3 presents the total scores of the 9 habitual aborters who were found to have isthmic hypotonia, as contrasted with those of the habitual-abortion group with no known organic basis for the abortions and those of the comparison group. When 5 or above was used again as the critical score, the difference between the habitual-abortion and isthmic-hypotonia groups was significant at the .01 level (χ^2, 9.68). The difference between the isthmic-hypotonia and comparison groups was not significant. Despite the small number of patients with sphincteric dysfunction of the isthmus, the data they provide are interesting in that they did not typically show the same personality pattern, as measured by the total score, characteristic of the habitual aborters without demonstrable pathologic findings. At present, very little is known about the development of isthmic hypotonia, but further research on the functioning of the uterine isthmus is now in progress.[17] In any event, these 9 women had a demonstrable impairment. The same total score which distinguished the habitual aborters without demonstrable pathologic changes from the comparison patients also discriminated between habitual aborters with and without an identifiable organic basis for the abortions.

RETEST OF HABITUAL-ABORTION GROUP

Table 4 presents the *only* significant changes found in the 109 test indicators calculated from the psychometric records of the 18 "successful" habitual aborters who were tested preconceptionally and retested at the thirty-fifth week of pregnancy. The measure used was the Sign-Rank test of Differences,[8] which provides a test of significance of the direction of change of paired observations. Since it was not possible to calculate the direction of change of the two indicators consisting of a proportion, the direction of change of each side of the proportion was calculated separately.

Seven test indicators changed significantly from one administration of the tests to the next. Four of these seven indicators had been found originally to discriminate between the habitual-abortion and comparison groups, and on all these the retested habitual aborters changed in the direction of the comparison group. The changes could be described as tending in the direction of greater emotional

TABLE 4   Test Indicators Showing Significant Changes in Habitual Aborters When Retested at the Thirty-fifth Week of Pregnancy (N = 18)

Test indicator	Direction of change	p-level, sign rank test
2. CF + C:FC		
CF + C%	No change	
FC%	+	.02
4. Hostility %	−	.01
5. Hh + %: Hor + %		
Hh + %	−	.05
Hor + %	No change	
10. Guilt themes	−	.05
Total Score	−	.01
No. R. Rorschach	−	.01
At %, Rorschach	−	.05
Neutral %, Rorschach	+	.05

TABLE 5   Total Scores of Habitual Aborters Tested Preconceptionally and Retested at the Thirty-fifth Week of Pregnancy (N = 18)*

Total score	First test	Retest
⩾ 5	14	6
⩽ 4	4	12

*χ^2, 6.13, significant at .02 level.

control, less build-up of tension in connection with feelings of hostility, and less guilt. In addition, the patients changed significantly in only three other respects, as shown at the bottom of the Table—giving fewer responses, showing less bodily preoccupation (even though they were approaching delivery), and evidencing more neutral content in their affective symbolism. Moreover, 16 of the 18 patients showed a sharp decrease in total score, a change that was significant at the .01 level. Thus the changes found in the aborters who had lost the symptom were chiefly in the characteristics which originally distinguished them from the comparison group.

When a total score of 5 was used again as the critical score, it can be seen in Table 5 that a majority of the 18 habitual aborters tested preconceptionally scored 5 or above, but that after treatment and a successful pregnancy the majority scored 4 or below. In no instance did a patient shift to a higher score. The difference in distribution is significant at the .02 level (reference 8, p. 240). The same total score which distinguished the whole habitual-abortion group tested preconceptionally from the comparison group also discriminated between the "successful" aborters before and after a term pregnancy.

In summary, a total score describing a pattern of personality characteristics was developed which significantly discriminated between: (1) habitual aborters and comparison patients, (2) habitual aborters with no known organic basis for their abortions and those having isthmic hypotonia, and (3) habitual aborters before and after successful treatment.

These results have not, of course, established that the psychological variables measured by the tests were the cause of the habitual abortions, nor do they explain the particular choice of target area or mechanism, nor the absence of the symptom in some women with seemingly similar personality characteristics. They do, however, constitute three lines of evidence that a certain set of personality characteristics typify a sizable group of abortion-prone women.

That the test indicators differentiating between the habitual aborters and comparison patients did not simply represent random differences is substantiated by the evidence that (a) parallel results were obtained from two different tests, (b) the personality characteristics as described are in close agreement with the independent clinical data, and (c) the same characteristics differentiating between the habitual aborters and comparison patients differentiate between habitual aborters with and without an organic basis as well as between habitual aborters before and after successful treatment.

The next question which arises is whether these characteristics are simply typical of women with some psychosomatic problem, especially one of an obstetrical-gynecological nature. That they probably are not is attested to by the fact that the half of the comparison group who had a range of gynecological or obstetrical difficulties of possible psychosomatic origin did not, as a group, show the same pattern as the habitual aborters and were not significantly different from the other comparison patients. The present investigators are currently using the same methods to study a group of infertility patients without identifiable pathologic changes who will provide an ideal comparison for the habitual aborters in that they have the same problem, i.e., inability to produce a child, but in whom vastly different mechanisms are operating. Thus far, the results point to a different personality pattern, but a definite answer will have to await completion of the study. Since a prospective prediction study is almost out of the question on practical grounds, it is thought that by studying sizable groups of women with the same presenting symptom and contrasting them with other comparable groups the relationship between psychological factors and physical symptoms can be better understood. To the degree that the psychological findings can be defined and stated in objectively measurable terms, not only will they be of assistance in the prognosis for an conduct of therapy but eventually perhaps may even be useful in preventive treatment.

Summary and conclusions

A battery of psychological tests including the Wechsler-Bellevue, Rorschach, and TAT was used to determine whether any identifiable personality characteristics distinguished women classified as habitual aborters (having had at least three successive spontaneous abortions) from other women seen in obstetrical-gynecological practice.

When a group of 61 habitual aborters with no discernible organic basis for their abortions was compared with a group of 35 patients who had no history of spontaneous abortion, 10 test indicators were found to discriminate between the two groups. According to these indicators, the habitual aborters as a group could be characterized as demonstrating an impairment of the ability to plan and anticipate, poorer emotional control, more emphasis on conformity and compliance with the conventional, greater tension about hostile affect, stronger feelings of dependency, and greater proneness to guilt feelings. A total score based on the test indicators discriminated between the two groups at the .01 level and a cut-off score correctly classified 77 per cent of the patients.

The same total score discriminated at the .05 level between the 61 habitual aborters with no discernible abortigenic pathologic changes and 9 habitual aborters whose abortions appeared to be based on isthmic hypotonia.

When 18 habitual aborters who had term pregnancies following psychotherapy were retested, there was found to be a significant change in the total score, in the direction of the comparison group. The changes found in the aborters who had been successfully treated were in those characteristics which originally distinguished them from the comparison group.

NOTE

*Picture 3BM is described in the manual as follows: "On the floor against a couch is the huddled form of a boy with his head bowed on his right arm. Beside him on the floor is a revolver:" 8BM: "An adolescent boy looks straight out of the picture. The barrel of a rifle is visible at one side, and in the background is the dim scene of a surgical operation, like a reverie-image;" 18GF: "A woman has her hands squeezed around the throat of another woman whom she appears to be pushing backwards across the banister of a stairway."[19] Card 8BM was included because such a large number of women in both groups developed the theme of the man being shot rather than the more usual one of the boy's daydreaming about becoming a doctor.

REFERENCES

1. Berle, B. B., and Javert, C. T. Stress and habitual abortion. *Obst. & Gynec.* 3:298, 1954.
2. Deutsch, H. *The Psychology of Women.* Grune, New York, 1945, vol. II.
3. De Vos, G. A quantitative approach to affective symbolism in Rorschach responses. *J. Proj. Tech. 16:*133, 1952.
4. De Vos, G. *Manual of Criteria for Scoring Affective Inferences.* 1955 (unpublished).
5. Dunbar, H. F. *Emotions and Bodily Changes,* ed. 4. Columbia, New York, 1954.
6. Eastman, N. J. *Williams Obstetrics,* ed. 11. Appleton-Century-Crofts, New York, 1956.
7. Eron, L. D. Responses of women to the Thematic Apperception Test. *J. Consult. Psychol. 17:*269, 1953.
8. Guilford, J. P. *Fundamental Statistics in Psychology and Education,* ed. 3. McGraw-Hill, New York, 1956.
9. Javert, C. T. *Spontaneous and Habitual Abortion.* McGraw-Hill, New York, 1957.
10. Klopfer, B., and Kelley, D. M. *The Rorschach Technique.* World Book Co., Yonkers, N. Y., 1942.
11. Klopeer, B., Ainsworth, M. D., Klopeer, W. G., and Holt, R. R. *Developments in the Rorschach Technique.* World Book Co., Yonkers, N. Y., 1954, vol. I.
12. Kroger, W. S., and Freed, S. C. *Psychosomatic Gynecology.* Saunders, Philadelphia, 1951.
13. Mandy, A. J., Mandy, T. E., Farkas, R., Scher, E., and Kaiser, I. The emotional aspects of obstetrics and gynecologic disorders. *Am. J. Obst. & Gynec. 60:*605, 1950.
14. Mann, E. C. Psychiatric investigation of habitual abortion, preliminary report. *Obst. & Cynec. 7:*589, 1956.
15. Mann, E. C. The role of emotional determinants in habitual abortion. *Surg. Clin. North America 37:*447, 1957.
16. Mann, E. C. Habitual abortion: A report in two parts on 160 patients. *Am. J. Obst. & Gynec. 73:*706, 1959.
17. Mann, E. C., McLarn, W. D., and Hayt, D. B. The physiology and clinical significance of the uterine isthmus (Part I). *Am. J. Obstet. & Gynec. 81:*209, 1961.
18. Mann, E. C., and Grimm, E. R. "Habitual abortion," in *Psychosomatics-Obstetrics, Gynecology, Endocrinology,* edited by William Kroger, Thomas, Springfield, Ill., 1961, in press.
19. Murray, H. A. *Thematic Apperception Test Manual.* Harvard, Cambridge, 1943.
20. Rapaport, D., Gill, M., and Schafer, R. *Diagnostic Psychological Testing.* Yr. Bk. Pub., Chicago, 1945, vol. I.
21. Rapaport, D., Gill, M., and Schafer, R. *Diagnostic Psychological Testing.* Yr. Bk. Pub., Chicago, 1946, vol. II.
22. Squier, R., and Dunbar, F. Emotional factors in the course of pregnancy. *Psychosom. Med. 8:*161, 1946.
23. Tupper, C., Moya, F., Stewart, D. C., Weil, R. J., and Gray, J. D. The problem of spontaneous abortion. I. A combined approach. *Am. J. Obst. & Gynec. 73:*313, 1957.
24. Wechsler, D. *The Measurement and Appraisal of Adult Intelligence,* ed. 4, Williams & Wilkins, Baltimore, 1958.
25. Weil, R. G., and Stewart, L. C. The problem of spontaneous abortion. III. Psychosomatic and interpersonal aspects of habitual abortion. *Am. J. Obst. & Gynec. 73:*322, 1957.
26. Weil, R. J., and Tupper, C. Personality life situation, and communication: A study of habitual abortion, *Psychosom. Med. 22:*448, 1960.

Part VII

Women and criteria of mental health

One of the consequences of the development of a more valid psychology of women will be an awareness of characteristic female qualities that have evolved because they are functional and adaptive. To the extent that they are qualities brought to achieving roles they will be "masculine"; to the extent that the role is nurturant, the same healthy woman will be "feminine." Besides acknowledging human adaptability and complexity, the most difficult professional task will be the recognition of how swayed we are by unconscious assumptions that what is masculine is healthy (except when they are found in women, who are then dominating, hostile, and castrating). According to the literature, to the extent that women are not masculine, their egos are mature. These judgments are implicit in our language and tacitly pervade the social sciences. Congruent with prejudiced theory, in the last section we saw that those who most closely, most rigidly adhere to stereotyped concepts of femininity are indeed dependent, passive, and masochistic. And sick. A more valid theory will develop when we acknowledge our vested interests, cease making value judgments, and are no longer impelled to demonstrate the superiority of one sex over the other.

Based on physical experiences and socialization norms, May predicted that men and women would have significantly different patterns of fantasy. Women, he expected, would respond initially with a negative theme followed by a positive one. For men, the reverse pattern is predicted. The hypotheses received very strong experimental support. In men's stories a decline or fall was abrupt, total, and irrevocable. In strong contrast, women fantasied a resurgence, indicating a quality or ego strength that enabled them to adapt to trauma. May found that women's stores were less tied to reality and less constrained by the here and now than men's. In addition, women were more likely to tolerate and use shifts in levels of psychic functioning. Healthy men have strong egos that are reality-bound; healthy women have strong egos that are not reality-bound. This observation is very similar to that of Gutmann,[1] who observed that success for men depends on their being able to perceive the real world objectively. Women, especially in the world of family, home, and neighborhood can personalize the world and see it without boundary. "In such a world porous ego boundaries might be a necessary precondition for contentment; and so-called strong ego boundaries could lead to alienation, a rupture of empathic bounds with one's children, and with the pleasant, self-confirming cycles of domestic life." Gutmann continues, explaining that the boundaryless mode for women is not regressive, but has its own style, with its own logic and sophistication. "This is not to say that women have no potential capacity for detached rationality nor men no potential for warm responsiveness; rather, women's affectional and response style is the one most relevant to the autocentric situation."

Hysteria is a psychopathology whose very name derives from the Greek work for uterus. Long believed to be a disease only of women, we now know that it is found in men, but is far more characteristic of female neurotics. A non-neurotic hysterical character is also more characteristic of women than men. Wolowitz analyzes the development and symptoms of hysteria and it is disconcerting to see how appropriate hysteric adaptations are for women.

The socialization of women emphasizes emotional expressiveness by girls, with the concomi-

tant emphasis by girls of emotional responsibility to them. Thus the base of a normal female identity rests on an ability to elicit approving emotional responses from other people. The hysteric is more extreme and competitive in the search for those affirmative responses than normal, healthy females, but the theoretic distinction is essentially quantitative.

Wolowitz describes the hysteric character: it uses exhibitionistic style of dress, speech or appearance in order to elicit responses. It is outwardly guided by an aim to please but it is superficial; it alters itself in order to gain love and thus feels phony. It is devastated by mild criticism, and manipulates others because they can't be trusted to respond as the hysteric needs, and uses sex to draw out self-confirming responses of love. The hysteric character wants to be marvelous but, preoccupied with eliciting responses, neither creates nor innovates.

The hysteric is a person who has become so altered in the pursuit of a reflected identity that there is no identity. Widespread reinforcement of emotional responses from others as the basis for self-esteem makes it more probable that females rather than males develop an hysteric character. As Gutmann indicated, emotional sensitivity in women is adaptive and healthy. As Wolowitz indicated, a dedicated, selfless pursuit of positive emotions assures the loss of self.

Some critics of Women's Lib have pointed to some of the more flamboyantly named groups (for example, SCUM: The Society for Cutting up Men), the participation by the Radical Lesbians, and the movement's assaults on cherished concepts of healthy sexuality, masculinity, and femininity, and have decided that the movement and the individuals within it are sick. The impetus for participation is then reduced to psychopathology. McNeill speculates that the extreme emotional outrage and hostility found in the movement may occur because long-suppressed feminine rage has suddenly been released. "Release phenomena" normally erupt in exaggerated form and become less extreme as society grows more accepting.

Even though some of the energies driving the movement originate in individual conflicts, the movement has raised larger, fundamental questions of the psychopathology of society and the positive characteristics of those who deviate from cultural sickness. Less charitably, McNeill observes that simultaneously the movement does provide a supportive milieu in which unacceptable impulses can be attributed to others. Having become conscious of their passivity and docility, how much of the rage vented against men springs from contempt for themselves? One can see the acting out of pathology and the dynamics of those who would change places with their oppressors. But pointing an accusatory finger citing the psychopathological movement intolerably and inaccurately belittles the importance of the movement. McNeill points out that pathology is deviation from social consensus and as the norms change because of confrontation, the next generation of neurotics will be those who clung to the old rules.

The paper by Broverman et al. is a stunning experimental indictment of the implicit value judgment within our culture and specifically within professional psychology and psychiatry. It is only recently that many voices are objecting to psychoanalytic concepts of normal femininity and the therapeutic goals that had evolved. (One can wonder: it is really a legitimate goal to become less resistant to, or even at ease with, one's presumed penis envy?) Broverman demonstrates powerfully that value-loaded clinical judgments are not limited to some core of classical psychoanalysts.

When male and female clinicians describe healthy women as having the socially undesirable qualities of being more submissive, less independent, less adventurous, more easily influenced, less aggressive, less competitive, more excitable in minor crises, more easily hurt, more emotional, more conceited about their appearance, and less objective than men, we have evidence of a widespread, internalized double standard of mental health. Healthy women are not optimally described by how they lack what healthy men are like. Because clinicians' concepts of adult psychological health are essentially identical with their ideas of the socially desirable characteristics of men, and because concepts of feminine health are very different, it follows that concepts of feminine health are essentially not healthy and are, instead, contemptuous.

[1] Gutmann, D. L., Women and the conception of ego strength, *Merrill-Palmer Quarterly*, **11:3** (1965), pp. 229-240.

44 *Sex differences in fantasy patterns*

Robert May

The social sciences have recently come under attack for propagating an inadequate, reactionary and socially harmful conception of women (Friedan, 1963; Rossi, 1964). These criticisms, although sometimes strident and rigid, cannot be dismissed. The female case has been often neglected, and too frequently forced into inappropriate male categories. As McClelland (1965) points out, psychologists have often set up dimensions where the female can only come out as "not male" (weak instead of strong, small instead of large, etc). And the persistent tendency to read "different" as "deficient" leads to less than rational controversy in this field, especially where it touches on delicate social balances and cherished mythologies. Freud was forced to conclude that "psychology cannot solve the riddle of femininity" (1933, p. 158).

The list of empirically validated sex differences is long and will not be recited here (good surveys are offered in Anastasi, 1958; Johnson & Terman, 1940; Tyler, 1956). The overall impression is one of tremendous diversity and heterogeneity, of many scattered and fortuitous findings. It is at least clear that the ramifications of maleness or femaleness go far beyond the "basics" of biological structure and function, extending into subtleties of thought, feeling, imagination and mannerism. But the lack of any broad directing theory makes the integration of findings a difficult task.

One broad theoretical framework is offered by psychoanalysis and its derivatives. This paper reports an attempt to test some hypotheses about sex-linked fantasy patterns drawn from analytically-oriented case studies, and to make some inferences about sex differences in personality. Although the investigation concerns both male and female fantasy patterns, more space will be devoted to the female case. Given our usual male-oriented baseline, it could be argued that the study of "sex differences" is in fact the study of women.

Theoretical background

THE FEMALE PATTERN

Most of Freud's thought about women centered around the concept of "penis-envy" (1924b, 1925, 1931). But in his final paper on women (1933) he expands his earlier formulation and introduces the idea of masochism: "We must not overlook one particularly constant relation between femininity and instinctual life. The repression of their aggressiveness, which is imposed on women by their constitutions and by society, favors the development of strong masochistic impulses, which have the effect of binding erotically the destructive tendencies which have been turned inwards. Masochism is then, as they say, truly feminine." (p. 158). This approach has been elaborated by Deutsch (1944). She sees three primary traits as making up the "femine core": passivity, masochism and narcissism. "Passivity" does not imply apathy or inactivity, but rather the tendency for the female to direct her activity inward, resulting in greater proneness to identification, stronger fantasy, subjectivity and inner perception.[1]

This passivity is assumed to stem from three factors: a) the female is constitutionally less active and aggressive, b) the female genital organ is not as appropriate as the male's for the expression of active or aggressive impulses and this leads to at least partial renunciation of this mode, and c) the social environment exerts pressures on the girl to inhibit activity and aggression. There seems to be clear empirical evidence for the existence of the first (Pratt, 1946; Terman & Tyler, 1946) and third (Kagan & Moss, 1962) factors, while the argument for the effect of different genital structures rests largely on clinical data.

Along with passivity goes masochism. The reasoning here (following the lines laid down by Freud, 1924a) is that activity and aggression are inextricably linked. As activity is inhibited and turned inwards, aggression follows the same course: "activity becomes passivity, and aggression is renounced for the sake of being loved. In this renunciation the aggressive forces that are not actively spent must find an outlet, and they do this by endowing the passive state of being loved with a masochistic character." Deutsch (1944, vol. 1, p. 251) feels that the father plays a decisive role in this transformation. He "bribes" the little girl to renounce further intensification of activity and aggression by offering her love and tenderness. In addition to rewarding "feminine passivity," the father actively promotes the "masochistic" mode: "He appears, without being conscious of it, as a seducer, with whose help the girl's aggressive instinctual

Reprinted from Robert May, "Sex Differences in Fantasy Patterns." Journal of Projective Techniques, 30:6, 1966, pp. 252-259. This work was supported by NIH grants MH-02980 to David McClelland and 2 F1 MH-21, 005-02 to the author. The author is indebted to Drs. David McClelland and Robert White for valuable advice and guidance, and to Peter Hunsberger for help in scoring protocols.

components are transformed into masochistic ones. The masochistic ingredient in the relation to the father appears in the active games with him, which later assume an increasingly erotic character. It is enough to observe the little girl's fearful jubilation when the father performs acrobatic tricks with her that are often painful, when he throws her up in the air, or lets her ride 'piggy back' on his shoulders" (Deutsch 1944, vol. 1, p. 252).

A complete definition of "feminine masochism" is not easy. Deutsch defines the term indirectly, by a succession of clinical examples. She seems to be pointing toward an unconscious association of pain and pleasure. "Pain" is here defined broadly, including psychological discomfort or a risking of the "self" emotionally or physically (e.g., the "fearful jubilation' in the above quote). Some of her own examples might be helpful here: subjecting oneself to a man's will, being attracted by suffering, a painful longing and wish to suffer for the lover, renunciation in favor of others, a feeling that suffering is compensated by love, rape fantasies, and the willingness to serve a cause or a human being with love and abnegation. This is obviously a wide range of behaviors and feelings, but there does seem to be a common theme of willingness to risk one's physical or psychological "integrity" in order to obtain something which is valued. "Integrity" here means the maintenance of a sharp boundary (or barrier) between the self and the environment, and the constant effort to maintain ascendancy (or conscious ego control) over the environment, both social and material. In Deutsch's examples the hoped-for or anticipated "reward" is usually love (loving or being loved), but this may be unnecessarily narrow.

Turning to the adult woman, Deutsch maintains that feminine masochism is an essential component of her role:

"Women's entire psychologic preparation for the sexual and reproductive functions is connected with masochistic ideas. In these ideas, coitus is closely associated with the act of defloration, and defloration with rape and a painful penetration of the body. The sexual readiness, the psychologic pleasure-affirming preparation for the sexual act, draws its masochistic components from two sources—one infantile, regressive, and dispositional and the other *real*. For defloration is really painful and involves the destruction of a part of the body. The rape fantasy reveals itself as only an exaggeration of reality. . . . A certain amount of masochism as psychologic preparation for adjustment to the sexual functions is necessary in woman" (1944, vol. 1, p. 276). The same argument is made regarding childbirth. Deutsch feels that the wish for a child acquires a masochistic character through association with fantasies of pain and danger and because of the reality of the birth process. Thus feminine masochism is a cumulative result of constitution, anatomy, social training, and biological role.

There are many ways one might try to identify a trait like feminine masochism. The approach taken in this study centers on fantasy. Deutsch, in commenting on masochistic fantasies, says that "often the fantasy is divided into two acts: the first, the masochistic act, produces the sexual tension, and the second, the amorous act, supplies all the delights of being loved and desired" (1944, vol. 1, p. 255). Expanding on this, feminine masochism could be defined as a typical *sequence* or pattern of action and feeling. Suffering following by joy, failure followed by success, risking oneself followed by love—these are the sorts of sequences one would expect in women's fantasy.

THE MALE PATTERN

What of the male case? Murray's clinical study, "American Icarus" (1955), offers some leads here. He outlines a syndrome involving, among other things, ascensionism (the wish to overcome gravity, rise, fly, be a spectacular success) and an underlying fear of falling (being injured, failing, losing one's self-confidence). This "Icarus complex" reveals itself in fantasies of flying, floating, rising, and of falling or precipitation (either directly or through metaphors of success and failure). The basic pattern is one of ascension followed by descension, "an archtypal thematic sequence against which we are warned by the ancient aphorism: 'Pride cometh before a fall' " (1955, p. 635). A strong dose of narcissism and a set of unrealistic goals result in an extreme and "immature" syndrome as Murray describes it in this particular case.

But the underlying pattern may be more general than this. Murray feels that one of the experiential bases of the ascension-descension cycle is the repeated sequence of phallic tumescene and detumescence. Federn (1948) states that an erection, with its apparent suspension of the laws of gravity, is perceived as flying by the infantile psyche, and this experience serves as a stimulus for dreams of flying and general ascendance (ambition, vanity, exhibitionism, etc.). Since most males have this biological experience over and over from the early years of life, it could be assumed that the ascension and decension sequence is a potentially powerful metaphor for them. Additional support is offered by Erickson's (1951, 1964) studies of play constructions in preadolescents. Concern with height and collapse emerged as a masculine theme: "While high structures are prevalent in the configurations of the boys, there is also much play with the danger of collapse or downfall" (1964, pp. 590-591). Erickson also relates this theme to the boy's experience of his body.

Switching to a more social level, it is possible to point to elements in the male role which could support this pattern. Males are typically trained to be active and aggressive (Barry, Bacon & Child. 1957; Kagan & Moss, 1962), to overcome the environment by frontal attack. As Fromm (1943) points out, this can lead to the male's being in a continual "test situation," always having to prove his ultimate endurance and superiority. The more this pressure is felt, consciously or unconsciously, the more anxiety about failure, about "falling down on the job." And there must always be an awareness that "decline" of one sort or another is inevitable, that the trajectory cannot be always upwards. In a more primitive economy, the loss of strength with increasing age might be the turning point; in any case, the more or less conscious awareness of death must temper the hope of rising forever.

Obviously many factors enter into this kind of patterning of life experience. One of the most blatant omissions here is the effect of age. Several of the studies cited in this section deal with adolescents or preadolescents, and thus it may be a phenomenon of youth. But since the sample to be dealt with below is a college group, this possibility will not affect the specific hypotheses to be tested, although it must obviously temper all attempts at generalization. Suffice it to say that there is reason to expect male fantasy to show a pattern of success followed by failure, gain followed by loss, high expectations followed by unsatisfying achievements.

Hypothesis

Males and females will exhibit different patterns of physical and emotional movement in TAT fantasy. The typical female theme will be one of relatively "negative" emotion or experience followed by more "positive" emotion or experience, while the typical male theme will be the reverse. This predicted difference is assumed to reflect sex differences in social role, including expectations concerning one's life cycle, and in the experience of one's own body.

Method

A scoring system was developed on the basis of stories written by Harvard and Radcliffe students to a picutre showing a male and female trapeze team performing in mid-air. The two general scoring categories are "deprivation" and "enhancement."[2] Deprivation refers to such things as physical tension or pain, injury, death, continued exertion, falling or losing control, growing old and weak, negative emotion (nervousness, fear, hate, etc.), negative press (being under compulsion, being trapped), self sacrifice without any mention of gain or gratification, failure, and dissatisfaction. Enhancement refers to satisfaction of physical need, physical excellence or accomplishment, rising (or cessation of fall), success, growth, positive emotion (happiness, love, excitement, etc.), positive anticipation, nurturant press, attention, revenge and insight or realization. These categories are intentionally very broad, ranging from specific physical rising or falling to diffuse emotional shifts.

Since the concern is with sequence, not just total occurrence, the first step in scoring is to establish an anchor point within the story. I have called this anchor point the "pivotal incident," and it is generally defined as the dramatic turning point of the story, the central act or feeling which mediates between the past and the future. Deprivation and enhancement units are weighted according to their position before or after the pivotal incident. The numerical weights were assigned such that: a story with one deprivation unit before the pivotal incident and one enhancement unit after scores +2; a story with the opposite pattern (one enhancement before and one deprivation after) scores −2; a story with equal numbers of the same kind of units before and after the pivotal incident scores 0. Many variations and combinations of these basic patterns occur, but the basic rule is that a positive score indicates a story with a positive shift and a negative score indicates a story with a negative shift. Thus the predicted male pattern (enhancement followed by deprivation) will score in the negative direction, while the predicted female pattern (deprivation followed by enhancement) will score in the positive direction. Whether

this difference is absolute or relative will depend on the particular numerical weights, pictures and subjects involved.

The following story is an example of the scoring process. Each scored unit is identified as deprivation (D) or enhancement (E) and is given a numerical weight depending on its position before or after the pivotal incident (P.I.):

The young lady is a *newcomer* (D, +1) *being caught* (E, −1) for the first time before an audience. The man is somewhat *older and experienced* (E, −1) in trapeze work. The girl and man *have been infatuated with one another* (E, −1), this providing incentive for the young lady, to *fly* (E, −1) — something she really *doesn't enjoy* (D, +1). While *flying* (E, -1) she thinks only of her *love* (E, −1, diverting her thoughts from the *agony* (D, +1) of this activity. He, in turn, *revels in his physical prowess* (E, −1). One day after *(E, −1) —his* love has dwindled *(D, +1) — he lets her fall* (P.I.) The net not securely fastened doesn't hold her and *she is killed* (D, −1). (Total score = −5).[3]

The subjects for this study were 104 college students, 60 female and 44 male. The relative homogeneity of this group in terms of age, social class and intelligence is both an advantage and a disadvantage. It limits the generality of any findings, but at the same time helps control for these factors in comparing males and females. This is a stringent test of the hypothesis in that many sex differences are narrowed in college populations (Johnson & Terman, 1940; Rabban, 1950). The easy availability of college students and their superior performance on the TAT (Veroff, 1961) finally determined the choice. The *Ss* were drawn from a large urban coed university, a private women's college, and an engineering college. They were all members of undergraduate psychology courses, were not paid for their participation, and did not initially volunteer for the study. It was a very compliant group of conscripts, with only one or two complete rejections of the TAT.

A group form TAT was used, with four pictures presented in a fixed order. The instructions emphasized the rapid production of a dramatic, creative and psychologically insightful story. The pictures were selected with the aim of including a broad, yet pertinent, range of people and situations. The first picture (A) was the same one on which the scoring system was developed. It shows a man and women doing a trapeze act in mid-air against a dark background. This picture could be expected to pull rather direct and dramatic stories of rising and falling. The second picture (B) shows a young bullfighter walking in the ring. He has an intense expression on his face and the picture is suggestive of some sort of crisis, either physical or spiritual. The third picture (C) presents a rather shabby man and a barefoot woman sitting on a stone bench. Their ages are unclear. The woman has her head on her hands, while the man is lying back with his eyes closed. Thie picture does not have the direct or implicit action of the first two and would seem more conductive to static, interpersonal stories (and insofar as the first picture represents a peak, this picture represents the valley, the bottom). The last picture (D) shows a child either leaping or running in a field, with a bird flying above. The sex of the child is not clear. This is another action picture, its main distinction being the age of the central figure.

TABLE 1   Reliability

		Picture A	Picture B	Picture C	Picture D
	N	71	47	41	54
Agreement on	Phi	.58	.48	.32	.65
Scorability	p	< .001	< .01	< .05	< .001
	N	49	41	23	36
Score	r	+.79	+.77	+.42	+.79
Correlations	p	< .0005	< .0005	< .05	< 0005

Note: N varies throughout according to the number of unscorable and doubtful stories.

TABLE 2   Pattern Differences in Total Scores

	Female		Male				
	N	Mean	N	Mean	diff.	t	p
Urban University	38	+ 0.812	31	− 0.221	1.033		
Engineering College			11	− 0.276			
Private Women's College	22	+ 0.790					
All Groups Combined	60	+ 0.801*	42	− 0.235**	1.039	3.578	< .0005

Note: Two males wrote from unscorable or unfinished stories in a row. Thus the total N is 102, not 101. Positive scores are predicted for females and negative scores for males.

$$*S^2 = 2.02 \qquad **S^2 = 2.18$$

Results

The 416 stories obtained were placed in a random order and were scored separately by two scorers. The reliability of the scoring system turned out to be acceptable (see Table 1).

The first step, that of deciding whether a story is scorable or not, was reliable beyond the .05 level for all four pictures. As Table 1 shows, the score correlations are also generally good. All four correlations are significant beyond the .05 level and, except for picture C (the man and woman on the bench), they are all respectably large. The author is at a loss to explain the low correlation for picture C, especially in view of the near unanimity of the other three. It might be that clear sequence judgments are more difficult with "non-action" pictures.

The most natural unit of analysis is the person. In order to approach the data this way, a total score was derived for each subject by averaging his or her scores on the separate pictures. This array of total scores can be looked at two ways: comparing male and female means, or comparing the number of positive (deprivation followed by enhancement) and negative (enhancement followed by deprivation) scores for each sex. Table 2 presents the first comparison.

The hypothesis is strongly supported. The difference between the combined male and female means is in the predicted direction and is significant beyond the .0005 level.

The second comparison of total scores asks how many Ss revealed the predicted male (negative scores) and female (positive scores) patterns (see Table 3).

Approximately 2/3 of the Ss score in the predicted direction. It is obvious that this is not a categorical effect. There is considerable overlap, as is the case with virtually all psychological sex differences (Anastasi, 1958) The chi square is significant well beyond the .001 level. Thus the hypothesis is confirmed both by comparison of means for each sex and by analysis of the number of Ss showing the predicted pattern.

Using only average scores may obscure worth-while information. In view of all the evidence for specific picture effects in the TAT (Murstein, 1961, 1963; Reitman & Atkinson, 1958), a separate analysis is in order. The hypothesis is confirmed for three out of the four pictures (see Table 4).

Pictures A and B perform "best," with the predicted sex difference significant beyond the .005 level. Picture C (man and woman on bench) also bears out the hypothesis, albeit not so strongly. But with picture D (child in field) there are no significant sex differences. Why does this picture fail to differentiate men and women? The most likely reason is that it features a child. There is evidence (Feshback, Singer & Feshbach, 1963; Reitman & Atkinson, 1958) to suggest that figures of children are not very effective projective stimuli for college students. Picture D may reveal this effect: a failure to identify with someone clearly younger than oneself and a tendency to describe childhood in stereotyped terms.

TABLE 3   Frequency of Positive and Negative Total Scores

	Positive Scores	Negative Scores
Female	43	16
Male	15	26

N = 100, X' = 11.64, p < .001

TABLE 4   Pattern Differences by Picture

Picture		N	Mean	S^2	t	p
A	Male	28	−0.714	5.38	2.729	< .005
	Female	47	+0.787	5.27		
B	Male	37	−1.635	7.54	3.039	< .005
	Female	57	+0.009	5.94		
C	Male	28	+1.695	2.60	2.506	< .01
	Female	46	+2.859	4.44		
D	Male	31	+0.032	6.35	−0.557	ns
	Female	48	−0.281	5.68		

Note: All differences are in the predicted direction except for Picture D.

It is obvious from the means given in Table 4 that the pictures used elicit different types of stories. The baseline for the sex difference shifts with each picture, so that in C, for example, both means are positive but the female mean is significantly greater than the male mean. Each picture has its own idiosyncratic baseline. Picture C is the most striking, with the overall mean shifting strongly in the positive (or female) direction. This is understandable since the picture almost dictates the mention of some past or present deprivation. The sex difference then comes in *how much* deprivation is stated and what the outcome is.

Several objections could be made to the findings at this point. In view of the evidence that women often tell stories with more sadness and unhappiness (Murstein, 1963), might we not be dealing with a simple trait of optimism or pessimism, rather than a pattern or sequence? The nature of the scoring system makes this unlikely, since the same kinds of references on both sides of the pivotal incident would cancel each other out. Nevertheless, this possibility was checked by testing for sex differences in the total number of deprivation or enhancement units used for each of the first three pictures (picture D will be dropped from further analysis since it showed no sex differences for anything). Of these six comparisons, only one is significant. Females do use more deprivation units with picture B ($p < .02$). It thus appears that the general emotional tone of the story cannot account for the bulk of the findings. Another possible objection is that the scoring system is only reflecting a general tendency for women to use happy endings and men to use sad endings. If this is the case, then the first part of the TAT stories (i.e., before the pivotal incident) should not differ across sex. A comparison was made, using the number of enhancement units minus the number of deprivation units. A sex difference in the predicted direction (relatively more D units for women) was found in all three cases, the effect being significant with pictures A and B ($p < .05$ and $p < .025$ respectively) and marginal ($p < .10$) with picture C. More is involved than simply happy or sad endings. Only a pattern hypothesis seems adequate to the data. Also, it might be objected that verbal fluency is confounding the whole business, since women often tell longer stories than men (Murstein, 1963). Again, the counterbalances scoring system makes this unlikely, but it was checked anyway. On only one picture (picture C) is there a significant sex difference in length of story, and for this

picture the correlation between length and score is an insignificant +.19. As a further check, a correlation was run between length and score on picture A. This yielded a correlation of the same magnitude ($r = +.15$, ns). Thus, length of story does not seem to be a factor, probably due in part to the nature of the scoring system.

Also in the area of verbal fluency or inclination: all Ss indicated their preferences for English or mathematics and it turns out that a preference for English over math is associated with scores farther in the predicted direction. Females preferring English have total scores significantly ($p < .05$) more positive than females preferring math, and males preferring English have total scores significantly more negative ($p < .025$) than males preferring math. Thus, it seems that an investment (and, assumedly, ability) in verbal expression goes along with a more clear and dramatic enactment of one's own pattern, the pattern characteristic of one's own sex.

Finally, it should be noted that the hypothesis in this study concerns relative rather than absolute shifts in emotional tone. In other words, the way the scoring system is set up, a story does not have to have an absolute change from positive to negative action and feeling in order to be scored as a "male" story. A story with one deprivation unit before the P.I. and three deprivation units after, for instance, is scored −2. Also, a story that has an enhancement unit before the P.I. and one enhancement plus one deprivation after, is scored as a shift in the negative, or male direction. There are two reasons why the hypothesis has been stated in this broader form. First, to demand an absolute pattern difference assumes that people have a baseline of "zero" or neutral feelings. It is reasonable that people differ in whether they tend to think in positive or negative terms. This difference is not necessarily sex-linked. Thus a person who thinks largely in enhancement terms could only express the "female" pattern by having more enhancement after the P.I. than before. Secondly, the overall level of feeling depends a lot on the stimulus. Thus picture C elicits stories that consist mostly of deprivation, but women give more deprivation before the P.I., while men give more after. The difference is a relative one, but still valid. Nonetheless, it seemed advisable to see what part these "deviant" patterns (stories with only one kind of unit throughout and stories with a sum of zero on either side of the P.I.) were playing in the overall results. Out of 416 stories, there are only 58 of the first type and 73 of the second type. And the means for these stories suggest that they are not contributing to the overall sex differences, since the mean difference between male and female stories with only one kind of unit is considerable smaller than the difference for all stories (0.404 versus 1.039) and the mean difference between male and female stories with a sum of zero on either side of the P.I. is in a direction contrary to the hypothesis.

Discussion

Men in this study tended to see any decline or fall as abrupt, total and final. The possibility of a resurgence or second change, which is implicit in the female pattern, does not seem very real for males. Perhaps an important meaning of the pattern difference in fantasy is that women can lose (or give up) control without panic—they are confident of recovery in the face of failure or suffering. The male, on the other hand, may be more prone to see any loss of conscious ego control as total and absolute ("once you slip, it's all over").

This approach can be followed on several levels. On the simplest physical level, one would expect women to show "an ability to stand (and to understand) pain as a meaningful aspect of human experience in general, and of the feminine role in particular" (Erikson, 1964, p. 594). And, going a few steps further, what about death, the ultimate deprivation or "fall?" Murray (1955) cites a desire for immortality as part of the Icarian syndrome, and one would suspect that many men, expecially when young, see death as the final and total collapse. The case may be very different for women. McClelland (1963b) has suggested that death has connotations of seduction for many women and that they are, if not excited and attracted by it, at least ambivalent. Greenberger (1965) lends support to this with her finding that critically ill women give more fantasy references to illicit sexuality ("death as lover") than do women hospitalized for minor complaints. This type of phenomenon can reveal itself strikingly in case studies. A young woman reports that one of her earliest memories is: "An older man tickling me on a big bed in the apartment upstairs. I thought I was going to die if he didn't stop. The implications were definitely sexual even then."[5] Another woman states that "around age 9 or 10 the idea of hanging by the neck inspired sexual stimulation," and she goes on to report trying to hang herself with her father's necktie.[4] Deutsch also reports cases of women for whom losing consciousness, or being tied up, caused intense excitment and arousal (e.g., 1944, vol. 1, p. 176 and p. 344).

All these experiences (pain, death, loss of consciousness, being bound) fit within the category of "deprivation" as it has been used in this study. Thus the expectation that women can see these experiences as leading to an exciting result is fully in line with the fantasy pattern that has been reported on. But some of the qualitative factors which were evident suggest that a broader interpretive framework would be useful. TAT stories written by women seem to be much less focused on the "here and now" reality than stories written by men. Females tend to include more often such phenomena as dreams, fantasy, forgetting, prayer and memory. These elements seem to represent, in the most general sense, shifts in the level of psychic functioning. If one takes conscious, action-oriented, ego functioning as the norm, then all the experiences which have been singled out above (death, loss of consciousness, capitivity, grief, fantasy, recollection, and perhaps even pain or fear) can be seen as alteration phenomena. In this light the hypothesis would be that women are more likely to tolerate, or make use of, shifts in level of psychic functioning.

This kind of sex difference even holds true in psychosis. Distler, May and Tuma (1964) report that male schizophrenics who get better are characterized by high scores on Barron's Ego Strength scale and low scores on Taylor's Manifest Anxiety scale. In contrast, female schizophrenics who improve have high manifest anxiety and low ego strength. The authors conclude that the female role permits "giving up" and the frank admission of symptoms, while males must maintain a facade of strength and control even under the onslaught of schizophrenia. Thus it is more appropriate, and more beneficial, for women to give themselves over to this radically altered state of consciousness, while men fare best when they attempt to retain their "normal" mode of ego functioning.

Within this broader framework, the sex difference in fantasy patterns which was the original focus of this study takes on another meaning. The categories of "deprivation" and "enhancement" seem to have been defined with the typical male mode of functioning as the implicit norm. The resultant patterns can then be seen as indicating that women can see these "deprivations," or shifts away from the mode of conscious ego control, as ultimately beneficial, while the male is more likely to see them as "lapses," or as leading to catastrophe, the beginning of the end. Because of the nature of the pictures used in this study, most stories contained some incidents of "deprivation," but both quantitative and qualitative factors indicate that males have less tolerance for this than females do. "Giving up" or suffering has overtones of finality for men, whereas for women it can be a means to an end, almost an opportunity. Or so it appears in fantasy.

NOTES

1. Here, as throughout, the psychoanalytic concepts may be easily translated into a more social-psychological or sociological approach. Note, for example, the similarity of Parsons' (1955) conception of sex roles, where he sees the male role as "instrumental" (involving activity in the material world) and the female role as "expressive" (involving concern with emotions and the "social world").

2. This approach was suggested by McClelland in a paper (1963a) which outlines the mythological and cultural aspects of the present hypothesis. Although the labels are "loaded" in the direction of male values (tending to equate "giving" with "giving up," etc.), I haven't been able to find any better descriptive terms.

3. A complete outline of the scoring system is available on request from the author.

4. Personal communication. Dr. Arthur Couch. Harvard University, June, 1964.

REFERENCES

Anastasi, A. *Differential psychology.* New York: Macmillan, 1958.
Barry, H., Bacon, M., & Child, I. A crosscultural survey of some sex differences in socialization. *Journal of Abnormal and Social Psychology,* 1957, 55 327-332.
Deutsch, H. *The psychology of women,* vols. 1 and 2. New York: Grune and Stratton, 1944.

Distler, L., May P., & Tuma, A. Anxiety and ego strength as predictors of response to treatment in schizophrenic patients, *Journal of Consulting Psychology*, 1964, *28* 17-177.

Erikson, E. Sex differences in the play configurations of pre-adolescents, *American Journal of Ortho-psychiatry*, 1951, *21*, 667-692.

Erikson, E. Inner and outer space: reflections on womanhood, *Daedalus*, Spring, 1964, 582-606.

Federn, P. Dreams of flying, in Fliess (Ed.), *The psychoanalytic reader*. New York: International Universities Press, 1948, 352-356.

Feshbach, S., Singer, R., & Feshbach, N. Effects of anger arousal and similarity upon the attribution of hostility to pictorial stimuli, *Journal of Consulting Psychology*, 1963, 248-252.

Friedan, B. *The feminine mystique*. New York: Norton, 1963.

Fromm, E. Sex and character, *Psychiatry*, 1943, *6*, 21-31.

Freud, S. The economic problem in masochism, *Collected papers*. New York: Basic Books (1959), 1924a, *vol. 2*, 255-268.

Freud, S. The passing of the oedipus-complex, *Collected papers*. New York: Basic Books (1959), 1924b, *vol 2*, 269-276.

Freud, S. Some psychological consequences of the anatomical distinction between the sexes, *Collected papers*. New York: Basic Books (1959), 1925, *vol. 5*, 186-197.

Freud, S. Female sexuality, *Collected papers*. New York: Basic Books (1959), 1931, *vol. 5*, 252-272.

Freud, S. The psychology of women. *New Introductory Lectures*. New York: Norton, 1933. 153-185.

Greenberger, E. Fantasies of women confronting death: a study of critically ill patients. *Journal of Consulting Psychology*, 1965, *29*, 3, 252-260.

Johnson, W., & Terman, L. Some highlights in the literature of psychological sex differences published since 1920. *Journal of Psychology*, 1940. *9*, 327-336.

Kagan, J., & Moss, H. *Birth to maturity*. New York: Wiley, 1962.

McClelland, D. Do women differ psychologically from men? Un-published paper. Center for Research in Personality, Harvard University, 1963a.

McClelland, D. The harlequin complex, in White (Ed.), *The study of lives*. New York: Atherton, 1963b, 94-119.

McClelland, D. Wanted: A new self-image for women, in R. J. Lifton (Ed.), *The woman in America*. Houghton Mifflin, Fall, 1965, 173-192.

Murray, H. American Icarus, in Burton & Harris, *Clinical studies of personality*. New York: Harper, 1955, 615-641.

Murstein, B. The role of the stimulus in the manifestation of fantasy, in Kagan & Lesser (Eds.), *Contemporary issues in thematic appreceptive methods*. Springfield, Ill.: Charles C. Thomas, 1961, 229-273.

Murstein, B. *Theory and research in projective techniques*. New York: J. Wiley and Sons, 1963.

Parsons, T., & Bales, F. (Eds.), *Family, socialization and interaction process*. New York: Free Press, 1955.

Pratt, K. The neonate, in Carmichael (Ed.), *Manual of child psychology*. New York: Wiley, 1946.

Rabban, M. Sex-role identification in young children in two diverse social groups. *Genetic psychology monographs*, 1950, *41*, 81-158.

Reitman, W., & Atkinson, J. Some methodological problems in the use of thematic appreceptive measures of human motives, in Atkinson (Ed.), *Motives in fantasy, action and society*. Princeton, N. J.: D. Van Nostrand, 1958, 664-683.

Rossi, A. Equality between the sexes: an immodest proposal, *Daedalus*, Spring, 1964, 607-652.

Terman, L., & Tyler, L. Psychological sex differences, in Carmichael (Ed.), *Manual of child psychology*. New York: Wiley, 1946.

Tyler, L. *The psychology of human differences*. New York: Appleton Century Crofts. 1956.

Veroff, J. Thematic apperception in a nationwide sample survey, in Dagan & Lesser (Eds.), *Contemporary issues in thematic apperceptive methods*. Springfield, Ill.: Charles C. Thomas, 1961, 83-111.

45 *Hysterical character and feminine identity*

Howard M. Wolowitz

Character and neurotic suffering

Psychoanalytic study of character has gradually evolved from its early emphasis on nuclear conflicts of particular psychosexual aims and particular defenses typical of certain character types (e.g. Abraham, 1921; Freud, 1908) to include characteristic cognitive-perceptual structures which are equally crucial to the understanding of particular personalities (e.g. Shapiro, 1965).

I will discuss character rather than style since "style" has been generally limited to the cognitive-perceptual patterns while "character" is more inclusive, denoting many aspects of personal being.

Regrettably, psychoanalytic references to both character and style have come to imply a neurotic quality as reflected in the widely used phrases "character disorder" and "neurotic style." If by neurotic we mean maladaptive consequences of character and style it seems likely that all styles have adaptive and maladaptive consequences,[1] hence it is misleading to imply that they are necessarily neurotic. Since clinical theorists base their observations primarily on neurotic patients, it is understandable that they have become particularly sensitized to maladaptive features of character types and miss the significance of the normative aspects of their findings.

While the description of hysterical character that follows is largely based on the more extreme and maladaptive examples observed in varying degrees in clinical practice much of the descriptive flavor and dynamic principles also apply to people who are not sufficiently troubled or unhappy to seek or need professional help. In fact an essential theme in this paper is the developmental appropriateness of an hysterical character in a nonpathological form in American women.

Reprinted from Howard M. Wolowitz, "Hysterical Character and Feminine Identity," unpublished paper, 1969.

On being female and hysteric

The word hysteric devived from the Ancient Greek "Husterikos," which meant uterus and implied the corresponding notion, long prevalent (Zilboorg and Henry, 1941), that such disturbances in bodily function were due to uterine suffering, in particular that an unmoored uterus wandered about the body and came to rest and obstruct whatever bodily organ was afflicted.

Whatever the demerits of this theory, it implied an extremely close, if overly direct, relationship between being hysteric and being female. In fact, so prevalent was this notion that Freud (1935) boasted in his autobiographical sketch of a demonstration to an incredulous audience of Viennese physicians, an actual case of male hysteria whereupon one member arose to exclaim "But my dear sir, how can you talk such nonsense? Hysteron (sic) means the uterus, so how can a man be hysterical?" (Actually, Frued's first detailed clinical publication on the subject "Studien Uber Hysteria" (Breuer and Freud, 1885) presented five case histories of the disorder, all of whom were female!)

Despite Freud's rightful objection to the presumption that hysteria was necessarily limited to women, the observation has strongly persisted even within psychoanalytic circles, that patients with hysterical symptoms and character are most often female (e.g. Shipiro, 1965). However, the observation has not been stated the other way around that (at least in our culture) females are often hysteric while the frequency is much less among males. With this emphasis we need no longer imply that females are therefore neurotic, but rather raise the issue of the reasons for the significant difference in the frequency of hysteria and hysterical character between the sexes. One of the aims of this paper is to explicate the common antededent determinants and consequent functions of both female identity and hysterical character.

Antecedents of character orientation and sex role differentiation

In so far as humans lack instinctively given, or genetically "wired-in," stimulus-response relationships, significant others must define (explicitly and implicitly, formally and informally) appropriate postures and orientations for children. Thus by parental attitude, definition, and action, involvement in various situations is set up as sets of rights and obligations which the child learns as regulatory. Hence even such basic activities as eating, sleeping, and talking are, in the case of human involvement, guaranteed to occur in particular ways not primarily by biological determinants, but initially by parental regulation of appropriate involvement.

To regulate the child's various involvements, socializing agents (parents, peers, relatives, etc.) make use of varying ratios of differing regulators including such things as rules, authority, physical restraint, intimidation, corporeal punishment, disapproval, respect, love, habit, material reward, approval, withdrawal, shame, guilt, emotional responsivity, and threats. While no parent employs merely one means of regulating involvement (several may be used at once and different means are employed depending on the type of involvement, child's age, etc.) there often occurs a major emphasis on a means of reacting that typifies or characterizes particular families, or members within the family, throughout particular periods of childhood or even its entirety.

Parsons and Bales (1955), among others, have noted that widespread in our culture is the allocation of females of a larger share of emotional-expressive functions than is deemed appropriate for males who correspondingly bear a greater allocation of the mastery-achievement responsibilities.

This particular orientation toward sex role differentiation enhances a different type of regulatory emphasis in reaction to, and defining of, involvement of female children from male children. *In the case of female children, there is observably a distinctly greater emphasis on the utilization of emotional responsivity on the part of others to define their involvements. As a consequence, there is a strong inclination for them to base their own sense of identity and worth as females on their ability to elicit strong positive emotional response from others.* While this quest for emotional responsivity varies quantitatively and qualitatively over all nuances of subtle meanings, its basic characteristics involve a continuum of approval through disapproval and another of intensity from extreme through mild to neutral.

The omnipresent tendency to manifest emotional reactions toward females is evident from earliest infancy. Thus if a mother takes her infant or baby out to a public place strangers express their intense positive sentiments. The child is admired and praised in the most extreme superlatives, smiled at, made the object of pleasant sounds, stroked, picked up often with an attempt to elicit a response to the stimulation.

As a consequence of the assymetrical allocation of emotional-expressive functions this kind of reaction is much more likely to occur with greater intensity on the part of women or girls rather than men or boys. In fact if a male exhibited what is tantamount to the normal fuss females make over children the mother would likely feel some uneasiness that he was acting peculiarly, just as appropriate females who failed to so react would be suspect. This "fuss over the child" is evoked more often and more intensely by younger rather than older and by female children than males. The immediate nutriment for the reaction is provided by more colorful, flamboyant manner in which baby girls are distinguishably dressed. This observation marks the beginning of a strong normative tendency which is pervasive in many relationships and situations.

Emotional responsivity and female-hysterical character aims

Instead of emphasizing the development of autonomy and achievement, emphasis on emotional reactivity as a means of defining, regulating and securing the child's involvements establishes the normative feminine component of character. The greater the reliance on this means, the more and more intense the responsivity, the more extremely weighted will be the feminine component which as it gets more extreme, shades into what we describe as the hysterical component of character. What is described as typical of the pathological hysteric may be observed in less extreme, and hence less maladaptive, form in the normal female.

In the more extreme hysterical instances the person's autonomy is severely undermined by the importance attached to emotional responses of others and the dedicated pursuit of those responses. This person pursues the attention of others against actual and potential claims of other real and imaginary contenders.[2]

Sometimes this competitiveness is pursued in an ostentatious, extravagant manner in a desperate attempt to pre-empt the attention and response of others. In this case, the amplifying paraphenalia of dramatic impact become important (e.g. certain styles of dress, make-up, hair-do, voice, tone, gestures, gait, and verbal expressions). These attention getting styles result in the widely recognized histrionic, exhibitionistic flavor of hysterics, especially those who have been rather successful in their past and who have become dependent on these props. Similar aims, however, can be discerned in the more desperate, less successful hysteric who utilizes real and imaginary suffering in the service of this quest for eliciting positive, although somewhat less desirable, tokens of other's responsivity such as concern, sympathy, attention, support, service and material tokens of worth.

Intense envy of those who receive more acclaim, attention and who get invested with greater importance by others dominates the threatened, competitive involvements of hysterics especially with like sexed siblings and peers. Sometimes this envy gets expressed in an over-generous or pseudoaltruistic manner when such a woman will heap extravagant, if superficial, praise on another woman's looks, dress or success.

Their underlying assumption is that attention is not something that another person freely chooses to give, but rather is legitimately demanded by those loudest in demand and distress.

There are many other direct and indirect manifestations of this competitive vying for attention, but one of the most annoyingly common ones is the person who, on being informed of another's misfortune or complaint, automatically attempts to deprive them of concern by saying, "That's nothing, you should have experienced what happened to me (or my friend, or neighbor)." Hysterics, inevitably feeling deprived of sufficient responsivity from others and vying for it competitively, cannot bear to express genuine concern for others although they are often quite expert in expressing pseudo-concern via stereotypical phrases such as "Oh, that's terrible!" or "How awful!" or, "You poor thing, I'm so sorry."

As a consequence of competitive unease, hysterics often have difficulty making close friends with others of the same sex (although they often have many acquaintances) and frequently don't wish to try. They achieve a relative sense of ease only in the company of men with whom they are less immediately competitive in the same way and who can provide what they seek unbegrudgingly.

Because this competitiveness has often been experienced earlier in childhood with their mothers, sisters, female cousins and peers, they turn to men to replace the sense of intimacy they might have gratified through other women, which is responsible for their classically intense and obvious oedipal complexes. Women of a strong hysteric character attempt to substitute the father, other male relatives and siblings or boys, for love from the mother, or other women, out of disappointment with them. However, since men are generally less suited than women to be emotionally expressive it is often an unsatisfying substitute for intimacy with other women and leads to an unconscious longing for reuniting with maternal figures as well as the premature cultivation of pseudosexuality which men value and respond to.

However, such attempted substitutions of other men are doomed, in part because of the guilt generated over incestuous object choice or over departure from idealized female sexual mores. This deep unconscious desire for maternal love may result in later demands on lovers and husbands to respond in ways that are more appropriate emotionally for a female than a male, and hence may generate disappointment and resentment when the man cannot fulfill these wishes. Deeper unconscious desire for such maternal love may generate homosexual interests.

The aim to please

The quest for other's responsivity results in an aim to be immediately (but often not deeply) pleasing which generates an other directedness, social charm and a radar-like (though often inaccurate) sensitivity to other's emotional states. In patients this is often evidenced by overconcerned inquiries (especially on beginning hours) such as "are you all right?" or "is everything o.k.?" in response to less than obvious signs from the therapist of his welcome or his readiness to intensively bestow attention immediately on the patient.

In moderate intensity these latter qualities seem particularly well suited to the complexities inherent in the roles of mother and wife (in our culture) whose major tasks focus on fulfilling the ever changing, conflicting daily round of complex emotional, interpersonally mediated needs of family members not unlike an orchestra leader who must be exquisitely sensitive to the individual needs of various instruments simultaneously and yet harmoniously coordinate his efforts in response to all of the players involved. Unlike the conductor, however, she is actively involved, as it were, in accompanying each of the players in performing their individual tasks! It is difficult to imagine, on hearing even the surface details of a typical day in the life of an involved wife and mother, how this all could be carried out successfully without a rather enormous investment in the wish to please others at the sacrifice of her own individual needs. It is not surprising then that the mother is often stereotyped as a masochistic martyr.

However, in the more extreme instances of hysterical character, this wish to please is heavily tied to the need for immediate repayment through the emotionally positive feedback reactions of others rather than satisfied by the experience and knowledge and perception that others are gratified. Hence, if intense demonstration of immediate emotional appreciation, value and gratitude are not reassuringly forthcoming (as evidenced by immediate, repeated, explicit verbalized superlatives) the attitude of caring to please is often rapidly succeeded by resentment, distress, anger, pouting, ambivalence and accusation of others' failure to appreciate. Inevitably this bewilders those who are less emotionally labile and who are also less cognizant of the psychological complexities underlying the motive to please in the hysteric. Equally confusing, but revealing, is the rapidity of the hysterical recovery upon token receipts of expressed appreciation from others which indexes the rather shallow, histrionic quality of hysteric emotional displays.

Likewise, of course, mild cirticism or anger from others is experienced as immediately devastating and intolerable bringing in its wake accusations of being hated, and unloved, followed often by reprisal threats of leaving, divorce, infidelity and even suicide.[3] These reactions tend, and are intended, to create an atmosphere of intimidation in order to blackmail others into submissively adopting responsive, placating postures to avoid antagonizing the hysteric. However, this results in counter-resentment and superficiality on the part of others which further endangers and undermines the hysteric's needs. One male patient described such a mother who constantly was dramatically exiting, luggage in hand, for the nearest train, bus or plane with the eventual result that he found himself resenting any of her emotional demands and withdrew entirely from her emotionally (as well, unfortunately, as others who symbolically reminded him of her). He recalled wishing finally that she would carry out her threats and leave forever. Similarly, the hysteric inclined to threaten suicide tragically generates similar feelings of resentment in others which may culminate in their actual wish for her to succeed at it. A husband of one such patient was in the practice of riding his bicycle to his office several miles from his residence and when called by a neighbor at work to inform him that his wife has just taken another large overdose of sleeping pills replied, "I'll be there as fast as I can pedal!"

The greatest fear and insult to an hysteric, therefore, is failure to evoke a reassuring, sufficiently intense, positive emotional response. The ability to attract an intense response or, as one patient phrased it, "to turn people on" becomes their most important and almost sole sense of worth. Hence, it is difficult for the hysteric to trust others to choose to respond in desired ways. Consequently they feel others must be manipulated to better guarantee obtaining the desired and necessary effects.[4]

Hysterical mothers and homosexual sons

So strong is this desire that it often acounts to a cavalier disregard of who is being manipulated to achieve the desired effect. Thus, while any male may serve this function he may also be a friend's husband, a husband's business associate, a minister, teacher, relative or even her own son. It is well known that sons of hysterical mothers who were chosen as targets to fulfill their needs for intense admiration and responsiveness have a strong disposition towards homo-

sexuality (Bieber, 1965). While the development of homosexuality in such sons is partly dependent on other factors, it can be related particularly to the mother's seductiveness which succeeds in generating intense sexual interests towards her, which results in extreme guilt and also fear of the father. Furthermore, the mother's demand for identificatory emotional response from her son tends to preempt the development of his complementary male attitudes and identity because it is his positive response to her psychic feminine attributes that she demands and he learns to value. Additionally, since she is vying competitively for attention and responsivity, this mother has a vested interest in distancing her son from potential rivals for his interest such as father, peers and other women.[5]

The witch identity

Frustration of this attempt to attain a desired responsivity as well as of the realization of being idealized leads the hysteric to wish to control and have power over other's reactions. This wish to manipulate, as it emerges during childhood, results in a fascination with the concept of the witch as a frustrated female who has obtained the power to command people to do what she wants them to by putting a magical spell over them for her own gratification. The hysteric learns to develop the kinds of informal skills that are designed to get others to respond and when this wish is realized, especially unexpectedly, there is a tendency to see this success as uncanny or weird, as a gratifying testament to unusual powers and as a defense against recognizing the manipulation. The manipulation generates guilt which, combined with the enhancement of mystery and a desire for omnipotence in creating an "influential effect" over others, leaves little room for the perception of fortuitous circumstance or the effects of skilled manipulation. Hence, occurrences which are at all out of the ordinarily expectable are categorized as inexplicable and therefore, attributable to one's personal mysterious power. More direct or obvious explanations tend to be acknowledged only with emotional disappointment. However, there is also a sense of discomfort over having such power with attendant fears of retributive punishment as in having such powers turned against oneself, being abandoned and set apart from others, and being transformed eventually into a weird, supernatural-like person. Thus, the hysteric often secretly envisions herself as having witch-like powers which are welcomed, but are also the source of discomfort and fear which victimize her as she cultivates beliefs in magical powers and the weird and supernatural.

Substitutions and the diminishment of self

The hysteric's willingness to replace genuine, more natural feelings, expression, and aims for those real personal attributes and role conceptions, in order to realize the goals of attention and love, results in feelings of ingenuousness, falseness and phoniness. Years of skillful cultivation of the abilities involved in simulating personal qualities designed to yield success in eliciting approval, positive emotional response and a glamorous image, crowd out the ability to feel what is genuinely oneself and drowns out the vividness of experience. The extreme of this results in a pervasive inner core sense of emptiness and loneliness. It is not uncommon for such patients to ask quite seriously, how one knows what one genuinely wants or feels apart from what others expect or approve.

A common example of this substitution of what appears desirable to evoke emotional response or to play a pleasing role is exemplified by the exaggerated display of positive feelings obviously unaccompanied by real feeling. Acting is itself a substitution of role for self. The fantasy therefore, of being an actress is often envisioned by the hysteric as the acme of an identity that would enable them to realize their aim of playing out desirable substitute roles and achieving public images and reputational value that would utilize their skill to win acclaim. The wish to win emotional acclaim also is frequently expressed in the desire to perform in front of other types of appreciative audiences as a dancer, singer or other type of solo performer. The ideal of being the focal center of a whole audience's appreciative attention is the most desired occurrence. Unfortunately, however, because this may not involve the expression of genuine self qualities and is highly dependent on props and transient situations the ensuing success of the hysteric whether formal or informal, does not affect the core sense or self in the form of an accumulated, dependable or stable feeling of self worth. Such applause and acclaim must therefore be continuously cultivated if it is be useful.

The root of this type of endeavor is to be observed in the ready encouragement little girls receive to pursue appreciation by performing informally for their family, peers and relatives. While it may be attached to more involved mastery, through lessons, of complex skills, the emphasis is more often on the acclaim received than on the experiential appreciation of the mastery achieved.

This eager willingness to incorporate substitutes for more genuine self qualities and expression led Angyal (1965) to postulate substitution as the central mechanism in hysterical development. Even the earliest socialization images involved in the differentiation of sex roles envision the female as ideally comprised of pleasing qualities in contrast to males as in the old nursery rhyme which avers that little girls are made of "sugar and spice and all that's nice" while little boys are made of "snaps and snails and puppy dogs' tails."

Undoubtedly this emphasis on the tradition of an idealized image of femininity lays the groundwork for the defensive reliance on repression and Pollyanish denial (Schafer, 1954) both of which are well recognized hallmarks of hysterical defense.

The covert ideals of the female hysteric

As we might expect, then, the kinds of fears and self complaints expressed in psychotherapy by female hysterics involve a sense of underlying worthlessness, falseness, emptiness, but also of being mundane, ordinary, uninteresting, stupid, dull and lack-luster. While these complaints and fears about the core self in part reflect the haunting, cumulative repercussions of not expressing and developing genu-

ine self qualities they also connote a pervasive, underlying, invidious discrepancy from their idealized self.

Typically the therapist hears directly voiced, or can unmistakably infer, wishes on their part to be desirable, exotic, brilliant, creative, sexy, famous, glamorous, alluring, charming, fascinating, irresistible, mysterious and even notorious. Obviously these qualities emphasize superlatives which place a premium not on self experiencing (one can hardly experience oneself as exotic, alluring, etc.), but on evoking intense positive reactivity of a reputational sort. Even something like brilliance is not experientially based; one can only experience the satisfaction of problem solving or thinking in various ways. This point can be demonstrated by contrasting them with apparently similar ones which are, however, more rooted in genuine, self experienced, undramatic involvements such as being worthwhile (vs. desirable), enjoying thinking or contemplation (vs. brilliance), spontaneously individual (vs. unique), productively expressive (vs. creative), sexual (vs. sexy), attractive (vs. glamorous), interested (vs. fascinating or interesting), open and transparent (vs. mysterious).

These hysterical versions of desirable personal qualities mirror the intense competitive impact they wish to achieve and, as such, represent superlatives which externalize their worth and, ideally if realized, place them beyond the pale of competitive comparison. Such aims are not only self-defeatingly unrealistic, but in fantasying about them, striving to attain or reaching them, the individual distances herself from what is experientially rewarding, substituting instead symbolic or reputational tokens of worth through others' or their own eyes. Small wonder then that little sense of actual self-gratification exists or that living has little intrinsic satisfaction inherent in experiencing. Often when hysterics tire of playing the game of pursuing others' positive response and acclaim or tire of self-perceived reputational value they become pessimistic, lethargic and depressed. There seems, to them, little point in going on living.

In despair over attempting to change, one female hysteric in her mid-thirties poignantly asked, "But what if there is nothing under all the pseudo-self . . . no real self that was ever allowed to emerge long enough to develop, to extend and to build on?" Such plaintive regrets are not easily answered except cavalierly or by wishful omnipotence on the therapist's part because indeed that may be, in no small part, an actuality.

While women in general tend to be more dependent on stimulation, companionship and others' responsiveness to feel emotionally satisfied, the hysteric may become so utterly dependent on responsivity that little can be experienced alone or without accompanying fantasies and exaggerations that confer a sense of significance without which everything seems lifeless, empty and lonely.

An example was expressed by a patient who realized that she constantly saw what was happening to her, while it was happening, as if it were a passage in a novel that both she and others were reading, thus guaranteeing not only an audience, but one whose stereotypic, prescribed responses could be utilized as a guide to feeling her own reaction.

Another hysteric reported that in order to supplement a

diminished experience of herself or anything when alone she hit on the practice of fantasying how she would seem to others if they could see her at that moment; what she was doing, how she had arranged the setting or how she was dressed and thus derived a modicum of experiencing somewhat more vividly through their reactions. She, as do most hysterics, hated being alone because she did not know how to experience or exist with herself in the absence of others and hence assiduously avoided it as much as possible.

Hysteric sexuality

Hysterics utilize sex to purchase companionship, responsivity and a sense of immediate worth and power. This leads to the cultivation of traits designed to interest others in them sexually such as charm, flirtatiousness, provocativeness, exhibitionism and suggestiveness, but is usually unaccompanied by genuine feelings of sexual or personal interest. This leads to the cultivation of pseudosexuality for the sense of being defined through others' responsiveness as sexually worthy. Other issues of conflict and guilt which are so pervasive in the hysteric's quest of an image tend to distance the self from deeper feeling and thus preclude the possibility of the kind of open abandonment to spontaneous feeling that promotes orgiastic climax. Naturally since the sexual partner is often not chosen himself on the basis of genuine feelings of involvement and of sexual attraction the whole basis of the possibility of deeper fulfillment is heavily tainted. Hysterics describe many reasons for their particular choice of husband except the presence of intense personal and sexual attraction. Consequently their ability to attain deeper sexual fulfillment with their husbands when they are better able to do so as a result of successful psychotherapy is often understandably very difficult or precluded by their feeling a lack of basic attraction to their spouses.

The shallowness of the hysteric's involvement or feelings towards a particular man or in their sexual relationships often results in rapid loss of interest as soon as other superficial needs have been satiated or some threat to their preferred image occurs. This may happen when they feel they have satisfied what they originally perceived as a challenge to get the man (usually one that is diffident or disdainful) to respond or when they fear their partner may get to know them more thoroughly and see their inner emptiness.

These feelings enhance short-lived relationships and generate bitterness, disappointment, pessimism and a fear of eventual loneliness. Eventually, a distaste develops for having to enact the complicated psychic requisites for genuine personal involvement and sexual interest. Not infrequently long periods of avoiding men and relationships occur accompanied by sexual abstinence which is experienced as a relief rather than frustrating.

Their history of sexual experience is characterized by such early, premature pseudo-involvement, disappointment and displeasure, it is difficult to establish any satisfactory basis on which they might build as a model of satisfaction and real feeling. Whatever modicum of actual arousal and gratification has been experienced is either extremely rare or heavily tainted by factors other than what Rogers (1961) has described as an independent valuing process leading to self-actualization.

After many years of an unsatisfying marriage and extramarital affairs one woman reported that she finally was enabled to feel intense sexual arousal by concentrating on the intensely excited expression on her partner's face which she could see was a response to her as a sexual object.

Hysterics are not merely repressing their sexuality as has been often observed, but, because of their early involvement in pleasing by internalizing a "sugar and spice and all that's nice" image, have developed a deeper feeling of distaste for sexuality and bodies (their own as well as men's) in spite of their apparent interest in sex. This has often been interpreted in psychoanalytic terms as a rejection of their female genitalia in the context of penis envy. However, this observation, while often accurate is insufficient because it fails to view the greater desirability of the penis in the larger context of their distaste for the "organicity" of their bodies as dirty, immoral and disgusting. Thus the preference for the penis is partly relative to the rejection of the female genitalia which is felt as more embarrassing because of its perceived greater organic nature as evidenced for example, by menstruation.

Penis envy and related problems in reaching sexual climax is determined by a variety of other factors, a few of which, however, are more easily anticipated as a result of our previous discussion. Diminishment of the role of actual sexual feeling, the concern to be pleasing to others and the wish to get them to respond positively lead hysterics to avoid making their own satisfaction a major focus of importance either to themselves or their partner. Hence, their goal sexually is to gratify the man rather than be gratified by him. This may be marked by the collusion with the choice of a male partner who is selfishly disinterested in her satisfaction, disapproves of it or is frightened of female sexual arousal. If the female hysteric feels, however, that she must abandon being guided by her own potential sexual feelings and gratification, and that sexual intercourse is to satisfy the man, she also resents her enslavement to his satisfaction and the masochistic surrender of her own demands. Therefore, she retaliates by withholding from the man (and herself) the satisfaction of feeling he has been able to gratify her thereby depriving him of masculine self-esteem.

The role of personal injustice

The dynamics described thus far have been based on the notion that certain antecedents of feminine character have been overabundantly and overexclusively present in the case of the female hysteric, resulting in a dysfunctional extreme development. In addition to this burden on self-fulfillment that these extreme involvements place on character functioning, an additional factor has been observed whose presence additionally leads to the emergence of neurotic, self-defeating trends in adaption. This factor has been referred to as a sense of personal injustice and its centrality to all types of neurotic involvement has been discussed extensively elsewhere (Wolowitz, 1971). In terms of the context of the present discussion, it is sufficient to state the case for the role of personal injustice in terms of two principles: 1) The experience of being unjustly treated in the pursuit of character aims and gratifications at the hands of the socializing agents themselves responsible for the character adaptations required leads to the covert wish to seek self-defeating forms of involvement in order to retaliate against them including their investment in oneself; 2) Different forms of psychopathology are a consequence in part of both different types of experienced injustices as well as of the depth of the perceived injustice.

In the case of female hysterics their sense of personal injustice is focused on feelings of unfairness over obtaining positive responsiveness, value and attention. This may stem from rather obvious features of their experience such as the presence of siblings whom they felt unfairly preempted their claims on one or both parents because of favoritism or differences in competence, age, goodness of conduct, sexual gender, physical appearance, etc. However, the injustice may also rest on less obvious features such as discrepancies between what they were led to believe and expect from their parents' attempt to respond, and what they actually experienced as insincere, insufficient, inconsistent, or inappropriate. The enormous discrepancies between one parent's evaluative response and another's or between parental and peer group evaluations can have similar effects.

One patient repeatedly recalled with anger and disappointment, her mother's apparently intense but superficial and feigned show of interest in her. Typically her mother would ask about her experiences or problems and if she attempted to express the details or her concerns she would experience a blank gaze, fleeting attention, an irrelevant question or an inane, stereotyped comment such as, "Well, don't let that worry you dear." or, "That's wonderful!" or, "But we love you." It was not so much the absolute level of deprivation of genuine responsivity she reacted to adversely, but rather to the false expectation that had been set up by her mother's attempt to be interested without actually being able to be so. If she expressed her anger it would be denied, along with the ostensible tokens of interest her mother so abundantly displayed which could not be confidently or effectively challenged without the cooperation of her mother's acknowledgement. Hence she grew up feeling on the one hand terribly spoiled, selfish, demanding and feeling insatiable in her need for response, while on the other hand, she felt deprived and needy of responsivity. Her compromise between retaliation against the experienced injustice, her sense of guilt and her fear of rejection was to refuse to express or share her deeper feelings with anyone, especially her mother.

Another extremely common example of the hysterical type of injustice involves the discrepancy between earlier experiences of physical and emotional intimacy with one or both parents, which is traumatically interrupted by the child's change with maturity into a more complex person who is less willing to please. This often puts immature, narcissistic parents off who respond to their loss of the sweet, cooperative and innocent little child by becoming significantly less intimate. The resulting sense of disappointment, bitterness, guilt and deprivation experienced by the child often instigates a deep, covert longing to regress to the innocence and guaranteed support of early childhood rather than become independent and mature, which is equated with a loss of intimacy and love.

This kind of trauma is often associated specifically with the development of sexual interests in the opposite sexed parent, who is prudish, moralistic or distrustful of his own control may reject the child's emerging sexual curiosity or expression of interest with alarming abruptness accompanied by explicit or implicit parental accusation or self-fantasy of one's evil or disgusting nature. This enhances inhibition and a fear of spontaneous self-expressiveness out of fear of being perceived as animalistic and, ipso facto, revolting, disgusting and rejectable. Such developments increase the intense strength of personal defense against awareness of sexual, aggressive and oedipal feelings. This feature is often found at the base of the hysterical sexual inhibitions. However, since as previously noted, sexual desirability is a major sphere of responsive worth and esteem, there is (as Angyal implies) a substitution of the image of being sexy, flirtatious or provocative for being sexual.

Since there is also a heavy cultural emphasis and premium placed on an idealized femininity, there develops an insidious and widespread collusion between the personal experiential basis of repression and the enhancement of the cultural ideal. This leads further and further away from the self becoming the basis for gratification and experience into a sense of emptiness, experiential deficiency and a wish to regress back into the dependency of early childhood as a haven.

Given the cultural ideal and the norms of socialization it is not surprising to find that hysterical character more frequently characterizes women than men and is widespread, comprehensible and almost predictable. The psychodynamics of the hysteric are uncomfortably close to the dynamics of the idealized normal feminine personality.

NOTES

1. The exception to this became known in psychoanalytic theory as the "genital character" which functions largely as a repository of ideal personal qualities and as the negative of neurotic orientations rather than as an empirically derived portrait of particular people encountered.
2. One of the reasons attention is approached competitively is that it is difficult to distribute other than successively one person at a time although other reasons will be discussed.
3. Although not frequently threatened, it is very often entertained privately as a response to disappointment by hysterics.
4. As an additional secondary guarantee of obtaining this responsiveness the hysteric's histrionic manner partly functions as self provided gratification or substitute positive feedback for what they so urgently seek from others. This is most apparent when they have temper tantrums even when no one else is around.
5. In addition to the mother, an older sister may succeed in utilizing her younger brother as a captive admirer with similar effects.

REFERENCES

Abraham, Karl. "Contribution to the Theory of Anal Character (1921)," Selected Papers on Psychoanalysis; Basic Books, 1957.
Angyal, Andreas. Neurosis and Treatment; Wiley, 1965.
Bieber, Irving. Homosexuality—A Psychoanalytic Study of Male Homosexuals; Vintage, 1965.
Breuer, Joseph and Freud, Sigmund. Studies in Hysteria (1885); Beacon, 1961.
Freud, Sigmund. An Autobiographical Study; Norton, 1935.
Freud, Sigmund. "Character and Anal Erotism (1908)," Vol. 2, Collected Papers; Basic Books, 1959.

Parsons, Talcott and Bales, Freed. Family Socialization and Interaction Process; Free Press, 1955.
Piaget, Jean. The Moral Judgment of the Child; Kegan Paul, 1932.
Rogers, Carl. On Becoming a Person; Houghton Mifflin, 1961.
Schafer, Roy. Psychoanalytic Interpretation of Rorschach Testing; Grune and Stratton, 1954.

Shapiro, David. Neurotic Styles; Basic Books. 1965.
Wolowitz, Howard. Personal Justice and Injustice: The Dynamics of Psychopathology and Psychotherapy as Evaluative Adaptation. Unpublished Manuscript, University of Michigan, 1971.
Zilboorg, Gregory and Henry, G. W. A History of Medical Psychology; Norton, 1941.

46 Women's lib—rational? or socially pathological?

Elton B. McNeil

We all suffer the curse of 'being born in an important age'—an age of transition and sudden change in the form of relationship between the sexes. As in no previous century, we are confronted by the angry, hatred-laden rhetoric of organizations such as WITCH (Women's International Conspiracy from Hell), SCUM (Society for Cutting up Men), NOW (National Organization for Women), and Radical Lesbians who demand an end to traditional definitions of maleness and femaleness. Some extreme subgroups of the women's liberation movement have demanded that we eliminate what they feel is extensive sexual repression in the society, cease to teach women to be dependent on male affectionate responses, and desist from defining love of the same sex as "sick" and "degenerate."

The Radical Lesbians, for example, call for a free choice of modes of sexual expression—a choice between homosexuality and bisexuality rather than a choice of homosexuality or heterosexuality. For them, this is a sick society—obsessed with a relentless persecution of those who choose other than heterosexuality. As radical lesbians maintain, if hostility to men causes lesbianism, then in a male-dominated society, lesbianism is a sign of health.

It is to assaults such as these on traditional views of proper relations between the sexes that the members of our society must respond. And, reasonable or not, the women's liberation movement must stand the social test of public judgment regarding normality or pathology.

The public response

Much of the public reaction to the comportment, rhetoric, and demands of the members of women's liberation has been less than charitable. The quest for liberation from male domination (and from the associated myths that have supported it for centuries) may be a legitimate goal but the means of achieving it have most often provoked antagonism, spoken or unspoken, rather than sympathy (Limpus, 1970).

The tenor of negative cultural response to the new feminist movement is summed up in the words of Helen Lawrenson,

You might have to go back to the Children's Crusade in 1212 A. D. to find as unfortunate and fatuous an attempt at manipulated hysteria as the Women's Liberation movement . . . a hair-raising emotional orgy of hatred as vicious as it is ludicrous, directed at love, marriage, children, the home, and encompassing en route, with wild catholicity, the penis, the Pill, false eyebrows, brassieres, Barbie dolls, Freud, Dr. Spock, the Old Left, the New Left, detergent advertisements. . . . (p. 83)

The aim of all this, according to Lawrenson, is not liberation for women but the absolute subjugation of men. And, according to her, these are not normal women. They are freaks who describe love as a debilitating, counterrevolutionary illusion and label men "superpig supremacists" or the "Hitlers in our homes." Thus, for the most extreme among them, one-half the species has suddenly become the oppressor and deadly enemy. Lawrenson concludes that many in their ranks are neurotic, inadequate women who are appallingly selfish.

Throughout history woman has been assigned exclusively to the kitchen, bed, and church (Weisstein, 1970). And some of the dynamic psychological theorists of this era have done little to revise the formula.

The eminent psychoanalyst Bruno Bettelheim (1965), for example, implied that women who sought careers as engineers or scientists really wanted most to be mothers and companions of men. Erik Erikson (1965) reinforced this sentiment by suggesting that female anatomy destined women primarily to bearing the offspring of their chosen male. And, Joseph Rheingold (1964) observed that only motherhood could bring a sense of fulfillment, a secure world, and what passes for the good life.

Social science has paid little heed to women and the bulk of the spare research it has accomplished has reinforced the popular mythology about women. Psychological research in

Reprinted from Elton B. McNeil, "Women's Lib—Rational? or Socially Pathological?" unpublished paper, 1969.

the past has regularly described the female as inconsistent, emotionally unstable, lacking in conscience, weak, "nurturant" rather than productive, and "intuitive" rather than intelligent.

Jo Freeman (1970) observed that women regularly describe themselves, in social science experiments, by using standard cultural stereotypes.

Women strongly felt that they could accurately be described as uncertain, anxious, nervous, hasty, careless, fearful, dull, childish, helpless, sorry, timid, clumsy, stupid, silly and domestic. On the more positive side women felt they were understanding, tender, sympathetic, pure, generous, affectionate, loving, moral, kind, grateful and patient. This is not a very favorable self-image, but it does correspond fairly well to the myths about what women are like. The image has some 'nice' qualities, but they are not the ones normally required for the kinds of achievement to which society gives its highest rewards. (p. 37)

The results of a study by Rosenkrantz, et al. (1968) are not very promising with regard to the hoped for liberation of females since they found that among college students sex-role stereotypes continue to exist—characteristics thought to be masculine still have a higher value than those associated with femininity. Women still learn to equate intellectual achievement with a loss of femininity and bright women are caught in a bind in which they worry not only about failure, but about success. If they fail, they are not meeting their own standards of performance; if they succeed they are not living up to social expectations about proper female behavior. The urge to achieve is often inhibited by the motive to avoid success and an unfortunately great number of women will explore their intellectual potential only when they do not need to compete with men (Horner, 1969).

The problem of the female role in our society is a deep-rooted one that is not likely to disappear in response to a shouted slogan.

Male chauvinism

Male chauvinism is by no means a recent invention. By one means or another males have always rationalized and justified their superior social position. In the past, as Una Stannard (1970) asserts, the males claimed that "women have babies, but men have the maternal instinct." To underscore her contention, she reminds us that, according to the Bible, Adam was the first mother and one of his ribs the basic component of the first female.

In isolated, primitive tribes, the Arapesh of New Guinea for example, the father was thought to be the only one capable of giving "life-soul" to a child. Indeed, as a father ages, his wrinkles wrought by the ravages of time are attributed in part to the burden of the many children he has borne. Historically, the husband has determined if the newborn will survive or perish and the destruction of "worthless" females was no more than an affirmation that while women can give birth to boys, only males can give birth to men. The female womb, according to this theory, is no more than a nest in which the baby grows. As the mythical Zeus bore Athena without female help, the role of the mother has been systematically ignored or demeaned in

the past since offspring must pass the test of acceptability to the male parent.

With the invention of the microscope in the 17th century, the live sperm in semen were discovered but they were viewed (by male scientists) as immature but fully formed babies entrusted by the male to nine months' nurturance in the female.

"It was not until 1861 that it was realized that the ovum was more than a source of nourishment for the embryo, but was the female sex cell, and it was not until 1875 that the actual union of the female and male gametes was observed. Mendel's discovery of the absolutely equal contribution of the sexes to the heredity of the child ought to have been the final blow to the male's illusion that he was the lord of creation." (Stannard, 1970, p. 28)

This "maternal instinct" of the male has enslaved the female. As Stannard notes,

If there is a maternal instinct, history reveals that it is men who have it, not women. For who were feeding their children roast pig at birth? Who were refusing to breast feed their children? Who doped infants with opium and gin? Who tossed illegitimate babies into sewers? Whose ignorance and neglect saw to it that most babies died? Who whenever possible hired servants to take their children off their hands? Who in the early years of this century were agitating for birth control? Who at the present time are clamoring for free abortions and child-care centers? Women. (Stannard, 1970, p. 31)

No part of modern culture is free of the suspicion of subtle male chauvinism. Even the musical accompaniment of the social upheaval of our times has become suspect. As some sensitive women's libbers complain, the rock music scene is dominated by sweaty, bearded men (who *allow* barefooted and bare breasted females to serve hot meals) as they shouted the praises of *Brother*-hood in song. The "rock music culture" is as degrading to females as any other social device invented and instrumented by males of any age—the rock culture simply reinforces age-old sex-role stereotypes disguised by "in" jargon that denies the truth of what is and always has been.

Rebellion, male long hair, and unisex clothes are, women's libbers note, no more than hip camouflage for very ancient sexism. Rock lyrics describe womankind as not much more than an easily available sex object bearing only traces of the basic humanity any living person has as a birthright. Woman is defined by the rock culture as hysterical, greedy, whining, hypocritical, servile, passive, and spiritless. The rock culture is a male phenomenon that condescends to admit a token handful of female exceptions (Pride of Women, Goldflower, Fanny, Joy of Cooking). Modern rock male chauvinists are as uncomprehending of female outrage as any establishment male who asks "What do these women want?"

It is not a new social problem

Hunt (1959) quotes a feminist of many years ago who stated "Woman was the earliest domestic animal of man." Woman, created as an afterthought, constructed of spare male parts, and designed solely as a companion for man is hardly an appetizing description of the female of the species. And, women in the recent past have reacted to such definitions of the self and have abandoned the traditional role demands in quest of something more fulfilling.

The problem of the women's role in society is neither recent nor limited to our society. In Japan, for example, Lifton (1965) observed that three general aspects of womanhood could be distinguished—those who nurture, those who provide sensual pleasure, and those "knowers" who convey social wisdom. In stable times these roles serve to delineate a path in life from birth onward. But,

During periods of rapid historical change, the social structuring of these three feminine identities become unstable and confused, and women most sensitive to such change experience considerable psychological discomfort. . . . Each woman tends to become a "generalist"—to become, in a new way, nurturer *and* temptress *and* knower. (p. 32)

Demands for excellence in a variety of roles leads inevitably to a faltering on the part of some coupled with a retreat to the sanctuary of earlier, less threatening cultural patterns. If a woman takes the alternate path and seeks to break the culturally established rhythms of male and female she invites self-destructive ambivalence and guilt since her "victories" each exact an exorbitant toll of her personal sense of well-being. She may experience, in adult form, the anxiety felt by the very young child separated from the mother as she abandons one role and self image for a new and yet untried one.

What we may be witnessing is what Lifton labels "release phenomenon." When psychological tendencies long suppressed by social custom suddenly emerge into behavior they may appear in extreme and exaggerated form. This visible excessiveness may dissipate as the new sense of freedom is adjusted to by our society. In this first phase some part of the rhetoric and behavior of the participants draws its energy not from the objective logic of woman's cultural status but from unresolved personal conflicts and anxieties for which the movement provides an elegant, nearly guilt-free outlet.

We have for a number of decades experienced what Degler (1965) has described as a "revolution without ideology"—a gradual loosening of male domination of the female until she is now freer than most women on this planet. But, for some women, the pace of change has not been rapid enough to match the tide of their rising expectations. And, in recent times, we have midwifed the birth of an ideology that has spawned a notable increase in socially deviant behavior.

Distinguishing between positive social deviance and collective pathology has occupied the attention of every society in history and the questions pondered have always been the same. Do the participants have special insight and critical faculties which make it possible for them to penetrate the obscuring veil of social sham and hypocrisy or are they merely suffering from personality and character disorders that destroy their capacity to internalize the values of the culture?

Over a decade ago Rigney and Smith (1961) explored these alternatives in their study of the "Bohemian" members of the "Beat Generation" living in the North Beach area of San Francisco. Smith (1969) described, for ex-

ample, the "angry young women" of that time in these terms,

. . . their behavior alternates between explosive, hostile outbursts and depression, hopelessness, and self-pity . . . Most of their rebelliousness and acting-out behavior is expressed in their sex lives. They appear to seek tenderness and love in their sexual relations, but they equate sexuality with violence, and their affairs end unhappily. They try to play the martyr role, frequently giving the impression that they have been put upon, taken advantage of, and hurt. (Smith, 1969 pp. 584-585)

Smith reports that the seeds of such maladjustment are planted early, blossom during adolescence, and leave some women feeling cheated and embittered by a life that traps them and twists their fate into an ugly shape—a shape they reject and rebel against. Rigney and Smith met the issue of positive social deviation versus collective pathology head on and concluded, as we must, that the only rational answer to the question must be that some are and some are not acting pathologically. If the social changes advocated by the most impatient and demanding members of women's lib were magically to occur tomorrow, an unpredictable number of women's libbers would still be hostile, depressed, angry, resentful, and their hatred for males would pulse strongly in their veins. For many it would mean the loss of an ideal catharsis for unresolved personal psychological problems.

The complaint is real

There is an indisputable factual basis for discontent among some women since the pattern of motherhood has shifted substantially since the late 1800s. Motherhood in 1890 occupied the average woman until her mid-fifties. In those days of shorter life expectancy, the typical mother could expect to live only 12 years after her last child married. Mothers of today, however, can anticipate living for a quarter century after their last child has been married and society has made no meaningful provision for retirement from motherhood. It is very much as if all males in our society were forced to retire at 40 years of age without preparation for meaningful alternative ways to absorb their creative, constructive energies. The female, early in life, must choose a social role that will withstand the test of time and it is not surprising that some members of this generation are being assailed by an erosive and severe anxiety about what the future may hold. The female is in trouble whether she blithely accepts the role prescribed for her, flatly rejects it, or vacillates between one or another alternative.

It is the man-made world that is the constant irritant to women whose newly sensitive perceptual nerve endings have been rubbed raw by constant encounter with the pervasive signs and symbols of rampant masculinity. Yet, it exceeds credibility to suggest that the course of social history has run so consistently guided only by a *deus ex machina* personified in the male. The female of the species must have played the cultural game and complied passively for centuries for this to have occurred. The luxury of being dependent has always been an alluring alternative to many females. There is little likelihood its psychological appeal will diminish in the years ahead.

Haunted by a culture-wide sense of guilt, the Jews of today ask why they walked quietly to the ovens of Belsen, obeyed in Dachau, and why they were so passively contained within the walls of the Warsaw ghetto in World War II. In much the same fashion, the radical feminists of today may react in an extreme fashion in order to expunge the bitter memory of their own past, passive acceptance of a now unconscionable social role. As Honoré de Balzac said, the revenge of sheep is horrible to behold; for some liberationists this may be the year the sheep is transformed into a wolf. This move to militancy has been apparent and undeniable in our time. Not too long ago (the 1950s) the female college students of Vassar were mindful only of June weddings, homes in the suburbs, and children. Identity in the 1950s was derived from the male, limited by the role of housewife-mother, finding a husband was the primary goal for the female, and little discontent was visible (Bushnell, 1962).

But, the seeds of change have been sown. In those years, an inquiry among fourth graders revealed that ten times as many girls expressed the wish to have been born boys than did boys wish to be females. In 1950, Pauline Wilson interviewed women college graduates 20 years following graduation and found 90 percent of them bothered by a sense of disappointment, frustration, or a sense of futility in their lives.

If blame for this condition is turned outwards with society and the male as prime targets, the college-educated female is ripe for membership in the women's liberation movement. But, if the self is seen as the source of one's social and personal troubles then a series of symptoms may develop when the period of reproductive functioning is ended and there is little left to provide self-esteem. No longer a mother or sex object, the retired mother is denied the satisfaction of the male as he moves up to accept the rewards of greater work responsibility and increased meaningfulness in his work. Our society provides no self-fulfilling assignment for women entering this phase of life. The male, then, may become an exceptionally visible, if not deserving, target for the outpouring of venom when life comes up empty for the woman. And, such women may seek to exact revenge on the male and the social system that accords greater personal satisfaction and a sense of well-being to the male.

Getting with the movement

How members get converted to the women's liberation point of view tells us something of the unfulfilled motives and needs of those most deeply involved in the movement. Anita Micossi (1970) interviewed members of women's lib to explore the basis of their conversion to the movement and found a number of preconditions that ready the candidate for the awakening. Each of the women studied had available alternative modes of self-expression and self-esteem (each was intelligent, highly educated, and had upwardly mobile goal orientations) which had been fostered throughout childhood (parental encouragement of achievement, advanced schooling, and a career). Such alternatives to the traditional role of women are, of course,

available only to a limited number, but they are a clear precondition to conversion to the movement.

Once the seed of a life style different from housewife-mother is implanted it requires only that individual women become aware of, and disturbed by, the discrepancy between aspirations, self-image, potential, and the realistic circumstances of life. From the discrepancy between what is and what could be come the feeling of being trapped, suffocated, and abused. And, the most visible perpetrator of such discomfort is, naturally, the male.

Once intellectual talent is coupled with an awareness of a stifling fate in life and coupled with a perspective that suggests the problem can be solved by action, we need only add what Micossi labels a "life-long pattern of defiance" to complete the list of ingredients that make a readiness for conversion to women's lib. A life-long pattern of defiance sensitizes the individual to translate life's many events (birth, divorce, job discrimination, etc.) into a crystallized conviction of who and what the enemy is.

The message of women's lib has, however, fallen on deaf ears among their black sisters. There is a near absolute absence of blacks from the ranks of the movement due to the incredible experiential gap between the "oppression" of the black man and woman who are unemployed and the "oppression" of the American white woman who is "sick and tired" of *Playboy* fold-outs, of Christian Dior lowering hemlines or adding ruffles or of Miss Clairol telling her that blondes have more fun. What does the black woman on welfare who has difficulty feeding her children have in common with the discontent of the suburban mother who has the luxury to protest washing the dishes on which her family's full meal was consumed? (La Rue, 1970, p. 60)

It is predictable that any group is tempted to align itself and its rhetoric to the more visible oppression of others. Women's libbers have indulged themselves freely of this commodity but black women can't resist pointing out that while white women may be suppressed, they are hardly unjustly, rigorously, cruelly, or harshly fettered by their husbands and their elevated station in life.

To the black female, the women's liberation movement reflects less of social progress and more of pathological discontent among those most favored socially. To most males, lower class women and men, black women and men, and members of the older generation, the movement is a pathological social upheaval.

Possibly the greatest single error of tactical judgment made by women's liberation forces is to overlook (or try to deny) the possibility that even the enslaved white, middle class housewife is positively rewarded by the condition of her servitude. It somehow seems inconceivable to the educated, intellectual, white, middle-class members of women's lib that the 28 million women who watch daytime soap operas are satisfied with the freedom of their home-bound refuge from the working world. Having children can provide an excellent social excuse for dependence on males and a life style in which one is cared for by another rather than fending for one's self.

A revolution, it is said, can only succeed if its issues strike a resonant chord in the ranks of the oppressed masses. In this instance it may be accurate to predict that any revolu-

318 WOMEN AND CRITERIA OF MENTAL HEALTH

tion initiated by an elite minority and designed primarily to gratify their needs and resolve their frustrations will have a limited appeal to the masses of housewives and equally limited achievement of its intended goals. The rhetoric of women's lib must seem alien and incomprehensible to those for whom their role in life is not only comfortable and natural but a positive defense against a less pleasant alternative.

Women's lib—rational or socially pathological?

There is little question that the traditional, time-honored definitions of proper male and female behavior have gone by the wayside and our middle-class urban young are freely mixing the gender symbols of hair and dress (Simon, 1969). The tenets of this 'new morality' suggest there will be radical shifts in the expression of sexuality on the contemporary scene. Winick (1968) concluded we are entering a Neuter age that will even further blur the line of demarcation between sexual roles—a unisex age in which names, clothing, appearance, leisure and work and home responsibilities will no longer be labeled masculine or feminine.

What will it mean in the future to be a male or female? According to Marshall McLuhan and George Leonard (1967), sex tomorrow may only vaguely resemble what it once was. We may, in fact, return to the sexual style of our primitive, hunting ancestors in which there could be little social or sexual differentiation since the hardships of basic survival placed men and women on a nearly equal basis. McLuhan and Leonard suggest that sex relationships in the future may again become a playful, casual activity as it once was in the tribal state. If so, the frequency of sexual intercourse should decrease since it will lose its surplus meaning, i.e., achievement, accomplishment, ego-reassurance, anxiety relief, etc. When the male is free of the need to be super masculine and the femal released from the bondage of emulating the youthful exaggerated breasts and buttocks in the center-fold of "men's" magazines, we may all be less anxious about male-female relationships and the institution of marriage will no longer be the same. There is little likelihood that life-long marital pacts will disappear even though John Watson, the father of modern behaviorism, predicted in 1925 that marriage would no longer exist by 1977. Marriage will, however, continue to be transformed into new and unusual shapes for some (Bernard, 1970).

Multilateral or group marriage in which three or more persons form a family unit, for example may increase radically (Constantine and Constantine, 1970). If sex roles and marriage forms change drastically we will all adjust eventually and perhaps painfully (despite our insistence we will not) to the new patterns. We will one day come to view them as the norm. But, the militant and radical demands for liberation from old style marriage will for many years be treated as a form of social pathology needing remedy rather than sanction. If we are to experience a social transformation in the relationship between the sexes it will be just one piece of a much larger transfiguration in the pattern of our social life.

Society and paranoia

Societies can experience a form of demoralization, conflict, and disintegration that closely resembles individual pathology. It is clear that for many of the members of women's liberation traditional conceptions of proper male-female role relationships no longer are acceptable. A by-product of this rejection of cultural values seems to have been an increase in paranoid thinking among the women who have newly found themselves an unaccustomed part of a militant minority group. Paranoid is too harsh and critical a term to apply but, despite its implication of pathology, it is richly descriptive of some aspects of the transformation some women have undergone.

The nature of paranoid reactions

According to classic psychodynamic theory, paranoid thinking is a delusional view of life that allows the individual to deny the existence of his own intolerable or unacceptable impulses by unconsciously attributing them to other persons and thus transferring blame away from the self. Most of us, of course, will react badly when exposed to severe tension or anticipation of some personal catastrophe (Swanson, Bohnert, and Smith, 1970) and are likely to become suspicious, misinterpret the motives and intentions of others, become hostile, and react aggressively or violently. Serious threats to security or self-esteem will produce immature, volatile, unpredictable, and paranoid behavior.

In paranoid thinking the suspicious person not only mistrusts the motives of others, he or she turns full attention to assembling proof of fixed and long-held convictions. The accompanying conviction of being center stage in life is a grandiose self-estimate that reassures the individual of his or her importance as a person.

When the person with a paranoid view of life finds a group of others who share his set of values and feelings they can have a multiplied impact on the course of social affairs. This form of almost normal social paranoia has increased in our society.

Paranoia and women's lib

In the militant, radical segment of the liberation movement are females who without question have donned a social mask to cover their personal pathology. They are angry, hostile, castrative, destructive, and they act out their individual inadequacies while wearing an assumed mask of logic, reality, and pristine-pure ideals of justice and equity. Their bitter and emotional rhetoric condemns one-half of the human species to eternal damnation at worst and perpetual reparations at best. They reject the possibility of intimacy, trust, and understanding between male and female and seem to desire the opportunity to become the new oppressors in an inverted social order. Their thinking is paranoid and their reactions are socially pathological.

But, perhaps, history has long made it clear that substantial social change has always required drastic, confrontational behavior if it is to succeed. And, since personal pathology is always defined in terms of deviation from the existing social consensus, it may be that feminist extremism of the sort we are witnessing in this era is absolutely necessary if change is to occur. It is equally reasonable to suggest that those females who irrationally deny the possibility of alteration of the male-female relationship may, in the course of history, be described in less than healthy terms.

These women of the movement are reacting against unpalatable norms and expectations for their style of life and are seeking to fulfill needs currently ungratified. They do this at some cost to their personal vulnerability since they are trying to redefine the traditional assumptions of psychological health and normality. Our judgment must be that this is a healthy protest that is exacting a high pathological toll among those at its forefront. The pathology can be uncharitably described as paranoid and at moments it uses defense mechanisms primitive as the denial of reality. Its driving force may well be a kind of pathetic search for someone to trust in a world that no longer trusts its fellow human being.

Sex has become the bone of contention in the modern world and the women's liberation movement has called for an end to arbitrary, constrictive, and coercive confinement of male and female to rigid, limited, and confining roles. If communal child rearing, total sexual freedom, new heterosexual combinations, and equality for the female become the norms of tomorrow, the radical feminists of today will appear to be the saintly martyrs of tomorrow.

REFERENCES

Bernard, Jessie. Women, Marriage and the Future. *The Futurist*, April 1970, Vol IV, #2, p. 41-43.

Bettelheim, B. The commitment required of a woman entering a scientific profession in present-day American society. *Woman and the Scientific Professions*, the MIT symposium on women in science and engineering, 1965.

Bushnell, J. Student culture at Vassar. In Sanford, N. (Ed.) *The American College*. New York Wiley, 1962.

Campbell, A. Measuring the quality of life. *The Michigan Alumnus*, 1971, Vol. 77, #7. March, p. 4.

Constantine, L. & Constantine, Joan, Where is Marriage Going? *The Futurist*. April 1970, Vol. IV, #2, p. 44-46.

Degler, C. Revolution Without Ideology: The Changing Place of Women in America. In R. Lifton (Ed.) *The Woman in America*. Boston Beacon Press. 1964, 1965, p. 193-210.

Erikson, E. Inner and outer space: Reflections on womanhood. *Daedalus*, 1964, 93, 582-606.

Freeman, Jo. Growing up girlish. *Transaction*, 8, Nov-Dec. 1970. P. 36-43.

Greer, Germaine. *The Female Eunich*. McGraw-Hill, 1971.

Horner, Matina. Fail: bright women. *Psychology Today*, 1969, 3, 36-cont.

Hunt, M. M. *The Natural History of Love*. New York: Knopf, 1959.

La Rue, Linda J. M. Black liberation and women's lib. *Transaction*, 8, Nov-Dec, 1970, Pp. 59-64.

Lawrenson, Helen. The Feminine Mistake. *Esquire*. January 1971, p. 83.

Lifton, R. J. "Woman as Knower: Some Psychological Perspectives. 27-51. In Lifton, R. J. (Ed.) *The Woman in America*. Boston, Mass. Beacon Press 1965.

McLuhan, M. and Leonard, G. B. The Future of Sex. *Look*. (July 25, 1967) 31 (15), 56-63.

Micossi, Anita Lynn. Conversion to women's lib. *Transaction*, 8, Nov-Dec., 1970, Pp. 82-90.

Rheingold, J. *The Fear of Being a Woman*. New York: Grune & Stratton, 1964.

Rigney, F. J. & Smith, L. D. *The Real Bohemia*. New York: Basic Books, Inc. 1961.

Rosenkrantz, P.; Vogel, Susan; Bee, Helen; Broverman, Inge; and Broverman, D. M. Sex role stereotypes and self concepts in college students. *J. consult. clin. Psychol.*, 1968, 32, 287-295.

Simon, W. Sex. *Psychology Today*. 1969 (July), 3, 23-27.

Smith, L. D. The "Beats" and Bohemia: Positive Social Deviance or a Problem in Collective Disturbance? In S. C. Plog & R. B. Edgerton (Eds.) *Changing Perspectives in Mental Illness*. Holt, Rinehart and Winston, Inc. 1969. Pp. 578-593.

Stannard, U. Adam's rib, or the woman within. *Transaction*, 8, Nov-Dec. 1970, Pp. 24-35.

Swanson, D. W., Bohnert, P. J., & Smith, J. A. *The Paranoid*. Boston: Little, Brown & Co. 1970.

Weisstein, Naomi. Kinder, Kuche, Kirche as scientific law: Psychology constructs the female. In Gadlin, H. and Garskof, B. E., *The Uptight Society: A Book of Readings*. Belmont, Calif.: Books /cole Publishing Co., 1970. Pp. 427-434.

Wilson, Pauline. College women who Express Futility. New York Teachers College, Columbia Bureau of Publications, 1950.

Winick, C. The Beige Epoch Depolarization of Sex Roles in America. In E. Sagarin (Ed.) *Sex and the Contemporary American Scene*, The Annals. 1968, #376, Pp. 18-24.

Wrightsman, L. S. and Baker, N. J. Where have all the idealistic, imperturbable freshmen gone? *Proceedings of the 77th Annual Convention of the American Psychological Association*, 1969, 4, 299-300.

47 Sex-role stereotypes and clinical judgments of mental health

Inge K. Broverman
Donald M. Broverman
Frank E. Clarkson
Paul S. Rosenkrantz
Susan R. Vogel

Evidence of the existence of sex-role stereotypes, that is, highly consensual norms and briefs about the differing characteristics of men and women, is abundantly present in the literature (Anastasi & Foley, 1940; Fernberger, 1948; Komarovsky, 1950; KcKee & Sherriffs, 1957; Seward, 1946; Seward & Larson, 1968; Wylie, 1961; Rosenkrantz, Vogel, Bee, Broverman & Broverman, 1968). Similarly, the differential valuations of behaviors and characteristics stereotypically ascribed to men and women are well established (Kitay, 1940; Lynn, 1959; McKee & Sherriffs, 1959; Rosenkrantz et al., 1968; White, 1950), that is, stereotypically masculine traits are more often perceived as socially desirable than are attributes which are stereotypically feminine. The literature also indicates that the social desirabilities of behaviors are positively related to the clinical ratings of these same behaviors in terms of "normality-abnormality" Cowen, 1961), "adjustment" (Wiener, Blumberg, Segman, & Cooper, 1959), and "health-sickness" (Kogan, Quinn, Ax, & Ripley, 1957).

Given the relationships existing between masculine versus feminine characteristics and social desirability, on the one hand, and between mental health and social desirability on the other, it seems reasonable to expect that clinicians will maintain parallel distinctions in their concepts of what, behaviorally, is healthy or pathological when considering men versus women. More specifically, particular behaviors and characteristics may be thought indicative of pathology in members of one sex, but not pathological in members of the opposite sex.

The present paper, then, tests the hypothesis that clinical judgments about the traits characterizing healthy, mature individuals will differ as a function of the sex of the person judged. Furthermore, these differences in clinical judgments are expected to parallel the stereotypic sex-role differences previously reported (Rosenkrantz et al., 1968).

Finally, the present paper hypothesizes that behavioral attributes which are regarded as healthy for an adult, sex unspecified, and thus presumably viewed from an ideal, absolute standpoint, will more often be considered by clinicians as healthy or appropriate for men than for women.

This hypothesis derives from the assumption that abstract notions of health will tend to be more influenced by the greater social value of masculine stereotypic characteristics than by the lesser valued feminine stereotypic characteristics.

The authors are suggesting, then, that a double standard of health exists wherein ideal concepts of health for a mature adult, sex unspecified, are meant primarily for men, less so for woman.

Method

SUBJECTS

Seventy-nine clinically-trained psychologists, psychiatrists, or social workers (46 men, 33 women) served as Ss. Of these, 31 men and 18 women had PhD or MD degrees. The Ss were all actively functioning in clinical settings. The ages varied between 23 and 55 years and experience ranged from internship to extensive professional experience.

INSTRUMENT

The authors have developed a Stereotype Questionnaire which is described in detail elsewhere (Rosenkrantz et al., 1968). Briefly, the questionnaire consists of 122 bipolar items each of which describes, with an adjective or a short phrase, a particular behavior trait or characteristic such as:

Very aggressive	Not at all aggressive
Doesn't hide emotions at all	Always hides emotions

One pole of each item can be characterized as typically masculine, the other as typically feminine (Rosenkrantz et al., 1968). On 41 items, 70% or better agreement occurred as to which pole characterizes men or women, respectively, in both a sample of college men and in a sample of college women (Rosenkrantz et al., 1968). These items have been classified as "stereotypic."

The questionnaire used in the present study differs slightly from the original questionnaire. Seven original items seemed to reflect adolescent concerns with sex, for example, "very proud of sexual ability ... not at all con-

Reprinted from Inge K. Broverman, Donald M. Broverman, Frank E. Clarkson, Paul S. Rosenkrantz, and Susan R. Vogel, "Sex-Role Stereotypes and Clinical Judgments of Mental Health," Journal of Consulting and Clinical Psychology, 34:1, 1970, pp. 1-7.

cerned with sexual ability." These items were replaced by seven more general items. Since three of the discarded items were stereotypic, the present questionnaire contains only 38 stereotypic items. These items are shown in Table 1.

Finally, in a prior study, judgments have been obtained from samples of Ss as to which pole of each item represents the more socially desirable behavior or trait for an adult individual in general, regardless of sex. On 27 of the 38 stereotypic items, the masculine pole is more socially desirable (male-valued items), and on the remaining 11 stereotypic items, the feminine pole is the more socially desirable one (female-valued items).

INSTRUCTIONS

The clinicians were given the 122-item questionnaire with one of three sets of instructions, "male," "female," or "adult." Seventeen men and 10 women were given the "male" instructions which stated "think of normal, adult men and then indicate on each item the pole to which a mature, healthy, socially competent adult man would be closer." The Ss were asked to look at the opposing poles of each items in terms of directions rather than extremes of behavior. Another 14 men and 12 women were given "female" instructions, that is, they were asked to described a "mature, healthy, socially competent adult woman." Finally, 15 men and 11 women were given "adult" instructions. These Ss were asked to describe a "healthy, mature, socially competent adult person" (sex unspecified). Responses to these "adult" instructions may be considered indicative of "ideal" health patterns, without respect to sex.

SCORES

Although Ss responded to all 122 items, only the stereotypic items which reflect highly consensual, clear distinctions between men and women, as perceived by lay people were analyzed. The questionnaires were scored by counting the number of Ss that marked each pole of each stereotypic item, within each set of instructions. Since some Ss occasionally left an item blank, the proportion of Ss marking each pole was computed for each item. Two types of scores were developed: "agreement" scores and "health" scores.

The agreement scores consisted of the proportion of Ss on that pole of each item which was marked by the majority of the Ss. Three agreement scores for each item were computed; namely, a "masculinity agreement score" based on Ss receiving the "male" instructions, a "femininity agreement score," and an "adult agreement score" derived from the Ss receiving the "female" and "adult" instructions, respectively.

The health scores are based on the assumption that the pole which the majority of the clinicians consider to be healthy for an adult, independent of sex, reflects an ideal standard of health. Hence, the proportion of Ss with either male or female instructions who marked that pole of an item which was most often designated as healthy for an adult was taken as a "health" score. Thus, two health scores were computed for each of the stereotypic items: a "masculinity health score" from Ss with "male" instructions, and a "femininity health score" from Ss with "female" instructions.

Results

SEX DIFFERENCES IN SUBJECT RESPONSES

The masculinity, femininity, and adult health and agreement scores of the male clinicians were first compared to the comparable scores of the female clinicians via t tests. None of these t tests were significant (the probability levels ranged from .25 to .90). Since the male and female Ss did not differ significantly in any way, all further analyses were performed with the samples of men and women combined.

AGREEMENT SCORES

The means and sigmas of the adult, masculinity, and femininity agreement scores across the 38 stereotypic items are shown in Table 2. For each of these three scores, the average proportion of Ss agreeing as to which pole reflects the more healthy behavior or trait is significantly greater than the .50 agreement one would expect by chance. Thus, the average masculinity agreement score is .831 ($z = 3.15$, $p < .001$), the average femininity agreement score is .763 ($z = 2.68$, $p < .005$), and the average adult agreement scores is .866 ($z = 3.73, p < .001$). These means indicate that on the stereotypic items clinicians strongly agree on the behaviors and attributes which characterize a healthy man, a healthy woman, or a healthy adult independent of sex, respectively.

RELATIONSHIP BETWEEN CLINICAL JUDGMENTS OF HEALTH AND STUDENT JUDGMENTS OF SOCIAL DESIRABILITY

Other studies indicate that social desirability is related to clinical judgments of mental health (Cowen, 1961; Kogan et al., 1957; Wiener et al., 1959). The relation between social desirability and clinical judgment was tested in the present data by comparing the previously established socially desirable poles of the stereotypic items (Rosenkrantz et al., 1968) to the poles of those items which the clinicians judged to be the healthier and more mature for an *adult.* Table 3 shows that the relationship is, as predicted, highly significantly ($t = 1.38, p < .10$), whereas a significant difconfirm the previously reported relationships that social desirability, as perceived by nonprofessional Ss, is strongly related to professional concepts of mental health.

The four items on which there is disagreement between health and social desirability ratings are: to be emotional; not to hide emotions; to be religious; to have a very strong need for security. The first two items are considered to be healthy for adults by clinicians but not by students; the second two items have the reverse pattern of ratings.

SEX-ROLE STEREOTYPE AND MASCULINITY VERSUS FEMININITY HEALTH SCORES

On 27 of the 38 stereotypic items, the male pole is perceived as more socially desirable by a sample of college students (male-valued items); while on 11 items, the feminine pole is seen as more socially desirable (female-valued items). A hypothesis of this paper is that the masculinity health scores will tend to be greater than the femininity health scores on the male-valued items, while the femininity health scores will tend to be greater than the masculinity health scores on the female-valued items. In other words, the relationship of the clinicians' judgments of health for

TABLE 1   *Male-valued and Female-valued Stereotypic Items*

Feminine pole	Masculine pole
Male-valued items	
Not at all aggressive	Very aggressive
Not at all independent	Very independent
Very emotional	Not at all emotional
Does not hide emotions at all	Almost always hides emotions
Very subjective	Very objective
Very easily influenced	Not at all easily influenced
Very submissive	Very dominant
Dislikes math and science very much	Likes math and science very much
Very excitable in a minor crisis	Not at all excitable in a minor crisis
Very passive	Very active
Not all all competitive	Very competitive
Very illogical	Very logical
Very home oriented	Very worldly
Not at all skilled in business	Very skilled in business
Very sneaky	Very direct
Does not know the way of the world	Knows the way of the world
Feelings easily hurt	Feelings not easily hurt
Not at all adventurous	Very adventurous
Has difficulty making decisions	Can make decisions easily
Cries very easily	Never cries
Almost never acts as a leader	Almost always acts as a leader
Not at all self-confident	Very self-confident
Very uncomfortable about being aggressive	Not at all uncomfortable about being aggressive
Not at all ambitious	Very ambitious
Unable to separate feelings from ideas	Easily able to separate feelings from ideas
Very dependent	Not at all dependent
Very conceited about appearance	Never conceited about appearance
Female-valued items	
Very talkative	Not at all talkative
Very tactful	Very blunt
Very gentle	Very rough
Very aware of feelings of others	Not at all aware of feelings of others
Very religious	Not at all religious
Very interested in own apperarance	Not at all interested in own appearance
Very neat in habits	Very sloppy in habits
Very quiet	Very loud
Very strong need for security	Very little need for security
Enjoys art and literature very much	Does not enjoy art and literature at all
Easily expresses tender feelings	Does not express tender feelings at all

men and women are expected to parallel the relationship between stereotypic sex-role behaviors and social desirability. The data support the hypothesis. Thus, on 25 of the 27 male-valued items, the masculinity health score exceeds the femininity health score; while 7 of the 11 female-valued items have higher femininity health scores than masculinity health scores. On four of the female-valued items, the masculinity health score exceeds the femininity health score. The chi-square derived from these data is 10.73 ($df = 1$, $p < .001$). This result indicates that clinicians tend to consider socially desirable masculine characteristics more often as healthy for men than for women. On the other hand, only about half of the socially desirable feminine characteristics are considered more often as healthy for women rather than for men.

On the face of it, the finding that clinicians tend to ascribe male-valued stereotypic traits more often to healthy men than to healthy women may seem trite. However, an examination of the content of these items suggests that this trite-seeming phenomenon conceals a powerful, negative assessment of women. For instance, among these items, clinicians are more likely to suggest that healthy women differ from healthy men by being more submissive, less independent, less adventurous, more easily influenced, less aggressive, less competitive, more excitable in minor crises, having their feelings more easily hurt, being more emotional, more conceited about their appearance, less objective, and disliking math and science. This constellation seems a most unusual way of describing any mature, healthy individual.

TABLE 2   *Means and Standard Deviations for Adult, Masculinity, and Femininity Agreement Scores on 38 Stereotypic Items*

Agreement score	M	SD	Deviation from chance	
			Z	p
Adult	.866	.116	3.73	< .001
Masculinity	.831	.122	3.15	< .001
Femininity	.763	.164	2.68	< .005

MEAN DIFFERENCES BETWEEN MASCULINITY HEALTH SCORES AND FEMININITY HEALTH SCORES

The above chi-square analysis reports a significant pattern of differences between masculine and feminine health scores in relationship to the stereotypic items. It is possible, however, that the differences, while in a consistent, predictable direction, actually are trivial in magnitude. A t test, performed between the means of the masculinity and femininity health scores, yielded a t of 2.16 ($p < .05$), indicating that the mean masculinity health score (.827) differed significantly from the mean femininity health score (.747). Thus, despite massive agreement about the health dimension per se, men and women appear to be located at significantly different points along this well-defined dimension of health.

CONCEPTS OF THE HEALTHY ADULT VERSUS CONCEPTS OF HEALTHY MEN AND HEALTHY WOMEN

Another hypothesis of this paper is that the concepts of health for a sex-unspecified adult, and for a man, will not differ, but that the concepts of health for women will differ significantly from those of the adult.

This hypothesis was tested by performing t tests between the adult agreement scores versus the masculinity and femininity health scores. Table 4 indicates, as predicted, that the adult and masculine concepts of health do not differ significantly ($t = 1.38$, $p < .10$), whereas a significant difference does exist between the concepts of health for adults versus females ($t = 3.33$, $p < .01$).

These results, then, confirm the hypothesis that a double standard of health exists for men and women, that is, the general standard of health is actually applied only to men, while healthy women are perceived as significantly less healthy by adult standards.

Discussion

The results of the present study indicate that high agreement exists among clinicians as to the attributes characterizing healthy adult men, healthy adult women, and healthy adults, sex unspecified. This agreement, furthermore, holds for both men and women clinicians. The results of this study also support the hypotheses that (a) clinicians have different concepts of health for men and women and (b) these differences parallel the sex-role stereotypes prevalent in our society.

Although no control for the theoretical orientation of the clinicians was attempted, it is unlikely that a particular theoretical orientation was disproportionately represented in the sample. A counterindication is that the clinicians' concepts of health for a mature adult are strongly related to the concepts of social desirability held by college students. This positive relationship between social desirability and concepts of health replicates findings by a number of other investigators (Cowen, 1961; Kogan et al., 1957; Wiener et al., 1959).

The clinicians' concepts of a healthy, mature man do not differ significantly from their concepts of a healthy adult. However, the clinicians' concepts of a mature healthy woman do differ significantly from their adult health concepts. Clinicians are significantly less likely to attribute traits which characterize healthy adults to a woman than they are likely to attribute these traits to a healthy man.

Speculation about the reasons for and the effects of this double standard of health and its ramifications seems appropriate. In the first place, men and women do differ biologically, and these biological differences appear to be reflected behaviorally, with each sex being more effective in certain behaviors (Broverman, Klaiber, Kobayashi, & Vogel, 1968). However, we know of no evidence indicating that these biologically-based behaviors are the basis of the attributes stereotypically attributed to men and to women. Even if biological factors did contribute to the formation of the sex-role stereotypes, enormous overlap undoubtedly exists between the sexes with respect to such traits as logical ability, objectivity, independence, etc.; that is, a great many women undoubtedly possess these characteristics to a greater degree than do many men. In addition, variation in these traits within each sex is certainly great. In view of the within-sex variability, and the overlap between sexes, it seems inappropriate to apply different standards of health to men compared to women on purely biological grounds.

TABLE 3   *Chi-square Analysis of Social Desirability Versus Adult Health Scores on 38 Stereotypic Items*

Item	Pole elected by majority of clinicians for healthy adults
Socially desirable pole	34
Socially undesirable pole	4

TABLE 4   *Relation of Adult Health Scores to Masculinity Health Scores and to Femininity Health Scores on 38 Stereotypic Items*

Health score	M	SD
Masculinity	.827	.130
		$t = 1.38*$
Adult	.866	.115
		$t = 3.33**$
Femininity	.747	.187

*$df = 74$, $p > .05$.
**$df = 74$, $p < .01$.

More likely, the double standard of health for men and women stems from the clinicans' acceptance of an "adjustment" notion of health, for example, health consists of a good adjustment to one's environment. In our society, men and women are systematically trained, practically from birth on, to fulfill different social roles. An adjustment notion of health, plus the existence of differential norms of male and female behavior in our society, automatically lead to a double standard of health. Thus, for a woman to be healthy, from an adjustment viewpoint, she must adjust to and accept the behavioral norms for her sex, even though these behaviors are generally less socially desirable and considered to be less healthy for the generalized competent, mature adult.

By way of analogy, one could argue that a black person who conformed to the "pre-civil rights" southern Negro stereotype, that is, a docile, unambitious, childlike, etc., person, was well adjusted to his environment and, therefore, a healthy and mature adult. Our recent history testifies to the bankruptcy of this concept. Alternative definitions of mental health and maturity are implied by concepts of innate drives toward self-actualization, toward mastery of the environment, and toward fulfillment of one's potential (Allport, 1955; Bühler, 1959; Erikson, 1950; Maslow, 1954; Rogers, 1951). Such innate drives, in both blacks and women, are certainly in conflict with becoming adjusted to a social environment with associated restrictive stereotypes. Acceptance of an adjustment notion of health, then, places women in the conflictual position of having to decide whether to exhibit those positive characteristics considered desirable for men and adults, and thus have their "femininity" questioned, that is, be deviant in terms of being a woman; or to behave in the prescribed feminine manner, accept second-class adult status, and possibly live a lie to boot.

Another problem with the adjustment notion of health lies in the conflict between the overt laws and ethics existing in our society versus the covert but real customs and mores which significantly shape an individual's behavior. Thus, while American society continually emphasizes equality of opportunity and freedom of choice, social pressures toward conformity to the sex-role stereotypes tend to restrict the actual career choices open to women, and, to a lesser extent, men. A girl who wants to become an engineer or business executive, or a boy who aspires to a career as a ballet dancer or a nurse, will at least encounter raised eyebrows. More likely, considerable obstacles will be put in the path of each by parents, teachers, and counselors.

We are not suggesting that it is the clinicians who pose this dilemma for women. Rather, we see the judgments of our sample of clinicians as merely reflecting the sex-role stereotypes, and the differing valuations of these stereotypes, prevalent in our society. It is the attitudes of our society that create the difficulty. However, the present study does provide evidence that clinicians do accept these sex-role stereotypes, at least implicitly, and, by so doing, help to perpetuate the stereotypes. Therapists should be concerned about whether the influence of the sex-role stereotypes on their professional activities acts to reinforce social and intrapsychic conflict. Clinicians undoubtedly exert an influence on social standards and attitudes beyond that of other groups. This influence arises not only from their effect on many individuals through conventional clinical functioning, but also out of their role as "expert" which leads to consultation to governmental and private agencies of all kinds, as well as guidance of the general public.

It may be worthwhile for clinicians to critically examine their attitudes concerning sex-role stereotypes, as well as their position with respect to an adjustment notion of health. The cause of mental health may be better served if both men and women are encouraged toward maximum realization of individual potential, rather than to an adjustment to existing restrictive sex roles.

NOTE

[1] Requests for reprints should be sent to Inge K. Broverman, Worcester State Hospital, Worcester, Massachusetts 01604.

REFERENCES

Allport, G. W. *Becoming.* Princeton: Yale University Press, 1955.
Anastasi, A., & Foley, J. P., Jr. *Differential psychology.* New York: Macmillan, 1949.
Broverman, D. M., Klaiber, E.L., Kobayashi, Y., & Vogel, W. Roles of activation and inhibition in sex differences in cognitive abilities. *Psychological Review,* 1968, 75, 23-50.
Bühler, C. Theoretical observations about life's basic tendencies. *American Journal of Psychotherapy,* 1959, 13, 561-581.
Cowen, E. L. The social desirability of trait descriptive terms: Preliminary norms and sex differences. *Journal of Social Psychology,* 1961, 53, 225-233.
Erikson, E. H. *Childhood and society.* New York: Norton, 1950.
Fernberger, S. W. Persistence of stereotypes concerning sex differences. *Journal of Abnormal and Social Psychology,* 1948, 43, 97-101.
Kitay, P. M. A comparison of the sexes in their attitudes and beliefs about women. *Sociometry,* 1940, 34, 399-407.
Kogan, W. S., Quinn, R., Ax, A. F., & Ripley, H. S. Some methodological problems in the quantification of clinical assessment by Q array. *Journal of Consulting Psychology,* 1957, 21, 57-62.
Komarovsky, M. Functional analysis of sex roles. *American Sociological Review,* 1950, 15, 508-516.
Lynn, D. B. A note on sex differences in the development of masculine and feminine identification. *Psychological Review,* 1959, 66, 126-135.
Maslow, A. H. *Motivation and personality.* New York: Harper, 1954.
McKee, J. P., & Sherriffs, A. C. The differential evaluation of males and females. *Journal of Personality,* 1957, 25, 356-371.
McKee, J. P., & Sherriffs, A. C. Men's and women's beliefs, ideals, and self-concepts. *American Journal of Sociology,* 1959, 64, 356-363.
Rogers, C. R. *Client-centered therapy; Its current practice, implications, and theory.* Boston: Houghton, 1951.
Rosenkrantz, P., Vogel, S., Bee, H., Broverman, I., & Broverman, D. Sex-role stereotypes and self-concepts in college students. *Journal of Consulting and Clinical Psychology,* 1968, 32, 287-295.
Seward, G. H. *Sex and the social order.* New York: McGraw-Hill, 1946.
Seward, G. H., & Larson, W. R. Adolescent concepts of social sex roles in the United States and the two Germanies. *Human Development,* 1968, 11, 217=248.
White, L., Jr. *Educating our daughters.* New York: Harper, 1950.
Wiener, M., Blumberg, A., Segman, S., & Cooper, A. A judgment of adjustment by psychologists, psychiatric social workers, and college students, and its relation to social desirability. *Journal of Abnormal Social Psychology,* 1959, 59, 315-321.
Wylie, R. *The self concept.* Lincoln: University of Nebraska Press, 1961.

Index

Index

75 76 9 8 7